A Cross-Section of Research Articles Classified by Design

Research Articles in Education and the Social & Behavioral Sciences

Compiled and Edited
by Thomas D. Kennedy and W. Alex Edmonds

Learning Solutions

New York   Boston   San Francisco
London   Toronto   Sydney   Tokyo   Singapore   Madrid
Mexico City   Munich   Paris   Cape Town   Hong Kong   Montreal

Pearson Learning Solutions, 501 Boylston Street, Suite 900, Boston, MA 02116
A Pearson Education Company
www.pearsoned.com

Printed in the United States of America

2 3 4 5 6 7 8 9 10 V3DZ 15 14 13 12 11 10

000200010270570218

LA/JR

ISBN 10: 0-558-64502-X
ISBN 13: 978-0-558-64502-1

Copyright Acknowledgments

Table of Contents

i. Introduction

Inclusion of Articles

Articles were included to cover a broad range of basic designs used in the field of education and the social and behavioral sciences.

How to Use the Book

This book is a supplement to the text *A Reference Guide to Basic Research Designs.* It allows for a deeper exploration and critical analysis of the designs discussed in the reference guide. Refer to the Annotated TOC on the following pages to see which design category each article falls into.

This book can also be used as a "stand alone" by professors and educators that teach in the field of education, sociology, psychology, nursing and the other human services. The book has been organized "by design." In other words, each article represents a different type of research design. There are no repeat designs used in the studies presented in this book. In fact, the book includes articles with 35 distinct basic quantitative, qualitative, and mixed methods research designs in education and the social and behavioral sciences. Students will learn how to review and critique these studies using the questions and guides included at the beginning of the book.

A critique of a journal article requires the student to analyze and evaluate, while a review is more of a summary. A review involves indentifying elements of the study and a follow-up discussion or summary of what was done. Alternatively, a critique, involves the analysis, interpretation and evaluation of a study, answering the questions how, why, and how well. Thus, a review might be more suited for undergraduate students, while a critique might be more appropriate for graduate students.

As a student progresses from conducting simple reviews to mastering complex critiques, they will progressively use higher level cognitive processes while demonstrating increased intellectual skills. Based on Bloom's (1956) taxonomy, a review may be conceptualized as a simple recall of data (knowledge) and demonstration of understanding (comprehension), while a critique involves synthesis and evaluation.

Guiding Questions and Prompts

These are provided to ensure that students are fully addressing all of the critical aspects of the study. The review questions are meant to provide support for students who are conducting an article review. The critique questions are meant for graduate students who are more familiar with the peer review process. A critique requires a greater understanding of the design and methodological issues. Critiquing the article involves high level critical analysis, as the student provides their own interpretations, criticisms and suggestions regarding the study. The questions included in this book may also be used to guide classroom discussions and for individualized assignments.

Rating Scale

Students can rate how they feel about different aspect of the article. These ratings should be well thought out and based on the prior review or critique of the article. The responses on this scale can be used to generate in class deliberations or discussion board postings for online classes. Students should be prepared to defend and explain their ratings of each statement.

Guides

There are two guides provided to help students with the organization and structure of their reviews and critiques.

Classification of the Articles

Articles were classified by the studies specific research design.

Annotated TOC

The annotated TOC is for students who are using this book in conjunction with the text *A Reference Guide to Basic Research Designs* by W. Alex Edmonds and Thomas D. Kennedy, ISBN 0-558-65201-8.

The articles in this book are grouped by different research designs as seen below. Please refer to the above text *A Reference Guide to Basic Research Design* for detailed information regarding these designs.

The following chart clarifies the levels of terms used in the following annotated TOC. The terms in the following chart may not be consistent with the terminology used in the actual article.

Level	Component	Definition
1	METHOD	The *method* refers to quantitative, qualitative, or mixed (e.g., a quantitative $method_1$).
2	RESEARCH	*Research* refers to experimental, quasi-experimental, or non-experimental (e.g., a quantitative $method_1$ and non-experimental $research_2$).
3	APPROACH	The *approach* is the first step to creating stucture to the design, and provides (a) a model of how the data will be collected, and (b) how many groups will be associated with the process (e.g., a quantitative $method_1$, non-experimental $research_2$ with a suvey $approach_3$).
4	DESIGN	The *design* is the actual structure of framework that indicates (a) the time frame(s) in which data will be collected, (b) when the intervention will be implemented (or not), and (c) how many groups will be involved (e.g., a quantitative $method_1$, non-experimental $research_2$ with a survey $approach_3$ and a longitudinal $design_4$).

Part I. Quantitative Methods Experimental and Quasi-Experimental Research

BETWEEN-SUBJECTS APPROACH

Pre and Posttest Designs

Pre and Posttest Control Group Design

Article 1.01 *Family-Centered Intervention for Young Children at-risk for Language and Behavior Problems.*

2-factor Pre and Posttest Control Group Design

Article 1.02 *Problem-Solving Skills Training and Relationship Therapy in the Treatment of Antisocial Child Behavior.*

2-factor Pre and Posttest Design

Article 1.03 *A Randomised Efficacy Study of Web-based Synthetic and Analytic Programmes Among Disadvantaged Urban Kindergarten Children.*

3-factor Pre and Posttest Design

Article 1.04 *The Effects of Visual Illustrations on Learners' Achievement and Interest in PDA- (Personal Digital Assistant) Based Learning.*

4-factor Pre and Posttest Design

Article 1.05 *Enhancing Mathematical Reasoning in the Classroom: The Effects of Cooperative Learning and Metacognitive Training.*

Posttest Designs

Posttest Control Group Design

Article 1.06 *Problem-Based Learning in Online vs. Face-to-Face Environments.*

2-factor Posttest Control Group Design

Article 1.07 *An Exploration of Online Environments Supporting Follow-up to Face-to-Face Professional Development.*

2-factor Posttest Design

Article 1.08 *Dog-Assisted Therapy in the Treatment of Chronic Schizophrenia Inpatients.*

3-factor Posttest Design

Article 1.09 *Endurance Exercise and Health-Related Quality of Life in 50-65 Year-Old Adults.*

WITHIN-SUBJECTS APPROACH

Repeated Measures Designs

Pre- and Posttest Design (one group)

Article 1.10 *Pilot Testing Okay With Asthma™: An Online Asthma Intervention for School-Age Children.*

Cross-over Design (multiple-group repeated measures)

Article 1.11 *Behavioral Treatment for Depressed Mood: A Pleasant Events Intervention for Seniors Residing in Assisted Living.*

Interrupted Time Series Design (one-group repeated measures)

Article 1.12 *Capturing the Cumulative Effects of School Reform: An 11-Year Study of the Impacts of America's Choice on Student Achievement.*

Factorial Designs

2 × 2 Factorial Pre- and Posttest Design (between-subjects)

Article 1.13 *Effects of Perceived Disability on Persuasiveness of Computer-Synthesized Speech.*

2 × 2 Factorial Posttest Design (between-subjects)

Article 1.14 *Perceptions of Leader Transformational Ability: The Role of Leader Speech and Follower Self-Esteem.*

2 × 2 Factorial Pre- and Posttest Design (within-subjects)

Article 1.15 *Effects of a Body Image Challenge on Smoking Motivation Among College Females.*

Part II: Quantitative Methods Continued: Non-Experimental Research

WITHIN-SUBJECTS

Posttest Design (within-subjects)

Article 2.01 *Evaluation of an Educational Intervention for Military Tobacco Users.*

CORRELATIONAL APPROACH

Explanatory Design

Article 2.02 *The Relations Between Student Motivational Beliefs and Cognitive Engagement in High School.*

Predictive Design 1

Article 2.03 *Exploring the Psychological Predictors of Programming Achievement.*

Predictive Design 2

Article 2.04 *The Longitudinal Relations of Teacher Expectations to Achievement in the Early School Years.*

SURVEY APPROACH

Cross-Sectional Design

Article 2.05 *A School-Based Survey of Recurrent Non-Specific Low-Back Pain Prevalence and Consequences in Children.*

Longitudinal Design

Article 2.06 *Social Capital, Self-Esteem, and Use of Online Social Network Sites: A Longitudinal Analysis.*

Part III. Qualitative Methods

GROUNDED THEORY APPROACH

Systematic Design

Article 3.01 *Ethnicity, Health and Medical Care: Towards a Critical Realist Analysis of General Practice in the Korean Community in Sydney.*

Emerging Design

Article 3.02 *Relationships and Their Potential for Change Developed in Difficult Type 1 Diabetes.*

Constructivist Design

Article 3.03 *Understanding Patterns of Commitment: Student Motivation for Community Service Involvement.*

ETHNOGRAPHIC APPROACH

Realist Design

Article 3.04 *The Dignity of Job-Seeking Men: Boundary Work among Immigrant Day Laborers.*

Critical Design

Article 3.05 *Harms and Benefits: Collecting Ethnicity Data in a Clinical Context.*

Case Study Design

Article 3.06 *Men Do Matter: Ethnographic Insights on the Socially Supportive Role of the African American Uncle in the Lives of Inner-City African American Male Youth.*

NARRATIVE APPROACH

Narrative Design

Article 3.07 *Autobiographical Memories of Early Language and Literacy Development.*

Part IV. Mixed Methods

TRIANGULATION APPROACH

Convergence Design

Article 4.01 *How Do Linguistically Diverse Students Fare in Full- and Half-Day Kindergarten? Examining Academic Achievement, Instructional Quality, and Attendance.*

Data Transformation Design

Article 4.02 *An Empirically Derived Taxonomy of Factors Affecting Physicians' Willingness to Disclose Medical Errors.*

Validating Quantitative Data Design

Article 4.03 *Transition Services for Incarcerated Youth: A Mixed Methods Evaluation Study.*

Multilevel Design

Article 4.04 *A Qualitative Evaluation of an Employee Counselling Service from the Perspective of Client, Counsellor and Organization.*

EMBEDDED APPROACH

Experimental Design

Article 4.05 *Cognitive Tools for Scaffolding Students Defining an Ill-Structured Problem.*

Correlational Design

Article 4.06 *Schizophrenia and the Motivation for Smoking.*

EXPLANATORY APPROACH

Follow-Up Explanations Design

Article 4.07 *The Effects of Pacing on the Academic Testing Performance of College Students with ADHD: A Mixed Methods Study.*

ii. Guides

The following may be used as a guide for writing a review of an article:

Review of an Article (3 sections)

Introduction

1) Give the title of the article and name of the author(s) and provide a full citation of the article.
2) Identify the author(s) by profession.
3) Identify the problem addressed in the article.
4) Identify the purpose of the article.
5) Present the research questions or hypotheses and explain how they address the purpose.
6) Include a statement which identifies the main points to be discussed in the body of the review.

Body

1) Briefly describe the participants, methods, design, procedures, what was measured, and where the research was conducted.
2) Discuss the type of data that was collected and the analysis.
3) Describe the results.
4) Write an analytical summary of the main findings, arguments, or conclusions of the author(s).
5) Discuss what you learned from the article.
6) Support your review with quotations or specific examples.

Conclusion

1) Summarize the information that was covered in the *Body*.
2) State what you learned from the article.
3) Comment on the implications of the research.

The following may be used as a guide for writing a critique of an article:

Critique of an Article (5 sections)

Introduction

Include a few opening sentences that declare the name of the author(s) and the title, and briefly explain the topic of the article. Present the aim of the article and summarize the main finding(s) or key argument(s). Conclude the introduction with a brief statement of your evaluation of the article. This can be a positive, negative or mixed appraisal of the study.

Summary

Present a summary of the key points along with specific examples to provide evidence of your assertions. Also, briefly explain the author(s) purpose throughout the article and describe how the study was conducted. The summary should only make up about a third of the critical review.

Critique

The critique should be a balanced discussion and evaluation of the strengths, weakness and notable features of the article. Remember to base the discussion on specific criteria. Thorough critiques also include other sources to support the evaluation (remember to reference). In long critiques, address each criterion chosen in a paragraph, including any negative and positive points. For very short critical reviews (one page or less), include a paragraph of the positive and another of the negative aspects of the article. Also include recommendations for how the manuscript could be improved in terms of ideas, research approach, method, design, and analyses. Theories or frameworks should also be described and evaluated in the critique section.

Conclusion

Restate your overall opinion. Briefly present recommendations. If necessary, include further qualifications or explanations of your judgment. Cleary defend the position you present. It is important to be fair and reasonable with any assertions and to support your opinions with data from other sources when possible.

Reference

If other sources are used in the critique include a list of references.

iii. Questions and Prompts

For Review

Identify

1) The main topic
2) The problem (usually in the Abstract or Introduction)
3) The purpose (usually in the Introduction)
4) The research question(s) (usually in the Introduction)
5) The hypothesis(es) (usually in the Introduction)
6) The participants and selection procedures (usually in the Methods)
7) The instruments or measures (usually in the Methods)
8) The design (usually in the Methods)
9) The test (data analyses) of the hypothesis or research questions (usually in the Methods)
10) The findings (in the Results section)

Explain and Interpret

1) How does the author(s) support the hypotheses or research questions?
2) What is the main objective of the article?
3) What were the most convincing arguments to justify the study?
4) Explain the methodology.
5) Discuss the design.
6) What were the major results?
7) Describe the tables and figures.
8) Discuss the author(s) conclusions?
9) How did this article impact your understanding of the topic?

For Critique

Analyze, Summarize and Evaluate

Introduction

1) Is the title of the article appropriate and clear?
2) Is the abstract specific, representative of the article, and well organized?
3) Is the purpose of the article made clear in the introduction?
4) Do you find errors of fact and interpretation? (Check on this by looking up the references cited by the author[s])
5) Has the author(s) cited the pertinent, and only the pertinent, literature?
6) Have any ideas been overemphasized or underemphasized?
7) Does the literature review include the current findings related to the topic?

Argument

1) Do you agree or disagree with the author(s) argument?
2) Is there anything about the author(s) logic that makes their argument questionable?
3) If the author(s) makes generalizations, do you feel these generalizations are justified?
4) Does the author(s) present counterevidence?
5) How does the author(s) treatment of counterevidence impact the effectiveness of their argument?
6) Is a theoretical framework presented? Is it appropriate? Can you think of a different or additional theoretical perspective that might have been useful?

Methods

1) What are the characteristics of the population studied?
2) What is the sample size? Is it sufficient?
3) Have the procedures been presented in enough detail to allow a reader to replicate them?
4) What instruments were used? How were they developed? What did they measure? Were the instruments valid, reliable, and appropriate? Describe any reliability and validity tests that were conducted? Was this sufficient?
5) How well is this design suited to the research question or hypothesis? Is the design modified in response to any constraints? Are there threats to the internal validity of the research design?
6) How were the variables utilized in the analysis? Were the statistics appropriate for the type of questions and the variables being used?

Findings

1) Is the discussion relevant and connected back to the literature?
2) Does the author(s) stay within the scope of the study?
3) What questions are left unanswered?
4) Do the unanswered questions limit the impact of the author's argument?
5) Do the author(s) adequately address the studies limitations?
6) Were there any confounding variables? If so, how might the research design have been improved to reduce interference from confounding variables?
7) Was the study conducted in an objective fashion? Is there any evidence of bias? Are there limitations to the generalizability of the findings?

Global

1) Should some sections of the manuscript be expanded, condensed or omitted?
2) Are the author(s) statements clear (appropriate transitions and well organized)?
3) What underlying assumptions does the author(s) have?
4) Has the author(s) been objective in his or her discussion of the topic?
5) How does the article contribute to the field?

iv. Rating the Article

Indicate the level of agreement with the following statements. <u>Circle the number</u> that is most accurate from 1 (*strongly agree*), to 5 (*strongly disagree*). Be prepared to discuss the ratings.

1. The title of the article accurately reflects the study.

    Strongly Agree   1   2   3   4   5   Strongly Disagree

2. The abstract provides an accurate synopsis of the study.

    Strongly Agree   1   2   3   4   5   Strongly Disagree

3. The introduction provides a clear problem statement.

    Strongly Agree   1   2   3   4   5   Strongly Disagree

4. The introduction provides a clear purpose statement.

    Strongly Agree   1   2   3   4   5   Strongly Disagree

5. The research questions or hypotheses are clearly stated.

    Strongly Agree   1   2   3   4   5   Strongly Disagree

6. The design is clearly explained.

    Strongly Agree   1   2   3   4   5   Strongly Disagree

7. There is enough data regarding the participants.

    Strongly Agree   1   2   3   4   5   Strongly Disagree

8. The procedures have been presented in a way to allow for replication of the study.

    Strongly Agree   1   2   3   4   5   Strongly Disagree

9. Ethical guidelines for a research study were followed.

    Strongly Agree   1   2   3   4   5   Strongly Disagree

10. The results are clearly presented.

    Strongly Agree   1   2   3   4   5   Strongly Disagree

11. The discussion is consistent with the results.

    Strongly Agree   1   2   3   4   5   Strongly Disagree

12. The conclusions are logical.

    Strongly Agree   1   2   3   4   5   Strongly Disagree

13. The conclusions are in agreement with the findings.

    Strongly Agree   1   2   3   4   5   Strongly Disagree

14. Study limitations are clearly presented.

    Strongly Agree   1   2   3   4   5   Strongly Disagree

15. The study was worthy of publication.

    Strongly Agree   1   2   3   4   5   Strongly Disagree

PART I

Quantitative Methods, Experimental and Quasi-Experimental Research

1.01

Family-Centered Intervention for Young Children at-risk for Language and Behavior Problems

Pen-Chiang Chao,* Tanis Bryan,* Karen Burstein,* and Cevriye Ergul*

ABSTRACT: This study investigated the effects of a family-centered intervention that involved parents in weekly assessments and daily routine activities for promoting young children's language and behavior. Forty-one 3–5-year-old children at-risk for language and behavior problems, recruited from three developmental pre-schools, were randomly assigned to a control and an intervention group that received parent–professional support. Analyses of covariance (ANCOVAs) were used to examine whether groups differed on post-test scores on the Test of Early Language Development—Third Edition and Eyberg Child Behavior Inventory, using pre-test scores as a covariate. Results showed that children in the intervention group out-performed children in the control group on both tests. The study indicated that family-centered intervention is an effective method for empowering parents to identify and implement concrete solutions to their children's problems, especially when done as part of a professional collaboration.

KEYWORDS: at-risk children; family-centered intervention; parent–professional collaboration; language; behavior.

Family-centered services, defined as professionals treating families with respect, sharing information with parents, and providing individualized, flexible services (Dunst, 2002), have been recommended practice in early intervention (Blue-Banning, Summers, Frankland, Nelson, & Beegle, 2004). Early intervention research has demonstrated that parent involvement produced positive effects on children's physical, cog-

nitive, social, and language skills (Baroff, 1986; Blasco, Hrncir, & Balsco, 1990; Odom & Karnes, 1988), tended to foster a sense of personal control and self-efficacy in parents (Trivette, Dunst, Boyd, & Hamby, 1995), and increased parents' satisfaction with services (Applequist & Bailey, 2000). Family-centered services have received strong support from federal legislation and policy. The Individuals with Disabilities Education Act (IDEA, 1997) mandated that assessments and interventions for young children with disabilities attend to families' capacities for supporting their children's development and be carried out within

*College of Education, Division of Curriculum and Instruction, Arizona State University, Chandler, AZ, USA.

authentic and typical learning experiences (Shonkoff, Hauser-Cram, Krauss, & Upshur, 1992).

In spite of federal legislation and research demonstrating that family-centered services are beneficial for child development, its implementation remains elusive (Bruder, 2000). Much of the research has not been translated into meaningful intervention plans and a gap remains between methods professionals use to support parents and actual family-centered practice (Blue-Banning et al., 2004). Professionals may continue to see their role as telling parents what is wrong with their child and family and what needs to be done to correct the deficits (Bernheimer, Gallimore, & Weisner, 1990; Dunst, 1985). Parents are not seen as equal partners and professionals maintain control (Blue-Banning, Turnbull, & Pereira, 2000). But even when plans are well thought out, many families fail to implement or to sustain the plans (Bernheimer & Keogh, 1995). Sometimes families do not conform to professional suggestions because the intervention plans are at odds with family values or do not fit into the family's daily routines (Bernheimer & Keogh, 1995).

The study presented here developed a family-centered early problem intervention program based on an ecocultural framework in which the family's life style is central in constructing intervention plans (Bernheimer et al., 1990; Dunst, 2002; Dunst, Trivette, & Deal, 1988; Gallimore, Weisner, Bernheimer, Guthrie, & Nihira, 1993b; Weisner & Gallimore, 1994). In this view, intervention is based on a partnership between families and professionals who work together to devise and implement plans (Dunst, 2002). Parents are empowered to make informed decisions and take control over their lives as professionals impart information, skills, and knowledge to the families.

The critical units of analysis in ecocultural theory are daily routines and activity settings (Bernheimer & Keogh, 1995; Gallimore, Goldenberg, & Weisner, 1993a; Weisner & Gallimore, 1994). Daily routines and activities provide children with opportunities to learn and develop through modeling, joint production, apprenticeship, and other forms of mediated social learning that are embedded in goal-directed interactions. Children's activities settings are the architecture of everyday life, familiar parts of a family's day (e.g., preparing meals, cleaning up, getting ready for school) (Bernheimer & Keogh, 1995). Parents use activities of daily routines as opportunities for teaching; for example, when they have children count dishes and silverware as they help to set the table. All families construct daily routines to meet the needs of family members although families differ in the ways routines are organized (Gallimore et al., 1993). The activities children engage in as an ordinary part of their daily lives have a profound impact on the cognitive and communicative functions they develop.

The purpose of this study was to examine whether active parent engagement in selecting and using routine-based activities has a positive effect on children's language and appropriate behavior development. The hypothesis was that parents are more likely to implement an intervention when it focuses on child issues of concern, and when they can select activities that are compatible with their goals and fit the family's daily routines. The assessments and interventions were conducted using a professional–parent partnership in which parents conducted weekly assessments of their children and selected activities that they believed would promote their children's language and behavior development. The goal was to empower parents to construct meaningful interventions for the child within the framework of daily family life. It allowed families to focus on helping their children develop the competencies they believed the child was ready for and needed.

METHOD

Subjects

Forty-one children (23 boys, 18 girls), ages 3–5 years ($M = 4.15$, $SD = .69$), were selected from three developmental pre-schools in the Phoenix metropolitan area. Children's ethnicity varied: Anglo American ($n = 34$), Hispanic ($n = 3$), African American ($n = 2$), Asian ($n = 1$), Native American ($n = 1$). This distribution reflects the demographics of the State of Arizona. All children spoke English as a primary language.

Subjects were identified as being at-risk for language and behavior problems because they exhibited at least one of the following two characteristics: (a) scoring at least one standard deviation below the mean on the Test of Early Language Development—Third Edition (TELD-3; Hresko, Reid, & Hammill, 1999) (i.e., Spoken Language Quotient < 85) and (b) scoring at least one standard deviation above the mean on the intensity scale of the Eyberg Child Behavior Inventory (ECBI; Ebyerg & Pincus, 1999) (i.e., intensity T-score > 60). Thirty-five children had only one problem (language = 24, behavior = 11), while 6 children demonstrated both characteristics. Individual child's language and/or behavior problems were unidentified because the standardized measures used for subject selection in this study summarized one's overall performance rather than specific problems.

Both language and behavior problems were assessed because they have been found to co-occur frequently. Forty to seventy percent of students with behavior disorders have been found to have concurrent language disorders (Donahue, Cole, & Hartas, 1994; Harrison, Gunter, Lee, & Reed, 1996; Sanger, Maag, & Shapera, 1994). Similarly, children referred for language problems have been shown to have significantly higher rates of inappropriate behaviors (Camarata, Hughes, & Ruhl, 1988; Ruhl, Hughes, & Camarata, 1992; Ylvisaker & Feeney, 1994).

Subjects were randomly assigned to a control and an intervention group. The control group included 19 children (9 boys, 10 girls), whereas the intervention group consisted of 22 children (14 boys, 8 girls). Children in the control group participated only in the pre- and post-testing phases of the study. Their parents did not receive training and were not required to attend regular meetings or submit weekly and monthly assessments of their children. Parents of children in the intervention group, however, were trained to use the Child Behavior and Language Assessment (CBLA). Parents were taught to complete weekly assessments of their children by recording positive and negative events and to submit monthly summaries to project staff. At the beginning of the intervention, parents completed the Problem Identification Checklist in the CBLA. The parent rated their child on health, motor skills, behavior, and receptive and expressive language items as 1 = need professional help, 2 = need some help with this problem, 3 = watch carefully and make notes, and 4 = no problem. The parent then selected activities in the Activities section of the CBLA and used the Problems Analysis Log to keep track of whether the activities helped. As parents conducted the assessment and defined the problems, parent denial of developmental issues did not become an issue.

In addition to using the CBLA, parents of the children in the intervention group participated in an ongoing "parent–professional dyad" relationship with project staff. Each parent was assigned a parent partner, a graduate student majoring in special education or speech and language pathology. The parent and parent partner met bi-monthly until the child matriculated into kindergarten or first grade. During these meetings, the pair reviewed the data parents had recorded, discussed problems parents wanted to resolve, and selected strategies for resolving the problems. They evaluated the effects of implementing the strategies parents had selected and when appropriate moved on to solving the next problem.

The underlying framework for the parent-professional partnership is a problem solving process that emphasizes parent choice and action within a collaborative relationship between parents and professionals. This relationship allows professional-parent teams to set goals and to jointly make programmatic decisions. Problem solving followed a sequence of stages: problem identification and clarification, problem analysis, goal setting, planning strategies and implementation, evaluation of outcome data, and consideration of need to modify plans.

Materials

The CBLA, based on the Child Health Status Assessment (CHSA; Bryan & Burstein, 2000), was the mainstay of the parent assessment and intervention. The CBLA has two parts: (1) a gated assessment of children's language and behavior and (2) routine-based activities for promoting language and appropriate behavior.

Gated Assessment

The gated assessment is nested in a Daily Planner, a calendar-notebook for recording family activities, a record of the child's health and development status, records of medical or education events, logs for tracking conversations with professionals, and the gated assessment.

At Gate 1, parents weekly record baseline data on typical activities, memorable events and milestones and their concerns related to the child's health, behavior, and language. When parents identify a problem they record the antecedent and consequent events surrounding the occurrence of the problem. If the problem is perceived by the parent as significant and persistent at Gate 1, parents move to Gate 2.

At Gate 2, the parent follows a series of problem-solving steps that include instructions on how to select strategies from the routine-based activities section, and how to record their child's responsiveness to the selected activities.

Parents move to Gate 3 when children are not responsive to parent intervention strategies or when events call for immediate responses. Gate 3 provides information on how to contact educational, psychological, and health resources.

Routine-Based Activities

These empirically derived activities are designed to promote children's language and behavior skills, as well as pre-reading and early literacy skills. Most of the activities are presented as part of typical daily routines (e.g., ways to promote language development and appropriate behavior during meals, watching television, bedtime, car trips, shopping). Additional sections include activities for promoting independence and self-help, getting along with siblings, phonemic awareness and pre-literacy skills. Information is included about why and how to establish routines, and space is provided for tracking the effectiveness of the activities.

Measures

Test of Early Language Development—Third Edition (Hresko et al., 1999)

The TELD-3 is an individually administered, standardized instrument for assessing receptive, expressive, and overall spoken language in young children aged 2–7 years. It has two forms (A and B), each of which contains 76 items of semantic and syntax questions. The TELD-3 produces scores with a mean of 100 and standard deviation of 15 for each subtest and the overall composite score. Reliabilities of the TELD-3 were reported: internal consistency (.80–.97), alternate form (.79–.94), test–retest (.80–.94), and inter-rater (.99). Criterion validity showed that the TELD-3 was highly correlated with a variety of widely recognized measures of language, academic ability, and intelligence.

Eyberg Child Behavior Inventory (Eyberg & Pincus, 1999)

The ECBI is a 36-item, parent-rating scale that assesses typical externalizing or conduct problem behaviors reported by parents of children and adolescents aged 2–16 years. Each behavior is rated on two scales: a 7-point intensity scale (1 = never, 7 = always) that indicates how often the behaviors occur and a yes-no problem scale that identifies whether the child's behavior is problematic or not for the parent. The ECBI's reliabilities were established: internal consistency (.88–.95), test–retest (.86–.88), and inter-rater (.79–.86). Its criterion validity was assessed and found to be acceptable (Eyberg & Pincus, 1999).

Procedures

Children and parents were administered the TELD-3 and ECBI respectively at the beginning (December 1999) and end (May 2002) of the project. A team of a psychologist/psychometrist, speech and language pathologist, and graduate assistant scheduled and tested the children at Arizona State University or at their homes when necessary. Consent forms were read to parents at the first test session. Parents were told that they could withdraw from the study at any time, that all information was confidential and that their relationship with the pre-school was unaffected by their decision.

After signing the consent form, parents completed a form on demographic variables (e.g., child's age, gender, primary language spoken at home). The assessments were then administered to the child and parent separately in different rooms.

Parents were given feedback on their child's performance and the opportunity to discuss any concerns they might have about their child in a third meeting within two weeks of the second assessment session. Additional information was provided in response to parents' questions and requests for information or referrals.

Data Analysis

Descriptive analyses were first conducted on both measures to summarize data. One-way analyses of covariance (ANCOVAs) were then used to examine whether groups differed on post-test scores on each measure, using pre-test scores as a covariate. Prior to conducting the ANCOVA, a preliminary analysis evaluating the homogeneity-of-slopes assumption examined whether the relationship between the pre-test and post-test differed significantly as a function of group assignment.

RESULTS

Results of the homogeneity-of-slopes analysis showed no significant interactions between pre-test and group assignment on any measure, indicating that ANCOVAs were appropriate for group comparisons. Means and standard deviations of the pretest and post-test on the TELD-3 and ECBI are presented in Table 1.

ANCOVA indicated significant group differences on the TELD-3 Receptive Language, $F(1, 38) = 4.68$, $p = .037$, partial $\eta^2 = .11$, Expressive Language, $F(1, 38) = 7.99$, $p = .007$, partial $\eta^2 = .17$, as well as Spoken Language Quotient, $F(1, 38) = 8.06$, $p = .007$, partial $\eta^2 = .18$. Children in the intervention group scored higher than children in the control group on all three categories.

Statistically significant differences were also found on the ECBI Intensity Scale, $F(1, 38) = 6.37$, $p = .016$,

Table 1. Means and Standard Deviations of Pre-test and Post-test on the Test of Early Language Development—Third Edition and Eyberg Child Behavior Inventory

Measure and Variable	Control Group (n = 19)		Intervention Group (n = 22)	
	Pre-test	Post-test	Pre-test	Post-test
Test of Early Language Development—Third Edition				
Receptive language quotient	103.6 (22.9)	102.9 (15.5)	101.3 (23.5)	109.4 (11.4)
Expressive language quotient	97.6 (27.7)	90.6 (17.3)	98.0 (19.6)	98.9 (12.6)
Spoken language quotient	101.7 (29.3)	96.3 (18.8)	100.7 (24.7)	104.9 (13.2)
Eyberg Child Behavior Inventory				
Intensity T-score	53.2 (5.6)	52.5 (4.8)	54.7 (7.4)	49.9 (6.9)
Problem T-score	46.9 (4.5)	47.4 (5.6)	49.1 (6.3)	45.7 (6.3)

Note: Values are means (SD).

partial η^2 = .14, and Problem Scale, F (1, 38) = 5.15, p = .029, partial η^2 = .12. Parents of the children in the intervention group scored significantly lower (i.e., better child behavior) than parents of the children in the control group on both scales.

DISCUSSION

As hypothesized, the family-centered intervention that involved parents in weekly assessments and daily routine activities was effective in promoting young children's language and behavior performance. On the TELD-3, results showed that children in the intervention group outperformed their peers in the control group on both subtests and the overall composite score. Similarly, parents who participated in parent–professional collaboration reported better behavior outcomes at the end of the project than parents in the control group. Investigation of the effect sizes ranging from .11–.18 indicated a moderate to strong relationship between the intervention and child performance. Traditionally, η^2 values of .01, .06, and .14 are regarded as small, medium, and large effect sizes, respectively (Green, Salkind, & Akey, 2000).

The family-centered intervention model appears to be a viable approach to enhancing at-risk pre-school children's language development and appropriate behavior. The family-centered intervention's emphasis on the parent–professional collaboration/partnership is empowering. Parents are empowered to establish the desired performance of their children, determine the characteristics and severity of a problem, and select appropriate problem-solving strategies based on the individual child's unique needs. Professionals serve as facilitators who impart needed knowledge and resources. In addition, when conducting weekly assessments, preparing monthly summaries, and attending regular meetings is part of a family–professional collaboration, parents are likely to be motivated to record children's trajectory of development with scrutiny and follow through with deliberate action. Nonetheless, sustaining parent participation over time was a significant issue and we did experience attrition in the condition where we met monthly. What worked best for maintaining parent participation was having graduate students assigned to families who met with families at their homes, or other designated sites, at a time named by the family. For example, one mother brought the whole family and they met at a local restaurant. It was family night out! This mother was having problems establishing independence from her family. The graduate assistant and parent would review the parent's Problems Analysis Log and talk about how well the activity worked and whether it was time to move onto another issue or try something else. This one-on-one

relationship worked very well even when the extended family showed up. As a staff, we met weekly to make sure we could support the graduate assistants and monitor what was happening.

This study presents a positive example of translating research into practice. Research generated by an ecocultural theoretical framework on early prevention/intervention was built into the program. However, the study has potential limitations with regard to subject recruitment which might affect its implementation. First, in public pre-schools (e.g., Head Start), children who have been identified with learning or behavior difficulties typically have already demonstrated obvious developmental problems. These children have Individualized Family Service Plans (IFSPs)/Individualized Education Programs (IEPs) that are responsive to family and child needs. It may well be that the activities in the family intervention program described here would enhance these efforts. But the primary concern in this study was children at risk who were less likely to be identified and provided services. These children often fall below the identification radar screen and are not identified until they show poor progress in early reading. Yet the results of this study show that significant gains can be made when families are involved in early intervention. Of course, until tested, it cannot be stated that the language progress children demonstrated would translate into fewer early literacy delays. Second, once children reach 3 years of age, special services are provided under IEPs and the relational emphasis is shifted from child–families to child–school. Typical family involvement consists of open houses, parent–teacher conferences, and informal parent–teacher communication. Yet, the study reported here demonstrated the advantage of active family participation and professional collaboration. IFSPs should be the norm through kindergarten, and perhaps beyond. Another limitation is related to the generalization of the results of this study. Although a sample size of 15 cases per group is large enough to yield valid results in ANOVA (Green et al. 2000), generalization of the results of this study should be cautious due to potential non-normal population distributions. Future research may need to include a larger sample size to increase statistical power.

In summary, the results of this study suggest that family-centered intervention is an effective method for empowering parents to identify and implement concrete solutions to their children's problems, especially when done as part of a professional collaboration. Intervention plans that are tailored to the individual family's cultural values and beliefs effectively meet the IDEA mandate to include parents in decision making of their children's education.

REFERENCES

Applequist, K. L., & Bailey, D. B. (2000). Navajo caregivers' perceptions of early intervention services. *Journal of Early Intervention, 23,* 47–61.

Baroff, G. S. (1986). *Mental retardation: Nature, cause, and management* (2nd ed.). New York: Hemisphere.

Bernheimer, L. P., Gallimore, R., & Weisner, T. S. (1990). Ecocultural theory as a context for the individual family service plan. *Journal of Early Intervention, 14,* 219–233.

Bernheimer, L. P., & Keogh, B. K. (1995). Weaving interventions into the fabrics of everyday life: An approach to family assessment. *Topics in Early Childhood Special Education, 15,* 415–433.

Blasco, P. M., Hrncir, E. J., & Blasco, P. A. (1990). The contribution of maternal involvement to mastery performance in infants with cerebral palsy. *Journal of Early Intervention, 14,* 161–174.

Blue-Banning, M., Summers, J. A., Frankland, H. C., Nelson, L. L., & Beegle, G. (2004). Dimensions of family and professional partnership: Constructive guidelines for collaboration. *Exceptional Children, 70,* 167–184.

Blue-Banning, M., Turnbull, A. P., & Pereira, L. (2000). Group action planning as a support strategy for Hispanic families: Parent and professional perspectives. *Mental Retardation, 38,* 262–275.

Bruder, M. B. (2000). Family-centered early intervention: Clarifying our values for the new millennium. *Topics in Early Childhood Special Education, 20,* 105–115.

Bryan, T., & Burstein, K. (2000). Parents as partners in the medical home: Parents monitor their child's health status. *Exceptional Parent, 30,* 104–110.

Camarata, S. M., Hughes, C. A., & Ruhl, K. L. (1988). Mild/moderate behaviorally disordered students: A population at risk for language disorders. *Language, Speech, and Hearing Services in the Schools, 19,* 191–200.

Donahue, M., Cole, D., & Hartas, D. (1994). Links between language and emotional/behavioral disorders. *Education and Treatment of Children, 17,* 244–254.

Dunst, C. J. (1985). Rethinking early intervention. *Analysis and Intervention in Developmental Disabilities, 5,* 165–201.

Dunst, C. J. (2002). Family-centered practices: Birth through high school. *Journal of Special Education, 36,* 139–147.

Dunst, C. J., Trivette, C. M., & Deal, A. G. (1988). *Enabling and empowering families: Principles and guidelines for practice.* Cambridge, MA: Brookline Books.

Eyberg, S., & Pincus, D. (1999). *Eyberg Child Behavior Inventory & Sutter-Eyberg Student Behavior Inventory* (Rev. ed.). Odessa, FL: Psychological Assessment Resources.

Gallimore, R., Goldenberg, C. N., & Weisner, T. S. (1993a). The social construction and subjective reality of activity settings: Implications for community psychology. *American Journal of Community Psychology, 21,* 537–559.

Gallimore, R., Weisner, T. S., Bernheimer, L. P., Guthrie, D., & Nihira, K. (1993b). Family responses to young children with developmental delays: Accommodation activity in ecological and cultural context. *American Journal of Mental Retardation, 98,* 185–206.

Green, S. B., Salkind, N. J., & Akey, T. M. (2000). *Using SPSS for windows: Analyzing and understand data* (2nd ed.). Upper Saddle River, NJ: Prentice Hall.

Harrison, J., Gunter, P. L., Lee, J., & Reed, T. M. (1996). Teacher instructional language and negative reinforcement: A conceptual framework for working with students with emotional and behavioral disorders. *Education and Treatment of Children, 19,* 183–196.

Hresko, W. P., Reid, D. K., & Hammill, D. D. (1999). *Test of early language development* (3rd ed.). Austin, TX: Pro-Ed.

Individuals with Disabilities Education Act Amendments of 1997, 20 U.S.C. § 1400 et seq.

Odom, S. L., & Karnes, M. S. (1988). *Early intervention for infants and children with handicaps: An empirical base.* Baltimore: Paul H. Brookes.

Ruhl, K. L., Hughes, C. A., & Camarata, S. M. (1992). Analysis of the expressive and receptive language characteristics of emotionally handicapped students served in public school settings. *Journal of Childhood Communication Disorders, 14,* 165–176.

Sanger, D., Maag, J., & Shapera, N. (1994). Language disorders among youngsters with emotional and behavioral problems. *Intervention in School and Clinic, 30,* 103–106.

Shonkoff, J. P., Hauser-Cram, P., Krauss, M. W., & Upshur, C. C. (1992). Development of infants with disabilities and their families. *Monographs of the Society for Research in Child Development, 57,* 1–163.

Trivette, C. M., Dunst, C. J., Boyd, K., & Hamby, D. W. (1995). Family-oriented program models, help-giving practices, and parental control appraisals. *Exceptional Children, 62,* 237–248.

Weisner, T. S., & Gallimore, R. (1994). Ecocultural studies of families adapting to childhood developmental delays: Unique features, defining, differences, and applied implications. In I. M. Leskimon (Ed.), *Family in focus: New perspectives on early childhood special education* (pp. 11–25). Jyvaskyla, Finland: University of Jyraskyla.

Ylvisaker, M., & Feeney, T. J. (1994). Communication and behavior: Collaboration between speech-language pathologists and behavioral psychologists. *Topics in Language Disorders, 15,* 37–54.

1.02

2-FACTOR PRE AND POSTTEST CONTROL GROUP DESIGN

Problem-Solving Skills Training and Relationship Therapy in the Treatment of Antisocial Child Behavior

Alan E. Kazdin,* Karen Esveldt-Dawson,* Nancy H. French,* and Alan S. Unis*

ABSTRACT: The present investigation evaluated the effects of cognitive–behavioral problem-solving skills training (PSST) and nondirective relationship therapy (RT) for the treatment of antisocial child behavior. Psychiatric inpatient children ($N = 56$, ages 7–13) were assigned randomly either to PSST, RT, or to a treatment–contact control condition (in which children met individually with a therapist but did not engage in specific activities designed to alter antisocial behavior). Children were hospitalized during the period in which treatment was administered and discharged thereafter. The PSST condition led to significantly greater decreases in externalizing and aggressive behaviors and in overall behavioral problems at home and at school and to increases in prosocial behaviors and in overall adjustment than the RT and contact-control conditions. These effects were evident immediately after treatment and at a 1-year follow-up. The RT and control children did not consistently improve over the treatment and follow-up periods. Comparisons with nonclinical (normative) levels of functioning revealed that a significantly higher proportion of PSST children, compared with those in other conditions, fell within the normative range for prosocial behavior at posttreatment and at follow-up. Even so, the majority of PSST children and almost all RT and control children remained outside the normative range of deviant behavior. The implications of the results for further research for antisocial youth are highlighted.

Antisocial behavior among children and adolescents is a significant clinical and social problem. The significance derives from findings that antisocial behaviors (particularly aggressive acts) are relatively prevalent among community samples, serve as the basis for one-third to one-half of clinical referrals among children,

*Western Psychiatric Institute and Clinic, University of Pittsburgh School of Medicine

Completion of this research was supported by Grant MH35408 and Research Scientist Development Award MH00353 from the National Institute of Mental Health. The efforts and support of several highly skilled staff, including Danielle Baum, Lisa DeCarolis, Louise Moore,

Stephanie Fuderich, Antoinette Rodgers, Debra Colbus, Todd Seigel, Rosanna Sherick, and Sherry Wilson, were pivotal to completion of this project. The authors are also very grateful to Thomas M. Achenbach and Philip C. Kendall, who provided valuable comments and suggestions on an earlier draft.

are relatively stable over the course of development, often portend major dysfunction in adulthood (e.g., criminal behavior, alcoholism, antisocial personality), and are likely to be transmitted to one's offspring (see Kazdin, in press; Loeber, 1985; Robins, 1981; Rutter & Giller, 1983). Several treatments have been implemented to alter antisocial behaviors, including diverse forms of individual and group therapy, family therapy, behavior therapy, residential treatment, pharmacotherapy, and a variety of community-based treatments (see Kazdin, 1985). To date, few treatments have been shown to alter antisocial behavior in clinical samples; none has been shown to controvert the poor long-term prognosis.

One of the most promising approaches is parent management-training, which has been shown to produce therapeutic change in children with aggressive and other antisocial behaviors (see G. Patterson, 1982). Unfortunately, parent management-training is not a viable option for many clinical cases when there is severe family dysfunction, parent psychopathology, and socioeconomic disadvantage (e.g., Dumas & Wahler, 1983) or, of course, when there is no available parent who can participate. Severity of the child's or parents' dysfunction, removal of the child from the home (e.g., due to abuse or neglect), or inability or unwillingness of the parents to participate in treatment obviously restrict the use of parent- or family-based approaches.

Other treatment options that focus on the resources of the child need to be considered. Among the more promising approaches are cognitive–behavioral treatments that train the child to use problem-solving skills in situations where interpersonal conflict and antisocial behavior emerge. Several studies have pointed to deficits in interpersonal cognitive problem-solving skills (e.g., generating solutions to problems), in level of cognitive development (e.g., moral reasoning), and in maladaptive cognitive strategies (e.g., impulsivity, attributional set) among aggressive children (see Dodge, 1985; Kendall & Braswell, 1985). Cognitive–behavioral treatments that focus on these processes have produced therapeutic change (e.g., Arbuthnot & Gordon, 1986; Kendall & Braswell, 1982; Lochman, Burch, Curry & Lampron, 1984). However, few studies have utilized clinic samples whose dysfunction was severe or have demonstrated changes on measures related to adjustment at home or at school (see Gresham, 1985; Kazdin, 1985). Thus, the clinical utility of these techniques for antisocial children warrants further attention.

Another approach that warrants evaluation is *nondirective psychotherapy*, a technique that focuses on the development of a close interpersonal relationship with the child. Treatment is designed to provide a corrective emotional experience and to permit self-exploration and the expression of feelings (C. Patterson, 1979; Reisman, 1973). Relationship-based treatment is one of the most frequently used variations of child counseling and is advocated for a broad range of child clinical problems, including antisocial behavior (C. Patterson, 1979). Although a few studies of individual or group nondirective therapy have shown improvements in adjustment among antisocial delinquent youths (e.g., Persons, 1966; Redfering, 1972), other studies have shown little or no change (Alexander & Parsons, 1973; Feldman, Caplinger, & Wodarski, 1983). Given the paucity of controlled studies with clinical populations, the technique warrants further study.

The present study evaluated the effectiveness of cognitive-behavioral problem-solving skills training (PSST) and nondirective relationship therapy (RT) for seriously disturbed antisocial children. The children were all referred to treatment for antisocial behaviors, primarily for aggression, and were hospitalized on an acute-care service. All children participated in a general ward program during the period in which they were also assigned randomly to one of three conditions in the present study. Children in the two treatment groups (PSST or RT) received individual sessions with a therapist while in the hospital. A control group was included in which children also received individual sessions with a therapist but did not engage in specific therapeutic processes designed to alter antisocial behavior.

METHOD

Subjects

Child Characteristics

The subjects consisted of 56 children (11 girls and 45 boys). The children were all inpatients of a psychiatric facility where children are hospitalized for 2–3 months. The facility houses 22 children (ages 5–13) at any one time. The children are admitted for acute disorders, including highly aggressive and destructive behavior, suicidal or homicidal ideation or behavior, and deteriorating family conditions.

Children were included if they (a) were referred for treatment for their antisocial behavior (including fighting, unmanageability at home or at school, stealing, running away, truancy, or related antisocial behaviors) as identified at intake assessment; (b) were rated by their parent at or above the 98th percentile on either the Aggression or Delinquency scale of the Child Behavior Checklist; (c) were 7–13 years of age; (d) received a full-scale Wechsler Intelligence Scale for Children–Revised (WISC-R; Wechsler, 1974) IQ score of 70 or above; (e) showed no evidence of neurological impairment, uncontrolled seizures, or dementia; and (f) were not receiving psychotropic medication.

Children were considered if there was no parent or guardian who could participate in treatment with the child.[1] Children were eligible if they were not in the custody of a parent or relative, if they were likely to be placed outside of the home (e.g., in foster care) after hospitalization, or if special family circumstances (e.g., excessive distance from the hospital) precluded parent contact with the treatment facility. Consent to participate was obtained from both child and parent (or legal guardian).

The children who met screening criteria ranged in age from 7 to 13 years ($M = 10.9$) and in full-scale WISC-R IQ score from 70 to 133 ($M = 92.9$). Forty-three (76.8%) children were white; 13 (23.2%) were black. Diagnoses of the children, based on *Diagnostic and Statistical Manual of Mental Disorders* (DSM-III; American Psychiatric Association, 1980) criteria, were obtained from direct interviews with the children and their parent(s) immediately before admission and psychiatric evaluation after the child had been admitted. On the basis of these sources of information, two staff members independently completed diagnoses for each child. Agreement on principal Axis I diagnosis yielded a kappa of .76. For any disagreement, the case was discussed to reach a consensus on the appropriate diagnosis. Principal Axis I diagnoses included conduct disorder ($n = 32$), attention deficit disorder ($n = 2$), depression ($n = 6$), adjustment disorder ($n = 4$), and other mental disorders ($n = 12$). For the entire sample, 39 (69.6%) of the children received a principal or secondary Axis I diagnosis of conduct disorder.

Parent Characteristics

The primary caretakers of these children included biological mothers ($n = 43$); step, foster, or adoptive mothers ($n = 6$); or other relatives ($n = 2$). They ranged in age from 24 to 55 years ($M = 33.1$). Five children (8.9%) were in the custody of youth service agencies and did not come from families; 25 children (44.6%) came from two-parent families; and 26 children (46.4%) came from single-parent families. Head-of-household social class, calculated with the Hollingshead and Redlich (1958) two-factor index, yielded the following breakdown: Class V (18.8%), Class IV (45.8%), Class III (27.1%), Class II (6.3%), and Class I (2.1%). Estimated monthly income for families ranged from $0 to $500 to more than $2,500 (median range = $500 to $1,000). Fifty-one percent of the families were on social assistance.

Parent psychiatric diagnoses were obtained by administering a standardized interview individually to each parent within 2–3 weeks of the child's admission. The Schedule for Affective Disorders and Schizophrenia (SADS-L; Endicott & Spitzer, 1978) was administered to measure current and lifetime parent psychopathology. Of the mothers, 62.2% met criteria for current mental disorder; 78.4%, for past mental dis-

order. Of the 18 fathers available for assessment, 50.0% met criteria for current mental disorder; 66.7%, for past mental disorder. Major depression and substance abuse were the most common diagnoses for mothers and fathers, respectively.

Assessment

The goals of treatment were to reduce antisocial behavior and to improve the children's functioning at home and at school. Consequently, treatment was evaluated with parent and teacher measures that were administered before and after treatment and up to a 1-year follow-up. Pretreatment measures were completed when the child was admitted to the hospital. Posttreatment measures were completed 1 month after the final treatment session after the child had returned home to permit parents and community teachers to base their evaluations on a sufficient sample of the child's behavior. Follow-up assessments were also conducted 4, 8, and 12 months after treatment had been completed. In addition, at the end of the final treatment session, therapists and children were asked to evaluate treatment and the progress that was made.

Parent Checklist Ratings

Parents completed the Child Behavior Checklist (CBCL; Achenbach & Edelbrock, 1983). The measure includes 118 items, each rated on a 0–2-point scale. The items constitute multiple behavior-problem scales (first-order factors) derived from factor analyses that were completed separately for boys and girls in different age groups (e.g., 6–11 years, 12–16 years). For the present investigation, the broad-band and summary scales were used because they are applicable to boys and girls of all age groups.

Two broad-band behavior problem scales (second-order factors) are Internalizing and Externalizing, which reflect inward-directed (e.g., schizophrenia, depression) versus outward-directed (e.g., aggression, delinquency) problems. The Total Behavior Problem score includes items loading on the first-order factors plus the items that do not load on specific scales. Of primary interest for present purposes was the impact of treatment on the Externalizing scale, which includes a broad array of antisocial behaviors (e.g., fighting, destroying property). In addition to the behavior problem scales, the CBCL includes three a priori social-competence scales: the Activities scale (child partici-

---

[1]Approximately 75% of the children in the psychiatric facility who met screening criteria did not have an available parent who could participate in treatment. The remaining 25% who did have an available parent participated in a separate project investigating the effects of parent management-training.

pation in activities), the Social scale (child interactions with others), and the School scale (child's academic performance at school), which together yield a Total Social Competence score.

Teacher Checklist Ratings

To evaluate performance at school, the children's teachers completed the School Behavior Checklist (SBCL-Form A2 Miller, 1977). The measure includes 96 items that assess behaviors among children 7–13 years old. Behavioral characteristics are rated by the child's teacher as true or false. Factor analyses have yielded six scales that include Low Need Achievement, Aggression, Anxiety, Academic Disability, Hostile Isolation, and Extraversion. Of these scales, the Aggression scale was selected because it reflects the central focus of treatment. In addition to this scale, the overall summary scale, Total Disability, was examined. This scale reflects a summary score of behavioral symptoms included in the six scales. The SBCL also includes five additional items in which the teacher rates, on 9-point Likert scales, the child's intellectual ability, academic skills and performance, emotional adjustment, and personal appeal. These ratings were summed and utilized for evaluation as the teachers' global ratings of school adjustment.

The CBCL and SBCL were selected for several reasons. First, the measures sample a broad range of childhood dysfunction, including aggressive behaviors and other antisocial behaviors that served as the basis for clinical referral. Second, each measure includes facets of prosocial behavior. The CBCL includes three social-competence scales; the SBCL includes overall ratings of school adjustment. Scales reflecting prosocial behaviors and adjustment were of interest because treatment was devoted to the development of prosocial behaviors as well as to the reduction of antisocial behavior. Finally, both the CBCL and SBCL have been carefully evaluated with clinic and nonclinic populations. Transformed scores facilitate interpretation of the measure in relation to normal (nonclinic) same-age peers.

Therapist Evaluations

Immediately after the final treatment sessions, therapists completed the Therapist Evaluation Inventory (TEI), a 15-item scale constructed for the present study and designed to evaluate progress made by the child. The measure includes two a priori subscales. The first subscale included 6 items in which the therapist evaluated the child's progress in treatment. The items, each rated on a 5-point Likert scale, required the therapist to evaluate how receptive the child was to treatment, how well the child grasped the strategies or approach, and how much was learned by

the child in the sessions. The second subscale included 9 items that focused on the likelihood that the child would show improvements in the future. Therapists rated the extent to which the child was likely to improve at home and at school, the degree of favorable impact that therapy was likely to have on the child's life, how well treatment affected the child's ability to handle interpersonal problems outside of treatment, and how well the child would be able to exert self-control. The purpose of the TEI was to examine the relation between the therapist's evaluations and the child's posttreatment functioning.[2]

Child Evaluations

At the end of the final treatment session, children completed a Child Evaluation Inventory (CEI). The measure included 19 items, each rated by the child on a 5-point scale, that constituted two subscales. The first subscale included 11 items in which the child was asked to evaluate his or her progress in treatment. The items were similar to those on the TEI. The questions in the child form were reworded and simplified but covered the same concepts (e.g., how treatment helped the child in handling problems, in interacting with others, and so on). The second subscale was designed to measure acceptability of treatment. Acceptability refers to judgments about the extent to which the treatment procedures are appropriate, fair, reasonable, and enjoyable to the patient. Eight items were included in this subscale and were drawn, in part, from previous work on the assessment and evaluation of acceptability of treatments for children (e.g., Kazdin, 1984). Items asked the child to evaluate how much they enjoyed treatment, looked forward to coming to the sessions, did not want the sessions to be over, and felt the sessions were interesting and fun.

Treatment Administration

Because all children were inpatients, the treatment and control conditions of the present study were superimposed upon the general milieu program.[3] This program included a variety of routine ward activities and day-to-day contact with direct-care workers and other staff. The ward activities and structure were directed toward care and management of the children rather than toward specific regimens to treat conduct disorders or other dysfunctions. Yet, time-out and seclusion contingencies were included routinely to manage uncontrollable behavior. There was no other general ward program (e.g., token economy) as part

---

[2] Copies of the Therapist Evaluation Inventory and the Child Evaluation Inventory are available from the authors.
[3] The term *milieu* here is used to denote a general ward-management program rather than milieu therapy.

of the management of the children, although there were structured routines, staff praise, and occasional loss of privileges. Therapeutic treatments, when deemed advisable for individual children (e.g., medication trials, psychotherapy, individualized behavioral programs) were superimposed on the general ward program. However, for all children in the present project, individualized programs or other specific treatments were not provided beyond those reported.

Treatment Conditions

Children who met criteria for participation were assigned randomly to one of four therapists and three conditions.

Problem-solving Skills Training

Children (*n* = 20) assigned to this condition received PSST, which was administered individually in 20 sessions. Sessions lasted approximately 45 min and were administered 2–3 times per week. Treatment was completed while the child was in the hospital. After completion of the sessions, the child was discharged. Therapy was modeled after the treatment procedures developed by Spivack, Platt, and Shure (1976) and by Kendall, Padawer, Zupan, and Braswell (in Kendall & Braswell, 1985). The modifications were made to emphasize interpersonal situations with significant others (e.g., parents, siblings, teachers, peers) and to include opportunities for individualizing content and addressing referral concerns and situations in which the child had engaged in antisocial and oppositional behavior. The treatment combines cognitive and behavioral techniques to teach problem-solving skills (e.g., generating alternative solutions, means–ends and consequential thinking, and taking the perspective of others) that the child can use to manage interpersonal situations.

Training began initially by teaching the child to use the problem-solving approach with academic tasks (selected at grade level) and games (e.g., checkers). The tasks became increasingly complex over the course of sessions. The bulk of treatment was devoted to enacting interpersonal situations through role playing where the child applied the approach (i.e., invoking specific problem-solving steps). In each session, practice, modeling, role playing, corrective feedback, and social reinforcement were used to develop problem-solving skills. Response cost (loss of chips) was also used for errors in carrying out the problem-solving approach (e.g., skipping a step). The chips, provided at the beginning of each session, could be exchanged for small toys and prizes at the end of each session. As part of treatment, children were assigned homework in which they identified situations in their daily lives in which the problem-solving approach could be

applied and eventually utilized the approach by themselves in real-life situations. Chips were also earned for completing homework assignments, based on information obtained through the child's report, on interviews, and on reenactments of homework situations within the sessions.

Relationship Therapy

Children (*n* = 19) in this condition received 20 individual treatment sessions of nondirective relationship therapy. The focus of the individual sessions, each lasting approximately 45 min, was on developing a close relationship with the child and providing empathy, unconditional positive regard, and warmth. Therapists focused on helping the child to express feelings. Therapy was modeled after principles and procedures outlined by C. Patterson (1979) and Reisman (1973). There were some important differences in the administration of RT that departed from administration with adults. Activities and play materials were available for early sessions so that child and therapist could talk in the context of playing a game. In later sessions, various themes were discussed, including interpersonal situations involving peers, parent(s), teachers, siblings, and individualized problem areas (based on referral concerns). Children in RT also received chips based on completion of their sessions, and these could be exchanged for prizes.

The games and activities used in early sessions, the emphasis on interpersonal themes, and the focus on individualized problem areas were similar across PSST and RT. In PSST, the games and tasks were the focus for teaching specific problem-solving skills; in RT, they were subservient to the goals of establishing a trusting relationship and discussing the child's feelings.

Treatment-contact Control

To partially control for repeated therapist contact and attendance at special sessions outside of the usual ward routine, a treatment-contact control group (*n* = 17) was included. The purpose was to provide an opportunity for children to have special treatment meetings with a therapist but not to provide problem-solving skills training or individual nondirective psychotherapy.

Children in this condition met with a therapist for 20 individual sessions. The number of sessions and their schedule were identical to those of the treatment groups. However, sessions were less than half the duration (20 min) of those of PSST and RT. The reason for the difference in duration was to adhere to the goals of the control group (i.e., individualized contact with a therapist) and to avoid in-depth discussion of affect-laden material likely to emerge in more protracted sessions. The critical feature of this condition was to provide the therapist and child with time together. The therapist's task in the sessions was to engage the child in discussion of routine activities (e.g., in class, with friends) on the unit. Although the primary medium of exchange was conversation, there was no attempt to probe the child's feelings or clinical problems or to develop insight, self-acceptance, or related processes. The therapist played games (e.g., checkers) if the child wished, as long as the child and therapist were together in a session without the interaction or interruption of others.

Therapists

Four female clinicians (ages 25–31) served as therapists. Each had completed postgraduate course work in child development or other mental-health-related fields and had 1–2 years of direct-care experience with children and families on the clinical service, prior to the study.

The therapists participated in an intensive training program for approximately 6 months to learn each treatment technique. The treatments were detailed in manual form in which the contents of each session, the materials, the order of presentation, and sample dialogues were detailed. Training utilized extensive role playing and modeling to master the treatment, at which point training cases were assigned. These initial training cases of children received close supervision, which included direct observation of each session, review of tapes with individual therapists on a session-by-session basis, discussion of the case, and group meetings to review cases. Therapist supervision continued throughout the course of the investigation with individual meetings with therapists, group meetings, and weekly case review. Treatment sessions were videotaped or audiotaped for supervision purposes.

Treatment Integrity

To sustain the integrity of treatment (Yeaton & Sechrest, 1981): (a) therapists followed a treatment manual that delineated each treatment on a session-by-session basis; (b) therapists saw two to three training cases in each condition before seeing cases for the study; (c) therapists were provided with several materials to foster the correct execution of each session, including checklists that prescribed the necessary materials for each session, the specific themes or tasks that needed to be covered, and related information; (d) therapists were required to provide documentation of the session, including summaries of what had transpired, any unique features, duration of session, and child progress; and (e) therapists were provided with ongoing clinical supervision, feedback, and training throughout the investigation.

Attrition

Fifty-six children were assigned randomly to treatment. Of these, 51 (91.1%) completed treatment. Of the 5 subjects who did not complete treatment, 2 were from the PSST condition; 1, from the RT condition; and 2, from the control condition. Reasons for failing to complete treatment included premature termination of hospitalization (against medical advice, $n = 2$) and child refusal to come to treatment ($n = 3$). The sample of 51 subjects was reduced further by the failure of four families to consent to or to provide assessment of child performance at home or at school after treatment. Posttreatment data analyses were based on 47 (83.9%) of the 56 originally assigned subjects, who included 17 of 20 (85.0%) PSST children; 14 of 19 (73.7%) RT children; and 16 of 17 (94.1%) control children. At the 1-year follow-up assessment, data were available from the parents and/or teachers of 42(75.0%) of the original 56 cases.

RESULTS

Preliminary Analyses

Factorial multivariate analyses of variance (MANOVAS) examined the effects of child age, gender, race, and IQ; diagnoses; and parent (or guardian) age, current or past mental disorder, welfare status, and Hollingshead class on CBCL and SBCL scales. For continuous variables (e.g., age, IQ), median splits were used to divide the sample and to test for differences on the dependent measures for these analyses. No differences were obtained as a function of subject and demographic variables at pretreatment, posttreatment, or follow-up assessment periods. The MANOVAS also revealed no significant differences among the treatment and control groups on subject or demographic variables or pretreatment CBCL and SBCL scores.

Treatment Effects

The MANOVAS revealed no significant differences as a function of therapist or of Therapist × Condition. Hence therapist was not included as a factor in the evaluation of treatment effects. Analyses of covariance (ANCOVAS) were used to evaluate treatment effects at each assessment period using pretreatment performance as the covariate. Multiple comparison tests of means (adjusted from covariance analyses) were computed where overall significant effects were obtained. Changes over the course of treatment and follow-up were evaluated by within-group t tests.

Posttreatment

Posttreatment assessment was conducted 1 month after completion of treatment and hospital discharge to allow parents and teachers the opportunity to evaluate the child's behavior. Means and standard deviations for parent and teacher measures are presented in Table 1; ANCOVAS appear in Table 2. At posttreatment, significant group differences were evident for the Internalizing scale, Externalizing scale, and Total Behavior Problem scale of the CBCL. Two CBCL social-competence scales, namely, the Activities scale and the School scale, also reflected group differences. On the SBCL, significant group differences were evident for Aggression, Total Disability, and overall ratings of school adjustment.

To evaluate the source of the differences for significant effects, multiple comparison tests were completed. Bonferroni t tests were conducted to control family-wise error rates for an alpha of .05 (Myers, 1979). The comparisons revealed a relatively consistent ordering of groups (see Table 3). Children who received PSST showed significantly less dysfunction on the CBCL and SBCL scales than RT and control children. The PSST children also showed significantly greater participation in social activities and progress at school (on the CBCL) and overall school adjustment (on the SBCL). Although the RT group showed lower

Table 1. Means and Standard Deviations for the Child Behavior Checklist (CBCL) and the School Behavior Checklist (SBCL) From Pretreatment Through Follow-Up

Measure	Pretreatment M	Pretreatment SD	Posttreatment M	Posttreatment SD	Follow-up M	Follow-up SD
Problem-solving skills training						
CBCL						
Internalizing	71.9	7.2	63.8	9.6	63.3	8.7
Externalizing	78.5	4.9	66.8	9.4	69.6	7.9
Total behavior problem	79.0	5.5	67.5	9.8	68.5	8.4
Activities	44.1	9.7	49.1	6.5	44.6	11.6
Social	26.9	12.6	32.3	11.9	33.5	11.1
School	32.8	9.9	42.2	10.5	38.3	10.5
SBCL						
Aggression	77.0	11.4	63.1	12.5	66.2	11.7
Total Disability	71.5	7.9	59.7	9.3	64.3	8.0
Global school adjustment	16.7	5.5	25.6	6.1	25.5	3.8
Relationship therapy						
CBCL						
Internalizing	70.8	11.2	70.9	6.0	68.9	6.4
Externalizing	77.6	6.6	73.8	5.4	77.5	5.8
Total behavior problem	77.9	7.9	75.4	7.1	78.0	7.8
Activities	44.0	11.3	42.2	9.6	42.3	8.3
Social	33.1	9.4	29.7	8.8	32.0	9.2
School	29.4	10.1	27.4	10.3	30.5	10.4
SBCL						
Aggression	76.8	10.7	71.6	10.8	76.1	11.7
Total Disability	72.9	9.5	69.0	7.1	70.9	6.8
Global school adjustment	18.9	5.7	21.4	5.0	20.6	5.6
Treatment-contact controls						
CBCL						
Internalizing	71.8	12.2	68.7	12.2	71.0	8.9
Externalizing	77.2	6.0	77.1	8.4	80.5	8.6
Total behavior problem	78.3	8.1	77.3	9.3	79.5	10.9
Activities	46.5	7.0	42.2	8.5	40.9	9.4
Social	31.8	11.8	30.5	10.1	28.8	11.7
School	32.0	7.6	28.0	7.4	27.9	6.9
SBCL						
Aggression	81.8	11.7	79.3	13.0	78.7	16.2
Total Disability	73.3	9.3	72.3	7.6	72.1	11.8
Global school adjustment	19.5	5.6	19.7	4.8	20.3	6.0

Note: Scores are normalized T scores derived from the Child Behavior Profile (see Achenbach & Edelbrock, 1983).

Table 2. Analyses of Covariance at Posttreatment and Follow-Up

Dependent Measure	Assessment Period	
	Posttreatment	Follow-up
CBCL[a]		
Internalizing	5.26**	3.60*
Externalizing	11.30***	8.24***
Total behavior problem	9.94***	6.76**
Activities	5.16**	1.70
Social	<1	<1
School	15.16***	10.63***
SBCL[b]		
Aggression	7.92***	3.86*
Total Disability	10.25***	3.19*
Global school adjustment	6.15**	7.31**

Note: CBCL = Child Behavior Checklist; SBCL = School Behavior Checklist.
[a]Posttreatment, $df = 2, 42$; Follow-up, $df = 2, 30$.
[b]Posttreatment, $df = 2, 40$; Follow-up, $df = 2, 36$.
* $p \leq .05$. ** $p \leq .01$. *** $p \leq .001$.

behavior-problem scores and higher prosocial behavior than the control group on all but one of the CBCL and SBCL scales, the differences did not attain statistical significance.

Within-group t tests were computed to evaluate change from pre- to posttreatment. The results (Table 4) indicated significant improvements for the children who received PSST on each of the behavior-problem scales and school performance on the CBCL and on Aggression, Total Disability, and overall adjustment on the SBCL. The RT children improved on externalizing

behavior on the CBCL and on the Aggression scale of the SBCL. Control children showed nonsignificant improvements in internalizing behavior and significant decrements in participation in social activities and school performance as measured by the CBCL.

One-year Follow-up

The CBCL and SBCL were readministered to parents and teachers 4, 8, and 12 months after treatment. The results for the different follow-up periods did not lead to different conclusions about the impact of treatment or about the relative standing of the treatment and control conditions. Consequently, for summary purposes and to evaluate the impact of treatment at the final assessment point, only results for the 1-year follow-up are presented and discussed (Tables 1 and 2).[4]

As is evident in Table 2, at the 1-year follow-up, significant group differences continued to be evident for the Internalizing scale, the Externalizing scale, and the Total Behavior Problem scale of the CBCL. Yet, group differences were no longer evident for the Activities scale at the end of 1 year. Of the social-competence scales, the School scale remained significantly different among groups. On the SBCL, Aggression, Total Disability, and global ratings of school adjustment also showed group differences at the 1-year follow-up.

Multiple-comparison tests were computed on the adjusted means from the ANCOVAS at the 1-year follow-up for those effects that attained significance. The results (Table 3) showed that PSST children were rated

[4]Additional tables and data analyses that include 4- and 8-month follow-up assessments are available on request.

Table 3. Multiple-Comparison Tests on Adjusted Means at Posttreatment and 1-Year Follow-Up

Measure	Posttherapy			Follow-up		
	PSST	RT	TC	PSST	RT	TC
CBCL						
Internalizing	63.6	71.4$_a$	68.5$_a$	62.9	69.4$_a$	71.0$_a$
Externalizing	66.3	74.0$_a$	77.5$_a$	69.7	77.7$_a$	80.2$_a$
Total behavior problem	67.0	76.0$_a$	77.3$_a$	68.1	78.6$_a$	79.4$_a$
Activities	49.3	42.6$_a$	41.6$_a$	—	—	—
School	39.9	29.3$_a$	28.4$_a$	39.7	31.2$_a$	27.7$_a$
SBCL						
Aggression	64.6	72.6$_a$	77.1$_a$	66.8	76.1$_a$	77.3$_a$
Total Disability	60.4	68.4$_a$	72.1$_a$	64.1	70.2$_a$	71.9$_a$
Global school adjustment	26.0	21.3$_a$	19.4$_a$	26.8	20.7$_a$	20.1$_a$

Note: PSST = problem-solving skills training; RT = relationship therapy; TC = treatment-contact control. CBCL = Child Behavior Checklist; SBCL = School Behavior Checklist. For a given measure at posttreatment or follow-up, means that share the same subscript are not significantly different. All differences are significant at $p < .05$, using Bonferroni t tests. Dash indicates that comparisons were not made because the overall test was not statistically significant.

Table 4. Within-Group t Tests From Pretreatment to Posttreatment and From Pretreatment to Follow-Up

Dependent Measure	PSST		RT		TC	
	Pretreatment to Post-treatment	Pretreatment to Follow-up	Pretreatment to Post-treatment	Pretreatment to Follow-up	Pretreatment to Post-treatment	Pretreatment to Follow up
CBCL	(16)	(12)	(12)	(10)	(15)	(9)
Internalizing	3.42**	3.23**	<1	<1	2.01	<1
Externalizing	6.03***	4.07**	2.36*	<1	<1	<1
Total behavior problem	5.46***	3.77**	1.20	<1	<1	<1
Activities	1.96	<1	<1	<1	−2.25*	−1.58
Social	1.14	<1	−1.17	−1.17	<1	<1
School	3.97**	3.28**	−1.62	<1	−3.16**	−2.49*
SBCL	(14)	(13)	(12)	(10)	(15)	(14)
Aggression	6.10***	5.18***	2.18*	<1	1.21	<1
Total Disability	5.17***	3.75**	1.92	1.13	<1	<1
Global school adjustment	5.72***	5.00***	1.82	1.95	<1	<1

Note: PSST = problem-solving skills training; RT = relationship therapy; TC = treatment-contact control. CBCL = Child Behavior Checklist; SBCL = School Behavior Checklist. Parentheses indicate degrees of freedom. Negative t values indicate that the change is in the direction of deterioration (increased deviance, decreased prosocial behavior).
*$p \leq .05$. **$p \leq .01$. ***$p \leq .001$.

as significantly less deviant than RT and control children on the behavior-problem scales of the CBCL and SBCL and higher in school performance and teacher-rated school adjustment. The results indicated that several of the group differences evident at posttreatment were sustained at the 1-year follow-up. The RT and control children were not significantly different from each other on any of the measures.

To examine behavior change after treatment, within-group t tests were computed from posttreatment to 1-year follow-up assessment. The PSST children showed no significant changes from posttreatment to the 1-year follow-up. The RT children showed a significant increase in externalizing behavior, $t(10) = -2.93$, $p < .05$, on the CBCL. Control children showed significant increases on the Externalizing scale, $t(9) = -2.80$, $p < .05$), and on the Total Behavior Problem scale, $t(9) = -2.46$, $p < .05$, of the CBCL. No significant changes were evident on the SBCL from posttreatment to follow-up for RT or control groups. Overall, the few changes that did transpire from posttreatment to 1-year follow-up were in the direction of increased deviant behavior for RT and control children.

Within-group t tests (Table 4) indicated that from pretreatment to 1-year follow-up, PSST children significantly improved on seven of the nine CBCL and SBCL scales. Within-group changes over this same period were not significant for RT and control children. Actually, at follow-up control children were significantly worse on the CBCL School scale relative to pretreatment.

Clinical Impact of Treatment

These results suggest that PSST produced significant changes and that this group was superior to RT and the contact-control condition at posttreatment and follow-up. Yet a major concern is the extent to which the treatment produced clinically important changes. Although there is no standardized way to assess clinical significance in outcome research, one way is to evaluate the extent to which treatments brought child behavior within the nonclinical range of functioning (Kazdin, 1977). Normative data are available for both the CBCL and the SBCL that permit delineation of a range of behavior for nonclinic samples. To reflect an overall level of dysfunction, CBCL Total Behavior Problem scale and SBCL Total Disability scale were examined for children who participated in the study relative to nonclinical samples within the same age range, as derived from normative data for these measures (see Achenbach & Edelbrock, 1983; Miller, 1977).

Using their analyses of clinic and nonclinic samples, Achenbach and Edelbrock (1983) identified the 90th percentile as a cutoff score for the upper limit of the normal range for the Total Behavior Problem score. Scores below this percentile fall within the nonclinical (normal) range. For present purposes, the 90th percentile criterion was used to define the upper limit of the normal range on the CBCL Total Behavior Problem scores and on the SBCL Total Disability score. Achenbach and Edelbrock (1983) also suggested the 10th percentile as the lower limit of the nonclinical range on the Total Social Competence score (the sum of the three CBCL social scales). Children below this percentile are more deviant in their prosocial behavior than 90% of children in nonreferred normative samples.

Group Means

The initial concern is the extent to which children in the alternative groups fell within the nonclinical range. To address this question, T scores that defined the boundary of the normal range were used as a criterion to evaluate performance for treatment and control children for CBCL Total Behavior Problem scale, SBCL Total Disability scale, and CBCL Total Social Competence scales. Figure 1 presents mean T scores for children in the PSST, RT, and contact-control groups as well as T score cutoffs based on data obtained from nonclinic samples. The figure shows that children who received PSST made marked changes on the CBCL (upper panel), but their mean remained well above the upper limit of the normative range at posttreatment and follow-up. For Total Disability from the teacher evaluations (lower panel), PSST children fell within the nonclinic range at posttreatment, but these gains were not sustained 1 year later. Finally, for social competence (Figure 2), the means for all groups were within the lower boundary of the nonclinical range before treatment. After treatment, PSST children showed greater penetration into this range, whereas the other groups moved in the direction of decrements in social behavior.

Individual Cases

The mean scores do not reflect the performance of individual children and their progress. Chi-square tests evaluated the proportions of group members who fell within the normative range for the Total Behavior Problem, Total Disability, and Total Social Competence scores. Two groups of children were delineated separately for each measure, namely those who fell within the nonclinic range (based upon the cutoff scores) and those who did not.[5] For each analysis, children were excluded if their pretreatment scores fell within the normal range.

Table 5 summarizes the proportion of children who fell within the nonclinic range at different assessment periods. The results indicated significant differences in proportions for the Total Disability scale at posttreatment. More children from the PSST group fell within the normal range at posttreatment than did RT or control children. However, these differences were no longer significant at the 1-year follow-up. For the social-competence measure, significant differences were evident in the proportions of children within the nonclinic range at both posttreatment and

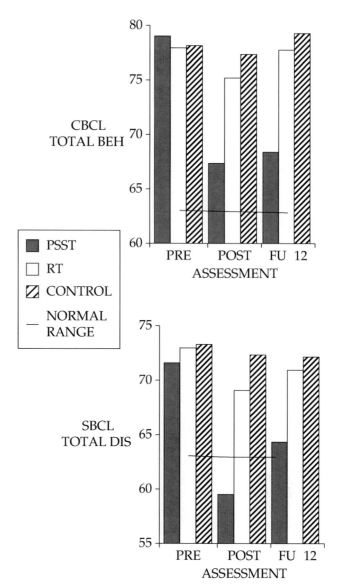

Figure 1. Mean T scores for the problem-solving skills training (PSST), relationship therapy (RT), and control groups for the Total Behavior Problem scale of the Child Behavior Checklist (CBCL, upper panel) and the Total Disability scale of the School Behavior Checklist (SBCL, lower panel). The horizontal line represents the upper limit of the nonclinical (normal) range of children of the same gender and age. The T scores below this line fall within the normal range. Note that *FU 12* designates 12-month follow-up.

follow-up. A significantly higher proportion of PSST children fell within the nonclinic range than RT and control children.

---

[5]Normative data and percentile equivalents are available from the assessment manuals for the CBCL (Achenbach & Edelbrock, 1983) and the SBCL (Miller, 1977). To compute whether a child's score falls within the normal range, raw scores must be examined because different raw scores may yield the same T scores (see Achenbach & Edelbrock, 1983).

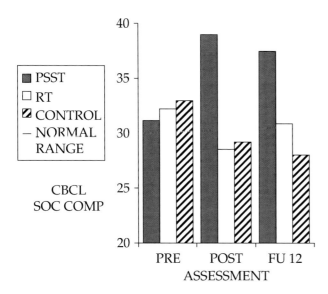

Figure 2. Mean *T* scores for the problem-solving skills training (PSST), relationship therapy (RT), and control groups for the Total Social Competence scales of the Child Behavior Checklist (CBCL). (The horizontal line represents the lower limit of the nonclinical [normal] range of children of the same gender and age for these prosocial behaviors. The *T* scores above this line fall within the normal range. Note that FU 12 designates 12-month follow-up.)

Supplementary Analyses

Therapist Evaluations

The TEI yielded measures from the two subscales, namely, the therapist's rating of the child's progress within the sessions and the prediction of posttreatment improvements. The ANCOVAS (3 × 4) were completed to evaluate whether progress or improvement ratings varied as a function of treatment condition or therapist. The results yielded a significant treatment effect for the improvement ratings, $F(2, 12) = 6.08$, $p < .05$. Multiple comparisons tests (Bonferroni *t* tests) indicated that PSST children ($M \simeq 28.8$) were considered by therapists to be more likely to improve in the future than were RT ($M = 22.5$) or control ($M = 20.6$) children. These latter groups were not different from each other.

Pearson product-moment correlations were computed between therapist evaluations and CBCL and SBCL summary scales at posttreatment and 1-year follow-up to examine if therapist ratings were related to child functioning at home and at school. Therapist ratings of child improvements correlated negatively with Total Disability scores at posttreatment and follow-up (*rs* = −.44 and −.53, both $p < .03$). Thus, the more favorable were therapist's predictions of improvement, the less deviant were children at school, as rated by classroom teachers who completed the SBCL. Therapist evaluations

of in-session progress or improvement were unrelated to CBCL scales at posttreatment and follow-up.

Child Evaluations

The Child Evaluation Inventory yielded two subscales reflecting the children's evaluations of progress they made in therapy and of treatment acceptability. Therapist × Condition ANCOVAS yielded no differences on these scales.[6] Pearson product-moment correlations were computed to examine if child evaluations of treatment correlated with the CBCL and SBCL scales. At posttreatment, child evaluations of progress correlated positively with parent ratings of social competence ($r = .41$, $p < .03$). The more the children viewed themselves as making progress, the more likely the parent rated them as socially competent on the CBCL. Child evaluations of progress tended to be negatively correlated ($r = −.29$) with total behavioral symptoms on the CBCL at posttreatment, but this failed to attain statistical significance ($p < .08$). Interestingly, at posttreatment acceptability was correlated negatively with CBCL Total Behavior Problem scores ($r = −.41$, $p < .03$) and positively with Total Social Competence ($r = .39$, $p < .04$). Children who viewed treatment as more acceptable scored lower in behavioral problem and higher in social competence at posttreatment. However, none of these relations was maintained at the 1-year follow-up assessments.

Convergence of Therapist and Child Ratings

Therapists and children both rated how much progress was made in treatment. Pearson product-moment correlations indicated a small and nonsignificant correlation between therapist and child evaluations of progress ($r = .36$, $p < .07$). Therapist evaluations of progress were correlated positively with child evaluations of treatment acceptability ($r = .40$, $p < .04$). The greater were therapist ratings of progress within sessions, the more acceptable was treatment viewed by the children. Therapist predictions of improvement were unrelated to the child's ratings of progress or acceptability.

---

[6]The absence of differences on the child acceptability ratings does not convey that the treatments were equally acceptable or unacceptable to the children. Each of the eight items on the Acceptability subscale of the CEI was scored on a 5-point scale, with a total possible score of 40. A moderate rating (score of 3 on each item) would yield a total score of 24. The means for PSST, RT, and control groups were 39.7, 37.2, and 36.7, respectively, which suggested a high degree of acceptability. Given that the means were all close to the maximum total score, it is possible that a ceiling effect precluded differences in acceptability ratings. Nevertheless, the results suggest that the children viewed the treatments as highly acceptable.

Table 5. Proportion of Children Who Fell Within Range of Nonclinic Samples at Posttreatment and Follow-Up

Measure	PSST		RT		TC		χ^{2b}
	n	%	n	%	n	%	
Posttreatment							
Total behavior problem	3/17	17.6	0/13	0.0	2/16	12.5	2.43
Social competence total	8/13	61.5	0/9	0.0	1/9	11.1	11.60**
Total Disability[a]	8/12	66.7	4/12	33.3	2/15	13.3	8.28*
One-year follow-up							
Total behavior problem	3/13	23.1	1/11	9.1	1/10	10.0	1.18
Social competence total	5/10	50.0	0/6	0.0	0/7	0.0	8.31*
Total Disability*	5/13	38.5	2/10	20.0	2/14	14.3	2.28

Note: PSST = problem-solving skills training; RT = relationship therapy; TC = treatment-contact control. Children with a raw score at or below the 90th percentile on the Total Behavior Problem scale or Total Disability scale or above the 10th percentile on the social-competence total at pretreatment were excluded from these proportions.
[a]Scale of the School Behavior Checklist. Other scales are from the Child Behavior Checklist. [b]$df = 2$.
*$p \le .05$. **$p \le .01$.

DISCUSSION

The results indicated that (a) problem-solving skills training led to significantly greater changes than relationship therapy and treatment-contact control conditions, (b) the between-groups differences and within-group changes of PSST were sustained up to 1-year follow-up, and (c) the effects of treatment were evident on measures of child behavior at home and at school. There was some evidence that treatment effects were attenuated over the course of follow-up. Nevertheless, at the 1-year follow-up, children who had received PSST evinced significant reductions in total behavioral problems at home and at school and improvements on measures of school performance rated by the parent and of overall school adjustment rated by the teacher. In contrast, children in the other groups made either few gains over the course of treatment and follow-up (the RT group) or became significantly worse on selected measures (the control group).

To evaluate the clinical impact of treatment, performance of treatment and control children was compared with normative data from nonclinic samples. The results indicated that the proportion of children who fell within the normative (nonclinic) range for behavioral problems was greater for the PSST group than for the other groups. The differences were especially marked for prosocial behavior (social competence) at posttreatment and follow-up. Even so, the majority of children in the PSST group remained outside (i.e., more deviant than) the upper level of the nonclinic range for CBCL Total Behavior Problem scale and SBCL Total Disability scale.

Although the magnitude of change produced with treatment leaves a great deal to be desired, the results from the PSST condition are noteworthy. The results suggest that cognitive–behavioral problem-skills training can effect changes in a seriously disturbed clinical population, that the changes are evident on community-based measures, and that changes are sustained at least up to 1 year. These findings are consistent with recent studies of impulsive, aggressive, and delinquent youths that show significant improvements following cognitive–behavioral interventions (e.g., Arbuthnot & Gordon, 1986; Kendall & Braswell, 1982; Lochman et al., 1984). These studies have also shown significant changes on measures of behavior at home, at school, and in the community, but the magnitude of the effects needs to be bolstered to achieve clinically significant outcomes.

Of interest were the findings for relationship therapy, which was found to produce effects no different from treatment-contact control conditions. Yet, children who received RT tended to fare somewhat better than control children. For example, control children became significantly worse on school performance over the course of follow-up, whereas RT children did not. Failure to obtain systematic improvements with relationship therapy in the present study is consistent with other studies that have examined similar modalities of treatment with antisocial youths (e.g., Alexander & Parsons, 1973; Feldman et al., 1983). In the treatment of antisocial youths, research suggests that relationship factors may be necessary but are insufficient to effect change (Alexander, Barton, Schiavo, & Parsons, 1976).

There are several possible explanations for the absence of differences between relationship and contact-control conditions. The hospital setting may, in some way, interfere with the efficacy of relationship therapy. Alternatively, the outcome measures may have been insensitive to the sorts of effects (e.g., changes in self-concept) that RT produces. Also, the critical conditions of treatment (e.g., empathy, unconditional positive regard) may not have been sufficiently high to produce change. These and other possible interpretations cannot be excluded on the basis of the present data. Few controlled trials of RT exist with antisocial children. Hence this treatment needs to be explored further, with improvements in design not evident here, before the impact can be evaluated definitively.

Therapist and child evaluations yielded interesting results. Child evaluations indicated that treatment and control interventions were both rated as highly acceptable. Child evaluations of acceptability were correlated negatively with parent ratings of deviant behavior and positively with prosocial behavior after treatment. Therapist evaluations of improvement at the end of therapy were negatively correlated with teacher ratings of deviant behavior after treatment and at the 1 year follow-up. These results suggest that both child and therapist evaluations can predict performance subsequent to treatment.

There are several limitations of the present study, both within the design and from the setting and circumstances of treatment. First, all children were inpatients and hence were exposed to another intervention, namely, hospitalization. Although there is no firm evidence that inpatient hospitalization improves antisocial behavior (see Kazdin, 1985), it is reasonable to consider its potentiating and interactive effects in applying other interventions. Thus, the present results may not extend to nonhospitalized youths.

Second, treatment effects were examined without evaluation of the role of child, parent, and family characteristics or scrutiny of treatment process variables. Because of the paucity of outcome studies with severely dysfunctional youths, the present investigation addressed a preliminary concern about whether therapeutic changes could be achieved with a relatively severe group of antisocial children. Further work is warranted that at once attempts to bolster the strength of treatment and to make and test predictions about child, family, and treatment variables that influence outcome (see Kazdin, in press). The findings of the present study suggest that cognitive–behavioral treatment can be applied to severely disturbed children and that it leads to reliable and sustained improvements, at least up to 1 year. The differences in statistical and clinical significance of the changes underscore the limitations of the results and the need for further work.

REFERENCES

Achenbach, T. M., & Edelbrock, C. S. (1983). *Manual for the Child Behavior Checklist and Revised Child Behavior Profile.* Burlington, VT: University Associates in Psychiatry.

Alexander, J. F., Barton, C., Schiavo, R. S., & Parsons, B. V. (1976). Systems-behavioral intervention with families of delinquents: Therapist characteristics, family behavior, and outcome. *Journal of Consulting and Clinical Psychology, 44*, 656–664.

Alexander, J. F., & Parsons, B. V. (1973). Short-term behavioral intervention with delinquent families: Impact on family process and recidivism. *Journal of Abnormal Psychology, 81*, 219–225.

American Psychiatric Association. (1980). *Diagnostic and statistical manual of mental disorders.* Washington, DC: Author.

Arbuthnot, J., & Gordon, D. A. (1986). Behavioral and cognitive effects of a moral reasoning development intervention for high-risk behavior-disordered adolescents. *Journal of Consulting and Clinical Psychology, 54*, 208–216.

Dodge, K. A. (1985). Attributional bias in aggressive children. In P. C. Kendali (Ed.), *Advances in cognitive-behavioral research and therapy* (Vol. 4, pp. 73–110). Orlando, FL: Academic Press.

Dumas, J., & Wahler, R. G. (1983). Predictors of treatment outcome in parent training: Mother insularity and socioeconomic disadvantage. *Behavioral Assessment, 5*, 301–313.

Endicott, J., & Spitzer, R. L. (1978). A diagnostic interview: The Schedule of Affective Disorders and Schizophrenia. *Archives of General Psychiatry, 35*, 837–844.

Feldman, R. A., Caplinger, T. E., & Wodarski, J. S. (1983). *The St. Louis conundrum: The effective treatment of antisocial youths.* Englewood Cliffs, NJ: Prentice-Hall.

Gresham, F. M. (1985). Utility of cognitive-behavioral procedures for social skills training with children: A critical review. *Journal of Abnormal Child Psychology, 13*, 411–423.

Hollingshead, A. B., & Redlich, F. C. (1958). *Social class and mental illness.* New York: Wiley.

Kazdin, A. E. (1977). Assessing the clinical or applied significance of behavior change through social validation. *Behavior Modification, 1*, 427–452.

Kazdin, A. E. (1984). Acceptability of aversive procedures and medication as treatment alternatives for deviant child behavior. *Journal of Abnormal Child Psychology, 12*, 289–302.

Kazdin, A. E. (1985). *Treatment of antisocial behavior in children and adolescents.* Homewood, IL: Dorsey Press.

Kazdin, A. E. (in press). *Conduct disorder in childhood and adolescence.* Beverly Hills, CA: Sage.

Kendall, P. C., & Braswell, L. (1982). Cognitive-behavioral self-control therapy for children: A components analysis. *Journal of Consulting and Clinical Psychology, 50,* 672–689.

Kendall, P. C., & Braswell, L. (1985). *Cognitive-behavioral therapy for impulsive children.* New York: Guilford Press.

Lochman, J. E., Burch, P. R., Curry, J. F., & Lampron, L. B. (1984). Treatment and generalization effects of cognitive-behavioral and goal-setting interventions with aggressive boys. *Journal of Consulting and Clinical Psychology, 52,* 915–916.

Loeber, R. (1985). Patterns and development of antisocial child behavior. In G. J. Whitehurst (Ed.), *Annals of child development* (Vol. 2, pp. 77–116). New York: JAI Press.

Miller, L. C. (1977). *School Behavior Checklist manual.* Los Angeles: Western Psychological Services.

Myers, J. L. (1979). *Fundamentals of experimental design* (3rd ed.). Boston: Allyn & Bacon.

Patterson, C. H. (1979). Rogerian counseling. In S. H. Harrison (Ed.), *Basic handbook of child psychiatry: Therapeutic interventions* (Vol. 3, pp. 203–215). New York: Basic Books.

Patterson, G. R. (1982). *Coercive family process.* Eugene, OR: Castalia.

Persons, R. W. (1966). Psychological and behavioral change in delinquents following psychotherapy. *Journal of Clinical Psychology, 22,* 337–340.

Redfering, D. L. (1972). Group counseling with institutionalized delinquent females. *American Corrective Therapy Journal, 26,* 160–163.

Reisman, J. M. (1973). *Principles of psychotherapy with children.* New York: Wiley.

Robins, L. N. (1981). Epidemiological approaches to natural history research: Antisocial disorders in children. *Journal of the American Academy of Child Psychiatry, 20,* 566–580.

Rutter, M., & Giller, H. (1983). *Juvenile delinquency: Trends and perspectives.* New York: Penguin Books.

Spivack, G., Platt, J. J., & Shure, M. B. (1976). *The problem solving approach to adjustment.* San Francisco: Jossey-Bass.

Wechsler, D. (1974). *Manual for the Wechsler Intelligence Scale for Children-Revised,* New York: The Psychological Corporation.

Yeaton, W. H., & Sechrest, L. (1981). Critical dimensions in the choice and maintenance of successful treatments: Strength, integrity, and effectiveness. *Journal of Consulting and Clinical Psychology, 49,* 156–167.

1.03

A Randomised Efficacy Study of Web-based Synthetic and Analytic Programmes Among Disadvantaged Urban Kindergarten Children

Erin M. Comaskey,* Robert S. Savage,* and Philip Abrami†

ABSTRACT: This study explores whether two computer-based literacy interventions – a 'synthetic phonics' and an 'analytic phonics' approach produce qualitatively distinct effects on the early phonological abilities and reading skills of disadvantaged urban Kindergarten (Reception) children. Participants ($n = 53$) were assigned by random allocation to one of the two interventions. Each intervention was generally delivered three times per week for 13 weeks as part of a reading centre approach in Kindergarten classrooms with small groups of children. In the synthetic programme children showed, as predicted, significant ($p < .05$) improvement in CV and VC word blending and the articulation of final consonants. The children in the analytic phonics programme showed, as predicted, significant ($p < .05$) improvements in articulating shared rimes in words. These results suggest that synthetic and analytic programmes have qualitatively different effects on children's phonological development. These phonological differences are not however immediately reflected in any qualitative differences in the way children undertook word reading or nonword decoding.

The purposes of this paper are twofold. Firstly, we briefly review the literature on the effectiveness of computer-based reading interventions and all intervention studies exploring the efficacy of synthetic and analytic phonics programmes. Secondly, we identify the need for, and then report the results of, a randomised intervention study using computers to deliver Web-based phonics interventions. We explore whether qualitatively different effects of synthetic and analytic phonics programmes were evident for disadvantaged children in an urban school.

THE EVIDENCE BASE FOR COMPUTER-BASED LITERACY INTERVENTIONS

What does the best evidence accumulated to date say on the effectiveness of computer-based literacy

*McGill University, Canada
†Centre for the Study of Learning and Performance, Concordia University, Canada

interventions? The most comprehensive review of studies of the impact of information and communication technology (ICT) on literacy was conducted by Torgerson and Zhu (2003). This meta-analysis used explicit criteria to select studies, limiting inclusion to randomised control trials (RCTs) of children aged 5–16. Twelve studies included for in-depth review were pared down from over 2,000 candidate studies initially identified on ERIC and PsychInfo databases. Analysis of these 12 studies showed mixed effects of interventions. Overall, effect sizes were not significantly different from zero. Torgerson and Zhu concluded firstly that teachers and policy-makers should be aware that there is not sufficient high-quality evidence available to justify the use of ICT to support literacy, and secondly that rigorously designed RCT studies of the impact of technology on literacy are urgently required. Similar results have been reported from a recent large-scale study in the United States by Dynarski et al. (2007). An RCT study of a range of commercially available ICT products was undertaken in 132 schools in 33 school districts and with a total of 4,389 teachers. Dynarski et al. showed that the effect size for interventions was not significantly different from zero on standard and local tests of reading in either Grade 1 or Grade 4.

Few studies to date however have explored the effects of technology in Kindergarten. It is also not clear to what extent the effects reported above reflect weaknesses in implementation of the individual programmes themselves rather than a more fundamental problem of ICT effectiveness. For example, in many studies teachers are given a single day's training in using technology and many have reported being unsure about using it in the classroom (e.g. Dynarski et al., 2007). Interventions run by well-trained facilitators rather than briefly trained teachers to establish *efficacy* of ICTs might be an important first step.

As Torgerson and Zhu identify, there is clearly a need for more randomised studies in this domain. In the medical sciences, there is growing consensus not only that well-designed RCT studies are needed but that such studies should be executed and reported following clear and consistent criteria such as the CONSORT criteria (Altman et al., 2001; Moher, Schulz & Altman, 2001). We thus sought to contribute a methodologically sound study of the effects of ICT on early literacy outcomes in Kindergarten reported closely following the CONSORT criteria for RCT trials.

WEB-BASED TECHNOLOGY

Most of the programmes described and evaluated by Torgerson and Zhu (2003) are commercially available packages that use CD or videotape as the medium of delivery. In contrast, almost no research exists on *Web-based* technologies. A series of recent studies (Abrami, Savage, Wade, Hipps & Lopez, 2008; Deault, Savage & Abrami, 2008; Savage, Abrami, Hipps & Deault, in press) from the ABRACADABRA literacy research and development programme has sought to fill this important gap in technology research using a free-access Web-based resource. A major advantage of Web-based tools compared with CDs or videotape is that they do not require individual installation and maintenance, often a problem in schools that seldom have comprehensive technical support.

ABRACADABRA is an acronym standing for A Balanced Reading Approach for Canadians Designed to Achieve Best Results for All. This software was developed by the Center for the Study of Learning and Performance, a multi-university research centre, based at Concordia University, Montreal, Canada. The version of ABRACADABRA used in this research can be found at (http://grover.concordia.ca/abra/ version1/ abracadabra.html).

The version of ABRACADABRA (hereafter, ABRA) used for this study was developed following a year-long pilot study conducted with first graders in 2004–2005. The activities used in ABRA were modelled after the National Reading Panel's (NRP) analysis of effective reading interventions (NRP, 2000), focusing specifically on letter–sound knowledge, phoneme blending and reading comprehension tasks involving prediction and sequencing.

In the ABRA studies to date, trained research facilitators have worked on basic literacy skills and story reading with small groups of students away from their classroom environment. These students were seen four times a week for between 9 and 12 weeks. As in the current study, previous studies have contrasted differences between a rime-based 'analytic' phonics intervention teaching children words in riming families (e.g. 'cat', 'hat', 'bat') and which encouraged the use of rime-analogy, and a phoneme-based 'synthetic' phonics intervention focusing on the blending and segmenting of phonemes (Johnston & Watson, 2004). Both were compared against regular classroom teaching.

The most recent RCT study by Savage et al. (in press) found significant improvements in letter knowledge in the analytic phonics programme and significant improvements in phonological awareness, listening comprehension and reading comprehension in the synthetic phonics programme at immediate post-test. Significant effects were evident for phonological awareness and reading fluency at a delayed post-test completed 8 months after the intervention, again favouring the synthetic programme. Effect size analyses confirmed that both interventions had a significant impact on literacy at both post-tests (effect sizes across all literacy measures were significantly different from zero at immediate and delayed post-test).

The ABRA studies reported to date have explored the impacts of interventions on typical children in Year 1. The present study thus sought to explore the effects of ABRA on children in Kindergarten classes (broadly equivalent to Reception in the United Kingdom). We also wished to add to a domain of research where there is very little evidence to date: the effectiveness of phonics programmes for children who experience English as an additional language. Studies by Stuart (1999, 2004) explored the impact of synthetic phonics instruction on Sylheti-speaking children of Bangladeshi origin in inner London, UK. Results of the study suggested that these children did indeed benefit from such early interventions. We wish to explore whether effects can be found using ABRA for children from other low-SES communities in a comparable urban social context where many children and their families experience English as an additional language.

CONTRASTING THE EFFECTS OF SYNTHETIC AND ANALYTIC PHONICS PROGRAMMES

There are only four randomised control studies to date contrasting the impacts of analytic and synthetic phonics approaches (three papers identified in a systematic review by Torgerson, Brooks & Hall, 2006 and Savage et al., in press). These studies have found non-significant advantages for synthetic over analytic approaches. Torgerson et al. (2006) however also identify the need for more research on this question using RCT studies before drawing any strong conclusions. One purpose of this study was to add a further RCT study to this field.

THE QUALITATIVELY DISTINCT IMPACTS OF SYNTHETIC AND ANALYTIC PHONICS

All of the studies of analytic and synthetic phonics to date have used standardised measures of reading ability and related skills. Such measures are a good way to identify whether one approach to phonics is quantitatively superior to another. Most literacy researchers have however assumed that the synthetic and analytic phonics teaching leads to *qualitatively* different ways of reading (Duncan, Seymour & Hill, 1997). For example skills in sounding out and blending of grapheme–phoneme correspondences are assumed to result from synthetic phonics interventions and rime-based analogy use is assumed to result from analytic phonics interventions. Thus a major purpose of the present study is to test this widely held assumption of qualitative differences in literacy cognition following synthetic and analytic phonics programmes.

In order to determine whether two different kinds of phonics interventions have qualitatively different effects on the reading strategies used by children, it is

necessary to use carefully designed and controlled experimental measures of rime- and phoneme-level phonological awareness and nonword and word decoding measures rather than standardised reading tests. The limited existing research using such tools is thus first described below firstly for phonological awareness and then for reading and decoding.

SYNTHETIC AND ANALYTIC PHONICS AND PHONOLOGICAL AWARENESS

Evidence exists that children benefit from brief rime-based instruction to rapidly improve explicit rime skills (Goswami & East, 2000). Outcomes here were measured in a common unit task where children were required to articulate the shared rimes in words pairs (e.g. 'cart' and 'heart') or pairs of words sharing codas (e.g. 'cart', 'boat'). In the Goswami and East intervention study, however, only a rime-based programme was implemented, so the *relative* ease and the specificity of the improvements noted in explicit rime awareness versus other subsyllabic units is unknown. Savage, Carless and Stuart (2003) thus evaluated the effects of a rime-based, a phoneme-based and a 'mixed' (rime- and phoneme-based) intervention on phonological onset-rime and phoneme manipulation skills. Results showed greater phonological onset-rime skills in *all* taught intervention groups. It was concluded that there was no simple association between rime- and phoneme-based teaching intervention and the phonological unit used by children following such interventions. However, as this latter study used an onset-rime blending task rather than the common unit task used by Goswami and East, it may be that task differences might explain different results. This issue is therefore revisited in the present study using a common unit task.

Other evidence has added complexity to the idea that children have a particular facility with rimes. Uhry and Ehri (1999) showed that the division of words into onsets and rimes is easier for words with a CVC structure but this does not hold true for shorter words. Uhry and Ehri found that VC words that broke up words within the rime unit (i-ce) were more easily segmented than CV words (s-igh) that respected the onset-rime boundary. Uhry and Ehri (1999) concluded that it is the position of the rime unit in a syllable and not the structure of the rime unit itself that makes it more accessible to children. This finding was replicated later by Guedens and Sandra (2002), who added an important methodological refinement by matching the CV words precisely with the VC words in terms of phonemes used in Dutch (e.g. 'to' as CV stimulus, 'ot' as VC stimulus). The impact of different kinds of intervention on these early phoneme manipulation abilities is unknown, and yet the measure is potentially a subtle index of the relative use of rime- and phoneme-based strategies. This issue is thus explored in the present study.

THE SPECIFIC IMPACTS OF SYNTHETIC AND ANALYTIC PHONICS ON READING AND DECODING

The way that children decode nonsense words with contrasting rime neighbourhood sizes is another way to explore qualitative differences between synthetic and analytic phonics programmes (e.g. Christensen & Bowey, 2005; Deavers, Solity & Kerfoot, 2000; Savage et al., 2003). Savage et al. (2003) therefore developed a nonword reading task in which high-rime neighbourhood (HRn) nonwords (e.g. 'dat' – with many real word rime neighbours) and low-rime neighbourhood (LRn) nonwords (e.g. 'tav' with few real word neighbours) were contrasted. Overall the HRn and LRn stimulus sets contained the same letter–sound correspondences, so any advantage for HRn words could only reflect use of a rime-based decoding strategy. In the Savage et al. (2003) intervention study all intervention groups performed better than the control on this task but there were no other significant effects for either high-rime or low-rime words for either of the analytic or synthetic intervention groups. On the other hand, Deavers et al. (2000) did find that a rime-based strategy influenced nonword reading for a distinct set of stimuli sharing real word analogues (e.g. the nonword 'dalk' pronounced so as to rhyme with 'talk', rather than pronounced via grapheme–phoneme rules). Given the mixed findings to date, this issue is therefore revisited here by measuring HRn and LRn decoding abilities at pre- and post-test.

Finally, it has been argued that a phoneme-based decoding strategy is useful to young readers because many English words cannot be deciphered by analogy to words sharing rimes. For example, 'unique' words such as *'soap'* cannot be read using an orthographic rime analogy strategy because they have no orthographic rime neighbours (Patterson & Morton, 1985). 'Soap' can however be read using grapheme-to-phoneme correspondences. Unique words are thus used as another outcome measure sensitive to different strategic approaches to decoding in the present study.

THE PURPOSE OF THE PRESENT STUDY, RESEARCH QUESTION AND SPECIFIC PREDICTIONS

The primary purpose of the present study was thus to explore the effectiveness of a Web-based literacy programme that delivered two distinct phonics programmes. The research question in this study was: *Does the ABRACADABRA literacy program produce qualitatively different effects for synthetic and analytic phonics interventions on phonological, word and nonword measures?*

Based on the literature it was predicted that the synthetic phonics group would show specific improve-ments on: (1) blending and segmenting tasks; (2) articulation of shared codas (final consonant); (3) decoding of nonsense words (low-rime neighbours); and (4) reading of unique words compared with the analytic phonics intervention group. The analytic phonics group was predicted to show gains in: (1) blending and segmenting only of CV words (those maintaining the onset–rime units); (2) articulation of shared rime units; and (3) decoding of nonsense words with high-rime neighbours only. No strong predictions were made regarding the overall *quantitative* effect of each intervention on reading abilities (e.g. in the WRAT reading test) given the existing literature to date showing few differences. All children in the interventions should improve equally on letter/sound knowledge tasks as both groups were taught these correspondences.

METHOD

Design

This study used a pre–post-test experimental intervention design. There was a full random allocation of participants within each classroom to each of two distinct reading interventions, so as to provide control for all extraneous variables such as teaching methods in the classrooms and unmeasured child characteristics. Data were collected over 2 years with two samples in the same school. The research team was given access to one intervention school located in one English language school board in an urban setting. The choice of school was made by senior officials in the participating school board who reported that this school was identified based on the board's perception of highest educational need.

There were five kinds of outcome measures that can distinguish qualitative effects of different phonics interventions: the three phonological awareness tasks (blending, segmenting and common unit tasks) and two decoding tasks (nonword reading and unique word reading tasks), so these are considered primary measures. WRAT reading and letter–sounds knowledge measures were considered secondary measures.

Participants

All children in four Kindergarten classes ($n = 65$) were initially approached to take part in the study. The final sample ($n = 53$) was based solely on whether formal written parental consent to participate was returned. There were no exclusions or other eligibility requirements for sample membership. Response rates for participation were also equal in each of the four classes (16, 16, 16 and 17). No children were excluded or refused to take part at subsequent phases of the study and all pre- and post-tests and both of the interventions themselves all involved the same $n = 53$ children initially identified

COMASKEY, SAVAGE and ABRAMI

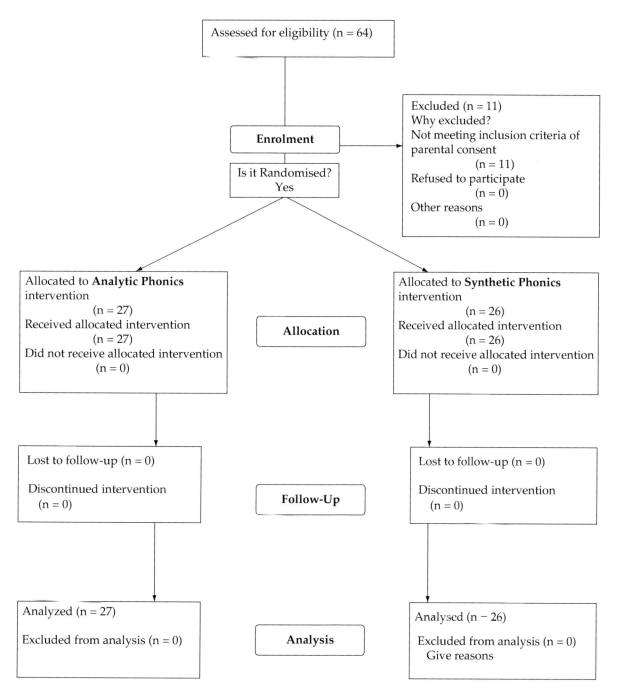

Figure 1. A CONSORT E-flowchart for the ABRACADABRA study.

as eligible to take part in the study. These details of the sample are specified in the CONSORT flow diagram (Figure 1).

A formal power calculation was made using Power and Precision V3 (Borenstein, Rothstein & Cohen, 2001). This showed that with α set at .05, *n* = 26 participants in each cell and one covariate, this design would yield a .80 power to detect a large effect size in analysis of covariance (where a large effect is

defined, following Cohen's 1988 effect size metric as *f* = .40). This level of power appeared reasonable given that a previous study using ABRA by Savage et al. (in press) had identified the presence of large effect sizes in standardised measures of phonological awareness.

Parent questionnaires were also distributed to obtain information about language spoken at home, and mother's education level. Of those 53 parents consenting for their child to take part, 47 responses

(88.7% of the total) to the additional parent questionnaire were returned. Analysis of these parental questionnaires revealed that 11% spoke only English at home. The majority of children (61%) spoke English plus another language, most often an East Indian language. The parents of 28% of children in this sample spoke no English at home at all.

Data on mother's educational level was coded using a 6-point scale from 0 = *no formal education* through high school completion to 6 = *completed postgraduate degree.* This scale was drawn from the 2006 census categories used by Statistics Canada. Only 45% of the mothers of children in this sample achieved a formal post-high school qualification. Scores for two elementary education categories and two post-secondary education categories were combined as the frequency count for two of these variables was below 5. This yielded four categories. Analysis of these scores against norms for women in Quebec from Statistics Canada (2006 census) showed that the levels of education in this sample were significantly lower than provincial norms, $\chi^2(3) = 8.31$, $p < .05$, confirming the presence of educational disadvantage.

The children within the two intervention classrooms were randomly assigned to either the synthetic or analytic phonics intervention group using a manual random allocation process (allocation cards pulled blind from a hat) by the first author. There were no restrictions or stratifications in this allocation process. This resulted in a total of $n = 27$ participants in the analytic phonics intervention group and $n = 26$ participants in the synthetic phonics intervention. The first author was also partly responsible for running the interventions as one of the facilitators, and was also responsible for pre- and post-test data collection. As in most educational research where interventions are visible no concealment of treatments was possible. All children in each of the intervention subgroups participated in the study. This sample size allowed the construction of two analytic and two synthetic phonics groups per intervention classroom in each of the 2 years of the study.

Procedure

Pre-testing was conducted at the beginning of the school year and was concluded in 3 weeks. Each child was screened individually by one of two trained facilitators away from their classroom. Following the pre-testing, interventions began immediately in the two assigned classrooms. Interventions were part of the 'centre activities' of the day. This means that the students were engaged in other learning centres and would rotate into the 'ABRA' centre during this designated time period. Small groups of (generally) four children working with ABRA would sit at the designated table in a quiet area in the room with the facilitator. The computer-based program was always the

focus for and source of learning activities. Children would engage in ABRA activities around a single computer supported by a facilitator. There was one mouse that rotated from child to child as each took turns.

There were two facilitators, one for each year the study was run. In both cases the facilitator was a trained Master's degree student who was also an experienced early years teacher. The facilitators each received detailed training in the use of ABRA and were highly familiar with and confident in using the system. Training included 2 days of formal training in assessment and intervention, practice time and ongoing weekly follow-up support by the second author and a devoted ABRA project manager. The primary role of the facilitator was to help children to navigate through the appropriate range of activities for each intervention while supporting the socio-academic functions of the group (e.g. maintaining on-task behaviour, observing peers' responses, turn-taking, offering of suggestions, responding appropriately as a group to ABRA prompts such as to blend a word). The facilitator would also judge when the group as a whole had reached mastery level for an activity and should move to the next level of task difficulty.

Every attempt was made to keep the two intervention conditions the same, apart from the different word attack strategies that were taught. Precisely specified lesson plans were developed by the ABRA team and reviewed weekly via reports from facilitators. These features alongside informal observation of interventions ensured high treatment integrity. For this reason, the same facilitator worked with both a synthetic phonics and an analytic phonics group so that teacher characteristics would be consistent. During the session, children not working with ABRA remained in the other centres in the classroom, thereby limiting any cross-contamination of intervention effects. Each small group of four children was generally seen three times a week, depending on school schedule, for 15 minutes. There were sometimes unavoidable delays due to other events taking place in a classroom. Thus it was not always possible to complete three sessions of ABRA every week for all groups. In a minority of cases therefore, the intervention was spread across 16 weeks. In all cases, a total of 40 sessions were completed resulting in 10 hours of instructional time per child.

Interventions for the synthetic and analytic phonics groups followed the same lesson structure, beginning with an Animated Alphabet followed by a 'core activity'. The Animated Alphabet normally took 2–3 minutes allowing 10 minutes to be spent on the core activity. The core activity for each lesson depended on the group. The analytic phonics group's core activities revolved around word families, identifying words that rhymed and manipulating and articulating words at the onset-rime level. The synthetic phonics group's core activities focused on blending and segmenting simple two-phoneme words, identifying words with shared initial and final consonants and forming new words by blending single phonemes. In general, all synthetic phonics groups mastered the CV and VC levels of their core blending activities. All analytic phonics groups showed rime word generation skills. In both interventions, children moved to the next level of difficulty in each activity when they reached 80% mastery.

Following the core activity, each group had a choice activity. The choice activity could be a story option, or a reinforcement game such as Letter Bingo (identifying the correct letter by its name) or letter-sound search (identifying the correct letter by its sound). Groups could also choose to do a different core activity as their choice. When time allowed, the core activity was repeated before ending each session.

General Session Components

The initial ABRA sessions included general literacy skills activities that were included in both analytic and synthetic phonics interventions with identical frequency and duration. Both groups were read ABRA stories, identified syllables in words and words in sentences and were taught letter–sound correspondences. All children in the classroom used ABRA so students whose parents did not submit consent were allowed to participate in the use of the software, but data were not collected.

Measures

Nine measurements were used in both the pre-screening and post-testing sessions. Most of these were based closely on those used in studies reviewed in the introduction. The PPVT (Peabody Picture Vocabulary Test) was only used at pre-test to assess general receptive verbal ability in the sample.

PPVT Vocabulary

The PPVT III (Dunn & Dunn, 1996) is a test of receptive vocabulary. On each item, the examiner reads aloud a target word and children are asked to select the picture that best illustrates the meaning of that target word. The median published split-half reliability of this test is $r = .94$. The mean standard score on the PPVT (Dunn & Dunn, 1996) was 93.11 ($SD = 14.89$), confirming that as a sample the children had slightly below-average vocabulary abilities.

Letter-sound Knowledge

In this task the children were shown the 26 letters of the English alphabet in upper-case letters in random order on one page. The children were instructed to say the sound that each letter makes. Words or letter names were not counted as correct answers. The Spearman–Brown internal reliability for this measure was $r = .93$.

Wide Range Achievement Test Word Recognition Subtest.

The first 12 words of the Wide Range Achievement Test Word Recognition Subtest (Wilkinson, 1993) were presented and children asked to read them. This approach was used to obtain a brief measure of reading ability suitable for children who were generally non-readers at pre-test. Standard scores could not be collected as norms do not exist for children this young. The Spearman–Brown internal reliability for this task was $r = .84$.

Experimental Phonological Awareness Tasks

Segmenting and Blending

This task consisted of a total of 16 monosyllabic words. The same 16 words were used for both the blending portion and the segmenting portion. There were two groups of eight words: consonant–vowel words (e.g. *Sigh*) or vowel–consonant (e.g. *Ice*) words. The words in each group were therefore matched exactly for phonemic similarity.

The tasks were fully counterbalanced during administration. Following a procedure described by Uhry and Ehri (1999), children were shown a prop of a funny character's face, 'Mrs Funnybunny'. Inside the character's mouth were two manipulatives. The participants were introduced to Mrs Funnybunny and then told, 'She likes to play with words and sounds. The facilitator would say, 'If Mrs Funnybunny says /z/ /oo/ what word could she be saying?' The facilitator would then move the manipulatives with each phoneme (e.g. /z/ /oo/ for zoo) and then prompt the child to blend those sounds together to figure out what word was trying to be said. When the word was blended the manipulatives would be pushed together to form the whole word. A total of four practice items were included. The Spearman–Brown internal reliability for this task was $r = .86$ for CV words and $r = .72$ for VC words. Using the same materials and procedure, children were asked to break the words down into their phonemic constituents. The Spearman–Brown internal reliability for this task was $r = .84$ for CV words and $r = .84$ for VC words.

Common Units Tasks

There were two common unit articulation tasks. One required participants to articulate the common 'rime unit' in two words (e.g. '*eet*' in *feet* and *sleet*). The other task required participants to articulate the common coda unit in two words (e.g. '*g*' in *dog* and *bag*). The order of presentation of these tasks was counterbalanced. In each task the children were given four practice items and picture prompts for each of the two words. Practice items could be repeated until the facilitator was sure that the child grasped the nature of the task. The Spearman–Brown internal reliability for the rime articulation was $r = .84$ and for the coda articulation was $r = .82$.

Experimental Word and Nonword Decoding Tasks

Nonsense Word Recognition

This list of 12 words was comprised of two types of stimuli: those words with high-rime neighbours (e.g. *lan*) and those words with low- or no rime neighbours (e.g. *pol*). The words were randomised and presented to the participant on one sheet in lower-case print. The instructions were to 'Name that monster'. The Spearman–Brown internal reliability for this task was $r = .91$.

Unique Word Recognition

This list consisted of eight words with no rime neighbours with the same spelling (e.g. soap). The children were asked to say them out loud. The Spearman–Brown internal reliability for this task was $r = .86$.

RESULTS

Preliminary Data Analyses

Preliminary data analysis was first performed to assure that the data set would meet statistical assumptions for multivariate analyses. The pre-test scores revealed three measures that had significant positive skew: WRAT sight vocabulary, nonsense word reading and articulation of rime units. Each of these measures showed patterns consistent with floor effects at pre-test. These variables were thus transformed using an inverse plus constant transformation following the standard procedures described by Tabachnick and Fidell (2001, pp. 82–83). This substantially improved the skew for these four samples.

No other transformations or manipulations of the data were necessary. There were no significant pre-test differences between either of the intervention subgroups in PPVT vocabulary, $F(1, 51) = 3.49$, $p = .07$, ns, $\eta_p^2 = .06$.

Main Analyses

A general linear model analysis was employed for each measure for each intervention group (synthetic vs analytic) univariate ANOVA. In order to closely control for any pretest differences between intervention groups, the corresponding pre-test measure was entered as a covariate in each analysis of post-test performance. We sought to test only a limited series of *specific* and theoretically driven predictions that were set out at the end of the Introduction for the phonological awareness, word reading and decoding measures, so conventional significance levels for α ($\alpha = .05$) were

used. Bonferonni's corrections were not used as they would tend to be overly conservative in data such as these where measures are highly correlated.

Finally, effect sizes for each analysis of covariance (ANCOVA) run were calculated using partial η^2 (η_p^2) which describes the percentage of variance accounted for by a given variable after controlling for differences at pre-test. Following conventional approaches, a small effect size is $\eta_p^2 = .01$, a medium effect size is $\eta_p^2 > .06$ and a large effect size is $\eta_p^2 > .10$. The obtained β in each ANCOVA for the effect of group is also reported alongside the associated 95% confidence intervals for β. All results are reported in Table 1.

Phonological Awareness Tasks

Blending and Segmenting

The blending CV words task yielded a significant result, $F(1, 50) = 9.05$, $p = .004$, $\eta_p^2 = .15$, with a significant advantage evident in comparisons for the synthetic phonics group over the analytic phonics group. The blending VC words task also yielded a significant result, $F(1, 50) = 4.93$, $p = .04$, $\eta_p^2 = .09$. The advantage here was again for the synthetic phonics intervention. The segmenting task yielded no significant effects either for CV or VC segmentation, $F(1, 50) < .02$, $p = .88$, ns, $\eta_p^2 = .000$ for CV words and $F(1, 50) = 3.78$, $p = .06$, ns, $\eta_p^2 = .07$ for VC words. This latter effect just escaped significance and showed a medium effect size favouring the synthetic phonics programme. Together then, advantages were evident for phoneme blending, but not segmentation, favouring the group taught synthetic phonics.

Common Unit Tasks

In the common unit rime articulation task, results showed a significant advantage for the analytic phonics subgroup over the synthetic phonics subgroup, $F(1, 50) = 6.38$, $p = .015$, $\eta_p^2 = .11$. There was also a significant effect for the common unit coda task, $F(1, 50) = 5.64$, $p = .02.$, $\eta_p^2 = .10$, this time favouring the synthetic phonics group. These findings suggest that students who are explicitly taught about rimes are able to identify and articulate that unit. Patterns appear to be specific to rime units in that particular intervention. The same specificity is evident in coda articulation after being taught about individual phonemes.

Word and Nonword Reading Tasks

For the unique word list there was no main effect of intervention group, $F(1, 50) = 0.11$, $p = .74$, ns, $\eta_p^2 = .002$. As the HRn and LRn nonwords were explicitly matched on shared grapheme-phoneme correspondences a 2 Intervention Group (synthetic vs analytic vs control) × 2 Nonword Type (HRn vs LRn words) ANCOVA was run with repeated measures on

Table 1. Means, standard deviations, statistical effects and 95% confidence intervals for all outcome measures

Task	Synthetic		Analytic		β of Effect and 95% Confidence Interval for β			F	P	η^2_p	Effect Source
	Pre	Post	Pre	Post	β	Lower Bound	Higher Bound				
Blending CV	1.07 (2.06)	6.27 (2.99)	1.48 (2.64)	3.93 (3.87)	2.61	0.87	4.35	9.05	.004**	.15	S > A
Blending VC	1.96 (2.09)	5.92 (3.02)	2.74 (2.81)	4.59 (3.40)	1.79	0.17	3.41	4.9	.03*	.0?	S > A
Segmenting CV	0.88 (2.36)	4.46 (2.82)	1.40 (2.75)	4.63 (3.94)	0.13	−1.62	1.87	0.02	.88	.00	
Segmenting VC	0.96 (1.97)	5.19 (2.83)	1.89 (3.32)	4.00 (3.65)	1.64	−0.06	3.32	3.77	.06	.07	
Rime articulation Coda	0.11 (0.59)	0.77 (1.92)	0.67 (2.11)	3.11 (3.72)	−1.74	−3.12	−0.36	6.38	.015**	.11	A > S
articulation WRAT word	0.96 (2.36)	6.31 (3.52)	2.26 (3.36)	4.70 (3.97)	2.31	0.36	4.25	5.64	.02*	.10	S > A
reading	0.62 (1.60)	2.65 (3.06)	0.63 (1.76)	3.22 (4.66)	−0.54	−2.07	0.99	0.51	.49	.01	
Unique words High N	0.56 (1.55)	2.12 (2.42)	0.93 (1.87)	2.15 (2.55)	0.18	−0.91	1.27	0.11	.74	.00	
nonwords Low N	0.04 (0.19)	1.27 (1.66)	0.19 (0.56)	1.22 (1.91)	0.32	−0.61	1.25	Group × Nonword:		***	
nonwords	0.11 (0.42)	1.12 (1.77)	0.31 (0.71)	1.44 (1.91)	−0.94	−1.08	0.89	2.49	.12	.05	
Letter-sounds	7.30 (7.24)	19.61(5.28)	6.22(6.27)	18.81(6.8)	0.26	−2.59	3.12	0.03	.86	.00	

Note: $^*p < .05$, $^{**}p < .01$. ***As the high-rime neighbourhood and low-rime neighbourhood nonwords are included in an omnibus 2 × 2 analysis, the Group × Nonword effect is the interaction predicted to be significant in research prediction 3, so the interaction effect rather than the main effect of Group is depicted for this effect. S = synthetic phonics intervention; A = analytic phonics intervention.

nonword type and with pre-test nonword type reading score as a covariate. This analysis also revealed no main effect of nonword type, $F(1, 49) = 0.16$, $p = .69$, ns, $\eta_p^2 < .003$, or group, $F(1, 49) = 0.06$, $p = .80$, ns, $\eta_p^2 < .001$ and no Intervention Group × Nonword Type interaction effect, $F(1, 50) = 2.49$, $p = .12$, ns, $\eta_p^2 = .05$. As the HRn and LRn nonwords are included in an omnibus 2×2 analysis, the Group × Nonword interaction effect is predicted to be significant in research prediction 3. That is to say, a specific improvement in reading of HRn nonwords and disadvantage in reading LRn nonwords at post-test should have been evident in the analytic phonics condition if children apply rime-based orthographic inferences to reading following rime-based intervention.

Secondary Analyses: Letter–Sound Knowledge and WRAT Reading

Analysis revealed no significant overall effects for letter–sound knowledge, $F(1, 50) = 0.03$, $p = .89$, ns, $\eta_p^2 = .001$. There were no differences between each intervention. On the WRAT word reading subtest assessment, no significant intervention group effect was found, $F(1, 50) = 0.51$, $p = .49$, ns, $\eta_p^2 = .01$.

DISCUSSION

The primary aim of this paper was to answer the question: does the ABRACADABRA literacy programme produce qualitatively different effects for synthetic and analytic phonics interventions on phonological awareness, word and nonword measures? Specific predictions for the synthetic phonics programme were superior blending and segmenting skills for both the VC and the CV words, superior abilities in articulating final consonant codas and superior decoding of all nonsense words irrespective of the number of riming neighbours they have.

The results provided partial support for these predictions as the children in the synthetic phonics subgroup showed specific improvements in both CV and VC phoneme blending tasks compared with children in the analytic phonics group. Children in the synthetic phonics programme also showed a significant and specific advantage for coda articulation in the common unit task and no advantage in the rime common unit tasks.

In contrast, there were no significant advantages for the synthetic phonics group in phoneme segmentation. Why was this? Firstly, there was a discernible trend in post-test improvement in VC segmentation, where a medium-sized effect (η_p^2) of .07 was evident. Such an effect could be practically important but is beyond the statistical power of the present study with $n = 53$ participants to detect as significant. Furthermore phoneme segmentation tasks are among the most difficult phonological tasks (Savage & Carless, 2005; Schatschneider,

Fletcher, Francis, Carlson & Foorman, 2004). Finally, children in the synthetic phonics programme here received only around 50 minutes of segmenting training, whereas they received 160 minutes of blending and decoding activity training.

Turning to the analytic phonics programme, this group was predicted to show superior segmentation and blending of CV words where phonemes represent onset and rime and to articulate the shared rime units in words. Similarly, strengths in decoding words with high-rime neighbours were predicted. Results provided only partial support for these predictions. Children showed significant and specific improvements in the common unit rime task. This finding replicates and extends the findings reported by Goswami and East (2000) to show intervention-specific effects of rime training on rime but not phoneme awareness using comparable tasks to those used by Goswami and East. Against this, there was no advantage in blending or segmenting CV over VC units suggesting that children's rime sensitivity is not reflected in intervention-specific rime blending and segmenting skill, as Savage et al. (2003) reported. This effect might be consistent with the view that the manipulation of CV onset–rime units is different in kind to that of onset–rimes in closed syllables (Guedens & Sandra, 2002; Uhry & Ehri, 1999), possibly reflecting specific perceptual characteristics of CV and VC stimuli.

Turning to the reading and decoding tasks, results here showed that children in the synthetic phonics teaching condition did not read more HRn than LRn nonsense words and read both at comparable levels to the children exposed to the analytic phonics intervention, suggesting instead that they all used grapheme-to-phoneme conversion to decode. This interpretation is also supported by the finding of no qualitative differences in levels of reading for unique words that have no rime neighbours.

These results are thus consistent with some of those reported previously in the literature (e.g. Savage et al., 2003). These results are on first glance not consistent with those reported by Deavers et al. (2000) who reported intervention-specific impacts of analytic phonics programmes. Deavers et al. studied somewhat older children (age 6 years 4 months) who were above-average readers (reading age 6 years 11 months), and who had been exposed to an intensive and daily rime-based phonics programme for nearly 2 academic years. It may be that a tendency to use orthographic rime strategies to pronounce nonsense words only emerges under such circumstances. Why might children in an analytic phonics programme emphasising rimes instead use grapheme-to-phoneme conversion to decode? Reasons for this are unclear, but the rime activities in ABRA may have implicitly directed children to attend to word onsets. It may also be that children preferred to use letter—sound correspondences that they had all been taught in ABRA to aid their early decoding.

There were also no overall advantages for the analytic over the synthetic phonics subgroup in reading sight words from the WRAT. This finding is consistent with and adds to several well-designed recent studies that have contrasted the decoding and reading abilities of young children exposed to synthetic and analytic phonics interventions in older children in Year 1 (Christensen & Bowey, 2005; Savage & Carless, 2005; Torgerson et al., 2006). According to Torgerson et al. (2006) there are only three well-designed RCT studies contrasting synthetic and analytic phonics programmes. They thus describe the evidence base here as 'weak'. This study represents a further contribution on this issue. It reinforces the existing view expressed by Torgerson et al. that there are not marked differences in the impact of synthetic and analytic phonics programmes on reading and decoding levels.

Our study also adds a new element to this literature by indicating that while synthetic and analytic phonics programmes provide quite large and significant early advantage in phoneme and rime phonological awareness, respectively, these qualitative phonological differences do not immediately translate into qualitative differences in the way that children approach word reading or decoding tasks in Kindergarten.

LIMITATIONS OF THE PRESENT STUDY

There are several limitations in the present study that need to be considered in evaluating our results. One limitation of the study was that the sample was relatively modest in size. Nevertheless, the study was sufficiently powerful to detect several large effects for phonological awareness. It is also possible that, as randomisation was not concealed from the researchers who were responsible for both running the study and administering the pre- and post-tests, this may have introduced subtle bias. In practice, it is not possible to disguise the nature of the content of these two interventions. The use of two distinct sub-teams of researchers with one to run the interventions and a second to pre- and post-test the children would however be a methodological improvement in future studies.

The conclusions are also limited to the specific approach used in this study: collaborative interventions in small groups in Kindergarten. This approach may have been effective because children could observe imitate and collaborate with peers. Implementation of ABRA in other ways such as one-to-one tutoring may lead to very different patterns of findings and different patterns may be evident in more experienced or older readers. There were also a limited number of very specific outcome measures in this study, focused as it was on phonics. Furthermore, as the study focused on very young children we were unable to measure reading com-

prehension growth. Reading comprehension is a key marker of literacy and probably requires children to have both good phonic and verbal comprehension skills.

The research was undertaken in a distinctive and multilingual urban Canadian context. The school was selected by our partner school board as being of particularly high need, so our capacity to generalise to other schools even in this community is unknown. It will therefore be important to replicate the effects in other pedagogical and linguistic contexts.

Another limitation was that the intervention was brief in duration. Our finding of significant effects with a 10-hour intervention is also, in some sense, a strength of the study, and is consistent with findings that brief interventions may be maximally effective (NRP, 2000). Nevertheless the possibility that distinct qualitative patterns might emerge with greater training cannot be ruled out. The current findings that distinct patterns of phonological awareness emerge but are not reflected in qualitative or quantitative differences in decoding are limited to our use of immediate follow-up. Differences between synthetic and analytic programmes might emerge in delayed follow-ups.

Finally, ABRA is also designed to be a tool for teachers. The focus of the present study was on whether technology can be *efficacious*. It is important to add ecological validity to these findings by placing the tool into the hands of well-trained classroom teachers to measure its *effectiveness* in the classroom. Work is currently under way to explore these issues. As ABRA is a free-access Web-based resource we also encourage other researchers and practitioners to take up these challenges with well-executed RCT studies and field trials. The latest version of ABRA consists of 35 graded English instructional activities linked to 17 stories designed to teach emerging readers alphabetics, fluency, comprehension and writing skills and associated subskills. ABRA also contains teacher professional development materials, just in time videos, assessment materials and a communication module (forthcoming) as well as an improved interface (see http://grover.concordia.ca/abra/current/index.php).

ACKNOWLEDGEMENTS

We would like to thank the staff, parents and children of our partner schools for their willingness to allow us to work with children in their schools for such extended periods of time. We would like to thank Stacy Altman for help in the collection of portions of these data undertaken as partial fulfilment of her MEd thesis. Erin Comaskey collected portions of these data as part of her MA thesis. This study was supported by grants from Fonds québécois de la recherche sur la société et la culture to the second and third author and the Social Sciences and Humanities Research Council of Canada to the second author.

REFERENCES

Abrami, P.C., Savage, R., Wade, A., Hipps, G. & Lopez, M. (2008). Using technology to assist children learning to read and write. In T. Willoughby & E. Wood (Eds.), *Children's learning in a digital world*. (pp. 129–172). Oxford: Blackwell Publishing.

Altman, D.G., Schulz, K.F., Moher, D., Egger, M., Davidoff, F., Elbourne, D. et al. (2001). The revised CONSORT statement for reporting randomized trials: Explanation and elaboration. *Annals of Internal Medicine*, 134, 663–694.

Borenstein, M., Rothstein, H. & Cohen, J. (2001). *Power and precision*. (Vol. 3). Englewood, NJ: BioStat.

Christensen, C.A. & Bowey, J. (2005). The efficacy of orthographic rime, grapheme–phoneme correspondence, and implicit phonics approaches to teaching decoding skills. *Scientific Studies of Reading*, 9, 327–349.

Deault, L., Savage, R.S. & Abrami, P. (2008). *Inattention and response to the ABRACADABRA Web-based literacy intervention*. Manuscript submitted for publication.

Deavers, R., Solity, J. & Kerfoot, J. (2000). The effect of instruction on early nonword reading strategies. *Journal of Research in Reading*, 23, 267–286.

Duncan, L.C., Seymour, P.H.K. & Hill, S. (1997). How important are rhyme and analogy in beginning reading? *Cognition*, 63, 171–208.

Dunn, L.M. & Dunn, L.M. (1996). *Peabody Picture Vocabulary Test*. (3rd edn). Circle Pines, MN: American Guidance Service.

Dynarski, M., Agodini, R., Heaviside, S., Novak, T., Carye, N., Campuzano, L. et al. (2007). *Effectiveness of reading and mathematics software products: Findings from the first student cohort*. Report to Congress, Institute of Educational Sciences National Centre for Educational Evaluation and Regional Assistance.

Goswami, U.C. & East, M. (2000). Rhyme and analogy in beginning reading: Conceptual and methodological issues. *Applied Psycholinguistics*, 21, 63–93.

Guedens, A. & Sandra, D. (2002). Beyond implicit phonological knowledge: No support for an onset-rime structure in children's explicit phonological awareness. *Journal of Memory and Language*, 49, 157–182.

Johnston, R.A. & Watson, J.E. (2004). Accelerating the development of reading, spelling and phonemic awareness skills in initial readers. *Reading and Writing: An Interdisciplinary Journal*, 17, 327–357.

Moher, D., Schulz, K.F. & Altman, D.G. (2001). The CONSORT statement: Revised recommendations for improving the quality of reports of parallel-group randomised trials. *Lancet*, 357, 1191–1194.

National Reading Panel (NRP) (2000). *Teaching children to read: Reports of the subgroups*. Retrieved 20 November 2008 from http://www.nichd.nih.gov/publications/nrp/report.cfm

Patterson, K.E. & Morton, J. (1985). From orthography to phonology: An attempt at an old interpretation. In K. Patterson, J.C. Marshall & M. Coltheart (Eds.), *Surface dyslexia*. (pp. 335–359). London: Erlbaum.

Savage, R., Abrami, P., Hipps, G. & Deault, L. (in press). A randomised control trial study of the ABRACADABRA reading intervention program in grade 1. *Journal of Educational Psychology*.

Savage, R. & Carless, S. (2005). Learning support assistants can deliver effective reading interventions for 'at-risk' children. *Educational Research*, 47, 45–61.

Savage, R., Carless, S. & Stuart, M. (2003). The effects of rime and phoneme based teaching delivered by learning support assistants. *Journal of Research in Reading*, 26, 211–233.

Schatschneider, C., Fletcher, J.M., Francis, D.J., Carlson, C.D. & Foorman, B. (2004). Kindergarten prediction of reading skills: A longitudinal comparative analysis. *Journal of Educational Psychology*, 96, 265–282.

Stuart, M. (1999). Getting ready for reading: Early phoneme awareness and phonics teaching improves reading and spelling in inner-city second language learners. *British Journal of Educational Psychology*, 69, 587–605.

Stuart, M. (2004). Getting ready for reading: A follow-up study of inner city second language learners at the end of Key Stage 1. *British Journal of Educational Psychology*, 74, 15–36.

Tabachnick, B.G. & Fidell, L.S. (2001). *Using multivariate statistics*. (4th edn). New York: Allyn & Bacon.

Torgerson, C., Brooks, G. & Hall, J. (2006). *A systematic review of the research literature on the use of phonics in the teaching of reading and spelling*. Department for Education and Skills Research Rep. No. RR711.

Torgerson, C. & Zhu, D. (2003). A systematic review and meta-analysis of the effectiveness of ICT on literacy learning in English, 5–16. In *Research evidence in education library*. London: EPPI-Centre, Social Sciences Research Unit Institute of Education. Retrieved 20 November 2008 from http://eppi.ioe.ac.uk/cms/default.aspx?tabid=198

Uhry, J. & Ehri, L. (1999). Ease of segmenting two- and three-phoneme words in Kindergarten: Rime cohesion or vowel salience? *Journal of Educational Psychology*, 91, 594–603.

Wilkinson, G.S. (1993). *The Wide Range Achievement Test*. Wilmington, DE: Wide Range Inc.

1.04

3-FACTOR PRE AND POSTTEST DESIGN

The Effects of Visual Illustrations on Learners' Achievement and Interest in PDA- (Personal Digital Assistant) Based Learning

Youngmin Lee,[*] Sanghoon Park,[†] Minjeong Kim,[†] Chanhee Son,[†] and Miyoung Lee[†]

ABSTRACT: PDAs (Personal Digital Assistants) have been used widely in educational settings. In this study, the visual illustration of a scientific text (cognitive-interest illustration, emotional-interest illustration, or no illustration) was manipulated to investigate its impact on student interest in instructional materials, achievement, and time spent on reading materials in PDA-based learning. Forty-five graduate students were randomly assigned to one of the three treatment groups: the cognitive-interest illustration group, emotional-interest illustration group, and the text only group. Each group was given instructional material corresponding to the treatments. Results revealed that the levels of post-interest across the groups were not significantly different among the three groups. However, the students in the cognitive-interest illustration group showed significantly higher achievement than those in the emotional illustration group and the text only group. Implications of the findings as a catalyst for further research in the development of instructional materials for PDA-based learning were discussed.

INTRODUCTION

New media technologies have been changing the ways of teaching and learning in the classroom. For example, multimedia computers have enabled teachers to incorporate audio and visual information into their materials and have helped students interactively acquire important knowledge. Of the new technologies that have impacted the classroom learning environments, PDAs (Person Digital Assistants), which have been called interchangeably Palmtop computers, Handheld computers, Palm Pilots, and Pocket PCs, are rapidly becoming a common technology because of their affordability and excellent portability (Bateman, Crystal, Davidson, Holzberg, McIntire, & McLester, 2001; Fasimpaur, 2002). The affordability and portability of handheld computers are the main factors that draw our attention to them as an alternative to conventional computers.

[*]Florida State University
[†]Korean Educational Research Institute

In addition to portability and affordability, there are other advantages that set PDAs apart from the desktop computer: accessibility, mobility, and adaptability (Pownell & Bailey, 2000). Pownell and Bailey differentiated between informational accessibility and portability, defining informational accessibility as the ability for users to get the information they need instantly, while portability refers to the physical device, which means PDAs are small enough to be taken anywhere. Mobility, on the other hand, refers to the user who has the ability for greater movement and is not tethered to one place. Finally, adaptability refers to the ability of the user to change his or her behavior because of this highly mobile technology. With great attention to PDAs, many educators and teachers have been trying to find out how to best use these devices for pedagogical purposes. For example, Son, Kim, and Park (2004) reported the eight categories of PDA utilizations in K-12 educational setting by analyzing cases collected from the website, which is being run by both Palm Inc. and Handspring Inc. K-12 schools. The PDAs were mainly used for the purpose of data transferring, evaluation, class management, visualization, scientific tool, data sharing, documentation, and data retrieving. In this case study, it was noticeable that PDAs were considered as a tool to support learning and teaching practice rather than as an instructional material for pedagogical purpose.

To fully utilize the advantages of PDAs for pedagogical purposes, however, there are still many pedagogical issues to be answered due to differences in a PDA's interface when compared with that of a desktop computer. One of the issues is related to the design of educational materials. Usually PDAs have a very small screen size with limited display capacity. Thus, it is difficult to deliver as much educational material as can be done on a computer screen. The learner's interest also decreases due to the lack of readability on the small sized screen.

Given the pitfalls of educational use of PDAs, two critical questions could be raised: 1) how to integrate the epitomes of educational materials for the purposes of PDA-based learning, and 2) how to represent those synthesized materials effectively to promote learner interest so that learners can attain higher achievement. Subject experts who are most familiar with the learning content may answer the first question. However, the second question, how to visually represent educational material for the purpose of PDA-based learning, is not easy to answer.

Regarding the second question, there have been a couple of studies investigating the best representation of educational material in PDAs. Usually, two factors were considered; text and graphics. In terms of the text, Park, Kim, Ryu, and Son (2003) investigated the effect of character spacing of text in PDA on learning performance and attitude. They conducted experiments with two treatments, PDA text with expanded character spacing and PDA text with condensed character spacing. However, there was no significant difference of the free recall test between expanded character spacing and condensed character spacing. Also, the comprehensive test did not show a significant difference between two different character spacing. In terms of the effect of graphics, Park and Lim (2004) investigated the effects of different types of visual illustrations in learner controlled multimedia material containing factual information as well as procedural information. In this study, he found that learners who were given illustrations feel more interest than the learners who were given only-text information. However, there was no significant difference between the mean score of cognitive interest illustration group and the mean score of emotional interest illustration group.

Therefore, in this article, the answer to the second question, how to represent instructional material effectively to promote learner interest and higher achievement in PDAs, was explored using two types of graphical representations, especially employing the concept of seductive detail/seductive augmentation. Regarding the presentation of educational materials, the effective use of graphical illustrations in designing instructional material has been considered an important facet of instructional message design (Anglin, Towers, and Levis, 1996). Using illustrations in instructional materials is an effective method for supporting learning because they can be used as interest-grabbing devices, and their use also helps learners interpret and acquire the context of the illustrated text. Based on the reviews of literature regarding the effects of illustration on knowledge acquisition in instructional settings, Anglin, Towers, and Levis (1996) pointed out that visual illustrations would facilitate the acquisition of knowledge when they are concurrently presented with textual information.

Levie and Lentz (1982) suggested that illustrations provided together with textual information could be classified based on how they impact learners in terms of their knowledge acquisition or how they function as instructional materials. The researchers classified illustrations into four major functional types: attentional, affective, cognitive, and compensatory (Levie & Lentz, 1982). The attentional function attracts or directs attention to the material given. The affective function enhances enjoyment or affects emotion and attitude. The cognitive function serves to facilitate learning textual content through improving comprehension, increasing retention, or providing additional information. The last function, the compensatory function, is used to accommodate poor readers. Among these four functional types of illustrations, previous studies usually focused on only the cognitive function of illustration. It has not been clearly answered what effect visual illustrations have on learners' emotions and attitudes.

Regarding the affective function of illustrations, Kintsch (1980) proposed the concepts of cognitive interest and emotional interest. Cognitive interest adjuncts, such as explanative summaries, influence the learner's cognition by promoting the structural understanding of the explanation. On the other hand, the emotional interest concept is explained by the addition of interesting, but only peripherally relevant, materials to a textbook lesson that serve to energize learners so that they pay more attention and learn more overall. Scholars have used the term "seductive detail" to refer to interesting but irrelevant details that are added to a passage to make it more interesting. This term has been used extensively in the reading education field in referring to those interesting yet unimportant text segments of expository texts added in order to increase the learner's interest.

Two opposite research suggestions have been made regarding the usefulness of seductive detail. The first suggestion asserts that such detail effectively promotes learning by energizing readers so that they pay more attention to the material and by influencing the learner's affect by promoting his/her enjoyment of the topic. Hence, it causes the learner to pay more attention to and encode more of the information from the material, thereby learning more overall (Izard & Ackerman, 2000; Kintsch, 1980). This suggestion includes using perceptual arousal techniques to increase the learner's attention as a motivational design guideline (Song, 1998). Researchers advancing the second suggestion take the completely opposite position. They argue that seductive detail disrupts the learner's construction of the cause-and-effect chain, so that adding seductive detail to the material will result in decreases on tests of retention and on solutions to transfer problems (Wade & Adams, 1990).

In multimedia learning environments such as PDA-based learning, seductive detail is usually called seductive augmentation because the term "seductive augmentation" refers not only to text but also graphics, narratives, voice, and animation accompanied in the multimedia learning environment for the purpose of increasing the learner's situational interest (Thalheimer, 2004).

Harp and Mayer (1997) examined the effects of emotional interest adjuncts and cognitive interest adjuncts on information retention, learning transfer, and learning interest. They reported that learners in the base text group recalled the most, whereas learners who read passages containing the base text along with emotional interest text and illustrations recalled the least. This result was consistent with the prediction

of cognitive interest theory and inconsistent with the prediction of emotional interest theory. However, the learners' achievement was measured based on the procedural information which explains the stage of a specific scientific phenomenon, not based on the factual information that contains several distinct scientific concepts. In addition, the instructional material was paper-based material and the participants were only allowed to read the passage once.

Therefore, the effects of these adjuncts are uncertain if the instructional material is delivered by PDAs and if a learner is allowed to read the text more than once. In PDA-based learning, learning material consists of text, graphics such as still illustrations and/or animation, and video clips. The learners can readily navigate the entire learning material using the navigation buttons. Thus, a learner can easily go back to previous content or go on to the next content page. A learner is also allowed to read the text more than once. In other words, the learner has greater control over the process of learning in the PDA setting than he or she does in the paper-based setting of the experiment described above.

Therefore, this study was designed with learner controlled PDA-based learning material containing scientific text. Two types of visual illustrations were implemented as independent variables for the research and were applied in designing the instructional materials from the perspective of cognitive interest and emotional interest. A total of three types of instructional materials were developed for this study. The first type was cognitive interest illustration and text. The second type was emotional interest illustration and text. The third type was text-only material without any illustrations, which was the material used in the control group. The experimental groups and control group were formed as follows:
1) Group 1 was presented text information and cognitive interest illustrations,
2) Group 2 was given text information and emotional interest illustrations, and
3) Group 3 was presented only text information.

Three dependent variables were examined in terms of post-interest, achievement, and time spent for reading the learning content. Since the learner's pre-interest and prior knowledge were assumed as important covariates that could affect learning interest and the learner's achievement, they were also measured before conducting research and considered as two covariates in data analysis. Three hypotheses were constructed and addressed on the basis of reviews of literature conveying previous study results and theoretical rationales: 1) Given the characteristics derived from the definition of cognitive interest and emotional interest, the learners in the emotional interest illustration group were predicted to show higher learning interest than those of the learners in the cognitive interest group and text-only group because of the affective function of illustration. 2) The learners in the emotional interest illustration group were predicted to show higher achievement than those of the learners in the cognitive interest group and text-only group. 3) The types of visual illustrations have positive impacts on time spent for reading the contents.

Four hypotheses were constructed and addressed on the basis of reviews of literature conveying previous study results and theoretical rationales: 1) There are no differences on prior knowledge among each group; 2) The types of visual illustrations have positive impacts on learners' achievement; 3) The types of visual illustrations have positive impacts on learners' interests; and 4) The types of visual illustrations have positive impacts on time spent for reading the contents.

METHODS

Participants

Participants included 45 graduate students who were enrolled in a public university in the Southeastern United States. Considering effect size, alpha level, and power, we performed power analysis to estimate the appropriate number of sample size. The minimum number of the sample size was 12 for each group. Among the 45 graduate students, 31 students were male, and the rest were female. Since most of them had no prior experience in using PDAs, a training session was given before conducting this study. Participation was voluntary, and participants were assured of the confidentiality of their responses.

Materials

The instructional material was developed using PDAs to teach the "Life Cycle of a Hurricane." The material contained six different parts: 1) unit overview, 2) origin of a hurricane, 3) the life cycle of hurricane development, 4) the eye and eyewall, 5) hurricane rotation, and 6) a hurricane's demise. In designing the material, only graphic and text information were applied in order to prevent the learners from learning content due to other variables such as sound or animation. The applied illustrations were all colored graphics describing the hurricane development process. The three types of instructional material were developed separately according to the differences among the three independent variable types.

The material contains two different types of illustrations and text only according to each group's condition. The figures below demonstrate how the illustrations were implemented in this study. Figure 1 shows an example of a cognitive interest illustration.

Figure 2 shows an example of an emotional interest illustration. (Figures are omitted in this edition). Lastly, Figure 3 is an example of text-only material.

> Several important ingredients are needed for a tropical disturbance to become a tropical cyclone and later strengthen into a tropical storm or hurricane: (1) A tropical disturbance with thunderstorms, (2) A distance of at least 500 kilometers (300 miles) from the equator, (3) Ocean temperatures of 26.5°C (80°F) or warmer to a depth of at least 50 meters (164 feet) below the surface, (4) Lots of moisture in the lower and middle part of the atmosphere, finally (5) Low moisture.

Measures

Independent Variables

The independent variable used for this study included the type of visual illustration used to deliver to learners the concept of the life cycle of the hurricane. The first type of independent variable was the cognitive interest illustration. The second type of the independent variable was the emotional interest illustration. The third type of the independent variable was text-only information without illustration. The instructional material containing cognitive interest illustrations consisted of a PDA-based presentation on the topic of the life cycle of the hurricane.

The design of the cognitive interest illustration was centered on Kintsch's cognitive interest theory (1980). In this study, cognitive interest illustrations were designed to improve the understanding of the four development stages of a hurricane, the required ingredients for a hurricane, and the location of the eye and eyewall. The illustrations were positioned immediately following the text information. Therefore the participants were able to read the text first and look at the illustration next. The instructional material including emotional interest illustrations was also portrayed on the screen of PDAs.

The design of the emotional interest illustrations was based on the emotional interest theory in Kintsch (1980). In the present research, emotional interest illustrations were designed to arouse the learner's interest in the four development stages of a hurricane, the required ingredients for a hurricane, and the location of the eye and eyewall. As in the case of the cognitive interest illustrations, emotional interest illustrations were positioned right after textual information. The position and the number of emotional interest illustrations were the same as those of cognitive interest illustrations.

The instructional material containing only text information consisted of a PDA-based presentation on the same topic as the cognitive/emotional interest illustration materials. However, it did not include any illustrations.

Dependent Variables

Three dependent variables for the study included learner's post-interest, achievement, and time spent in reading the instructional material.

Pre- and Post-Interest

A multiple-choice test was used to measure pre- and post-interest. The pre- and post-interest test consisted of seven items measured using a 7-point Likert scale. The test was conducted to see how interested the learners were in the content of hurricanes. Participants were asked to indicate their interest level about instructional material by selecting one of seven choices ranging from "Not at all true" through "Very true." The reliability coefficient was .84.

Prior Knowledge and Achievement

In order to measure cognition levels, a prior knowledge test and an achievement test were conducted. Prior knowledge was measured on a 7-point Likert scale, and its reliability coefficient was .86. It consisted of 10 question items. On the other hand, the achievement test was designed to assess the learner's ability to solve the given problems using what they have learned from the instructional material. The total number of items was ten, including five short-answer items and five multiple-choice items. These items were designed to ask questions about the following topics: a) The four development processes of hurricanes, b) Meteorological factors necessary for forming hurricanes, c) Identification of hurricanes from real weather pictures, and d) The structure of a hurricane.

Time Spent

The amount of time spent was recorded during the participants' reading of the material about the life cycle of hurricanes and compared among the three conditions.

Procedures

Participants were randomly assigned to one of three treatment groups: the cognitive interest illustration group, the emotional interest illustration group, and the text-only group. Participants were asked to fill out the prior knowledge and pre-interest survey before processing instructional material. Then they were informed that they would be studying an instructional material on the life cycle of hurricanes and that after they finished reading, they would be asked a series of questions about what they had read. They were

instructed to read the material carefully according to their normal reading rates.

Each participant was given the material corresponding to his/her treatment group and told to start studying. They were not allowed to take notes or refer to other resources. The amount of time spent was recorded during their reading of the material. The experimenter then handed them the post-interest survey inventory for each to fill out at his or her own rate. After completing the post-interest inventory, participants were given achievement test sheets and allowed 10 minutes to work on the test. After this, the participants were thanked for their participation. We took the PDA participants' homes to conduct the study individually over the three weeks.

Data Analysis

Pre- and Post-Interest

One-way analysis of variance (ANOVA) setting the alpha level at .05 was conducted to compare the level of pre-interest among the three groups. Also, one-way analysis of variance (ANOVA) setting the alpha level at .05 and LSD were conducted to compare the level of post-interest among each group.

Prior Knowledge and Achievement

One-way analysis of variance (ANOVA) setting the alpha level at .05 was conducted to compare the level of prior knowledge among each group. Achievement test data was collected by grading the number of correct answers provided on each achievement test. The scoring procedure for the achievement test was administrated as follows. Achievement tests were graded based on a pre-determined answer sheet. The total number of questions was 10, but each question had different weight depending on the difficulty of question. Since there are correct answers for all of the questions, the answer sheet was prepared based on the information from the hurricane learning material. Total scores ranged from 0 through 19. The results of achievement were analyzed based on the analysis of covariance (ANCOVA) setting the alpha level at .05. The analysis of covariance (ANCOVA) setting the alpha level at .05 was conducted to determine whether the achievement test scores of the three groups differed after adjustments were made for prior knowledge differences. LSD was conducted to compare the achievement scores across the three groups.

Time Spent

One-way analysis of variance (ANOVA) setting the alpha level at .05 and LSD were conducted to compare the time spent among each group.

RESULTS

Preliminary Analysis

The five variables of prior knowledge, pre-interest, post-interest, recall, achievement, and time spent were measured. Only one missing value was found in the post-interest inventory and the EM (Expectation-Maximization) method for missing value analysis was used to fill in the missing value with the estimated mean. Descriptive statistics for the scores of each dependent variable are presented in Table 1.

Kolmogorov-Smirnov's test of the normality setting with alpha levels at .05 for prior knowledge ($z = .11$, $p > .05$), pre-interest ($z = .10$, $p > .05$), post-interest ($z = .14$, $p > .05$), achievement ($z = .14$, $p > .05$), and time spent ($z = .14$, $p > .05$) indicated that the scores of the dependent variables were normally distributed. In addition, skewness and its standard deviation for each dependent variable are between –2 and +2. Therefore, the data are normal based on skewness. Kurtosis and its standard deviation for each dependent variable are between –2 and +2. Therefore, the data are also normal based on kurtosis.

The Levene's test of the homogeneity of variance setting with alpha levels .05 for prior knowledge ($F = 1.26$, $p > .05$), pre-interest ($F = 1.66$, $p > .05$), post-interest ($F = .06$, $p > .05$), achievement ($F = 2.28$, $p > .05$), and time spent ($F = .17$, $p > .05$) indicated that there was no evidence to reject the assumption of homogeneity of variances across the dependent variables.

Findings

Correlation Test

Bivariate correlation for five variables was conducted to measure if each variable was related. There was no significant correlation among variables.

Pre- and Post-Interest

One-way analysis of variance (ANOVA) setting the alpha level at .05 was conducted to compare the level of pre-interest among the three groups. The result was there was no significant difference among the groups, $F(2, 42) = 1.168$, $p > .05$, $\eta^2 = .053$. This result indicated that there was no significant difference among the pre-interest levels of each group.

One-way analysis of variance (ANOVA) setting the alpha level at .05 and post-hoc LSD were conducted to compare the level of post-interest among each group. The result was there was no significant difference among the groups, $F(2, 42) = .433$, $p > .05$, $\eta^2 = .020$. The result indicated that the levels of post-interest across the groups were also not significantly different among the three groups.

Prior Knowledge and Achievement

One-way analysis of variance (ANOVA) setting the alpha level at .05 was conducted to compare the level of prior knowledge among each group. The result was there was no significant difference among the groups, $F(2, 42) = .864$, $p > .05$, $\eta^2 = .040$. Although the result indicated that the levels of prior knowledge across the groups were not significantly different, previous researchers have found that there is a significant relationship between prior knowledge and achievement. In fact, prior knowledge has been suggested as related to both individual interest and situational interest. However, regarding the form of the relationship between knowledge and interest, Tobias (1994) concluded that personal interest and prior knowledge are related in a linear manner.

In contrast, Kintsch (1980) proposed that prior knowledge is related to situational interest via an inverted U-shaped function unlike individual interest. That is, exceptionally low or high levels of knowledge led to low interest, whereas moderate amounts of knowledge may lead to higher interest because it creates a desire on the part of learners to learn more about

Table 1. Descriptive Statistics for Each Dependent Variable

	Post-interest		Achievement		Time spent (in seconds)	
	M	SD	M	SD	M	SD
Cognitive-Interest Illustration Group (n = 15)	4.61	1.11	11.87	1.60	617	177
Emotional-Interest Illustration Group (n = 15)	4.88	0.90	9.73	3.53	556	164
Text-Only Group (n = 15)	4.79	0.98	9.53	3.20	618	222

the topic. Therefore, in this study, prior knowledge served as a covariate to adjust the means of achievement and was measured using a five 7-point Likert scale. Its reliability coefficient was .86.

Achievement test data was collected by grading the number of correct answers on the achievement test. An analysis of covariance (ANCOVA) setting the alpha level at .05 was conducted to determine whether the achievement test scores of the three groups differed after adjustments were made for prior knowledge differences. Post-hoc LSD was conducted to compare the achievement scores across the three groups.

The covariate, prior knowledge, was not significantly related to the students' achievement test scores, $F(2, 42) = 2.12$, $p > 0.05$, $\eta^2 = .05$. However, there was significant effect of types of illustration on student achievement after controlling for the effect of prior knowledge, $F(2, 42) = 3.64$, $p < 0.05$, $\eta^2 = .15$. Multiple comparisons revealed that those students who received the cognitive illustrations showed significantly higher achievement compared to both those who received emotional illustrations, $t(29) = -2.31$, $p < .05$, and those receiving text-only material, $t(29) = -2.64$, $p < .05$.

Time Spent

One-way analysis of variance (ANOVA) setting the alpha level at .05 and post-hoc LSD were conducted to compare the time spent among the three groups. The result was there was no significant difference among the groups, $F(2, 42) = .519$, $p > .05$, $\eta^2 = .024$. The result indicated that the levels of time spent across the groups were not different.

DISCUSSION

This study extended past research by examining several factors related to visual illustrations within the context of PDA-based learning. Students in the cognitive interest group earned significantly higher achievement scores than did students in both the emotional interest group and the text-only group. In addition, students in the emotional interest group had more learning interest in the learning content than did students in the cognitive interest and text-only groups.

The key finding of the study provides support for the same results from the previous researches. Cognitive interest-improved illustrations were found to have a significant impact on the learners' achievement. However, the emotional interest-improved illustrations did not serve to improve the learners' achievement. This finding is in line with the concept of seductive detail effect. The term "seductive detail effect" is used to describe the cognitive consequences of adding seductive details to

text (Harp, 1997). Garner et al. (1989) explained that the reason for the seductive effect detail is because of the proficient recall of seductive details within a passage but poor recall of important ideas. As shown from Harp and Mayer's study (1997), seductive details diminish a learner's ability to solve problems based on main ideas. Since emotional interest-improved illustrations were created based on seductive detail augmentation, the seductive detail effect could be a cause for the low achievement scores of students in the emotional interest group.

The result of this study also indicated learners who were given emotional interest illustrations felt more interest than did the learners who were given cognitive interest illustrations and text-only material. However, there was no significant difference between the mean score among those three conditions. This finding affirms that when the learner is given an emotional interest illustration, he/she is aroused and feels positive emotion and interest in the instructional material.

There were several limitations to the findings of this study. First, the learner's individual characteristic regarding preference for illustrations was not considered. Because learners did not have control over the illustration type, they had to receive illustrations along with the text information when the condition of their group called for it. Second, the effect of the multimedia authoring program was not considered. Since the program was totally new to participants in this research, all participants could be motivated on the same level no matter what illustrations they were given.

Additional research is needed to fill the gaps in our understanding of the interaction between a learner's characteristic and the type of illustration in a multimedia setting. Future research should also attempt to determine different functions of an illustration in terms of cognitive function as well as affective function. Then it would be possible to compare the different research results on the same topic based on the function of the illustration.

The implication of this study involves the influence of visual illustrations in PDA-based instructional material on a learner's affect, even though this study did not prove that has a positive effect on visual illustration on learner's achievement. However, it is clear that using illustrations in PDA-based instructional material increases the learning interest of the learner. Learner interest is a very complex psychological construct (Krapp, Hidi, & Renninger, 1992). Instructional designers or educators need to consider the potential benefits of using different types of illustrations when they develop PDA-based instructional material.

REFERENCES

Anglin, G. J., Towers, R. L., & Levis, W. H. (1996). Visual message design and learning: The role of static and dynamic illustrations. In D. H. Jonassen (Ed.), *Handbook of research for educational communications and technology* (pp. 755–794). New York: Simon & Schuster Macmillan.

Bateman, B., Crystal, J., Davidson, H., Holzberg, C. S., McIntire, T., & McLester, S. (2001). Top ten technologies breaking through for schools. *Technology and Learning, 22,* 22–32.

Fasimpaur, K. (2002, May). The Power of Using "Palm Size" Handheld Computers in Education. *Paper presented at the computer using in education (CUE)*, Anaheim, California.

Garner, R., Gillingham, M., & White, C. (1989). Effects of "seductive details" on macroprocessing and microprocessing in adults and children. *Cognition and Instruction, 6*(1), 41–57.

Harp, S. F. (1997). *How seductive details do their damage: A cognitive theory of interest in science learning.* Unpublished Doctoral Dissertation, University of California, Santa Barbara.

Harp, S. F., & Mayer, R. E. (1997). The role of interest in learning from scientific text and illustrations: On the distinction between emotional interest and cognitive interest. *Journal of Educational Psychology, 89*(1), 92–102.

Izard, C. E., & Ackerman, B. P. (2000). Motivational, organizational, and regulatory functions of discrete emotions. In M. Lewis & J. M. Haviland-Jones (Eds.), *Handbook of emotion* (Vol. II, pp. 253–264). New York: Guilford Publications, Inc.

Kintsch, W. (1980). Learning from text, levels of comprehension. *Poetics, 9*(9), 87–98.

Krapp, A., Hidi, S., & Renninger, A. (1992). Interest, learning, and development. In A. Krapp, S. Hidi, & A. Renninger (Eds.), *The role of interest in learning and development* (pp. 3–25). Hillsdale, NJ: Lawrence Erlbaum Association.

Levie, J. R., & Lentz, R. (1982). Effects of text illustrations: A review of research. *Educational Communication and Technology Journal, 30*(4), 195–232.

Park, S., Kim, M., Ryu, J., & Son, C. (2003). The effect of character spacing on reading in personal digital assistants (PDAs), *Proceedings of the Association for the Advancement of Computing in Education (AACE) E-Learn 2003 World Conference*, Phoenix, Arizona.

Park, S., & Lim, J. (2004). The effect of graphical representation of science text on the learner's learning interest and achievement in multimedia learning. *Proceedings of the Association for Educational Communications and Technology (AECT) World Conference*, Chicago, Illinois.

Son, C., Kim, M., & Park, S. (2004). The case analysis of PDA integrated classroom. *Proceedings of the Association for the Advancement of Computing in Education (AACE) SITE 2004 World Conference*, Atlanta, Georgia.

Song, S. H. (1998). *The effects of motivationally adaptive computer-assisted instruction developed through ARCS model.* Unpublished Doctoral Dissertation, Florida State University, Tallahassee.

Thalheimer, W. (2004, April). *Bells, whistles, neon, and purple prose: When interesting words, sounds, and visuals hurt learning and performance—A review of the seductive-augmentation research.* Retrieved December 16, 2004, from http://www.work-learning.com/seductive_augmentations.htm

Tobias, S. (1994). Interest, prior knowledge, and learning. *Review of Educational Research, 64,* 37–54.

Wade, S. E., & Adams, B. (1990). Effects of importance and interest on recall of biographical text. *Journal of Literacy, 22,* 331–353.

1.05

4-FACTOR PRE AND POSTTEST DESIGN

Enhancing Mathematical Reasoning in the Classroom: The Effects of Cooperative Learning and Metacognitive Training

Bracha Kramarski and Zemira R. Mevarech

ABSTRACT: The purpose of this study was to investigate the effects of four instructional methods on students' mathematical reasoning and metacognitive knowledge. The participants were 384 eighth-grade students. The instructional methods were cooperative learning combined with metacognitive training (COOP + META), individualized learning combined with metacognitive training (IND + META), cooperative learning without metacognitive training (COOP), and individualized learning without metacognitive training (IND). Results showed that the COOP + META group significantly outperformed the IND + META group, which in turn significantly outperformed the COOP and IND groups on graph interpretation and various aspects of mathematical explanations. Furthermore, the metacognitive groups (COOP + META and IND + META) outperformed their counterparts (COOP and IND) on graph construction (transfer tasks) and metacognitive knowledge. This article presents theoretical and practical implications of the findings.

KEYWORDS: Argumentation; graphs; mathematical reasoning; metacognition; transfer task.

Most research on mathematical education emphasizes the importance of mathematical reasoning as an integral part of doing mathematics (National Council of Teachers, of Mathematics [NCTM], 1989, 2000; Cai, Lane, & Jakabcsin, 1996). According to the NCTM standards, mathematical reasoning requires the attainment of abilities to construct mathematical conjectures, develop and evaluate mathematical arguments, and select and use various types of representations. To help students meet the standards, the NCTM emphasizes the importance of mathematical discourse in the classroom. Students not only should discuss their reasoning on a regular basis with the teacher and with one another but also should explain the basis for their mathematical reasoning, both in writing and in their mathematical discourse.

Bracha Kramarski is a Lecturer and Head of the Teacher Training Department, School of Education, Bar-Ilan University, Ramat-Gan 52900, Israel. Her areas of special interest are mathematical education, metacognitive instruction, advanced educational technologies, and teachers' professional development.

Zemira R. Mevarech is the Head of the School of Education, Bar-Ilan University, Ramat-Gan 52900, Israel. Her areas of special interest are mathematical education, metacognitive instruction, quantitative methods of education research, and advanced educational technologies.

Research on the NCTM standards has moved beyond identifying their elements to focusing on the treatments, or conditions, under which they can be optimally enhanced in the classroom. In the literature two methods have been suggested: One focuses on cooperative learning (e.g., Slavin, 1996), the other on metacognitive training (e.g., Schoenfeld, 1985). The following paragraphs briefly describe the effects of each method on mathematical reasoning.

COOPERATIVE LEARNING AND MATHEMATICAL REASONING

Research in cognitive psychology has shown that learning occurs when the learner is engaged in some sort of cognitive restructuring or elaboration (Wittrock, 1986). One of the most effective means of elaboration is explaining the material to someone else. Slavin proposes that "(a) through mutual feedback and debate, peers motivate one another to abandon misconceptions and search for better solutions; (b) the experience of peer interaction can help a child master social processes, such as participation and argumentation, and cognitive processes, such as verification and criticism; (c) collaboration between peers can provide a forum for discovery learning and can encourage creative thinking; and (d) peer interaction can introduce children to the process of generating ideas" (1996, pp. 49–50).

On the basis of this research, several cooperative learning programs have been designed to replace the traditional teaching of mathematics. The following are examples of programs for teaching mathematics in cooperative settings: the Interactive Mathematics Program, a 4-year program for learning algebra through precalculus (Fendel et al., 1996); the Core-Plus Mathematics Project (Hirsch et al., 1997) for high school students; Connect Mathematics for Grades 6–8 (Lappan et al., 1996); IMPROVE for Grades 7–9 (Mevarech & Kramarski, 1997a); and Number Power for Grades K–6 (Robertson et al., 1996). For an excellent review of cooperative programs for the teaching of mathematics, see Davidson, 1990.

The use of small groups, however, requires fundamental changes not only in the organization of the classroom but also in ways of learning. From a cognitive perspective, students who have poor communication skills are less likely to benefit from cooperative learning because they are not able to communicate their mathematical reasoning to others, nor do they know how to ask questions, reflect on their solution process to explain it to their peers, or offer constructive criticism (Webb, 1989, 1991; Webb & Farivar, 1994).

Cohen (1996), Webb and Farivar (1994), Meloth and Deering (1994), and Mevarech and Kramarski (1997a) suggest that developing mathematical reasoning in small-group activities must be structured to maximize the opportunities for each student to be engaged in questioning, elaboration, explanation, and other verbal communication through which students can express their ideas and group members can give and receive feedback. Researchers (Cohen; Cobb, Boufi, McClain, & Whitenack, 1997) have indicated that features of discourse are new behaviors that students can learn through practice and reinforcement. Using arguments for mathematical reasoning, for example, can become a norm for behavior that enhances mathematical reasoning. Participation in reflective discourse in which mathematical activity is objectified can be an explicit topic of conversation. Thus, students need to be exposed to explicit metacognitive training that focuses on skills for high-level discourse.

METACOGNITIVE TRAINING AND MATHEMATICAL REASONING

Several studies (e.g., Mevarech & Kramarski, 1997a; Schoenfeld, 1985; Lester, Garofalo, & Kroll, 1989) have examined the effects of metacognitive training on mathematics reasoning. In all of these studies, the metacognitive training was based on Polya's (1945) approach for solving mathematical problems. A major common element of these programs is training students who work in small groups to formulate and answer a series of self-addressed metacognitive questions that focus on (a) the nature of the problem or task, (b) the construction of relationships between previous and new knowledge, and (c) the use of strategies appropriate for solving the problem or task.

Mevarech and Kramarski (1997a) examined the effects of metacognitive training embedded in small groups. The program is called IMPROVE, the acronym of all the teaching stages: *I*ntroducing the new concepts, *M*etacognitive questioning, *P*racticing, *R*eviewing and reducing difficulties, *O*btaining mastery, *V*erification, and *E*nrichment. Mevarech and Kramarski reported that IMPROVE students who studied in heterogeneous classrooms without tracking or grouping outperformed their counterparts in nontreatment control groups who studied in small groups. In particular, observation showed that IMPROVE had positive effects on students' mathematical achievement and ability to explain their reasoning. These findings are in line with those of King (1989, 1991, 1994), who showed that students in various age groups (e.g., fourth-graders, sixth-graders, and college students) who were trained to formulate and answer metacognitive questions similar to the ones described earlier outperformed their counterparts in control groups on various measures of achievement and problem solving outside the area of mathematics.

Although these findings are promising, they all focus on combined cooperative learning and metacognitive training. Thus there remains the interesting question,

What is the unique contribution by each component to students' mathematical reasoning? For example, one may convincingly argue that students exposed to metacognitive training in individualized settings perform similarly to or even better than students exposed to metacognitive training in cooperative learning settings because the former are trained to analyze the problem or task, to construct connections between new and previous knowledge, and to use strategies that are appropriate for solving the problems or completing the tasks. According to this view, metacognitive training is an effective method for enhancing mathematical reasoning regardless of classroom organization. By comparing the mathematical reasoning of students who learned in cooperative settings (with or without metacognitive training) and that of students who learned in individualized settings (with or without metacognitive training), better evidence can be provided regarding the conditions appropriate for attaining standards in mathematics (NCTM, 1989, 2000). To our knowledge, no previous study has addressed this issue.

It is particularly important to examine the differential effects of the four instructional methods on the completion of transfer tasks. Many studies have indicated that students' ability to transfer their knowledge to new situations is quite limited (e.g., Salomon & Perkins, 1987). One of the factors that contribute to that limitation is students' inability to identify the essential elements that are similar or different in the already-completed and targeted tasks. Cecil and Roazzi (1994) reported that training students to describe the similarities and differences between problems facilitated their ability to succeed at transfer tasks. On the basis of that study, we hypothesized that regardless of classroom organization, students who are trained to formulate and answer metacognitive questions such as those described earlier will be better able to transfer their knowledge to new situations than students who are not exposed to such metacognitive training.

Finally, there is a need to investigate the metacognitive knowledge that students acquire under the various conditions. Since the late 1970s, when Flavell (1979) first coined the term *metacognition*, much research has focused on the nature of metacognition (e.g., Schoenfeld, 1987), how it develops as a function of students' age (e.g., Schneider & Sodian, 1990), and how it can be used in the classroom (e.g., Garofalo & Lester, 1985). In particular, research has focused on various kinds of metacognition, including metamemory, metalanguage, metasolving, and metareading (Forrest-Pressley, Makinnon, & Gary Waller, 1985). These studies led us to suggest a distinction between general and domain-specific metacognitive knowledge, similar to the distinction made between cognitive processes (Salomon & Perkins, 1987). *General metacognitive knowledge* is knowing about and being able to control and regulate problem-solving processes regardless of the specific domain from which problems or tasks are drawn. *Domain-specific metacognitive knowledge* focuses on the unique features of each domain and therefore varies among domains. Schoenfeld indicated that in mathematics, metacognitive knowledge includes knowledge about one's own thought processes (e.g., accuracy in describing your own thinking), control or self-regulation (e.g., keeping track of what you are doing when solving problems or tasks), and beliefs and intuitions (e.g., ideas about mathematics that you bring to your work in mathematics). There is reason to suppose that different instructional methods may have different effects on students' general and specific metacognitive knowledge. Students who are exposed to metacognitive training are expected to be better at reflecting on solution processes (general and specific) than students who are not exposed to such training. Discussing metacognitive issues with others is expected to enhance metacognitive knowledge.

The present study addressed these issues. We compared students' mathematical reasoning, transfer ability, and metacognitive knowledge under four instructional methods: cooperative learning combined with metacognitive training (COOP + META), cooperative learning without metacognitive training (COOP), individualized learning combined with metacognitive training (IND + META), and individualized learning without metacognitive training (IND).

METHOD

Participants

The participants were 384 students (181 boys and 203 girls) who studied in 12 eighth-grade classrooms randomly selected from 4 junior high schools. The 4 schools were randomly selected from a pool of 15 schools located in one district, where mathematics was taught in heterogeneous classrooms without groupings or ability tracking. The schools were similar in size, average socioeconomic status as defined by the Israel Ministry of Education, students' mean age, and levels of mathematics achievement assessed before the beginning of the study. Within schools classes were normally distributed in terms of students' ability and prior knowledge. The average students' age was 13.3 years.

Twelve teachers participated in the study, each teaching in one classroom. All teachers were female and had more than 5 years of experience in teaching mathematics, and all had taught in heterogeneous classrooms. All teachers had a degree in mathematics education. The teachers were exposed to a 2-day inservice training program (to be described later).

Conditions

All classes studied a linear graph unit. That unit was selected for three reasons: First, it introduced various kinds of mathematics representations. Second, comprehending graphs was one of the mathematical skills that were emphasized by the NCTM standards (1989, 2000). Finally, comprehending graphs is a central skill in the study of sciences and mathematics.

The main purpose of the unit was to develop students' understanding of linear graphs. In particular, all of the students studied (a) the concepts of slope, intersection point, and rate of change; (b) quantitative and qualitative methods of graph interpretation; and (c) transformation of algebraic expressions of the form $y = mx + b$ into graphic representations.

In all classrooms mathematics was taught five times a week, in accordance with the mathematics curriculum suggested by the Israel Ministry of Education. The linear graph unit was taught for 2 weeks. At the beginning of the unit the teacher introduced strategies of graph interpretation such as using tables, algebraic formulas, steps, and verbal explanations. All students in all conditions practiced those strategies with the same problems or tasks, and all used the same textbook. In addition, the teachers used the same problems or tasks when they introduced new concepts. In addition to the textbook, students under each condition used learning materials that covered the same kinds of exercises as those presented in the textbook but that emphasized the unique components of each condition. An example of an open-ended task and how it related to the instruction is provided in Appendix A.

The differences among the groups were in the instructional method. Because each condition was defined by the presence or absence of two components—metacognitive training and cooperative learning—we first describe the components separately and then describe how they were combined.

Metacognitive Training

The metacognitive training used in the present study was based on the techniques suggested by Schoenfeld (1985) and Mevarech and Kramarski (1997a). The metacognitive training used three sets of self-addressed metacognitive questions: *comprehension questions*, *strategic questions*, and *connection questions*. The comprehension questions were designed to prompt students to reflect on a problem before solving it. In addressing a comprehension question, students had to read the problem, describe the relevant concepts in their own words, and try to understand what the concepts meant. In graph interpretation, the comprehension questions guided students to interpret problems on both the local-to-global dimension and the quantitative-to-qualitative

dimension (Leinhardt, Zaslavsky, & Stein, 1990). The comprehension questions included the following: What does the x-axis represent? What does the y-axis represent? What is the trend of the graph? What are the specific points on the graph? To assist students in remembering the comprehension questions, students used the acronym DATA: *D*escribe the x-axis and the y-axis; *A*ddress the units and the ranges of each axis; *T*ell the *T*rend(s) of the graph or parts of the graph; and *A*nalyze specific points.

The strategic questions were designed to prompt students to consider which strategies were appropriate for solving or completing a given problem or task and for what reasons. In addressing the strategic questions, students had to describe the "what" (e.g., What strategy, tactic, or principle can be used to solve the problem or complete the task?), the "why" (e.g., Why is this strategy, tactic, or principle most appropriate for this problem or task?); and the "how" (e.g., How can the suggested plan be carried out?). Possible strategies for interpreting graphs were adding steps to a graph to calculate the slope, using data tables, and referring to the algebraic representation of the graph.

The connection questions were designed to prompt students to focus on similarities and differences between the immediate problem or task and problems or tasks that they had already completed successfully. Connection questions regarding graphs guided students to find similarities and differences between the graph at hand and graphs they had already interpreted, or to compare different intervals on the same graph.

The metacognitive questions were printed in the students' working sheets and in the teacher guide. Students used the metacognitive questions in their small groups or individualized activities and in writing when they used their booklets. In addition, the teachers modeled the use of the metacognitive questioning when they introduced new concepts to the whole class, reviewed the materials, and helped students in their small groups or individualized activities. Students were told that asking and answering the metacognitive questions would help them to understand and remember the material presented in mathematics classes.

Cooperative and Individualized Learning

Generally speaking, both cooperative and individualized learning sessions included three parts: teacher introduction to the whole class (about 10 minutes), cooperative or individualized seatwork (about 30 minutes), and teacher review with the whole class (about 5 minutes).

Each session started with a teacher's short presentation of the new materials to the whole class using the question-answering technique described by Marx and Walsh (1988). The teacher began by providing answers to two questions: What am I supposed to do in this task? (What's in the problem or task?) and, What do I already know about it? (What are the differences and similarities between . . . and . . .?). Next, the teacher modeled strategies for completing the task and explained why the strategies were likely to succeed. Last, the teacher explained how to check the answer and what to do if the plan did not work.

After the introduction, students began work in small groups or individually, using the materials designed by us. The cooperative technique followed the method suggested by Brown and Palincsar (1989): Students learned in heterogeneous teams of four, each team including one high-achieving student, two middle-achieving students, and one low-achieving student. To ensure team heterogeneity, all students were tested on mathematics achievement before the beginning of the study and teams were constructed on the basis of students' performance on that test. The learning in teams was implemented as follows: Each student, in turn, read a problem or task aloud and tried to complete it. Whenever there was no consensus, the team discussed the issue until the disagreements, were resolved. In talking about the problem or task, explaining it to each other, approaching it from different perspectives, balancing the perspectives against each other, and proceeding according to what seemed to be the best option at the time, students used the diversity in their prior knowledge to self-regulate their learning. When all team members agreed on a solution, they wrote it down on their answer sheets. When none of the team members knew how to complete a problem or task, they asked for teacher assistance. At the end of the period the teacher reviewed the main ideas of the lesson with the entire class. When common difficulties came to light, the teacher provided additional explanations to the whole class.

Components Combined to Form the Four Conditions

The metacognitive training and the cooperative or individualized components were combined as follows.

COOP + META Condition

The COOP + META condition resembled the IMPROVE procedure (Mevarech & Kramarski, 1997a). Students in that condition studied in small heterogeneous groups using the metacognitive questions described earlier: comprehension questions, strategic questions, and connection questions. The metacognitive questions were used by students individually when their turn arrived to solve a problem or complete a task aloud, by the group as a whole in mathematical discourse, and by the teacher when introducing the new concepts to the whole class, reviewing, the lesson at the end of the class, and providing help in the small groups.

IND + META Condition

Under the IND + META condition, the metacognitive training was exactly the same as in the COOP + META condition, except that it was implemented in individualized rather than cooperative settings. As in the COOP + META condition, each period in the IND + META condition started with a 10-minute teacher introduction for the whole class. The teacher introduced the new concepts using the metacognitive question-answering technique and modeling the use of the questions. The students then began to work individually on problems or tasks by using the same metacognitive questions described earlier, and the metacognitive questions were printed in the students' booklets. Students had to answer the questions in writing. Finally, at the end of the period, the teacher reviewed the new concepts by using the question-answering technique and modeling the use of the metacognitive questions. When students worked on the problems individually, the teacher provided help to individual students as needed. When helping students, the teacher also modeled the use of the metacognitive questions.

COOP Condition

Under the COOP condition, students studied in small heterogeneous groups as in the COOP + META condition, but they were not exposed to metacognitive training. Each session started with a short presentation of the new materials to the whole class using the question-a-nswering technique. The students then started work on the problems or tasks. The teachers encouraged students to discuss mathematical ideas in their small groups and to provide explanations to one another, but no explicit metacognitive guidance was provided. Each student, in turn, read a problem or task aloud and tried to solve or complete it. When students failed to solve a problem or did not agree on the solution, the team discussed the components of the problem until consensus was achieved. When all team members agreed on a solution, they recorded it in their notebooks. When no team members knew how to solve a problem, the team asked for teacher assistance. At the end of the lesson, the teacher reviewed the main ideas of the lesson with the entire class. When common difficulties were observed, the teacher provided additional explanations to the whole class. In each period the teacher worked with two to three groups.

IND Condition

Under the IND condition, students learned individually and without metacognitive training. Each class started with a 10-minute teacher introduction of the new concepts to the whole class. Students then worked on the problems or tasks individually without using the metacognitive questions. While the students worked, the teacher provided help to those who needed it. At the end of the class, the teacher reviewed the new concepts with the whole class. That group served as a control group.

Learning Materials and Teacher Training

We designed two sets of learning materials for the purposes of the present study. One set included the metacognitive questions and the other did not. Instead of metacognitive questions, the learning materials of the non-metacognitiye groups (COOP and IND) included general, instruction (e.g., Explain your answer in writing; or, Discuss your mathematical ideas with your classmates). Otherwise, the two sets of learning materials were identical.

Before the beginning of the study, all 12 teachers were exposed to a 2-day inservice training, which focused on pedagogical issues related to the teaching of the linear graph unit. Teachers were told that they were participating in an experiment in which new learning materials would be tried out.

Teachers in each learning condition were exposed separately to the theoretical background of their learning method and its practical implications. The teaching guides included explict lesson plans, learning materials, and use of examples. One set of learning materials included the metacognitive questions; the other, general instructions (e.g., Discuss your mathematical ideas with your classmates; or, Explain your answers). The mathematical problems that were used as examples were identical in all conditions. The teachers who were assigned to the metacognitive groups (COOP + META and IND + META) were introduced to the rationale and techniques of the metacognitive method. The COOP and the COOP + META teachers were introduced to the rationale of cooperative learning and how to implement it. The IND and IND + META teachers were introduced to the rationale of individualized learning and how to implement it. Otherwise, the training of all teachers was identical.

Measurements

We used three measures to assess students' mathematical reasoning and metacognitive knowledge: a graph interpretation test, a graph construction test, and a metacognitive questionnaire.

A 36-item test, adapted from the studies of Mevarech and Kramarski (1992, 1993), assessed students' ability to interpret graphs, particularly linear graphs. The test included items that required qualitative and quantitative graph interpretation skills. According to Leinhardt et al. (1990), qualitative interpretation of a graph requires "looking at the entire graph (or part of it) and gaining meaning about the relationship between the two variables and, in particular, their pattern of covariation" (p. 11). Quantitative interpretation is often associated with local and specific features, based on point identification and a lower level of graph processing (Wainer, 1992).

The test contained two kinds of items, presented in a mixed order. Twenty-seven were based on traditional evaluation procedures; they included multiple-choice and short, open-ended items regarding basic knowledge about the Cartesian system and linear-graph interpretation (e.g., In which months were the temperatures equal?). Nine items did not require (or invite) local interpretations or computations but rather were designed specifically to assess students' mathematical reasoning. These were open-ended items that asked students to give a final answer and explain their reasoning in writing. They required students to (a) draw conclusions and make algebraic generalizations on the basis of a given graph; (b) evaluate graphs representing the same story and decide which graph better represented the story; (c) resolve mathematical conflicts regarding linear graphs; (d) identify, misconceptions regarding linear graphs (see, for example, Leinhardt et al., 1990; Mevarech & Kramarski, 1997b); (e) analyze graphs and decide whether certain mathematical expressions always, never, or sometimes represented the given graphs and vice versa; and (f) analyze the structure of graphs. An example of an open-ended task is presented later.

Students received a score of either 1 (correct answer) or zero (incorrect answer) for each item and a total score ranging from zero to 36. The Kuder Richardson reliability coefficient was .91. In addition, we analyzed the mathematical explanations that students provided, in response to the nine open-ended items, as described in the next section.

Mathematical explanations could be correct or incorrect and could be expressed in formal or informal mathematical language. We considered an explanation to be correct if the argument fit the conventions, even if it was not expressed in a formal mathematical language.

Students could use one or more arguments to explain their reasoning. We analyzed their explanations by focusing on two dimensions: fluency and flexibility (California Learning Assessment System, 1993).

Fluency refers to the number of correct arguments provided by students. In addition, students also provided incorrect arguments. No significant differences were found between groups on the number of incorrect arguments before the beginning and at the end of the study, $F(3, 372) < 1$, $p > .05$; therefore, we will not report further on fluency of incorrect arguments. Hereinafter, fluency refers only to the total number of correct arguments. *Flexibility* refers to a student's providing more than one kind of correct argument to justify his or her reasoning.

We classified the arguments into four categories: logical-formal, numerical-computational, visual, and drawing. Definitions and examples are provided below. All examples refer to the following task, in which students were directed to examine the graph shown in Figure 1:

> The graph below represents the income of two companies between the years 1990 and 2000. Until the year 1994, was the change rate in the income of Company B greater than, smaller than, or equal to the change rate in the income of Company A? After 1994, did the change rates in the companies' incomes become different? Please explain your reasoning.

Student responses were classified as *logical-formal* (based on logical-mathematical arguments), *numerical-computational* (based on numerical computations or algebraic formulas), *visual* (based on intuitive, visual analysis of the graph), or *drawing* (based on drawings that students added to the graph). Here are examples of correct and incorrect responses of each type:

Logical-formal

> *Correct:* "The change rate of line A is greater because its slope is steeper than that of line B"; "The change rate of line A is greater because the angle it creates with the *x*-axis is bigger than the angle that line B creates with the *x*-axis."
>
> *Incorrect:* "The change rate of line A is smaller because it starts from the origin (0, 0)."

Numerical-computational

> *Correct:* "The change rate of line A is 3 times greater than the change rate of line B."
>
> *Incorrect:* "The change rate of line A is 5 times greater than the change rate of line B."

Visual

> *Correct:* "Line A is steeper, line A is more diagonal."
>
> *Incorrect:* "At M the line breaks"; "Line A is above line B."

Drawing

> *Correct:* Adding one-unit steps to the graph and calculating the change rate by using the steps.
>
> *Incorrect:* Adding lines that do not assist in finding the change rate.

Because students could use more than one kind of argument in explaining their reasoning, one explanation could be classified in several categories. Figure 2 presents a diagram of the categories used in the present study to classify students' mathematical explanations.

Two judges who were experts in mathematics education analyzed the students' explanations. The interjudge reliability coefficient was 88.

Graph Construction Test (Transfer Tasks)

The graph construction test, adapted from the study by Mevarech and Kramarski (1997b), assessed students' ability to construct graphs. That test was regarded as assessing transfer knowledge because in none of the classrooms did the students study graph construction. According to Leinhardt et al., "con-struction is quite different from interpretation. Where as interpretation relies on and requires reaction to a given piece of data (e.g., a graph, an equation, or a data set) construction requires generating new parts that are not given" (1990, p. 12). Graph construction requires interpretation skills and involves more difficulties than does graph interpretation (Mevarech & Kramarski).

The graph construction test contained 7 items, each presenting a verbal description of a situation. The situations represented increasing, decreasing, constant, and curvilinear functions. Students were asked to transform the verbal descriptions into graphic representations. They could choose any kind of representation and were allowed to construct the graphs freehand, without using a ruler. Appendix B provides several examples.

For each item, students received a score of either 1 (correct answer) or zero (incorrect answer), and a total score ranging from zero to 7. A graph was considered correct if it followed the conventions of the Cartesian system and represented correctly the situation described, regardless of the kind of graph used (e.g., histogram, bar graph, or line graph). Two judges who are experts in mathematics education scored students' responses. The interjudge reliability coefficient was .92.

Income (thousands)

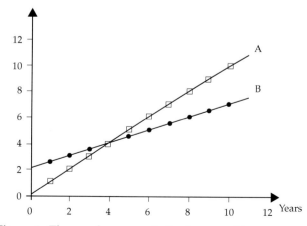

Figure 1. The graph represents the income of two companies between the years 1990 and 2000.

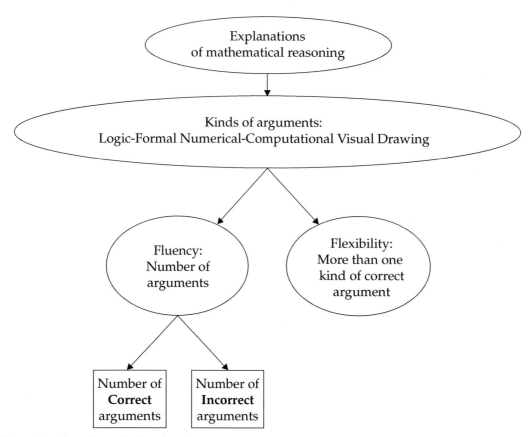

Figure 2. Categories of mathematical explanations.

Metacognitive Questionnaire

The metacognitive. questionnaire, adapted from a study by Montague and Bos (1990), assessed students' general and specific metacognitive knowledge regarding graph comprehension. The questionnaire included 20 items: 7 items referred to general strategies (e.g., "When I solve a math problem I read the problem several times before attempting a solution"); 4 items referred to strategies for transformation from one kind of representation to another (e.g., "When I see a graph", I try to find out the algebraic expression it presents"); and 9 items referred to specific quantitative and qualitative graph interpretation strategies (e.g., "When I see a graph, I first look at specific points" [quantitative interpretation]; "When I see a graph, I first try to find out the general trend of the graph" [qualitative interpretation].

Each item was constructed on a 5-point Likert-type scale, ranging from 1 (never) to 5 (always). Thus students received scores on each item, ranging from 1 to 5, and a total score from 20 to 100. The alpha Cronbach coefficient was .86.

Procedure

As indicated, 12 classrooms from four schools participated in the study. Schools were randomly assigned to conditions, and in each school 3 classrooms (out of 6 parallel eighth-grade classrooms) were randomly selected to participate in the present study. We did not assign classrooms to different conditions within one school because our experience shows that teachers in the same school tend to share materials and talk to each other about their teaching activities.

About a month after the beginning of the school year, all students were administered the examinations described earlier: Graph Interpretation Test, Graph Construction Test, and Metacognitive Questionnaire. Then, each teacher began teaching the unit according to the instructional method to which she was assigned, using the materials specially designed, for that condition. To ensure that the instruction was properly implemented as designed, all classrooms were observed twice a week by one of the authors of this article. At the end of the study, the same battery of tests was readministered.

RESULTS

Mathematical Reasoning

The first purpose of the present study was to investigate the differential effects of COOP + META, IND + META, COOP, and IND on students' mathematical reasoning. Because a significant correlation was found between graph interpretation and graph construction scores ($r = .48$), a MANCOVA (Wilks's lambda test) was carried out on the posttreatment scores of those two variables simultaneously with classrooms nested in conditions and controlling for pretreatment on graph interpretation and graph construction. Before carrying out the MANCOVA, we checked the prerequisites for running it, $MS_e = 2.3$, $F(6, 743) < 1$, $p > .05$.

The results indicated significant differences between conditions on the posttest scores of graph interpretation and graph construction simultaneously, $MS_e = 10.7$, $F(6, 744) = 6.17$, $p < .001$.

Graph Interpretation

Given the MANCOVA findings, we carried out a one-way analysis of variance (ANOVA) on the pretest scores and a one-way analysis of covariance (ANCOVA) on the posttest scores with classrooms nested in conditions and with the corresponding pretest scores used as a covariant.

Table 1 presents the mean scores, adjusted mean scores, and standard deviations on graph interpretation by time and condition. The ANOVA with classrooms nested in conditions indicated no significant differences between conditions before the beginning of the study, $MS_e = 38.4$, $F(3, 372) = .71$, $p > .05$. Significant differences between treatment groups, however, were found at the end of the study after controlling for pretreatment differences, $MS_e = 44.6$, $F(3, 371) = 3.98$, $p < .05$.

Post hoc analyses of the adjusted mean scores based on the pairwise comparison t test technique indicated that the COOP + META group significantly outperformed the IND + META group, which in turn significantly outperformed the COOP and IND groups. No significant differences were found between the two groups that had not been exposed to the metacognitive training.

Students' Mathematical Explanations

In addition to analyzing the total scores on graph interpretation, we also analyzed students' explanations of their mathematical reasoning. As was indicated earlier, two dimensions of mathematical explanations were investigated: fluency (number of correct arguments) and flexibility (provision of more than one kind of correct argument).

Fluency

Table 2 presents the mean scores, adjusted mean scores, and standard deviations of students' fluency

Table 1. Scores on Graph Interpretation Test (by Time and Condition)

	COOP + META $n = 105$	IND+META $n = 95$	COOP $n = 91$	IND $n = 93$	F
Pretest M	15.5	14.4	14.2	16.0	< 1
SD	6.4	6.4	5.9	6.2	
Posttest M	24.4	20.9	19.2	19.8	3.98**
Adjusted M	24.0	21.4	19.8	19.1	
SD	7.2	6.9	6.4	6.6	

Note: Scores ranged from zero to 36.
**$p < .01$.

Table 2 Scores for Fluency in Providing Correct Arguments (by Time and Condition)

	COOP + META $n = 105$	IND + META $n = 95$	COOP $n = 91$	IND $n = 93$	F
Pretest					
M	3.2	2.8	2.7	3.7	1.38
SD	2.4	2.2	2.1	2.6	
Posttest					
M	8.9	6.5	4.9	4.6	7.53*
Adjusted M	8.9	6.7	5.2	4.2	
SD	5.0	4.4	3.2	2.9	

Note: Fluency was scored by the number of correct arguments provided by a student. Scores ranged from zero to 21 for COOP + META, from zero to 18 for IND + META, from zero to 15 for COOP, and from zero to 13 for IND.
*$p < .05$.

in providing correct arguments by time and condition. Although no significant differences were found between groups before the beginning of the study, $MS_e = 5.25$, $F(3, 372) = 1.38$, $p > .05$, significant differences were found at the end of the study with classrooms nested in conditions and with the corresponding pretest scores used as a covariant, $MS_e = 11.95$, $F(3, 371) = 7.53$, $p < .01$.

Post hoc analyses of the adjusted mean scores based on the pairwise comparison t test technique indicated that the COOP + META group outperformed the IND + META group, which, in turn, significantly outperformed the COOP and IND groups. However, no significant differences were found on that measure between the two groups that had not been exposed to metacognitive training.

Table 3 presents the number of students in each condition (percentages are in parentheses) who used each type of correct argument, by time and treatment. As can be seen from the table, under all conditions most students (60%) relied on numerical-computational arguments in justifying their reasoning. It is interesting to note that in the individualized groups (with or without metacognitive training), even more students (64%) did so than in the cooperative groups, where 51% with metacognitive training used such arguments and 60% without such training did so. In addition to using numerical-computational arguments, students quite often used logical-formal arguments. The frequency of using logical-formal arguments, however, was significantly larger under the COOP + META condition (29.5%) than under all other conditions (15.3%, 14.3%, and 20.4% for the IND + META, COOP, and IND conditions, respectively). These differences were statistically significant ($\chi^2 = 27.0$, $p < .001$). Further

analyses showed that under all conditions, students used the visual and drawing arguments quite infrequently (fewer than 8%), of the students under each condition).

Flexibility

As indicated earlier, the term *flexibility* refers to a student's provision of more than one kind of correct argument to justify his or her reasoning. For example, referring to the task described earlier, a student responded as follows: "The rate of change of Company A is greater because its rate of change is 1 and that of Company B is 1/3. We can also see it by looking at the slopes. The slope of line A is steeper than the slope of line B."

Initial analysis of students' arguments indicated that students very rarely provided more than two kinds of argument to explain their ideas regarding the solution of a given task. Under each condition this kind of response occurred two or three times. Therefore, in further analysis we distinguished between students who provided one kind of correct argument and those who provided more than one kind of correct argument to justify their reasoning on each task. Table 4 presents that information. Although before the study there had been no significant differences ($\chi^2 = 9.3$, $p > .05$) between conditions on flexibility, at the end of the study the chi-square analyses showed significant differences on all tasks but two. According to Table 4, on average about 27%, 12%, 6%, and 4% of the students under the COOP + META, IND + META, COOP, and IND conditions, respectively, justified their mathematical ideas by basing their explanations on more than one kind of correct argument.

Table 3. Frequency of Four Types of Correct Arguments (by Time and Condition)

	COOP + META $n = 105$	IND + META $n = 95$	COOP $n = 91$	IND $n = 93$
Logical-formal				
Pretest	19 (18.1)	16 (16.8)	6 (6.6)	18 (19.4)
Posttest	31 (29.5)	14 (15.3)	13 (14.3)	19 (20.4)
Numerical-computational				
Pretest	50 (47.6)	46 (48.4)	47 (51.6)	40 (43.0)
Posttest	54 (51.4)	61 (64.2)	55 (60.4)	60 (64.5)
Visual				
Pretest	6 (5.7)	3 (3.2)	4 (4.4)	5 (5.4)
Posttest	7 (6.6)	7 (7.4)	5 (5.5)	0
Drawing				
Pretest	0	0	0	1 (1.1)
Posttest	6 (5.7)	5 (5.3)	0	0

Note: Percentages (the s in parentheses) for each answer category were calculated by dividing the number of students who gave answers in that category by the total number of students in the same condition.

Table 4. Percentages of Students Who Displayed Flexible Reasoning (by Task and Condition)

	COOP + META $n = 105$		IND + META $n = 95$		COOP $n = 91$		IND $n = 93$		
	One Argument	More than one Argument	One Argument	More than one Argument	One Argument	More than one Argument	One Argument	More than one Argument	χ^2
Task 1	22.3	35.9	26.8	16.4	30	14.5	24.7	7.5	57.9***
Task 2	32.1	39.8	37.6	20.3	37.8	21.1	26.6	21.5	22.1**
Task 3	15.5	24.3	18.3	11.8	12.2	4.4	19.4	3.2	22.0**
Task 4	30.6	15.6	29.0	12.4	26.7	5.6	31.2	3.2	23.0**
Task 5	25.2	31.1	23.7	16.2	16.7	5.6	18.3	1.1	46.2***
Task 6	35.9	28.2	38.7	14.0	21.1	3.3	24.7	2.2	30.0**
Task 7	38.8	20.4	31.2	14.0	17.8	1.1	32.3	2.2	40.3***
Task 8	15.8	1.3	14.0	0	11.6	0	11.1	0	0.7
Task 9	38.8	1.9	13.9	1.1	14.4	0	11.5	1.0	1.2

Note: A student was said to display flexibility when he or she provided more than one type of correct argument to justify a solution to a problem. The percentages in each argument category were calculated by dividing the number of students who gave arguments in that category by the total number of students in the same condition.
**$p < .01$. ***$p < .001$.

Significant differences between conditions were also found among the students who provided one kind of correct argument to explain their reasoning, but the differences were not as large as those among students who provided more than one kind of argument to explain their reasoning. According to Table 4, on average about a quarter of the students under COOP + META (28%) and IND + META (26%) provided one kind of correct argument, as compared with 21% and 22% of the students under the COOP and IND conditions, respectively.

Graph Construction (Transfer Task)

The second purpose of the present study was to investigate the differential effects of COOP + META, IND + META, COOP, and IND on students' ability, in graph construction, to which they were not exposed in the classroom. Table 5 presents the mean scores, adjusted mean scores, and standard deviations on graph construction by time and condition. An ANOVA of classrooms nested within conditions indicated no significant differences between conditions before the beginning of the study, $MS_e = 5.22$, $F(3, 372) = .2$, $p > .05$, but at the end of the study, significant differences were found between conditions controlling for pretreatment differences, $MS_e = 2.95$, $F(3, 371) = 7.19$, $p < .01$.

Post hoc analyses of the adjusted mean scores based on the pairwise comparison *t* test technique indicated significant differences between the metacognitive

groups (COOP + META and IND + META) and the non-metacognitive groups (COOP and IND), but no significant differences were found between the two metacognitive groups or between the two non-metacognitive groups.

Metacognitive Knowledge

The third purpose of the present study was to investigate the differential effects of COOP + META, IND + META, COOP, and IND on students' metacognitive knowledge. A one-way MANCOVA (Wilks's lambda test) on the two criteria (general strategy and specific strategy), which were used as dependent variables with classrooms nested in conditions and with the pretest scores used as a covariant, indicated significant differences between conditions on both general and domain-specific metacognitive criteria simultaneously, $MS_e = .29$, $F(6, 744) = 2.97$, $p < .01$. Before carrying out the MANCOVA, we checked the prerequisites for running it, $MS_e = 2.8$, $F(6,743) < 1$, $p > .05$.

Table 6 presents the mean scores, adjusted mean scores, and standard deviations by time and condition on general and domain-specific metacognitive knowledge. As one may see from Table 6, no significant differences were found between conditions on any aspect of the metacognitive measure before the beginning of the study (F values ranged from .65 to 0.94, all p values > .05). Yet at the end of the study, significant differences were found between conditions on domain-specific metacognitive knowledge with classrooms nested in conditions, $MS_e = 0.64$, $F(3, 371) = 7.75$,

Table 5. Scores on Graph Construction Test (by Time and Condition)

	COOP + META n = 105	IND + META n = 95	COOP n = 91	IND n = 93	F
Pretest M	3.4	3.3	3.5	3.5	< 1
SD	2.3	2.5	2.1	2.4	
Posttest M	5.3	5.0	4.5	4.6	7.19*
Adjusted M	5.4	5.1	4.4	4.5	
SD	2.3	2.2	2.0	2.1	

Note: Scores on the graph construction test ranged from zero to 7. This was a transfer task.
*p < .05.

Table 6. Scores on Metacognitive Knowledge of General and Domain-Specific Strategies (by Time and Condition)

	COOP + META n = 105	IND + META n = 95	COOP n = 91	IND n = 93	F
General strategies					
Pretest					< 1
M	3.0	3.0	2.9	3.0	
SD	.6	.6	.6	.6	
Posttest					< 1
M	3.1	3.1	3.0	3.0	
Adjusted M	3.1	3.1	2.9	3.0	
SD	.6	.5	.5	.5	
Domain-specific strategies					
Pretest					< 1
M	3.2	3.3	3.3	3.3	
SD	.6	.6	.6	.6	
Posttest					7.75
M	3.5	3.5	3.3	3.3	
Adjusted M	3.5	3.5	3.2	3.3	
SD	.6	.5	.6	.5	

Note: Scores ranged from 1 to 5.
*p < .05.

$p < .01$, controlling for pretreatment differences, but not on general metacognition, $F(3, 371) < 1, p > .05$.

Post hoc analyses of the adjusted mean scores based on the pairwise comparison t test technique indicated significant differences between the metacognitive groups (COOP + META and IND + META) and the non-metacognitive groups (COOP and IND), but no significant differences were found between the two metacognitive groups or between the two non-metacognitive groups.

In sum, students who were exposed to the metacognitive training in either cooperative or individualized settings significantly outperformed the other students on graph interpretation (total scores), fluency and flexibility of correct explanations, use of logical-formal arguments to justify their reasoning, and transfer tasks (graph construction). In addition, the metacognitive groups attained higher levels of domain-specific metacognitive knowledge than the non-metacognitive groups. Table 7 summarizes these findings.

DISCUSSION

The present study compared the effects of the four instructional methods (COOP + META, IND + META, COOP, and IND) on mathematical reasoning, transfer of knowledge, and metacognitive knowledge. Although all four methods focused on promoting mathematical comprehension, each method was based on a different theoretical and operational approach. Therefore, the results should not be used to draw conclusions about which method is more "efficient." Rather, the purpose is to increase understanding of how each program operates relative to the others on these measures.

Table 7. Summary of Students' Performance
(by Dependent Variable and Condition)

Dependent Variable	Findings
1. Mathematical reasoning	
Graph interpretation (total score)	$4 > 3 > 2 = 1$
Mathematical explanations	
Fluency	$4 > 3 > 2 = 1$
Logical-formal	$4 > 3 > 2 = 1$
Numerical-computational	$4 = 3 = 2 = 1$
Visual	$4 > 3 = 2 > 1$
Drawing	$4 = 3 > 2 = 1$
Flexibility	$4 > 3 > 2 = 1$
2. Graph construction (transfer task)	$4 = 3 > 2 = 1$
3. Metacognitive knowledge	
General strategies	$4 = 3 = 2 = 1$
Specific strategies	$4 = 3 > 2 = 1$

Note: 1 = IND, 2 = COOP, 3 = IND + META, 4 = COOP + META. Use of the equals sign (=) indicates that there are no significant differences between two groups. The greater-than sign (>) indicates a significant difference in the mean scores of two groups.

It should also be emphasized that the present study focused on only one instructional unit: linear graphs. Although that unit is essential in the mathematics curriculum (NCTM, 2000), longitudinal investigations and large-scale studies that focus on other instructional units are needed to document the changes in other schooling outcomes. Moreover, methods for cooperative learning (e.g., Slavin, 1996) and metacognitive instruction (e.g., King, 1994; Schoenfeld, 1985) vary. Therefore, the generalizability of our findings may be limited to cooperative settings and metacognitive training that are similar to the ones we explored in this study.

Mathematical Reasoning

In the present study we analyzed mathematical reasoning in two complementary ways: One focused on the final answers, and the other on the written explanations provided by students to justify their mathematical ideas. The dual focus enabled us to develop a better understanding of how students learn to think flexibly about linear relationships and their representations in tables, graphs, and equations. Sometimes the final answers, were correct but based on wrong lines of reasoning, as seen in the following example of a student's response to the question about the graph in Figure 1: "The change rate in the income of company A is greater [the conclusion is correct] because its line is above Company B [the explanation is incorrect]." In other cases the final answers were incorrect but the explanations were correct. That happened most frequently when students made mistakes

in the calculations or in the solution of the equations. By formulating written explanations, students learned valuable lessons about the need for accuracy, precision, and completeness in their answers.

The data further showed that the average numbers of correct arguments were 4.2, 5.2, 6.7, and 8.9 for IND, COOP, IND + META, and COOP + META students, respectively. These data indicate that the number of arguments provided by IMPROVE students was almost double the number of arguments provided by IND students. Furthermore, IMPROVE students frequently used more logical-formal arguments, whereas other groups based their explanations mainly on numerical-computational arguments. The reason may be that, when studying the unit, IMPROVE students not only had to explain their strategies to their peers and the reasons for using those strategies but also had to analyze, compare, and contrast the meaningfulness of the tasks and their solutions.

The emphasis on fluency and flexibility, two important elements of mathematical discourse, has several implications. First, students tend to conceive of mathematics as a rigid subject based on arbitrary rules that allow only one correct answer and one correct argument to explain the answer (Schoenfeld, 1985). By contrast, it seems that IMPROVE teachers (and students) succeeded in building a mathematical community where students expressed their mathematical ideas fluently and flexibly, using various kinds of arguments to justify their ideas. Second, according to cognitive psychologists, elaboration is an important means for enhancing understanding (Wittrock, 1986). Our study confirmed that students who were exposed to metacognitive training did attain a higher level of mathematics achievement and were better able to explain their mathematical ideas in writing. In comparison with the written explanations of all other groups, those of IMPROVE students were longer, more accurate, and more frequently embedded with the new mathematical terms that had been introduced in the unit. Often their explanations included mathematical arguments and rationales, not just procedural descriptions or summaries (e.g., "The change rate of line A is greater because the angle it creates with the x-axis is larger then the angle that line B creates with the x-axis"). These findings are in line with the New Standards (NCTM, 2000), as well as with current studies showing that fluency and flexibility are essential components of mathematical thinking (Nohda, 2000; Brenner, Herman, Ho, & Zimmer, 1999; Dreyfus & Eisenberg, 1996).

Finally, beyond context and content, there is the role of the teacher. The study illustrates several important facets of teachers' roles, pertaining to metacognitive guidance, organization of the classroom, and the selection and use of worthwhile mathematical tasks that allow significant mathematical discourse to occur. Such tasks should include complex situations that present quantitative information in different contexts, allow multiple representations, or afford students opportunities to resolve mathematical conflicts (Mevarech & Kramarski, 1997a; NCTM, 2000). For example, the task described earlier, answering questions about the change rates of Companies A and B, was in many ways quite simple. It provided students with an opportunity to use their understanding of linear graphs, rate of change, slopes, and speed—important mathematical ideas in the middle grades. The task was simple enough that all students could perform it in a test situation, difficult enough to challenge students to think and reason about the properties of linear graphs and the applications of abstract mathematical ideas to everyday situations, and rich enough to allow students to engage in various levels of thinking—using quantitative or qualitative interpretations (Wainer, 1992) or computational or logical-formal arguments (Leinhardt et al., 1990).

Transfer Knowledge

The findings indicate that students who were exposed to metacognitive training were better able to transfer their knowledge from graph interpretation, which was taught in all classrooms, to graph construction, which was new to all students. Salomon, Globerson, and Gutterman (1989) reported similar findings, which showed that students who were exposed to metacognitive training in the area of reading comprehension improved their scores not only in reading comprehension but also in writing tasks

(e.g., writing compositions). These findings also support earlier conclusions (Mevarech, 1999; Hoek, Eeden, & Terwel, 1999; Kramarski, Mevarech, & Liberman, 2001) that metacognitive training leads students to link new and existing knowledge.

It is interesting that on the transfer task we found no significant differences between students who were exposed to the metacognitive training in cooperative settings and those who were exposed to the training in individualized settings (COOP + META and IND + META). Two plausible explanations are that (a) a seven-item test and scoring procedure based on correct and incorrect responses is not sensitive enough to assess students' transfer ability; and (b) the metacogitive questions were internalized by both groups to such an extent that students' interactions could have only a small additional impact on transfer performance. Indirect support for the latter explanation comes from the analysis of students' metacognitive knowledge, which showed no significant differences between the COOP + META and the IND + META groups on several aspects of metacognitive knowledge.

Metacognitive Knowledge

The findings also showed that the two groups that were exposed to metacognitive training (COOP + META and IND + META) scored higher on the metacognitive questionnaire than the two groups that were not exposed to metacognitive training, (COOP and IND).

It is interesting to note, however, that the differences between the metacognitive and non-metacognitive groups were observed only on domain-specific metacognitive knowledge but not on general metacognitive knowledge. That finding points to the importance of broadening the distinction between general and domain-specific knowledge (e.g., Salomon & Perkins, 1987) in the area of metacognition. Future research based on interviews and observations may explore the development of general and specific metacognitive knowledge under various conditions.

Comparisons Among the Conditions

Several issues relating to the comparison among the conditions need further consideration.

First, why did the COOP + META students outperform the IND + META students on graph interpretation (total scores), fluency, and flexibility in providing correct mathematical explanations? Two factors may explain these findings. One, it is possible that the type of metacognitive training used in the present study is more appropriate for cooperative than for individualized settings because learning in small groups provides a natural setting for students to formulate and discuss questions such as those used in the present study (Mevarech & Susak, 1993). Future research may focus on metacognitive training programs that are explicitly designed to be used in individualized settings. Two, cognitive psychologists (e.g., Sweller, Merrienboer, & Paas, 1998) indicate that the use of dual presentation techniques involving both auditory and visual-writing forms increases cognitive performance more than does the use of one form. Because students in the COOP + META condition more often used dual presentation forms, they were likely to outperform their counterparts in the IND + META condition who used mainly the visual-writing form.

Second, why did the COOP + META students outperform the COOP group on both aspects of mathematical reasoning? A partial answer relates to the quality of the mathematical discourse in the two cooperative conditions: Students who had been exposed to the metacognitive training in cooperative settings were better able to express their mathematical ideas in writing than were students who had studied, in cooperative settings without metacognitive training. That finding was also consistent with studies by Yager, Johnson, Johnson, and Schneider (1986), and Webb (1989, 1991), who showed that the quality of discourse in the groups related to students' mathematical achievement. In particular, Webb indicated that giving and receiving elaborated help is more strongly related to mathematics achievement than is giving or receiving final answers without elaboration or asking for help and not receiving it. To gather further information on this question, students' interactions under both conditions should be videotaped and analyzed.

Third, why did the IND + META students outperform the COOP students? The cooperative learning approach is rooted in cognitive theories assuming that elaboration is an important means for enhancing understanding and that cooperative settings are appropriate contexts for encouraging students to elaborate information. The present study indicated that placing students in cooperative groups is not sufficient for enhancing mathematical reasoning. According to the present study, metacognitive training is an effective means of facilitating mathematical reasoning, even when the training is implemented in individualized settings.

Finally, why did the COOP students not outperform the IND students on mathematical reasoning? From a cognitive perspective, students who have poor communication skills are less likely to benefit from cooperative learning because they are not able to communicate their mathematical ideas and the strategies they have used, nor do they know how to ask questions, reflect on their reasoning to explain it

to their peers, or specify what they do not understand. These findings support earlier studies arguing that there is a need to structure learning in small groups and that features of discourse such as "given reasons" must be practiced and reinforced (Webb, 1991; Webb & Farivar, 1994; Cohen, 1996; Mevarech & Kramarski, 1997a).

Practical Implications and Future Research

Assuming that these findings generalize to other settings, the study, suggests several important practical implications. First, it appears that under certain conditions students in junior high schools can learn to provide mathematical arguments to justify their ideas. In particular, IMPROVE students under the COOP + META condition were more fluent and flexible than the other students in explaining their ideas in writing. These findings call for the design of additional learning environments based on similar components. Such environments are desirable at all grade levels and for all mathematical topics. There is a need, therefore, to adapt IMPROVE and other COOP + META programs to the needs of primary school children. The issue of how children's mathematical explanations develop under various conditions merits future research.

A second issue relates to the exposure of students to the COOP + META program in various classrooms, not only in mathematics classrooms. There is reason to suppose that if students study under the COOP + META condition in mathematics as well as in other subjects (e.g., languages), they will be better able to internalize and activate metacognitive processes. This issue is open for future research.

A third issue relates to the norms for evaluating mathematical reasoning in junior high school classrooms. Our study emphasizes the importance of changing classroom organization when providing metacognitive training. The study also describes the kinds of arguments that students use in their mathematical explanations. At present, many state proficiency tests and international examinations (e.g., TIMSS-1999 and PISA; administered by OECD [Organisation for Economic Co-operation and Development] countries) include tasks that require students to explain their, reasoning in writing. To acquaint students with such tasks and the scoring procedure, teachers may prepare guidelines and ask students to score one another's explanations by using the guidelines and activating metacognitive processes. Thus students will learn how to construct explanations that are coherent, clear, and precise. Researchers in mathematics education may design "task banks" that challenge students to provide explanations. The task banks may be followed by analyses of students' correct and incorrect arguments.

REFERENCES

Brenner, M. E., Herman, S., Ho, H. Z., & Zimmer, M. J. (1999). Cross-national comparison of representational competence. *Journal for Research in Mathematics Education, 30*(5), 541–557.

Brown, A., & Palincsar, A. (1989). Guided cooperative learning and individual knowledge acquisition. In L. Resnick (Ed.), *Knowing, learning, and instruction: Essays in honor of Robert Glaser* (pp. 393–451). Hillsdale, NJ: Lawrence Erlbaum.

Cai, J., Lane, S., & Jakabcsin, M. S. (1996). The role of open-ended tasks and holistic scoring rubrics: Assessing students' mathematical reasoning and communication. In P. C. Elliott & M. J. Kenney (Eds.), *Communication in mathematics, K–12 and beyond* (pp. 137–145). Reston, VA: Academic Press.

California Learning Assessment System. (1993). *Portfolio assessment: Final report.* San Diego: CA: Center for Performance Assessment, Educational Testing Service.

Cecil, S. J., & Roazzi, A. (1994). The effects of context on cognition: Postcards from Brazil In J. S. Sternberg & R. K. Wagner (Eds.), *Mind in context: Interactionist perspectives on human intelligence* (pp. 74–100). Cambridge, UK: Academic Press.

Cobb, P., Boufi, A., McClain, K., & Whitenack, J. (1997). Reflective discourse and collective reflection. *Journal for Research in Mathematics Education, 28,* 28–47.

Cohen, E. G. (1996). *A sociologist looks at talking and working together in the mathematics classroom.* Paper presented at the annual meeting of the American Educational Research Association, New York.

Davidson, N. (1990). *Cooperative learning in mathematics: A handbook for teachers.* Menlo Park, CA: Addison-Wesley.

Dreyfus, T., & Eisenberg, T. (1996). On different facets of mathematical thinking. In R. J. Stermberg & T. Ben-Zeev (Eds.), *The Nature of Mathematical Thinking* (pp. 253–284). Mahwah, NJ: Lawrence Erlbaum.

Fendel, C., Resek, D., Alper, L., & Fraser, S. (1996). *Interactive mathematics program (IMP).* Berkley, CA: Key Curriculum Press.

Flavell, J. H. (1979). Metacognition and cognitive monitoring: A new area of cognitive developmental inquiry. *American Psychology, 34,* 906–911.

Forrest-Pressley, D. L., Makinnon, T., & Gary Waller, T. (1985). *Metacognition, cognition, and human performance.* Orlando, FL: Academic Press.

Garofalo, J., & Lester, F. K. (1985). Metacognition, cognitive monitoring, and mathematical performance. *Journal for Research in Mathematics Education, 16,* 163–176.

Hirsch, C., Coxford, A., Fey, J., & Schoen, H. (1997). *Contemporary mathematics in context: A unified approach.* (Core-Plus Mathematics Project). Chicago, IL: Janson.

Hoek, D., Van den Eeden, P., & Terwel, J. (1999). The effects of integrated social and cognitive strategy instruction on the mathematics achievement in secondary education. *Learning and Instruction, 9*(5), 427–448.

King, A. (1989). Effects of self-questioning training on college students' comprehension of lectures. *Contemporary Educational Psychology, 14,* 366–381.

King, A. (1991). Effects of training in strategic questioning on children's problem-solving performance. *Journal of Educational Psychology, 83,* 307–317.

King, A. (1994). Guiding knowledge construction in the classroom: Effects of teaching children how to question and how to explain. *American Educational Research Journal, 31,* 338–368.

Kramarski, B., Mevarech, Z. R., & Liberman, A. (2001). The effects of multilevel—versus unilevel—metacognitive training on mathematical reasoning. *Journal for Educational Research, 94*(5), 292–300.

Lappan, G., Fey, J., Fitzgerald, W., Freil, S., & Phillips, E. (1996). *Connected mathematics (Grades 6–8).* Palo Alto, CA: Dale Seymour.

Leinhardt, G., Zaslavsky, O., & Stein, M. K. (1990). Functions, graphs, and graphing: Tasks, learning, and teaching. *Review of Educational Research, 60,* 1–64.

Lester, F. K., Garofalo, Jr, & Kroll, D. L. (1989). *The role of metacognition in mathematical problem solving: A study of two grade-seven classes,* pp. 1–126. (ERIC Document Reproduction Service No. ED314255)

Marx, R. W., & Walsh, J. (1988). Learning from academic tasks. *Elementary School Journal, 88,* 207–219.

Meloth, M. S., & Deering, P. D. (1994). Task talk and task awareness under different cooperative learning, conditions. *American Educational Research Journal, 31,* 138–165.

Mevarech, Z. R. (1999). Effects of metacognitive training embedded in cooperative settings on mathematical problem solving. *Journal of Educational Research, 92*(4), 195–205.

Mevarech, Z. R. & Kramarski, B. (1992). How and how much can cooperative Logo environments enhance creativity and social relationships? *Learning and Instruction, 2,* 259–274.

Mevarech, Z. R., & Kramarski, B. (1993). Vygotsky, and Papert: Social-cognitive interactions with Logo environments. *British Journal of Educational Psychology, 63,* 96–109.

Mevarech, Z. R., & Kramarski, B. (1997a). IMPROVE: A multidimensional method for teaching mathematics in heterogeneous classrooms. *American Educational Research Journal, 34,* 365–394.

Mevarech, Z. R., & Kramarski, B. (1997b). From verbal descriptions to graphic representations:

Misconceptions regarding the construction of linear graphs. *Educational Studies in Mathematics, 32,* 22–263.

Mevarech, Z. R., & Susak, Z. (1993). Effects of learning with cooperative-mastery learning method on elementary students. *Journal of Educational Research, 86,* 197–205.

Montague, M., & Bos, C. S. (1990). Cognitive and metacognitive characteristics of eighth-grade students' mathematical problem solving. *Learning and Individual Differences, 2,* 371–388.

National Council of Teachers of Mathematics. (1989). *Curriculum and evaluation standards for school mathematics.* New York: Routledge & Kegan Paul.

National Council of Teachers of Mathematics. (2000). *Principles and standards for school mathematics.* Reston, VA: Author.

Nohda, N. (2000). Teaching by open-approach method in Japanese mathematics classroom. In T. Nakahara & M. Koyama (Eds.), *Proceedings of the 24th Conference of the International Group for the Psychology of Mathematics Education* (pp. 1–39). Hiroshima, Japan: Academic Press.

Organisation for Economic Co-operation and Development. (2000). Measuring students' knowledge and skills. *The PISA 2000 assessment of reading, mathematical and scientific literacy.*

Polya, G. (1945). *How to solve it?* Garden City, NY: Doubleday.

Robertson, L., Regan, S., Contestable, J., & Freeman, M. (1996). *Number power: A cooperative approach to mathematics and social development (Grades K–6).* Menlo Park, CA: Addison Wesley.

Salomon, G., Globerson, T., & Gutterman, E. (1989). The computer as a zone of proximal development: Internalizing reading-related metacognition from a reading partner. *Journal of Educational Psychology, 81,* 620–627.

Salomon, G., & Perkins, D. N. (1987). Transfer of cognitive skills from programming: When and how? *Journal of Educational Computing Research, 3,* 149–169.

Schneider, W., & Sodian, B. (1990). Children's understanding of cognitive cueing: How to manipulate to fool a competitor. *Child Development, 1*(3), 697–704.

Schoenfeld, A. H. (1985). *Mathematical Problem Solving.* San Diego, CA: Academic Press.

Schoenfeld, A. H. (1987). What's all the fuss about metacognition? In A. H. Schoenfeld (Ed.), *Cognitive Science and Mathematics Education* (pp. 189–215). Hillsdale, NJ: Erlbaum.

Slavin, R. E. (1996). Research on cooperative learning and achievement: What we know, what we need to know. *Contemporary Educational Psychology, 21,* 43–69.

Sweller, J., Van Merrienboer, J.J.G., & Paas, F. G. W. C. (1998). Cognitive architecture and instructional design. *Educational Psychology Review, 10*(3), 251–296.

Wainer, H. (1992). Understanding graphs and tables. *Educational Researcher, 21*(1), 14–23.

Webb, N. (1989). Peer interaction and learning in small groups. *International Journal of Educational Research, 13,* 21–40.

Webb, N. (1991). Task-related verbal interaction in mathematics learning in small groups. *Journal for Research in Mathematics Education, 22,* 366–389.

Webb, N., & Farivar, S. (1994). Promoting helping behavior in cooperative small groups in middle school mathematics. *American Educational Research Journal, 31,* 369–396.

Wittrock, M. C. (1986). Students' thought processes. In M. C. Wittrock (Ed.), *Handbook of research on teaching* (3rd ed., pp. 315–327). New York: Macmillan.

Yager, S., Johnson, R. T., Johnson, D. W., & Schneider, B. (1986). The impact of group processing on achievement in cooperative learning. *Journal of Social Psychology, 126,* 389–397.

APPENDIX A

Presentation of an Open-Ended Graph Task in the Metacognitive and Non-Metacognitive Conditions

The task:

The following graph describes the distance that seventh-grade students traveled in 7 hours on an end-of-school-year trip. Was the speed during the trip constant? Explain your reasoning in writing.

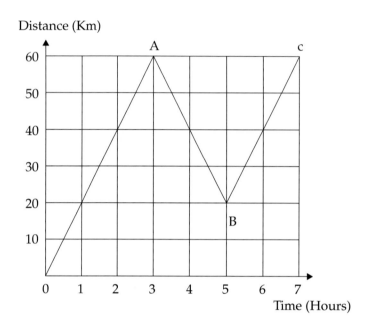

META Conditions	Non-META Conditions
COOP + META:	COOP
Discuss the task with your classmates.	Discuss the task with your classmates.
IND + META:	IND:
What is the problem/task about?	What are the students' speeds
Comprehension question:	(a) During the first 3 hours?
Use the acronym *DATA* to describe the graph:	(b) Between the 3rd and 5th hours?
Describe the *x*-axis and the *y*-axis.	(c) After the 5th hour?
Address the units and ranges of each axis.	
Tell the *T*rend(s) of the graph or parts of the graph.	
*A*nalyze specific points.	
Strategic question:	
Which strategy or principle is appropriate	
for solving or addressing the problem or task?	
Connection question:	
How is this problem or task different	
from what you have already solved?	

APPENDIX B

A Sample Graph Construction Task: Increasing, Decreasing, Constant, and Curvilinear Graphs

The task:

Construct the following graphs:

(a) The more time a student prepares for tests, the better her grades on the tests are.

(b) The more time a student prepares for tests, the lower her grades on the tests are.

(c) No matter how much time a student spends preparing for tests, her grades on the tests are always the same.

(d) When a student prepares for tests for up to 3 hours, the more time she prepares for tests the better her grades on the tests are; but if she prepares for more than 3 hours, she becomes tired and her grades on the tests decline.

1.06

POSTTEST CONTROL GROUP DESIGN

Problem-Based Learning in Online vs. Face-to-Face Environments

Jancis K. Dennis*

ABSTRACT: This study compared outcomes of problem-based learning between synchronous online groups and face-to-face tutorial groups. Specifically, the study compared learning outcomes, time-on-task and learning issue generation.

Methods and procedures: A post-test only control group design was used to investigate the effects of learning conditions on learning outcomes and processes. The experimental learning condition was defined as computer-mediated problem-based learning (CMPBL) and the control condition was traditional problem based learning in face-to-face groups (TPBL). The learning process consisted of four elements: an initial tutorial, a period of self-directed learning, a second tutorial and a laboratory session. During the initial tutorial students generated learning issues that they submitted to the research assistant. In the self-directed learning phase, students researched their learning issues and returned for the second tutorial with their findings. Students in the CMPBL groups interacted with the resource person electronically via email, chat room or bulletin board. At the second tutorial, groups shared information related to their learning issues and completed their products for the problem.

Results: There was no difference in learning outcomes between groups. The CMPBL group spent significantly more time on learning than the TPBL group. There was no overall difference between groups on generation of learning issues; however, there was a significant relationship between number of learning issues generated and higher score on the examination regardless of tutorial medium.

KEYWORDS: Problem based learning; online; synchronous; learning issues.

INTRODUCTION

Technological innovations of the past decade are enabling the proliferation of distance education programmes. By the end of 2002, it is estimated that 85% of 2 and 4-year colleges in the USA will be offering dis-

tance education (International Data Corporation, 1999). Indeed universities and corporations worldwide are planning to deliver education via distance all around the globe (van der Wende & Beerkens, 1999; Maslen, 2000; Overland, 2000; Michau *et al.*, 2001; van de Bunt-Kokkus, 2001). In this context, questions arise about educational infrastructures, learning models and instructor skills that will facilitate successful outcomes. There is concern that distance education is becoming a market commodity in which the essential interplay

* California State University, Sacramento, Solano Hall 4011, 6000 J Street, Sacramento, CA 95819, USA

between professor and student is in danger (Cremer, 2001). This underscores the need for examining models of online education in which real-time communication is preserved.

In the late 90s the Masters of Physical Therapy (MPT) programme at The Medical College of Georgia (MCG) was a problem-based learning (PBL) curriculum with a satellite campus in Albany, GA. The campuses were connected daily using Georgia Statewide Academic and Medical System (GSAMS) and continuously by WebCT™ This study investigated the effects of conducting PBL online. Specifically, the study compared outcomes between online and face-to-face (FTF) tutorial groups in relation to time-on-task and learning issue (LI) generation. Transcripts of the online tutorials were analysed to identify factors influencing LI generation. Online PBL has been minimally reported; two studies reported the use of asynchronous PBL for continuing medical education (Chan *et al.*, 1999; Sargeant *et al.*, 2000).

Background

Physical Therapy (PT) programmes have used both PBL and technology in their curricula. PBL is a recognized alternative to traditional lecture-laboratory approaches in health professions education. Many PT programmes are structured as PBL curricula while others utilize a combination of traditional courses in the first year and PBL approaches for patient care courses. (Solomon *et al.*, 1996; Saarinen-Rahiika & Binkley, 1998). Educational technologies have enabled PT programmes to offer degree upgrades, continuing education, or entry-level education using web-based courseware.

METHODS

A post-test only control group design was used to investigate the effects of learning conditions on learning outcomes and processes. The experimental learning condition was defined as computer-mediated problem-based learning (CMPBL) and the control condition was traditional problem based learning in FTF groups (TPBL). The results for three dependent variables are reported: learning outcomes, (measured by performance on course examination); time-on-task, (the self-reported time spent in and out of class on learning activities related to the course); and generation of LIs (recorded by each group during the first tutorial as recommended by Barrows (1986)). LIs are key products of the tutorial process since they are believed to contribute to self-directed learning (Barrows, 1986; Dolmans *et al.*, 1995).

Procedures

The CMPBL groups met in an online chat room. The tutorial began when all group members and the

facilitator were logged in. The discussion appeared as text that could be saved and emailed to students for reference. Two of the traditional face-to-face (FTF) tutorial groups met on campus, and the third met in the GSAMS classroom, with the facilitator at the main campus and the students at the remote site.

The sample of 34 was drawn from 54 second-year students. The sample size was a trade-off between availability of facilitators and ideal group size. Three faculty members were available as facilitators and the recommended group size for PBL is five to six students, with a maximum of seven (Barrows, 1992). Thus 17 students were randomly assigned to each of the learning conditions (17 to CMPBL and 17 to TPBL) with proportional representation of the remote campus students in each of the learning conditions. The three facilitators were each assigned a CMPBL and a TPBL group, and one worked exclusively with the Albany campus students. The principal investigator (PI) acted as "expert" for all students and as facilitator for the non-study groups.

Data were collected to assess the equivalence of the samples. The variables included the learning style elements of the Myers Briggs Type Indicator (MBTI). Functional pairs were used since these relate to learning style (Briggs Myers, 1998). Additional measures included GRE, gender, and computer skills as measured by Patrikas (1995). Students maintained logs to record time spent on learning activities. Entries were recorded in units, with one unit equal to 15 min.

Participants had the right to withdraw from the study at any time. All students provided a pseudonym to be used for both study instruments and tests, and this guaranteed anonymity when grading examinations.

The study was conducted during the Women's Health (WH) component of a medical and surgical conditions course. The learning activities consisted of two problems, one addressing pregnancy and the other urinary incontinence. The learning process for each problem consisted of four elements: an initial tutorial, a self-directed learning activity, a second tutorial and a laboratory session.

During the initial tutorial, students generated LIs. In the self-directed learning phase, students researched their LIs and returned for the second tutorial with their findings. Students could seek and ask experts, explore on-line or library resources, use their own texts or interact with the faculty resource person. Students in the TPBL learning mode could ask for specific information to be provided in a FTF resource session. Students in the CMPBL groups interacted with the resource person via email, chat room or bulletin board. At the second tutorial, groups shared information related to their LIs and completed the problem. TPBL groups met FTF and shared information in hard copy, CMPBL groups shared information via the bulletin board. The final activity for all groups was a clinical laboratory session. Assessment of learning consisted of a 30-item multiple choice test based on key LIs identified by the PI and two case-based short answer questions designed to evaluate students' clinical reasoning and coherence of explanation.

Training sessions for learning the course software were scheduled for the CMPBL group before commencement of the WH module. Students received an introductory packet explaining WebCT™ and were invited to visit the site maintained by the University of British Columbia to acquaint students with the programme. They attended an introductory session for accessing and using the chat room, using the bulletin board and email, and received an activity log. Facilitators were instructed to distribute activity logs to the TPBL group at the first tutorial session. A research assistant distributed and collected all other instruments. All facilitators had been trained in a 3-day workshop in which they practiced questioning skills and learned to guide the tutorial session rather than direct the learning.

RESULTS

Description of Sample

The two groups were similar in all characteristics as shown in Table 1.

Learning Outcomes

A *t*-test was used to investigate the hypothesis that student learning outcomes, as measured by final course grade, were not different between groups. Descriptive statistical analyses indicated the assumptions of normality of distribution and equality of variances were met. Table 2 displays the means, range and standard deviations of the two groups on the course grade. There was no statistical difference between the means of the students based on the conditions of learning ($p > 0.05$).

Table 1. Comparison of the Samples

Parameters of Comparison	TPBL	CMPBL
Female to male ratio	13:4	14:3
GRE	1082	1089
Myers-Briggs Type		
Feeling: Thinking types	15:2	14:3
Sensing: Intuiting types	9:8	10:7
Knowledge of computer	3.5 (2.3–4.5)	3.44 (2.8–4.4)
Computer operating		
system skills	1.38 (1–1.9)	1.51 (1–1.8)

Time-on-Task

The independent out-of-class learning activities were categorized into five major types: use of electronic resources, use of text-based resources, use of class peers as resources, (for example an extra group meeting or working with a study partner), use of expert resources and independent review. A sixth category, technology problems, was identified for the CMPBL group only. These data are represented in Figure 1 (omitted in this edition).

Proportional units of time were allocated across categories by both groups. The CMPBL group appeared to expend greater time-on-task in all categories except individual study. A Kolmogorov-Smirnov test indicated that there was a significant difference in time-on-task between the two groups, CMPBL and TPBL (alpha = 0.0012).

Learning Issues

A master list of LIs was developed by the PI and categorized as (a) critical to be identified, (b) important but not critical, and (c) appropriate but neither important nor critical and (d) other. Tables 3 and 4 show the LIs identified by the groups for each problem. In problem 1, the CMPBL groups identified more learning issues than the TPBL groups. In problem 2, the TPBL groups identified more LIs than the CMPBL groups. In both problems most LIs were generated about issues the instructor considered critical with a gradient through the important and appropriate but not critical issues.

Inspection of LIs from individual groups identified an apparent difference in group productivity. In problem 1, CMPBL3 named more LIs and covered both the pre- and post-partum elements of the problem while at the other end of the scale TPBL3 named very few LIs and covered a critical but narrow range of issues. The other four groups fell between the extremes. When each group's LIs were tabulated for problem 2, CMPBL group 3 identified more LIs than the other two CMPBL groups. Within the TPBL cohort, TPBL group 3 generated the least number of LIs. These observations prompted *post hoc* analyses.

A chi square analysis was performed to test the relationship between the number of LIs identified and course grade. Grades were divided into A (over 89) and B (up to 89), and LI identification was divided into two groups based on the median of total LIs identified across the two problems (22 and above, below 22). Chi square was 5.8456, df 1, $p = 0.0156$, indicating a significant relationship between the two.

Chat room logs were analysed to identify factors that might have resulted in different LI identification. No transcripts of FTF processes were available for comparison. Rabow *et al.* (1994) described four types of interaction occurring when small groups learn

Table 2. Comparison of Means and Standard Deviations of the TPBL Group and the CMPBL Group on Overall Grade in the Course

Variable	Count	Mean	Standard Deviation	Standard Error	95% LCL of Mean	95% UCL of Mean
TPBL	17	87.01176	5.345078	1.296372	84.26358	89.75995
CMPBL	17	88.47647	4.42133	1.07233	86.20323	90.74971

Table 3. Number of Learning Issues Identified by CMPBL Groups and TPBL Groups compared to Learning Issues Identified by the Problem Developer (problem 1)

Problem Developer Learning Issues	CMPBL Learning Issues	TPBL Learning Issues
Critical to identify		
Physiology of pregnancy	8	6
Change = > minor discomforts of pregnancy	10	1
Exercise prescription issues	20	14
Pathologies to screen	7	2
Total critical identified	45	23
Important to identify		
High risk pregnancy	4	3
Identify post partum complications	2	1
Normal post partum	1	1
Post partum exercise prescription	1	1
Total important identified	8	6
Appropriate to identify		
Normal birth process	1	0
Indications for Cesarean birth	1	2
Total appropriate identified	2	2
Other learning issues	2	4
Total	57	35

Table 4. Number of Learning Issues Identified by CMPBL and TPBL Groups Compared to Learning Issues Identified by the Problem Developer (problem 2)

Learning Problem Developer Issues	CMPBL Learning Issues	TPBL Learning Issues
Critical to identify		
Types/causes of incontinence	10	12
Anatomy of pelvic floor	2	2
PT evaluations	0	5
Pelvic relaxations	0	2
Normal micturition	0	1
PT treatment options	8	2
Total critical identified	20	24
Important to identify		
Medical interventions	3	3
Surgical interventions	1	1
Behavioural interventions	1	2
Nerve supply	0	1
Total important identified	5	7
Appropriate to identify		
Medical investigations	1	5
Total appropriate identified	1	5
Other learning issues	3	2
Total	29	38

through discussion: conventional, assertive, speculative, and confrontive. Conventional and assertive statements do not promote deep understanding of concepts. Conventional statements are social in nature ("Thank you for acknowledging that X."), while assertive statements are those in which students voice opinions, not necessarily associated with the topic of discussion ("This is the most unorganized thing I've done. It's like seven people are talking at once about different issues."). The transcripts were screened for statements that did not contribute to deep processing by adding conventional statements, assertive statements and technology-related statements (e.g., "My computer is really slow at this. Sorry!"). All other inputs were classified as on-task. CMPBL 3 had only 24.5% of off-task exchanges compared to CMPBL 2 whose exchanges were off-task 37.8% of the time (Table 5).

DISCUSSION

Learning Outcomes

The hypothesis that the CMPBL group would have a different level of academic achievement was not supported. Results of research in this area vary. Some studies report that CMC is no different from, or is at least as effective as traditional classroom learning (Straus, 1996; Hiltz, 1998). This is in contrast to other research that has shown superior performance by groups engaged in online discussion (Kekkonen-Moneta & Moneta, 2002), but many of those studies have used on-line learning activities as an adjunct to regular classes (Althaus, 1997). It is not surprising that added opportunities for learning result in superior outcomes. This is the only study reporting the use of a chat room for PBL tutorials. Two studies reported asynchronous PBL using the bulletin board for discussion, but postings were low in number and student interaction less than desired (Chan *et al.,* 1999; Sargeant *et al.,* 2000).

Table 5. Tally of Types of Input to the Tutorial Compared for Tutors and Students and for Students by on-task and off-task Contributions

Student Inputs

| Group | Total Inputs | Total tutor Inputs | Total on-task Inputs | Total Inputs that Discourage Deep Processing | | | |
				Social	Method	Assertions Unrelated to Task	Total off-task
CMPBL 1	646	192 (29.7%)	260 (40.2%)	78 (12.1%)	111 (17.2%)	5 (0.01%)	30%
CMPBL 2	732	97 (13.3%)	358 (48.9%)	149 (20.4%)	109 (14.9%)	19 (0.03%)	37.8%
CMPBL 3	620	107 (17.3%)	361 (58.2%)	81 (13.1%)	68 (10.9%)	3 (0.004%)	24.5%

The study was approved by the Medical College of Georgia Human Assurance Committee 98-09-091.

Time-on-Task

For this cohort of students, and this approach to PBL, computer-mediated communication resulted in significantly longer time-on-task for the same learning outcomes as the FTF group. The CMPBL group spent approximately 23% more time-on-task than the TPBL groups. It would have been appropriate had the finding been associated with superior outcomes. However, evidence that online students expended more time for outcomes similar to the FTF group is a matter for concern.

Previous studies have attributed longer time-on-task to the slowness of the asynchronous medium (Strauss, 1996; Weisenberg, 1999), or difficulty managing online materials (Rodd & Coombs, 1998). However, these were small components of the online activities required in this study and the reported time-on-task for the CMPBL group was increased across all categories. The mechanism for sharing learning issue research via the bulletin board accounted for only 16 units of extra time for the CMPBL group, which equates to approximately 15 min. per student. Technological problems accounted for a further 40 min. per student leaving 3 h. and 30 min. that cannot be attributed directly to the electronic medium.

A possible explanation is that the CMPBL tutorials were less productive than FTF groups (Straus & McGrath, 1994). In this situation students would need more study time to complete the problem. Analysis of chat room transcripts did not support early research that on-line discussion would be more focused and less personal, thus leading to a more efficient process (Philips & Santoro, 1989; Althaus, 1997). Rather, transcripts revealed considerable social exchange predicted to occur when students know each other (Romiszowski & Mason, 1996; Muffoletto, 1997). Some exchanges were frankly unprofessional—an example of "electronic normlessness" as described by Hiltz and Wellman (1997).

Technology

Technological problems played a role in the percentage of off-task time for CMPBL 1. Some of this group connected to the chat room through the Internet using telephone lines. These students complained of slow connectivity and repeated disconnections which impeded communication. This has ramifications for the use of real-time discussion, since the disconnections were highly disruptive to the tutorial. The infrastructure must be robust if education is to be delivered electronically with real-time interaction between students and professors. It is of concern that pedagogy might be driven by bandwidth. (Lloyd, 2000). At this time, cable and DSL serve less than 20% of all US Internet connections and considerably less in other nations. The promise of satellite connection in countries with poor telephone systems may be negated by its costs, estimated at $400–$1000 per installation (Wolff, 1999).

Learning Issues

Students in both learning conditions developed a satisfactory number of LIs compared to the instructor's expectations. The level of overlap between student and instructor LIs ranged between 70 and 100% depending on the problem. These percentages are similar to those reported by Dolmans et al. (1995).

CMPBL3 was highly successful in developing LIs in the online environment. It is worth noting that all groups, except for CMPBL3, were composed of a balance between sensing and intuitive, judging and perceiving types. CMPBL3 was made up exclusively of sensing types, and five were judging types and one a perceiving type. This would suggest that the group would be data driven and on task. The group composition might have contributed to its superior performance in LI generation, but the study was too small to make this assertion with confidence.

Although each group's ability to generate LIs differed, those differences were not associated with conditions of learning. *Post hoc* analysis revealed a positive association between numbers of LIs and course grade. This is one of the first studies to identify a positive relationship between the two, but results must be interpreted with caution since the study sample was extremely small.

CONCLUSIONS

The use of a chat room for PBL tutorials online proved to be as effective for learning outcomes as the FTF tutorial, but the process was less efficient. The use of PBL using CMC should be implemented cautiously since the students needed more learning time for the same outcomes. Regardless of the medium, the number of LIs developed by a group was associated with a higher grade. The study size was small but the suggested relationship between learning issue generation and course grade warrants further investigation.

The role of facilitator in PBL is the subject of much speculation. In FTF groups the facilitator plays a role modeling scientific inquiry and challenging students metacognitively. In the online environment the facilitator role may need to be modified since non-verbal cues available in the FTF environment might need to be replaced with textual techniques that promote student contribution, challenge thinking and keep the group on task.

REFERENCES

Althaus, S. (1997). Computer-mediated communication in the university classroom: An experiment with online discussions. *Communication Education, 46,* 158–174.

Barrows, H. (1986). A taxonomy of problem-based learning methods. *Medical Education,* 20, 481–486.

Barrows, H. (1992). *The Tutorial Process.* Springfield IL. Southern Illinois Medical School.

Briggs Myers, I. (1998). *Introduction to Type* (6th ed). Rev. by Kirby, L.K. & Myers K., Palo Alto, CA: Consulting Psychologists Press.

Chan, D.H., Le Clair, K. & Kaczorowski, J. (1999). Problem-based small-group learning via the Internet among community family physicians: A randomized controlled trial. *MD Computing, 16*(3), 54–58.

Cremer, D. (2001). Education as Commodity: The Ideology of Online Education and Distance Learning. *Journal of the Association for History and Computing. IV* (2). http://mcel.pacificu.edu/JAHC/JAHCiv2/ARTICLES/ArticlesIV2.HTML

Dolmans, D., Schmidt, H. & Gijselaers, W. (1995). The relationship between student-generated learning issues and self-study in problem-based learning. *Instructional Science, 22,* 251–267.

Hiltz, S.R. (1998). Collaborative learning in asynchronous learning networks: Building learning communities. Paper. In *Proceedings: WebNet 98 World Conference of the WWW, Internet and Intranet.* Orlando, FL. (ERIC Document Reprododuction Service ED 427705).

Hiltz, S.R. & Wellman, B. (1997). Asynchronous learning networks as a virtual classroom. *Communications of the ACM, 40*(9), 44–49.

International Data Corporation (1999). Online distance learning in higher education 1998–2002. Cited in Council for Higher Education Accreditation, *CHEA* Update #2. June 1999.

Kekkonen-Moneta S. & Moneta, G.B. (2002). E-learning in Hong Kong: comparing learning outcomes in online multimedia and lecture versions of an introductory computer course. *British Journal of Educational Technology, 33*(4), 423–434.

Lloyd, A. (2000). Pedagogy versus competition in higher education distance learning. *Educational Technology and Society, 3*(2), ISSN 1436–4522.

Maslen, G (2000). RMIT signs up for the e-education push. *Campus Review* June 21–27.

Michau, F., Gentil, S. & Barrault, M. (2001). Expected benefits of web-based learning for engineering education: examples in control engineering. *European Journal of Engineering Education, 26*(2), 151–168.

Muffoletto, R. (1997). Reflections on designing and producing an internet-based course. *TechTrends, 42*(2), 50–53.

Overland, M.A. (2000). India's new telecommunications policy may speed the growth of distance education. *Chronicle of Higher Education, 47*(2), A63.

Patrikas, E.O. (1995). Computer literacy among students entering the health information management programs. *J Ahima, 66*(1), 29–33.

Phillips, G.M. & Santoro, G.M. (1989). Teaching group discussion via computer-mediated communication. *Communication Education, 38,* 151–161.

Rabow, J., Charness, M., Kipperman, J. & Radcliffe-Vasile, S. (1994). *Learning Through Discussion.* Thousand Oaks, CA: Sage Publications.

Rodd, J. & Coombs, S. (1998). Distance learning with a difference: Using the Internet to deliver higher education. Paper. In *Proceedings ED-MEDIA/ED-TELECOM World Conference on Educational Multimedia and Hypermedia and World Conference on Educational Telecommunications.* Freiburg, Germany. (ERIC Document reproduction Service No. ED 428716).

Romiszowski, A.J. & Mason, R. (1996). Computer-mediated communication. In D.H. Jonassen (Ed.),

Handbook of Research for Educational Communications and Technology. New York, NY: Simon & Schuster MacMillan.

Sargeant, J.M., Purdy, R.A., Allen, M.J., Nadkarni, S., Watton, L. & O'Brien, P., (2000). Evaluation of a CME problem-based learning internet discussion. *Academic Medicine.* 75(10 Suppl.), S50–2.

Saarinen-Rahiika, H. & Binkley, J. (1998). Problem-based learning in physical therapy: A review of the literature and overview of the McMaster University experience. *Physical Therapy, 78*(2), 195–206, 210–211.

Solomon, P.E., Binkley, J. & Stratford, P. (1996). A descriptive study of learning processes and outcomes in two problem-based curricular designs. *Journal of Physical Therapy Education, 10*(2), 72–76.

Straus, S.G. (1996). Getting a clue: The effects of communication media and information distribution on participation and performance in computer-mediated and face-to-face groups. *Small Group research, 27*(1), 115–141.

Straus, S.G. & McGrath, J.E. (1994). Does the medium matter? The interaction of task type and technology on group performance and member reactions. *J Applied Psychology, 79*(1), 87–97.

Van de Bunt-Kokhus, S. (2001). Online learning at universities in developing countries: from leap-frogging to antelope jumping – Specific needs and solutions. *Higher Education in Europe.* XXVI (2), ISSN 0379–7724.

Van der Wends, M. & Beerkens, E. (1999) An international orientation on institutional strategies and governmental policies for the use of ICT in higher education. *Interactive Learning Environments, 7*(2/3), 283–322.

Wiesenberg, F. (1999). Teaching on-line: One instructor's evolving 'theory of practice'. *Adult Basic Education, 9*(3), 149–161.

Wolff, L. (1999). High speed Internet access: The future for the world and the implications for developing countries. Summary of five articles published in Scientific American, October 1999). http://www.iadb.org/sds/doc/Edu&Tech6.pdf

1.07

2-FACTOR POSTTEST CONTROL GROUP DESIGN

An Exploration of Online Environments Supporting Follow-Up to Face-to-Face Professional Development

Marybeth Green[*] **and Lauren Cifuentes**[†]

ABSTRACT: In this study we examined the effects of online follow-up and online peer interaction following a face-to face professional development workshop on attitudes towards that professional development and completion of a professional development task. School librarians were invited to work online on a three page plan outlining interventions a library program would undertake to address student weaknesses on the state mandated test. The study used a posttest-only control group experimental design with randomly assigned self-selected participants. Three online environments were compared: (a) an environment that provided Follow-up with Peer Interaction, (b) one that provided Follow-up without Peer Interaction, and (c) a control environment that provided a traditional post workshop environment with Only Solicited Follow-up/No Peer Interaction. Online follow-up with or without peer interaction positively affected attitudes towards the professional development program. In addition, online Follow-up with Peer Interaction increased the likelihood of completion of the professional development task. No difference was found between the completion rates for participants in the follow-up group that did not have peer interaction and those in the Only Solicited Follow-up/No Peer Interaction. environment. Our findings indicate that teacher educators are well advised to provide online Follow-up with Peer Interaction in their professional development programs.

Information communication technologies in schools create new opportunities for professional developers to provide follow-up to their face-to-face workshops. Web-based learning management systems enable extended

[*]University of Texas San Antonio, San Antonio, TX USA, marybeth.green@utsa.edu
[†]College Station, TX USA, laurenc@tamu.edu

online teacher professional development (oTPD) with high degrees of interactivity among educators spread across vast geographic landscapes. Most importantly, oTPD programs allow participants to choose the time and place of their involvement.

In her introduction to the special issue on online teacher professional development in the Journal of Technology and Teacher Education, Sprague (2006) recommended investigating "... the value of 'blended' learning [.] What does online add to face-to-face programs?" (p. 660). This study investigated the potential for online environments to provide for follow-up and peer interaction that would not be available in the traditional face-to-face workshop form of professional development.

Follow-up to face-to-face professional development has long been established as essential to sustaining teacher change (Joyce & Showers, 1988). Participants' initial enthusiasm for content presented in a professional development workshop may be reassuring to organizers, but has relatively little influence on changing teaching practices (Showers, Joyce, & Bennett, 1987). Beeby (1980) summarized the need for follow-up to professional development saying: "Without continuing encouragement and support [upon completion of workshops and courses], the average teacher has a remarkable capacity for reverting back to old practices" (p. 466). Teachers need time beyond the professional development workshop to (a) build competence in new tasks or strategies, (b) create new structures, (c) try new roles in safe environments, and (d) engage in discussions regarding beliefs and assumptions about issues related to practice (Fullan & Stiegelbauer, 1991; Garmston, 2003; Lieberman, 1995).

Previous research (Lance, Rodney, & Hamilton-Pennell, 1999, 2000, 2002) has established the importance of school librarians and school library programs to student achievement making professional development of these librarians critical. The ultimate goal for librarians' professional development is to promote positive change in their knowledge, understanding, behaviors, skills, values, and beliefs as demonstrated by completion of professional development tasks and implementation of those tasks with students in schools (Hord, 1994).

The greatest challenge to providing follow-up to professional development is simply finding time in a teacher's day. Time for teacher learning is an elusive commodity in American schools. Teachers' days are filled with countless tasks leaving little time to think about, much less plan for innovation. Moving teacher-learning to meetings at the end of already crowded days breeds resentment. Providing release time through substitutes so that teachers can meet during the day is costly.

Online environments allow educators to access professional development at their own convenience and potentially address the problem of lack of time. For this study, online follow-up environments were provided to Texas school librarians following a face-to-face professional development workshop to investigate the efficacy of online follow-up and online peer interaction as support for professional development. The researchers anticipated that online follow-up and use of online interactive tools would both positively affect teachers' attitudes toward professional development and would increase the likelihood of completion of professional development tasks after a face-to-face session. The purpose of the professional development program was to help school librarians develop a plan to support student performance on identified weaknesses on the Texas Assessment of Knowledge and Skills (TAKS), the state standardized assessment taken by students at various grade levels. After identifying TAKS weaknesses at each librarian's school, the librarian would create a plan for activities, programs, or instruction that would support student performance on those weaknesses. The online follow-up for the treatment groups included a variety of resources, opportunities for reflection and encouragement to support completion of each part of the TAKS Support Plan.

THEORETICAL FRAMEWORK

There is growing consensus that effective professional development is grounded in social constructivist theories (Sparks & Hirsch, 1997). Constructivist methods enable teachers to "apply current understandings, note relevant elements in new learning experiences, judge the consistency of prior and emerging knowledge, and based on that judgment . . . modify knowledge" (Hoover, 1996, ¶ 14). Four constructs are central to the constructivist professional development paradigm: learning is developmental; disequilibrium facilitates learning; reflective abstraction is the driving force of learning and may be accomplished through discussions, and discourse within a community engenders further thinking (Fosnot & Perry, 2005).

Research studies provide evidence that follow-up is an important factor in professional development. Showers et al.'s (1987) meta-analysis compared the effect sizes of professional development with inclusion of differing combinations of the following components: (a) instruction in theory, (b) demonstration, (c) practice, (d) feedback, and (e) coaching. Those professional development workshops that included all five components had an effect size of 1.68 for transfer of training to the classroom. Inclusion of only the first four yielded an effect size of .39 for transfer of training to the classroom. Use of fewer components yielded a negligible effect for transfer of training. Without follow-up, or what Showers et al. (1987) called "coaching," the traditional model of professional development overrates the teacher's capacity for change (Fullan & Stiegelbauer, 1991).

Professional development programs that result in educators developing the knowledge and skills that improve student outcomes are rated favorably by educators (Guskey, 2000). Teacher attitudes towards professional development ultimately impact completion and implementation of professional development tasks (Bradley, 1991). Traditional professional development programs based on stand-alone workshops are not as well received by educators as professional development programs that include follow-up to support the ongoing process of educator change (McBride, Reed, & Dollar, 1994). Such follow-up enhances educators' feelings of competence (Guskey), and educators value professional development that enhances their effectiveness with students (Fullan & Stiegelbauer, 1991). Conversely, professional development programs that fail to develop the requisite knowledge and skills are viewed negatively and considered a waste of time by teachers (Lindstrom & Speck, 2004).

Delivery of professional development to groups of librarians is more complex than for subject matter teachers. Although school librarians work as part of an instructional team, there is usually only one librarian at most campuses, leaving few opportunities for discourse among librarians regarding the unique issues in their practice. In large school districts, the majority of peer interaction for professional growth among school librarians is limited to professional development workshops scheduled by the school districts six times per year at best. School librarians in small school districts must travel to offerings at regional service centers and by professional organizations. Therefore, school librarians are typically eager to interact with peers on professional tasks. Online follow-up, including peer interaction appears to be a logical way to address the issue of school librarian isolation.

The purpose of this controlled study was to examine the effects of online follow-up and online peer interaction on school librarians' attitudes towards professional development and completion of a professional development program. Therefore, the researchers asked two questions:

1. Is there a significant difference in participant attitudes towards the professional development program between oTPD environments including Follow-up with Peer Interaction, Follow-up without Peer Interaction, and Only Solicited Follow-up/No Peer Interaction?
2. Does the likelihood of participant completion of a TAKS Support Plan, the professional task following a face-to-face workshop, improve as a result of being provided Follow-up with Peer Interaction with or Follow-up without Peer Interaction?

Findings inform professional developers regarding design for effective oTPD.

METHOD

The researchers applied quantitative methods to investigate the questions and conducted the study in the natural work life setting of school librarians in Texas. Professional development follow-up was provided to an archipelago of school librarians who were as far as 747 miles apart.

Participants

Participants for this study were identified through a purposive sample of independent school districts in Texas. Purposive sampling of 12 large school districts created a potential participant list of 812 school librarians who resided in Texas elementary, middle, and secondary public education institutions. The 12 sampled school districts—Aldine, Austin, Dallas, El Paso, Fort Bend, Fort Worth, Houston, Hurst-Euless-Bedford, Mesquite, Plano, and Round Rock—represented 15% of the 1,266 school districts in Texas. These 12 school districts were purposively selected as they represented a large percentage of Texas student populations (21.6%), underprivileged student populations (25%), and minority student populations (27.2%).

The 812 potential participants attended a face-to-face professional development workshop on how to develop a TAKS support plan and were invited to join in the study. The final list of volunteers for this study included 450 librarians who represented all 12 school districts in the original purposive sample of Texas school districts. The other 362 potential participants chose not to participate. Participants were stratified by level of service (elementary school, middle school, high school) and by socioeconomic status of the school. Socioeconomic status was measured by the percentage of students classified as economically disadvantaged at each school. This information is available by school on the Academic Excellence Indicator System on the Texas Education Agency website (Academic Excellence Indicator System, n.d.).

The 450 participants were stratified by level of service and socioeconomic status and randomly assigned to one of three groups. Following assignment, there was some attrition of volunteers leaving 280 who participated in one of three online environments: (a) Follow-up with Peer Interaction ($n = 94$), (b) Follow-up without Peer Interaction ($n = 98$), and a (c) Control group, Only Solicited Follow-up/No Peer Interaction ($n = 88$). In addition to applying stratification as a safeguard for matched groups, chi-square tests were used to determine if there were significant differences across the groups of stratification in service level and socioeconomic status of school. No significant difference was found for level of service ($\chi^2 = 1.356$ $df = 4$, $n = 280$, $p = 0.852$) or socioeconomic status ($\chi^2 = 3.759$, $df = 4$, $n = 280$, $p = 0.440$). Gender representation was consistent with representation in the profession and the same across environments with 96% female and 4% male librarians.

The need to control for differences in instructional approaches of teachers necessitated that one instructor deliver follow-up instruction to the three treatment groups. The instructor was one of the researchers in this study. This could be viewed as a limitation of the study, but due to the expertise required for delivery of workshop content, this could not be avoided. The instructor divided her daily time equally among the two experimental groups and responded promptly to any solicitations from the control group. The instructor provided feedback by responding to parts of students' plans as they were submitted rather than working from a script. The instructor gave direction to enable progress towards completion of as many plans as possible.

Design and Procedures

A posttest-only control group experimental design with self-selected participants was used to determine the effects of the independent variable online follow-up environment, on the dependent variables attitudes towards the professional development, and course completion. One of the researchers trained 12 Library Services Directors or their designee during the summer in workshop content and delivery so that all workshops would be consistent. At the beginning of the 2004–2005 school year, all school librarians in 12 school districts across the state of Texas participated in a three hour face-to-face workshop in their district presented by their district's Library Services Director or a designee. Each presenter used an agenda and a PowerPoint presentation developed by one of the researchers.

The workshop content focused on training librarians to create a plan for the library at their school to support weaknesses in student performance on the TAKS, the state standardized test. During the workshop, school librarians explored: (a) case studies illustrating the need for evidence based practice as it applies to school library media centers, (b) the need for a TAKS support plan at their school, (c) student weaknesses at their school provided in the Summary Report of Student Performance by the Texas Education Agency, (d) components of the plan for intervention, and (e) resources available to help them complete the plan.

The TAKS support plan that the librarians were expected to complete as a product of the professional development was written by each participating school librarian detailing his or her strategy for supporting student weaknesses identified on the TAKS at their school. It was to consist of six-sections totaling three pages: (a) background of the school, (b) plan for collaborating within the school to achieve goals, (c) Texas Essential Knowledge and Skills objectives selected as

weaknesses, (d) library plan for addressing weaknesses, (e) evaluating resources, and (f) communicating with the school community.

At the end of the workshop, librarians were offered the opportunity to continue working on creating their TAKS support plans through oTPD and were told that the follow-up would require approximately one hour of time online each week. Those who chose to continue working were randomly assigned to one of the three online environments. For participants in all three environments, the TAKS Support Plan was due to be turned in to the workshop instructor eight weeks later.

Treatment Environments

Each group was provided with separate WebCT Vista courses that were configured to support their environment. Content for the six modules provided to the two groups whose members received follow-up drew from readings from various journals, school library web sites, and PowerPoints providing further guidance for creating each section of the TAKS Support Plan. Modules were released weekly using the selective release tool of WebCT Vista. Each module was designed to require an average of one hour per week in online time and two to three hours on-the-job.

Follow-up without Peer Interaction Environment

Follow-up in this environment consisted of access to readings from professional journals and relevant Web sites, tasks within the school relevant to TAKS Plan completion, and opportunities for reflection by independently preparing a journal response to the same discussion questions as in the follow-up including peer interaction environment. This environment provided follow-up through: (a) six modules with objectives, readings to support the themes, discussion questions, and an assignment for development of the TAKS Support Plan, (b) individualized feedback from the instructor, (c) examination of student TAKS data from the participating librarian's school, (d) development and submission of sections of the TAKS Support Plans weekly through the WebCT Vista assignment tool, (e) weekly cueing messages in the form of announcements welcoming them to each week's work sent to their school email at the beginning of the week and messages alerting them to new resources as needs developed, and (f) opportunities for reflection through journal assignments and selective release of course materials over time. Journal assignments were identical to discussion questions posted in the Follow-up with Peer Interaction. The question from Week 1, for example, asked librarians to reflect on the importance of creating a TAKS Support Plan.

In a typical week, a school librarian in this environment might log on and take part in online activities involving interactivity with content and with the instructor (Moore & Kearsley, 1996). Content interaction included reading the objectives and journal articles and viewing the PowerPoint presentations chosen. Student interaction included checking for announcements that were made approximately twice a week, reading feedback from the instructor on his or her previous week's TAKS Plan section submission, and communicating with the instructor regarding course issues. However, all communication tools were blocked eliminating the ability to have any contact with peers. Librarians in this environment received the same discussion question as the Follow-up with Peer Interaction, but as a journal assignment.

Follow-up with Peer Interaction Environment

For this group, follow-up experiences were similar to the Follow-up without Peer Interaction group. However, this group differed from the other treatment group in that participants interacted weekly with their peers. Peer interaction included (a) reviewing the parts of colleagues' TAKS Support Plans as they were posted, (b) providing feedback to peers regarding their progress on their TAKS Support Plan, (c) reading feedback from peers on the previous week's TAKS Support Plan section submission, (d) reading and sending email, (e) participating in the weekly discussion that featured the same question that was journaled by the Follow-up without Peer Interaction, and (f) participating in a chat. Librarians in this environment were randomly divided into online discussion groups with no more than 15 per discussion group. A discussion question was posted by the instructor in each module that was relevant to the weekly topic. The librarians were asked to respond to the question and to respond to each other's comments. The instructor posted frequent comments in the initial discussions and fewer as learners took charge of their own learning.

Only solicited online follow-up/no peer interaction environment. This group received the typical post workshop treatment for professional development including guidance from the instructor when solicited from participants and access to face-to-face workshop materials. Participants had online access to the instructor for questions regarding completion of the report by way of an email address and telephone number posted on the welcome page and online access to all face-to-face workshop materials. In addition, the welcome page had a link to face-to-face workshop materials. However, the instructor did not offer unsolicited information, encouragement, or support. Participants in this control environment received only administrative messages from the instructor to their personal email accounts. School librarians were given a link to instructions for using the assignment tool to upload

their TAKS Support Plans whenever the participant deemed it was completed.

Instrumentation

Attitudes Towards the Professional Development Program, a survey instrument developed by the researcher, measured course satisfaction in five categories drawn from Guskey's (2000) professional development evaluation model: (a) participant reactions, (b) participant learning, (c) participant's use of new skills, (d) organizational culture, and (e) student outcomes. The seven items related to "participant reactions" were intended to assess whether participants felt that the program was well organized, that time was well spent, and that learning activities were useful (see Table 2 in results). The four items related to "participant learning" were intended to assess how well the participants felt they had learned the concepts, ideas, and/or pedagogies included in the professional development program. The two items related to "participants' use of new skills" were intended to assess the extent to which participants were implementing new concepts, ideas, and/or pedagogies in the professional development program in their educational situation. The one item related to "organizational culture" assessed the participants' perceptions of support by their school for their plan. The one item related to "student outcomes" measured the extent to which librarians believed that their TAKS Support Plan would impact student performance on the TAKS. The survey included 15 items regarding participation in the overall professional development program. This survey used a 5-point Likert scale to indicate the degree to which participants agreed or disagreed with the item. Higher scores corresponded with a positive response. Mean survey responses ranged from 1–5. In reporting scores, mean ratings of 1.00–2.00 were classified as very negative, 2.01–2.99 were classified as mildly negative, 3.0 was classified as neutral, 3.01–4.00 were classified as mildly positive, and 4.01 to 5.00 were classified as very positive. Content validity was established by closely tying to Gusky's model and by evaluation of the instrument by three educational psychologists.

Attitude survey responses were collected through an online tool in WebCT at the beginning of the sixth week of the program. At the beginning of the seventh week, library directors sent email requests to participants to complete the Attitude Survey. After two additional weeks, paper copies of the Attitude Survey were sent to approximately 50 participants who had failed to respond previously to electronic requests with an addressed, stamped envelope.

Course completion was measured by completion and submission of all six parts of the TAKS Support Plan to the WebCT site. Plans that met this criterion were given a 1 and plans that were not completed or submitted were given 0. As with the survey, participants in all three groups were encouraged to submit their TAKS Support Plans through an email message that included directions on how and when to submit.

Data Analyses

In the Follow-up with Peer Interaction environment, a total of 70 surveys were returned, representing a 74.4% return rate. Of the surveys returned, 53 were returned by librarians who had completed the TAKS Plan. In the follow-up without Peer Interaction, a total of 68 surveys were returned, representing a 68.4% return rate. Of the surveys that were returned, 43 were returned by librarians who had completed the TAKS Plan. In the Only Solicited Follow-up/No Peer interaction, a total of 61 surveys were returned representing a 70% return rate. Of the surveys that were returned, 27 were returned by librarians who had completed the TAKS Plan. To establish reliability of the Attitudes Towards Professional Development Survey, a coefficient alpha was generated to determine the relationship between individual test items and the test as a whole. The coefficient for the Attitudes Towards the Professional Development Program survey was .92.

An analysis of variance (ANOVA) was conducted to determine the effects of professional development environments on attitudes towards the professional development experience across environments. In this analysis, the dependent variable was mean scores from the Attitudes Towards the Professional Development Program, and the independent variable was the professional development online environment. Post hoc comparisons were completed through Tukey HSD to identify specific statistical differences between the professional development environments.

Binary logistic regression analysis was employed to estimate the probability of course completion as a function of the professional development environment. The dependent variable, course completion, was binomial with 1 indicating that the participant completed requirements for the course and 0 indicating that the participant failed to complete course requirements. The predictor variable was online environment. There were two phases to this analysis. In the first phase, the group that received Only Solicited Follow-up/No Peer Interaction was the referent environment, while in the second phase, the group that received follow-up including peer interaction, was the referent environment (Afifi, Clark, & May, 2004).

RESULTS

The findings reported here are organized according to the two research questions posed earlier. First,

evidence is presented regarding the comparative effects of environments that provide Follow-up with Peer Interaction, Follow-up without Peer Interaction, and Only Solicited Follow-up/No Peer Interaction on attitudes toward the professional development program. Second, evidence is presented regarding differences in likelihood of completion of professional development task across environmental experiences.

Frequency of Interactions

A Tool Usage Summary report was generated in WebCT Vista to determine the type and extent of interactions in each of the two experimental environments. The two treatment environments did not differ much in their amount of interaction through announcements (Follow-up with Peer Interaction, 360 and Follow-up without Peer Interaction, 362) and assignments (Follow-up with Peer Interaction 2253, and Follow-up without Peer Interaction, 2188). However, the Follow-up with Peer Interaction participants interacted in chat 53 times, discussions 2005 times, and participants' interactions email 614 times. Emails included 43 received by the instructor and 54 sent by the instructor. The majority of emails, 517 were exchanged by participants.

The Follow-up without Peer Interaction group had zero interactions through chat and discussion. The email tool was blocked and email to the instructor was available through an email address on the welcome page. Their email interactions were only with the instructor and totaled approximately 280. These emails originated from less than half of the Follow-up without Peer Interaction.

Attitudes

Participant attitudes towards the professional development program differed according to environment. Participants in the Follow-up with Peer Interaction environment gave the highest ratings followed by the ratings of participants in the Follow-up without Peer Interaction environment. The least positive ratings were given by participants in the Only Solicited Follow-up/No Peer Interaction environment. Although significant differences occurred between groups, all participants mean scores reflected mildly positive attitudes. Means and standard deviations for the attitudinal survey items are reported by professional development environment in Table 1. The mean rating for participants on the Attitudinal Survey was 3.71(SD .77). The mean rating for participants in the Follow-up with Peer Interaction was 3.94(SD .68). The mean rating for participants in the Follow-up without Peer Interaction was 3.77(SD .68). The mean rating for participants in Only Solicited Follow-up/No Peer Interaction was 3.36(SD .84).

Table 1. Results of the ANOVA on Attitudes Towards the Professional Development Program

Source	df	SS	MS	F	p
Attitudes between groups	2	1.199	.599	10.098	.001*
Within groups	201	11.932	.059		
Total	203	13.131			

*Significant at $p \leq .05$.

One-way analysis of variance (ANOVA) indicated that the differences in attitudes towards the professional development program were statistically significant among the three professional development environments $F(2,203) = 10.098$, $p < .001$ (Table 1). Post hoc Tukey HSD Tests indicated that the participants who received follow-up with peer interaction had more positive attitudes than the participants in the control environment ($p < .001$). Likewise, participants in the Follow-up without Peer Interaction environment had more positive attitudes than participants in the control environment ($p < .007$). Effect sizes were calculated by using Cohen's d (1977). A moderate effect size of $d = .76$ was found between the Follow-up with Peer Interaction environment and the control environment. A moderate effect size of $d = .54$ was found between the Follow-up without Peer Interaction environment and the control environment.

Means and standard deviations of responses to individual items are reported in Table 2. Questionnaire items are reported according to their contribution to the variance from most to least contribution. The table also shows the category from Guskey's (2000) professional development evaluation framework addressed by each item. Participants in the three environments voiced differing opinions regarding the actual experience of professional development (item 1) and items which dealt with the belief that the professional development had some impact (items 2–7). The value of the content of the professional development experience (items 8–15) made little or no contribution to the differences in attitudes, meaning that all groups valued the content.

Completion

One-hundred-and-twenty-five librarians completed their TAKS Support Plans. Table 3 displays the chi-square comparison for completion percentage based on environment.

The overall chi-square test was significant $\chi^2 = 14.79$, $df = 2$, $n = 280$, $p < .001$. The completion percentage was higher for Follow-up with Peer Interaction (58.5%) than for either Follow-up without Peer Interaction (43.9%) or Only Solicited Follow-up/No Peer Interaction (30.7%). As post hoc analyses, two-by-two chi-square tests were performed for the completion percentage based on each pair of environments. It was found that Follow-up with Peer Interaction had a significantly higher completion percentage than either Follow-up without Peer Interaction ($\chi^2 = 4.11$, $df = 1$, $n = 192$, $p < 05$) or Only Solicited Follow-up/No Interaction ($\chi^2 = 14.21$, $df = 1$, $n = 182$, $p < .001$). No significant differences were found between Follow-up without Peer Interaction and Only Solicited Follow-up ($\chi^2 = 3.44$, $df = 1$, $n = 186$, $p < .06$).

Logistic regression was used to predict the probability of completion of a TAKS Support Plan. Differences in completion using logistic regression were significantly predicted ($\chi^2 = 14.474$, $df = 2$, $p < .001$) Nagelkerke $r^2 = .07$. Table 4 presents the results of the logistic regression with Only Solicited Follow-up/No Peer Interaction as the referent group. Membership in the Follow-up with Peer Interaction condition was significantly associated with greater likelihood of course completion when Only Solicited Follow-up/No Interaction participants were the referent group ($OR = 3.186$, $p < .001$).

A second logistical regression was conducted using the Follow-up with Peer Interaction as the referent group to determine whether there was a difference between the participants in the Follow-up with Peer Interaction environment and the participants in the Follow-up without Peer Interaction environment in predicting the likelihood of course completion (Table 5).

Results showed that participants in the Follow-up without Peer Interaction environment were significantly less likely to complete when compared with participants in the Follow-up with Peer Interaction environment ($OR = 0.554$, $p < .05$). In addition, participants in the Only Solicited Follow-up/No Peer Interaction group were significantly less likely to complete the course when compared to the Follow-up with peer interaction group ($OR = 0.31$, $p < .001$).

DISCUSSION

The purpose of this controlled study was to examine the effects of online follow-up and online peer interaction on attitudes towards professional development and completion of a professional development program, in this case a Support Plan for supporting students' achievement on the TAKS. We found that, with a substantial sample of Texas school librarians, effective professional development includes extended follow-up support and interaction with peers and other professionals.

Table 2. Means and Standard Deviations of Responses to Individual Survey Items on the Attitudes Towards the Professional Development Survey by Environment

Statement	Follow-up with Peer Interaction		Follow-up without Peer Interaction		Only Solicited Follow-up/ No Peer Interaction		Guskey Model
	Mean	SD	Mean	SD	Mean	SD	
1. Setting my own schedule for involvement in professional development worked well for me.	4.21	.92	3.80	1.23	3.31	1.41	Participant Reactions
2. The professional development program helped me acquire the intended knowledge and skills to create a TAKS Support Plan.	3.82	.97	3.70	.94	3.03	1.20	Participant Learning
3. I will communicate the TAKS Support Plan to the various community stakeholders in my school community.	3.96	.84	3.59	.94	3.18	1.15	Participant Use of New Skills
4. The professional development program enhanced my contributions to the school community.	3.96	.89	3.64	.99	3.20	1.17	Participant Learning
5. I will put the TAKS Support Plan I developed into use this school year to support achievement in my school.	4.01	.93	3.89	.89	3.31	1.19	Participant Use of New Skills
6. The professional development activities helped me integrate evidence-based practice into my situation.	3.87	.89	3.64	.95	3.23	1.16	Participant Learning
7. I believe that my learning is likely to increase student performance.	3.79	.81	3.70	.91	3.16	1.05	Student Outcomes
8. The professional development program was well organized	3.92	1.14	3.97	.93	3.31	1.09	Participant Reactions
9. The professional development program helped me develop a greater understanding of evidence-based practice for school libraries.	3.79	.98	3.66	.98	3.20	1.15	Participant Learning
10. Working with other faculty at my school helped create a more meaningful plan.	4.06	.82	3.93	.89	3.54	.98	Participant Reactions
11. Goals and objectives of the professional development program were clear	4.03	.95	4.01	.94	3.57	1.09	Participant Reactions

(Continued)

Table 2. (Continued)

Statement	Follow-up with Peer Interaction		Follow-up without Peer Interaction		Only Solicited Follow-up/ No Peer Interaction		Guskey Model
	Mean	SD	Mean	SD	Mean	SD	
12. Creating a TAKS Support Plan was supported by my community.	3.99	.92	3.63	.89	3.58	.98	Organizational Culture
13. The professional development program content was relevant and with consistent overall objectives	4.15	.78	4.17	.70	3.79	.99	Participant Reactions
14. The TAKS support plan [As designated by the instructor] was appropriate in length and format.	3.89	.98	3.67	.91	3.57	1.09	Participant Reactions
15. The time required for the professional development was appropriate.	3.65	1.00	3.62	1.04	3.44	.99	Participant Reactions

Follow-up to professional development, with and without peer interaction, led to more positive attitudes by the treatment groups toward the professional development experience. This may be attributed in part to the enhanced feelings of competence in the treatment groups as a result of the participation in the online follow-up experience. Educators who experienced follow-up to professional development believed that the professional development program helped them acquire the intended knowledge and skills, they would communicate the plan to their school communities, and the professional development program enhanced their contributions to their school communities. Consistent with constructivist principles that learning is developmental, the sustained professional development format experienced by the treatment groups in this study provided extensive support over time. This allowed school librarians to deepen their understanding of evidence-based practice and to continue learning about the process of constructing a TAKS Support Plan. The problem presented, "What are student weaknesses on the TAKS at my school and what library interventions can the library program provide in support of student learning with regard to those weaknesses," proved to be an intimidating task. Participating in the discussions and the critiques in the Follow-up with Peer Interaction environment and the journals in the Follow-up without Peer Interaction environment provided school librarians with an opportunity to re-examine their current understandings of evidence-based practice as it related to their practice and for that understanding to evolve in strength and complexity. Through emails and phone calls, school librarians in the environment with Only Solicited Follow-up/No Peer Interaction frequently shared that they felt that the task was too hard to complete on their

Table 3. Chi-Square Comparison for Completion Percentage Based on Environment

	Follow-up with Peer Interaction		Follow-up without Peer Interaction		Only Solicited Follow-up/ No peer Interaction	
	n	%	n	%	n	5
Dropped Out	39	41.5	55	56.1	61	69.3
Completed TAKS Plan	55	58.5	43	43.9	27	30.7
Totals	94	100.0	98	100.0	88	100.0

Table 4. Logistic Regression Predicting Completion with Only Solicited Follow-up/No Peer Interaction as Referent Group

Variable	β	SE	Odds Ratio	p
Follow-up with peer interaction	1.159	.312	3.186	.000*
Follow-up without peer interaction	.569	.308	1.766	.065
Constant	−.815	.231	.433	.000

*Significant at p < .05.

Referent: Group for calculating Odds Ratio was Only Solicited Follow-up/No Peer Interaction.

Table 5. Logistic Regression with Follow-up with Peer Interaction as Referent Group

Variable	β	SE	Odds Ratio	p
Follow-up without peer interaction	−.590	.292	.554	.043*
Only Solicited Follow-up/No Peer Interaction	−1.159	.312	.314	.000*
Constant	.344	.209	1.410	.101

*Significant at $p < .05$.

Referent: Group for calculating Odds Ratio was Follow-up with Peer Interaction.

own leading to their less positive ratings of the professional development program. These findings are consistent with previous theory and research that asserts that educators prefer professional development that provides ongoing encouragement and guidance and learn best when professional development learning is sustained over time through follow-up (McBride et al., 1994; Garet, Porter, Desimone, Birman, & Yoon, 2001; Showers et al., 1987).

The finding of the significant difference in completion and the higher likelihood of completion by the Follow-up with Peer Interaction participants is consistent with Lou, Abrami, and d'Appolonia's (2001) meta analysis that found that participants were likely to persevere in socially mediated technology environments. Higher completion rates of the TAKS Support Plans by those librarians in the Follow-up with Peer Interaction group can be attributed to application of social constructivist theory in the design of that environment. Environments that provide for developmental learning, disequilibration, reflective abstraction, and discourse are most effective. In their research, Joyce and Showers (1988) found that without follow-up, only 5% of teachers will implement professional development training.

Completion rates in the professional development program were impacted by follow-up provided through the eight-week long course. Further, the discussions and critiques in the Follow-up with Peer Interaction environment enabled school librarians to build upon the shared expertise of the group in resolving difficulties in creating the plan. Using the Publish tool in WebCT Vista, these librarians were able to view their colleagues' developing plans as they were posted week-by-week. Viewing and critiquing their colleagues work enabled them to glean ideas for their own plan as well as reflect on the quality of their plan. Many librarians also found creating a TAKS Support Plan involved moving beyond their comfort zone and taking risks in connecting in new ways with their faculties. They found support in their online peer group in taking this step.

An alternative explanation to the differences in completion could be that treatment groups had the opportunity to receive more instruction than the control group. Online follow-up does successfully provide for extended instruction when it includes peer interaction. The goal of this study was to investigate the comparative effect of typical professional development practices including the added value of extended online access to materials and the instructor to professional development including follow-up and peer interaction. The findings presented here provide strong evidence that implementing online follow-up programs including online peer interaction following professional development workshops positively affects attitudes towards the professional development and increases the likelihood that educators will complete professional development tasks.

The randomized controlled trial with experimental groups receiving online follow-up while the control group did not, included valid measures of completion and attitudes toward the professional development experience. The online intervention was implemented in the natural settings of librarians' schools or homes (Coalition for Evidence-Based Practice, 2003). A limitation of the study was that only 34% of the possible participants chose to participate in the study, and there was no outcome data for those workshop participants who did not volunteer to participate in follow-up.

CONCLUSIONS

New technologies hold the promise of surmounting old problems. Providing oTPD in learning environments founded on constructivist principles including (a) viewing teacher learning as developmental, (b) focusing on illstructured problems in authentic contexts, (c) providing opportunities for reflection, and (d) making time for discourse creates powerful new opportunities for teacher learning. Online teacher professional development offers flexibility of time and space to participants as well as greater opportunities for involvement and peer interaction.

This study supports the inclusion of opportunities for online interaction in online follow-up to face-to-face professional development. Online delivery of professional development is a fast-growing industry. Course management systems such as WebCT Vista and Moodle offer increasingly sophisticated platforms for online interaction. Professional development designers should consider applying the tools in these platforms to support interaction with others rather.

An important area for follow-up investigation would provide insight regarding how the TAKS Support Plans created by this cohort of school librarians impacted the schools in which they were created. We suggest asking questions such as: (a) To what extent were TAKS support plans implemented? (b) What were the impacts on student learning? (c) What were the impacts on school culture? and (d) What were the impacts on the perceived leadership ability of the school librarian? In addition, participants in the Interactive Follow-up environment were the most successful in completing the course. However, even this environment sustained losses. Survival analysis statistical modeling techniques could be applied to oTPD to learn what trigger points cause learners to drop out. Finally, further investigation of the Attitudes towards Professional Development instrument may be warranted through Factor Analysis.

REFERENCES

Abdal-Haqq, I. (1996). *Making time for teacher professional development.* (ERIC Document Reproduction Service No. ED400259.)

Academic Excellence Indicator System. (n.d.). Retrieved August 1, 2004, from Texas Education Agency Web site: http://www.tea.state.tx.us/perfreport/aeis/

Afifi, A., Clark, V.C., & May, S. (2004). *Computer-aided multivariate analysis* (4th ed.). Boca Raton, FL: Chapman & Hall/CRC.

Beeby, C.E. (1980). The thesis of the stages fourteen years later. *International Review of Education, 26*(4), 451–474.

Bradley, H. (1991). *Staff development.* London: Falmer Press.

Coalition for Evidence-Based Practice. (2003). *Identifying and implementing educational practices supported by rigorous evidence: A user friendly guide.* Retrieved March 30, 2006, from http://www.excelgov.org/evidence

Cohen J. (1977). *Statistical power analysis for the behavioral sciences* (Rev. ed.). New York, Academic Press.

Fosnot, C.T, & Perry, R.S. (2005). Constructivism: A psychological theory of learning. In C.T. Fosnot (Ed.), *Constructivism: Theory, perspectives, and practice* (2nd ed.). New York: Teachers College Press.

Fullan, M.F. & Stiegelbauer, S. (1991). *The new meaning of educational change.* New York: Teachers College Press.

Garet, M.S., Porter, A.C., Desimone, L., Birman, B.F., & Yoon, K.S. (2001, Winter). What makes professional development effective? Results from a national sample of teachers. *American Educational Research Journal, 38*(4), 915–945.

Garmston, R.J. (2003). Group wise. *Journal of Staff Development, 24*(4), 65–66.

Guskey, T.R. (2000). *Evaluating professional development.* Thousand Oaks, CA: Corwin Press.

Hoover, W.A. (1996, August). *The practice implications of constructivism. SEDLetter, 9*(3). Retrieved February 1, 2005, from http://www.sedl.org/pubs/sedletter/v09n03/practice.html

Hord, S.M. (1994). Staff development and change process: Cut from the same cloth. Issues. *About Change, 4*(2), 1–6.

Joyce, B., & Showers, B. (1988). *Student achievement through staff development.* New York: Longman.

Lance, K.C., Rodney, M.J., & Hamilton-Pennell, C. (1999). *Measuring up to standards: The impact of school libraries & information literacy in Pennsylvania schools.* Retrieved March 8, 2004, from http://www.statelibrary.state.pa.us/libraries/lib/libraries/measuringup.pdf

Lance, K.C., Rodney, M.J., & Hamilton-Pennell, C. (2000). *How school librarians help kids achieve standards: The second Colorado study.* San Jose, CA: HiWillow.

Lance, K.C., Rodney, M.J., & Hamilton-Pennell, C. (2002). *Oregon school librarians collaborate to improve academic achievement.* Retrieved December 19, 2006, from http://www.oema.net/Oregon_Study/OR_Study.htm

Lieberman, A. (1995). Practices that support teacher development. *Phi Delta Kappan, 76*(8), 591–596.

Lindstrom, P.H., & Speck, M. (2004). *The principal as professional development leader.* Thousand Oaks, CA: Corwin Press.

Lou, Y., Abrami, P.C., & d'Appolonia, S. (2001). Small group and individual learning with technology: A meta-analysis. *Review of Educational Research, 71*(3), 449–521.

McBride, R.E., Reed, J., & Dollar, J. (1994). Teacher attitudes toward staff development: A symbiotic relationship at best. *Journal of Staff Development, 15*(2), 36–41.

Moore, M.G. & Kearsley, G. (1996). *Distance education: A systems view*. Belmont, CA: Wadsworth.

Showers, B., Joyce, B., & Bennett, B. (1987). Synthesis of research on staff development: A framework for future study and a state-of-the-art analysis. *Educational Leadership, 45*(3), 77–87.

Sparks, D., & Hirsch, S. (1997). *A new vision for staff development*. Alexandria, VA: Association for Supervision and Curriculum Development and National Staff Development Council.

Sprague, D. (2006). Research agenda for online teacher professional development. *Journal of Technology and Teacher Education, 14*(4), 657–661.

APPENDIX A

Attitudes Towards the Professional Development Program

Attitudes Towards Professional Development

Please indicate your response to the following items as

1 = **Strongly disagree**
2 = **Disagree**
3 = **Undecided**
4 = **Agree**
5 = **Strongly Agree**

Participant Reactions (Asked to all participants)

1.   Goals and objectives of the professional development program were clear.

   1   2   3   4   5

2.   The professional development program content was relevant and consistent with overall objectives.

   1   2   3   4   5

3.   The professional development program was well organized.

   1   2   3   4   5

4.   The time required for professional development was appropriate.

   1   2   3   4   5

5.   Setting my own schedule for involvement in professional development worked well for me.

   1   2   3   4   5

6.   The TAKS support plan was appropriate in length and format.

   1   2   3   4   5

7.   Working with other faculty at my school helped me create a more meaningful plan

   1   2   3   4   5

Participant's Learning (Asked to all participants)

8.   The professional development program helped me develop a greater understanding of evidence-based practice for school libraries.

   1   2   3   4   5

9.   The professional development activities helped me integrate evidence-based practice material into my situation.

   1   2   3   4   5

10. This professional development program helped me acquire the intended knowledge and skills to create a TAKS Support Plan.

   1   2   3   4   5

11. The professional development program enhanced my contributions to the school community.

   1   2   3   4   5

Participant Use of New Skills (Asked to all participants)

12. I will put the TAKS Support Plan I developed into use this school year to support achievement in my school.

           1   2   3   4   5

13. I will communicate the TAKS Support Plan to the various community stakeholders in my school community.

           1   2   3   4   5

Organizational Culture (Asked to all participants)

14. Creating a TAKS Support Plan was supported by my campus.

           1   2   3   4   5

Outcomes (Asked to all participants)

15. I believe my new learning is likely to increase student performance.

           1   2   3   4   5

1.08

2-FACTOR POSTTEST DESIGN

Dog-Assisted Therapy in the Treatment of Chronic Schizophrenia Inpatients

Victòria Villalta-Gil,[*,†,‡] Mercedes Roca,[†] Nieves Gonzalez,[*] Eva Domènec,[§] Cuca,[§] Ana Escanila,[†] M. Rosa Asensio,[†] M. Elisa Esteban,[†] Susana Ochoa,[*,†,‡] Josep Maria Haro,[*,†,‡] and Schi-Can group

ABSTRACT: Patients with a diagnosis of schizophrenia living in long-term care units show high levels of disability. The present study aimed to assess the effectiveness of including a trained therapy dog in an intervention program applied to institutionalized patients with chronic schizophrenia. A randomized, controlled study with blind assessment was conducted. Twenty-four persons with chronic schizophrenia were randomly selected from a register that included all inpatients at Saint John of God's psychiatric hospital in Spain. Patients who agreed to participate ($n = 21$) were randomly assigned to one of the two treatment groups: one group received an intervention assisted by a therapy dog (IG + D) (12 patients), while the other received the same intervention but without a therapy dog (IG) (9 patients). The assessment items included the Positive and Negative Symptoms Scale (PANSS), the Living Skills Profile (LSP), the Brief World Health Organization Quality of Life Assessment (WHOQOL-BREF), and the Satisfaction with Treatment Questionnaire (STQ). Mann Whitney U tests and Wilcoxon signed-rank tests were conducted. Patients in the IG+D group showed significant improvements in the LSP social contact score ($p = 0.041$), in the positive ($p = 0.005$) and negative symptom dimensions ($p = 0.005$) and total score of the PANSS ($p = 0.014$), and in quality of life related with social relationships ($p = 0.024$). Patients in the IG group showed significant positive changes in positive ($p = 0.027$) and general symptoms ($p = 0.046$) and total PANSS score ($p = 0.027$). No differences were found between the two groups before and after the application of the intervention. Introducing a dog into the psychosocial intervention for patients with schizophrenia produced some positive outcomes. However, the results of the study are not conclusive and must be interpreted cautiously.

KEYWORDS: Animal-assisted therapy; dog; psychosocial interventions; randomized controlled study; schizophrenia.

[*]Saint John of God's Research and Teaching Foundation, Esplugues de Llobregat, Spain
[†]Saint John of God-Mental Health Services, St. Boi de Llobregat, Spain
[‡] CIBERSAM, Instituto de Salud Carlos III, Spanish Ministry of Health, Spain
[§] Bocalan Foundation, Sant Cugat del Vallès, Spain

In the last few decades, a progressive deinstitutionaliza-
tion of psychiatric patients has occurred. This process
has selected patients with mild disabilities for community health services, while those with severe disabilities
have remained in psychiatric institutions (Ochoa et al.
2003). It has been described that institutionalized
patients perceive their quality of life as worse than their
community analogues; as well, their social network
decreases and their daily life abilities worsen (Leff,
Trieman and Gooch 1996).

Patients with a diagnosis of schizophrenia constitute the majority of individuals in long-term care facilities. This disorder may have a very heterogeneous
clinical presentation and course, but frequently leads
to a high degree of disability in several daily life activities (Meise and Fleischhacker 1996). Several intervention programs have been designed and applied to
patients with schizophrenia in order to improve their
social functioning and reduce their disability (Garety
et al. 1994; Hodel and Brenner 1994; Kuipers et al. 1998;
Penades 2002). However, patients with schizophrenia
still show high degrees of social disability (Usall et al.
2002; Ochoa et al, 2003; Villalta-Gil et al. 2006). Training
in social abilities and treatments that try to improve
social functioning usually show diminished success,
given the limited social access and support of inpatients. This social support must be regular and must
be provided by the rehabilitation services, among others. These services must readjust constantly their intervention in an appropriate manner in order to promote
the provision of social support (Sheperd 1996).

For some time now, some therapists have introduced animals into their therapy sessions. Even though
the presence of animals in institutionalized settings has
a long history (Serpell 2003; Macauley 2006), the active
participation of the animal in the therapy sessions is
quite new. It was Levinson (1962) who first described
that the presence of his dog eased the interaction with
many children who were withdrawn and uncommu-
nicative. Since then, some experiments with people with
several disorders have been conducted, most of them
reporting positive results in different areas, but particularly in social functioning (Mader, Hart and Bergin
1989; Barak et al. 2001; Banks and Banks 2002; Kovacs
et al. 2004). However, the results mainly come from clinical observations; very little empirical research has been
conducted on the effectiveness of animal-assisted therapy. Following a literature review (Villalta-Gil and
Ochoa 2007), we found a few studies conducted on people with schizophrenia undergoing animal-assisted therapies. They have shown that interventions assisted by
an animal result in improvements in social and daily life
skills (Barak et al. 2001; Kovacs et al. 2004), negative
symptoms (Mayol-Pou 2002), quality of life (Nathans-
Barel et al. 2005) and mood symptoms (Barker and
Dawson 1998). Unfortunately, most of these studies were
not controlled and had small sample sizes. No previous

studies have randomized either the selection or allocation of patients, nor have they used blind assessment.

The present study aimed to assess the effectiveness of including a trained therapy dog in an intervention program applied to institutionalized patients with
a diagnosis of chronic schizophrenia. Specifically, we
hypothesized that patients receiving the intervention
assisted by a dog will improve their social competence,
quality of life, and negative symptoms more than
those patients receiving the same intervention program without the assistance of a therapy dog.

METHODS

Design, Patients Selection and Allocation

A randomized, controlled study with blind assessment of outcome was used. The patients included in the
study were inpatients at Saint John of God-Mental
Health Services Hospital and came from different socio-
demographic environments from the city of Barcelona
and its surroundings. Only those patients staying at
Long Term Care facilities were included; these patients
cannot live in the community, due to their social and
clinical characteristics. A long course of the disorder and
cognitive or social deficits characterize patients staying
in these facilities.

Inclusion criteria were: a) primary diagnosis of
schizophrenia (DSM-IV criteria; APA 1994) with more
than 10 years since onset; b) age over 18 years; and
c) be institutionalized during the application of the
program. Patients with mental retardation, neurological disorders, or having adverse psychological or
physical reactions to animals were excluded. All
patients were stable on medications. In accordance
with these criteria, 24 patients with chronic schizophrenia were randomly selected from a computerized
register that included all inpatients at Saint John of
God's Hospital.

Selected individuals were informed by their psy-
chiatrist of the objectives and methodology of the study,
and they provided informed consent to participate.
Patients did not receive any incentive to participate in
the study. Three decided not to take part. The study was
previously approved by the Saint John of God-Mental
Health Services Ethics Committee, which follows the
Helsinki Declaration of ethical standards.

Once a patient accepted inclusion in the study, the
baseline assessment was administered. Afterwards,
patients were randomly assigned to one of two novel
treatment groups: one group received an intervention
assisted by a therapy dog (IG + D; 12 patients assigned),
while the other received the same intervention, but
without the therapy dog (IG; 9 patients assigned).

The IG + D group was divided into three groups
of four people each, of which 11 completed the full
program. The IG group was divided into two groups

of four and five people, respectively, of which seven completed the full program.

Interventions

The intervention program was applied by a trained psychologist. It consisted of 25 sessions of 45 minutes each; two sessions were given per week. The intervention group with therapy dog (IG + D) was directed by the psychologist, who was assisted by a two-year-old, female Labrador, certified as a therapy dog. The dog was accompanied by her handler. The group without a dog (IG) was directed by the same psychologist. The intervention was based on Integrated Psychological Treatment (IPT) designed by Brenner et al. (1994). This treatment for patients with schizophrenia has been developed to work as much on cognitive functioning as on social functioning. It is a group-intervention structured program with five subprograms: cognitive differentiation, social perception, verbal communication, social skills training, and interpersonal problem solving. They are hierarchically ordered, so the first interventions are directed to basic cognitive skills, the next interventions transform the cognitive skills into social and verbal behaviors, and the last ones train the patients in the solution of more complex interpersonal problems. In our study, it was partially modified, in order to bring dogs into the therapy sessions (Table 1).

Table 1. Description of the Intervention Program

Subprogram*	Intervention Focus	Intervention Techniques	
		IG + D	IG
Cognitive Rehabilitation (6 sessions)	Attention Abilities	• Classifying objects brought by dog • Sustained attention: Stimulus being a particular dog action (e.g., wave tail)	• Classifying objects handled by therapist • Sustained attention: Stimulus being a particular therapist action (e.g., touch leg)
	Memory	• Short- and long-term recall of the dog's story • Sequences with dog	• Short- and long-term recall of a story • Sequences
Social Perception (3 sessions)	Social Stimulus Analysis	• Description and interpretation of a social interaction in which the dog participated • Discussion about the above social situation	• Description and interpretation of a social interaction • Discussion about the above social situation
Verbal Communication (4 sessions)	Conversation Abilities	• Repetition of verbal orders for the dog • Questions generation implying the dog • Conversation about a topic limited to the dog • Free conversation	• Repetition of verbal stimulus • Questions generation • Conversation about current news • Free conversation
Social Abilities (5 sessions)	Competence in Social Abilities	• Cognitive training in low and high emotional risk abilities always related to the dog (e.g., asking the bus driver to let the dog get in) • Role-play	• Cognitive training in low and high emotional risk abilities • Role-play
Interpersonal Problem Solving (5 sessions)	Practicing Problem Solving Strategies	• Identification and analysis of a problem (e.g., ask the dog to bring a ball which is inside a drawer) • Generating solutions • Generating alternative solutions • Practicing those solutions • Evaluate the exercise	• Identification and analysis of a problem • Generating solutions • Generating alternative solutions • Practicing those solutions • Evaluate the exercise

*Two more sessions were conducted: one to introduce the program to the patients and one to end the program.
IG = intervention group (no therapy dog); IG + D = intervention group with therapy dog.

Sessions for the IG+D group were designed so that the handler interacted with the dog and the therapist, the therapist interacted with the patient and the handler, and patients interacted with the dog and the therapist. This design was used in order to minimize interactions between handler and patients, as the handler was not present in the IG group. Sessions were also designed so that materials used in the IPT (cards, sentences, etc . . .) were substituted by, or were referenced to, the dog (sample exercises are described in Table 2). The dog had an active role within the sessions, so certification of the dog as a therapy dog was mandatory.

Saint John of God Hospital does not have resident pets. Thus, interactions with dogs were limited to exposures during sessions. Exposures during "leave" (when patients could leave the institution for a few hours) could not be controlled; we assume equal chance for patients of both groups to be exposed to dogs during these periods.

Patients received their usual pharmacological treatment during the course of the study.

Assessment Procedures and Instruments

All patients were evaluated by a trained psychologist blind to the patient's intervention group at baseline and after the intervention program (patients were asked not to mention details about the therapy sessions and the psychologist was also not supposed to gather information about their intervention group). Socio-demographic and clinical variables were gathered. Symptoms were assessed with the Positive and Negative Syndrome Scale (PANSS) (Kay, Fiszbein and Opler 1987), Spanish version (Peralta and Cuesta 1994); higher scores indicate more severity of symptoms. Social competence was assessed with the Living

Table 2. Two Sample Exercises From the Program, Describing the Role of Each Participant for Each Group

Aim	Exercise	Therapist	Dog	Handler	Group
Accommodate the tone of voice according the message given	Repetition of commands for the dog , (*i.e., Cuca bring the ball; Cuca, touch the cone, etc . . .*)	The therapist indicated the command/ sentence to be said Correct patients until said correctly	Execution of the command when allowed by handler	Agree with therapist the commands that can be used Inhibited the behavior of the dog until the verbal command had been given appropriately (according to therapist criteria)	IG + D
	Repetition of sentences (*i.e., Pass me the jacket*)		—	—	IG
Attention functions	Classify several items regarding some characteristics (*i.e., Please, give me five yellow, animal-related objectcards*)	Specify characteristics to be searched Help patients to focus attention on those characteristics	Hold the object-cards and carry the selected object-cards to the therapist	Supervise that the dog does not drop the object-cards given by patients all the way until the dog reaches the therapist	IG + D
		Checks whether objects selected have the characteristics specified	—	—	IG

IG = intervention group (no therapy dog); IG + D = intervention group with therapy dog.

Skills Profile (LSP) (Rosen, Hadzi-Pavlovic and Parker 1989); this scale gives information of five areas of functioning: self-care, personal social behavior, social contact, non personal social behavior, and autonomous life. Subjective perception of quality of life was assessed with the Brief World Health Organization Quality of Life Assessment-Spanish version (WHO-QOL-BREF) (Lucas 1998), which gives us information on perception of quality of life in four domains: physical health, psychological, social relationships, and environment. Higher scores in either the LSP and the WHOQOL-BREF indicate better social competence. The post-intervention assessment also included the Satisfaction with Treatment Questionnaire (STQ) (Larsen et al. 1979); higher scores indicate more satisfaction. Only the WHOQOL-BREF and the STQ were self-administered. A schedule assessing adverse reactions to animals, the Wechsler Adult Intelligence Scale (Wechsler 1999), and the Mini Mental State Examination (Folstein, Folstein and McHugh 1975; Lobo and Ezquerra 1979) were used as screening instruments, in order to confirm inclusion of patients into the sample.

Data Analysis

Due to the sample size, non parametric statistical tests were performed. In order to assess differences between groups, Mann Whitney U tests were conducted. In order to assess differences before and after the application of the program in both groups,

Table 3. Sample Characteristics for Each Intervention Group

		IG + D	IG
Mean Age (*SD*)		49.08 (9.37)	48.88 (8.62)
Mean Years Since Onset (*SD*)		28.55 (9.43)	29.03(9.06)
Male Gender (%)		91.7	77.8
Years of Education (%)			
	1–4	25.0	11.1
	5–8	33.3	33.3
	9–12	25.0	55.6
	>12	16.7	0.0
Marital Status (%)			
	Single	100.0	77.8
	Married	0.0	22.2
Schizophrenia Subtype (%)			
	Paranoid	58.3	44.4
	Catatonic	0.0	0.0
	Disorganized	8.3	22.2
	Undifferentiated	8.3	0.0
	Residual	25.0	33.3

IG = intervention group (no therapy dog); IG + D = intervention group with therapy dog.

Wilcoxon signed-rank tests were used. Cohen's d for effect size was also computed.

All statistical analyses were conducted using SPSS for Windows 10.0 (Chicago, IL, USA).

RESULTS

Table 3 shows the socio-demographic and clinical characteristics of the patients included in each of the two groups. Patients' mean age was almost 50 years and the mean time since the onset of the illness was nearly 30 years. Most patients were men who had never been married. None of them were illiterate. Most patients had a diagnosis of chronic paranoid schizophrenia. No significant differences were found in these variables between the two groups.

Patients in the IG + D group showed significant improvements in the area of social contact (assessed with the LSP; higher scores mean better functioning: $p = 0.041$), in positive ($p = 0.005$) and negative symptoms ($p = 0.005$) and total score of the PANSS ($p = 0.014$), and they also perceived their quality of life related to social relationships significantly better ($p = 0.024$). On the other hand, their non-personal social behavior, assessed with the LSP, significantly worsened ($p = 0.049$) (Table 4). Regarding the patients in the IG group, we only found significant positive differences in positive ($p = 0.027$) and general symptoms ($p = 0.046$) and total score of the PANSS ($p = 0.027$) (Table 4). The effect sizes for all the significant results were over 0.80, indicating that the mean scores of those variables were over the 79 percentile of the basal measure.

No differences were found between the two groups of patients (Mann Whitney U tests) in any of the variables assessed at baseline or after the application of the intervention.

DISCUSSION

Our results partially support the use of animals in the therapy of patients with schizophrenia. However, the study has important limitations. First, the sample size is small, which decreases the ability to detect differences between groups. Second, 14.3% of the patients dropped out of the treatment before the end of the sessions. Third, the characteristics of the intervention prevented double-blind design to be implemented. Fourth, the handler was not present in the intervention group which didn't have the dog. Finally, a large number of statistical comparisons were performed, which increases the possibility of finding spurious results.

The two groups of inpatients included in the study improved with the intervention based on the Integrated Psychological Treatment designed by Brenner et al. (1994). Both groups showed significant improvements

Table 4. Mean Scores (Wilcoxon signed signed-rank test) Before and After the Intervention in Both Groups and Value of Cohen's d for Those Variables Showing Significant Differences

	IG + D Basal Mean (SD)	IG + D Post-Intervention Mean (SD)	Z	d	IG Basal Mean (SD)	IG Post-Intervention Mean (SD)	Z	d
LSP								
Self-Care	32.00 (5.29)	31.81 (6.03)	−0.12		32.67 (4.33)	31.57 (5.77)	−0.17	
Social Behavior	33.33 (4.54)	32.73 (3.85)	−0.12		32.89 (3.48)	34.57 (2.37)	−1.47	
Social Contact	13.67 (2.67)	18.00 (4.40)	−2.04*	−1.19	14.56 (2.88)	18.57 (4.65)	−1.57	
Non Social Behavior	22.50 (1.38)	20.55 (2.94)	−1.97*	0.85	23.11 (0.93)	21.71 (1.80)	−1.22	
Autonomous Life	14.50 (4.42)	15.64 (5.26)	−1.49		13.56 (2.65)	15.29 (4.54)	−0.85	
PANSS								
Positive symptoms	20.83 (5.46)	15.64 (4.03)	−2.81**	1.08	22.67 (7.71)	17.00 (6.07)	−2.21*	0.82
Negative Symptoms	28.92 (5.25)	19.36 (6.34)	−2.81**	1.64	25.44 (4.42)	16.67 (4.32)	−1.89	
General Symptoms	38.50 (3.66)	34.91 (6.80)	−1.74		38.11 (5.82)	28.50 (5.58)	−1.99*	1.69
Total PANSS	88.25 (12.17)	73.64 (18.69)	−2.45*	0.93	86.22 (10.03)	61.83 (12.69)	−2.21*	2.13
WHOQOL-BREF								
Physical Health	3.11 (0.56)	3.40 (0.46)	−0.96		3.27 (0.84)	3.21 (0.46)	−0.13	
Psychological	2.97 (0.67)	3.12 (0.65)	−0.45		3.37 (0.54)	3.53 (0.60)	−0.27	
Social Relationships	2.08 (0.79)	2.85 (0.56)	−2.26*	−1.12	2.81 (1.02)	3.22 (0.69)	−0.27	
Environment	3.01 (0.82)	3.11 (0.51)	−0.85		3.10 (0.67)	2.85 (0.71)	−1.84	
STQ	–	24.36 (3.47)	–		–	25.17 (4.87)	–	

LSP = Living Skills Profile; PANNS = Positive and Negative Syndrome Scale; WHOQOL-BREF = Brief World Health Organization Quality of Life Assessment – Spanish version; STQ = Satisfaction with Treatment Questionnaire.

IG = intervention group (no therapy dog); IG+D = intervention group with therapy dog.

*$p < 0.05$ **$p < 0.01$.

in positive symptoms, as well as in the total PANSS score. Although there were no statistical differences between the group which received therapy assisted by a dog and the group which received the treatment without the assistance of a therapy dog, before and after comparisons within each group indicated some extra benefits for the group assisted by the dog.

While the patients who didn't have the therapy dog also improved their general symptoms, patients in the therapy-dog group also improved in the areas related to social contact. It is noticeable that patients improved in severity of negative symptoms which, as assessed by PANSS, include the evaluation of social functioning (Addington and Addington 1999; Dickinson and Coursey 2002). Previous studies found similar results regarding improvements of negative symptoms (Mayol-Pou 2002). The improvement in negative symptoms is significant, as pharmacological treatments have been described to be more effective for positive symptoms (Feldman et al. 2003; Miller 2004; Rueter et al. 2004), and negative symptoms have also been defined to be more predictive of disability than other clinical variables (Dickerson et al. 1999; Villalta-Gil et al. 2006). Thus, psychosocial interventions successful in reducing severity of negative symptoms should be taken into account.

The other area in which patients with the therapy dog improved refers to objective and subjective assessment of social contact. Thus, patients perceived a significantly better quality of life related to social relationships; as well, objective social contact abilities improved. Pets not only interact directly with people but, through their presence alone, may also modify the social behavior between two or more people (Messent 1985). This is what could have happened with the patients in this group: they benefited not only from the intervention and the direct contact with the dog but also from focusing the attention of other people in the institution. The same reaction has been found in people with other disabilities; for instance, Mader, Hart and Bergin (1989) found that children with physical disabilities who had a service dog had more positive social contacts with non-disabled people than children with disabilities who didn't have a service dog. These results led them to conclude that service dogs facilitate social acknowledgement for children with disabilities. We should acknowledge that the handler in our study was not present in the IG group, thus the effect of the handler on the social variables is unknown. However, this effect was minimized by using a design where the interaction between handler and patients within the sessions was reduced.

We found that non-personal social behavior significantly worsened in the patients who were assisted by the therapy dog. A similar trend was seen in the patients who didn't have the therapy dog. This behavior refers mainly to disruptive behaviors directed towards public objects, spaces, or themselves. The intervention program did not focus on these behaviors, so therefore future interventions should take non-personal social behaviors into account.

Besides the problem of having a small sample size, the small number of differences we found in our study could be due to the sample characteristics. Patients had over 28 years since the onset of illness, coupled with a chronic disorder diagnosis and high levels of disability. Therefore even though there were significant within group differences, improvements in the areas assessed were not big enough to give statistical significance between the groups.

People with a diagnosis of chronic schizophrenia living in institutionalized settings have very low levels of social functioning and social activity (Kovacs et al. 2004). Negative symptoms have not been much reduced by antipsychotic medication and this group of symptoms is frequently associated with a chronic course of the disorder and with high levels of social disability (Hammer, Katsanis and Iacono 1995; Liddle 2000; Grawe and Levander 2001; Penades et al. 2001). Results from our study regarding improvement of negative symptoms and social functioning give support to previous studies (Barker and Dawson 1998; Barak et al. 2001; Mayol-Pou 2002; Kovacs et al. 2004; Nathans-Barel et al. 2005) and also suggest that introducing a dog into some intervention programs could be beneficial for inpatients with chronic schizophrenia.

Interventions aimed to improve social abilities and support can help people with chronic disorders to improve their community functioning (Farkas 1996). Outpatients with schizophrenia show social withdrawal and this withdrawal increases if patients are institutionalized. Introducing dogs into some psychosocial interventions may facilitate the patients' social abilities, thus improving their ability to function in the community.

ACKNOWLEDGEMENTS

This project received the financial help of the La Caixa Foundation and was supported by the Spanish Ministry of Health, Instituto de Salud Carlos III, CIBERSAM. The authors declare that no competing interests exist.

REFERENCES

Addington, J. and Addington, D. 1999. Neurocognitive and social functioning in schizophrenia. *Schizophrenia Bulletin* 25: 173–182.

American Psychiatric Association. 1994. *Diagnostic and Statistical Manual of Mental Disorders*. 4th edn. Washington, DC: Author.

Banks, M. R. and Banks, W. A. 2002. The effects of animal-assisted therapy on loneliness in an elderly population in long-term care facilities. *Journals of Gerontology Series A: Biological Sciences and Medical Sciences* 57: M428–M432.

Barak, Y., Savorai, O., Mavashev, S. and Beni, A. 2001. Animal-assisted therapy for elderly schizophrenic patients: a one-year controlled trial. *American Journal of Geriatric Psychiatry* 9: 439–442.

Barker, S. B. and Dawson, K. S. 1998. The effects of animal-assisted therapy on anxiety ratings of hospitalized psychiatric patients. *Psychiatric Services* 49: 797–801.

Brenner, H., Roder, V., Hodel, B., Kienzie, N., Reed, D. and Liberman, R. 1994. *Integrated Psychological Therapy for Schizophrenic Patients*. Seattle: Hoegreffe & Huber.

Dickerson, F., Boronow, J. J., Ringel, N. and Parente, F. 1999. Social functioning and neurocognitive deficits in outpatients with schizophrenia: a 2-year follow-up. *Schizophrenia Research* 37: 13–20.

Dickinson, D. and Coursey, R. D. 2002. Independence and overlap among neurocognitive correlates of community functioning in schizophrenia. *Schizophrenia Research* 56: 161–170.

Farkas, M. 1996. Avances en Rehabilitación psiquiátrica: Una perspectiva norteamericana. In *Esquizofrenia: Fundamentos Psicológicos y Psiquiátricos de la Rehabilitación*, 167–186, ed. J. A. Aldaz and C. Vázquez. Madrid: Siglo XXI.

Feldman, P. D., Kaiser, C. J., Kennedy, J. S., Sutton, V. K. Tran, P. V., Tollefson, G. D., Zhang, F. and Breier A. 2003. Comparison of risperidone and olanzapine in the control of negative symptoms of chronic schizophrenia and related psychotic disorders in patients aged 50 to 65 years. *Journal of Clinical Psychiatry* 64: 998–1004.

Folstein, M. F., Folstein, S. E. and McHugh, P. R. 1975. "Mini-mental state". A practical method for grading the cognitive state of patients for the clinician. *Journal of Psychiatric Research* 12: 189–198.

Garety, P. A., Kuipers, L., Fowler, D., Chamberlain, F. and Dunn, G. 1994. Cognitive behavioural therapy for drug-resistant psychosis. *British Journal of Medical Psychology* 67: 259–271.

Grawe, R. W. and Levander, S. 2001. Neuropsychological impairments in patients with schizophrenia: stability and prediction of outcome. *Acta Psychiatrica Scandinavica* 104: 60–64.

Hammer, M. A., Katsanis, J. and Iacono, W. G. 1995. The relationship between negative symptoms and neuropsychological performance. *Biological Psychiatry* 37: 828–830.

Hodel, B. and Brenner, H. D. 1994. Cognitive therapy with schizophrenic patients: conceptual basis, present state, future directions. *Acta Psychiatrica Scandinavica Supplementum* 384: 108–115.

Kay, S. R., Fiszbein, A. and Opler, L. A. 1987. The positive and negative syndrome scale PANSS for schizophrenia, *Schizophrenia Bulletin* 13: 261–276.

Kovacs, Z., Kis, R., Rozsa, S. and Rozsa, L. 2004. Animal-assisted therapy for middle-aged schizophrenic patients living in a social institution. A pilot study. *Clinical Rehabilitation* 18: 483–486.

Kuipers, E., Fowler, D., Garety, P., Chisholm, D., Freeman, D., Dunn, G. et al. 1998. London-east Anglia randomised controlled trial of cognitive-behavioural therapy for psychosis. III: Follow-up and economic evaluation at 18 months. *British Journal of Psychiatry* 173: 61–68.

Larsen, D. L., Atkinson, C. C., Hargreaves, W. A. and Nguyen, T. D. 1979. Assessment of client satisfaction: Development of a general scale. *Evaluation and Program Planning* 2: 197–207.

Leff, J., Trieman, N. and Gooch, C. 1996. Team for the Assessment of Psychiatric Services TAPS Project 33: Prospective follow-up study of long-stay patients discharged from two psychiatric hospitals. *American Journal of Psychiatry* 153: 1318–1324.

Levinson, B. M. 1962. The dog as a "co-therapist." *Mental Hygiene* 46: 59–65.

Liddle, P. F. 2000. Cognitive impairment in schizophrenia: its impact on social functioning. *Acta Psychiatrica Scandinavica* 101: 11–16.

Lobo, A. and Ezquerra, J. 1979. El Mini Examen Cognoscitivo: Un test sencillo, práctico para detectar alteraciones intelectivas en pacientes médicos. *Actas Luso-Españolas de Neurología, Psiquiatría y ciencias afines* 3: 189–202.

Lucas, R. 1998. *Versión Española del WHOQOL*. Madrid: Ergon.

Macauley, B. L. 2006. Animal-assisted therapy for persons with aphasia: A pilot study. *Journal of Rehabilitation Research and Development* 43: 357–366.

Mader, B., Hart, L. A. and Bergin, B. 1989. Social acknowledgements for children with disabilities: Effects of service dogs. *Child Development* 60: 1529–1534.

Mayol-Pou, A. 2002. Teràpia Facilitada per animals de companyia en pacients psicòtics greument deteriorats. Ph.D. thesis, Universitat de les Illes Balears, Spain.

Meise, U. and Fleischhacker, W. W. 1996. Perspectives on treatment needs in schizophrenia. *British Journal of Psychiatry Supplement*: 9–16.

Messent, P. R. 1985. Pets as social facilitators. *Veterinary Clinics of North America: Small Animal Practice* 15: 387–393.

Miller, A. L. 2004. Combination treatments for schizophrenia. *CNS Spectrums* 9: 19–23.

Nathans-Barel, I., Feldman, P., Berger, B., Modai, I. and Silver, H. 2005. Animal-assisted therapy ameliorates anhedonia in schizophrenia patients. A controlled pilot study. *Psychotherapy and Psychosomatics* 74: 31–35.

Ochoa, S., Haro, J. M., Autonell, J., Pendas, A., Teba, F. and Marquez, M. 2003. Met and unmet needs of schizophrenia patients in a Spanish sample. *Schizophrenia Bulletin* 29: 201–210.

Penades, R. 2002. La rehabilitació neuropsicológica del pacient esquizofrènic. Ph.D. thesis, Departament de Psiquiatria i Psicobiologia clinica, Universitat de Barcelona, Spain.

Penades, R., Gasto, C., Boget, T., Catalan, R. and Salamero, M. 2001. Deficit in schizophrenia: the relationship between negative symptoms and neurocognition. *Comprehensive Psychiatry* 42: 64–69.

Peralta V. C. MJ. 1994. Validación de la escala de los síndromes positivo y negativo PANSS en una muestra de esquizofrénicos españoles. *Actas Luso-Españolas de Neurología, Psiqulatría y ciencias afines* 22: 171–177.

Rosen, A., Hadzi-Pavlovic, D. and Parker, G. 1989. The life skills profile: a measure assessing function and disability in schizophrenia. *Schizophrenia Bulletin* 15: 325–337.

Rueter, L. E., Ballard, M. E., Gallagher, K. B., Basso, A. M., Curzon, P. and Kohlhaas, K. L. 2004. Chronic low dose risperidone and clozapine alleviate positive but not negative symptoms in the rat neonatal ventral hippocampal lesion model of schizophrenia. *Psychopharmacology Berl* 176: 312–319.

Serpell, J. A. 2003. Animales de compañía y bienestar humano: un análisis histórico del valor de las relaciones persona-animal. In *Manual de Terapia Asistida por Animales. Fundamentos Teóricos y Modelos Prácticos*, 3–22, ed. A. H. Fine. Barcelona: Fundación Affinity.

Sheperd, G. 1996. Avances recientes en la rehabilitación psiquiátrica. In *Esquizofrenia: Fundamentos Psicológicos y Psiquiátricos de la Rehabilitación*, 1–22, ed. J. A. Aldaz and C. Vázquez. Madrid: Siglo XXI.

Usall, J., Haro, J. M., Ochoa, S., Marquez, M. and Araya, S. 2002. Influence of gender on social outcome in schizophrenia. *Acta Psychiatrica Scandinavica* 106: 337–342.

Villalta-Gil, V. and Ochoa, S. 2007. La Terapia Facilitada por Animales de Compañía como programa de Rehabilitación Adjunto para personas con diagnóstico de Esquizofrenia crónica. *Papeles del Psicólogo* 28: 49–56.

Villalta-Gil, V., Vilaplana, M., Ochoa, S., Haro, J. M., Dolz, M., Usall, J. et al. 2006. Neurocognitive performance and negative symptoms: Are they equal in explaining disability in schizophrenia outpatients? *Schizophrenia Research* 87: 246–253.

Wechsler, D. A. 1999. *WAIS-III Escala de Inteligencia de Wechsler para Adultos III*. Madrid: TEA Ediciones.

1.09

3-FACTOR POSTTEST DESIGN

Endurance Exercise and Health-Related Quality of Life in 50–65 Year-Old Adults[*]

Anita L. Stewart, PhD,[†] Abby C. King, PhD,[††] and William L. Haskell, PhD[§]

ABSTRACT: Health-related quality of life was evaluated in relation to endurance exercise over the prior year for 194 previously sedentary, healthy men and women aged 50–65 using a posttest-only design. Three exercise regimens were studied that varied in format (class-based vs home-based) and intensity (higher vs lower). In all regimens, subjects who participated more had better physical health 12 months after program initiation (p values < .05); no differences were observed in general psychological well-being. Extent of participation, rather than format or intensity of exercise, was associated with better physical health in this population.

KEYWORDS: Physical activity; health; functioning; well-being; physical fitness.

Exercise and physical fitness have been found to provide a number of benefits for older adults in health areas spanning cardiovascular, respiratory, neuromuscular, and metabolic functions (Bortz, 1984; Paffenbarger & Hyde, 1987; Stamford, 1988). For instance, fitness has been associated with reduced mortality from all causes in a large sample of men and women (Blair et al., 1989), with the decline in death rates with increased levels of fitness being most pronounced in older persons. Currently, however, the majority of the exercise-related health outcomes that have been evaluated tend to be distal to the exercise behavior itself (e.g., reduced risk of heart disease or premature mortality). Determining the more immedi-

[*]Preparation of this work was supported by PHS grant HL36272, awarded to Dr. Haskell by the National Heart, Lung, and Blood Institute; by PHS grant AG00440, awarded to Dr. King by the National Institute on Aging; by PHS grant AG09931, awarded to Dr. Stewart by the National Institute on Aging; and by a grant to Dr. Stewart from the University of California San Francisco Academic Senate Committee on Research.

The authors would like to acknowledge Dr. Helena Kraemer for her assistance with statistical analysis, Steven Preston for his assistance with data analysis, and the citizens of the city of Sunnyvale, CA, for their support and participation.

Address correspondence to: Anita L. Stewart, PhD, University of California San Francisco, Institute for Health & Aging, Box 0646, San Francisco, CA 94143-0646.
[†]University of California San Francisco, Institute for Health & Aging, School of Nursing.
[††]Stanford Center for Research in Disease Prevention, Department of Medicine, and Department of Health Research and Policy, Stanford Medical School.
[§]Stanford Center for Research in Disease Prevention, Division of Cardiology, Department of Medicine, Stanford Medical School.

ate quality of life benefits obtained with regular exercise could serve to motivate older adults to become more regularly active, thereby facilitating advances toward the current national health objectives in the exercise area (U.S. Department of Health and Human Services, 1992; U.S. Preventive Services Task Force, 1989). Most of the research in this area to date has been limited to psychological outcomes (Stewart & King, 1991), with mixed findings (Emery & Blumenthal, 1991). Much less is known about the potential benefits in terms of a broader array of quality of life domains such as physical functioning, functioning in daily activities, fatigue, pain, and health perceptions (Stewart & King, 1991).

Much of the research that is available on exercise and health-related quality of life in older adults tends to evaluate higher-intensity exercise (Emery & Blumenthal, 1990; Minor, Hewett, Webel, Anderson, & Ray, 1989). Although lower-intensity programs may not result in substantial increases in maximal oxygen uptake, they could contribute to improved day-today functioning and other aspects of quality of life (Minor, 1991). Because few studies of older adults have included both physiologic measures and measures of health-related quality of life (Stewart & King, 1991), it remains unclear whether exercise has any direct effects on health-related quality of life independent of improvements in physiological parameters, which for some older adults may be difficult to attain. Regular exercise could improve physical functioning, for example, through improvements in underlying physical fitness parameters such as aerobic capacity, flexibility, or muscle strength (Buchner, Beresford, Larson, LaCroix, & Wagner, 1992). It could also improve physical functioning and other physical health indicators through enhancing confidence in one's ability to be more active or through improving mood, and thereby also through motivation.

Different intensities of exercise need to be evaluated in relation to health-related quality of life outcomes. Similarly, virtually all programs that have evaluated the effects of exercise on quality of life outcomes in older adults have utilized group formats, making it impossible to differentiate effects due to the exercise itself, independent of group influences (Stewart & King, 1991).

The purpose of this study was to determine the relationship between participation in different intensities and formats of exercise engaged in over a one-year period and health-related quality of life in a sample of initially sedentary, healthy adults aged 50–65 years. In addition, we examined whether associations between exercise and health-related quality of life would be explained by level of exercise participation (adherence). The specific features of the exercise programs evaluated were intensity (higher- vs lower-

intensity) and format (supervised home-based vs group). Finally, we examined whether changes in physiologic parameters such as aerobic capacity or body weight that may accompany exercise training programs explain any health-related quality of life changes. This is an important age group for study, for several reasons: (a) it is during these years that the incidence of the major chronic diseases of aging rises significantly; (b) these individuals are somewhat younger than the over 65 age group that has traditionally been labeled as older adults and thus have typically been overlooked in studies of exercise and health-related quality of life; and (c) given the relatively large number of years remaining to persons in this age group, hygienic changes made at that age could have important effects on health for a number of years to come. In addition, this age group had been designated as senior citizens for purposes of receiving services in the community from which the study sample was drawn.

METHODS

Sample

The sample consisted of 194 men and women aged 50–65 and represented a subset of participants from a larger randomized, controlled trial evaluating the effects of endurance exercise on health outcomes (King, Haskell, Taylor, Kraemer, & DeBusk, 1991). A goal of the major trial was to include only subjects who were reasonably healthy and previously sedentary. Subjects were eligible for the trial if they were free of cardiovascular disease, diabetes, or stroke, not currently taking medication for the treatment of hypertension or hyperlipidemia, did not have any musculoskeletal problems that would prevent moderate exercise, and were sedentary for the previous 6 months. Sedentary was defined as not having engaged in regular exercise two or more times a week for at least 20 minutes per session, or engaging in a participative sport at least twice a week. All women were postmenopausal and not taking hormone-replacement medications. Subjects were recruited for the trial through a random digit dial telephone survey of residents of Sunnyvale, CA (King, Taylor, & Haskell, 1990) and through a media-based community-wide promotion. The sample of 194 subjects reported here represent the final group of the 357 participants entering the trial. This group received a quality of life questionnaire after 12 months of the exercise program, in addition to the standard assessment protocol. Thus, they represent a sample of convenience.

Design

Because of the limited window of opportunity that was available to us for administration of this questionnaire, we were unable to obtain baseline measures of health-related quality of life on this sample. No control group was available for these analyses, because by this time the original control group had begun their exercise program. However, the presence of three types of regimens allowed for comparisons of whether higher vs lower intensity exercise, or group vs home-based formats, were associated with health-related quality of life. Although not ideal, this posttest design did include a comprehensive, prospective assessment of physical activity levels over the prior year using stringent methods (e.g., including physiologic verification).

Procedures

Eligible subjects were subsequently randomized to one of three exercise training regimens: group-based training of higher intensity (i.e., 73–88% of peak heart rate achieved during symptom-limited treadmill testing), supervised home-based training of comparable intensity, or supervised home-based training of lower intensity (60–73% of peak heart rate achieved) (King et al., 1991).

The group-based sessions were provided at a local community college and senior center. Sessions were taught by trained exercise instructors 6 days a week, 3 times a day, to provide the opportunity for all participants to take part relatively easily. For the two home-based programs, following an initial individually-based instructional session, written information was provided and a project staff member telephoned the subject at home weekly for the first 4 weeks, biweekly for the following 4 weeks, and then once monthly through 12 months to monitor progress, answer questions, and provide individualized feedback to subjects. Subjects randomized to the home-based programs thus received only one initial face-to-face counseling session with study staff, with subsequent instructional episodes occurring via telephone and mail. The major endurance activity performed was brisk walking or walking-jogging for both group- and home-based programs. Prescribed activity for the two higher intensity conditions consisted of 120 minutes of endurance exercise per week (3 sessions of 40 minutes each). Subjects were instructed to exercise to achieve 73–88% of the peak heart rate achieved during treadmill exercise testing. To standardize caloric expenditure across the three training regimens, based on known relationships between intensity (i.e., heart rate) and energy expenditure levels (American College of Sports Medicine, 1986), subjects in the lower intensity condition were prescribed 150 minutes of exercise per week (5 sessions of 30 minutes each). The lower intensity subjects were instructed to exercise to achieve 60–73% of the peak heart rate achieved during treadmill exercise testing, a level that could be reached by brisk walking for most

subjects. The estimated caloric expenditure per week across all three exercise groups was approximately 900 kilocalories. Because kilocalories per week were highly correlated with number of sessions completed per week for all exercise regimens, and sessions/week is the most frequently used and readily understandable index of physical activity adherence among professionals as well as the public, sessions/week was used as the measure of interest. All subjects were trained to measure and record their exercise heart rates through palpation of the radial or brachial artery. In addition, exercise heart rate levels were evaluated in approximately half of subjects randomly selected from each condition, through use of a solid-state portable microprocessor (Vitalog Corporation, Redwood City, CA) that recorded heart rate and movement continuously for a 3-day period at baseline, 6 months, and 12 months. This device provides a valid and reliable indicator of adherence to prescribed exercise (Mueller et al., 1986). Activity logs were provided to subjects to determine exercise participation rates; these were returned by mail each month in the two home-based conditions, and were completed with the aid of instructors in the group condition.

Subjects received regular instruction and support related to exercising in their assigned conditions over the year. Within 6 weeks of completing their one-year evaluation, subjects completed the self-administered quality of life questionnaire for the current investigation.

Measures of Level of Participation, Physiologic Parameters, and Health-Related Quality of Life

Level of Participation

Level of participation in the exercise regimens over the first year was determined through class attendance sheets and subject activity logs, which were validated through a variety of techniques including the use of an ambulatory heart rate and activity monitor as well as changes in treadmill exercise performance (King et al., 1991). Participation in exercise was calculated as the number of sessions completed over the one-year period divided by the number of sessions prescribed, times 100. In addition to the continuous score of exercise participation, four groups were defined in terms of level of participation: 0–33%, 34–66%, 67–100%, and >100%. The latter group was included because some persons exercised more than the prescribed amount.

Physiologic Parameters

At baseline and at 12 months, measures of maximal oxygen uptake and body mass index were administered. Body mass index (BMI) was calculated using the formula weight (kg)/height^2 (meters). BMI has been found to be strongly correlated with body fat measured by precise laboratory techniques, and thus provides a more accurate measure of obesity than is provided by weight alone (King & Tribble, 1991; Stewart, Brook, & Kane, 1980). Maximal oxygen uptake ($\dot{V}O_2$ max) was assessed at baseline and 12 months during a symptom-limited treadmill exercise test using a Balke-type protocol with workloads increased approximately two METS every 3 minutes (American College of Sports Medicine, 1986). A 12-lead electrocardiogram was recorded at rest and monitored continuously during the test. ECG tracings were recorded at the end of each workload and at peak exercise. Oxygen uptake during exercise was determined each minute using a semiautomatic computer-based system (Gossard et al., 1986). $\dot{V}O_2$ max was defined as the highest oxygen uptake value determined during the last two minutes of exercise. Missing data for the $\dot{V}O_2$ max measure at 12 months (17%) were due primarily to treadmill test contraindications (e.g., medical reasons such as infectious diseases, minor musculoskeletal injuries, or resting ECG indicating heart disease progression). Potential differences between those subjects who were missing this measure and those who were not were evaluated using t-tests.

Health-related Quality of Life

Eight components of health-related quality of life were assessed: physical functioning, role limitations due to health, social activity limitations due to health, current health perceptions, pain, psychological distress/well-being, energy/fatigue, and sleep problems. These have been identified as factors most likely to be affected by exercise (Stewart & King, 1991). The first 6 scales constitute the Medical Outcomes Study (MOS) 20-item Short-Form General Health Survey (Stewart, Hays, & Ware, 1988; Stewart et al., 1989). The remaining two scales were developed for the longitudinal portion of the MOS (Hays & Stewart, 1992; Stewart, Hays, & Ware, 1992). The eight measures are summarized in Table 1, including their definitions, number of items, internal-consistency reliability in both the MOS sample and the current sample, and the mean and standard deviation.

A statistically conservative approach was taken in which the quality of life scales were factor analyzed

Table 1. Summary of Health-Related Quality of Life Outcome Measures and Descriptive Statistics (N = 194)

Concept/Measure[a]	Definition	Number of Items	Reliability MOS[b]	Reliability Current Sample	Mean[c]	SD
Physical Functioning (+)	Extent to which health limits physical activities such as self-care, walking, climbing hills/stairs, bending, lifting, and moderate and vigorous activities	6	.86	.68	74.4	23.0
Role Functioning (+)	Extent to which health interferes with usual daily activities such as work, housework, schoolwork	2	.81	.82	82.3	35.1
Social Functioning (+)	Limitations in normal social activities during past 4 weeks due to health	1	.67[d]	—	95.3	11.6
Current Health Perceptions (+)	Ratings of overall current health (e.g., I have been feeling bad lately; my health is excellent	5	.87	.85	80.7	17.5
Pain (-)	Extent of bodily pain in past 4 weeks	1	.76[d]	—	29.3	25.3
Psychological distress/Well-being (+)	Feelings of depression, anxiety, positive affect during past month	5	.88	.83	80.7	13.5
Energy/fatigue (+)	Amount of time past month full of pep, energetic, worn out, tired, had enough energy to do things	5	.88	.90	67.5	18.1
Sleep Problems Index (-)	Sleep disturbance, adequacy, somnolence, and awaken short of breath during past 4 weeks	6	.78	.73	20.7	13.8

[a](+) High score is better health, (-) High score is poorer health.
[b]Medical Outcomes Study.
[c]Scores range from 0–100.
[d]Alternate forms reliability.

to determine the most parsimonious manner of representing these outcomes. Two factors, physical health and psychological well-being, were identified using an oblique rotation (Ford, MacCallum, & Tait, 1986). Physical functioning, role functioning, current health perceptions, and pain loaded significantly on the physical health index, and psychological distress/well-being, energy/fatigue, and sleep problems loaded on the psychological well-being index. To score the two indices, responses on the pain and sleep problems scales were first reversed to ensure that the direction of scoring was compatible for all scales. Scores were then standardized and summed. The two index scores were considered as the primary dependent variables. The individual scales were also evaluated descriptively to provide additional clinical information on the precise pattern of effects.

Covariates

Smoking status was assessed at baseline and one year, and remained the same for all participants. It was scored dichotomously (current smoker vs not). Chronic conditions were assessed as a count of the number of patient-reported conditions at one year. These included arthritis; asthma or other lung problems (such as chronic bronchitis, emphysema); back problems (including disc or spine); ulcer, chronic inflamed bowel, enteritis, or colitis; allergies; kidney disease; neurologic problems; trouble seeing (even with glasses or contacts), and recently diagnosed cancer. These conditions were those likely to cause functional limitations, as taken from the MOS screening survey. No attempt was made to weight the conditions, because of the problem of identifying weights that are replicable across studies and because unit weights are robust and tend to cross-validate as well as non-unitary weights (Dawes, 1979; Stanley & Wang, 1970). Injuries were assessed at one year in terms of whether subjects had experienced a bruise/scrape, sprain/strain, or break/fracture of the hip, leg, knee, foot, ankle, toe, arm/wrist/hand/elbow, shoulder, face, head, or other body part during the previous 6 months. For this analysis, we counted the number of sprains, strains, breaks, and fractures.

Methods of Analysis

Given the lack of baseline measurement of quality of life, analysis of covariance methods were used to control for several variables which could influence the physical and psychological well-being indices, independent of exercise participation or fitness levels (i.e., threats to internal validity). These variables were: gender, assignment to type of exercise program, chronic conditions, injuries in the last 6 months, and smoking status. Age and education were not included as covariates because the sample was found to be homogeneous on these characteristics (King et al., 1991). Other major

chronic conditions were controlled for through the initial eligibility criteria for the major trial.

In addition to the covariance procedures, analyses were also conducted using multiple regression, with similar results. In that analysis, level of participation was included as a continuous measure. Because the analysis of covariance using the four-level exercise participation variable allows a clearer graphic display of the results, the analysis of covariance findings are reported here.

To evaluate whether any differences were mediated by physical fitness, change in $\dot{V}O_2$ max was subsequently added to the above analyses as a covariate. The analysis including $\dot{V}O_2$ max was conducted on the portion of the sample performing the treadmill test at 1 year ($n = 164$). Similarly, change in body mass index was added as a covariate in a separate analysis ($n = 183$). To assure noncollinearity between exercise participation and physical fitness, correlations between these measures were calculated and found to be satisfactory (Pearson product-moment correlations between exercise participation and change in $\dot{V}O_2$ max, $r = -.30$; between exercise participation and change in BMI, $r = -.14$.). The correlation between changes in $\dot{V}O_2$ max and changes in body mass index ($r = -.19$) indicated that these two physical fitness measures were reasonably independent and thus could be treated as separate indicators of physical fitness.

Preplanned comparisons were conducted to determine more precisely where the significant differences were between groups differing in exercise participation level. The Tukey test was used (Keppel, 1973),

Table 2. Sample Characteristics (N = 194)

Education:		
Range in years	1–18+	
Completed high school	95%	
Have a college degree	57%	
Gender:		
Male	57%	
Female	43%	
Race:		
Nonwhite	10%	
Age in years:		
Range	50–65	
Mean (SD)	58.8	(4.3)
Household income > $35,000	80%	
Current cigarette smokers	16%	
Number of chronic conditions:		
Range	0–6	
Mean (SD)	1.48	(1.28)
Number of serious injuries:		
Range	0–4	
Mean (SD)	.35	(.73)
Number of injuries:		
Range	0–4	
Mean (SD)	.48	(.89)

based on the harmonic mean, which adjusts results for the unequal sample sizes among the four groups representing the different exercise participation levels.

RESULTS

Sample characteristics are described in Table 2. As shown, the sample was relatively well educated and reasonably healthy. This sample was found to be comparable to the larger trial sample on all variables except for smoking status (King et al., 1991). The smoking rates in this sample were approximately 5% lower than those for the sample as a whole.

In general, measurement reliability in the current sample was similar to that achieved in the MOS sample on which the measures were originally developed. The only exception was the physical functioning scale, which had a somewhat lower reliability in the current sample (0.68 compared to 0.86 in the MOS). Inspection of item distributions suggests that this lower reliability could be due to the more limited item variability in this sample, which was relatively healthy. Nevertheless, this reliability is acceptable for group comparisons. One measure — social activity limitations — was highly skewed (98% of the sample scored in the two highest response categories), and thus was omitted from subsequent analyses.

The covariates (e.g., smoking status, injuries, chronic conditions) were found to be modestly correlated with participation levels for all three exercise regimens (r values ranged from −.13 to .19).

Exercise Participation and Physical and Psychological Well-Being

Analysis of covariance, with the number of chronic conditions, injuries, gender, and smoking status used as covariates, showed no differences in the physical health or psychological well-being indices as a function of study assignment to type of exercise program — either by intensity (higher vs lower) or format (group vs class) (p values ≥ .10). Level of exercise participation during the year was associated with the physical health index at one year ($F = 8.35$, $p < .001$). Physical health scores were greater with higher levels of exercise participation. Post-hoc tests indicated that physical health was significantly better for the > 100% participation group than for the 0–33% or the 34–66% participation groups; physical health was also significantly better for the 67–100% participation group than for the 0–33% group (all p values < .05). In contrast, the psychological well-being index was not related to exercise participation levels throughout the year ($F = 0.66$, n.s.).

The number of chronic conditions was significantly negatively associated with both health indices (for physical health, $F = 52.82$, $p < .001$; for psychological well-

being, $F = 21.00$, $p < .001$). Gender was also significantly associated with rated physical health and psychological well-being as measured by the quality of life questionnaires; women had poorer rated physical health ($F = 10.69$, $p < .01$) and somewhat poorer psychological well-being scores $F = 3.74$, $p - .055$). Smoking status was not significantly associated with either index.

When change in $\dot{V}O_2$ max was added as a covariate to the analyses of the two indexes, this variable did not reach statistical significance ($p > .10$) and the previous results did not change. Similarly, when change in body mass index was added as a covariate to the analyses, this variable did not reach statistical significance ($p > .10$). The association between exercise participation and physical health was thus found to be independent of these physiological parameters as well as the chronic conditions, gender, injuries, study assignment, and smoking status variables noted above.

Those who did not participate in the one-year treadmill test (and thus were missing the $\dot{V}O_2$ max measure) were found to have somewhat poorer rated health and physical functioning, more pain and chronic conditions, and lower exercise participation rates than those who did complete this treadmill test (p values < .05). However, these two groups were not different in terms of age, gender, energy/fatigue, psychological distress/well-being, or sleep problems. This suggests that analyses including $\dot{V}O_2$ max were conducted on a somewhat healthier portion of the sample, which is expected since the treadmill was not administered if health problems suggested that it was contraindicated.

Exercise Participation and Components of Health

To understand further the nature and magnitude of changes in rated physical health and exercise participation level, we determined the mean scores on each of the four components of the physical health index separately (physical functioning, role functioning, pain, and current health perceptions) in association with the four exercise participation levels (i.e., 0–33%, 34–66%, 67–100%, and >100%). The mean scores on the four physical health index components by exercise participation level (including N's for each participation level) are shown in Figure 1. Mean differences between the lowest and highest levels of exercise participation were large — between .5 and 1.0 standard deviation. Post-hoc tests indicated that physical functioning was significantly better for the >100% group than for the 0–33% group or the 34–66% group; it was also significantly better for the 67–100% group than for the 0–33% group (p values < .05). For pain and for current health perceptions, the >100% group was significantly better than the 0–33% group (p values < .05). No statistically significant differences were found among participation groups for role func-

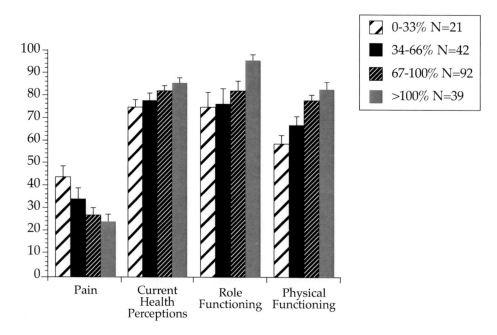

Figure 1.   Health-related quality of life by exercise participation level.
Note: All scores range from 0–100. High scores indicate better health, except for pain, which is scored so that a higher score indicates more pain. Bars = standard error. Participation level is scored using the following formula:

$$\frac{\text{Number of exercise sessions completed}}{\text{Number of exercise sessions Prescribed}} \times 100$$

Pain: Group 0–33% vs Group > 100% (*p* < .05); Group 0–33% vs Group 67–100% (*p* < .05).
Current Health Perceptions: Group 0–33% vs Group > 100% (*p* < .05).
Physical Functioning: Group 0–33% vs Group > 100% (*p* < .05); Group 0–33% vs Group 67–100% (*p* < .05); Group 34–66% vs Group > 100% (*p* < .05).

tioning, although the pattern of results by category of exercise participation was similar to those for the other three variables. This is most likely due to the large variation in this measure.

Similar analyses for the components of psychological well-being indicated that none of the components were statistically significant.

DISCUSSION

We found that greater levels of endurance exercise participation over a one-year period were significantly associated with better ratings of physical health at the end of the year, defined in terms of physical functioning, role functioning, pain, and current health perceptions, regardless of the intensity (higher- vs lower-intensity) or format (group- vs home-based) of the exercise program assigned. The magnitude of the association was notable, as indicated by the mean quality of life differences between the lowest and highest levels of exercise participation. These findings were not explained by changes in either functional capacity ($\dot{V}O_2$ max) or body weight (body mass index) across the one-year period.

In contrast, exercise participation levels were not significantly associated with psychological distress/well-being, energy/fatigue, and sleep problems as measured by the MOS scales. The finding of no association with psychological distress/well-being is in contrast to findings on other measures of stress, anxiety, and depression at one year (King, Taylor, & Haskell, 1993), suggesting that these three MOS measures may be insensitive to group differences in this population. It thus remains to be determined to what extent these particular psychological outcomes are influenced by endurance exercise.

Most prior studies attempting to evaluate the effects of exercise on quality of life outcomes in older adults have been cross-sectional in nature, evaluating levels of exercise with quality of life at one point in time (Stewart & King, 1991). This study represents the next step — a study in which the quality of life outcomes were assessed at the end of a one-year controlled intervention. Although other posttest-only studies have been reported, most do not include a range of both physical and psychological outcomes such as were included in the current study. Further, many of the available posttest studies evaluate exercise regimens of relatively short duration, do not provide comparisons among several different exercise regimens, and do not adequately measure extent of exercise participation. Subsequent studies can further contribute to our knowledge in this area by using randomized longitudinal designs with pretest-posttest evaluation. This point notwithstanding, because of the general lack of pretest-posttest designs evaluating a wide range of physical and psychological outcomes in this age group, the current study contributes useful information with respect to the potential utility of participating in a variety of exercise programs on such outcomes.

The posttest-only study design used with this sample of opportunity does not allow us to state conclusively that participation in exercise caused these physical health outcomes to be enhanced. The most commonly proposed alternative explanation in such studies is that people with more health problems exercised less. While the current design precludes the ability to rule out this alternative explanation completely, there are several aspects of the data that make this explanation less likely (Paffenbarger, 1988). First, the sample was screened thoroughly prior to study entry to ensure that participants had no serious health problems that would preclude exercising. Second, there were no significant differences in the number of chronic conditions or injuries across the four exercise participation levels, suggesting that the differences in exercise participation rates were not due to poorer health on the part of subjects. Finally, all analyses controlled for the effects of chronic conditions, recent injuries, smoking status, and other variables that could potentially influence quality of life. These points notwithstanding, there could be additional unmeasured health variables that we were unable to control for. In addition, because we did not have baseline measures of physical functioning, it is conceivable that those with better physical functioning were able to participate at higher levels throughout the study. These points suggest that caution should be applied in interpreting our study findings.

The key factor associated with better-rated physical health was the extent of exercise participation, rather than the type of exercise program persons were involved in (i.e., home- vs group-based, higher vs lower intensity). Further, we found that these effects were not mediated by physical fitness changes, although in the original trial fitness levels were improved significantly for all three exercise training programs across the year, relative to assessment-only controls (King et al., 1991). These findings are not uncommon; $\dot{V}O_2$ max is not always related to perceived ratings of physical or psychological functioning (King, Taylor, Haskell, & DeBusk, 1989). It is also possible that the associations were mediated by other fitness parameters not measured, such as muscle strength, flexibility, or balance. Our finding that exercise participation was associated with better health *regardless* of whether fitness parameters were modified over the one year period is important, since it is likely that many middle-aged and older adults lack the interest or ability to exercise vigorously enough to achieve large increases in such fitness measures (U.S. Preventive Services Task Force, 1989).

One advantage of the current sample is that it was drawn from a defined population and consisted of as representative a community sample as has been reported in the exercise training area to date (King et al., 1991). We can thus infer that these findings might generalize to other persons in this age group in the community, at least to those who might similarly volunteer. Other advantages of this sample include the fact that unlike many studies, multiple formats and intensities of exercise regimens were studied and both women and men were included.

We conclude that exercise participation may have important quality of life benefits in terms of rated physical health in older populations. Because physical functioning is one of the important factors leading to increased health care utilization (Branch et al., 1981), such participation could in turn lead to reduced costs of care. Because many previous studies of the benefits of exercise have focused only on psychological outcomes (Stewart & King, 1991), future studies need to incorporate a more comprehensive definition of quality of life that includes physical components, as well as providing pretest to posttest comparisons. These physical components remain an important though understudied dimension of quality of life, a dimension that may be significantly influenced by even moderate levels of physical exercise.

REFERENCES

American College of Sports Medicine. (1986). *Guidelines for exercise testing and prescription* (3rd ed.). Philadelphia: Lea & Febiger.

Blair, S. N., Kohl, H. W., Paffenbarger, R. S., Clark, D. G., Cooper, K. H., & Gibbons, L. W. (1989). Physical fitness and all-cause mortality: A prospective study of healthy men and women. *Journal of the American Medical Association, 262*, 2395–2401.

Bortz, W. M. (1984). The disuse syndrome. *The Western Journal of Medicine, 141*, 691–694.

Branch, L. G., Jette, A. M., Evashwick, C. J., Polansky, M., Rowe, G., & Diehr, P. (1981). Toward understanding elders' health service utilization. *Journal of Community Health, 7*, 80–92.

Buchner, D. M., Beresford, S. A. A., Larson, E. B., LaCroix, A. Z., & Wagner, E. H. (1992). Effects of physical activity on health status in older adults

II: Intervention studies. *Annual Review of Public Health, 13,* 469–488.

Dawes, R. M. (1979). The robust beauty of improper linear models. *American Psychologist, 34,* 571–582.

Emery, C. F., & Blumenthal, J. A. (1990). Perceived change among participants in an exercise program for older adults. *The Gerontologist, 30,* 516–521.

Emery, C. F., & Blumenthal, J. A. (1991). Effects of physical exercise on psychological and cognitive functioning of older adults. *Annals of Behavioral Medicine, 13,* 99–107.

Ford, J. K., MacCallum, R. C., & Tait, M. (1986). The application of exploratory factor analysis in applied psychology: A critical review and analysis. *Personnel Psychology, 39,* 291–314.

Gossard, D., Haskell, W. L., Taylor, C. B., Mueller, J. K., Rogers, F., Chandler, M., Ahu, D. K., Miller, N. H., & DeBusk, R. F. (1986). Effects of low- and high-intensity home-based exercise training on functional capacity in healthy middle-aged men. *American Journal of Cardiology, 57,* 447–449.

Hays, R. D., & Stewart, A. L. (1992). Sleep measures. In A. L. Stewart & J. E. Ware Jr. (Eds.), *Measuring functioning and well-being: The Medical Outcomes Study approach* (pp. 235–259). Durham, NC: Duke University Press.

Keppel, G. (1973). *Design and analysis: A researcher's handbook.* Englewood Cliffs, NJ: Prentice-Hall, Inc.

King, A. C., Haskell, W. L., Taylor, C. B., Kraemer, H. C., & DeBusk, R. F. (1991). Group- vs home-based exercise training in healthy older men and women: A community-based clinical trial. *Journal of the American Medical Association, 266,* 1535–1542.

King, A. C., Taylor, C. B., & Haskell, W. B. (1990). Smoking in older women: Is being female a "risk factor" for continued cigarette use? *Archives of Internal Medicine, 150,* 1841–1846.

King, A. C., Taylor, C. B., & Haskell, W. L. (1993). The effects of differing intensities and formats of twelve months of exercise training on psychological outcomes in older adults. *Health Psychology, 12,* 292–300.

King, A. C., Taylor, C. B., Haskell, W. L., & DeBusk, R. F. (1989). The influence of regular aerobic exercise on psychological health: A randomized, controlled trial of healthy middle-aged adults. *Health Psychology, 8,* 305–324.

King, A. C., & Tribble, D. L. (1991). The role of exercise in weight regulation in nonathletes. *Sports Medicine, 11,* 331–339.

Minor, M. A. (1991). Physical activity and management of arthritis. *Annals of Behavioral Medicine, 13,* 117–124.

Minor, M. A., Hewett, J. E., Webel, R. R., Anderson, S. K., & Ray, D. R. (1989). Efficacy of physical conditioning exercise in patients with rheumatoid arthritis and osteoarthritis. *Arthritis and Rheumatism, 32,* 1396–1405.

Mueller, J. K., Gossard, D., Adams, F. R., Taylor, C. B., Haskell, W. L., Kraemer, H. C., Ahn, D. K., Burnett, K., & DeBusk, R. F. (1986). Assessment of prescribed increases in physical activity: Application of a new method for microprocessor analysis of heart rate. *American Journal of Cardiology, 57,* 441–445.

Paffenbarger, R. S. (1988). Contributions of epidemiology to exercise science and cardiovascular health. *Medicine and Science in Sports and Exercise, 20,* 426–438.

Paffenbarger, R. S., & Hyde, R. T. (1987). Exercise and the aging process. In R. J. Carlson & B. Newman (Eds.), *Issues and trends in health* (pp. 242–253). St. Louis: C.V. Mosby.

Stamford, B. A. (1988). Exercise and the elderly. In *American College of Sports Medicine Series, Exercise and Sport Sciences Reviews* (Vol. 16). New York: MacMillan.

Stanley, J. C., & Wang, M. D. (1970). Weighting test items and test-item options, an overview of the analytical and empirical literature. *Educational and Psychological Measurement, 30,* 21–35.

Stewart, A. L., Brook, R. H., & Kane, R. L. (1980). *Conceptualization and measurement of health habits for adults in the Health Insurance Study: Vol. II. Overweight (R-2374-2-HEW).* Santa Monica CA: The Rand Corporation.

Stewart, A. L., Hays, R. D., & Ware, J. E., Jr. (1988). The MOS Short-form General Health Survey: Reliability and validity in a patient population. *Medical Care, 26,* 724–735.

Stewart, A. L., Hays, R. D., & Ware, J. E., Jr. (1992). Health perceptions, energy/fatigue, and health distress measures. In A. L. Stewart & J. E. Ware, Jr. (Eds.), *Measuring functioning and well-being: The Medical Outcomes Study approach* (pp. 143–172). Durham, NC: Duke University Press.

Stewart, A. L., & King, A. C. (1991). Evaluating the efficacy of physical activity for influencing quality of life outcomes in older adults. *Annals of Behavioral Medicine, 13,* 108–116.

Stewart, A. L., Greenfield, S., Hays, R. D., Wells, K., Rogers, W. H., Berry, S. D., McGlynn, E. A., & Ware, J. E., Jr. (1989). Functional status and well-being of patients with chronic conditions: Results from the Medical Outcomes Study. *Journal of the American Medical Association, 262,* 907–913.

U.S. Department of Health and Human Services. (1992). *Healthy people 2000: National health promotion and disease prevention objectives.* Boston: Jones and Bartlett.

U.S. Preventive Services Task Force. (1989). Recommendations for physical exercise in primary prevention. *Journal of the American Medical Association, 261,* 3588–3589.

1.10

PRE- AND POSTTEST DESIGN (ONE GROUP)

Pilot Testing *Okay With Asthma*™: An Online Asthma Intervention for School-Age Children

Tami H. Wyatt, RN, PhD, CNE and Emily J. Hauenstein, RN, PhD, LCP

ABSTRACT: Asthma is the leading cause of missed school days despite advancements in asthma treatment. This may be, in part, due to a lack of understanding about asthma. *Okay With Asthma*™, an online story with psychosocial management strategies for school-age children, was pilot tested to measure its effect on asthma knowledge and attitude. The online program delivers content about asthma through a digital story and story-writing program. Using a one-group pretest-posttest quasi-experimental design, 35 children with moderate to severe asthma completed a pretest measure of asthma knowledge and attitudes and then completed *Okay With Asthma*™. At 1 week and 2 weeks after the intervention, the children completed the measures again. There were significant improvements in asthma knowledge scores at the 1- and 2-week evaluations and significant improvements in attitude scores 2 weeks after the program. *Okay With Asthma*™ specifically targets school-age children and teaches them how to use school resources and peers while managing their asthma.

KEYWORDS: Asthma; digital story; psychosocial management; storytelling; story writing.

INTRODUCTION

Asthma, an obstructive airway disease characterized by recurrent episodes of breathlessness and wheezing, is one of the most prevalent chronic illnesses among children in the United States. Approximately 13% of American children between 0 and 17 years of age have been diagnosed with asthma during their lifetime, and 9% currently have asthma (Federal Interagency Forum on Child and Family Statistics, 2007). Low-income and African American children have incidence rates almost two times that for children of other races and backgrounds. Although the incidence of asthma rose rapidly during the early 1990s, the rate increases have stabilized since 1997. Although the stable prevalence rates are encouraging and in part

Tami H. Wyatt, RN, PhD, CNE, is an assistant professor at the University of Tennessee Knoxville, College of Nursing.

Emily J. Hauenstein, RN, PhD, LCP, is the Thomas A. Saunders III Family Professor and director of the Southeastern Rural Mental Health Research Center, University of Virginia, School of Nursing, Charlottesville.

attributable to improved asthma medications and intervention programs, a large number of children continue to be affected by this disorder.

Asthma is the leading cause of missed school days and the third leading cause of hospitalizations in children (U.S. Environmental Protection Agency, Indoor Environments Division, 2007). Asthma requires ongoing management. Because children spend approximately half of their weekday waking hours in school, the school nurse often participates in the management of their asthma.

Okay With Asthma™, developed for school nurses to use in health offices, encourages children to become active participants in their own asthma management. It is an online asthma management program for children 8 to 11 years of age. The program is unique because it incorporates the traditional content of asthma management along with psychosocial strategies for managing asthma. The program uses a unique interactive and media-rich method, digital story, and story writing to deliver the curriculum. Because the program is published on the Internet, it is free and accessible to any school with Internet access. The self-guided program can be completed independently by a child visiting the health office without dedicated instructional time by the school nurse. Once the program was developed, it was pilot tested to measure the effect of the *Okay With Asthma*™ program on asthma knowledge and attitudes about having asthma in school-age children.

BACKGROUND

Although the exact cause of asthma is unknown, factors known to trigger episodes include infections, allergic reactions, exercise, and stress. Approximately 75% to 80% of children with asthma have allergies (Kemp & Kemp, 2001). Because children spend a significant amount of their weekdays in schools, they are susceptible to asthma attacks during school. Children with asthma may experience psychosocial stress, leading to negative attitudes about asthma and low self-esteem, which affects school performance, family and peer relationships, and asthma management (Wood & Miller, 2002). Therefore, it is important to integrate psychosocial management strategies into asthma education programs.

Many programs for children with asthma are based on the guidelines of the National Asthma Education and Prevention Program (NAEPP) developed by an expert panel representing the National Heart, Lung and Blood Institute (NHLBI; 2007), but they do not necessarily address the emotional component of children's experience with asthma. Recent programs recognize this shortcoming and include strategies for coping with asthma. For example, Quest for the Code™ by Starbright™, an interactive CD-ROM game for children, describes how to talk with peers about asthma as well as provides information about the medical management of asthma.

Asthma education programs for children are traditionally based on a family model and focus on the family's role in managing the child's asthma. Although family involvement is essential, a child involved in his or her own care will assume more responsibility and ultimately feel more in control, promoting a more positive attitude about having asthma (Wood & Miller, 2002). Children in school or engaged in after-school activities must identify their own symptoms during an asthma attack and seek help outside the family, relying on school, peer, and community interactions to assist with self-management.

Some asthma programs for school-age children are designed for classroom settings, such as Open Airways for Schools™ (American Lung Association, 1997), Kick-in' Asthma (American Public Health Association, 2006), and Asthma Awareness: Curriculum for the Elementary Classroom™ (NHLBI, 1993), whereas others are designed to be fully integrated in the community, such as the Asthma-Friendly Schools Initiative (American Lung Association, 2007). Because of increasing curricular demands, such labor and time-intensive programs are difficult to implement, often not integrated into the curriculum, and may be taught by persons who do not have sufficient knowledge or experience with the management of asthma.

Other asthma programs use multimedia, which is effective in increasing health-promoting behavior (Huss, Winkelstein, Crosbie, Stanton, & Huss, 2001). Children typically become more involved in multimedia activities than traditional educational activities because they have grown accustomed to learning in audiovisual environments (Mayer, 2001). One useful role-modeling strategy for school-age children is story. *Okay With Asthma*™, the intervention tested and reported in this study, uses story and story-writing techniques to teach children about asthma and ways to cope with having asthma.

Story is the communication of information through a storyline with characters, conflict, and resolution of the conflict. There are two components of story: storytelling (receiving a story) and story writing (making a story). Information that is presented in a story format may be more effective in improving knowledge and changing behavior because knowledge and information are processed and stored in one's memory as a story (Egan, 1997). *Okay With Asthma*™ aims to fill the gap in asthma programs for school-age children by including traditional asthma management content as well as psychosocial management strategies in a multimedia innovative technique using digital story. The psychosocial management strategies are based on the biobehavioral family model (Wood & Miller, 2002) that engages not just the family in asthma management but also peers, the health care system, and the community such as schools. It is believed that children who engage their friends in asthma management are less likely to hide their condition from peers. Furthermore, peers are less likely to tease children with asthma if they share the responsibility of identifying symptoms or getting assistance during an asthma episode.

METHODS

This study used a one-group pretest-posttest quasi-experimental design to pilot test the effectiveness of *Okay With Asthma*™ in increasing asthma knowledge and improving children's attitudes toward their illness. A child's knowledge and attitude about asthma were measured at baseline and 1 and 2 weeks after completing *Okay With Asthma*™. Once the study was approved by the Institutional Review Board, 169 letters requesting participation in this study were sent to families of children with asthma who were between the ages of 8 and 11 years and enrolled in 1 of 16 participating rural public elementary schools. Fifty-three families returned a self-addressed postcard indicating interest in the study. Sixteen children were excluded from the study because they did not meet inclusion criteria, which were (a) ability to complete assent forms; (b) children without cognitive, psychiatric, or behavioral disturbances identified by the school nurse; and (c) children with moderate to severe asthma based on the NAEPP-recommended rating scale. Thirty-seven children enrolled in the study, completing pretests and visiting the *Okay With Asthma*™ program. Thirty-five children completed all measures; 2 withdrew from the study after the first measure because of scheduling conflicts.

Instruments

The Asthma Information Quiz (AIQ) measured asthma knowledge (Wade et al., 1997). This is a 23-item true-false questionnaire testing a child's knowledge of asthma triggers, symptoms, medication management, and prevention. This measure was modified by simplifying the language to reflect a Flesch-Kincaid Grade Level Score of 3.0, changing double-negative language in the items and adding four items pertaining to the psychosocial management of asthma. The AIQ is scored by calculating the percentage of items answered correctly.

The Child Attitude Toward Illness Scale (CATIS) was used to measure the participants' attitudes toward having asthma. This 13-item, 5-point Likert-type scale instrument is a self-report scale developed

for children aged 8 to 12 years. The CATIS is scored by summing the numerical responses and dividing by 13. High scores reflect positive attitudes (Austin & Huberty, 1993). The alpha reliability coefficient for this scale was .91, with an interitem correlation ranging from .04 to .71 with a mean of .44.

Procedures

Upon receipt of the postcard from parents indicating interest in the study, the investigator met with each child and his or her caregiver(s) to obtain parental consent and child assent and to collect descriptive data. Descriptive data were obtained to identify factors that might influence the results. These included the child's learning preferences, access to a computer, family structure, current asthma care, and demographics such as gender, age, race, and number of years diagnosed with asthma.

This study took place during school or after school hours in computer labs of public elementary schools. Data were collected over a 10-week period during the spring season; all children in the study reported asthma symptoms during the course of the study. None of the children participated in other asthma intervention programs during the study. At the participating schools, children completed pretests, the *Okay With Asthma*™ program, and posttests. Because of existing public school curriculum requirements, children in this study had the basic computer skills necessary to participate in the *Okay With Asthma*™ program.

During the first session, children completed the pretests and *Okay With Asthma*™ program under the supervision of the investigator. The investigator conducted a debriefing with each child after viewing the multimedia program, asking questions such as, "Is there anything that you saw in the story that upsets you or makes you feel bad?" One week and 2 weeks after completing the program, children completed the posttests under the supervision of the investigator. The participating children received a $10 certificate after completing the posttests at the 2-week interval. The two participants who withdrew from the study received their $10 gift certificate by mail.

Data Analyses

To determine if *Okay With Asthma*™ improved knowledge scores on the AIQ and attitude scores on the CATIS, scores were calculated and analyzed using *t* tests and Wilcoxon signed rank tests, pairing pretests with 1-week scores and pretests with 2-week scores. The alpha for significance was set at $p < .05$. Descriptive data collected during the interviews were analyzed using descriptive statistics. Data from the two children who withdrew were not included in the analyses.

RESULTS

The number of boys and girls who participated in the study was nearly equal. The convenience sample yielded an ethnic representation equal to that of the geographic region in a rural community in central Virginia where the study took place. Demographic data are listed in Table 1. Only 4 (11%) of the 35 participants received care from an asthma specialist; the remaining children received care from either a pediatrician or a family practice physician. Two children (6%) had previously participated in an asthma education program.

In measuring the effects of the *Okay With Asthma*™ program on knowledge and attitude 1 week after completing the program, a significant difference was found between the knowledge pretest and 1-week posttest scores ($t = 3.107$, $p = .004$) but not between attitude pretest and 1-week posttest scores ($t = 1.636$, $p = .111$). Two weeks after completing the program, both knowledge and attitude scores were significantly improved.

Table 1. Demographics of Study Participants ($n = 35$)

Characteristic	n (%)
Gender	
Male	19 (54)
Female	16 (46)
Age (years)	
8	15 (43)
9	7 (20)
10	9 (26)
11	4 (11)
Race	
American Indian or Alaskan	0 (0)
Asian or Pacific Islander	1 (3)
Black, not Hispanic origin	12 (34)
Hispanic	2 (6)
White, not Hispanic origin	20 (57)
Asthma severity	
Moderate	25 (71)
Severe	10 (29)
Activity limitations	
Minimal	18 (52)
Moderate	12 (34)
Severe	5 (14)
Asthma duration	
Less than 1 year	5 (14)
1–3 years	10 (29)
3–5 years	20 (57)
Family history of asthma	
Asthma history	24 (69)
No asthma history	11 (31)
Learning styles	
Auditory	12 (34)
Visual	10 (29)
Kinesthetic	13 (37)

Children scored higher on 2-week posttest knowledge scores ($z = 2.705$, $p = .007$) and attitude scores ($z = 2.554$, $p = .011$).

Overall, the attitude scores improved at either 1 week posttest or 2 week posttest in 31 of 35 participants (highest possible score = 5). The knowledge scores improved at either 1-week posttest or 2-week posttest when compared to pretest in 30 of 35 participants (highest possible score = 35). See Figures 1 and 2 for mean scores and differences between boys and girls during each evaluation. Ten-year-old participants scored significantly higher on knowledge pretest scores than the 8-, 9-, and 11-year-old children ($t = -2.351$, $p = .025$).

Overall, the mean attitude scores of both boys and girls improved at each evaluation (highest possible score = 5), but boys scored consistently higher on the attitude measure than girls did (Figure 2). Participants with severe asthma had a significantly greater change in attitude scores from pretest to 1-week posttest compared with children with moderate asthma ($t = 2.13$, $p = .041$). Lastly, novice Internet and computer users, as rated by parents, had significantly greater increases in attitude scores between pretest and 2-week posttest scores than proficient Internet users ($t = 2.74$, $p = .010$) and proficient or advanced computer users ($t = 2.41$, $p = .021$).

DISCUSSION

Okay With Asthma™ used digital story to deliver asthma management strategies, including psychosocial strategies to adjust to asthma as well as the role of

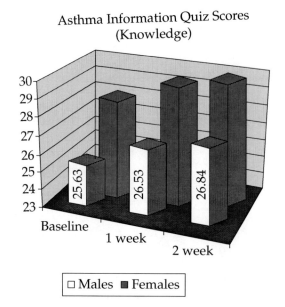

Asthma Information Quiz Scores (Knowledge)

Figure 1. Comparison of Male and Female Asthma Knowledge Scores ($n = 35$).

Child Attitude Toward Having Illness Scores
(Attitude)

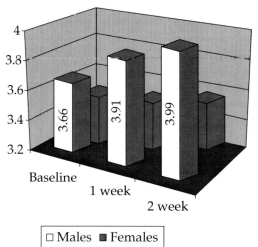

Figure 2. Comparison of Male and Female Attitude Toward Asthma Scores (*n* = 35).

school personnel and peers in helping a child adjust to asthma. The program reinforced family, peer, and school involvement in managing asthma by role-modeling effective strategies such as eliciting help from others and talking with friends about feelings associated with asthma.

Attitude, which is widely documented as difficult to change, was significantly improved in as little as 2 weeks. The greatest change in attitude scores occurred in children with severe asthma, because of their lower attitude baseline scores, and children 8 years of age, possibly because of their enthusiastic interest in the program. Children with fewer computer and Internet skills, as rated by their parents, scored better on attitude measures than did children with more computer skills, indicating that *Okay With Asthma™* is useful regardless of computer skills and, in fact, may be suitable for younger children with fewer computer skills.

There are limitations to this study. The knowledge tool was challenging for some participants. It was selected because it had been used in previous pediatric asthma studies (Wade et al., 1997). In some cases, it was necessary for the investigator to read items aloud and explain questions or concepts so the child could respond to the item. Despite these shortcomings, knowledge scores improved and were sustained for 2 weeks.

More research is needed to determine the efficacy of *Okay With Asthma™* and the retention of changes in knowledge and attitude using larger samples of children with asthma. Furthermore, to generalize these findings and determine the program's efficacy, the intervention must be tested with larger samples of children and over a longer period of time to determine the

retention of asthma knowledge and attitude toward having asthma.

IMPLICATIONS FOR SCHOOL NURSING PRACTICE

School nurses consistently report spending more of their school days providing care to children with asthma. In a survey conducted in one public county school, school staff reported not only providing more immediate care during asthma episodes but also administering asthma maintenance medications that in the past were administered at a child's home (Knox County Public School Report, 2007). This increased responsibility of school staff is time intensive and leaves less time and resources to teach children about health and wellness and how to manage their conditions. *Okay With Asthma™* helps deal with time restrictions of school staff because the program is self-guided, requiring little to no school staff guidance. The program, which is available at www.okay-with-asthma.org, includes a 20-minute animated story about a school-age girl with asthma. While playing outside with her friends during recess, she pets a stray dog. This initiates an asthma attack that requires medication. She visits the health office, where she learns about her triggers, an action plan, and how important it is to include peers and school staff in her asthma care. At the end of the story, users may write their own story by adding text to a prewritten story. The asthma content is presented in an interactive and animated movie-style story that is entertaining while teaching children ways to manage their asthma and the importance of including friends and peers in asthma care.

The program is designed for school-age children with asthma but also can be used to teach children who do not have asthma. This is an important aspect of effective programs because children who are supported by their peers are less likely to hide their condition. Because *Okay With Asthma™* is a self-guided program, school staff may encourage children to preview the program while waiting for their asthma medication to relieve their symptoms. It may also be used in a lesson plan to introduce asthma, asthma triggers, and treatment. The program may also serve as a resource for children who must learn about various chronic disorders in the health curriculum.

CONCLUSION

Okay With Asthma™ has promise for children with asthma. The use of stories as an instructional method has long been used in education, and the use of interactive technologies in health education is emerging. Prior interventions have not incorporated story and psychosocial asthma management strategies using interactive technologies in a self-guided Internet-based program. The testing of *Okay With Asthma*™ provides information about an innovative computer-based program using novel health education strategies. It contributes to knowledge in health care research by suggesting innovations that have promise in promoting health in children with chronic illnesses.

ACKNOWLEDGMENTS

This study was funded by the National Institutes of Health, National Institute of Nursing Research Service Award 5 F31 NR07692-02, Sigma Theta Tau International, Beta Kappa Chapter Verhonick Research Award, and the University of Virginia Barbara Brodie Scholar Award.

REFERENCES

American Lung Association. (1997). *Open airways in schools*. In cooperation with the City of New York, the New York City Department of Health and Mental Hygiene, the New York City Department of Education, GlaxoSmithKline, and the New York City Council. Retrieved October 30, 2007, from http://www.alaw.org/asthma/open_airways_for_schools

American Lung Association. (2007). *Asthma-Friendly Schools Initiative® toolkit*. Retrieved October 18, 2007, from http://www.lungusa.org/site/apps/s/content.asp?c=dvLUK9O0E&b=34706&ct=67480#toolkit

American Public Health Association. (2006). "Kickin' asthma": School-based asthma education in an urban community. *School Health Education and Services Section Newsletter: Student Corner*. Retrieved October 18, 2007, from http://www.apha.org/membergroups/newsletters/sectionnewsletters/school/fall06/2877.htm

Austin, J. K., & Huberty, T. J. (1993). Development of the Child Attitude Toward Illness Scale. *Journal of Pediatric Psychology, 18*, 467–480.

Egan, K. (1997). *The educated mind: How cognitive tools shape our understanding*. Chicago: University of Chicago Press.

Federal Interagency Forum on Child and Family Statistics. (2007). *America's children: Key national indicators of well-being, 2007*. Washington, DC: Government Printing Office.

Huss, K., Winkelstein, M. L., Crosbie, K., Stanton, C. I., & Huss, R. W. (2001). "Backpack adventures in asthma": Interactive multimedia computer game piques children's interest in asthma. *Journal of Allergy and Clinical Immunology, 107*, 239.

Kemp, J. P., & Kemp, J. A. (2001). Management of asthma in children. *American Family Physician, 63*, 1341–1348, 1353–1354.

Knox County Public Schools Report. (2007). *School health indices, 2006–2007*. Knox, TN: Coordinated School Health Program.

Mayer, R. E. (2001). *Multi-media learning*. New York: Cambridge University Press.

National Heart, Lung and Blood Institute (NHLBI). (1993). *Asthma Awareness: Curriculum for the elementary classroom*. Retrieved October 18, 2007, from http://www.nhlbi.nih.gov/health/prof/lung/asthma/school/index.htm

National Heart, Lung and Blood Institute (NHLBI). (2007). *Expert panel report 3 (EPR2): Guidelines for the diagnosis and management of asthma*. Retrieved October 18, 2007, from http://www.nhlbi.nih.gov/guidelines/asthma/asthgdln.htm

U.S. Environmental Protection Agency, Indoor Environments Division. (2007). *Asthma facts*. Retrieved October 18, 1997, from epa.gov/asthma/pdfs/asthma_fact_sheet_en.pdf

Wade, S. L., Weil, C., Holden, G., Mitchell, H., Evans, R., Kruszon-Moran, D., et al. (1997). Psychosocial characteristics of inner-city children with asthma: A description of the NCICAS psychosocial protocol. *Pediatric Pulmonology, 24*, 263–276.

Wood, B. L., & Miller, B. D. (2002). *A biopsychosocial approach to child health*. In Kaslow F (Ed.), *Comprehensive handbook of psychotherapy* (4th ed., pp. 59–77). Hoboken, NJ: John Wiley & Sons.

1.11

CROSS-OVER DESIGN (MULTIPLE-GROUP REPEATED MEASURES)

Behavioral Treatment for Depressed Mood: A Pleasant Events Intervention for Seniors Residing in Assisted Living

Paul A. Cernin, PhD[*] and Peter A. Lichtenberg, PhD[†]

ABSTRACT: This pilot study examined a pleasant events focused treatment for depressed mood (Lichtenberg, Kimbarow, Wall, Roth, & MacNeill, 1998) in frail older adults. Using a cross-over design, 15 individuals from two suburban assisted living settings were randomly assigned to either the immediate treatment group ($n = 8$) or the wait-list control group ($n = 7$). Data from all participants were collected at baseline, 3 months, and 6 months. Trained staff delivered the treatment sessions to residents over a 3-month period for 30-minute sessions. Mood ratings ($p < .05$) and depression scores ($p < .09$) tended to improve for both treatment groups. Overall, 37% (4 of 11) of those who initially scored above the cutoff for depression scored below it following the treatment package; all of these four remained below threshold at final follow-up. This type of behavioral treatment appears promising for assisted living residents with mild to moderate levels of depressed mood.

KEYWORDS: Behavioral treatment; depressed mood; assisted living.

The prevalence of depression in nursing home residents and other frail populations is extremely high (Meeks & Depp, 2002), with nearly 50% of the nursing home population experiencing significant depressive symptoms. Although less is known about the general prevalence of depression in assisted living facilities, two recent studies have documented the point prevalence of clinical depression in these set-

tings. One study found the point prevalence to be 15% (Cummings & Cockerham, 2004); another found it to be 24% (Watson et al., 2006). Given these relatively high rates, developing and testing intervention strategies for treating depression in assisted living facilities remains a priority.

Behavioral treatment of depression in frail older adults has become increasingly identified as an effective non-pharmacological intervention. In this population, the stimulation of an increase in pleasant events is thought to be a key part of successful treatment. At least two groups have demonstrated the effectiveness of this type of intervention for this population. Teri,

*University of California at Los Angeles, Los Angeles, California, USA
†Institute of Gerontology, Wayne State University, Detroit, Michigan, USA

Logsdon, Uomoto, and McCurry (1997) demonstrated its success for treating depression in persons with dementia. Lichtenberg, Kimbarow, Morris, and Vangel (1996) demonstrated similar success for treating depression in older medical rehabilitation patients.

Both the Teri and Lichtenberg groups used innovative integrated care methods by partnering with lay and non-mental health professionals to deliver treatment. Integrated care, also known as interdisciplinary care, relates to a model of treatment where multiple practitioners across different provider backgrounds plan and implement care in a coordinated fashion. Teri's group worked directly with family caregivers, while Lichtenberg's group worked with occupational therapists. The current study sought to provide a preliminary exploration utilizing personal care attendants as the source of behavioral treatment for older adults with depressive problems who reside in assisted living facilities.

METHODS

Participants

Participants in this study were recruited from two senior assisted living communities affiliated with Jewish Apartments and Services in metropolitan Detroit, Michigan. Seniors were recruited through flyers as well as through referrals from social workers. Twenty-five individuals were enrolled in the study. Of those, seven attrited (i.e., one expired, two transferred to nursing homes, and four dropped out due to time constraints), and three were removed because of cognitive impairment (i.e., scoring >3 on the Benton Temporal Orientation Test [BTOT] and <10 on Animal Naming). The final treatment sample numbered 15 individuals from whom data was collected at baseline, 3 months, and 6 months.

Measures

Geriatric Depression Scale (GDS)

The GDS (Yesavage et al., 1983) is a 30-item measure used to screen for depressed mood. This measure has demonstrated good reliability and validity in older adults (Stiles & McGarrahan, 1998) as well as good sensitivity and specificity in nursing home patients (Jongenelis et al., 2005). Respondents answer yes or no to questions about mood over the last 2 weeks. Total scores range from 0 to 30, with higher scores indicating greater depressive symptoms. Scores ranging from 0 to 9 indicate no to minimal depressive symptoms, scores ranging from 10 to 19 indicate mild depressive symptoms, and scores ranging from 20 to 30 indicate moderate to severe depressive symptoms.

MacNeill-Lichtenberg Decision Tree (MLDT)

The MLDT (MacNeill & Lichtenberg, 2000) is a screening measure that assesses orientation (BTOT), verbal fluency (Animal Naming), mood (three items from the GDS), and psychosocial factors. For the purpose of the current study, only the neurocognitive items were used to screen for cognitive impairment. Scores >3 on the BTOT and <10 on Animal Naming are suggestive of cognitive impairment.

Pleasant Events Schedule for Alzheimer's Disease (PES-AD)

The PES-AD (Teri & Logsdon, 1991) is a 53-item questionnaire of pleasant event activities, ranging from quiet activities (e.g., watching TV) to mild physical activities (e.g., taking a walk). More items endorsed indicates a greater number of activities of interest to the resident. The PES-AD was administered by a staff member to the senior resident during the initial intervention session to stimulate ideas about potential activities for the treatment period.

Global Mood

This measure (Lewinsohn & Graf, 1973) consists of a single question about global mood status. Participants rate their mood from 1, "Worst I've ever felt," to 10, "Best I've ever felt." This measure was administered at the beginning of each treatment session.

Procedure

Participants were randomly assigned to either the immediate treatment ($n = 8$) or wait-list treatment condition ($n = 7$) using a cross-over design (see Table 1). Participants were enrolled at various time points during the 3-year study period. Data were collected by the project coordinator for all participants at baseline, 3 months, and 6 months. Data collection periods included a brief interview as well as neurocognitive (MLDT; MacNeill & Lichtenberg, 2000) and depression (GDS; Yesavage et al., 1983) screens. Participants enrolled in the immediate treatment condition received the intervention after baseline data collection in the first 3 months of the study design. Participants

Table 1. Cross-Over Study Design

	Baseline	3 months	6 months
Immediate Trt	X [Treatment]	X	X
Wait-List Trt	X	X [Treatment]	X

Note: X, data collection point.

enrolled in the wait-list treatment condition received the intervention between 3 and 6 months. Treatment consisted of pleasant event activities mutually agreed upon with residents and was delivered in 30-minute sessions with a target goal of 3 sessions per week (i.e., 36 total sessions). Written consent was obtained and documented for each resident.

Assisted living staff were trained by the project coordinator on treatment delivery as described in the treatment manual by Lichtenberg et al. (1998). In addition, prior to the start of each new intervention phase, training staff received booster training sessions, which included role-plays and education about the study.

RESULTS

Treatment participants (n = 15) were 83.27 (SD = 9.3) years old, had 13.73 (SD = 1.7) years of education, named 10.73 (SD = 4.8) words on Animal Naming, obtained a BTOT score of 0.40 (SD = 0.9), had an average GDS score of 12.0 (SD = 6.9), and indicated an average of 35.2 (SD = 4.0) pleasant event activities on the PES. The attrition sample (n = 10) reported significantly fewer years of education (M = 11.40, SD = 2.4), $F(1,24)$ = 8.23, p = .009, achieved greater BTOT scores (M = 10.8, SD = 15.1), $F(1,24)$ = 7.26, p = .013, named fewer items on Animal Naming (M = 7.30, SD = 4.4), $F(1,24)$ = 3.27, p = .08), and indicated fewer activities on the PES (M = 31.2, SD = 5.6), $F(1,24)$ = 4.4, p = .048, compared with the treatment sample.

Individuals in the immediate treatment condition (n = 8) were female (100%), 82.9 (SD = 10.9) years old, and reported 13.8 (SD = 2.1) years of education. Individuals in the wait-list condition (n = 7) were not statistically different in terms of age (M = 83.7, SD = 8.0), education (M = 13.7, SD = 1.4), or gender (71.4%). Pre-treatment GDS scores for both treatment groups were, on average, in the mildly depressed range. The wait-list group indicated more depressive symptoms (M = 15.4, SD = 6.1), however, compared with the immediate treatment group (M = 9.6, SD = 6.2), $F(1,14)$ = 3.36, p < .05, suggesting that the wait-list group had a greater level of depressed mood. Complete demographic characteristics by treatment group are presented in Table 2.

Treatment Implementation and Mood Ratings

A total of 367 out of a possible 540 treatment sessions were delivered during the intervention phase, resulting in a 68% implementation rate. The implementation rate was slightly greater in the immediate treatment group (73%) than the wait-list treatment group (63%). There was no statistical difference in the number of treatment sessions delivered to the immediate treatment group (M = 26.1, SD = 7.2) and the

Table 2. Treatment Sample Characteristics

Characteristic	Immediate (n = 8) % Mean (SD)	Wait-List (n = 7) % Mean (SD)
Age	82.9 (10.9)	83.7 (8.0)
Gender Female	100.0	71.4
Education	13.8 (2.1)	13.7 (1.4)
Pre GDS[a]	9.6 (6.2)	15.4 (6.1)*
Post GDS	8.9 (5.0)	12.7 (6.5)*
Initial Mood[b]	6.6 (1.7)	6.1 (1.9)
End Mood	8.4 (1.1)	7.7 (0.9)
Treatment Sessions	26.1 (7.2)	22.6 (11.8)

Note: [a]Geriatric Depression Scale, 30-item version. [b]Mood Rating, 1 (worst) to 10 (best) taken at beginning and end of sessions.

*p < .05.

wait-list group (M = 22.6, SD = 11.8). A total of 670 pleasant event activities over the 367 treatment sessions were recorded and coded throughout the intervention period. The pleasant event activities generally fell into three of the five following categories: Social (51%), Physical (28%), Quiet (15%), Reminiscing (0%), Pampering (0%).

For the immediate treatment group, average global mood ratings at the beginning of the session (M = 6.6, SD = 1.7) improved significantly (M = 8.4, SD = 1.1) by the end of treatment $t(7)$ = −.43, p = .004. For the wait-list treatment group, average global mood ratings also improved significantly from 6.1 (SD = 1.9) to 7.7 (SD = 0.9), $t(6)$ = −3.6, p = .012.

Depression Scores

Post-treatment GDS scores were significantly related to mood ratings at both the beginning [$r(15)$ = −.74, p = .002] and end [$r(15)$ = −.61, p = .015] of treatment sessions, demonstrating an intimate link between global subjective mood and depressed mood. In the entire treatment sample, there was a strong trend for pre-treatment GDS scores (M = 12.33, SD = 6.6) to decrease (M = 10.66 SD = 5.9) following the intervention $t(14)$ = 1.80, p = .093. Post-treatment GDS scores were not related to age, gender, education, BTOT score, or number of treatment sessions.

For the immediate treatment sample (n = 8), three individuals moved from the mildly depressed range to the minimally depressed range on the GDS following the treatment phase. An additional three individuals who were initially in the minimally depressed range remained in that range. Although the difference in average GDS scores between pre-treatment (M = 9.6) and 3 months (M = 8.85) was not statistically significant, this difference indicated that individuals remained in the minimally depressed range. Difference in GDS scores between 3 and 6 months was not statistically signifi-

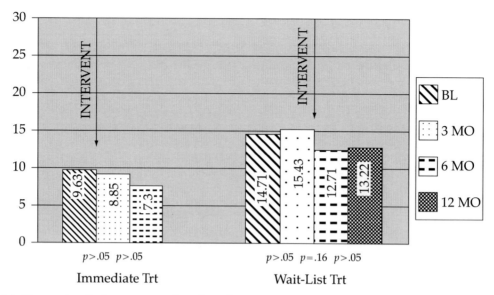

Figure 1. Geriatric Depression Scale scores as a function of treatment.

cant, although GDS scores continued to improve as evidenced by a decrease in GDS score at 6 months ($M = 7.30$, $SD = 4.9$), $t(7) = 1.9$, $p = .10$. Figure 1 shows the GDS scores as a function of treatment.

For the wait-list sample ($n = 7$), one individual moved from the mildly depressed to the minimally depressed range on the GDS following the treatment phase and one individual who was initially in the minimally depressed range on the GDS remained minimally depressed. As expected, during the wait-list period, there was no significant change in GDS score between baseline ($M = 14.7$, $SD = 7.1$) and 3 months ($M = 15.4$, $SD = 6.1$), $t(6) = -0.44$, $p = .67$. Although the difference in average GDS scores between pretreatment ($M = 15.4$, $SD = 6.1$) and 6 months ($M = 12.7$, $SD = 6.5$) was not statistically significant ($t[6] = 1.6$, $p = .16$) scores tended to decrease.

Taken together, there were 11 individuals above the cutoff score for mild depression. Of these, 37% (4/11) moved below the cutoff score following treatment. All of the 4 individuals who were below the GDS cutoff for mild depression remained below it following the intervention.

DISCUSSION

This pleasant events intervention delivered by assisted living staff to senior residents over a three-month treatment period resulted in a decrease in depressive symptoms as well as a significant increase in subjective global mood. Taken together, these findings demonstrate that a pleasant events intervention in an assisted living sample of older adults may result in improved affective functioning. In other words, increas-

ing pleasant events in older adults who live in this setting may be one way to improve or maintain healthy levels of affective functioning. The findings from this study are consistent with findings in other settings (Quijano et al., 2007; Sood, Cisek, Zimmerman, Zaleski, & Fillmore, 2003).

This intervention proved to be a practical way to engage assisted living residents. At the same time, the slightly greater implementation rate in the immediate treatment group (73%) versus the delayed treatment group (63%) may indicate greater difficulty in consistently applying behavioral intervention programs for more depressed individuals (individuals in the delayed treatment group had slightly higher depression scores). Nevertheless, individuals in both groups received on average between two and three sessions weekly, which approached the target goal of three weekly sessions. Future studies may examine the ways to improve implementation of behavioral interventions in assisted living.

There are several limitations to this pilot study. First, the study employed a limited sample size and results are considered only preliminary evidence of the effectiveness of behavioral treatment for seniors residing in assisted living. Second, the project coordinator was responsible for all data collection points and as such was not blind to participants' treatment group status. Third, the treatment sample was not exclusively depressed; no depression score was employed for participants to be included in the study. In fact, there were four individuals who were in the minimally depressed range (0 to 9) before treatment and who remained in that range following treatment. Although this could be considered a limitation of the study, it also may be considered a strength of the study. Maintenance of affective functioning among minimally depressed seniors residing in assisted living may assist in helping achieve a prophylaxis and less vulnerability for depressed mood. Despite the limitations of this study, this study appears to be one of the first to examine a pleasant events intervention in an exclusively assisted living setting. Future studies are needed to document more comprehensively the effectiveness of this intervention in this population.

ACKNOWLEDGEMENTS

We would like to acknowledge the generous help of Karen Voytas, LPN, Administrator, and Steve Popkin, LMSW, ACSW in coordinating this project. The staff who delivered this intervention (Shawjuan Austin, Sheila Ellis, Emma Kelly, Meredith Goldberg, Rosemary Hughes, and Hilary Rotenberg) made this research possible. This study was supported by a generous research grant from the Jewish Federation of Detroit.

REFERENCES

Cummings, S.M. & Cockerham, C. (2004). Depression and life satisfaction in assisted living residents: Impact of health and social support. *Clinical Gerontologist, 27,* 25–42.

Jongenelis, K., Pot, A.M., Eisses, A.M.H., Gerritsen, D.L., Derksen, M., Beekman, A.T.F., et al. (2005). Diagnostic accuracy of the original 30-item and shortened versions of the Geriatric Depression Scale in nursing home patients. *International Journal of Geriatric Psychiatry, 20,* 1067–1074.

Lewinsohn, P.M. & Graf, M. (1973). Pleasant activities and depression. *Journal of Consulting and Clinical Psychology, 41,* 261–268.

Lichtenberg, P.A., Kemp-Havican, J., MacNeill, S.E., & Schafer Johnson, A. (2005). Pilot study of behavioral treatment in dementia care units. *The Gerontologist, 45,* 406–410.

Lichtenberg, P.A., Kimbarow, M.L., Morris, P., & Vangel, S.J. (1996). Behavioral treatment of depression in predominantly African-American medical patients. *Clinical Gerontologist, 17,* 15–33.

Lichtenberg, P.A., Kimbarow, M.L., Wall, J.R., Roth, R.E., & MacNeill, S.E. (1998). *Depression in geriatric medical and nursing home patients: A treatment manual.* Detroit, MI: Wayne State University Press.

MacNeill, S.E., & Lichtenberg, P.A. (2000). The MacNeill Lichtenberg decision tree: A unique method of triaging mental health problems in older medical rehabilitation patients. *Archives of Physical and Medical Rehabilitation, 81,* 618–622.

Meeks, S. & Depp, C.A. (2002). Pleasant events-based behavioral intervention for depression in nursing home residents: A conceptual and empirical foundation. *Clinical Gerontologist, 25,* 125–148.

Quijano, L.M., Stanley, M.A., Petersen, N.J., Casado, B.L., Steinberg, E.H., Cully, J.A., et al. (2007). Healthy IDEAS: A depression intervention delivered by community-based case managers serving older adults. *Journal of Applied Gerontology, 26,* 139–156.

Sood, J.R., Cisek, E., Zimmerman, J., Zaleski, E.H., & Fillmore, H.H. (2003). Treatment of depressive symptoms during short-term rehabilitation: An attempted replication of the DOUR project. *Rehabilitation Psychology, 48,* 44–49.

Stiles, P.G., & McGarrahan, J.F. (1998). The Geriatric Depression Scale: A comprehensive review. *Journal of Clinical Geropsychology, 4,* 89–110.

Teri, L. & Logsdon, R.G. (1991). Identifying pleasant activities for Alzheimer's disease patients: The Pleasant Events Schedule-AD. *The Gerontologist, 31,* 124–127.

Teri, L., Logsdon, R.G., Uomoto, J., & McCurry, S.M. (1997). Behavioral treatment of depression in dementia patients: A controlled clinical trial. *Journals of Gerontology, 52B,* P159–P166.

Watson, L.C., Lehmann, S., Mayer, L., Samus, Q., Baker, A., Brandt, J., et al. (2006). Depression in assisted living is common and related to physical burden. *American Journal of Geriatric Psychiatry, 14,* 876–883.

Yesavage, J.A., Brink, T.L., Rose, T.L., Lum, O., Huang, V., Adey, M.B., et al. (1983). Development and validation of a geriatric depression screening scale: A preliminary report. *Journal of Psychiatric Research, 17,* 37–49.

1.12

INTERRUPTED TIME SERIES DESIGN (ONE-GROUP
REPEATED MEASURES)

Capturing the Cumulative Effects of School Reform: An 11-Year Study of the Impacts of America's Choice on Student Achievement

Henry May* and Jonathan A. Supovitz†

ABSTRACT: This article presents the results of an 11-year longitudinal study of the impact of America's Choice comprehensive school reform (CSR) design on student learning gains in Rochester, New York. A quasi-experimental interrupted time-series approach using Bayesian hierarchical growth curve analysis with crossed random effects is used to compare the annual gains in test performance of students attending America's Choice schools to those of students attending other Rochester schools and to those of students attending America's Choice schools before they adopted this CSR model. Findings reveal significant annual effects, which accumulate over time, in elementary and middle grades reading and mathematics.

KEYWORDS: Comprehensive school reform; growth curve analysis; student achievement; time series.

Education is a cumulative process. Children typically spend 13 years of their early lives, from the ages of 6 to 18, progressing through the American educational system. Over these years, a host of influences combine to affect each student's rate of learning. These include circumstances internal to the student—their developmental state, home life, and psychological circumstances, among others—and external factors such as

*HENRY MAY is a Research Assistant Professor, Graduate School of Education, University of Pennsylvania, and a Researcher and Statistician, Consortium for Policy Research in Education, 3440 Market Street, Suite 560, Philadelphia, PA 19104; hmay z@gse.upenn .edu. His areas of specialization are multilevel modeling, impact evaluation, and school reform.

†JONATHAN A. SUPOVITZ is an Associate Professor, Graduate School of Education, University of Pennsylvania, and a Senior Researcher, Consortium for Policy Research in Education, 3440 Market Street, Suite 560, Philadelphia, PA 19104; jons@gse. upenn.edu. His areas of specialization are program evaluation, instructional improvement, and educational policy and leadership.

schools, teachers, and educational programs. Yet evaluations of educational policies and programs rarely account for the additive nature of the learning process. Although most educational research is cross-sectional or involves no more than two years of data, we believe that the most powerful educational research involves longitudinal study of student progress over several years. Such research can investigate the sustained effects of interventions on students' developmental trajectories.

Numerous methodological arguments support longitudinal over cross-sectional analyses. On this issue, Rogosa (1982, p. 744) points out, "Two waves of data are better than one, but maybe not much better." This is especially true for program impact evaluations because two waves of data from an intervention group cannot control for the problem of natural maturation (Campbell & Stanley, 1963). If improvement is already happening before an intervention is implemented, then pre–post analyses may cause the researcher to attribute this improvement incorrectly to the intervention because the preintervention trend is unknown. Even when pre–post data are collected from both treatment and comparison groups, Bryk and Weisberg (1977) point out how analyses of pre–post data using various statistical models, including analysis of raw gains and analysis of covariance (ANCOVA), are highly susceptible to bias under most situations. Those authors conclude that explicit models of growth over multiple time points are the best way to estimate differences in growth (Bryk & Weisberg, 1977, p. 960). Since then, it has become widely accepted that the best way to estimate change accurately is to use several time points to model the trajectory of change (Raudenbush & Bryk, 2002; Rogosa, 1995; Singer & Willett, 2003).

The growth analysis approach is also attractive from a more practical perspective. Given that students in every school and classroom should be learning, the objective in an educational impact study is to determine whether an intervention caused an increase in students' rates of learning. A pre–post analysis is the simplest way to accomplish this without the use of randomization. Unfortunately, strong assumptions about the nature of achievement growth are required to choose a statistical model for the pre–post analysis. However, if data are available for three or more time points, the growth trajectory can be modeled explicitly, and assumptions about the nature of growth can be tested.

In this article we use growth models to estimate more accurately the longitudinal effects of a major educational reform initiative on student learning. Specifically, we present the results of a longitudinal study of the impact of the America's Choice comprehensive school reform (CSR) design on student learning gains in Rochester, New York. This study is noteworthy both for its findings of significant annual effects that accumulate over time and for the use of a modeling approach that allows us to reflect more precisely the reality of students' academic experiences over time. As the No Child Left Behind Act (NCLB) of 2002 spurs states toward annual testing, individual student-level data become increasingly available. Consequently, longitudinal methods can become powerful mechanisms to measure more appropriately the effects of complex educational interventions on the learning gains of students over multiple years.

PREVIOUS RESEARCH ON IMPACTS OF CSR

The CSR movement represents one of the most concerted efforts at broad-scale school improvement in American educational history. Following the theory that coherence among programs and policies is more effective than individual programmatic reforms (Smith & O'Day, 1991), CSR providers offer a comprehensive set of instructional expertise, school reorganization techniques, curriculum materials, and improvement strategies that are designed to build school capacity and improve student learning (Supovitz & Taylor, 2005). Federal funding for CSR is substantial, peaking at more than $300 million annually in 2004 (U.S. Department of Education, 2005). CSR models have been implemented in thousands of schools over the past decade (Datnow, Borman, Stringfield, Overman, & Castellano, 2003), serving millions of students (Borman, Hewes, Overman, & Brown, 2003).

CSR is also one of the most intensely studied reform movements. Thousands of evaluations of the effects of CSR models on student performance have taken place (see Herman et al., 1999 and Northwest Regional Educational Laboratory, 2005, for compendiums). Perhaps the most extensive and exhaustive examination of CSR impact evaluations was conducted by Borman, Hewes, Overman, and Brown (2003). These authors conducted a meta-analysis of CSR studies of 29 widely implemented models. Most of their data were collected by the beginning of 2001, and therefore few studies after that date were included in their analyses. Overall, they examined more than 800 studies and identified a subset of 232 that assessed models' effects on student test performance. They found that the "the overall effects of CSR are statistically significant, meaningful, and appear to be greater than the effects of other interventions that have been designed to serve similar purposes and students and school populations" (p. 164).

More to the point for our purpose were the data from the 232 studies upon which the meta-analysts based their conclusions. Only 28, or 12%, of the 232 studies that Borman et al. (2003) analyzed used three or more time points (G. Hewes, personal communication, June 30, 2005). An analysis of these 28 studies indicates that while the data presented contained more than two time points, they were often analyzed cross-sectionally.

The authors went beyond cross-sectional analyses in few of these studies, even if they had longitudinal data available. Several studies analyzed longitudinal achievement data sequentially, rather than cumulatively. For example, Madden, Slavin, Karweit, Dolan, & Wasik (1993) conducted separate multivariate analyses of covariance (MANCOVAs) for first, second, and third graders on a series of reading outcomes controlling for entering first-grade achievement. Thus, each of their models incorporated a different length of exposure to the treatment of interest, but analyses contained only two time points. Jones, Gottfredson, and Gottfredson (1997); MacIver and Kemper (2002); and Ross, Smith, and Casey (1997) adopted similar approaches in analyzing CSR program effects on elementary grade students.

Some studies used multiple data points descriptively rather than analytically. Meyer (1983) separately presented second- and third-grade test performance of students in a New York Direct Instruction school relative to a matched comparison school from the same neighborhood. She then traced students who received Direct Instruction in grades K–3 in a single New York school in the late 1960s, to high school a dozen years later to examine their relative dropout, graduation, and college-going rates. Ligas and Vaughan (1999) presented graphics of student performance trends for the same cohort of students over 4 years, but used ANCOVA to predict performance on the fourth time point controlling for the first time point.

Others adopted unorthodox approaches to handle multiple data points. For example, using a unique approach, Becker and Gersten (1982) conducted separate ANCOVAs for student performance data from five Direct Instruction cities and compared them to schools in the same city over a 2-year period. They then tallied the number of values that were significant ($p < .05$), "suggestive of a trend" ($.05 < p < .15$), and nonsignificant ($p > .15$), and conducted chi-square meta-analyses of differences between groups by year.

In a more recent study of the long-term effects of Success for All (SFA), Borman and Hewes (2002) analyze student achievement scores at the eighth grade to determine whether participation in SFA during elementary school leads to improved outcomes in later years. Although their cross-sectional analysis worked well for establishing sustained effects of SFA at eighth grade, the findings may have been even more powerful if the data had allowed an analysis of student learning gains over the years from first to eighth grade.

One true longitudinal approach, repeated measures multivariate analysis of variance (MANOVA), was used in two studies. Ligas (2002) used four data points and used MANOVA to examine program-by-year effects of Direct Instruction. Ross, Smith, and Casey (1997) used a similar approach that also included a covariate (MANCOVA) in their study of SFA. Still, these approaches treat time discretely and do not model explicitly the trajectory of growth in student achievement, as suggested by Bryk and Weisberg (1977) and Rogosa (1995).

One study that stands out as a true longitudinal design with an explicit model of achievement growth was an interrupted time series analysis conducted by Bloom, Ham, Melton, and O'Brien (2001). The authors examined 10 years of school-average third-grade performance data for eight schools that adopted the Accelerated Schools reform model. Each school had at least 5 years of baseline data before implementation of Accelerated Schools and 5 years of follow-up data. Using regression analysis of the baseline data, the authors predicted performance trajectories through the follow-up years and estimated the effect of the program as the difference between observed performance after adopting the reform and the predicted performance from the growth trajectory prior to adopting the reform.

Based on this work, Bloom (2001) also produced a methodological paper describing the benefits of longitudinal designs for producing better quasi-experimental estimates of the causal impacts of CSR models. He describes an interrupted time series analysis that compares the achievement score trajectories of students before and after the implementation of a CSR model. The proposed model incorporates fixed effects for the impacts each year the program is in place. The annual impact estimates show the degree to which achievement scores each year exceed, or fall below, the expected scores as projected by the preintervention trend in scores. Bloom also describes how multiple treatment and control schools could be included in the same analysis to produce a better picture of the counterfactual (i.e., what would happen in the absence of the intervention). The resultant model is able to address the issues of maturation, history, and selection bias (Bloom, 1999, p. 5; see also Campbell & Stanley, 1963).

In his concluding sections, Bloom (2001, p. 43) describes how his proposed model using fixed effects could be improved by including random effects for students and schools to allow estimation of separate achievement trajectories for each student within a sample of schools. This is the general approach we have taken in this research; however, we have also incorporated one additional enhancement, crossed random effects, to account for student mobility over time. The resulting analysis represents a strong quasi-experimental approach for producing an unbiased estimate of the causal impacts of a whole school intervention over several years.

ABOUT THE AMERICA'S CHOICE COMPREHENSIVE SCHOOL REFORM DESIGN

The America's Choice School Design is a K–12 comprehensive school reform model developed by the National Center on Education and the Economy (NCEE). America's Choice is a well-established school reform model that has been implemented in thousands of schools nationwide over the past decade. America's Choice focuses on raising academic achievement by providing a rigorous standards-based curriculum and safety nets for all students.

Two key elements support America's Choice's ambitious expectations for student learning. First are the New Standards Performance Standards, internationally benchmarked expectations for students performance including examples of student work that meet the standards. The second key element is a belief that all students can meet these standards.

The centerpiece of the America's Choice instructional program is an extended daily literacy block. In elementary schools, for example, students receive daily intensive reading instruction, writing instruction, and skills development for a total of 2 to 2-1/2 hours. The reading component concentrates on oral language development, vocabulary instruction, phonemic awareness, phonics, comprehension, and the development of fluency in reading. The daily session includes rituals and routines such as reading to children, shared or choral reading, and teacher-led instruction to small and large groups, as well as partner reading and independent reading with guidance and feedback.

The America's Choice approach to writing includes whole-class and small-group instruction and one-on-one conferencing to teach students about writing strategies and styles. Students have daily occasions to learn and practice the craft of writing, editing, and revision. They are given opportunities to write in various genres for a range of purposes closely connected to the classroom curriculum and their own interests. Skills development in the early grades provides systematic instruction in the essential components of literacy: phonemic awareness, phonics, and vocabulary. Assessment is ongoing, systematic, and provides information to teachers about what students can do at that point in time, both independently and with teacher support.

In mathematics, Rochester's America's Choice support was built upon the district's adoption of Harcourt Brace's *Math Advantage* textbook. Teachers were trained on the textbook by the district and expected to implement textbook lessons and use state and district standards to guide the topics and concepts they covered. In America's Choice schools, the district training was supplemented through the use of core assignments, Accountable Talk, and the America's Choice lesson structure. The America's Choice mathematics cluster leader regularly monitored implementation through meetings with school leadership teams, focus walks, and school visitations.

Teachers are trained via school-embedded, ongoing, teacher professional development, led by a full-time instructional coach, designed to strengthen teachers' knowledge of the America's Choice approach to teaching and learning. This includes learning how to conduct a close analysis of their students' work in relation to standards, and using this knowledge to develop lessons calibrated to the needs of different students.

A school leadership team coordinates time, resources, and other organizational implementation issues through a variety of means. These include setting performance targets, adjusting school schedules, and setting up and monitoring safety net programs designed to provide students with extensive support and multiple opportunities to achieve the standards. Many of these elements of the America's Choice design are generally associated with characteristics of effective schools (Purkey & Smith, 1983; Reynolds & Teddlie, 2000).

Several previous Consortium for Policy Research in Education (CPRE) studies have documented both the implementation and impacts of America's Choice on students, teachers, and schools. In a comparison of 159 America's Choice schools in Georgia to a matched comparison group of demographically similar schools, CPRE researchers found significantly greater gains in the 2002 fifth- and eighth-grade writing performance of America's Choice schools when compared with other Georgia schools, after adjusting for differences in prior school performance and a variety of school-level demographic characteristics (May, Supovitz, & Lesnick, 2004). A study of student test performance from 1999 to 2001 in Duval County, Florida, found effects on student writing performance associated with America's Choice, but few effects in mathematics, and no effects in reading (Supovitz, Taylor, & May, 2002). Supovitz and May (2004) examined the relationship between teacher implementation of the America's Choice literacy design in Plainfield, New Jersey, in the 2001–2002 school year, as measured by survey responses, and linked those data to the reading and writing test performance of students taught by those teachers. They found statistically significant positive relationships between teacher implementation of America's Choice and gains in student test performance.

THE CONTEXT OF ROCHESTER, NEW YORK

Rochester—located in the northwestern part of New York on Lake Ontario, about one hour from the Canadian border—is a midsized urban district. The home of once corporate giants Kodak, Xerox, and Bausch and Lomb, Rochester has long been a thriving metropolis. The Rochester City School District currently educates just over 35,000 students from pre-K to grade 12. In stark contrast to surrounding wealthy and suburban Monroe County, the city has become increasingly poor and minority. Over the past 25 years, the schools increasingly have educated high numbers of poor and minority students. From 1980 to 2004, the percentage of students in the district with free or reduced-price lunch increased from 22% to 81%. Minority population in the city increased from 69% in 1990 to 85% in 2004. Rochester ranks 11th nationally in per-capita child poverty, ahead of large urban districts such as New York City, Washington, D.C., Chicago, and Los Angeles. Rochester schools are projected to face enrollment declines of 30% by the end of the decade.

The district has a long history of educational innovation and partnerships. The Rochester teachers' union has long been considered one of the most innovative in the nation, pioneering such efforts as teacher mentor programs and initiatives to professionalize the teaching staff. The district has one of the most highly acclaimed pre-K systems in the nation and several professional development initiatives with local colleges and universities. Rochester also has a long record of experimenting with school reform models.

Manuel Rivera, the current superintendent, is the only person to have held the superintendency twice.

He was Rochester superintendent from 1992 to 1994, before becoming a vice president for Edison Schools. Rivera returned to the district in 2002. His second tenure has focused on reducing and aligning the array of reforms in the district, developing and aligning accountability systems with these initiatives, and navigating the district through declining funding and enrollment.

America's Choice took root in Rochester between Rivera's two tenures. The program was introduced to Rochester in fall 1998, when six elementary schools began to implement the design. In fall 2000, one middle school adopted America's Choice. An additional five elementary schools and four middle schools began implementing America's Choice in fall 2001. About one-third of the elementary and middle schools in Rochester had experience with America's Choice by the 2002–2003 school year.

Table 1 shows the demographics of the district for the years before and after the implementation of America's Choice. The America's Choice students represent a more disadvantaged student group when compared to their peers not receiving America's Choice. America's Choice students were more likely to receive free or reduced-priced lunch and were somewhat more likely to receive special education services or be classified as limited English proficient (LEP) students. Schools using America's Choice also enrolled a greater proportion of minority students. Almost 90% of America's Choice students were either African American or Hispanic, compared with 78.5% of students not receiving America's Choice. America's Choice schools were also slightly larger than comparison schools, with an average of 506 students versus 438 students.

Table 1. Demographic Characteristics of Students (Grades 1–8) in Rochester City School District by America's Choice Participation Status

Student Characteristic	1993–1998 all Students (%)	1998–2003	
		America's Choice Students (%)	Other Rochester Students (%)
Female	49.9	49.8	49.4
Male	50.1	50.2	50.6
African American	59.5	71.7	58.9
Hispanic	17.5	17.8	19.6
White	21.1	8.9	19.1
Other	2.6	1.6	2.4
Special education	13.7	16.6	15.3
Limited english proficient	6.6	8.8	8.6
Receiving free/ reduced-price lunch	87.4	95.2	89.2

RESEARCH QUESTIONS

This research was guided by three central questions. These questions were derived directly from the primary goal of the America's Choice model—the goal that all students meet or exceed the same high standards in reading and mathematics. In working to meet this goal, the America's Choice teacher is expected to use ongoing assessment to evaluate individual student progress, and to provide extra assistance and resources to students in need. One can imagine how this increased support could lead to substantial gains for lower-performing students. An important question is whether an America's Choice teacher is able to provide this extra support to students in greater need, while also providing enough support to more advanced students to maintain their previous rates of learning. In line with this notion, our three major research questions in evaluating the impacts of America's Choice are:

1. Is there evidence that America's Choice increases students' rates of learning and, if so, how big is the increase?
2. Does America's Choice improve the performance of particularly low-achieving students? If so, is this accomplished at the expense of higher-performing students?
3. Does America's Choice make education more equitable for minority students? If so, is this accomplished at the expense of nonminority students?

METHODS

Sample

We analyzed 11 years of student performance data from Rochester, New York: 6 years of data before schools' adoption of America's Choice in 1998, and up to 5 years after (depending on the year a school introduced the reform). The data include all student test scores from the 1992–1993 school year to the 2002–2003 school year. During this period, more than 55,000 students in Grades 1 through 8, in 42 elementary and 10 middle schools, were tested in reading and mathematics.[1] Because Rochester tested nearly every student in every grade, these data constitute a near census of the population of students enrolled in Rochester elementary and middle schools from 1993 to 2003. Figure 1 shows the cohorts of students included in these analyses and dates of implementation of America's Choice in Rochester.

Additional demographic data were collected for each student, including age, race or ethnicity, poverty status, special education status, and LEP status.

---

[1]The sample size of 55,000 students is much larger than the size of the district (i.e., 35,000) because the sample in this study includes multiple cohorts of students.

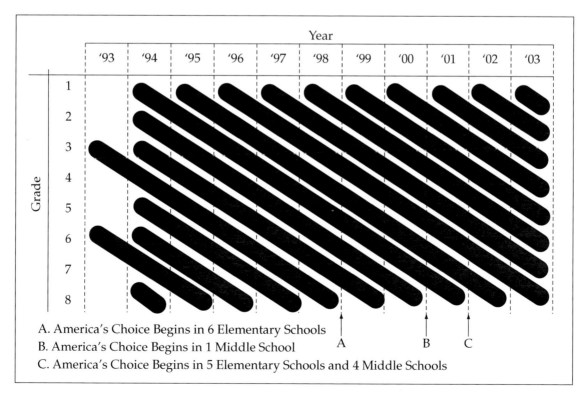

A. America's Choice Begins in 6 Elementary Schools
B. America's Choice Begins in 1 Middle School
C. America's Choice Begins in 5 Elementary Schools and 4 Middle Schools

Figure 1. Cohorts of students and America's Choice implementation.

Inclusion of these demographic variables in statistical models allowed us to control for differences in students' backgrounds.

The demographic and annual test score data for each student were linked across years, so that achievement scores could be tracked over time for each student. This enabled us to estimate the amount of learning (i.e., as represented by increases in test scores) that occurred for each student during each year. However, as a result of student mobility in and out of the district and matriculation beyond eighth grade, most students had less than 8 years of data. Figure 2 shows the number of students and test score points available. The final sample included 56,693 students in reading and 55,932 students in mathematics, with approximately 50% of the students having 4 or more years of data, and with more than 6,000 students having 7 or 8 years of data.[2] No single student had data for all 11 years of this study.

Participation in America's Choice was concentrated in the elementary grades from 1998 to 2000–2001, with approximately 2,500 students per year in Grades 1 through 5. By the 2001–2002 school year, the program had expanded to almost 4,300 elementary students and had added more than 3,400 students in Grades 6 through 8. Across all cohorts and grades, 12,306 students attended an America's Choice school during the period 1998 to 2003. The average length of time a student attended an America's Choice school was 2 years, with 1,175 students attending for 3 years, 783 students attending for 4 years, and 420 students attending for 5 years.

Measures

Rochester used multiple achievement tests during the 11-year span covered by this study. These included the Stanford Achievement Test (SAT-9), the California Achievement Test (CAT-5), the Degrees of Reading Power test (DRP), the New York State assessments (NYS), the New York Pupil Evaluation Program tests (PEP), and the New York Preliminary Competency Test (PCT). The SAT-9, CAT, and DRP are nationally normed standardized tests. The NYS, PEP, and PCT are New York state assessments. In Rochester, the SAT-9 was the most widely used test in recent years, used in Grades 1 through 3 and Grades 5 through 7 from the 1999–2000 school year to the present.

To track changes in individual student performance over time, the achievement scores from the different tests were rescaled to the same metric on a vertical scale.[3] Because the majority of test scores from the 1999–2000 school year onward were from districtwide

---

[2]The sample size is slightly lower for mathematics because the NYS Grade 4 and Grade 8 mathematics scores for 2003 were not yet available at the time of this analysis.

[3]Vertical scaling simply means that the test scores at each grade level are on the same metric, and that scores from one year to the next can be subtracted to create an estimate of growth. Vertical scaling allows growth in student performance to be charted across grades in a manner similar to that shown in Figure 2. This is not possible if the average score is the same for each grade (e.g., average fourth-grade score = 500, average fourth-grade score = 500). If scores are not vertically scaled, then a student who learns at an average rate will have the same score from one year to the next, and subtracting the two scores produces a gain of zero (which says nothing about actual learning). It is possible to conduct longitudinal analyses using test data that are not vertically scaled, but the resultant effects are expressed relative to the overall variance in student achievement at a single point in time. Having vertically scaled test data allows the researcher first to calculate the baseline rate of growth, against which the program effects are compared. Therefore, while vertically scaled test data are not imperative for longitudinal analyses, vertical scaling helps greatly to improve the interpretation of effect sizes. Because assessments at different grade levels typically emphasize different knowledge and skills, vertical scaling is often considered a form of calibration (Mislevy, 1992; Linn, 1993), which implies limitations for this analysis as described in the discussion section of this article.

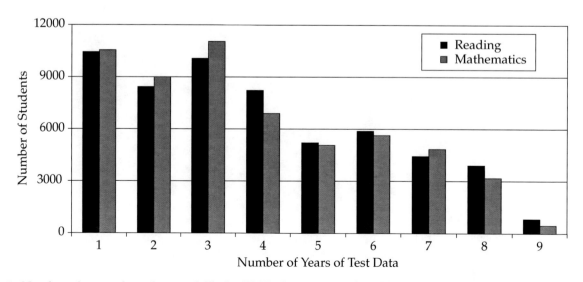

Figure 2. Number of years of test data available for RSCD elementary and middle grades students.

administrations of the SAT-9 and already vertically scaled, the other tests were rescaled to the metric of the SAT-9 so that growth in student performance could be charted over time.[4] Traditional equating methods were not possible in this context because tests were not administered simultaneously and there were no common items across the tests used in Rochester. Instead, the test scores were linked using a linear rescaling within each grade based on the mean and standard deviation of the scores on the SAT-9 for each grade level during the 2002–2003 school year. This type of linking is in the category of calibration defined by Linn (1993). This process imposes the assumption that test scores are distributed similarly over time and across tests, and that the only difference between the tests is the scale of the scores (e.g., a 100-point scale versus a 500-point scale). In other words, it is assumed that a student would show similar performance relative to other students in the district, regardless of which test was used to measure performance. Although these assumptions will never be met perfectly, the key question is whether the linking of these five assessments to the SAT-9 is adequate to support a growth curve analysis that will produce unbiased estimates of the effects of America's Choice.

Linking different educational assessments is not a new subject. In 1997, Congress commissioned the National Academy of Sciences (NAS) to conduct a feasibility study to determine if scores from commercially developed tests could be linked to the National Assessment of Educational Progress (NAEP) and to each other. Whereas the committee found this was not universally feasible, members concluded the following:

> Under limited conditions it may be possible to calculate a linkage between two tests, but multiple factors affect the validity of inferences drawn from the linked scores. These factors include the content, format, and margins of error of the tests; the intended and actual uses of the tests; and the consequences attached to the results of the tests. When tests differ on any of these factors, some limited interpretations of the linked results may be defensible while others would not (Feuer, Holland, Green, Bertenthal, & Hemphill, 1999, p. 5).

All the assessments used in this analysis were similar in content, format, reliability, use, and consequences.

Previous research cited in the NAS report provides empirical evidence that meaningful links can be made between assessments that measure the same constructs (e.g., reading comprehension) with similar types of items (e.g., multiple choice) (Loret, Seder, Bianchini, & Vale, 1972). Fortunately, the multiple tests used in Rochester are similar in this regard. The vast majority of math test scores are from administrations of the SAT-9, the CAT-5, and the NYS Math test. The SAT-9 is a nationally normed test developed by Harcourt Educational Measurement. Both the CAT-5

and the NYS Math tests are developed by CTB/McGraw-Hill. All three of these tests and the PEP have roughly similar distributions of items focusing on mathematical procedures and computation and on concepts and problem solving. All four tests use multiple choice items exclusively.

The vast majority of reading test scores are from administrations of the SAT-9, the DRP, and the NYS English Language Arts test. The DRP is a nationally normed test of reading comprehension developed by Touchstone Applied Science Associates. The SAT-9, the NYS-ELA, and the PEP include items that cover reading comprehension and vocabulary. All the reading tests use multiple choice exclusively.

With these issues and details in mind, we linked the multiple tests while also conducting multiple validity checks to determine whether the linkages were accurate. The process by which different tests were linked across years and grades was as follows. First, the distribution of test scores was examined for each test by year and grade to verify approximate normality (i.e., bell-shaped curve). Next, the means and standard deviations of SAT-9 scores were calculated for each grade and year from 2000 to 2003. These means and standard deviations were nearly identical across years for a given grade, so only the means and standard deviations for 2003 were used from this point forward. It is important to note that linking was done separately for reading and mathematics scores. In other words, reading scores were not used to predict mathematics scores, or vice versa.

The SAT-9 was administered in May of each year to students in first, second, third, fifth, sixth, and seventh grades. Therefore, expected scores for tests administered at other times during the year and in Grades 4 and 8 had to be interpolated based upon the growth curve for observed mean SAT-9 scores. This was accomplished using piecewise linear regression models of district mean reading and mathematics scores over time. The fit of these models to the data was quite good, with all but one explaining more than 99% of the variance in district mean achievement scores over time.

The last step in the equating process was to rescale the scores for each cohort of students within each subject and grade so that the mean and standard deviation of scores for each year and within a particular grade equaled the mean and standard deviation of the observed SAT-9 scores for that grade in 2003. The resultant scores were plotted again for each year and

---

[4]The New York State assessments were scaled with equal mean scores at each grade level. Therefore, average growth using this metric would be represented by a gain of 0 points. Use of the SAT-9 metric allows comparison of program effects to typical rates of annual growth in test scores.

grade to verify consistency in the distribution and to identify unreasonable score values or outliers. No outliers or other abnormalities were found.

Because the district mean of the rescaled scores for any given grade did not vary across time, any districtwide acceleration or deceleration of achievement growth was removed from the data. However, as noted above, there was no evidence of any districtwide changes in annual growth, given that the observed SAT-9 district means for any one grade were nearly identical from 1999 to 2003. For example, the district average SAT-9 score for third grade was 601 for 4 years straight. Similarly, the district average SAT-9 score for fifth grade was 640 for 4 years straight. This suggests that the performance of third graders in Rochester in 2000, on average, was nearly identical to that of third graders in Rochester in any other year, and that the same is true for fifth graders (i.e., the cohorts are interchangeable). Similar stability was found for scores on the other nationally normed tests (i.e., CAT-5, DRP) during the period 1993 to 1998. Therefore, it is unlikely that the results of these analyses would be different if districtwide changes in growth rates were included in these analyses.

To evaluate further the plausibility of the equating assumptions using empirical methods, we estimated correlations between students' scores as they progressed through the grades and compared the correlations from the years in which the tests changed to correlations from the following year. For example, if the correlation between a cohort of second graders' reading scores in 1999 (i.e., DRP scores) and their scores as third graders in 2000 (i.e., SAT-9 scores) was similar to the correlation between the next cohort of second graders' reading scores in 2000 (i.e., SAT-9 scores) and their scores as third graders in 2001 (i.e., SAT-9 scores), then there is evidence to suggest that the two tests have a similar linear relationship and that the DRP from 1999 can be substituted as a similar pretest measure when SAT-9 scores are unavailable. The results of our analyses of grade-to-grade correlations suggest remarkable consistency among the six tests in both reading and mathematics. Table 2 shows correlations between test scores from 1999 to 2001. The analysis is restricted to these years because this was the major transition period in which previously used tests were replaced with the SAT-9.

In Table 2 the correlations for adjacent cohorts taking different combinations of tests are similar (i.e., there is little difference within each column and subject). In addition, the lower-grade to upper-grade correlations increase as grade level increases (i.e., the correlations increase from left to right within each row). This suggests that the tests share similar pretest–posttest relationships, and the differences between pretest and posttest are smaller in later grades.

Visual inspection of the distribution of scores on the six tests for each grade and year in this study also support the equating assumptions. For example, the shapes of the distributions of scores for all grades on all relevant tests in all years were similar and approximately normal. Figure 3 shows box plots of the

Table 2. Grade-to-Grade Correlations for 1999–2000 and 2000–2001 Reading and Mathematics Tests

Test	Grade Levels						
	1→2	2→3	3→4	4→5	5→6	6→7	7→8
Reading							
1999 lower-grade test	CAT-5	DRP	PEP	NYS	DRP	PEP	DRP
2000 upper-grade test	SAT-9	SAT-9	NYS	SAT-9	SAT-9	SAT-9	NYS
2000 lower-grade test	SAT-9	SAT-9	SAT-9	NYS	SAT-9	SAT-9	SAT-9
2001 upper-grade test	SAT-9	SAT-9	NYS	SAT-9	SAT-9	SAT-9	NYS
1999–2000 lower-grade → upper-grade correlation	0.61	0.69	0.70	0.75	0.76	0.75	0.71
2000–2001 lower-grade → upper-grade correlation	0.69	0.69	0.71	0.73	0.79	0.83	0.75
Mathematics							
1999 lower-grade test	n/a	CAT-5	PEP	NYS	CAT-5	PEP	CAT-5
2000 upper-grade test	SAT-9	SAT-9	NYS	SAT-9	SAT-9	SAT-9	NYS
2000 lower-grade test	SAT-9	SAT-9	SAT-9	NYS	SAT-9	SAT-9	SAT-9
2001 upper-grade test	SAT-9	SAT-9	NYS	SAT-9	SAT-9	SAT-9	NYS
1999–2000 lower-grade → upper-grade correlation	n/a	0.60	0.73	0.77	0.72	0.73	0.73
2000–2001 lower-grade → upper-grade correlation	0.65	0.65	0.71	0.76	0.78	0.81	0.75

Note: Lower and upper grade refer to the two grades listed at the top of each column.
n/a = not available (no test given).

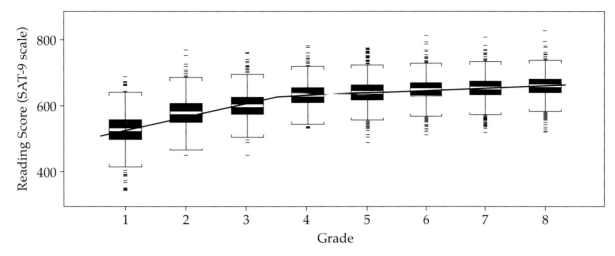

Figure 3. Boxplots of rescaled reading achievement scores.

rescaled reading achievement scores by grade. This plot shows consistent variance from grade to grade; however, the rate of growth is much steeper from first to third grade compared with the rate of growth from fourth to eighth grade. A similar difference in the growth rates from first to third grade and fourth to eighth grade is present in the national norms for the SAT-9 in both reading and mathematics (Harcourt, 1997, Table 72). This may be due to actual differences in rates of learning or may be an artifact of the scaling methodology for the SAT-9. As described below, separate growth trajectories are fit for these two grade spans.

Statistical Models

Building on the work of Bloom (1999, 2001) on interrupted time series, and extending it to incorporate Bayesian hierarchical growth curve analysis with crossed random effects, we compared the longitudinal gains in test performance of students attending America's Choice schools with those of students attending other Rochester schools and with students in the America's Choice schools before they adopted this CSR model. This technique enabled us to model the annual growth in individual students' reading and mathematics performance, while adjusting for differences in students' demographic characteristics. This method also allowed us to determine the extent to which differences in students' performance and growth were due to particular individual factors (e.g., minority status) and school-level factors (e.g., participation in America's Choice). Although America's Choice did not start in Rochester schools until 1998, having data from 1993 permitted us to examine differences in the rates of growth of students from before America's Choice began in Rochester until deep into and after the program's implementation.

The time series models for these analyses were three-level hierarchical growth curve models (Raudenbush & Bryk, 2002) using crossed random effects and Bayesian estimation. SAT-9 reading or mathematics scores were the dependent variables, with test scores nested within students, and students nested within schools. Separate models were fit for the early-elementary grades (first through third grades) and the upper-elementary and middle grades (fourth through eighth grades) to reflect the change in growth trajectories from the early-elementary grades to later grades.[5] This was done to improve the fit of the model, given that increases in SAT-9 scores were rapid during Grades 1 through 3, then slowed after third grade. This two-stage trend can be seen in Figure 2; growth is linear in Grades 1 through 3 and continues at a slower linear pace in Grades 4 through 8. This piecewise approach using two linear growth models was selected instead of a curvilinear growth model to maintain simple interpretation of the growth parameters. For example, it is simpler to interpret the linear growth estimate of points gained per year, while it is not simple to interpret the quadratic growth estimate of points per year-squared.

Student age, centered around 9 years, was used to represent time. Student gender, minority status, free or reduced-price lunch eligibility, LEP status, and special education status were included as control variables

---

[5]We attempted to estimate growth models for both time periods using a single piecewise growth model (Raudenbush & Bryk, 2002, p. 178), but high collinearity between the two slope components for the two time periods created massive inflations in the standard errors for the growth curve estimates. Therefore, we chose to estimate separate models for the two time periods to maintain adequate precision of students' score trajectories. The downside of this approach is that the individual growth trajectories are restricted to three data points for the early grades model and five data points for the upper grades model.

predicting student status at age nine, and the slope of the growth curve. All control variables, including dummy variables, were centered around the grand mean for America's Choice students to enable interpretation of the intercepts as representing the growth curve for a student with demographic characteristics similar to the average America's Choice student. To estimate the impact of America's Choice, one of two measures of exposure to the design was added to the model. The first was a time-varying covariate indicating the number of years a student had been in an America's Choice school. The estimate for this variable shows the change in growth of SAT-9 scores for each year in an America's Choice school (i.e., the impact of the program on learning rates while attending an America's Choice school). The second measure was a set of five dummy variables indicating whether each student had been in an America's Choice school during each of the 5 years of implementation. The estimates for this second set of variables show the year-by-year impact of the America's Choice program.

It is important to note that the first method of analysis produces a time-averaged estimate of the effect of America's Choice on student achievement growth. In other words, a linear model including the number of years each student has attended an America's Choice school is unable to detect differences in the effect of the program during the early stages of implementation compared to later stages. The estimate of annual impact on student performance is the same regardless of the number of years the school has been implementing the design. The time-averaged effect is also representative of the effect of America's Choice on those students while they attended an America's Choice school. In other words, the time-averaged effect is an estimate of the effect of the "treatment on the treated."

Unfortunately, the production of year-by-year estimates of effect is complicated by the high mobility of students in the Rochester district.[6] More specifically, effects after the first year of implementation may be mitigated by the fact that many students are being exposed to the program for the first time. Still, a year-by-year estimate of the treatment effect is important because it provides information about the effect of America's Choice in the presence of high student mobility. These estimates show the impact of America's Choice each year of implementation regardless of whether the students attending America's Choice schools continued in those schools in future years or were enrolled in the America's Choice school for only part of the time the program was implemented. In contrast to the time-averaged impact estimate, the year-by-year estimates of the impact of America's Choice are "intent-to-treat" estimates; that is, they are estimates of the impact uncorrected for partial participation by students.

An added benefit of estimating the intent-to-treat impact estimates is that we can compare these year-by-year estimates to the time-averaged estimates to assess the assumption of consistent effects across cohorts and implementation years. Additional analyses used to check the fit of the statistical models (e.g., residual analysis) can also help to determine whether changes in achievement are unusually large or small for any given year.

Although both the intent-to-treat and the time-averaged models include time-varying measures of student exposure to the America's Choice program (i.e., the variables are measured at the lowest level in this hierarchy, the year), the use of random effects for students and schools adjusts these estimates and their standard errors for nesting in these data. Stated another way, these time-varying measures produce estimates of the program impact on each student, and the multilevel structure of the statistical model combines these individual estimates across students, schools, and cohorts into an overall treatment effect, much like a meta-analysis.

Because many students switched schools during the study, the data did not have a pure nested structure; that is, not all the observations for a single student were nested within the same school. Therefore, traditional hierarchical linear modeling methods could not be used. This is because the assumption of nesting, when applied to longitudinal data, presumes that students do not switch classrooms or schools at any time during the study. When mobility does occur, a traditional hierarchical growth curve model would break students' growth curves into independent pieces, one for each school attended. This can result in serious bias of coefficient estimates (Browne, 2002; May, 2004).

Fortunately, the use of crossed random effects (Rasbash & Goldstein, 1994; Raudenbush, 1993) combined with Bayesian estimation techniques (see Browne, 2002, p. 165) made possible analyses of data with complex nesting structures. Crossed random effects are similar to the random effects used to distinguish levels in a traditional hierarchical linear models analysis, except that crossed random effects do not necessarily imply a neatly nested structure to the data (e.g., students can be nested in more than one school across time). This approach results in a model that pro-

---

[6]Explicitly modeling mobility effects using growth curves is a significant challenge from a statistical standpoint (see Dunn, Kadane, & Garrow, 2003). Our attempts to model mobility explicitly resulted in poor convergence of the models. Thus, we chose not to include explicit mobility effects in our models. This decision may bias the estimated effects of America's Choice toward zero, due to the negative effect of mobility occurring simultaneously with the positive effect of America's Choice for any student moving into an America's Choice school.

duces a single growth trajectory for each student and correctly attributes annual gains along each student's growth curve to the school attended at each point in time. Without this approach, it would be impossible to measure the change in the rate of learning that occurs when a student switches schools. Failure to use crossed random effects in this analysis would translate to an underestimation of program effects if students moving into America's Choice schools had slower rates of learning while attending a previous school. This is because without crossed random effects, it would be impossible to link a student's trajectory of prior performance to his or her trajectory of performance after enrolling in an America's Choice school.

Within-district mobility was a fairly common occurrence in Rochester. Of the nearly 6,100 students who attended an America's Choice school in first through third grades from the 1998–1999 to the 2002–2003 school year, approximately 700 students (12%) moved to a non-America's Choice elementary school within the district. Of the nearly 9,000 students attending America's Choice schools in fourth through eighth grades during the years of this study, approximately 1,200 students (13%) moved to a non-America's Choice school before finishing elementary school, and approximately 1,300 students (14%) naturally matriculated from an America's Choice elementary school to a non-America's Choice middle school.

Using the notation of Browne, Goldstein, and Rasbash (2001) for cross-classified models, the mathematical form of the model estimating the time-averaged impact of attending an America's Choice school was[7]:

$$
\begin{aligned}
y_1 = {} & \beta_0 + \beta_1 \text{MALE} + \beta_2 \text{MINORITY} + \beta_3 \text{SPCED} \\
& + \beta_4 \text{LEP} + \beta_5 \text{FRL} + \beta_6 \text{AGE}' \\
& + \beta_7 (\text{AGE}' \times \text{MALE}) \\
& + \beta_8 (\text{AGE}' \times \text{MINORITY}) \\
& + \beta_9 (\text{AGE}' \times \text{SPCED}) + \beta_{10} (\text{AGE}' \times \text{LEP}) \\
& + \beta_{11} (\text{AGE}' \times \text{FRL}) + \beta_{12} (\text{YEARS IN AC}) \\
& + \left(\text{AGE}' \times u^{(3)}_{1,\text{School}(t)} \right) + \left(\text{AGE}' \times u^{(2)}_{1,\text{Student}(t)} \right) \\
& + u^{(3)}_{0,\text{School}(t)} + u^{(2)}_{0,\text{Student}(t)} + e_t
\end{aligned}
$$

$$
\begin{bmatrix} u^{(3)}_{1,\text{School}(t)} \\ u^{(3)}_{0,\text{School}(t)} \end{bmatrix} N\left(0, \Omega^{(3)}_u\right) : \Omega^{(3)}_u = \begin{bmatrix} \Omega^{(3)}_{u0,0} \\ \Omega^{(3)}_{u0,1} & \Omega^{(3)}_{u1,1} \end{bmatrix}
$$

$$
\begin{bmatrix} u^{(2)}_{1,\text{Student}(t)} \\ u^{(2)}_{0,\text{Student}(t)} \end{bmatrix} N\left(0, \Omega^{(2)}_u\right) : \Omega^{(2)}_u = \begin{bmatrix} \Omega^{(2)}_{u0,0} \\ \Omega^{(2)}_{u0,1} & \Omega^{(2)}_{u1,1} \end{bmatrix}
$$

$$
[e_1] \, N(0, \Omega_e)
$$

The mathematical form of the model estimating the year-by-year impact of America's Choice was:

$$
\begin{aligned}
y_1 = {} & \beta_0 + \beta_1 \text{MALE} + \beta_2 \text{MINORITY} + \beta_3 \text{SPCED} \\
& + \beta_4 \text{LEP} + \beta_5 \text{FRL} + \beta_6 \text{AGE}' \\
& + \beta_7 (\text{AGE}' \times \text{MALE}) \\
& + \beta_8 (\text{AGE}' \times \text{MINORITY}) \\
& + \beta_9 (\text{AGE}' \times \text{SPCED}) + \beta_{10} (\text{AGE}' \times \text{LEP}) \\
& + \beta_{11} (\text{AGE}' \times \text{FRL}) \\
& + \sum_{year=1}^{5} \beta_{(11+year)} \text{IN AC}_{year\,t} \\
& + \left(\text{AGE}' \times u^{(3)}_{1,\text{School}(t)} \right) + \left(\text{AGE}' \times u^{(2)}_{1,\text{Student}(t)} \right) \\
& + u^{(3)}_{0,\text{School}(t)} + u^{(2)}_{0,\text{Student}(t)} + e_t
\end{aligned}
$$

$$
\begin{bmatrix} u^{(3)}_{1,\text{School}(t)} \\ u^{(3)}_{0,\text{School}(t)} \end{bmatrix} N\left(0, \Omega^{(3)}_u\right) : \Omega^{(3)}_u = \begin{bmatrix} \Omega^{(3)}_{u0,0} \\ \Omega^{(3)}_{u0,1} & \Omega^{(3)}_{u1,1} \end{bmatrix}
$$

$$
\begin{bmatrix} u^{(2)}_{1\,\text{Student}(t)} \\ u^{(2)}_{0,\text{Student}(t)} \end{bmatrix} N\left(0, \Omega^{(2)}_u\right) : \Omega^{(2)}_u = \begin{bmatrix} \Omega^{(2)}_{u0,0} \\ \Omega^{(2)}_{u0,1} & \Omega^{(2)}_{u1,1} \end{bmatrix}
$$

$$
[e_1] \, N(0, \Omega_e)
$$

As mentioned previously, the age variable is centered around nine years of age, and all control variables are centered around the grand mean for America's Choice schools. Therefore, β_0 shows the expected achievement score for a 9-year-old from a comparison school who has characteristics similar to the average America's Choice student. This is referred to as baseline in the tables of results. The estimate for β_6 shows the expected annual gain in achievement score for a student from a comparison school who has characteristics similar to the average America's Choice student. This is referred to as annual change in the tables of results. The estimates for β_{12-16} show the additional gain in achievement score for an America's Choice student. This is referred to as additional annual growth while in America's Choice or as the year-by-year effect of America's Choice in the tables of results.

The Bayesian estimation technique used here is a simulation-based method called Markov Chain Monte Carlo using Gibbs Sampling (Geman & Geman, 1984). The model was estimated via MLwiN 2.0 (Browne, 2002; Rasbash, Browne, Healy, Cameron, & Charlton, 2003). Due to the complexity of the models, a long burn-in period of 10,000 iterations preceded a chain of 50,000 iterations in which plausible values were drawn from the posterior distributions of parameters at every fifth iteration, yielding 10,000 plausible values for each parameter. Point estimates and standard errors are calculated as the mean and standard deviation, respectively, of the plausible values from each posterior distribution.

---

[7]The structure of the error term implies the random effects are assumed to be independent across schools and not involved in an interaction with other random effects. This indicates that a school's effect on a student is independent of other school's effects on that student and on other students.

In accordance with our research questions, we conducted a staged analysis. The first stage focused on overall effects on achievement growth, and is separated into effects on individual student growth and year-by-year effects of the program. These analyses include all students in the sample. The second stage explores the effects of the program on the achievement growth of students with different initial performance levels (i.e., the data are reanalyzed by initial performance quartile). Finally, the third stage involves the estimation of different effects for students of different ethnicities through the inclusion of cross-level interactions between student ethnicity indicators and the treatment effect. Whereas the first stage of analysis seeks to answer the overarching question of general program effectiveness, the second and third stages seek to determine the degree to which America's Choice is successful in closing the gaps between low and high performers and between minority and White students.

All Rochester public schools in existence from 1992 to 2003 were included in the analyses. Alternative education programs were combined into a single cluster. The total school-level sample size for each model was 43 schools for Grades 1 through 3 and 50 schools for Grades 4 through 8. The student-level sample sizes ranged from about 10,000 students in the quartile analyses, to more than 40,000 students in the overall models. The number of test scores included in the analyses ranged from about 25,000 individual scores in the quartile models to more than 130,000 in the overall models. In each model, individual test scores were treated as cross-classified within students and schools.

Three key pieces of information are produced by the growth-curve models, and all are adjusted to control for differences in the demographic characteristics of America's Choice students and students in other schools. First, the models produce an estimate of the typical annual growth in achievement. In the simplest terms, this shows the average number of points gained per year over multiple years. Second, the models produce estimates of the additional annual growth experienced by students participating in America's Choice. In other words, this shows the number of extra points students gain per year on average while they attend an America's Choice school. Third, by dividing the additional growth attributable to America's Choice by the baseline growth estimate and multiplying by 10 months,[8] we produce an estimate of the number of additional months of learning that students experience each year they attend an America's Choice school.

RESULTS

In this section we describe the average annual test score gain for students in Rochester and compare this to the national norms for the SAT-9. We then present results of analyses designed to answer the three research questions presented earlier. First, we examine the effect of America's Choice on students' annual gains in general (i.e., the effect of the treatment on the treated) and for each year schools implemented the program (i.e., the intent-to-treat effect). Second, we look more specifically at the effect of America's Choice on the annual gains of students with different initial performance. Third, we look at the effects of America's Choice on the annual gains of students from different ethnicities. In the sections that follow, we report the impact estimates for each analysis. Because of the complexity of the analysis and the number of models run, only program effects are presented in tabular form within this article, and full results for the complete set of models with control variables are presented in an online appendix available at http://www.cpre.org/Publications/Publications_Journal.htm.

Baseline Test Score Gains for All Rochester Students

To interpret the meaning of the impact estimates, it is helpful to know the magnitude of typical annual growth in reading and mathematics achievement scores at different grade levels for all students in Rochester. Differences in rates of growth in the early grades versus the later grades could be due to differences in the amount of learning that is typically experienced for different subjects at different grade levels, or they could simply be artifacts of the scale of the test. Either way, knowledge about the expected rate of growth in SAT-9 scores for all students in the nation helps in benchmarking both the annual rates of learning for Rochester students in general, and also in benchmarking the effects of America's Choice on student learning gains.

In Grades 1 through 3, Rochester students gained 29.7 points per year in reading and 27 points per year in mathematics, on average. These rates of growth are smaller than national norms for the SAT-9 during grades one through three, which has expected annual growth rates of 49.9 points in reading and 36.7 points in mathematics.[9] This suggests that Rochester students in Grades 1 through 3 are learning at a rate that is 40%

---

[8]The school year in Rochester runs from the first week in September to the last week in June, or 9.75 months. We rounded to 10 months for simplicity.

[9]The annual growth rates for the national norming sample were calculated using grade equivalents and scale scores published in the Stanford-9 Spring Norms Book (Harcourt, 1997). The average annual growth rate for grades one through three and grades four through eight were calculated by averaging the differences in scale scores at subsequent grade equivalents. For example, the scale score in reading associated with a grade equivalent of 2.0 is 540, and it is 588 for a grade equivalent of 3.0. Therefore, the national average expected gain from second to third grade in reading is 48 points.

slower than national norms in reading and 26% slower than national norms in mathematics.

In fourth through eighth grades, Rochester students gained 8.6 points per year in reading and 6.2 points per year in mathematics, on average. These rates of growth are also smaller than national norms for the SAT-9 during fourth through eighth grades, which have expected annual growth rates of 14.1 points in reading and 14.8 points in mathematics (see note 7). This suggests that Rochester students in fourth through eighth grades are learning at a rate that is 39% slower than national norms in reading and 58% slower than national norms in mathematics.

Although the number of points gained on the SAT-9 in Grades 1 through 3 is much larger than in Grades 4 through 8, the comparison to national norms shows that, in reading, the difference in the number of points gained is not an indication that Rochester students in Grades 4 through 8 are performing worse than Rochester students in Grades 1 through 3. In fact, the annual gains in reading are equally poor for Grades 1 through 3 and Grades 4 through 8 (both about 40% below national norms). In mathematics, however, there is evidence that Rochester students perform worse while in Grades 4 through 8 (58% below national norms) compared to performance during Grades 1 through 3 (26% below national norms).

Mean Effects of America's Choice on Student Achievement Growth

Overall, students attending America's Choice schools in Rochester experienced significantly greater annual gains in both reading and mathematics performance than did similar students in other schools in the district. Table 3 shows annual gains by grade level and subject. It also shows the additional annual gains made by America's Choice students in terms of months of schooling. For both reading and mathematics, students attending America's Choice schools in first through third grades experienced an additional 7/10 of a month of learning each year compared to similar students in other Rochester schools (e.g., $[2.0 \div 29.7] \times 10 = 0.7$). In fourth through eighth grades, students in America's Choice schools experienced an additional 1.7 months of learning each year in reading, and an additional 2.6 months of learning each year in mathematics, compared to similar students in other Rochester schools.

In terms of points gained on the SAT-9, reading scores for fourth-through eighth-grade students in non–America's Choice schools increased by 8.6 points per year, and reading scores for fourth-through eighth-grade students attending America's Choice schools increased by 10.1 points per year (1.5 points in addition to the baseline 8.6 points per year).

Using the standardized effect size formulas for growth curve models described by Raudenbush and Liu (2001), the effect sizes were 0.16 for reading in Grades 1 through 3; 0.36 for reading in Grades 4 through 8; 0.28 for math in Grades 1 through 3; and 0.39 for math in Grades 4 through 8. These standardized effect sizes show the change in growth rate in standard deviation units. This effect size is similar to a standardized effect size from an analysis of difference scores (i.e., the difference in average gains between the treatment and control groups divided by the standard deviation of the gains); however, these effect sizes are not comparable to Cohen's D, as these effect sizes are based on variance in rates of growth instead of overall variance in the population.

It is important to recognize that these estimates of impact on achievement growth are averaged across years. In the next section, we present year-by-year estimates to determine the degree to which the mean estimates accurately represent a consistent trend, and the degree to which student mobility moderates the impact of the program.

Table 3. Baseline Growth in Achievement and Effects of America's Choice in Rochester, NY

| | Annual Achievement Growth (Standard Errors in Parentheses) | | | |
| | Reading | | Mathematics | |
Growth Estimate	Grades 1–3	Grades 4–8	Grades 1–3	Grades 4–8
Baseline annual growth of SAT-9 scores	29.7***	8.6***	27.0***	6.2***
	(0.6)	(0.2)	(0.7)	(0.4)
Effect of America's Choice				
Additional SAT-9 points per year	2.0***	1.5***	1.9***	1.6***
	(0.3)	(0.1)	(0.3)	(0.2)
Standardized effect size	0.16	0.36	0.28	0.39
Additional months of learning per year	+0.7	+1.7	+0.7	+2.6

*$p < .05$, **$p < .01$, ***$p < .001$.

Year-by-Year Effects of America's Choice

Efforts to separate the overall effect of America's Choice into year-by-year effects suggested there is variation in the program impact across years; however, the effects were neither concentrated in the early years of implementation, nor in the later years. Table 4 shows annual impact by grade level and subject. There is some indication that program effects dropped off in the fifth year, especially in reading, where the impact estimate is negative. However, without an in-depth qualitative study or a 6th year of test score data, it is unclear whether this is the result of a systematic downward trend or just another dip in a somewhat random process. It is also interesting to note that only six schools in this study used the America's Choice design for 5 years, and that these schools began implementing the design under a 3-year implementation plan. After the 3rd year as an America's Choice school, the program was maintained in these schools through a less involved relationship with NCEE. During this time, according to one district official, "The original prescribed design started to erode in many places." The degree to which the effects of comprehensive school reform can be sustained under maintenance contracts is an important issue for future research.

Across the 5 years of program implementation, the impact estimates are predominantly positive and statistically significant. Therefore, linear projections of student achievement growth based on a time-averaged estimate of program impact can serve as a relatively accurate approximation of changes in individual student performance during the first few years of implementation.

Averaging these effects across the 5 years of implementation produces an intent-to-treat impact estimate that can be compared to the treatment-on-the-treated estimates shown in Table 3. The average intent-to-treat effects are as follows. In reading, the effects were 1.4 points per year in Grades 1 through 3 and 1.1 points per year in Grades 4 through 8. In math, the effects were 1.5 points per year in Grades 1 through 3 and 1.1 points per year in Grades 4 through 8. These intent-to-treat estimates are all approximately 70% smaller than the impact estimates of the treatment on the treated. This is not surprising given Rochester's intradistrict mobility rate near 20% and interdistrict mobility rate near 10% annually.

Visual Projections of Student Achievement Growth

In this section we introduce visual plots of individual student achievement growth using time-averaged impact estimates from Table 3. In these plots, two lines are used to represent typical achievement trends for America's Choice students (gray line) and similar students in other Rochester schools (black line). In these graphs the estimated trajectory for comparison students (i.e., preintervention) and the America's Choice trajectory are shown starting at the same grade. This helps improve the perspective for interpreting the size of the impact estimates, and for gauging the cumulative effects of the program over time.

Figure 4 offers a visual depiction of two prototypical Rochester students with similar demographics who start first grade with identical reading achievement scores. The student in an America's Choice

Table 4. Baseline Growth in Achievement and Year-by-Year Effects of America's Choice in Rochester, NY

| | Annual Achievement Growth (Standard Errors in Parentheses) | | | |
| | Reading | | Mathematics | |
Growth Estimate	Grades 1–3	Grades 4–8	Grades 1–3	Grades 4–8
Baseline annual growth of SAT-9 scores	29.7***	8.6***	26.9***	6.0***
	(0.6)	(0.3)	(0.7)	(0.4)
Effect of America's Choice				
Additional SAT-9 points in year 1	2.2***	2.8***	3.3***	2.9***
	(0.6)	(0.3)	(0.6)	(0.3)
Additional SAT-9 points in year 2	−0.5	1.6***	−0.8	1.2***
	(0.7)	(0.3)	(0.7)	(0.4)
Additional SAT-9 points in year 3	2.6**	−0.3	2.7***	−0.4
	(0.9)	(0.6)	(0.9)	(0.6)
Additional SAT-9 points in year 4	4.6***	2.6***	1.9*	2.5***
	(0.9)	(0.7)	(0.9)	(0.7)
Additional SAT-9 points in year 5	−1.9*	−1.4*	0.2	−0.7
	(1.0)	(0.7)	(1.0)	(0.8)

*$p < .05$, **$p < .01$, ***$p < .001$.

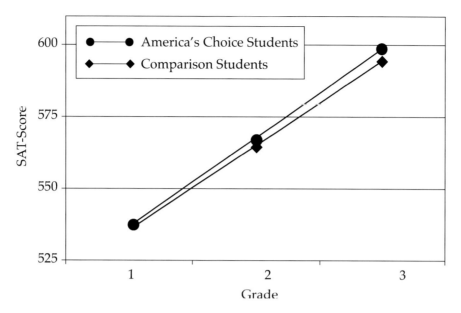

Figure 4. Growth in reading achievement of America's Choice students and similar students in other Rochester schools during Grades 1–3.

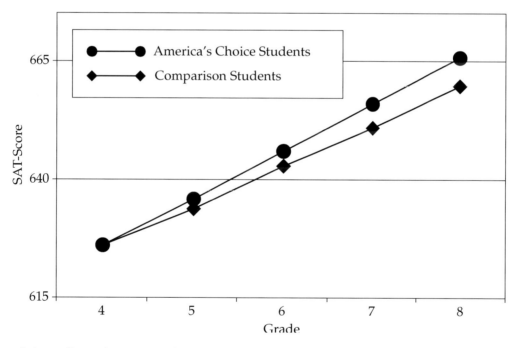

Figure 5. Growth in reading achievement of America's Choice students and similar students in other Rochester schools during Grades 4–8.

school experiences a slightly faster rate of growth than the student in a non–America's Choice school. After 2 years, a student attending an America's Choice school would have gained 63.4 points (31.7 points × 2), while a student in a non–America's Choice school would have gained only 59.4 points (29.7 points × 2).

Figure 5 gives a visual depiction of two prototypical Rochester students with similar demographics

who start fourth grade with identical achievement scores. The student in an America's Choice school experiences a considerably faster rate of growth than the student in a non-America's Choice school. After 4 years, a student attending an America's Choice school would have gained 40.4 points (10.1 points × 4), whereas a student in a non-America's Choice school would have gained only 34.4 points (8.6 points × 4).

Effects of America's Choice on Students With Different Initial Performance Levels

The results presented in this section serve to answer our second research question, "Does America's Choice improve the performance of particularly low-achieving students? If so, is this accomplished at the expense of higher performing students?"

Results showed the lowest performing students in America's Choice schools typically experienced the greatest gains relative to similar students in other Rochester schools, although effects of America's Choice were present at all performance levels. To determine the effects of America's Choice on students at different performance levels, we grouped students into four performance groups (quartiles) to compare students in America's Choice schools to those in other Rochester schools within each of the performance quartiles. Students were grouped into performance quartiles based on their first available achievement score. Because test scores within each grade were dis-tributed similarly across years, the same grade-specific cutoff scores were used for all years. Details of these results are given in Table 5.

America's Choice students in the lowest quartile (percentile rank less than 25) gained significantly more than did the lowest performing students in other district schools. The lowest quartile students in America's Choice schools gained nearly 1 additional month in reading during Grades 1 through 3 and an additional 3.4 months per year in reading during Grades 4 through 8 during the years they attended an America's Choice school. These lowest performing students also gained an additional 1.4 months in mathematics during Grades 1 through 3 and an additional 3.8 months in mathematics during Grades 4 through 8 for every year they attended an America's Choice school.

America's Choice students in the second quartile (percentile rank between 25 and 50) had significantly greater gains in both reading and mathematics in Grades 4 through 8, but not in Grades 1 through 3.

Table 5. Baseline Growth in Achievement and Effects of America's Choice by Initial Performance

| | Annual Achievement Growth (Standard Errors in Parentheses) | | | |
| | Reading | | Mathematics | |
Quartile	Grades 1–3	Grades 4–8	Grades 1–3	Grades 4–8
First (lowest initial performance)				
Baseline annual growth of SAT-9 scores	38.0***	8.7***	30.7***	6.3***
	(0.6)	(0.4)	(0.5)	(0.3)
Effect of America's Choice				
Additional SAT-9 points per year	3.6***	3.0***	4.4***	2.4***
	(0.6)	(0.3)	(0.6)	(0.3)
Additional months of learning per year	+0.9	+3.4	+1.4	+3.8
Second				
Baseline annual growth of SAT-9 scores	31.5***	8.6***	26.4***	5.4***
	(0.4)	(0.3)	(0.4)	(0.4)
Effect of America's Choice				
Additional SAT-9 points per year	−0.5	1.7***	0.8	1.8***
	(0.5)	(0.2)	(0.5)	(0.2)
Additional months of learning per year	~	+2.0	~	+3.3
Third				
Baseline annual growth of SAT-9 scores	27.3***	8.4***	24.3***	5.8***
	(0.4)	(0.3)	(0.5)	(0.5)
Effect of America's Choice				
Additional SAT-9 points per year	−0.6	0.3	−0.6	0.6*
	(0.5)	(0.2)	(0.5)	(0.3)
Additional months of learning per year	~	~	~	+1.0
Fourth (highest initial performance)				
Baseline annual growth of SAT-9 scores	17.5***	8.2***	18.7***	6.0***
	(0.5)	(0.3)	(0.7)	(0.7)
Effect of America's Choice				
Additional SAT-9 points per year	−1.2	−0.3	0.2	1.4***
	(0.6)	(0.3)	(0.6)	(0.4)
Additional months of learning per year	~	~	~	+2.3

*$p < .05$, **$p < .01$, ***$p < .001$.
~ = no significant difference in annual gains.

While in the earlier grades, second-quartile students gained similarly in both America's Choice and other district schools; however, these students gained an additional 2 months in reading and an additional 3.3 months in mathematics while in fourth through eighth grades, compared with counterparts in other district schools.

Gains for students in the third quartile (percentile rank between 50 and 75) were generally similar between those in America's Choice schools and those in other Rochester schools. Only America's Choice students in Grades 4 through 8 mathematics exhibited greater learning gains, an additional 1 month per year during the years they attended an America's Choice school.

For the highest performing students, those in the fourth quartile (percentile rank greater than 75), there were few differences between those in America's Choice schools and those in other Rochester schools. Only in mathematics during Grades 4 through 8 did students in America's Choice schools have greater gains, an additional 2.3 months per year.

There were no cases in any quartile, in either reading or mathematics, in which students in other Rochester schools had faster growth rates than students in the America's Choice schools, after adjusting for differences in student demographics between the two student populations.

Figure 6 presents a visual depiction of four pairs of prototypical Rochester students with similar demographics who start fourth grade with a reading achievement score at the average value for each of four quartiles. The students in America's Choice schools who start out with lower achievement scores experience a faster rate of growth than their counterparts in non-America's Choice schools. This can be seen by the steeper slope of the lines representing America's Choice students from quartiles 1 and 2. Furthermore, the growth of higher-performing students in America's Choice schools is equivalent to the growth rates for their counterparts in non-America's Choice schools. This shows that students with lower initial performance experience significant benefits from America's Choice, but not at the expense of higher-performing students.

Effects on Students of Different Ethnicities

The results presented in this section answer our third research question, "Does America's Choice make education more equitable for minority students? If so, is this accomplished at the expense of nonminority students?"

Results showed that minority students exhibited the largest learning gains from their involvement in America's Choice relative to minority students in Rochester's non-America's Choice schools. Both Hispanic and African American students in America's Choice schools typically gained significantly more than their ethnic counterparts in non-America's Choice schools. These results are shown in Table 6.

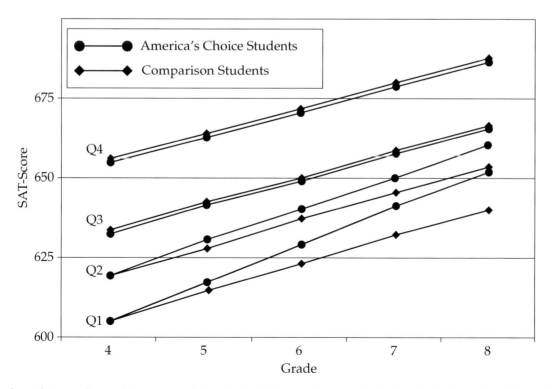

Figure 6. Growth in reading achievement of America's Choice students and similar students in other Rochester school during Grades 4–8 by initial performance quartile.

Table 6. Baseline Growth in Achievement and Effects of America's Choice by Ethnicity

| | Annual Achievement Growth (Standard Errors in Parentheses) | | | |
| | Reading | | Mathematics | |
Student Ethnicity	Grades 1–3	Grades 4–8	Grades 1–3	Grades 4–8
White				
Baseline annual growth of SAT-9 scores	29.6***	8.6***	26.9***	6.1***
	(0.7)	(0.3)	(0.7)	(0.4)
Effect of America's Choice				
Additional SAT-9 points per year	−0.4	0.8	−0.4	1.3*
	(1.0)	(0.5)	(1.0)	(0.5)
Additional months of learning	~	~	~	+2.1
African American				
Baseline annual growth of SAT-9 scores	29.0***	8.4***	25.9***	6.0***
	(0.6)	(0.3)	(0.5)	(0.4)
Effect of America's Choice				
Additional SAT-9 points per year	1.2***	1.2***	1.3**	1.1***
	(0.4)	(0.2)	(0.4)	(0.2)
Additional months of learning	+0.4	+1.4	+0.5	+1.8
Hispanic				
Baseline annual growth of SAT-9 scores	29.0***	8.4***	25.9***	6.0***
	(0.6)	(0.3)	(0.5)	(0.4)
Effect of America's Choice				
Additional SAT-9 points per year	3.6***	2.4***	3.1***	1.6***
	(0.6)	(0.3)	(0.7)	(0.3)
Additional months of learning	+1.2	+2.9	+1.2	+2.7

$*p < .05$, $**p < .01$, $***p < .001$.
~ = no significant difference in annual gains.

White students in America's Choice schools did not experience significant additional gains in reading compared with White students in other Rochester schools. In mathematics, they gained an additional 2.1 months per year during Grades 4 through 8.

African American students in America's Choice schools gained an additional two-fifths of a month per year in reading during Grades 1 through 3 and an additional 1.4 months per year in reading during fourth through eighth grades. They also gained an additional one-half of a month per year in mathematics during first through third grades and an additional 1.8 months per year in mathematics during fourth through eighth grades.

Hispanic students in America's Choice schools gained an additional 1.2 months per year in reading during first through third grades, and an additional 2.9 months per year in reading during fourth through eighth grades. They also gained an additional 1.2 months per year in mathematics during the earlier grades and an additional 2.7 months per year in mathematics during the later grades.

Figure 7 shows three pairs of prototypical White, Hispanic, and African American Rochester students during Grades 4 through 8. The minority students in America's Choice schools experience a faster rate of growth than their counterparts in non–America's Choice schools. This can be seen by the steeper slope of the lines representing Hispanic and African American America's Choice students. Furthermore, the growth of White students in America's Choice schools is equivalent to the growth rates for their counterparts in other schools. This shows that minority students experience significant benefits from America's Choice, but not at the expense of nonminority students.

DISCUSSION

These analyses reveal several important findings about the effectiveness of America's Choice in Rochester. Most important, the overall results indicate that, on average, students in America's Choice schools learned significantly more than did other students in the district, even after adjusting for differences in student demographics. Each year, the magnitude of these results is small to moderate, but they accumulate over the time that students attend America's Choice schools.

Furthermore, the impact of America's Choice seems to be larger in the later grades than in the early grades. In fact, the results are two to three times

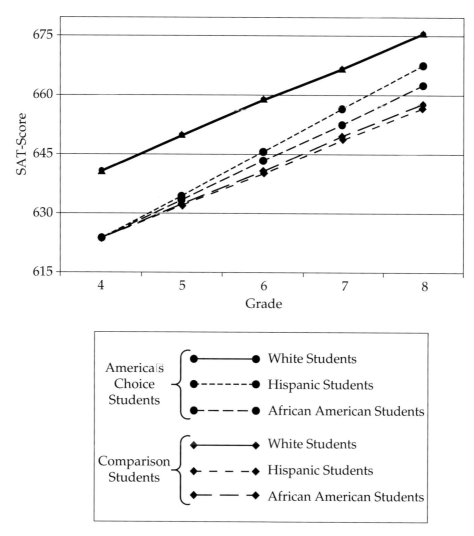

Figure 7. Growth in reading achievement of America's Choice students and similar students in other Rochester schools during Grades 4–8, by ethnicity.

stronger in the later grades (1.7 months in reading and 2.6 months in mathematics in Grades 4 through 8) than in the early grades (0.7 months in both reading and mathematics in Grades 1 through 3). This could be due to more powerful programmatic influences in the later grades; however, the very small baseline gains for students in Grades 4 through 8 suggest another possible interpretation. If Rochester students are learning very little each year during Grades 4 through 8, the proportional effect of America's Choice may be an overstatement of its actual effectiveness. That is, even though Rochester students in America's Choice schools are learning more than their counterparts in other Rochester schools, they are by no means learning an overwhelming amount each year. Even with the added growth associated with America's Choice, rates of learning are still below the average growth rate for the SAT-9 national norming sample.

Given that the America's Choice approach to instruction emphasizes ongoing assessment and differ-

entiation of instruction, one objective of this research was to explore whether America's Choice was successful in helping low-performing students catch up to their higher-performing peers, and whether the program was successful in reducing the minority achievement gap. The results of this study suggest that America's Choice is effective in both these regards. The performance gains are particularly dramatic for students in the lowest quartile and African American and particularly Hispanic students who attend America's Choice schools, relative to their counterparts in non–America's Choice schools in the district. It could be that the ethnicity effect and the effect on the lowest achieving students result from the same phenomenon, given the correlation between low performance and minority status. Regardless, the America's Choice strategies of identifying and paying substantial attention to bringing lower-performing students up to standard and differentiating instruction for learners at all levels appears to result in substantial achievement gains for the most disadvantaged students. More importantly, while America's Choice appears to be particularly powerful for low-performing and minority students, there is no evidence to suggest that these closures in achievement gaps were obtained at the expense of higher-performing or non-minority students.

These findings are consistent with other research on America's Choice in several respects. First, significant impacts on student reading performance have been found in evaluations in several other sites. Supovitz, Poglinco, and Snyder (2001) conducted a cross-sectional study of America's Choice in 1999 to 2000 in several districts, including Rochester. They found significantly greater reading gains for students in America's Choice schools compared with students in other schools in their district. Consistent with this study, the reading effects also appeared to be most pronounced in the upper elementary and middle school grades. Supovitz, Taylor, and May (2002) examined the test performance of students in America's Choice schools after 2 years of implementation of the design compared with other district schools in Duval County, Florida, from 1999 to 2001, and found results most pronounced in writing, with some smaller effects in reading and mathematics.

Other research supports the finding that the America's Choice approach to improving instruction may be more powerful for the upper elementary and middle grades. Specifically, analyses of student achievement data under the Study of Instructional Improvement (Rowan & Miller, 2006) found the effects of America's Choice were more pronounced in the upper elementary grades. The authors attribute this consistent difference in effects on instruction and achievement to what they describe as a "professional control" model of organizing schools for improvement. The foundation of this approach is through professional development of teachers and coaching designed to enhance teachers' skills for making instructional decisions and using data to target instruction to the needs of their students.

Based on the results presented here and on previous research on America's Choice, we believe the impacts of the design are accomplished primarily through improvements in teachers' capacity to (a) promote and maintain ambitious expectations for student learning, (b) provide instruction that is more targeted to the needs of individual students, and (c) modify the supporting organizational structures within schools to better facilitate this work, and provide additional time and learning opportunities for individual students. We hypothesize that the positive impact on student achievement of America's Choice is determined to a great extent by the effectiveness of the design in bringing about these specific changes in how students are taught.

At the most global level, the instructional approach of America's Choice could be described as a strategy to treat students as individual learners who are members of a classroom community, rather than as a homogeneous group, to teach them more effectively and thus improve their learning. This view assumes that students enter the classroom with different kinds and amounts of prior knowledge, and different background experiences and strengths, and that it is the teacher's job to match instructional decisions to the different learning needs of individual students and to the classroom group as a whole. America's Choice seeks to provide teachers with the skills and tools to assess students' current developmental levels, contrast these to standards, and apply appropriate instructional strategies to improve student learning. This concept is relatively simple, but its ramifications on classroom processes are profound. The implications of this way of thinking about teaching and learning reach into the organization of classroom time, the choice and structure of activities, the grouping of students, and perhaps most importantly, the expertise of teachers to enact this vision of instruction.

Finally, this study also contributes to the evidence base suggesting that strong district support is a critical factor in the success of whole school reform. Within Rochester, district leaders provided substantial and steady support to the America's Choice program beyond the services the program delivered to individual schools. The district resources and the opportunity for participating schools to engage with their peers who were undergoing the same experience may have contributed to the performance gains of students in America's Choice schools. This is important because much of the research on the impacts of America's Choice occurs in districts in which the design is implemented in at least a substantial proportion of the schools, with consonant priority and attention from the district. These include studies in Duval County, Florida, (Supovitz & Taylor, 2003; Supovitz & Taylor, 2005; Supovitz, Taylor, & May, 2002) and Plainfield, New Jersey (Supovitz & May, 2004). The importance of district support is also well noted in other studies of CSR (Bodilly, 1996; Datnow & Stringfield, 2000).

Although the results of this study provide significant evidence that America's Choice has positive effects on student performance, the results also suggest that the effects of America's Choice on student achievement are not nearly large enough to compensate for inequities in educational outcomes. Even with the positive effects of America's Choice, and possibly any CSR model, our longitudinal analyses suggest that the annual learning gains of economically disadvantaged students in urban districts are still likely to fall short of the national average. Under such conditions, poor urban students will continue to fall further behind each year. Although achievement gaps within a district may shrink, the only way for low-performing urban schools to catch up to high-performing suburban schools is for urban students to experience annual rates of learning that far exceed the national average.

Limitations of This Study

Although this study provides strong evidence of the longitudinal effects of the America's Choice program, the study has limitations. First, schools in Rochester were not randomly assigned to America's Choice. Without such an experimental design, we must rely on statistical models to adjust for preexisting differences between America's Choice schools and comparison schools. The methods used in this study are thought to be effective in accomplishing this goal (Bloom 2001; Bryk & Weisberg, 1977; Shadish, Cook, & Campbell, 2002); however, the study would be even stronger if America's Choice schools had been selected at random from a pool of eligible schools (see Borman et al., 2005a and 2005b, for an example of a randomized evaluation of CSR).

Second, this study does not attempt to connect improvements in performance directly to implementation of specific components of the America's Choice design (as was done in May, Supovitz, and Lesnick, 2004, and in Supovitz and May, 2004). Therefore, while the study suggests the program has positive impacts, it does not provide specific evidence of how and why these positive results were achieved.

Other limitations of this study arise from the issue of linking different sources of assessment data. The linkages in this study were from two sources, calibration of different tests and vertical scaling across grades, and the limitations implied by these two sources are similar. The goal of both cross-assessment linkage and vertical scaling is to place scores from different tests on the same continuous scale for the purposes of estimating growth. If the linkages are faulty, then estimates of growth may be biased. This would happen if there were substantial differences in the constructs measured by the assessments and the different constructs were not highly correlated (Martineau, 2006). This situation may be likely to occur when vertical scaling is used to link assessments over wide grade spans (Yen, 1986). The content of a third-grade test likely would be considerably different from the content of an eighth-grade test. In fact, it is more likely that the linkages between the SAT-9, CAT-5, NYS, and other tests within each grade are more valid than the linkages between SAT-9 forms from first to eighth grade. Perhaps the more serious issue in this study is not the use of multiple tests, but the use of a vertical scale to illustrate growth. Recent research by Martineau (2006)

suggests that vertical scales may be ineffective at capturing real learning gains over more than a couple of years. However, even if the idea that a vertical scale is a valid measure of student learning is dismissed, it is difficult to dismiss the value of reliable test scores as indicators of relative performance (i.e., the ability to discriminate between levels of performance on a single test). So at the very least, the growth curve models in this study are able to capture changes in the performance of individual students relative to their peers as they progress from first to eighth grade.

Implications for Future Research

This research study helps to illustrate the value of long-term longitudinal research in education. Through its ability to represent program effects relative to baseline rates of learning (e.g., as additional months of learning), the growth curve modeling approach can characterize program effects in terms that are easy to understand and that represent the effects of programs and interventions in a more concrete metric than the esoteric "standardized effect size." The quasi-experimental interrupted time series approach also provides more valid impact estimates than traditional cross-sectional analyses. This translates to better information for policymakers and educators regarding the potential effects of programs and regarding the time necessary to establish desired effects.

Another benefit of longitudinal analysis is increased statistical power that comes from having more data to support estimates of treatment effects. The typical educational study includes only 1 or 2 years of data from a limited number of schools. This suggests that most educational studies have sufficient statistical power to detect only relatively large effects. This study, along with previous research, suggests that 1-year effect sizes in education are usually small by Cohen's standards (e.g., $\delta \approx 0.20$). Yet this study also reveals that whereas the standardized effect size may seem small because overall variation in student achievement at a single point in time is large, the effect size relative to the baseline rate of learning is much larger. Therefore, important and substantial effects of programs and policies may be doomed to remain undetected because the typical educational research study is not longitudinal. On the other hand, the research community now has a much greater opportunity to conduct longitudinal studies because annual testing data are now quite prevalent.

The keys to successful implementation of this kind of analysis are data availability and data quality. NCLB requirements have resulted in annual test data available for Grades 3 through 8, and longitudinal studies across those grades are easy to design. Unfortunately, from the researchers' perspective, annual test data are not readily available for early elementary grades, or for high schools.

When longitudinal data are available, it is important that reliable linkages of individual data over time can be made. Within a single district, this can usually be done with a single student identifier. In a larger context, additional data including student demographics and even names can be used to make probabilistic linkages, even when student IDs change as a result of mobility or data errors. CPRE has been successful using Link-King, a free package of SAS macros, to do probabilistic matching of students across statewide annual datasets (see http://www.the-link-king.com).

The final contribution of the method used in this study is its ability to handle student mobility through crossed random effects. This includes mobility due to relocations, along with the inevitable mobility that results from matriculation from elementary to middle and then to high school. The cross-classified growth curve model approach allows learning trajectories of individual students to be tracked, regardless of how many times they change schools. At the same time, the degree to which each school influences the learning rates of its students is reflected in the school-level effects. The advantages of this approach, and the availability of at least a few multilevel statistical software packages to do cross-classified modeling, makes this kind of interrupted time series approach a powerful option for longitudinal quasi-experimental impact evaluation.

REFERENCES

Becker, W. C., & Gersten, R. M. (1982). A follow-up of follow-through: The later effects of the direct instruction model on children in fifth and sixth grades. *American Educational Research Journal, 19*(1), 75–92.

Bloom, H. (2001). *Measuring the impacts of whole-school reforms: Methodological lessons from an evaluation of accelerated schools.* New York: Manpower Demonstration Research Corporation.

Bloom, H. S. (1999). *Estimating program impacts on student achievement using "short" interrupted time-series.* New York: Manpower Demonstration Research Corporation.

Bloom, H., Ham, S., Melton, L., & O'Brien, J. (2001). *Evaluation of the Accelerated Schools approach: A look at early implementation and impacts in eight elementary schools.* New York: Manpower Demonstration Research Corporation.

Bodilly, S. (1996). *Lessons from New American Schools Development Corporation's demonstration phase.* Santa Monica, CA: Rand.

Borman, G., & Hewes, G. (2002). Long-term effects and cost-effectiveness of Success for All. *Educational Evaluation and Policy Analysis, 24,* 243–266.

Borman, G. D., Hewes, G. M., Overman, L. T., & Brown, S. (2003). Comprehensive school reform and achievement: A meta-analysis. *Review of Educational Research 73*(2), 125–230.

Borman, G. D., Slavin, R. E., Cheung, A., Chamberlain, A. M., Madden, N. A., & Chambers, B. (2005a). Success for All: First-year results from the national randomized field trial. *Educational Evaluation and Policy Analysis, 27,* 1–22.

Borman, G. D., Slavin, R. E., Cheung, A., Chamberlain, A. M., Madden, N. A., & Chambers, B. (2005b). The national randomized field trial of Success for All: Second-year outcomes. *American Educational Research Journal, 42*(4), 673–696.

Browne, W. J. (2002). *MCMC estimation in MLwiN.* London: Centre for Multilevel Modelling, University of London.

Browne, W. J., Goldstein, H., & Rasbash, J. (2001). Multiple membership multiple classification (MMMC) models. *Statistical Modelling 1,* 103–124.

Bryk, A., & Weisberg, H. (1977). Use of the non-equivalent control group design when subjects are growing. *Psychological Bulletin, 84*(5), 950–962.

Campbell, D. T., & Stanley, J. C. (1963). Experimental and quasi-experimental designs for research on teaching. In N. L. Gage (Ed.), *Handbook of research on teaching* (pp. 171–246). Chicago: Rand McNally.

Datnow, A., Borman, G. D., Stringfield, S., Overman, L. T., & Castellano, M. (2003). Comprehensive school reform in culturally and linguistically diverse contexts: Implementation and outcomes from a four-year study. *Educational Evaluation and Policy Analysis, 25,* 143–170.

Datnow, A., & Stringfield, S. (2000). Working together for reliable school reform. *Journal of Education for Students Placed at Risk, 5*(2), 183–204.

Dunn, M., Kadane, J. B., & Garrow, J. R. (2003). Comparing Harm Done by Mobility and Class Absence: Missing Students and Missing Data. *Journal of Educational and Behavioral Statistics, 28*(3), 269–288.

Feuer, M. J., Holland, P. W., Green, B. F., Bertenthal, M. W., & Hemphill, F. C. (1999). Uncommon measures: Equivalence and linkage among educational tests. Washington, DC: National Academy Press.

Geman, S., & Geman, D. (1984). Stochastic relaxation Gibbs distributions and the Bayesian restoration of images. *IEEE Transactions on Pattern Analysis and Machine Intelligence, 6*(6), 721–741.

Harcourt. (1997). *Stanford Achievement Test Series, ninth edition, spring norms book.* San Antonio, TX: Author.

Herman, R., Aladjem, D., McMahon, P., Masem, E., Mulligan, I., O'Malley, A., et al. (1999). *An educator's guide to schoolwide reform.* Washington, DC: American Institutes for Research.

Jones, E. M., Gottfredson, G. D., & Gottfredson, D. C. (1997). Success for some: An evaluation of a Success for All program. *Evaluation Review, 21*(6), 643–670.

Ligas, M. R. (2002). Evaluation of Broward County Alliance of Quality Schools Project, *Journal of Education for Students Placed at Risk, 7*(2), 117–139.

Ligas, M. R., & Vaughan, D. W. (1999). *Alliance of quality schools: 1998–99 evaluation report.* Broward, FL: Broward County Schools.

Linn, R. L. (1993). Linking results of distinct assessments. *Applied Measurement in Education, 6*(1), 83–102.

Loret, P. G., Seder, A., Bianchini, J. C., & Vale, C. A. (1972). *A description of the Anchor Test Study.* Princeton, NJ: Educational Testing Service.

MacIver, M. A., & Kemper, E. (2002). The impact of Direct Instruction on elementary students' reading achievement in an urban school district. *Journal of Education for Students Placed at Risk, 7*(2), 197–220.

Madden, N. A., Slavin, R. E., Karweit, N. L., Dolan, L. J., & Wasik, B. A. (1993). Success for All: Longitudinal effects of a restructuring program for innercity elementary schools. *American Educational Research Journal, 30*, 123–148.

Martineau, J. A. (2006). Distorting value added: The use of longitudinal, vertically scaled student achievement data for growth-based, value-added accountability. *Journal of Educational and Behavioral Statistics, 31*(1), 35–62.

May, H. (2004, April). *Practical longitudinal analysis of student achievement using cross-classified Bayesian hierarchical linear modeling.* Paper presented at the annual meeting of the American Educational Research Association, San Diego, CA.

May, H., Supovitz, J. A., & Lesnick, J. (2004). *The impact of America's Choice on writing performance in Georgia: First-year results.* Philadelphia: Consortium for Policy Research in Education, University of Pennsylvania.

Meyer, L. A. (1983). *Long-term academic effects of direct instruction follow through.* Technical Report No. 299. Champaign, IL: University of Illinois at Urbana-Champaign, Center for the Study of Reading. (Eric Document Reproduction Service No. ED 237932.)

Mislevy, R. J. (1992). *Linking educational assessments: Concepts, issues, methods, and prospects.* Princeton, NJ: Educational Testing Service.

Northwest Regional Educational Laboratory. (2005). *Catalog of school reform models.* Portland, OR: Author. Retrieved August 1, 2005, from http://www.nwrel.org/scpd/catalog/guide.shtml

Purkey, S. C., & Smith, M. S. (1983). Effective schools: A review. *Elementary School Journal, 83*(4), 426–452.

Rasbash, J., & Goldstein, H. (1994). Efficient analysis of mixed hierarchical and cross-classified random structures using a multilevel model. *Journal of Educational and Behavioral Statistics, 19*, 337–350.

Rasbash, J., Browne, W., Healy, M., Cameron, B., & Charlton, C. (2003). MLwiN (Version 2.00) [Computer Software]. London: Centre for Multilevel Modelling, University of London.

Raudenbush, S. W. (1993). A crossed random effects model for unbalanced data with applications in cross-sectional and longitudinal research. *Journal of Educational and Behavioral Statistics, 18*, 321–349.

Raudenbush, S. W., & Bryk, A. S. (2002). *Hierarchical linear models: Applications and data analysis methods* (2nd ed.). Thousand Oaks, CA: Sage.

Raudenbush, S. W., & Liu, X. (2001). Effects of study duration, frequency of observation, and sample size on power in studies of treatment effects on polynomial change. *Psychological Methods, 6*, 387–401.

Reynolds, D., & Teddlie, C. (2000). The processes of school effectiveness. In C. Teddlie & D. Reynolds (Eds.), *The international handbook of school effectiveness research* (pp. 134–159). London: Falmer Press.

Rogosa, D. R. (1995). Myths and methods: "Myths about longitudinal research," plus supplemental questions. In J. M. Gottman (Ed.), *The analysis of change* (pp. 3–65). Hillsdale, NJ: Erlbaum.

Rogosa, D. R., Brandt, D., & Zimowski, M. (1982). A growth curve approach to the measurement of change. *Psychological Bulletin, 92*, 726–748.

Ross, S. M., Smith, L. J., & Casey, J. P. (1997). Preventing early school failure: Impacts of Success for All on standardized test outcomes, minority group performance, and school effectiveness. *Journal of Education for Students Placed at Risk, 2*(1), 29–53.

Rowan, B. P., & Miller, J. M. (2006, April). *Organizing schools for instructional improvement: A longitudinal study of three CSR models.* Paper presented at the annual meeting of the American Educational Research Association, San Francisco, CA.

Shadish, W. R., Cook, T. D., & Campbell, D. T. (2002). *Experimental and quasi-experimental designs for generalized causal inference.* New York: Houghton Mifflin.

Singer, J. D., & Willett, J. B. (2003). *Applied longitudinal data analysis: Modeling change and event occurrence.* New York: Oxford University Press.

Smith, M. S., & O'Day, J. A. (1991). Systemic school reform. In S. Fuhrman & B. Malen (Eds.), *The politics of curriculum and testing.* Bristol, PA: Falmer Press.

Supovitz, J. A., & May, H. (2004). A study of the links between implementation and effectiveness of the America's Choice comprehensive school reform design. *Journal of Education for Students Placed at Risk, 9*(4), 389–419.

Supovitz, J. A., Poglinco, S. M., & Snyder, B. A. (2001). *Moving mountains: successes and challenges of the America's Choice comprehensive school reform design.* Philadelphia: Consortium for Policy Research in Education.

Supovitz, J. A., & Taylor, B. S. (2003). *The impact of standards-based reform in Duval County, Florida, 1999–2002.* Philadelphia: Consortium for Policy Research in Education.

Supovitz, J. A., & Taylor, B. S. (2005). Systemic education evaluation: Evaluating the impact of systemwide reform in education. *American Journal of Evaluation, 26*(2), 204–230.

Supovitz, J. A., Taylor, B. S., & May, H. (2002). *Impact of America's Choice on student performance in Duval County, Florida.* Philadelphia: Consortium for Policy Research in Education.

U.S. Department of Education. (2005). *Department of Education, 2005.* Retrieved August 1, 2005 from http://www.ed.gov/programs/compreform/funding.html

Yen, W. M. (1986). The choice of scale for educational measurement: An IRT perspective. *Journal of Educational Measurement, 23*(4), 399–325.

1.13

2 × 2 FACTORIAL PRE- AND POSTTEST DESIGN (BETWEEN-SUBJECTS)

Effects of Perceived Disability on Persuasiveness of Computer-Synthesized Speech

Steven E. Stern, John W. Mullennix, and Stephen J. Wilson

ABSTRACT: Are perceptions of computer-synthesized speech altered by the belief that the person using this technology is disabled? In a 2 × 2 factorial design, participants completed an attitude pretest and were randomly assigned to watch an actor deliver a persuasive appeal under 1 of the following 4 conditions: disabled or nondisabled using normal speech and disabled or nondisabled using computer-synthesized speech. Participants then completed a posttest survey and a series of questionnaires assessing perceptions of voice, speaker, and message. Natural speech was perceived more favorably and was more persuasive than computer-synthesized speech. When the speaker was perceived to be speech-disabled, however, this difference diminished. This finding suggests that negatively viewed assistive technologies will be perceived more favorably when used by people with disabilities.

Ranging from the use of prosthetics and mobility aids to special computer applications, assistive technologies aid disabled people in performing everyday tasks and overcoming their disabilities (Seelman, 1993). Researchers have examined the social perceptions of disabled people (e.g., Gething, 1992), but there is little known about how the use of assistive technologies by disabled people moderates those effects.

Much of the research on perceptions of disabled people suggests that they are perceived differently than nondisabled people. Interestingly enough, the empirical literature (e.g., Elliot & Frank, 1990; Makas, 1988) often reports the existence of a positive prejudice. Unlike other stigmatized groups (e.g., African Americans), disabled people are often rated more favorably than nondisabled people are. Research

Steven E. Stern, John W. Mullennix, and Stephen J. Wilson, Department of Psychology, University of Pittsburgh at Johnstown.

This research was funded by grants from the University of Pittsburgh–Johnstown Research Council and the University of Pittsburgh Central Research Development Fund. We acknowledge Marissa Andolina, Heather Clark, Melissa Guntrum, and Erin King for their assistance on this project.

Correspondence concerning this article should be addressed to Steven E. Stern or John W. Mullennix, Department of Psychology, University of Pittsburgh at Johnstown, Johnstown, Pennsylvania 15904. E-mail: sstern@pitt.edu or mullenni@pitt.edu generally suggests that the likelihood of positive reactions to disabled people increases with prior contact (Esposito & Reed, 1986), when disabled people exhibit socially appropriate responses to contact (Elliot & Frank, 1990), and for certain types of disabilities over others (MacDonald & Hall, 1969). The present study seeks to examine whether people using a technology designated as an assistive aid will be perceived differently if they are disabled.

Text-to-speech (TTS) systems are computerized systems that "speak" the words that are typed into a computer terminal. Often used as a talking aid for people with hearing and speaking impairments, this assistive technology makes it possible for people to speak who otherwise could not do so (Syrdal, 1995). In a recent study focusing on TTS in situations in which extended communication was used, Stern, Mullennix, Dyson, and Wilson (1999) examined the persuasiveness of computer-synthesized speech compared with human speech. They found that when people listened to a persuasive argument via either computer-synthesized speech or human speech, they perceived human speech as softer, higher pitched, less accented, less lengthy, less nasal, and more lively. More important, they perceived the human speaker as more knowledgeable, truthful, and involved, though less powerful. However, there were no statistically significant findings that suggested that synthetic speech was less persuasive than human speech.

In the present study, we expanded on this research by examining whether listeners' perceptions of synthesized speech would be affected by whether participants believed the person delivering the message was speech-disabled. We examined how the listener evaluated the speaker and the message as well as the degree to which the listener was persuaded.

We addressed four hypotheses. Hypotheses 1A and 1B address effects of speech type and disability on participants' ratings of perceptions of speech, message, and speaker. Hypotheses 2A and 2B address effects of speech type and disability on the persuasiveness of the message. The four hypotheses follow:

Hypothesis 1A: Synthesized speech will be rated less favorably than human speech.

Hypothesis 1B: Synthesized speech will be rated less favorably than human speech with this effect minimized when participants are led to believe that the person delivering the persuasive appeal is disabled.

Hypothesis 2A: Synthesized speech will be less persuasive than human speech.

Hypothesis 2B: Synthesized speech will be less persuasive than human speech with this effect minimized when participants are led to believe that the person delivering the persuasive appeal is disabled.

METHOD

Participants

Participants in this study were 189 undergraduates (41 men and 148 women) with an average age of 19.42 years. All participants were enrolled in introductory psychology classes at the University of Pittsburgh at Johnstown and were given course credit for their participation.

Materials

Apparatus

Two versions of a persuasive appeal were presented via VHS videotape. In the natural human speech condition, the actor read the message in a natural voice. The synthetic speech was presented via DECtalk Express V2.4C, a commercially available, high-quality TTS system. The actor used a keyboard to simulate outputting the message via the DECtalk TTS system. Participants watched the videotapes on a commercial quality television monitor.

Stimulus Materials

To increase the realism of our design, we used a videotaped persuasive appeal instead of an audiotaped appeal as we had used previously. The persuasive argument was a passage in favor of university-wide comprehensive exams and was adapted from models of strong arguments provided by Petty and Cacioppo (1986).

The human speech message was recorded by a male actor using his natural voice. The actor was a local college student who had acting experience. We chose this particular actor to emulate as closely as possible the way in which a persuasive speech on this topic would be actually recorded and used in the local college environment. For the synthetic TTS systems, default values for speech output were used. For DECtalk, the default male voice ("Paul") was used, along with default values for speech rate and all other parameters.

The second independent variable was disability. Level of disability was manipulated through the instruction set. In the nondisabled condition, researchers did not mention disability. In the disabled condition, if the speaker was using the TTS system, researchers told the participants that the speaker had a speech disability. If participants watched the video of the speaker using his own voice, they were told that he had a speech disability and was in the process of losing his ability to speak.

Dependent Measures

To measure various perceived qualities of speech, perceptions toward the message, and perceptions of the speaker, we used a series of three questionnaires containing a total of 25 semantic differential items developed by Leathers (1997) and Lucia (1998). The items examining perceived speech qualities consisted of seven scales (i.e., *loud voice–soft-spoken voice, deep voiced–squeaky voiced, fast speaking–slow speaking, heavy accent–faint accent, talked too long–didn't talk long enough, heavy nasality–faint nasality,* and *monotone–lively*). The items examining perceptions of the message consisted of six scales (i.e., *stimulating–boring, vague–specific, unsupported–supported, complex–simple, convincing–unconvincing,* and *uninteresting–interesting*). The items examining perceptions of the speaker consisted of 12 scales (i.e., *incompetent–competent, honest–dishonest, unassertive–assertive, uninformed–informed, untrustworthy–trustworthy, timid–bold, unintelligent–intelligent, straightforward–evasive, active–inactive, qualified–unqualified, sincere–insincere,* and *meek–forceful*).

To rate the effectiveness of the argument, we administered a series of 9-point semantic differential scales used by Baker and Petty (1994). This questionnaire consisted of six scales (i.e., *bad–good, foolish–wise, negative–positive, beneficial–harmful, effective–ineffective,* and *convincing–unconvincing*).

Persuasion was measured through the use of a pretest–posttest attitudinal measure developed after Rosselli, Skelly, and Mackie's (1995) Initial Attitude Questionnaire. Our measure consisted of 12 items rated on a 7-point Likert-type item scale (1 = *disagree completely*, 7 = *agree completely*). Three items were designed to measure attitudes relevant to the stimulus argument about comprehensive exams, and the other 9 items measured attitudes toward animal rights, environmentalism, and a proposed tuition raise.

Procedure

The experimenter randomly assigned participants to watch the persuasive appeal in one of the four experimental conditions: nondisabled–natural speech, nondisabled–synthetic speech, disabled–natural speech, or disabled–synthetic speech. Participants were told that the experiment concerned the topic of comprehensive exams in college and that they would listen carefully to a passage and answer some questions about it afterward. Participants in all conditions observed the videotaped message through the television monitor and were permitted to adjust the volume. The experimenter began the tape and requested that the participant signal when the tape was finished.

Participants completed the attitude measure as a pretest prior to the presentation of the message and as a posttest after the completion of the persuasive message. After completing the posttest attitude measure, participants completed the measures assessing speech characteristics, attitudes toward the message, attitudes toward the speaker, and effectiveness of the message. At the conclusion of the session, the experimenters debriefed each participant about the purpose of the study.

RESULTS

The data from the scales used to assess perceptions of the speech qualities, attitudes toward the message and the speaker, and effectiveness of the argument were analyzed using a series of 2 × 2 (Speech Type × Disability) factorial analyses of variance (ANOVAs). Speech type referred to whether the speech was human or synthetic. The data from the scales used to assess attitudes toward the message and the speaker were collapsed into five factors and four factors, respectively, on the basis of a factor loading analysis using the same scales conducted by Stern et al. (1999). Only significant results for each type of perception or attitude are listed below.

Effects of Speech Type on Ratings

We found support for Hypothesis 1A. For all of the dependent variables except for one (perception of the message as simple), human speech was perceived significantly more favorably than computer-synthesized speech. The mean ratings for human versus computer-synthesized voice for all of the variables and the significance levels can be seen in Table 1. Readers should note that the variables reflecting perception of the speaker and perceptions of the message are composite measures derived from summations of factor loadings. Not all of the factors have the same number of items aggregated into them.

Differential Effects of Speech Type by Disability on Ratings

Hypothesis 1B predicted that the degree to which human speech was favored over synthetic speech would be minimized when participants believed that the person delivering the appeal was disabled. This hypothesis was tested through a series of planned comparisons. Although we could have examined the interactions between disability and type of speech, the comparisons were chosen because they more directly tested the specific hypothesis.

The contrast *t*s were calculated by comparing the difference between the mean ratings of the two voice ratings in the nondisabled condition with the difference between the mean ratings of the two voice ratings in the disabled condition. Specifically, we expected that the difference between the speech conditions would be lower when the speaker was disabled than when he was not disabled. The mean square error

Table 1. Effects of Human Versus Synthetic Speech on Perceptions of Speaker, Message, Effectiveness of Message, and Speech Characteristics

Measure	Speech		F	p	r
	Human	Synthetic			
Perceptions of speaker ($N = 188$)					
Knowledgeable	16.25	14.84	15.89	<.001	.28
Truthful	10.79	9.87	8.19	.005	.21
Involved	15.31	12.61	35.47	<.001	.41
Powerful	9.51	8.21	16.93	<.001	.29
Accurate	12.09	11.46	6.46	.01	.18
Perceptions of message ($N = 188$)					
Captivating	9.44	7.05	36.07	<.001	.40
Clear	11.81	11.05	6.13	.01	.18
Convincing	5.33	4.57	15.36	<.001	.28
Simple	4.15	3.88	1.75	ns	.09
Effectiveness of message ($N = 188$)					
Good	6.80	5.80	23.77	<.001	.34
Wise	6.77	5.90	34.90	<.001	.30
Positive	6.91	6.26	8.40	.004	.21
Harmful	2.70	3.32	11.88	.001	.41
Unconvincing	3.12	4.27	21.75	<.001	.33
Ineffective	3.21	4.45	24.54	<.001	.34
Speech characteristics ($N = 189$)					
Soft	3.24	3.64	4.97	.03	.16
Squeaky	3.26	3.82	14.42	<.001	.27
Slow	4.10	2.72	51.09	<.001	.46
Unaccented	5.51	4.01	48.36	<.001	.45
Not long enough	3.69	2.84	27.72	<.001	.36
Less nasal	5.16	3.41	64.96	<.001	.51
Lively	4.27	1.44	235.61	<.001	.75

Note: The degrees of freedom were 1, 184 for all F values for perceptions of speaker, perceptions of message, and effectiveness of message. The degrees of freedom were 1, 185 for all F values for speech characteristics.

and degrees of freedom from the factorial ANOVA were used (Rosenthal & Rosnow, 1991). Table 2 provides the t values, significance levels, effect sizes (reported as rs), and contrast weights.

The predicted effect was found for the following four of the seven speech characteristics: soft, squeaky, not long enough, and lively (see Figure 1). The predicted effect was found for all four factors relating to perceptions of the message (captivating, clear, convincing, and simple; see Figure 2). The effect was also found for four of the five factors relating to perceptions of the speaker: knowledgeable, truthful, involved, and accurate (see Figure 3). Finally, four of the six scales assessing argument effectiveness (Baker & Petty, 1994) were also affected (see Figure 4). These were wise, positive, unconvincing, and ineffective.

Effect of Speech Type on Persuasion

We also found support for Hypothesis 2A, that computer-synthesized speech would be less persuasive than human speech. To assess this hypothesis, we conducted a three-way ANOVA with type of speech (human or synthetic), pretest versus posttest, and the topic on the attitudinal questionnaire. Although we expected that there would be no attitudinal change on the topics of tuition increase, animal rights, and environmentalism, we expected that a shift would be seen for the topic of comprehensive exams if persuasion occurred. More specifically, we expected that the shift would be more pronounced for human speech. We did find support for this hypothesis, $F(3, 185) = 5.36$, $p = .001$, $\eta^2 = .17$ (see Table 3 for the means for all conditions).

A more focused comparison was calculated that compared the difference between posttest human speech and posttest computer-synthesized speech scores on attitudes toward comprehensive exams with the combined difference between posttest human and computer-synthesized speech scores for the three irrelevant topics (i.e., tuition raise, animal rights, and environmentalism). Using the mean square error for between groups as a conservative (high) error term, the finding was sustained, $F(1, 185) = 1.96$, $p = .03$, one tailed, $r = .14$.

Table 2. Contrast t Values, Significance Levels, and Effect Sizes Examining Interactions Between Speech and Disability

Measure	Contrast		
	t	*p*	*r*
Speech characteristics (N = 189)			
Soft	1.65	.05	.12
Squeaky	2.48	.007	.18
Slow	1.14	*ns*	.08
Unaccented	0.72	*ns*	.05
Not long enough	4.99	<.001	.34
Less nasal	1.15	*ns*	.13
Lively	3.75	<.001	.27
Perceptions of message (N = 188)			
Captivating	1.63	.05	.12
Clear	2.24	.01	.16
Convincing	2.70	.004	.19
Simple	2.68	.004	.19
Perceptions of speaker (N = 188)			
Knowledgeable	7.12	<.001	.46
Truthful	4.30	<.001	.30
Involved	5.00	<.001	.34
Powerful	0.63	*ns*	.05
Accurate	3.00	.001	.22
Effectiveness of message (N = 188)			
Good	1.11	*ns*	.08
Wise	3.81	<.001	.27
Positive	3.48	<.001	.25
Harmful	0.60	*ns*	.04
Unconvincing	2.07	.02	.15
Ineffective	4.09	<.001	.29

Note: Contrast weights of 1 and −1 were used to make the comparisons. The degrees of freedom were 185 for all *t* values for speech characteristics. The degrees of freedom were 184 for all *t* values for perceptions of message, perceptions of speaker, and effectiveness of message.

Differential Effects of Speech Type by Disability on Persuasion

There was no support for Hypothesis 2B, that there would be a differential effect due to disability for persuasion. Multivariate analyses examining pretest and posttest attitudinal measures across all conditions failed to reveal the expected result.

Finally, although we did not make specific predictions of main effects for disability, we found two significant effects for disability. When the speaker was disabled, the message was perceived as more simple, $F(1, 184) = 4.04$, $p = .05$, $r = .14$, and the speech as more accented, $F(1, 185) = 5.72$, $p = .02$, $r = .17$.[1]

DISCUSSION

This study supported the hypothesis that the differential evaluations of human versus computer-synthesized speech would diminish when the person presenting the argument was perceived as disabled. As the data show, when the person delivering a persuasive appeal is perceived as disabled, his or her use of synthetic speech is viewed more positively than when the person is not perceived as disabled. In addition, we found support for our hypothesis that synthetic speech would be less persuasive than human speech.

What are the implications of the present study? We have demonstrated that TTS systems are perceived differently from human speech. Synthetic speech arguably affects the listener's perceptions of the speaker. The speaker is seen as knowing less, being less honest, and caring less. Furthermore, the person using TTS is at risk of being less persuasive than a speaking person.

We have also demonstrated that this disadvantage is mitigated when the observer believes the speaker to be disabled. This finding is encouraging inasmuch as listeners appear to shed some of the bias that they hold against computer-synthesized speech when they feel that the person needs to be using the synthesized voice to communicate. More generally, the use of the technology that people dislike is forgiven when it is seen as necessary.

Evaluations of people, the arguments that they make, and how persuasive they are are part of our everyday interactions. If any stigmatized group of people, such as individuals with disabilities, are viewed as less persuasive, this should be a matter of concern. Our findings are encouraging; inasmuch as this technology appears to be viewed negatively in general, disabled people appear to receive little negative bias when using this speech technology. Hence, we have no evidence from our data to suggest that speech-disabled people who use TTS systems to communicate will be less persuasive in their everyday social encounters.

One issue that deserves attention is that because of the sample size (N = 189), the study is statistically powerful. This large sample permits us to detect small effects that may not have practical significance. For many of the variables, there were statistically significant differences, although there was less than a 1-point difference on a 7-point scale between the groups.

In conclusion, social perception is clearly affected by the use of synthesized speech. That is, the effect of using this technology is moderated by listeners understanding of circumstances and attributions

---

[1] The degrees of freedom decreased to 184 because 1 participant failed to complete all the scales.

Table 3. Comparison of Pre- and Posttest Attitude Scores Comparing Attitudes Toward Comprehensive Exams With Alternative Topics by Type of Speech

Speech Type	Comprehensive Exams		Tuition Increase		Animal Rights		Environmentalism	
	Pretest	Posttest	Pretest	Posttest	Pretest	Posttest	Pretest	Posttest
Human	13.15	16.27	9.72	11.25	9.83	9.74	13.17	12.73
Computer-synthesized	13.51	15.17	9.57	11.46	9.93	9.71	12.86	12.42

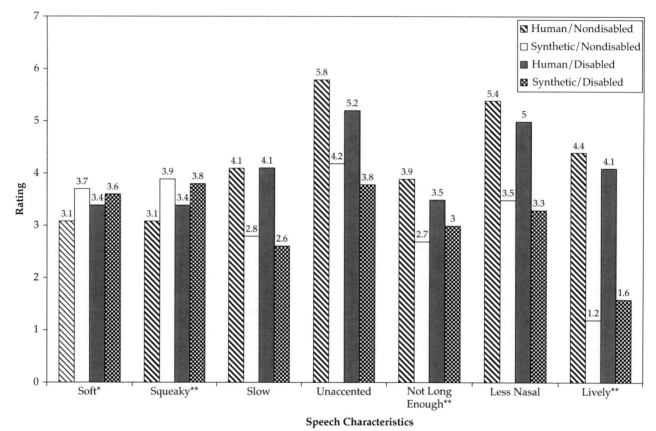

Figure 1. Mean ratings across speech and disability conditions for speech characteristics. $^*p < .05.$ $^{**} p < .01.$

for the use of TTS. Having found substantial effects on social perception for the use of TTS, it would seem worthwhile to investigate whether similar effects are ound with other assistive technologies. Furthermore, these findings underscore the degree to which technologies used in everyday life can affect how people form impressions of one another under a variety of circumstances.

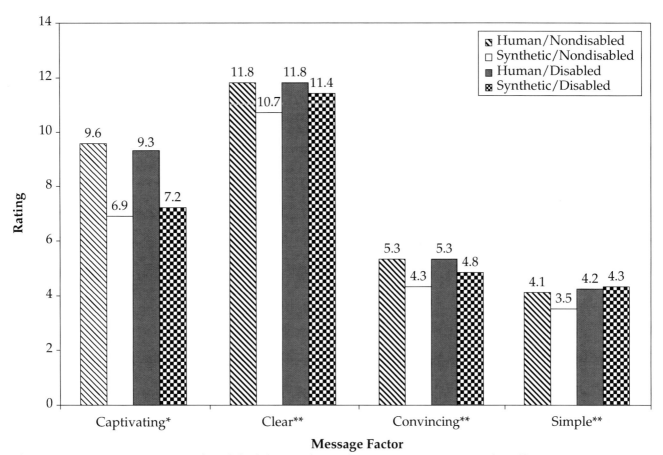

Figure 2. Mean ratings across speech and disability conditions for perceptions of message. *$p < .05$. ** $p < .01$.

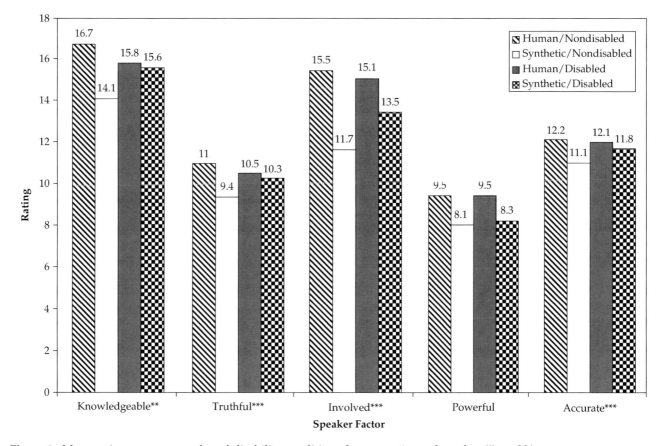

Figure 3. Mean ratings across speech and disability conditions for perceptions of speaker. ***$p < .001$.

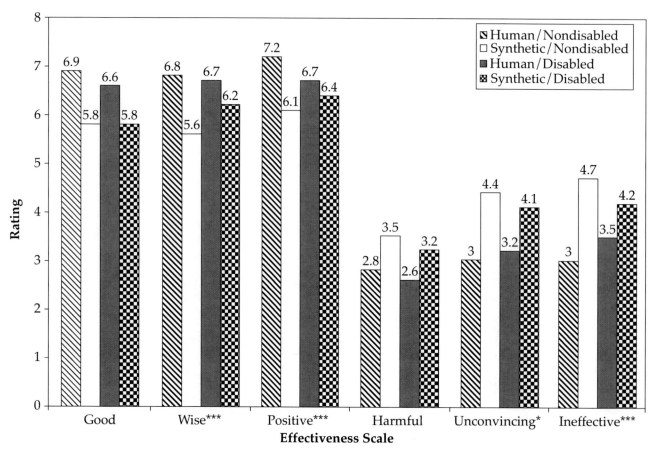

Figure 4. Mean ratings across speech and disability conditions for effectiveness of message. *p < .05. ***p < .001.

REFERENCES

Baker, S. M., & Petty, R. E. (1994). Majority and minority influence: Source position imbalance as a determinant of message scrutiny. *Journal of Personality and Social Psychology, 67,* 5–19.

Elliot, T., & Frank, R. (1990). Social and interpersonal reactions to depression and disability. *Rehabilitation Psychology, 35,* 135–147.

Esposito, B., & Reed, T. (1986). The effects of contact with handicapped persons on young children's attitudes. *Exceptional Children, 53,* 224–229.

Gething, L. (1992). Judgements of health professionals of personal characteristics of people with a visible physical disability. *Social Science and Medicine, 34,* 809–815.

Leathers, D. G. (1997). *Successful nonverbal communication: Principles and applications* (3rd ed.). Boston: Allyn & Bacon.

Lucia, V. C. (1998). *The effects of speech rate and speaker–listener congruence on persuasion.* Unpublished master's thesis, Wayne State University, Detroit, MI.

MacDonald, A., & Hall, J. (1969). Perception of disability by the nondisabled. *Journal of Consulting and Clinical Psychology, 33,* 654–660.

Makas, E. (1988). Positive attitudes toward disabled people: Disabled and nondisabled persons' perspectives. *Journal of Social Issues, 44,* 49–62.

Petty, R. E., & Cacioppo, J. T. (1986). *Communication and persuasion.* New York: Springer-Verlag.

Rosenthal, R., & Rosnow, R. L. (1991). *Essentials of behavioral research: Methods and data analysis* (2nd ed.). New York: McGraw-Hill.

Rosselli, F., Skelly, J. J., & Mackie, D. M. (1995). Processing rational and emotional messages: The cognitive and affective mediation of persuasion. *Journal of Experimental Social Psychology, 31,* 163–190.

Seelman, K. D. (1993). Assistive technology policy: A road to independence for individuals with disabilities. *Journal of Social Issues, 49,* 115–136.

Stern, S. E., Mullennix, J. W., Dyson, C., & Wilson, S. J. (1999). The persuasiveness of synthetic speech versus human speech. *Human Factors, 41,* 588–595.

Syrdal, A. K. (1995). Text-to-speech systems. In A. K. Syrdal, R. Bennet, & S. Greenspan (Eds.), *Applied speech technology* (pp. 99–126). Boca Raton, FL: CRC Press.

1.14

2 × 2 FACTORIAL POSTTEST DESIGN (BETWEEN-SUBJECTS)

Perceptions of Leader Transformational Ability

The role of leader speech and follower self-esteem

Yusuf Munir Sidani

ABSTRACT: Purpose – The purpose of this paper is to assess the role of speech on transformational leadership attributions and the role of follower self-esteem in fostering the relationship between followers and their leaders.

Design/methodology/approach – Survey research was used testing specific relationships. A 2-by-2 experimental design was conducted including treatments of leader speech and attributes with follower self-esteem acting as a covariate.

Findings – Significant relationships between most attributions of transformational leadership and follower self-esteem were found. Inspirational leader speeches were found to lead to higher levels of attributed transformational abilities.

Research limitations/implications – It is suggested that there are contextual differences between different types of transformational relationships. Researchers are invited to distinguish between different types of charisma (social charisma vs business charisma).

Practical implications – Although the use of appropriate speech is an influential asset for the transformational leader, effective leadership does not solely depend on it. Organizations may benefit from inculcating communication training programs into their training agenda towards elevating their trainees to a higher level of leadership capability.

Originality/value – Leadership research has been heavily dominated by an overriding focus on leader attributes. This study concentrates on a specific leader impression management behavior (speech) and inculcates a follower variable (self-esteem) into the equation towards a better understanding of the leadership phenomenon.

KEYWORDS: Transformational leadership; Charisma; Personality; Leaders; Language; Self esteem.

Olayan School of Business, American University of Beirut, Beirut, Lebanon

Yusuf Munir Sidani is a member of the management and marketing track at the Olayan School of Business. His research interests include leadership and business ethics.

THEORETICAL FOUNDATIONS

Charismatic and Transformational Leadership

Charismatic leadership concepts have passed through several developmental cycles over the past few years (e.g. House, 1977; Conger and Kanungo, 1998; Shamir et al., 1993; Pearce et al., 2003). Earlier studies concentrated on attributes and behaviors of leaders. Later, charismatic leadership was seen as a "relationship" encompassing many parties, all of which are necessary for the development of such phenomenon. Klein and House (1995) described charisma as a "fire" which is the product of a spark (leader), flammable material (followers), and oxygen (a conducive environment). Later, the concept of transactional versus transformational leaders gained much popularity with charisma now regarded as one component in transformational leadership.

Bass (1985), extending the work of Burns (1978), described transactional leaders as those who deal with subordinates based on an exchange process. Transactional leaders show followers the kinds of rewards/penalties associated with compliance/noncompliance. The more exciting transformational leadership, on the other hand, elevates the individual motives of their followers while inspiring them to higher levels of performance (Pounder, 2003; Tickle et al., 2005). Revisions of transformational leadership led to the development of several components. These include attributed charisma, idealized influence, inspiration (or inspirational motivation), individualized consideration, and intellectual stimulation (Bass and Avolio, 1990, 1993; Bass, 1998). Charisma refers to visionary leaders who are admirably seen as displaying behaviors of sacrifice and group benefit. Idealized influence involves leaders with whom followers identify and who are able to talk followers into commitment to their beliefs. Inspiration results from the ability to raise followers' enthusiasm through providing meaning and challenge. Individualized consideration refers to the ability to recognize followers' needs – caring for them on an individual basis. Finally, intellectual stimulation refers to instances where followers perceive their leaders as able to develop their capacity to look at old problems in new ways.

Much of the research to follow tackled the whole concept of transformational leadership instead of just focusing on charisma alone. One question for researchers became how much effectiveness can be attributed to charisma alone, or to other components of transformational leadership? In other words, can a charismatic leader, who lacks the other transformational qualities, lead the organization into higher degrees of effectiveness and performance? Other related questions revolve around the impressions that such leaders foster among their followers and the role of such impressions on follower behavior in their organizations.

Leaders and Impression Management Tactics

House (1977) indicated that charismatic leaders employ image building in their behavioral repertoire. Bass (1985) referred to the use of impression management techniques by charismatic leaders to gain followers' admiration. Conger and Kanungo (1998) contended that charismatic leaders use such behaviors in inspiring followers and getting their commitment. Gardner and Avolio (1998) presented a model of the processes where leaders use impression management behaviors in creating and sustaining their heroic image. Howell and Frost (1989) conducted an experiment where they found that impression management behaviors yielded higher satisfaction and task performance from subjects. Shamir et al. (1994) studied the rhetoric of the charismatic leader and found elevated enthusiasm among the participants exposed to clever verbal cues. Gardner and Cleavenger (1998) found that exemplification, a major impression management technique, was positively related to transformational leadership components of charisma, inspiration, intellectual stimulation, and individualized consideration. Willner (1984) noted how leaders make extensive use of their rhetorical abilities and figurative expression leading to astounding effects on followers. Conger (1991) emphasized how attributed charisma can be enhanced through the use of rhetorical techniques such as alliteration, repetition, and rhythm. Den Hartog and Verburg (1997) examined communicative techniques of international business leaders and noted that charisma could be elevated through use of such rhetorical tools. Awamleh and Gardner (1999) found that the use of symbolic language appealing to followers' higher level values, leads to attributions of leader charisma and effectiveness.

Those studies have been continuously emphasizing the role of impression management techniques in fostering transformational images. The transformational leader is now perceived to be an expert in managing others perceptions of himself or herself. To do that, the leader uses a host of tools including body language, verbal cues, and artifactual tools (Gardner and Avolio, 1998). The impact of impression management techniques on fostering the transformational relationship has thus become widely accepted. The task before researchers has become which factors contribute to what impressions and how do these impressions help in forming the transformational image.

Followers' Attributes

Klein and House (1995) and Conger and Kanungo (1998) noted how the traits of followers have mostly been neglected in empirical research. Nevertheless, some studies have addressed the roles of followers in framing the charismatic relationship. Weierter (1997), for example, analyzed the effect of follower characteristics in framing the leadership phenomenon. Gardner and Avolio (1998) proposed that the self-systems of the followers play major roles in building such effects. Lord *et al.* (1999) suggested that followers impact leaders' self-schema. Jung and Avolio (1999) found that followers with a certain cultural orientation (collectivists) generated more ideas with a transformational leader as opposed to a transactional leader. Conger *et al.* (2000) found a strong relationship between follower reverence and charismatic leadership. Ehrhart and Klein (2001) conducted a laboratory study in which participants' values and personality dimensions were used to predict their preferences for certain leadership styles. Wofford *et al.* (2001) established that some followers are more susceptible to the efforts of transformational leader compared to other followers. Wong and Law (2002) found that the emotional intelligence of followers affected job performance and job satisfaction. Dvir and Shamir (2003) tested follower developmental traits as predictors of transformational leadership. These studies, though testifying to the increasing interest in the followers' part of the equation, do not negate the fact that the study of transformational leadership remains centered along leader attributes. Thus a key task for researchers is to study how do follower attributes contribute to enhancing or weakening the transformational relationship.

Self-esteem

Wells and Marwell (1976) indicated that self-esteem has been used in the social sciences to explore such areas as conformity, responses to threats or stress, dishonest behavior, social participation, competitive behavior, interpersonal attraction, group attraction, cognitive dissonance, equity-maintenance, helping and help-seeking behavior, and causal attributions. Self-esteem has been suggested as being one variable impacting the relationship between followers and charismatic leaders. Gardner and Avolio (1998) speculated that followers of personalized leaders (self-serving charismatic leaders) tend to be low-esteem individuals who are psychologically distressed. Low self-esteem individuals have been found to be very prone to join religious cults (Galanter, 1982). On the other hand, individuals with high self-esteem are less likely to follow a personalized leader. These individuals are more likely to follow a socialized leader through which they can achieve their own goals, and not merely identify with the leader's personal goals.

It should be noted that it is expected that low self-esteem individuals may attribute more transformational

qualities to leaders in general. In other words, they may be more receptive to the influence of the transformational leader. This study attempts to empirically test one follower trait – self-esteem – as a moderator in attributions of charisma and other transformational leadership measures. In addition, it attempts to address the impact of specific leadership styles and impression management techniques on the transformational relationship.

HYPOTHESES

Based on the above review, some research hypotheses are presented, along with the rationale relating to them.

Self-esteem

Are individuals with low self-esteem more prone to the transformational relationship? Previous studies have proposed that low self-esteem individuals are more likely to assign higher transformational qualities to leaders. Thus, it is hypothesized that:

H1. Individuals with low self-esteem attribute higher levels of transformational attributes to leaders.

Speech Content

This section addresses the impact of the content of the leader's speech in fostering leader's charisma and attributed transformational abilities. Conger (1991) distinguished between two types of rhetorical skills used by transformational leaders: framing and rhetorical crafting. Framing refers to the way a leader portrays the purpose of the organization or task at hand in a way that is energizing and motivating (Awamleh and Gardner, 1999). Rhetorical crafting is related to the usage of rhetorical devices to impact listeners, such as the use of metaphors, analogies, repetition, balance, and alliteration. It is suggested here that leaders who invoke such devices in their speeches are perceived to be more transformational than others. Accordingly it is hypothesized that:

H2. Leader speeches characterized by a good use of rhetorical devices will lead to higher levels of attributed transformational abilities.

Interaction of Leader Speech and Attributes

The above review suggested that both the leader's attributes and the leader's behaviors combine to influence the charismatic relationship. It has also been argued that impression management behaviors play a key role in this process. Of particular interest is the role of the content of the leader's speech as indicated by the previous hypothesis. The interaction of the transformational leader's attributes with high articulation skills leads to greater perceptions of transformational qualities. Therefore, the following hypotheses are advanced:

> H3. The interaction of the transformational leader style with inspirational speech leads to greater attributions of transformational leadership than is the case when either or both of these components are absent.

> H4. The interaction of the non-transformational leader style with non-inspirational speech leads to the lowest attributions of transformational leadership compared to other interactions.

METHODS

Participants and Research Design

The respondents were students (junior and senior) enrolled in undergraduate business courses in a North American University that has an enrollment exceeding 10,000 students. A total of 340 subjects participated in the study: 73 percent of the respondents were between 18 and 22 years of age and 65 percent were males. The raters were provided with some background information relating to a certain company's performance. They were given a general portrait of the organization with some financial data portraying a mild crisis in progress. The respondents were then divided into four groups and each group was exposed to a different treatment. As 27 responses were not usable, the final number of responses was 313 out of the original 340.

The study thus utilized a two-by-two experimental design (inspirational speech/non-inspirational speech by transformational/non-transformational leadership). Leadership style was manipulated by the development of two written leader profiles – one describing a transformational leader while the other described a transactional leader. The profiles were written following the literature relevant to those styles, as explained in the above sections. Speeches were developed through an extensive content analysis of speeches of transformational leaders as explained below.

The use of speeches as a treatment within an experiment is not a novel idea. Smith (1982) used recorded speeches to assess subordinates' responses. Holladay and Coombs (1993) examined the impact of delivery on perceptions of the leader's charisma. Written speeches have also been used in organizational research. Winter (1987) used the inaugural speeches of 34 US presidents, from Washington to Reagan, to measure presidential affiliation, power, and achievement motives. In their study of personality and charisma in the US presidency, House et al. (1991) used four sources to measure activity inhibition including president speeches.

Two kinds of leader speeches were presented to the subjects in this study. The first (inspirational speech) contained words reflecting high linguistic ability. This speech was constructed by compiling excerpts from speeches made by Steven Jobs, founder of Apple Computers, and Arch McGill, an AT&T top executive, as presented by Conger (1989). In addition, a portion of this speech came from John F. Kennedy's Inaugural Address on January 20, 1961, and his Commencement Address at American University in Washington on June 10, 1963. The passages borrowed from Kennedy's speech pertained to the importance of building and pursuing a vision for the future; those passages would also apply to the business context and could be expected to be heard from a charismatic business leader. The second speech was direct and reflected no extensive use of any of the above-mentioned techniques. Both speeches had virtually the same length, just above 300 words. The design yielded four cell sizes which were roughly equal. The respondents were exposed to the different treatments as follows ($n_{i,tm} = 81$; $n_{i,ts} = 76$; $n_{ni,tm} = 77$; $n_{ni,ts} = 79$; i = inspirational; ni = non-inspirational; tm = transformational; ts = transactional).

Measures

The Multifactor Leadership Questionnaire (MLQ-Form 5X) developed by Bruce Avolio, a widely-used measure, was used to measure respondents' perceptions of leadership. The MLQ has undergone a series of revisions and there are several slightly different versions that apply to the specific requirements of different organizations (Bryman, 1992). The MLQ's validity and reliability have been established in earlier studies (Hater and Bass, 1988; Avolio et al., 1988; Komives, 1991). The factors included attributed charisma, idealized influence, inspiration, individualized consideration, and intellectual stimulation for transformational leadership, and contingent reward and management by exception, active and passive, for transactional leadership. The covariate, self-esteem, was measured via the Rosenberg self-esteem scale (Rosenberg, 1979). Sample items of this scale include "I feel that I have a number of good qualities" and "I take a positive attitude toward myself".

RESULTS

A Multivariate Analysis of Covariance (MANCOVA) procedure was conducted with speech content and leadership style serving as factors and the subscales of the MLQ (Attributed charisma, idealized influence, inspiration, intellectual stimulation, individualized consideration, contingent reward, management by exception – active, management by exception – passive, laissez faire) acting as dependent variables

Table 1. Reliabilities of the Measures Used

Measure	Cronbach's Alpha
Attributed charisma	0.80
Idealized influence	0.80
Inspiration	0.87
Intellectual stimulation	0.85
Individualized consideration	0.87
Contingent reward	0.86
Management-by-exception – active	0.77
Management-by-exception – passive	0.86
Laissez-faire management	0.83

and self-esteem as a covariate. Reliability measures were calculated for all the sub-scales used in this study and the results were acceptable (Table 1).

The multivariate tests summarized in Table 2 indicate that there is a significant relationship ($p < 0.001$) between the covariate self-esteem and the combined dependent variables. Univariate analysis indicates significant relationships between all of the dependent variables (except intellectual stimulation and management by exception-active) and the covariate self-esteem. Correlations between self-esteem and the different measures (Table 3) indicate positive relationships between self-esteem and transformational leadership measures thus leading to the rejection of *H1*. A relationship was indeed established but, contrary to expectations, high – as opposed to low – self-esteem individuals assigned higher transformational qualities to leaders.

Multivariate analysis also indicates that there is a significant main effect for speech content ($p < 0.001$) on the combined dependent variables (Table 4). The univariate analysis indicates that contributions to this effect were made by attributed charisma, inspiration, intellectual stimulation, contingent reward, management by exception – active, and management by

Table 2. General MANCOVA Model: the Effects of Speech Content, Leader Attributes on Transformational Leadership Measures and Effectiveness with Self-esteem as a Covariate

Covariate Analysis	F
Self-esteem	
Model	3.80**
Attributed charisma	27.3**
Idealized influence	7.32**
Inspiration	7.64**
Intellectual stimulation	5.08
Individualized consideration	8.65**
Contingent reward	20.46**
Management by exception – active	0.68
Management by exception – passive	2.38**
Laissez-faire	2.45**

Note: *$p < 0.05$; ** $p < 0.01$

Table 3. Correlations – Self-esteem and Select Factors

	Self Esteem
Attributed charisma	0.24**
Idealized influence	0.27**
Inspiration	0.25**
Intellectual stimulation	0.09
Individualized consideration	0.13*
Contingent reward	−0.20**
Management by exception – active	−0.11*
Management by exception – passive	−0.20**
Laissez-faire	−0.28**

Note: *$p < 0.05$; ** $p < 0.01$

exception – passive. No significant contributions were found for the idealized influence, individualized consideration, and *laissez-faire* measures. The results of this study provide support for *H2 vis-à-vis* attributed transformational qualities as the main effect of speech was significant for most measures.

The results also indicate that the interaction effect of leader style and leader speech content was significant ($p < 0.001$) – Table 5. In addition, there were significant univariate contributions for six of the dependent variables (attributed charisma, idealized influence, inspiration, intellectual stimulation, individualized consideration, contingent reward). There were no significant effects for management by exception – active, management by exception – passive, and *laissez-faire* measures. The MANCOVA procedure leads to the conclusion that the treatments, controlled for the effect of self-esteem, lead to significantly different attributions of transformational qualities.

Post hoc Procedures

The MANCOVA procedure does not tell which groups were most responsible for the significant results generated. To obtain this information, the current study performed univariate *F* tests (one-way

Table 4. General MANCOVA Model – Main Effect (speech)

Speech Main Effect	F
Speech content	
Model	4.54**
Attributed charisma	6.84**
Idealized influence	2.69
Inspiration	9.31**
Intellectual stimulation	10.65**
Individualized consideration	3.61
Contingent reward	5.68*
Management by exception – active	7.51**
Management by exception – passive	4.96*
Laissez-faire	0.4

Note: * $p < 0.05$; ** $p < 0.01$

Table 5. General MANCOVA Model – Interaction Effect

Interaction Effect	F
Speech content *leadership style	
Model	2.27**
Attributed charisma	8.69**
Idealized influence	6.06*
Inspiration	6.88**
Intellectual stimulation	4.46*
Individualized consideration	7.81**
Contingent reward	19.13**
Management by exception – active	0.39
Management by exception – passive	1.56
Laissez-faire	1.46

Note: * $p < 0.05$; ** $p < 0.01$

ANOVAs) for each dependent variable on an individual basis (Table 6). The results of the *post hoc* procedure indicate that the treatment most responsible for the overall significant group differences is the non-transformational, non-inspirational treatment. There are no significant differences across the first three treatments for the dependent variables. The transformational inspirational treatment did not lead to significantly higher attributions of transformational qualities revealing lack of support for *H3*. On the other hand, the non-transformational, non-inspirational treatment led to significantly lower attributions for most transformational qualities lending support to *H4*. These

Table 6. *Post hoc* Procedures
(one way analysis of variance)

	F-value	Cases Where the Non-transformational, Non-inspirational Treatment was Responsible for most Group Differences
Attributed charisma	18.39**	✓
Idealized influence	6.84**	✓
Inspiration	9.79**	✓
Intellectual stimulation	8.22**	✓
Individualized consideration	13.11**	✓
Contingent reward	13.18**	–
Management by exception – active	9.39**	✓
Management by exception – passive	7.35**	✓
Laissez-faire	2.12	–

results indicate that speech content may be very important for leaders who do not otherwise exhibit transformational behaviors or skills.

DISCUSSION

It should be added that some may question the issue of using students as surrogates for potential followers in a job environment. While relying on student samples could pose potential weaknesses (Moskowitz, 1971), they have been extensively utilized in prior research. Wyld and Jones (1997) indicate that student demographics seem to overcome earlier objections to their use as they possess similar traits to the population of interest. They contend that students – as a survey group – are increasingly approximating practicing managers. Greenberg (1987, p. 158) argues "that student and non-student samples may be equally useful sources of information about the processes underlying organizational phenomena". The student respondents in this study were business students and the scenarios developed were business scenarios that students are commonly expected to experience soon after graduation. Accordingly, the results obtained could suggest as to how typically will business people behave in business situations given their personalities and the context within which they are working.

Based on the results of this study, it can be argued that effective speech can help to create an image of trustworthiness and credibility. Respondents who were exposed to an inspirational speech attributed more transformational abilities to the leader. These respondents felt that they were inspired more and that they were intellectually stimulated. When the leader's behavior was described as being non-transformational, the inspirational speech had a sizable impact. Due to the effect of speech, attributions of charisma were still assigned unto the leader whose behavior was not described as being transformational. This indicates that the inspirational message was most effective when the leader was not perceived as exhibiting transformational behaviors in the profile given. What this essentially means is that for leaders who display a lot of heroic behaviors, their speech does not necessarily add significantly to their perceived charisma and other transformational abilities. However, for those who do not display such behavior, the speech does indeed add to their perceived transformational abilities.

The role of self-esteem in the charismatic relationship has been discussed primarily in the sociological literature, which analyzed cults and similar groups. The premise has been that such groups usually revolve around a charismatic leader who is able to attract low self-esteem individuals. This assumption is sometimes generalized to all kinds of relationships. It is important to note that there are important differences between various contexts. Based on the results of this study, a distinction could be made between "social charisma" and "business charisma." Social charisma is mostly dominant in religious and political arenas. Business charisma is the charisma one finds in business settings. The emergence of the charismatic phenomenon becomes dependent on things that go beyond the traits or behaviors of the leader. This study has shown that what is being said is important; but the context of what is being said becomes – at least – as important.

Followers in social contexts include, among others, those low self-esteem individuals who yearn for a leader to direct them into a better world. In some cases, especially in personalized charismatic relationships, low self-esteem individuals may be actively sought and recruited. Many social movements can tolerate, sometimes encourage, the existence of such individuals. The very existence and continuation of the charismatic relationships in such movements may depend on the degree that these followers stay within that movement.

In the business arena, however, this is not necessarily true. The business setting cannot normally tolerate such a relationship with low self-esteem followers, since many may be wholly or partially unproductive. Business organizations depend upon effective results, both in the short and the long term. As a consequence, individuals who cannot perform their required tasks are normally forced, one way or another, out of the group. The role of leadership in these situations is to produce momentum, motivation, and enthusiasm for the organization's goals. Thus, it is suggested here that followers of transformational business leaders are much more likely to possess moderate to high levels of self-esteem. Organizational researchers need to be alert to instances where business settings differ from other social settings. That is, followers in business environments do not necessarily hold the same attributes as followers of other social movements. Self-esteem represents one such follower attribute which is likely to differ across various settings. More research is evidently needed to delineate other distinctions between business and social charisma.

IMPLICATIONS FOR PRACTICE

The last few years have witnessed an increasing awareness of the importance of leadership and the possibilities of teaching it. Delineating the exact process of learning is not an easy task since leadership theorists have been more involved in constructing theories of leadership rather than techniques of leadership (Wright and Taylor, 1985). Conger (1989) describes how skills-training programs may be implemented focusing on building visionary, communication, trust-building, and empowerment skills. Special attention, relevant to this study, could be given to transformational communication skills. This is important as subordinates will respond most favorably to what they perceive to be honest and authentic dialogue that reflects the true feeling of the leader. The secret sometimes in a leadership situation could be related to leader's ability to foster an impression of trustworthiness.

This study has been mainly concerned with words and their impact on persuasion. This is a very specific skill, albeit an important one, that could be used very effectively if found in the leader's repertoire. The use of appropriate speech is a very influential asset for the transformational leader. Leaders are continuously faced with opportunities to sell their ideas and their vision to their employees, clientele, and other stakeholders. In some cases, as the results of this study would suggest, leaders with strong inspirational messages are more likely to gain the attention and trust of their listeners. An inspirational message would deliver the leader's message more effectively. This act of trusting and admiring the organizational leader could also lead to trust in, and commitment to, the organization.

Effective leadership builds on inspirational messages but does not solely depend on it. It is true that organizations may benefit from inculcating communication training programs into their training agenda for the purpose of elevating their trainees to a higher level of leadership capability. Skills building should, however, be part of a much larger leadership program that not only helps participants to acquire new skills, but teaches trainees new ways of thinking and new ways of approaching problems. Even a perfect program in communication skills will not single-handedly produce influential leaders. A proper choice of words in communicating with others is fundamental, yet it is not sufficient – on its own – in building trust or elevating organizational performance.

REFERENCES

Avolio, B.J., Waldman, D.A. and Einstein, W.O. (1988), "Transformational leadership in a management game simulation", *Group & Organization Studies*, Vol. 13 No. 1, pp. 59–80.

Awamleh, R. and Gardner, W.L. (1999), "Perceptions of leader charisma and effectiveness: the effects of vision content, delivery, and organizational performance", *Leadership Quarterly*, Vol. 10 No. 3, pp. 345–73.

Bass, B.M. (1985), *Leadership and Performance Beyond Expectations*, Free Press, New York, NY.

Bass, B.M. (1998), *Transformational Leadership: Industrial, Military, and Educational Impact*, Lawrence Erlbaum Associates, Mahwah, NJ.

Bass, B.M. and Avolio, B.J. (1990), "The implications of transactional and transformational leadership for individual, team, and organizational development", in Woodman, R.W. and Passmore, W.A. (Eds), *Research in Organizational Change and Development*, JAI Press, Greenwich, CT, Vol. 4, pp. 231–72.

Bass, B.M. and Avolio, B.J. (1993), "Transformational leadership: a response to critiques", in Chemers, M.M and Ayman, R. (Eds), *Leadership Theory and Research: Perspectives and Directions*, Academic Press, San Diego, CA, pp. 49–80.

Bryman, A. (1992), *Charisma and Leadership in Organizations*, Sage, London.

Burns, J.M. (1978), *Leadership*, Harper & Row, New York, NY.

Conger, J.A. (1989), *The Charismatic Leader: Behind the Mystique of Exceptional Leadership*, Jossey-Bass, San Francisco, CA.

Conger, J.A. (1991), "Inspiring others: the language of leadership", *Academy of Management Executive*, Vol. 5 No. 1, pp. 31–45.

Conger, J.A. and Kanungo, R.N. (1998), *Charismatic Leadership in Organizations*, Sage Publishers, Thousand Oaks, CA.

Conger, J.A., Kanungo, R.N. and Menon, S.T. (2000), "Charismatic leadership and follower effects", *Journal of Organizational Behavior*, Vol. 21 No. 7, pp. 747–67.

Den Hartog, D.N. and Verburg, R.M. (1997), "Charisma and rhetoric: communicative techniques of international business leaders", *Leadership Quarterly*, Vol. 8 No. 4, pp. 355–91.

Dvir, T. and Shamir, B. (2003), "Follower developmental characteristics as predictors of predicting transformational leadership: a longitudinal field study", *Leadership Quarterly*, Vol. 14 No. 3, pp. 327–44.

Ehrhart, M.G. and Klein, K.J. (2001), "Predicting followers' preferences for charismatic leadership: the influence of follower values and personality", *Leadership Quarterly*, Vol. 12 No. 2, pp. 153–79.

Galanter, M. (1982), "Charismatic religious sects and psychiatry: an overview", *American Journal of Psychiatry*, Vol. 139 No. 12, pp. 1539–48.

Gardner, W.L. and Avolio, B.J. (1998), "The charismatic relationship: a dramaturgical perspective", *Academy of Management Review*, Vol. 23 No. 1, pp. 32–58.

Gardner, W.L. and Cleavenger, D. (1998), "The impression management strategies associated with transformational leadership at the world-class level: a psychohistorical assessment", *Management Communication Quarterly*, Vol. 12 No. 1, pp. 3–41.

Greenberg, J. (1987), "The college sophomore as guinea pig: setting the record straight", *Academy of Management Review*, Vol. 12 No. 1, pp. 157–9.

Hater, J.J. and Bass, B.M. (1988), "Superiors' evaluations and subordinates' perceptions of transformational and transactional leadership", *Journal of Applied Psychology*, Vol. 73 No. 4, pp. 695–702.

Holladay, S.J. and Coombs, W.T. (1993), "Communicating visions: an exploration of the role of delivery in the creation of leader charisma", *Management Communication Quarterly*, Vol. 6 No. 4, pp. 405–27.

House, R.J. (1977), "A 1976 theory of charismatic leadership", in Hunt, J.G. and Larson, L.L. (Eds), *Leadership: The Cutting Edge*, Southern Illinois University Press, Carbondale, IL, pp. 189–207.

House, R.J., Spangler, W.D. and Woycke, J. (1991), "Personality and charisma in the US presidency: a psychological theory of leader effectiveness", *Administrative Science Quarterly*, Vol. 36 No. 3, pp. 364–96.

Howell, J.M. and Frost, P.J. (1989), "A laboratory study of charismatic leadership", *Organizational Behavior and Human Decision Processes*, Vol. 43 No. 2, pp. 243–69.

Jung, D.I. and Avolio, B.J. (1999), "Effects of leadership style and followers' cultural orientation on performance in group and individual task conditions", *Academy of Management Journal*, Vol. 42 No. 2, pp. 208–18.

Klein, K.J. and House, R.J. (1995), "On fire: charismatic leadership and levels of analysis", *Leadership Quarterly*, Vol. 6 No. 2, pp. 183–98.

Komives, S.R. (1991), "The relationship of hall directors' transformational and transactional leadership factors to resident assistant's perceived outcomes", *Journal of College Student Development*, Vol. 32 No. 6, pp. 509–15.

Lord, R.G., Brown, D.J. and Freiberg, S.J. (1999), "Understanding the dynamics of leadership: the role of follower self-concepts in the leader/follower relationship", *Organizational Behavior & Human Decision Processes*, Vol. 78 No. 3, pp. 167–203.

Moskowitz, H. (1971), "Managers as partners in business decision research", *Academy of Management Journal*, Vol. 14 No. 3, pp. 317–25.

Pearce, C.L., Sims, H.P. Jr, Cox, J.F., Ball, G., Schnell, E., Smith, K.A. and Trevino, L. (2003), "Transactors, transformers and beyond: a multimethod development of a theoretical typology of leadership", *Journal of Management Development*, Vol. 22 No. 4, pp. 273–307.

Pounder, J.S. (2003), "Employing transformational leadership to enhance the quality of management development instruction", *Journal of Management Development.*, Vol. 22 No. 1, pp. 6–13.

Rosenberg, M. (1979), *Conceiving the Self*, Basic Books, New York, NY.

Shamir, B., House, R. and Arthur, M.B. (1993), "The motivational effects of charismatic leadership: a self-concept based theory", *Organizational Science*, Vol. 4 No. 4, pp. 577–94.

Shamir, B., Arthur, M.B. and House, R.J. (1994), "The rhetoric of charismatic leadership. A theoretical extension, a case study, and implications for research", *Leadership Quarterly*, Vol. 5 No. 1, pp. 25–42.

Smith, B.J. (1982), "An initial test to a theory of charismatic leadership based on the response of subordinates", unpublished PhD dissertation, University of Toronto, Toronto.

Tickle, E.L., Brownlee, J. and De Nailon, D. (2005), "Personal epistemological beliefs and transformational leadership behaviours", *Journal of Management Development*, Vol. 24 No. 8, pp. 706–19.

Weierter, S.J.M. (1997), "Who wants to play 'follow the leader'? A theory of charismatic relationships based on routinized charisma and follower characteristics", *Leadership Quarterly*, Vol. 8 No. 2, pp. 171–93.

Wells, L.E. and Marwell, G. (1976), *Self-Esteem: Its Conceptualization and Measurement*, Sage Publications, Beverly Hills, CA.

Willner, A.R. (1984), *The Spellbinders: Charismatic Political Leadership*, Yale University Press, New Haven, CT.

Winter, D.G. (1987), "Leader appeal, leader performance, and the motive profiles of leaders and followers: a study of American presidents and elections", *Journal of Personality and Social Psychology*, Vol. 52 No. 1, pp. 196–202.

Wofford, J.C., Whittington, J.L. and Goodwin, V.L. (2001), "Follower motive patterns as situational moderators for transformational leadership effectiveness", *Journal of Managerial Issues*, Vol. 13 No. 2, pp. 196–211.

Wong, C.S. and Law, K.S. (2002), "The effects of leader and follower emotional intelligence on performance and attitude: an exploratory study", *Leadership Quarterly*, Vol. 13 No. 3, pp. 243–74.

Wright, P. and Taylor, D. (1985), "The implications of a skills approach to leadership", *Journal of Management Development*, Vol. 4 No. 3, pp. 15–28.

Wyld, D.C. and Jones, C.A. (1997), "An empirical look at the use of managerial and non-managerial student subjects for inquiries into ethical judgement", *Management Research News*, Vol. 20 No. 9, pp. 18–30.

1.15

2 × 2 FACTORIAL PRE- AND POSTTEST DESIGN (WITHIN-SUBJECTS)

Effects of a Body Image Challenge on Smoking Motivation Among College Females

Elena N. Lopez,* David J. Drobes,* J. Kevin Thompson,* and Thomas H. Brandon*

OBJECTIVE: Previous correlational and quasi-experimental research has established that weight concerns and negative body image are associated with tobacco smoking, cessation, and relapse, particularly among young women. This study examined the causal influence of body image upon smoking motivation by merging methodologies from the addiction and body image literatures. *Design:* Using a cue-reactivity paradigm, the study tested whether an experimental manipulation designed to challenge women's body image—specifically, their weight dissatisfaction—influenced their motivation to smoke. Female college smokers ($N = 62$) were included in a 2 X 2 factorial, within-subjects design (body image cues X smoking cues). *Main Outcome Measures:* Self-reported urge to smoke was the primary dependent measure, with skin conductance as a secondary measure. *Results:* As hypothesized, the presentation of smoking images and thin model images produced greater urges to smoke than control images. Additionally, trait weight concerns moderated the effect of the body image manipulation such that those women with greater weight concerns produced greater craving to the thin model image (when smoking cues were not present). *Conclusion:* These findings provide initial evidence that situational challenges to body image are causally related to smoking motivation.

KEYWORDS: Tobacco smoking; weight concerns; body dissatisfaction; cue reactivity; women.

*University of South Florida and the H. Lee Moffitt Cancer Center & Research Institute

Elena N. Lopez and J. Kevin Thompson, Department of Psychology, University of South Florida. Tampa, and the H. Lee Moffitt Cancer Center & Research Institute, Tampa, Florida; David J. Drobes and Thomas H. Brandon, Departments of Psychology and Interdisciplinary Oncology, University of South Florida, and the H. Lee Moffitt Cancer Center & Research Institute.

This study was supported in part by National Cancer Institute Grant R01 CA80706. We thank Michael Brannick and Erika Litvin for their helpful suggestions.

Correspondence concerning this article should be addressed to Thomas H. Brandon, Tobacco Research & Intervention Program, H. Lee Moffitt Cancer Center & Research Institute, 4115 E. Fowler Avenue, Tampa, FL 33617. E-mail: thomas.brandon@moffitt.org

Tobacco smoking is the leading cause of preventable mortality and morbidity in women (Husten, 1998; U.S. Department of Health and Human Services, 2001). The decline in smoking prevalence over the past three decades has been slower among women than among men (Escobedo & Peddicord, 1996, 1997; National Center for Health Statistics, 1993; Ockene, 1993), with 19.2% of women smoking as of 2003 (Centers for Disease Control and Prevention [CDC], 2005). Females are not only initiating at higher rates than males, but they appear to have more difficulty in quitting and remaining abstinent (Bjornson et al., 1995; Blake et al., 1989; Centers for Disease Control and Prevention, 1994; Cepeda-Benito, Reynoso, & Erath, 2004; Ockene. 1993; Ortner, Schindler, Kraigher, Mendelsohn, & Fischer, 2002; Swan, Ward, Carmelli, & Jack, 1993; Ward, Klesges, Zbikowski, Bliss, & Garvey, 1997; Wetter et al., 1999).

Gender differences are also found among smokers' outcome expectancies. Outcome expectancies are beliefs about the consequences of one's actions, and are posited to play a motivational role in behavior (Bandura, 1977). Smoking outcome expectancies, specifically, are beliefs about the consequences or effects of smoking, and there is substantial correlational and experimental evidence that these expectancies influence smoking behavior (Brandon, Juliano, & Copeland. 1999). One key gender difference concerns expectancies regarding weight and body image. Women report weight control as a perceived benefit of smoking (CepedaBenito & Reig-Ferrer, 2000; Ward et al., 1997). Women, more so than men, appear to tie their smoking behavior to reasons of weight control, weight loss, fear of weight gain, or actual, post-cessation weight gain (Killen, 1998; Klesges & Klesges, 1988; Klesges et al., 1998; M. D. Levine, Perkins, & Marcus, 2001; Ogden, 1994; Perkins, Levine, Marcus, & Shiffman, 1997; Ward et al., 1997). Thoughts about weight, eating disorder symptoms, weight control attempts, body image disturbances, and general weight concerns are predictive of females – but not males – initiating smoking (French, Perry, Leon, & Fulkerson. 1994; Killen, 1998; Stice & Shaw. 2003). Younger women smokers are up to 4 times more likely than men to report weight gain as a cause of relapse (Swan et al., 1993). And in general, women hold higher outcome expectancies than men of cigarette's utility for controlling appetite and weight (Brandon & Baker, 1991).

Whereas these relationships appear across women of all ages, college students represent a particularly important subpopulation. First, individuals in the age group of 18–24 have not decreased their prevalence of smoking and continue to have among the highest smoking prevalence (CDC, 2002). In addition, the prevalence of current smoking increased among those aged 20–24 with 13 or more years of education. There

is also evidence suggesting that university females report greater body dissatisfaction and beliefs of being overweight than they had as high school seniors (Vohs. Heatherton, & Herrin, 2001). Within the college student population, it is a high priority to achieve and maintain an ideal weight, and the use of dieting strategies of all types are extremely high in this group (Klesges & Klesges, 1988; Thompson, Heinberg, Altabe, & Tantleff-Dunn, 1999). In addition to these risk factors, college females are often transitioning from occasional to regular smoking (Lantz, 2003: Ling & Glantz, 2002); thus, understanding this specific population may lead to the development of secondary prevention interventions.

Although the descriptive, correlational, and quasi-experimental findings reviewed above suggest a general relationship between smoking and weight concerns among women, direct evidence of a causal relationship between weight concerns or body image and smoking motivation is lacking. Moreover, it is not known whether phasic fluctuations in body image influence situational cravings for cigarettes, and if this relationship is moderated by a woman's general body satisfaction. Such a relationship would be consistent with a causal influence of body image on smoking motivation.

THE CURRENT STUDY

The current study was designed to address the causality gaps in the literature noted above by examining the role of state body dissatisfaction in the situational motivation to smoke among college women. State body dissatisfaction refers to the transitory dimension of one's body image, which may fluctuate over time and vary in intensity (Thompson, 2004). For example, studies have found that women, immediately following exposure to images of thin models, report increased shame, body and weight dissatisfaction, and weight concern (e.g., Birkeland et al., 2005; Cattarin, Thompson, Thomas, & Williams, 2000; Groesz, Levine, & Murnen, 2002; see M. Levine & Harrison, 2004 for a review; Pinhas, Toner, Ali, Garfinkel, & Stuckless, 1999; Posavac, Posavac, & Posavac, 1998). In contrast, trait body dissatisfaction refers to a relatively stable individual difference in the evaluation of one's body, upon which state body dissatisfaction is superimposed (Thompson, 2004).

The primary aim of this study was to test if state body dissatisfaction would lead to a situational increase in smoking motivation among young college females. Thus, we examined whether a body image manipulation (BIM) affected self-reported urge to smoke and physiological responses associated with smoking motivation. The study also included a more traditional smoking cue manipulation (SCM) that has repeatedly been shown to produce subjective, physiological, and behavioral reactivity, thought to reflect prior classical conditioning (Brandon, Piasecki, Quinn, & Baker, 1995; Carter & Tiffany, 1999; Niaura et al., 1988; Rohsenow, Niaura, Childress, Abrams, & Monti, 1990). Cue reactivity can help identify the stimuli and situations that provoke ongoing smoking and relapse (e.g., Tiffany. 1990). The most robust indices of cue-reactivity have been self-reported urge to smoke and skin conductance response (Carter & Tiffany, 1999). The SCM was included in this initial study because we were unsure as to whether a smoking cue might be necessary to evoke an effect of the BIM on smoking motivation. This was based on Lang's theory (1984) that the probability of accessing an affective state (urge, in this case) appears to be a function of the number of propositions that are matched to the emotion prototype. Thus, because we did not know if a smoking cue would have an additive or synergistic effect upon the effect of the body image cue, or alternatively if it might mask an effect of the BIM, we presented the body image cue both with and without a simultaneous smoking cue. We hypothesized that greater urges to smoke would be found for both the SCM (replicating previous research) and the BIM. In addition, we tested for interactions between the two factors, although we had no a priori hypotheses about the relationship.

In past research on body image satisfaction, greater effects of BIMs were found among participants with greater trait body dissatisfaction (Groesz et al., 2002; Thompson et al., 1999). Therefore, our second aim was to evaluate level of trait body dissatisfaction as a moderating variable in the BIM, hypothesizing that those individuals with greater trait body dissatisfaction would show the greatest impact of the body image challenge on smoking urge. Because weight appears to be the dimension of body image most closely associated with smoking, we focused specifically on weight dissatisfaction with both our state and trait measures.

METHOD

Experimental Design and Overview

The study used a randomized 2 (BIM) X 2 (SCM) crossed factorial, within-subjects design. Pairs of cues associated with each factor were presented simultaneously on a split screen. Thus, the four conditions were thin models/smoking cues (T/S), thin models/ neutral cues (T/N), neutral cues/smoking cues (N/S), and neutral cues/neutral cues (N/N). Participants completed measures assessing basic demographics, smoking history, smoking expectancies, and weight dissatisfaction. The primary dependent measure was self-reported smoking urge, with skin conductance response as the secondary dependent measure.

Participants

Participants were 62 college females recruited through fliers posted on local college campuses, freshman orientation screenings, classroom recruitment, and psychology courses that offered extra credit for participating in research. Potential participants were screened over the telephone for the following inclusion criteria: female, currently attending college, aged 18–24, smoking at least 10 cigarettes per day for at least 1 year. Aside from those receiving extra course credit, participants were paid $20.00.

Measures

Smoking Status Questionnaire (SSQ)

This form was used to assess the participants' smoking status and nicotine dependence. Along with questions assessing years smoked and frequency of inhaling when smoking, it included the Fagerström Test for Nicotine Dependence (FTND), the standard, validated measure of nicotine dependence (Heatherton, Kozlowski, Frecker, & Fagerström. 1991).

Short Smoking Consequences Questionnaire (Short SCQ; Myers, MacPherson, McCarthy, & Brown, 2003)

This is a 21-item version of the original 50-item Smoking Consequences Questionnaire (SCQ; Brandon & Baker, 1991), a standard instrument for measuring smoking expectancies among college students. We were interested in only the Appetite/Weight Control factor ($\alpha = .94$), although we administered the entire short form.

Eating Disorders Examination-Questionnaire Version-Weight Concern subscale (EDEQ-WC; Fairburn & Beglin, 1994)

The EDEQ is a self-report measure based on the Eating Disorders Examination clinical interview (Cooper & Fairburn, 1987), with excellent psychometric properties. We administered only the Weight Concern subscale ($\alpha = .88$, for the current sample), which served as our measure of trait weight dissatisfaction.

Urge to Smoke Visual Analogue Scale (Smoke VAS)

Participants used a computerized system to rate their urge to smoke. A computer trackball was mounted on the arm of the recliner in which the participant sat, on the side with the dominant hand. The trackball controlled a computer-generated horizontal bar graph that was displayed on a computer screen following each trial. The bar-graph rating provided a score between 0 and 20, with higher numbers indicating a greater urge to smoke. This scale assessed participants' immediate urge to smoke following the experimental trials. The alpha coefficient was greater than .93 in each condition.

Weight Dissatisfaction Visual Analogue Scale (Weight Dissatisfaction VAS)

This state measure of weight dissatisfaction was administered in a similar fashion as the Smoke VAS, above, and was included as a manipulation check for the BIM (i.e., the ascertain that the body image cues produced changes in degree of weight dissatisfaction). The bar-graph rating provided a score between 0 and 20, with higher numbers indicating greater satisfaction with their weight. This scale was then reverse-coded so that higher scores indicated greater dissatisfaction. This type of state body dissatisfaction measure has been widely used in body image exposure studies (Birkeland et al., 2005; Thompson, 2004). The alpha coefficient was above .98 in each condition.

Object Desirability Form

On this form the participant indicated whether she wanted to own the items displayed in each image, including the clothing worn by the thin models. The instructions asked the participant to imagine using the item. This instrument served to reinforce the cover story as a study on consumer preferences, and it also encouraged social comparison to the thin models.

Other Materials

Carbon monoxide (CO) Monitor

A BreathCo carbon monoxide recorder (Vitalograph. Inc., Lenexa. KS) was used to measure the participants' level of expired CO in parts per million (ppm). This measurement was taken immediately following informed consent. (This measure was not available for the first 7 participants.)

Body-related Images

Six images of thin models, taken from fashion-oriented websites, were used in the experimental condition of the BIM. All models appeared to be in the age group of the participants, and a sampling of ethnically/racially diverse individuals was chosen. A separate sample of thirty college females evaluated these six images along with six images of average-weight models and six images of overweight models, in random order. Participants made their evaluations on a 1 to 7 Likert scale. Each image was evaluated on the model's appearance from *very underweight* to *very overweight* and the model's attractiveness from *very*

attractive to *very unattractive*. The three sets of models were rated as equivalent on attractiveness, but the thin model images were rated significantly lower in weight than either the normal-weight models or the overweight models ($ps < .001$).

Smoking Cue Images

Six images were used in the experimental condition of the SCM. The images were of standard smoking cues, such as lit cigarettes (e.g., Carter et al., 2006).

Neutral Images

Thirty-six neutral images were selected as control images for the BIM and the SCM. Images chosen were inanimate objects with no obvious relation to eating, grooming, body weight, physical body image, or smoking, and thus were not expected to trigger any body or weight evaluation nor smoking urges. The images were devoid of any human figures. These neutral images (e.g., household appliances, furniture) were selected from the International Affective Picture System (IAPS; Center for the Study of Emotion and Attention [CSEA], 1995), and have been previously demonstrated to produce low arousal: Also used were comparable images taken with a digital camera of similar objects (e.g., office supplies, household objects). Such neutral images represent the most common control images used in experimental research on body image (Groesz et al., 2002). Although images of average size models offer a potentially cleaner design by controlling for human images, they are less often used in this research due to difficulties in obtaining such images and because female participants often perceive average sized models as being overweight (Groesz et al., 2002). Therefore, for this initial study, we chose to use inanimate objects rather than average weight women as control images.

Physiological Measure

Skin conductance has been found to be a reliable index of cue-reactivity in previous drug studies, and it provides an objective measure of cue reactivity (Carter & Tiffany, 1999; Niaura et al., 1988). Skin conductance responses provide an index of sympathetic arousal (e.g., Raskin, 1973). To measure skin conductance, two large (8mm) Ag-AgCl electrodes filled with K - Y Jelly were attached to the hypothenar eminence on the participant's non-dominant hand. For each trial, skin conductance was recorded for a two-second baseline period and for 10 seconds from the beginning of the image onset. Skin conductance was sampled and stored at 20 Hz and later reduced to the median for each half-second interval. These values were converted from A/D units to microsiemens and then normalized via log-transformation.

Procedure

Pre-manipulation

All participants who met inclusion criteria were scheduled for an individual appointment in the afternoon or evening. Upon their arrival, participants were informed that they were participating in a study to understand smokers' feelings and reactions to images of different consumer products. Participants provided a breath sample for the CO analysis and then were instructed to step outside to smoke one of their own cigarettes. This was done in an attempt to minimize and standardize nicotine withdrawal. Upon returning inside, the participant was asked to complete the demographic questionnaire, the SSQ, the Short-SCQ, and the TBD measures.

Manipulation

The participant was seated in a comfortable chair in front of a 17" color computer monitor. A female researcher attached the electrodes to the participant and then left her alone for 4 minutes to acclimate to the testing situation. Upon returning, the researcher explained the procedure of the study, including instructions on how to evaluate the images, complete the Object Desirability Form, and use the trackball to make VAS ratings. The participant then was left alone to complete the session.

The participant was exposed to a series of slides containing paired images. Each slide, or trial, was comprised of a photo representing the BIM (thin model or neutral image) displayed next to an image representing the SCM (smoking cue or neutral image), with the two manipulations counterbalanced with respect to the two sides of the screen. One of each of the four trial types comprised a block, and participants were randomly exposed to a total of three blocks. An additional Neutral/Neutral slide was displayed after each of the experimental trials to allow the data collection to be a fluid process, while also producing some distraction to reduce carry-over effects from one experimental trial to the next.

The participant was instructed to view each slide for the entire 17 s presentation. A tone was presented 10 s into the trial, at which point the participant made her ratings on the Object Desirability Form. The VAS ratings then were displayed consecutively and followed by 7 s of black screen, during which a 2 s baseline for the next trial was collected.

Post-manipulation

Upon completion of the session and removal of electrodes, participants' height and weight were measured. The participants were asked to guess the purpose of the study (to confirm that the cover story was successful), debriefed, and paid.

Overview of Analyses. With skin conductance data, deviation scores were created by subtracting the 2-second baseline for each trial from each of the other 20 half-second time points for that trial. These scores were then averaged across the three trials of each type. Mean scores per trial type were also calculated for the VAS measures. These resultant means were used in subsequent analyses. The main analyses were conducted with a 2×2 (body image vs. neutral cues × smoking cues vs. neutral cues) repeated measure analyses of variance (ANOVA).

RESULTS

Participant Characteristics

Demographic and smoking history characteristics are presented in Table 1. Although all participants met the inclusion criteria of smoking a minimum of 10 cigarettes per day for at least one year, the mean score on the FTND (3.29) indicates a relatively low level of nicotine dependence, as would be expected in a college student population.

Manipulation Check

No participants reported during debriefing that they disbelieved the cover story, and none guessed the purpose of the study. To confirm that the thin images increased weight dissatisfaction, we conducted a 2×2 repeated measure ANOVA with Weight Dissatisfaction VAS as the dependent variable. As expected, the thin images ($M = 10.30$, $SE = .82$) produced greater weight dissatisfaction than the neutral images ($M = 9.77$, $SE = .79$). indicating

Table 1. Participant Characteristics

Variable	%	M	SD
Age		20.03	1.50
Smoking history			
Years smoked		4.58	2.37
Cigarettes smoked per day		15.65	4.89
Fagerström score		3.29	2.00
Carbon monoxide level (ppm)*		15.16	8.74
Race			
Caucasian	91.9		
African American	3.2		
Other	4.8		
Hispanic ethnicity	8.1		
Year in school			
Freshman	32.3		
Sophomore	29.0		
Junior	22.6		
Senior	16.1		
Body Mass Index		23.93	6.35

*Breath CO was collected from 55 participants.

that the manipulation was successful, $F(1, 61) = 13.02$, $p = .001$. No effect was found for the smoking images on Weight Dissatisfaction VAS, $F(1, 61) = .42$, $p = .52$.

Primary Analyses

Urge ratings. A 2 × 2 repeated measures ANOVA was conducted to test the effects of the manipulations on the VAS smoking urge ratings. As expected, a main effect of the SCM was found, $F(1, 61) = 17.13$, $p < .001$, $\eta_p^2 = .22$. Smoking images produced greater urges to smoke ($M = 8.97$, $SE = .77$) than neutral images ($M = 8.00$, $SE = .69$), replicating previous cue-reactivity research. The hypothesized main effect for the BIM was also found, $F(1, 61) = 5.80$, $p = .02$, $\eta_p^2 = .09$. As predicted, the thin model images produced greater urges to smoke ($M = 8.62$, $SE = .73$) than neutral images ($M = 8.35$, $SE = .72$). There was no interaction between the two manipulations ($p = .42$), indicating that they had independent, additive effects rather than synergistic effects (see Table 2).

Skin conductance

As shown in Figure 1, there was a clear initiation of a skin conductance response at 3 seconds after stimulus onset. The deviation scores were averaged across seconds 3 to 8 to create a mean response magnitude for each trial type per participant. A main effect was found

for the SCM, $F(1, 61) = 11.27$, $p = .001$, $\eta_p^2 = .16$, with smoking images producing greater skin conductance reactivity ($M = -.004$, $SE = .002$) than neutral images ($M = -.011$, $SE = .002$), again replicating previous cue-reactivity research. As predicted, a main effect was also found for the BIM, $F(1, 61) = 6.39$, $p = .01$, $\eta_p^2 = .10$, indicating the thin model images produced greater skin conductance reactivity ($M = -.006$, $SE = .002$) than neutral images ($M = -.010$, $SE = .001$). However, a significant interaction was also found, $F(1, 61) = 5.64$, $p = .02$, $\eta_p^2 = .09$, indicating that the smoking cue and the thin model images had a synergistic effect on skin conductance. That is, the condition with both a smoking cue and a thin model cue produced a greater response than any of the other three conditions. Although main effects of both factors were found for urge and skin conductance, the two measures were not correlated within any of the four conditions ($rs = -0.04 - 0.19$, ns).

Moderators

For our second aim, we had hypothesized that the level of trait weight dissatisfaction would moderate the effect of the BIM on smoking urge, such that the manipulation would have the greatest impact among women with higher trait weight dissatisfaction. The hypothesized moderator effect was tested as the interaction between the BIM and the EDEQ-WC ($M = 11.08$,

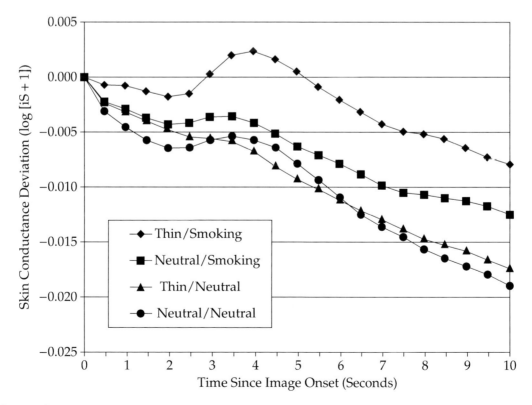

Figure 1. Skin conductance response for each trial type displayed as deviation scores from the trial baseline.

Table 2. Means (Standard Deviations) of Smoking Urge Ratings

Smoking Cue ($p < .001$)	Body Image Manipulation ($p = .02$)	
	Thin	Neutral
Smoking	9.06 (6.10)	8.88 (6.13)
Neutral	8.19 (5.57)	7.82 (5.36)

$SD = 8.30$), which approached significance, $F(1, 60) = 2.125$, $p = .15$. Moreover, a significant three-way interaction was found between the two within-subjects factors and trait weight dissatisfaction, $F(1, 60) = 6.70$, $p = .01$. Separate ANOVAs were conducted within each condition of the SCM factor to determine the nature of the three-way interaction. In the absence of the smoking cue, a significant interaction effect with EDEQ-WC was found, $F(1, 60) = 7.58$, $p < .01$. In the presence of the smoking cue, there was no interaction with EDEQ-WC, $F(1, 60) = .69$, $p = .41$. Thus, only when smoking images were *not* present did trait weight dissatisfaction moderate the effect of the BIM. That is, in the absence of smoking cues, individuals with high trait weight dissatisfaction, as measured by the EDEQ-WC, reported the greatest differential urge responses to the images of thin models versus the neutral images.

We also tested both body mass index (BMI: kg/m²), which was correlated with EDEQ-WC, $r(60) = .38$, $p < .01$, and the Appetite/Weight Control factor of the Short-SCQ as potential moderator variables. However, neither variable moderated the main effects of either the manipulations or their interaction.

DISCUSSION

Given the wide range of descriptive and correlational evidence associating smoking with body image and weight-related variables among women, the overarching goal of the present experiment was to test the causal nature of this association in a controlled setting. That is, it examined how phasic fluctuations in one's weight dissatisfaction might influence motivation to smoke among college student women, a key demographic for body image distortion, weight-control behaviors, and associated disorders.

This study had two specific aims: to test the effects of a body image challenge and a traditional smoking cue presentation on smoking motivation, as indexed by self-reported urges to smoke and skin conductance response; and to test if trait body dissatisfaction moderated the relationship between the BIM and the reported urge to smoke. As we hypothesized, we replicated past studies finding that smoking cues

produced greater urges to smoke than neutral images. More novel, however, was our hypothesis that the presentation of images of thin models would also produce stronger smoking urges compared to neutral images. This hypothesis was also supported, although the effect size was smaller than that achieved with the smoking cues. The effects of the two manipulations were independent and additive, but not synergistic.

Results for the skin conductance response were similar to those found for the self-reported urges in that main effects were found for both the SCM and the BIM. However, in this case, we found an interaction indicating a synergistic effect. Indeed, the presence of a smoking cue appeared to potentiate the reaction to the thin body image. No significant association was found between the two reactivity measures, urge and skin conductance. Such response dysynchrony is a common finding in studies of cue-reactivity or affect in general (Abrams & Wilson, 1979; Drobes & Tiffany, 1997; Lang, 1979; Tiffany, 1990), and it may be more likely among samples that are low in nicotine dependence and not experiencing withdrawal effects during testing, such as the present sample (Sayette, Martin, Hull, Wertz, & Perrott, 2003). Similarly, dysynchrony may be more likely in studies such as the current one that do not induce intense affective states among participants (Hodgson & Rachman, 1974; Lang, 1984; Sayette et al., 2003).

Because a main effect of the BIM on craving was found, we tested trait weight dissatisfaction as a potential moderating variable. Other studies have demonstrated that women with greater baseline body dissatisfaction are more affected by BIMs (Groesz et al., 2002). Our hypothesis that those women with higher trait body dissatisfaction would be most affected by the thin model image, and thus show greater urge responses, was supported, but only in the absence of the smoking image. It may have been that the more potent smoking images overpowered or masked the more nuanced moderating effect of trait weight dissatisfaction on the presentation of body image cues. Nevertheless, the finding of any moderating effect, together with the main effect of the BIM, is consistent with a causal role of body image on smoking motivation. Moreover, it reinforces the evidence from earlier studies that trait body image dissatisfaction is a risk factor for smoking onset and maintenance (Bruckner, Spring, & Pingitore, 1994; Feldman, Hodgson, & Corber, 1985; King, Matacin, Marcus, Bock, & Tripolone, 2000; Stice & Shaw, 2003). In contrast with trait weight dissatisfaction, we found that participants' actual body mass, indexed by the BMI, although correlated with weight dissatisfaction, did not moderate the relationship between the BIM and reported urge to smoke. Thus, it was women's subjective weight dissatisfaction rather then their actual weight that appeared to influence their urge to smoke in response to images of thin models. This finding is consistent with a treatment study for women smokers that found that cognitive-behavioral therapy to reduce weight concerns was more effective at producing tobacco abstinence than a behavior program to prevent actual weight gain (Perkins et al., 2001). In this context, perception appears to be a stronger motivator than reality.

LIMITATIONS

The most notable limitation of this study is that, although hypotheses were largely supported, the effect sizes were modest. These include the group differences in weight dissatisfaction caused by the body image manipulation, as well as the main dependent variable of urge rating. There are several possible explanations for this. First, we selected an ethnically and racially diverse set of images of thin models as stimuli for the BIM, yet the participant sample was primarily Caucasian. This mismatch may have attenuated the intended social comparison (Birkeland et al., 2005; Brewer & Weber, 1994; Cattarin et al., 2000; Major, Sciacchitano, & Crocker, 1993; Miller, Turnbull, & McFarland, 1988), as found in a recent study of African American women presented with multi-race images (Frisby, 2004). Despite the advantages of standardization, it may be beneficial to tailor the images to participants' apparent ethnic and racial characteristics in future studies.

A second barrier to larger experimental effects may have been the use of a within-subjects design. We chose such a design because we wished to maximize the statistical power of this first study on the causal role of body dissatisfaction on smoking urges. However, in their meta-analysis, Groesz et al. (2002) found a greater effect size for BIMs that used between-subjects designs. A reasonable explanation for the relative weakness of within-subjects designs is that carry-over effects occur, even when distracter trials are used between experimental trials. The half-life of body image threats is unknown and may be longer than the inter-trial interval of this study.

The effects of the manipulations may have also been attenuated by our requirement that participants smoke a cigarette near the start of the session, about 30 minutes before beginning the exposure to the stimuli. We did this in an effort to standardize participants with respect to nicotine withdrawal. However, because college students tend to be light smokers, that single cigarette may have dampened subsequent urge responding. Future studies might either increase the interval between the baseline smoking and the stimulus presentation, or raise the inclusion criterion for number of cigarettes smoked per day. The latter would

likely increase the nicotine dependence and conditioning histories of the sample, which could produce greater cue-reactivity (Niaura et al., 1988). However, the cost would be a less representative sample of college-aged smokers.

Additionally, our cue-exposure methodology was unique in that we paired stimuli together to test for additive and synergistic effects. However, the use of the side-by-side images may also have reduced effect sizes by diffusing the participant's attention to any given stimulus. This might have been particularly the case with the body image stimuli, which may have been less salient in this context than were the smoking stimuli. Future studies could examine the effects of body image stimuli alone, or experiment with other techniques used to elicit body dissatisfaction that may be more potent (e.g., Fredrickson, Roberts, Noll, Quinn, & Twenge, 1998).

Ultimately, we cannot discount the possibility that the effect size is genuinely small. However, this does not negate the theoretical or public health significance of the finding. That we were able to elicit even a small increase in smoking motivation merely by displaying an image of a thin model for 17 seconds suggests the potential impact of a more powerful manipulation. Moreover, the compounding of relatively small risk factors may produce larger effects (c.f., Forehand, Biggar, & Kotchick, 1998), as seen by the additive effect of thin models and smoking cues. Similarly, cumulative effects over time may aggregate to produce significant impact on real-world outcomes (Abelson, 1985). In the case of threats to body image and its effect on smoking motivation, college women are constantly exposed to images of the thin ideal. Therefore, although our brief laboratory-based presentations of images of thin women may indeed model the immediate naturalistic effects of challenges to young women's body image, it cannot be expected to capture fully the totality and cumulative impact of repetitive real-world exposure to body image threats. A naturalistic study that maximizes external validity rather than internal validity — possibly using ecological momentary assessment (Stone & Shiffman, 1994) to examine the correspondence between body dissatisfaction and smoking motivation—would compliment the present experiment.

Finally, although we included multimodal assessment of situational smoking motivation (self-report and physiological reactivity), we did not measure actual smoking behavior. The findings from urge ratings and skin conductance supported our hypothesis that a body image challenge would increase responding on these measures, but we do not know the degree to which our laboratory paradigm models naturalistic smoking by young women. Nevertheless, several studies have demonstrated that smoking and alcohol cue reactions are predictive of subsequent self-administration behavior, particularly post-cessation relapse (e.g., Abrams, Monti, Carey, Pinto, & Jacobus, 1988; Cooney, Litt, Morse, Bauer. & Gaupp, 1997; Drummond & Glautier, 1994; Niaura, Abrams, Demuth, Pinto, & Monti, 1989; Rohsenow et al., 1994), which underscores the clinical significance of cue reactivity. Moreover, our paradigm, which was designed to maximize internal validity, produced results that were consistent with the descriptive and correlational studies reviewed earlier that emphasized external validity over internal validity. Thus, the studies complement each other and together support the causal role of body image and weight control in the motivation of smoking. Our findings, however, do not address whether state body dissatisfaction exerts its influence on smoking motivation through a direct route (e.g., due to expectancies that smoking will control weight) or via a mediator such as negative affect. It is possible that the presentation of thin models induced negative affect in participants, which in turn increased motivation to smoke (Baker, Piper, McCarthy, Majeskie, & Fiore, 2004; Brandon, 1994). Future research will need to examine mediators more closely.

In summary, this study drew upon theory and methodology from both addiction research and body image/eating disorder research to examine the role of phasic body dissatisfaction in motivating situational tobacco smoking. Through the use of an experimental design, the findings build upon and complement past descriptive and correlational research that has suggested a relationship between body image and smoking. It is the first study, to our knowledge, to manipulate body image in the laboratory and observe concomitant changes on indices of smoking motivation consistent with a causal relationship. Future research will need to examine how this relationship impacts smoking frequency and intensity, leading to the development or maintenance of tobacco dependence. Finally, downstream treatment implications include the possibility of using images of thin women or other cues for body dissatisfaction as stimuli for extinction-based cue-exposure therapies, as well as the more general conclusion that body dissatisfaction and weight concerns should be direct targets of cognitive-behavioral treatments for smoking cessation (c.f. Perkins et al., 2001). Our findings are most relevant to the population sampled — young college women — because of their high prevalence of body dissatisfaction as well as the clinical potential for intervening before they become more tobacco dependent. However, because body dissatisfaction is common throughout the general population, it will be important to examine the generalizability of the findings.

REFERENCES

Abelson, R. P. (1985). A variance explanation paradox: When a little is a lot. *Psychological Bulletin, 97*(1), 129–133.

Abrams, D. B., Monti, P. M., Carey, K. B., Pinto, R. P., & Jacobus, S. I. (1988). Reactivity to smoking cues and relapse: Two studies of discriminant validity. *Behaviour Research and Therapy, 26*(3), 225–233.

Abrams, D. B., & Wilson, G. (1979). Effects of alcohol on social anxiety in women: Cognitive versus physiological processes. *Journal of Abnormal Psychology 88*(2), 161–173.

Baker, T. B., Piper, M. E., McCarthy, D. E., Majeskie, M. R., & Fiore, M. C. (2004). Addiction motivation reformulated: An affective processing model of negative reinforcement. *Psychological Review, 111*(1), 33–51.

Bandura, A. (1977). *Social learning theory*. Englewood Cliffs, N.J: Prentice Hall.

Birkeland, R., Thompson, J. K., Herbozo, S., Roehrig, M., Cafri, G., & van den Berg, P. (2005). Media exposure, mood, and body image dissatisfaction: An experimental test of person versus product priming. *Body Image: An International Journal of Research, 2*, 53–61.

Bjornson, W., Rand, C., Connett, J. E., Lindgren, P., Nides, M., Pope, F., et al. (1995). Gender differences in smoking cessation after 3 years in the Lung Health Study. *American Journal of Public Health, 85*(2), 223–230.

Blake, S. M., Klepp, K. I., Pechacek, T. F., Folsom, A. R., Luepker, R. V., Jacobs, D. R., et al. (1989). Differences in smoking cessation strategies between men and women. *Addictive Behaviors, 14*, 409–418.

Brandon, T. H. (1994). Negative affect as motivation to smoke. *Current Directions in Psychological Science, 3*(2), 33–37.

Brandon, T. H., & Baker, T. B. (1991). The Smoking Consequences Questionnaire: The subjective expected utility of smoking in college students. *Psychological Assessment, 3*(3), 484–491.

Brandon, T. H., Juliano, L. M., & Copeland, A. L. (1999). Expectancies for tobacco smoking. In I. Kirsch (Ed.), *How expectancies shape experience* (pp. 263–299). Washington, DC: American Psychological Association.

Brandon, T. H., Piasecki, T. M., Quinn, E. P., & Baker, T. B. (1995). Cue exposure treatment in nicotine dependence. In D. Colin Drummond, Stephen T. Tiffany, S. Gautier, & B.Remington (Eds.), *Addictive behaviour: Cue exposure theory and practice* (pp. 211–227). Brisbane, Queensland, Australia: John Wiley and Sons.

Brewer, M. B., & Weber, J. G. (1994). Self-evaluation effects of interpersonal versus intergroup social comparison. *Journal of Personality and Social Psychology, 66*(2), 268–275.

Bruckner, E., Spring, B., & Pingitore, R. (1994). Weight consciousness and food intake during smoking cessation. *Annals of Behavioral Medicine, 16*(Suppl.), S118.

Carter, B. L., Robinson, J. D., Lam, C. Y., Wetter, D. W., Tsan, J. Y., Day, S. X., et al. (2006). A psychometric evaluation of cigarette stimuli used in a cue reactivity study. *Nicotine & Tobacco Research, 8*(3), 361–369.

Carter, B. L., & Tiffany, S. T. (1999). Meta-analysis of cue-reactivity in addiction research. *Addiction, 94*(3), 327–340.

Cattarin, J. A., Thomspon, J. K., Thomas, C., & Williams, R. (2000). Body image, mood, and televised images of attractiveness: The role of social comparison. *Journal of Social and Clinical Psychology, 19*(2), 220–239.

Center for the Study of Emotion and Attention. (1995). *The international affective picture system* [Photographic slides]. Center for Research in Psychophysiology. University of Florida, P.O. Box 112766, Gainesville, FL 32611.

Centers for Disease Control and Prevention. (1994). Surveillance for selected tobacco-use behavior—United States, 1900–1994. *Morbidity and Mortality Weekly Report, 43*(Suppl.), 1–43.

Centers for Disease Control and Prevention. (2002). Cigarette smoking among adults—United States, 2000. *Morbidity and Mortality Weekly Report, 51*(29), 642–645.

Centers for Disease Control and Prevention. (2005). Cigarette smoking among adults—United States, 2003. *Morbidity and Mortality Weekly Report, 54*(20), 509–513.

Cepeda-Benito, A., & Reig-Ferrer, A. (2000). Smoking Consequences Questionnaire—Spanish. *Psychology of Addictive Behaviors, 14*(3), 219–230.

Cepeda-Benito, A., Reynoso, J. T., & Erath, S. (2004). Meta-analysis of the efficacy of nicotine replacement therapy for smoking cessation: Differences between men and women. *Journal of Consulting and Clinical Psychology, 72*(4), 712–722.

Cooney, N. L., Litt, M. D., Morse, P. A., Bauer, L. O., & Gaupp, L. (1997). Alcohol cue reactivity, negative-mood reactivity, and relapse in treated alcoholic men. *Journal of Abnormal Psychology, 106*(2), 243–250.

Cooper, Z., & Fairburn, C. (1987). The eating disorder examination: A semi-structured interview for the assessment of the specific psychopathology of eating disorders. *International Journal of Eating Disorders, 6*(1), 1–8.

Drobes, D. J., & Tiffany, S. T. (1997). Induction of smoking urge through imaginal and in vivo procedures: Physiological and self-report manifestations. *Journal of Abnormal Psychology, 106*(1), 15–25.

Drummond, D., & Glautier, S. (1994). A controlled trial of cue exposure treatment in alcohol dependence. *Journal of Consulting and Clinical Psychology, 62*(4), 809–817.

Escobedo, L. G., & Peddicord, .J. P. (1996). Smoking prevalence in US birth cohorts: The influence of gender and education. *American Journal of Public Health, 86*(2), 231–236.

Escobedo, L. G., & Peddicord, J. P. (1997). Long-term trends in cigarette smoking among young U.S. adults. *Addictive Behaviors, 22*(3), 427–430.

Fairburn, C. G., & Beglin, S. J. (1994). Assessment of eating disorders: Interview or self-report questionnaire? *International Journal of Eating Disorders, 16*(4), 363–370.

Feldman, W., Hodgson, C., &. Corber, S. (1985). Relationship between higher prevalence of smoking and weight concern amongst adolescent girls. *Canadian Journal of Public Health, 76*, 205–206.

Forehand, R., Biggar, H., & Kotchick, B. A. (1998). Cumulative risk across family stressors: Short- and long-term effects for adolescents. *Journal of Abnormal Child Psychology, 26*(2), 119–128.

Fredrickson, B. L., Roberts, T.-A., Noll, S. M., Quinn, D. M., & Twenge, J. M. (1998). That swimsuit becomes you: Sex differences in self-objectification, restrained eating, and math performance. *Journal of Personality and Social Psychology, 75*(1), 269–284.

French, S. A., Perry, C. L., Leon, G. R., & Fulkerson, J. A. (1994). Weight concerns, dieting behavior, and smoking initiation among adolescents: A prospective study. *American Journal of Public Health, 84*, 1818–1820.

Frisby, C. M. (2004). Does race matter? Effects of idealized images on African American women's perceptions of body esteem. *Journal of Black Studies, 34*(3), 323–347.

Groesz, L. M., Levine, M. P., & Murnen, S. K. (2002). The effect of experimental presentation of thin media images on body satisfaction: A meta-analytic review. *International Journal of Eating Disorders, 31*(1), 1–16.

Heatherton, T. F., Kozlowski, L. T., Frecker, R. C., & Fagerström, K.-O. (1991). The Fagerström Test for Nicotine Dependence: A revision of the Fagerström Tolerance Questionnaire. *British Journal of Addiction, 86*(9), 1119–1127.

Hodgson. R., & Rachman. S. (1974). Desynchrony in measures of fear. *Behaviour Research and Therapy, 12*, 319–326.

Husten, C. G. (1998). Cigarette smoking. In E. A. Blechman & K. D. Brownell (Eds.), *Behavioral medicine and women: A comprehensive handbook* (pp. 425–430). New York: Guilford Press.

Killen, J. D. (1998). Smoking prevention. In E. A. Blechman & K. D. Brownell (Eds.), *Behavioral medicine and women: A comprehensive handbook* (pp. 228–232). New York: Guilford Press.

King, T. K., Matacin, M., Marcus, B. H., Bock, B. C., & Tripolone, J. (2000). Body image evaluations in women smokers. *Addictive Behaviors, 25*(4), 613–618.

Klesges, R. C., & Klesges, L. M. (1988). Cigarette smoking as a dieting strategy in a university population. *International Journal of Eating Disorders, 7*(3), 413–419.

Klesges, R. C., Ward, K. D., Ray, J. W., Cutter, G., Jacobs, D. R., Jr., & Wagenknecht, L. E. (1998). The prospective relationships between smoking and weight in a young, biracial cohort: The Coronary Artery Risk Development in Young Adults study. *Journal of Consulting and Clinical Psychology, 66*(6). 987–993.

Lang, P. J. (1979). A bio-informational theory of emotional imagery. *Psychophysiology 16*(6), 495–512.

Lang, P. J. (1984). Cognition in emotion: Concept and action. In C. Izzard, J. Kaga, & R. Zajonc (Eds.), *Emotions, cognition, and behavior* (pp. 128–200). New York: Cambridge University Press.

Lantz, P. M. (2003). Smoking on the rise among young adults: Implications for research and policy. *Tobacco Control, 12*, 60–70.

Levine, M., & Harrison, K. (2004). Media's role in the perpetuation and prevention of negative body image and disordered eating. In J. K. Thompson (Ed.), *Handbook of eating disorders and obesity* (pp. 695–717). New York: Wiley.

Levine, M. D., Perkins. K. A., & Marcus, M. D. (2001). The characteristics of women smokers concerned about postcessation weight gain. *Addictive Behaviors, 26*, 749–756.

Ling, P. M., & Glantz, S. A. (2002). Why and how the tobacco industry sells cigarettes to young adults: Evidence from industry documents. *American Journal of Public Health, 92*(6), 908–916.

Major, B., Sciacchitano, A. M., & Crocker, J. (1993). In-group versus out-group comparisons and self-esteem. *Personality and Social Psychology Bulletin, 19*(6), 711–721.

Miller, D. T., Turnbull, W., & McFarland, C. (1988). Particularistic and universalistic evaluation in the social comparison process. *Journal of Personality and Social Psychology, 55*(6), 908–917.

Myers, M. G., MacPherson, L., McCarthy, D. M., & Brown, S. A. (2003). Constructing a short form of the Smoking Consequences Questionnaire with adolescents and young adults. *Psychological Assessment, 15*(2), 163–172.

National Center for Health Statistics. (1993). *Healthy People 2000 Review, 1992.* Hyattsville, MD: Public Health Service.

Niaura, R., Abrams, D. B., Demuth, B., Pinto, R., & Monti, P. M. (1989). Responses to smoking-related stimuli and early relapse to smoking. *Addictive Behaviors, 14*(4), 419–428.

Niaura, R., Rohsenow, D. J., Binkoff, J. A., Monti, P. M., Pedraza, M., & Abrams, D. B. (1988). Relevance of cue reactivity to understanding alcohol and smoking relapse. *Journal of Abnormal Psychology, 97*(2), 133–152.

Ockene, J. K. (1993). Smoking among women across the life span: Prevalence, interventions, and implications for cessation research. *Annals of Behavioral Medicine, 15*, 135–148.

Ogden, J. (1994). Effects of smoking cessation, restrained eating, and motivational states on food intake in the laboratory. *Health Psychology, 13*(2), 114–121.

Ortner, R., Schindler, S. D., Kraigher, D., Mendelsohn, A., & Fischer. G. (2002). Women addicted to nicotine. *Archives of Women's Mental Health, 4*(4), 103–109.

Perkins. K. A., Levine, M. D., Marcus. M. D., & Shiffman, S. (1997). Addressing women's concerns about weight gain due to smoking cessation. *Journal of Substance Abuse Treatment, 14*(2), 173–182.

Perkins, K. A., Marcus, M. D., Levine, M. D., D'Amico, D., Miller, A., Broge. M., et al. (2001). Cognitive-behavioral therapy to reduce weight concerns improves smoking cessation outcome in weight-concerned women. *Journal of Consulting and Clinical Psychology, 69*(4), 604–613.

Pinhas, L., Toner, B. B., Ali, A., Garfinkel, P. E., & Stuckless, N. (1999). The effects of the ideal of female beauty on mood and body satisfaction. *International Journal of Eating Disorders, 25*(2), 223–226.

Posavac, H. D., Posavac, S. S., & Posavac, E. J. (1998). Exposure to media images of female attractiveness and concern with body weight among young women. *Sex Roles, 38*(3–4): 187–201.

Raskin. D. C. (1973). Attention and arousal. In W. F. Prokasy & D. C. Raskin (Eds.), *Electrodermal activity in psychological research* (pp. 125–155). New York: Academic Press.

Rohsenow, D. J., Monti, P. M., Rubonis, A. V., Sirota, A. D., Niaura, R. S., Colby, S. M., et al. (1994). Cue reactivity as a predictor of drinking among male alcoholics. *Journal of Consulting and Clinical Psychology, 62*(3), 620–626.

Rohsenow, D. J., Niaura, R. S., Childress, A. R., Abrams, D. B., & Monti, P. M. (1990). Cue reactivity in addictive behaviors: Theoretical and treatment implications. *International Journal of the Addictions, 25*(7A–8A), 957–993.

Sayette, M. A., Martin, C. S., Hull, J. G., Wertz, J. M., & Perrott, M. A. (2003). Effects of nicotine deprivation on craving response covariation in smokers. *Journal of Abnormal Psychology, 112*(1), 110–118.

Stice, E., & Shaw, H. (2003). Prospective relations of body image, eating, and affective disturbances to smoking onset in adolescent girls: How Virginia slims. *Journal of Consulting and Clinical Psychology, 71*(1), 129–135.

Stone, A. A., & Shiffman, S. (1994). Ecological momentary assessment (EMA) in behavorial medicine. *Annals of Behavioral Medicine, 16*(3), 199–202.

Swan, G. E., Ward, M. N., Carmelli, D., & Jack, L. M. (1993). Differential rates of relapse in subgroups of male and female smokers. *Journal of Clinical Epidemiology, 46*, 1041–1053.

Thompson, J. K. (2004). The (mis)measurement of body image: Ten strategies to improve assessment for applied and research purposes. *Body Image: An International Journal of Research, 1*, 7–14.

Thompson, J. K., Heinberg, L. J., Altabe, M., & Tantleff-Dunn, S. (1999). *Exacting beauty: Theory, assessment, and treatment of body image disturbance*: Washington, DC: American Psychological Association.

Tiffany, S. T. (1990). A cognitive model of drug urges and drug-use behavior: Role of automatic and nonautomatic processes. *Psychological Review, 97*(2), 147–168.

U.S. Department of Health and Human Services. (2001). *Women and smoking: A report of the surgeon general*. Rockville, MD: Author. Vohs, K. D., Heatherton, T. F., & Herrin, M. (2001). Disordered eating and the transition to college: A prospective study. *International Journal of Eating Disorders, 29*(3), 280–288.

Ward, K. D., Klesges, R. C., Zbikowski, S. M., Bliss, R. E., & Garvey, A. J. (1997). Gender differences in the outcome of an unaided smoking cessation attempt. *Addictive Behaviors, 22*(4), 521–533.

Wetter, D. W., Kenford, S. L., Smith, S. S., Fiore, M. C., Jorenby, D. E., & Baker, T. B. (1999). Gender differences in smoking cessation. *Journal of Consulting and Clinical Psychology, 67*(4), 555–562.

PART II

Quantitative Methods Continued: Non-Experimental Research

2.01

POSTTEST DESIGN (WITHIN-SUBJECTS)

Evaluation of an Educational Intervention for Military Tobacco Users

Guarantor: CPT Beverly J. Morgan, NC USA
Contributor: CPT Beverly J. Morgan, NC USA

ABSTRACT: This study evaluated the short-term effect of a one-time tobacco hazard education intervention on tobacco use and intention to quit among military tobacco users. Of the 151 Army infantry soldiers who received the intervention, 60 (40%) participated in a 1-month follow-up survey. Respondents' reported pre-intervention tobacco habits included 51% smoking, 22% smokeless tobacco use, and 27% both. A one-group, posttest-only design demonstrated a decline in tobacco use in more than half of tobacco users: 14% quit, and 37% decreased use. However, 46% stayed the same, and 3% increased use. A statistically significant difference in tobacco use existed among the three subgroups of tobacco users ($p = 0.004$). Smokeless-tobacco-only users were more likely to quit than smoking-only or combined users. Eighty percent had positive thoughts or actions toward quitting tobacco use after the intervention. Results suggest that a one-time tobacco education intervention can positively influence tobacco use in the short term and motivate tobacco users toward quitting.

INTRODUCTION

Tobacco use, both smoking and smokeless, among military personnel continues despite cessation efforts by military health officials, including work-site smoking restrictions, prohibition of tobacco use in basic and advanced individual training, and the provision of tobacco cessation programs. Although a decrease in cigarette smoking by military personnel has been noted, decreasing from 51% in 1980 to approximately 30% in 1998,[1] rates continue to be higher than targeted goals. Current tobacco use patterns of military personnel indicate that 29.9% smoke cigarettes and

Family Nurse Practitioner Program, Graduate School of Nursing, Uniformed Services University of the Health Sciences, 4301 Jones Bridge Road, Bethesda, MD.

Presented in part at the Combined Army Preventive Medicine Conference, U.S. Army Center for Health Promotion and Preventive Medicine, Kansas City, MO, August 24–28, 1998.

32.6% smoke cigars and pipes.[1] Additionally, smokeless tobacco use has recently demonstrated a resurgence.[2] Overall, smokeless tobacco use by military members is 11.7%, with the highest use at 19% among males aged 18 to 24 years. The Healthy People 2000 objectives for military personnel was 20% for cigarette smoking and 4% for smokeless tobacco use by males age 24 years and younger.[3] Healthy People 2010 objectives, however, seek to achieve a further decrease in tobacco use, with targeted goals at 12% for all adults.[4]

The Department of Defense (DoD) estimated that smoking among the military cost the DoD approximately $930 million in 1995.[5] Of this amount, $584 million was for U.S. military health care expenditures, with an additional $346 million in lost productivity among active duty personnel. Tobacco use among military personnel also constitutes a major readiness issue for the U.S. armed forces, particularly among Army infantry soldiers. Cigarette smoking and smokeless tobacco use has been shown to adversely affect the athletic performance of soldiers.[6,7] Several studies have demonstrated that seasoned infantry soldiers and basic trainees who smoked were more likely to sustain injuries during training and occupational activities, including sprains, musculoskeletal pain, strains, and other overuse injuries.[8-10] One study found that daily use of smokeless tobacco was one of the risk factors associated with blister formation in U.S. Military Academy cadets in basic training.[11]

Knowledge of the health risks associated with tobacco use may be a factor in cessation, and it has been cited as a reason for a decline or cessation of tobacco use among Navy personnel.[12] Burns and Williams[13] reported that 45% of active duty military tobacco users had limited knowledge of one or more of the hazards associated with tobacco use. And Army smokers have been found to be less knowledgeable than their civilian counterparts regarding the likelihood of contracting seven smoking-related diseases.[14]

Numerous smoking cessation methods have been used during the past four decades with wide ranges of efficacy.[15-18] Although several community-based studies have demonstrated the efficacy of education as the sole intervention for tobacco cessation, studies among military personnel are limited or have reported mixed results.[19,20]

The purpose of this study was to examine tobacco use behaviors and intention to quit in a selected group of military tobacco users after a tobacco hazard education intervention. It was hypothesized that there would be differences in tobacco use behaviors and intention to quit among three groups of tobacco users (smoking only, smokeless tobacco only, and combined use) after tobacco education. Both the study purpose and hypothesis were intended to confirm previous research.

METHODS

Subjects and Setting

The study was conducted at Fort Campbell, Kentucky, an Army installation, after the request of a U.S. Army infantry brigade commander for tobacco use awareness training for tobacco users. A convenience sample of 151 male soldiers assigned to one specific infantry brigade participated in the education program. Study inclusion criteria were current tobacco use, either smoking or smokeless products, and attendance at the tobacco education presentation. (A copy of the tobacco use presentation, including slides and lesson plan, may be obtained from the author.)

Intervention

A tobacco hazard education presentation, specifically targeting the needs of the group, was developed. The presentation goals were primarily to inform military tobacco users about tobacco health hazards and effects on military readiness. Physical changes resulting from tobacco use were depicted, with numerous visual graphic images. Reasons to quit, preparing and approaches to quitting, maintaining abstinence, and resources for quitting also were provided.

Education was conducted by the author, a community health nurse trained and certified as an American Cancer Society (ACS) Freshstart facilitator. The education content was structured from session one of the ACS Freshstart program, a four-session quit-smoking program. The ACS has reported quit rates of 37% at 1 year with four sessions of the Freshstart smoking cessation program and one- to three-session quit rates of 30%.[21] Glover[22] found an abstinence rate of 38% among smokers at 6 months after the ACS Freshstart smoking cessation program. However, when he adapted the Freshstart smoking cessation program for smokeless tobacco users, he found only a 2.3% abstinence rate at 6 months, much lower than his 38% abstinence rate for smokers.

The 1-hour tobacco hazard education presentation was supplemented with a question-answer period, written educational and resource information, and the opportunity to enroll in the installation's Commit to Quit smoking cessation program. After the formal presentation, the unit command reinforced tobacco's negative effects on personal readiness and encouraged the participants to consider quitting.

Post-Intervention Survey

One month after the educational intervention, participants were surveyed and asked to complete a one-page pencil-and-paper questionnaire consisting of five questions to determine (1) the type of tobacco products used before the education program, (2) post-education tobacco use, and (3) post-education intention to quit. The questionnaire also allowed for written comments by the respondents. Participants indicated post-education tobacco use by selecting one of four responses: quit, decreased, stayed same, or increased.

Post-education intention to quit tobacco was categorized according to the transtheoretical model of behavior change.[23] This well-recognized model, developed by Prochaska[23] and widely used for smoking cessation, describes the five-stage process of change an individual passes through when changing a high-risk behavior. The five stages are precontemplation (no serious consideration of quitting within the next 6 months), contemplation (serious consideration of quitting in the next 6 months), preparation (recent quit attempts/intends to quit in the next month), action (quit for 6 months), and maintenance (continued quitting after 6 months). The content validity of the questionnaire was established using the transtheoretical model. However, definitions of intention to quit varied slightly from the stages of change described in the model. Face validity was established before survey of the participants.

The post-intervention study used a pre-experimental, one-group, post-test-only design. This design is commonly used to evaluate health promotion interventions, particularly when the researcher does not have an opportunity to pre-test subjects. Data were analyzed using χ^2 tests.

RESULTS

Tobacco Habit of Respondents

Sixty usable questionnaires were returned for a 40% participation rate in the post-intervention survey.

All participants were male. Participants were categorized by type of tobacco product used before and after the intervention: smoking only (cigarettes/cigars), smokeless only (chew/dip), and combined use (smoking and smokeless). Figure 1 shows the classification of the post-intervention survey respondents according to type and combination of tobacco use before the intervention.

Tobacco Use (Post-Intervention)

Table 1 represents respondents' reported tobacco use after the intervention. Thirty respondents (51%) reported decreasing or quitting tobacco use, whereas 29 respondents (49%) reported either an increase or no change in tobacco use. Respondents who reported decreased use were primarily smoking only ($N = 15$) and constituted 68% of those with decreased use. Respondents who reported having quit were primarily smokeless tobacco users ($N = 6$), accounting for 75% of those quitting tobacco. Respondents who were combined users ($N = 16$) reported the least improvement in tobacco use, with 13% reporting an increase in use.

Using a χ^2 test likelihood ratio, a significant difference ($p = 0.004$) was found among the three groups of tobacco users. When grouped by no improvement in tobacco use (increase use or no change) vs. an improvement in tobacco use (decreased use or quit), most respondents ($N = 30$) reported a positive change.

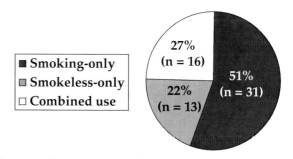

Figure 1. Pre-intervention habits of respondents by type of tobacco use ($N = 60$).

Table 1. Post-Intervention Activity by Type of Tobacco Use

Group	Increased		Same		Decreased		Quit	
	N	%	N	%	N	%	N	%
Smoking only ($N = 30$)	–	–	14	47	15	50	1	3
Smokeless only ($N = 13$)	–	–	5	39	2	15	6	46
Combined use ($N = 16$)	2	13	8	50	5	31	1	6
Total ($N = 59$)[a]	2	3	27	46	22	37	8	14

[a]One questionnaire was excluded because of incomplete data.

Intention to Quit (Post-Intervention)

Although the study did not specify time criteria (i.e., 6 months for precontemplation and contemplation, and quit plan in next month for preparation) for several stages, the study definitions closely represent the stages of change as defined by Prochaska.[23] Table 2 outlines respondents' intention to quit after the tobacco education intervention. Using a χ^2 test likelihood ratio, a significant difference ($p = 0.007$) was found among the three groups of tobacco users. Although 12 of the respondents (20%) reported not considering quitting tobacco since the intervention, the majority of respondents ($N = 47$, 80%) reported some positive level of intention to quit. Most of the respondents were in either the contemplation stage or the preparation stage (36% and 31%, respectively). The smoking-only respondents ($N = 31$) were primarily in either the contemplation stage (39%) or the preparation stage (39%), but more respondents of the smokeless-only group ($N = 13$) were in the action stage (46%). Combined users were more likely to be in the precontemplation stage (33%) or the contemplation stage (47%) of intention to quit tobacco use.

Participant Comments

Unstructured written remarks by several of the respondents who "quit" revealed their efforts: "Quit the day of the class. . . still quit," "The class gave me a reason to quit. . . sometimes that's all it takes," "Quit the day of the briefing," and "it was hard." One respondent signaled his intent to quit, noting: "On May 1st I retire and I'm shooting for that date to quit."

The educational content was highlighted in several statements: "The information was very helpful to help me determine a course of action to quit," "The graphic images were effective and inspiring" and "The scare tactics work." Several of the remarks revealed the challenge nicotine addiction represents for both the addict and the interventionists, "I like nicotine," "For health reasons I would like to quit, but realistically I enjoy smoking too much," "Quitting is admitting to fear," and "It's a hard obstacle to overcome." Finally, a non-tobacco user who responded to the survey commented: "Although I don't use tobacco products, after attending this class, I know I won't start to use them either."

DISCUSSION

Data from this study indicated that Army infantry personnel use both smoking and smokeless forms of tobacco, either alone or in combination. The results indicated that most tobacco users were motivated to quit 1 month after the intervention, with 80% of respondents reporting contemplating, preparing, or actively quitting. Although the majority of tobacco users surveyed in this study were smokers, a large percentage also used smokeless tobacco products. The fact that the respondents were primarily young males may reflect the increase in smokeless tobacco use seen nationally among this age group; however, other factors may be involved. Dipping snuff has been associated with the infantry and other military subcultures, because in the field environment the sight and smell of cigarette smoke or the flame of a cigarette at night could give away a position.[24] Smokeless tobacco also is used for its stimulant effect to stay awake on night patrol. Use of smokeless tobacco products by military personnel could reflect institutionalized nonsmoking policies in certain government buildings and in the use of certain equipment.[25,26]

Nonetheless, the respondents demonstrating the most significant behavior change after the intervention in this study were in the smokeless-tobacco-only group. Sixty-one percent reported improvement in their smokeless tobacco use, with 15% reporting a decrease in use and 46% reporting quitting. These findings are similar to those of Anantha et al.,[16] who found that an anti-tobacco education program had a greater impact on male smokeless tobacco users than male smokers, with an approximate 10% difference in quit rates among smokeless tobacco users. Although the reason for the greater improvement in smokeless tobacco users is unknown, graphic images of the oral consequences of smokeless tobacco use may have played a role in this study. Subjects in a previous study cited graphic images to be the most helpful component

Table 2. Post-Intervention Intention to Quit Tobacco Use by Stages of Change

Group	Precontemplation		Contemplation		Preparation		Action	
	N	%	N	%	N	%	N	%
Smoking only ($N = 31$)	6	19	12	39	12	39	1	3
Smokeless only ($N = 13$)	1	8	2	15	4	31	6	46
Combined use ($N = 15$)	5	33	7	47	2	13	1	7
Total ($N = 59$)[a]	12	20	21	36	18	31	8	14

[a] One questionnaire was excluded because of incomplete data.

of a dental office-based intervention for smokeless tobacco users.[27]

Different abstinence rates for smokeless tobacco users might be expected at later follow-up, as reported in previous studies. Using variations of behavioral modification and nicotine gum, Hatsukami and colleagues demonstrated 1-month post-treatment quit rates of 22% to 55% among smokeless tobacco users. However, quit rates decreased slightly to 20% to 47% at 6 months.[28] Studies using dental office-based interventions, on the other hand, report abstinence rates of 32% at 3-month follow-up and from 34% to 35% at 1-year follow-up.[27,29]

Combined tobacco users appeared to be the least influenced by the intervention in that they were the least likely to report any improvement in tobacco use and were the only group to report an increase in tobacco use. The use of multiple forms of tobacco products may be a more complex addiction needing to be addressed by more intensive therapy.

This study had several limitations. Generalization of the findings is limited because of the small sample size and the homogenous makeup of the sample of all male infantry soldiers. Future studies should use a sample more representative of the variety of tobacco users in the military population. In addition, the one-group post-test-only design has inherent weaknesses and threats to validity that limits its use for making causal inferences.[30] There was no control group; therefore, it is unknown if tobacco users who had not received the intervention would have provided similar responses to a post-test survey. Because time constraints prohibited pre-testing of participants, reported change as a result of the intervention should be viewed with caution. However, the data can provide useful information with which to design later studies. Future studies should use a randomized, pre-test/post-test experimental design, allowing for greater control and increasing the ability to generalize results.

Follow-up survey data collection was limited to 1 month after the intervention as a result of deployments, yielding only short-term results. Future studies at periodic time intervals would yield important data on the long-term effect of the intervention on behavior change. An improvement in tobacco use, either decreasing use or quitting, was found among all categories of tobacco users at 1 month. These results suggest some short-term improvement in behavior change after the tobacco education intervention. They also support earlier findings of ex-smokers reporting that information on the dangers of smoking was relatively important in their decision to quit.[14]

Although the content and face validity of the survey questionnaire was established based on the transtheoretical model of behavior change,[23] reliability was not determined. Future studies might apply more rigor to instrument development by obtaining estimates of reliability or use an instrument with documented reliability estimates.

Finally, although extraneous variables were neither examined nor controlled in this study, the influence of the command unit on changing behavior was evident. The unit initiated tobacco awareness training for all tobacco users and encouraged users to quit for the benefit of the unit.

CONCLUSION AND IMPLICATIONS FOR PRACTICE

This study suggests that a one-time tobacco hazard education intervention can have a positive impact on tobacco use behaviors, at least in the short term. Overall, most tobacco users were motivated toward quitting after tobacco education, either by contemplating, preparing, or actively quitting.

A one-time tobacco education intervention for tobacco users is particularly well suited for the military because it can be targeted to a larger population. The military environment provides unique opportunities to encourage healthy choices and offer health promotion programs to at-risk individuals. The military structure provides and often mandates periodic training for high-risk activities and scenarios, and it can regulate environments to favor healthy lifestyle behaviors.

Because the vast majority of individuals with high-risk behaviors, including smokers, are not prepared to take action on their behavior, with 40% to 60% in the precontemplation stage and only 10% to 20% in the preparation stage, many smokers clearly are not planning to quit in the near future.[31] Yet, recent data from a DoD survey demonstrated that one-third to one-half of Army smokers are in the preparation stage of behavior change. Of those surveyed, 32% reported that they planned to quit within 30 days and another 47% reported that they tried to quit within the past year.[1] This suggests that Army tobacco users may be more motivated to quit than the majority of at-risk individuals. Periodic tobacco education to military tobacco users might capture these individuals, perhaps motivating them to change their behavior and serving as an efficient and cost-effective means of secondary prevention for tobacco users.

Because the majority of tobacco cessation programs are action-oriented for tobacco users who are ready and actively seeking assistance to quit, health promotion specialists have little opportunity to intervene with the majority of tobacco users, who studies have shown will attempt to quit on their own without attending formal tobacco cessation programs.[32] One-time tobacco education intervention may effectively target all tobacco users, enhancing cessation efforts.

Health promotion specialists must remain proactive and creative in targeting high-risk behaviors in military personnel. Currently, most tobacco cessation programs have a smoking focus, and smokeless tobacco interventions are not as well studied or established.[28] Future emphasis should be placed on tobacco hazard awareness training for all military tobacco users, with a special emphasis on smokeless tobacco users, who constitute a significant portion of tobacco users and for whom few effective cessation programs exist. Health care providers and other tobacco cessation interventionists also should consider the prevalence of combination tobacco use by certain military personnel.

ACKNOWLEDGMENTS

The author expresses gratitude for the support, guidance, and critical review provided by Dr. Barbara Sylvia, Dr. Eugene Levine, and Dr. Barbara Goldrick (Uniformed Services University of the Health Sciences) and Dr. Kathleen Lopez-Bushnell (University of New Mexico).

REFERENCES

1. Bray RM, et al: 1998 Department of Defense Survey of Health Related Behaviors among Military Personnel. Research Triangle Park. NC, Research Triangle Institute, 1999.
2. Smith SS, Fiore MC: Tobacco use and cessation: the epidemiology of tobacco use, dependence, and cessation in the United States. Prim Care 1999; 26: 434–61.
3. National Center for Health Statistics: Healthy People 2000 Review 1997. DHHS publication PHS 98-1256. Hyattsville, MD, Public Health Service, 1998.
4. Healthy People 2010 (Conference Edition, in two volumes). Washington, DC, US Department of Health and Human Services, January 2000.
5. Helyer AJ, Brehm WT, Perino L: Economic consequences of tobacco use for the Department of Defense, 1995. Milit Med 1998: 163: 217–21.
6. Zadoo V, Fengler S, Catterson M: The effects of alcohol and tobacco use on troop readiness. Milit Med 1993; 158: 480–4.
7. Bahrke MS, Baur TS, Poland DF. Connors DF: Tobacco use and performance on the U.S. Army physical fitness test. Milit Med 1998; 153: 229–35.
8. Reynolds KI. Heckel HA, Witt CE. et al: Cigarette smoking, physical fitness, and injuries in infantry soldiers. Am J Prev Med 1994; 10: 145–9.
9. Jones BH, Cowan DN, Tomlinson P. Robinson JR. Polly DW, Frykman PN: Epidemiology of injuries associated with physical training among young men in the army. Med Sci Sports Exercise 1993; 25: 197–203.
10. Reynolds KL. White JS. Knapik JJ. Witt CE, Amoroso PJ: Injuries and risk factors in a 100-mile (161-km) infantry road march. Prev Med 1999: 28: 167–73.
11. Knapik JJ, Barson J, Reynolds K: Risk factors for foot blisters during road marching: tobacco use, ethnicity, foot type, previous illness, and other factors. Milit Med 1999: 164: 92–7.
12. Forgas LB, Meyer DM, Cohen ME: Tobacco use habits of naval personnel during Desert Storm. Milit Med 1996; 161: 165–8.
13. Burns JC, Williams LN: A survey to determine the knowledge of military members about the hazards of tobacco use, and a resulting tobacco-hazard education project. J Cancer Educ 1995: 10: 37–40.
14. Carroll DA, Lednar W, Carte WB: The short-term impact of Army smoking policies. Milit Med 1989; 154: 603–7.
15. Schwartz JL: Methods for smoking cessation. Clin Chest Med 1991; 12: 737–53.
16. Anantha N, Nandakumar A. Vishwanath N, et al: Efficacy of an anti-tobacco community education program in India. Cancer Causes Control 1995; 6: 119–29.
17. Perine JL, Schare ML: Effect of counselor and client education in nicotine addiction on smoking in substance abusers. Addict Behav 1999; 24: 443–7.
18. Tracy J, Hosken R: The importance of smoking education and preventative health strategies for people with intellectual disability. J Intellect Disabil Res 1997; 41: 416–21.
19. Cronan TA, Conway TL, Hervig LK: Evaluation of smoking interventions in recruit training. Milit Med 1989; 154: 371–5.
20. Pokorski TL, Chen WW, Pigg RM, Dorman SM: Effect of educational intervention on smoking prevalence of U.S. Navy recruits. Health Values 1995; 19: 48–55.
21. American Cancer Society: Freshstart. Available at http://www.cancer.org/tobacco/freshstart.html.
22. Glover ED: Conducting smokeless tobacco cessation clinics. Am J Public Health 1986; 76: 207.
23. Prochaska JO, Goldstein MG: Process of smoking cessation: implications for clinicians. Clin Chest Med 1991; 12: 727–35.
24. Tsimekles D: The skinny on dipping. Army Times November 1. 1999, pp 14–6.
25. Department of Defense Directive 1010:10: Health Promotion. March 11, 1986.
26. Department of Defense Directive 1010:15: Smokefree Workplace. March 7, 1994.
27. Walsh MM. Hilton JF. Masouredis CM. Gee L, Chesney MA, Ernster VL: Smokeless tobacco ces-

sation intervention for college athletes: results after one year. Am J Public Health 1999; 89: 228–34.

28. Hatsukami D. Jensen J, Allen S, Grillo M. Bliss R: Effects of behavioral and pharmacological treatment on smokeless tobacco users. J Consult Clin Psychol 1991; 64: 153–61.

29. Stevens VJ, Severson H, Lichtenstein E, Little SJ, Leben J: Making the most of a teachable moment: a smokeless tobacco cessation intervention in the dental office. Am J Public Health 1995: 85: 231–5.

30. Burns N, Grove SK: The Practice of Nursing Research: Conduct, Critique, and Utilization, Ed 3. Philadelphia, WB Saunders. 1997.

31. Prochaska JO: Strong and weak principles for progressing from precontemplation to action on the basis of twelve problem behaviors. Health Psychol 1994; 13: 47–51.

32. Adult Use of Tobacco, 1975. Washington, DC. US Department of Health, Education, and Welfare, 1976.

2.02

EXPLANATORY DESIGN

The Relations Between Student Motivational Beliefs and Cognitive Engagement in High School

Christopher O. Walker[*] and Barbara A. Greene[†]

ABSTRACT: The authors examined relations among student perceptions of classroom achievement goals, self-efficacy, perceived instrumentality of classroom work, and sense of belonging within a classroom. Participants were 249 high school students. The authors also examined how cognitive engagement was predicted by those variables along with personal achievement goals (mastery and performance approach). The results indicate that the adoption of mastery goals was predicted by perceived instrumentality, self-efficacy, and belonging, whereas cognitive engagement was predicted by belonging and perceived instrumentality. Last, the authors found that a classroom promoting a mastery orientation was predictive of a student's sense of belonging. They discuss the importance of mastery-oriented classrooms.

KEYWORDS: Achievement goals; cognitive engagement; perceived instrumentality; self-efficacy, student belonging.

Even as the majority of researchers in the field of educational psychology have moved beyond the examination of race, gender, and socioeconomic status as the causal determinants of academic success or failure, the focus of research has been consistently split along two lines (Furrer & Skinner, 2003). Furrer and Skinner argued that the first line of research has focused on student-centered cognitive–motivational factors such as self-efficacy (Bandura, 1986, 1994; Schunk, 1989), achievement goals (Ames, 1992; Ames & Archer, 1988; Urdan, 1997), and, more recently, perceived instrumen-

tality (Miller, DeBacker, & Greene, 1999), with each of the previously mentioned variables considered a distinct facet of student motivation. The common thread of this first line of research is the focus on the students' perceptions of their academic competency, their attitudes toward the academic material, and how those perceptions of personal ability and interest guide their behavior. Although this first line of research has yielded significant findings, another important line of research has traditionally focused on a variety of environment-centered factors.

Research on environmental influences is exemplified in literature on the perception of care (Wentzel, 1996, 1997, 1998), person–environment fit (Eccles & Midgley,

*University of Science and Arts of Oklahoma
†University of Oklahoma

1989; Eccles, Wigfield, & Schiefele, 1998), and student perceptions of classroom goal structures (Anderman & Midgley, 1997; Wolters & Daugherty, 2007). This research focuses primarily on how perceptions of a classroom or social environment impact student behavior and influence their achievement. As with the first line of inquiry, this line of research has added to our understanding of what encourages students to put forth effort and be successful. Because both lines of research are concerned with student perceptions, though varying in terms of the focus of the perception, it seems reasonable to assume that theoretical and empirical research that examines student- and environment-related factors lead to a more complete understanding of student motivation and achievement.

Studies have found that schools have the ability to provide adolescents with opportunities to experience social support while simultaneously developing the level of academic knowledge and understanding of their students (Midgley, Anderman, & Hicks, 1995; Roeser, Midgley, & Urdan, 1996). Unfortunately, during the crucial developmental period of adolescence, schools have been found to emphasize social comparisons of ability (Midgley et al.) and deemphasize the relational quality between teachers and students (Midgley, Feldlaufer, & Eccles, 1989), thus potentially limiting the overall positive role school can play in the lives of students (Eccles et al., 1993). Studies have indicated that the net results of this narrowly focused academic framework are declines in academic motivation and engagement in academically adaptive behaviors throughout adolescence (Eccles et al.; Harter, Whitesell, & Kowalski, 1992). As a result, Hargreaves, Earl, and Ryan (1996) stated, "One of the most fundamental reforms needed in secondary and high school education is to make schools into better communities of caring and support for young people" (p. 77). Therefore, the purpose of the present study was to go beyond the work that has examined perceptions of classroom environments that support mastery learning and autonomy (e.g., Greene, Miller, Crowson, Duke, & Akey, 2004) to include perceptions of belonging to see if those perceptions are also important for encouraging student motivation.

Researchers have argued that by establishing a supportive and inclusive environment, schools are able to foster and support student perceptions of belonging and thereby increase student engagement and achievement (Goodenow, 1993; Osterman, 2000; Voelkl, 1996, 1997). It should be noted that investigations pertaining to a personal perception of belonging and the subsequent behavioral response is not new within the fields of social, developmental, personality, and educational psychology (Baumeister & Leary, 1995; Osterman). Maslow (1968) argued that only food and shelter take precedence over the need for love and

belonging, whereas attachment theories have long held that taking part in a mutually beneficial relationship plays a vital role in personal growth and development (Bowlby, 1969, 1973). Furthermore, theorists and researchers such as Horney (1945), Fromm (1956), and Epstein (1992) have all articulated the significance of perceiving oneself to be a valued member of a wider group. However, although the need to belong is likely to be pervasive throughout a person's life, research has suggested that during the period of adolescence the need to connect with others through mutually supportive relationships is at its peak (Midgley et al., 1989). Therefore, even though research regarding belonging has an established place in the wider field of psychology, it seems especially germane to the study of adolescent attitudes and behavior within the context of school.

Within the context of academics, Goodenow (1993) defined *belonging* as "the extent to which students feel personally accepted, respected, included, and supported by others in the school social environment" (p. 80) and used the term *belonging* synonymously with the term *psychological membership*. Other authors have defined *belonging* in a similar manner. Voelkl (1996) defined *school belonging* as an internalized perception that "one is an important part of the school environment" (p. 296). Finn (1989) conceptualized *belonging* as a student's perception of there being mutually beneficial relationships in a school and found that when a sense of belonging was absent, students were likely to have a higher rate of truancy, disruptive behavior, and dropping out. As stated previously, student perception of a supportive environment has been found to be especially relevant during adolescence when students begin to consider their capabilities, aspirations, and, as a result, the utility value of engaging in academic pursuits (Goodenow).

Garmezy (1991) has noted that student perceptions of supportive relationships are primary protective factors in schools and the wider community. A *protective factor*, as defined by Garmezy, included any factor that mediated or suppressed negative effects that could be associated with poverty or other factors associated with being characterized as an at-risk student. Specifically, Garmezy argued that the perception of a warm and cohesive family unit (i.e., a family unit that fosters and maintains the perception of belonging among its members) was the primary predictor of resiliency in adolescence.

Studies in grade school (Batcher, 1981) and college settings (Tinto, 1987) have also found that when a lack of belonging or sense of membership persists, negative outcomes (i.e., lack of persistence and commitment) result. Trusty and Dooley-Dickey (1993) found that when students reported a sense of alienation toward school, their grades in reading and mathematics were negatively impacted. Furthermore, Wentzel and Asher (1995) reported that children categorized as rejected or controversial were more likely to break school rules. This work suggests that when an environment is perceived to be uninviting or non-supportive, students are likely to distance themselves, either psychologically, physically, or both, from that environment. However, when an environment is perceived to be inclusive or accepting, a person is likely to behave prosocially and engage in the activities presented in that environment (Solomon, Battistich, Watson, Schaps, & Lewis, 2000; Solomon, Watson, Battistich, Schaps, & DeLucci, 1996). For example, Sletta, Valas, and Skaalvik (1996) reported that student perception of peer support was linked to perceptions of social competence and interest in academics.

In summary, the perception of belonging, as fostered by the recognition of a supportive environment, has been found to positively impact engagement and achievement within school and community settings. These findings further suggest that resiliency and learning do not occur in isolation. Instead, learning is a complex process that must take into account the central role of personal interactions and the perceptions that stem from those interactions.

The Present Study

The purpose of the present study was to build on previous research by examining the relations among student perceptions of belonging and other motivation variables (i.e., self-efficacy, perceived instrumentality, personal achievement goals, and perceptions of the classroom goal orientation) that have consistently demonstrated positive relations with student engagement. Although each of the variables to be addressed has been supported in literature (Bandura, 1986, 1994, 1997; Eccles & Wigfield, 1995; Miller & Brickman, 2004; Pajares & Miller, 1994; Wigfield & Eccles, 2002; Wolters, 2004; Zimmerman & Bandura, 1994), it is the confluence of student- and environment-related variables in the present study that provided the unique contribution to our understanding of student motivation and achievement. In the subsequent sections we provide a brief overview of the theory and findings relating to self-efficacy, perceived instrumentality, and achievement goals.

Self-Efficacy

Self-efficacy is the extent to which an individual perceives that he or she possesses the ability necessary to manage a given set of circumstances (Bandura, 1977, 1994). In other words, does a person

perceive that they have the prerequisite skills necessary to successfully complete a given task? Self-efficacy beliefs are shaped over time through a blend of personal experiences, vicarious experiences, social persuasion, and interpretations of physical and emotional condition (Bandura, 1994). Research has demonstrated that students with high self-efficacy are more likely to seek challenge, persist in the face of challenge, and adopt effective strategies to mediate challenges when compared with their classmates with low self-efficacy (Bandura, 1994; Eccles et al., 1998; Schunk, 1989; Zeldin & Pajares, 2000). In addition, there has been a great deal of research that has demonstrated a positive link between student self-efficacy and the resulting use of meaningful learning strategies (e.g., Greene & Miller, 1996; Pintrich & DeGroot, 1990), as well as links between self-efficacy and achievement (Pajares & Miller, 1994; Zimmerman & Bandura, 1994).

Perceived Instrumentality

Although Bandura (1986) argued that proximal goals and appraisals are the key to promoting self-regulation, other researchers have stressed the "importance of personal future for present motivation and learning" (Simons, Dewitte, & Lens, 2000, p. 356). In fact, several researchers have suggested that perceiving a current task as instrumental in attaining one's future goals enhances not only student motivation but also subsequent performance (Eccles & Wigfield, 1995; Miller & Brickman, 2004; Miller, Greene, Montalvo, Ravindran, & Nichols, 1996; Vansteenkiste et al., 2004; Wigfield & Eccles, 2002). Without some future orientation, the importance and relevance attached to current tasks would be limited to their short-term appeal (Miller & Brickman). However, once a distal goal is established, relevant proximal subgoals are likely to be established and perceived as instrumental. Research has shown a link among the perceived instrumentality of a task and the adoption of mastery goals (DeBacker & Nelson, 1999; Greene, DeBacker, Ravindran & Krows, 1999; Miller et al., 1999; Miller et al., 1996), course achievement (Greene et al., 2004; Miller et al., 1996), and persistence and effort (Miller et al., 1996). These findings support earlier research by Raynor (1970, 1974), DeVolder and Lens (1982), and Markus and Nurius (1986), which stressed the impact that a future frame of reference can have on present engagement and achievement.

Achievement Goals

Achievement goal theory focuses on the reasons students have for engaging in achievement-related tasks and how those reasons can impact the type and amount of effort used (Ames & Archer, 1988; Midgley et al., 1995). Initially, achievement goal theorists posited two types of achievement goals (performance and mastery). On the one hand, theorists argued that students who adopted mastery goals would focus on increasing competence and understanding while basing their judgments of success on "self-referenced standards" (Ames, 1992, p. 262). On the other hand, students adopting performance goals would focus on the accomplishment of a task rather than the task itself and judge their performance relative to others (Midgley, Kaplan, & Middleton, 2001). For over a decade, Elliot, Harackiewicz, and colleagues have worked to revise achievement goal theory by examining performance goals within the dichotomous framework of approach and avoidance (Elliot & Church, 1997; Elliot & Harackiewicz, 1996; Elliot & McGregor, 1999; Harackiewicz, Barron, Pintrich, Elliot, & Thrash, 2002). Despite these efforts, in the present study, we followed the work of Greene et al. (2004) and chose to include only approach-oriented goals to streamline measures so that all motivation variables had positive connotations based on theory.

Mastery goals have often been linked to positive academic behaviors such as effort and persistence while studying, the adoption of self-regulated learning strategies, willingness to seek help, the use of meaningful cognitive processing strategies, long-term retention, and intrinsic motivation (Anderman, Griesinger, & Westerfield, 1998; Anderman & Young, 1994; Elliot & Church, 1997; Elliot & Harackiewicz, 1996; Middleton & Midgley, 1997; Miller, Behrens, Greene, & Newman, 1993; Miller et al., 1996; Schraw, Horn, Thorndike-Christ, & Bruning, 1995; Wentzel, 1996). Performance-approach goals have been empirically linked to maladaptive academic behaviors (Church, Elliot, & Gable, 2001; Elliot, McGregor, & Gable, 1999; Greene & Miller, 1996; Meece, Blumenfeld, & Hoyle, 1988; Miller et al., 1993; Miller et al., 1996; Nolen, 1988; Pintrich & Garcia, 1991), but they have also been positively related to academic performance (Barron & Harackiewicz, 2001; Elliot & Church, 1997; Elliot & McGregor, 1999, 2001; Harackiewicz, Barron, Carter, Letho, & Elliot, 1997; Harackiewicz, Barron, Tauer, & Elliot, 2000; Skaalvik, 1997).

Classroom Achievement Goals

Ames (1992) stated that "considerable research and writings have addressed how classroom learning environments influence student learning, but more recent attention has focused on how classroom environments influence students' views about the nature and purposes of learning" (p. 261). Thus, although students adopt personal achievement goals, they do so within the context of a classroom environment that has its own preexisting "goal structure" (Urdan, 2004, p. 222). Urdan suggested that these classroom (or school)

goal structures are likely to make some goals personally relevant to students while minimizing others. For example, if teachers promote competition in their classrooms, it would be likely that students would adopt corresponding performance goals. Conversely, if a teacher emphasizes the development of understanding and personal mastery, students are more likely to adopt corresponding mastery goals. In short, theory suggests that students are likely to adopt a parallel goal orientation in keeping with what exists in their classrooms.

Urdan, Midgley, and Anderman (1998) found that when students perceived a prevailing performance-goal orientation within their classroom, they were more likely to adopt self-handicapping strategies. In contrast, Turner et al. (2002) determined that within mastery-oriented classrooms, students were less likely to utilize self-handicapping strategies and more likely to seek help when needed. Finally, research findings suggest that if students were to move into a different class, they would be likely to adopt the goal orientation of that classroom, despite their experience in previous classrooms (Urdan & Midgley, 2003). This last finding is encouraging in that it shows the malleability of student motivation and the potentially positive influence that an academic environment can have on students if and when they were to move into a mastery-oriented classroom.

Research Questions

On the basis of the theory and findings previously described, we developed the following four research questions and a set of related predictions. Research Question 1 addressed the correlations with the belonging variable.

Research Question 1: What student and classroom motivation variables are related to student sense of belonging in the classroom?

We predicted that sense of belonging would be positively related to all of the motivation variables except for the individual and classroom performance goals. Research Question 2 concerned the role of belonging in the prediction of student mastery goals.

Research Question 2: Does the student sense of belonging score add uniquely to the prediction of mastery goals after classroom goals and student motivation variables have been entered into the prediction equation?

We predicted that there would be unique variance explained after entering the individual and classroom motivation variables. Research Question 3 regarded whether self-efficacy, perceived instrumentality, and sense of belonging each offered statistically significant contributions to the prediction of cognitive engagement of high school students in their English classes.

Research Question 3: Do self-efficacy, perceived instrumentality and sense of belonging scores provide unique prediction of scores on the cognitive engagement variable?

On the basis of theory and some prior research, we predicted that all three of the variables would contribute to the explanation of variance in cognitive engagement scores. Research Question 4 concerned classroom goals.

Research Question 4: Do classroom goals predict student sense of belonging?

We predicted that classroom mastery goals but not classroom performance goals would predict sense of belonging scores.

METHOD

Participants

Participants were 249 students between the ages of 14–19 years from three high schools in the midwestern United States. To reduce the likelihood of redundancy and maximize overall participation, we used English classes to recruit students. However, intact classes were not obtained as samples and could not be used as a unit of analysis. Instead, students were the unit of analysis.

Caucasian students constituted 48.2% of the sample, while 28.5% were African-American, 4.4% were Hispanic, 6.8% were Native American, and 12% categorized themselves as "bi-racial" or "other." Juniors and seniors each comprised 36.5% (73% collectively) of the sample, whereas sophomores accounted for 26.1%. Because two of the three high schools used in the present study started at Grade 10, and because there was a poor return rate of parental consent forms at the only high school that comprised Grades 9–12, freshmen composed less than 1% of the sample. Students enrolled in English I composed 0.9% of the sample, with 25.7% of participating students

enrolled in English II, 26.1% enrolled in English III, and 23.3% enrolled in English IV. Also, 10.8% were enrolled in Advanced Placement (AP) or Honors English III, with 13.2% enrolled in AP or Honors English IV. These demographic data are intended to describe the sample, but they are not relevant to our research questions.

Measures

Students completed a questionnaire packet containing four questionnaires and a demographic sheet. We used the demographic sheet to collect basic information including participant age, grade, gender, and race or ethnicity; however, as we considered only malleable predictors of mastery goals and cognitive engagement, we did not use the demographic data for any subsequent analysis. Each of the four questionnaires had items that were oriented to the classroom level of specificity (i.e., the phrase "in this class" appeared in each item). Bandura (2006) argued that motivation variables are best measured at a consistent level of specificity in a given study. We chose the classroom level because much of the research that supports the present study examined variables at the classroom level (e.g., Greene et al., 2004). Also consistent with the prior motivation research, the unit of analysis was still the individual, not the class. Each item required a response on a 6-point Likert-style agreement scale ranging from 1 (*strongly disagree*) to 6 (*strongly agree*). Table 1 presents the descriptive data for each subscale on the questionnaires, including the number of items per subscale.

We derived the perceived instrumentality and the self-efficacy items from the Approaches to Learning Survey developed by Miller and colleagues (Miller et al., 1999; Miller et al., 1996). For example, two perceived instrumentality items were "I do the work assigned in this class because my achievement is important for attaining my dreams" and "I do the work assigned in

Table 1. Descriptive Statistics (*N* = 249)

Variable	*n*	α	M	*SD*	Min-Max
Cognitive engagement	11	.86	4.16	0.975	1–6
Mastery goals	5	.86	4.75	1.06	1–6
Performance-approach goals	5	.87	3.27	1.33	1–6
Self-efficacy	8	.89	4.81	0.90	2–6
Perceived instrumenrality	5	.92	4.84	1.18	1–6
Belonging	18	.90	4.69	0.85	2–6
Classroom mastery goals	5	.85	4.81	0.99	1–6
Classroom performance-approach goals	5	.73	4.34	1.17	1–6

Note: Min = minimum: Max = maximum.

this class because learning the content plays a role in reaching my future goals." An example of a self-efficacy item was "I am confident about my ability to do the assignments in this class."

We measured student and classroom achievement goal orientations using the *Patterns of Adaptive Learning Survey* (PALS; Midgley et al., 1996). The PALS provides a three-factor, 17-item goal-orientation measure that includes sub-scales for mastery goals (6 items), performance-approach goals (5 items), and performance-avoidance goals (6 items). As previously stated, we did not use the performance-avoidance scale. An example of a mastery goal item stated, "An important reason why I do my schoolwork is because I like to learn new things." An example of a performance-approach item read, "I want to do better than other students in my class." There were also parallel items that asked about the goal structures in the classroom.

We measured student sense of belonging via Goodenow's (1993) Psychological Sense of School Membership (PSSM) scale. The PSSM comprises 18 items and contains a single-factor latent structure (Goodenow). Belonging items were oriented to the classroom level of specificity matching the self-efficacy, achievement goal, and perceived instrumentality items. Thus, we substituted the word *class* where the word *school* was used in the original version of the PSSM. Belonging items included "I feel like a real part of this class" and "people in this class are friendly to me."

Procedure

We used standard protocols for the protection of human participants starting with the approval by the appropriate institutional review board of all the methods used in the present study. An official at each school gave permission for student volunteers to be solicited from English classes. Only students returning a signed parental permission form were eligible to complete the research packet. Questionnaires were distributed and completed in English classes at midsemester. The classroom teachers were asked to read a set of instructions to their students who were then told to sign and date the student assent form if they wished to complete the research packet. Participants were instructed to read each item carefully and reflect on their current English class as they answered each item. It took students approximately 30 min to complete the entire packet.

RESULTS

Instrument and Subscale Statistics

We calculated Cronbach's alpha reliability coefficients for each scale and subscale to provide evidence for internal consistency. We found alpha reliability scores for each scale to be adequate, ranging from .73 to .92 (see

Table 1). From examining the means, it can be seen that except for performance-approach goals, all of the means for the motivation variables and the cognitive-engagement variable were above a 4 on the 6-point scale, suggesting that students' motivation was relatively positive for their English classes in these high schools.

Subscale Intercorrelations

To address Research Question 1, we created a correlation matrix that included each of the variables in the present study (see Table 2). As expected, we found student sense of belonging to have a significant positive relation with self-efficacy, perceived instrumentality, cognitive engagement, and mastery goals. It is interesting to note that the only variable that was not correlated with sense of belonging was personal performance-approach goals, and the weakest correlation was with classroom performance-approach goals. In fact, as shown in the table, the weakest correlations were those involving performance-approach and classroom performance-approach goals. Self-efficacy, mastery goals, and perceived instrumentality were related to one another and other variables in a theoretically consistent manner. To address Research Questions 2 and 3, we conducted two regression analyses with mastery goals and cognitive engagement serving as the dependent variables, respectively.

Prediction of Mastery Goals

We selected hierarchical regression analysis to determine whether the student sense-of-belonging variable contributed additional explained variance in mastery goals beyond variance accounted for by self-efficacy and perceived instrumentality. To determine whether student sense of classroom belonging would significantly add to the explained variance of mastery goal adoption, perceived instrumentality and self-efficacy were simultaneously entered in Equation 1, with sense of belonging entered in Equation 2. The initial regression equation with self-efficacy and perceived instrumentality serving as the predictor variables yielded a significant R^2 of .42, $F(2, 246) = 89.71$, $p < .0001$, whereas the addition of belonging into the model accounted for an additional 4.8% of variance that was also statistically significant, $F(1, 245) = 22.29$, $p < .0001$. The final regression equation explained 47% of the variance, $R^2 = .47$, $F(3, 245) = 72.41$, $p < .0001$. As can be seen in Table 3, once all three independent variables were entered into the regression equation, each yielded a statistically significant beta value.

Prediction of Cognitive Engagement

We computed the second regression analysis with cognitive engagement serving as the dependent variable and belonging, self-efficacy, and perceived instrumentality simultaneously entered as the predictor

Table 2. Bivariate Correlations Among Cognitive Engagement and Motivation Variables

Variable	1	2	3	4	5	6	7	8
1. Cognitive engagement	—							
2. Mastery goals	.55**	—						
3. Performance-approach goals	.18**	.20**	—					
4. Self-efficacy	.34**	.47**	.13*	—				
5. Perceived instrumentality	.42**	.615**	.15**	.47**	—			
6. Belonging	.34**	.49**	.02	.49**	.38**	—		
7. Classroom mastery goals	.47**	.79**	.15**	.38**	.51**	.52**	—	
8. Classroom performance-approach goals	.275**	.33**	.47**	.20**	.28**	.13*	.35**	—

*$p < .05$.** $p < .01$

variables. We obtained a statistically significant R^2 of .224, $F(23, 245) = 23.63$, $p = .0001$. As can be seen in Table 4, perceived instrumentality and sense of belonging had statistically significant beta values, but self-efficacy did not. That self-efficacy did not contribute a significant prediction was contrary to what we predicted on the basis of other research.

Prediction of Sense of Belonging

Our final analysis was conducted to answer Research Question 4 regarding whether or not the two classroom goal variables would predict the sense-of-belonging scores. We entered both classroom mastery and classroom performance goals simultaneously to predict the sense-of-belonging score. The overall equation was significant, with 27% of the variance explained, $F(2, 246) = 46.41$, $p = .0001$, but only the beta value for classroom mastery goals was significant ($\beta = .54$, $p = .0001$). In fact, the beta value for classroom performance-approach goals was essentially zero.

DISCUSSION

Research has indicated that student perceptions of belonging are related to and predictive of several important cognitive—motivational constructs (Baumeister & Leary, 1995; Osterman, 2000). The results of the present study support and extend previous research by suggesting that high school students who report a sense of belonging are more likely to focus on the development of understanding and then use cognitive effort to make that understanding possible. This is important for several reasons. First, because mastery goals have been shown to predict a host of positive academic outcomes (Elliot & Church, 1997; Urdan, 1997), it is important to understand the factors that promote their adoption. With a recent inclusion of belonging into the mix of factors associated with the adoption of mastery goals (Patrick, Ryan, & Kaplan, 2007) combined with the results of the present study, there is growing evidence that suggests teachers who wish to emphasize the development of understanding and comprehension would do well to consider how the classroom environment can encourage their students' perceptions of belonging.

Second, cognitive engagement has been found to predict achievement in a number of studies (e.g., Graham & Golan, 1991; Greene et al., 1999; Greene & Miller, 1996; Greene et al., 2004; Kardash & Amlund, 1991; Nolen, 1988; Pintrich & Garcia, 1991), so knowing that belonging, along with perceived instrumentality, is important for understanding cognitive engagement means also knowing what positively, if indirectly, influences achievement.

Table 3. Summary of Hierarchical Regression Analysis for Variables Predicting the Adoption of Mastery Goals, by Perceived Instrumentality, Self-Efficacy, and Student Sense of Belonging

Variable	B	SE B	β
Equation 1			
Perceived instrumentality	0.452	0.049	.503***
Self-efficacy	0.281	0.065	.238***
Equation 2			
Perceived instrumentality	0.407	0.048	.454***
Self-efficacy	0.161	0.067	.136***
Belonging	0.318	0.067	.256***

***$p < .001$.

Table 4. Summary of Hierarchical Regression Analysis for Variables Predicting Cognitive Engagement, by Perceived Instrumentality, Self-Efficacy, and Student Sense of Belonging

Variable	B	SE B	β
Perceived instrumentality	0.244	0.054	.295***
Self-efficacy	0.130	0.075	.120
Belonging	0.199	0.075	.174**

**$p < .01$. ***$p < .001$

The findings from the present study also suggest that a student's perception of classroom belonging is not a fixed property that is immune to appropriate and targeted intervention. This is consistent with Osterman's (2000) suggestion that quality of instruction, which included teacher support as a component, is a major factor in predicting student perceptions of belonging. Teacher support has also been found to affect such factors as the utilization of self-regulated learning strategies (Ryan & Patrick, 2001) and student willingness to seek help (Newman & Schwager, 1993). Again, the impact of such findings is that teacher support is clearly an element in every classroom that falls under the direct and immediate control of the classroom teacher and, given its relation with perceptions of belonging, could be utilized to effect positive change in student effort and achievement.

It is also important to note that belonging, along with perceptions of instrumentality, accounted for unique variance in the prediction of mastery goals and cognitive engagement in addition to that provided by self-efficacy, a variable that has a long established place in motivation research. These findings are notable because they suggest that perceptions of belonging and instrumentality provide additional avenues through which mastery goals can be fostered and supported. It is important to note that self-efficacy, although certainly important, is not the singular motivational factor that facilitates learning. A major contribution of the present study is the fact that two cognitive—motivational variables, in addition to self-efficacy, were important predictors of motivational outcomes.

It should also be noted that the student-perception-of instrumentality variable was found to be a significant predictor of mastery-goal adoption within a high school sample. This finding underscores the importance of teachers' articulating, and students' being able to understand, why and how learning is personally relevant to their future. Although some people may worry that this sort of utility focus undermines the intrinsic nature of learning (i.e., learning for the sake of learning), the results of the present study suggest that understanding the relevance and meaningfulness of course content directly relates to students' willingness to develop a meaningful understanding of that material through the adoption of mastery goals. These findings support previous work (Greene et al., 2004; Miller et al., 1999) that has also shown benefits of students' considering academic material as relevant and meaningful to their future.

Finally, it should be noted that in the present study, performance-approach goals were not predictive of cognitive engagement. Harackiewicz and colleagues (Harackiewicz et al., 2002; Harackiewicz et al., 2000) suggested several potentially positive effects that

performance-approach goals can have on student behaviors, but they did so uniformly using college samples. The lack of a predictive relation to cognitive engagement in the present study using a high school sample supports Midgley et al.'s (2001) argument that the positive effects of performance-approach goals, if present, are not likely to apply to all students. More specifically, Midgley et al. argued that factors such as age and culture could hinder any positive effects of performance-approach goals, which the results of the present study support.

Limitations

First, the correlational nature of the study meant that we did not study effects, but rather relations. By using the classroom and student goal measures from the PALS, we ended up with subscales that were very highly correlated, making it difficult to analyze for differential relations between the classroom and student goals. Future researchers should consider measures of classroom goals more carefully so that their shared variance with student goals is not artificially inflated. Our intention was to include one or more measures of achievement. However, we found that measures of achievement were not similar enough across the schools and classes used in the present study. Additionally, we did not collect enough information to use class as the unit of analysis. In future work, we would strive for true multilevel data and devise a measure of achievement that can be consistent across contexts.

CONCLUSION

Student adoption of mastery goals and the use of cognitive engagement strategies are primary factors when trying to understand and predict student achievement. The major contribution of the present study is that its findings support the inclusion of student perceptions of belonging and perceived instrumentality in the range of factors known to affect both. More specifically, the results of the present study indicate that when students believe that they are valued members of their classroom community, feel supported by both teachers and peers, and believe that the current work is instrumental to their future, they are more likely to focus on the development of understanding and, simultaneously, to use the cognitive strategies that support each aim. These findings support Osterman's (2000) contention that "students who experience acceptance are more highly motivated and engaged in learning and more committed to school" (p. 359). The question now becomes the following: Are schools ready to establish and support the "values, norms, policies, and practices" (Osterman, p. 360) that facilitate a student's desire to belong?

REFERENCES

Ames, C. (1992). Classrooms: Goals, structures, and student motivation. *Journal of Educational Psychology, 84*, 261–271.

Ames, C., & Archer, J. (1988). Achievement goals in the classroom: Students' learning strategies and motivation processes. *Journal of Educational Psychology, 80*, 260–270.

Anderman, E. M., Griesinger, T., & Westerfield, G. (1998). Motivation and cheating during adolescence. *Journal of Educational Psychology, 90*, 84–93.

Anderman, E., & Midgley, C. (1997). Changes in personal achievement goals and perceived classroom goal structures across the transition to middle level schools. *Contemporary Educational Psychology, 22*, 269–298.

Anderman, E. M., & Young, A. J. (1994). Motivation and strategy use in science: Individual differences and classroom effects. *Journal of Research in Science Teaching, 31*, 811–831.

Bandura, A. (1977). Self-efficacy: Toward a unifying theory of behavioral change. *Psychological Review, 84*, 191–215.

Bandura, A. (1986). *Social foundations of thought and action: A social cognitive theory*, Englewood Cliffs, NJ: Prentice-Hall.

Bandura, A. (1994). *Self-efficacy: The exercise of control.* New York: Freeman.

Bandura, A. (1997). Self-efficacy: Toward a unifying theory of behavioral change. *Psychological Bulletin, 84*, 191–215.

Bandura, A. (2006). Guide for constructing self-efficacy scales. In F. Pajares & T. Urdan (Eds.), *Self-efficacy beliefs of adolescents* (Vol. 5., pp. 307–337). Greenwich, CT: Information Age.

Barron, K. E., & Harackiewicz, J. M. (2001). Achievement goals and optimal motivation: Testing multiple goal models. *Journal of Personality and Social Psychology, 80*, 706–722.

Batcher, E. (1981). *Emotions in the classroom: A study of children's experience.* New York: Praeger.

Baumeister, R. F., & Leary, M. R. (1995). The need to belong: Desire for interpersonal attachments as a fundamental human motivation. *Psychological Bulletin, 117*, 497–529.

Bowlby, J. (1969). *Attachment and loss: Vol. 1. Attachment.* New York: Basic Books.

Bowlby, J. (1973). *Attachment and loss: Vol. 2. Separation anxiety and anger.* New York: Basic Books.

Church, M. A., Elliot, A. J., & Gable, S. L. (2001). Perceptions of classroom environment, achievement goals and achievement outcomes. *Journal of Educational Psychology, 93*, 43–54.

DeBacker, T, & Nelson, R. M. (1999). Variations on an expectancy-value model of motivation in science. *Contemporary Educational Psychology, 24*, 71–94.

De Volder, M. L., & Lens, W. (1982). Academic achievement and future time perspective as a cognitive-motivational concept. *Journal of Personality and Social Psychology, 42*, 566–571.

Eccles, J. S., & Midgley, C. (1989). Stage/environment fit: Developmentally appropriate classrooms for early adolescents. In R. E. Ames & C. Ames (Eds.), *Research on motivation in education* (Vol. 3, pp. 139–186). New York: Academic Press.

Eccles, J. S., Midgley, C., Wigfield, A., Miller-Buchanan, C., Reuman, D., Flanagan, C., et al. (1993). Development during adolescence: The impact of stage-environment fit on young adolescents' experiences in schools and in families. *American Psychologist, 48*, 90–101.

Eccles, J. S., & Wigfield, A. (1995). In the mind of the actor: The structure of adolescent achievement task values and expectancy related beliefs. *Society for Personality and Social Psychology Bulletin, 21*, 215–225.

Eccles, J. S., Wigfield, A., & Schiefele, U. (1998). Motivation to succeed. In N. Eisenberg & W. Damon (Eds.), *Handbook of child psychology* (5th ed., pp. 1017–1095). New York: Wiley.

Elliot, A., & Church, M. (1997). A hierarchical model of approach and avoidance achievement motivation. *Journal of Personality and Social Psychology, 72*, 218–232.

Elliot, A., & Harackiewicz, J. (1996). Approach and avoidance achievement goals and intrinsic motivation: A mediational analysis. *Journal of Personality and Social Psychology, 70*, 968–980.

Elliot, A., & McGregor, H. A. (1999). Test anxiety and the hierarchical model of approach and avoidance achievement motivation. *Journal of Personality and Social Psychology, 76*, 628–644.

Elliot, A. J., McGregor, H. A., & Gable, S. L. (1999). Achievement goals, study strategies, and exam performance: A meditational analysis. *Journal of Educational Psychology, 91*, 549–563.

Epstein, S. (1992). The cognitive self, the psychoanalytic self, and the forgotten selves. *Psychological Inquiry, 3*, 34–37.

Finn, J. D. (1989). Withdrawing from school. *Review of Educational Research, 59*, 117–142.

Fromm, E. (1956). *The art of loving.* New York: Harper & Brothers.

Furrer, C., & Skinner, E. (2003). Sense of relatedness as a factor in children's academic engagement and performance. *Journal of Educational Psychology, 95*, 148–162.

Garmezy, N. (1991). Resilience and vulnerability to adverse developmental outcomes associated with poverty. *American Behavioral Scientist, 34*, 416–430.

Goodenow, C. (1993). The psychological sense of school membership among adolescents: Scale development and educational correlates. *Psychology in the Schools, 30*, 79–90.

Graham, S., & Golan, S. (1991). Motivational influences on cognition: Task involvement, ego involvement, and depth of information processing. *Journal of Educational Psychology, 83*, 187–194.

Greene, B. A., DeBacker, T. K., Ravindran, B., & Krows, A. J. (1999). Goals, values, and beliefs as predictors of achievement and effort in high school mathematics classes. *Sex Roles, 40*, 421–458.

Greene, B. A., & Miller, R. B. (1996). Influences on achievement: Goals, perceived ability, and cognitive engagement. *Contemporary Educational Psychology, 21*, 181–192.

Greene, B. A., Miller, R. B., Crowson, H. M., Duke, B. L., & Akey, K. L. (2004). Predicting high school students' cognitive engagement and achievement: Contributions of classroom perceptions and motivation. *Contemporary Educational Psychology, 29*, 462–482

Harackiewicz, J., Barron, K. E., Carter, S., Letho, A., & Elliot, A. J. (1997). Determinants and consequences of achievement goals in the college classroom: Maintaining interest and making the grade. *Personality and Social Psychology, 73*, 1284–1295.

Harackiewicz, J. M., Barron, K. E., Pintrich, P. R., Elliot, A. J., & Thrash, T. M. (2002). Revision of achievement goal theory: Necessary and illuminating source. *Journal of Educational Psychology, 94*, 638–645.

Harackiewicz, J. M., Barron, K. E., Tauer, J. M., & Elliot, A. J. (2000). Short-term and long-term consequences of achievement goals in college: Predicting continued interest and performance over time. *Journal of Educational Psychology, 92*, 316–330.

Hargreaves, A., Earl, L., & Ryan, J. (1996). *Schooling for change: Reinventing education for early adolescents.* Bristol, PA: Falmer.

Harter, S., Whitesell, N. R., & Kowalski, P. (1992). Individual differences in the effects of educational transitions on young adolescents' perceptions of competence and motivational orientation. *American Educational Research Journal, 29*, 777–807.

Horney, K. (1945). *Our inner conflicts: A constructive theory of neurosis.* New York: Norton.

Kardash, C. M., & Amlund, J. T. (1991). Self-reported learning strategies and learning from expository text. *Contemporary Educational Psychology, 16*, 117–138.

Markus, H. R., & Nurius, P. (1986). Possible selves. *American Psychologist, 41*, 954–969.

Maslow, A. H. (1968). *Toward a psychology of being.* New York: Van Nostrand.

Meece, J. L., Blumenfeld, P. C., & Hoyle, R. H. (1988). Student's goal orientations and cognitive engagement in classroom activities. *Journal of Educational Psychology, 80*, 514–523.

Middleton, M., & Midgley, C. (1997). Avoiding the demonstration of lack of ability: An underexplored aspect of goal theory. *Journal of Educational Psychology, 89*, 710–718.

Midgley, C., Anderman, E., & Hicks, L. (1995). Differences between elementary and middle school teachers and students: A goal theory approach. *Journal of Early Adolescence, 15*, 90–113.

Midgley, C., Feldlaufer, H., & Eccles, J. S. (1989). Change in teacher efficacy and student self-and task-related beliefs in mathematics during the transition to junior high school. *Journal of Educational Psychology, 81*, 247–258.

Midgley, C., Kaplan, A., & Middleton, M. (2001). Performance-approach goals: Good for what, for whom, under what circumstances, and at what cost? *Journal of Educational Psychology, 93*, 77–86.

Miller, R. B., Behrens, J. T., Greene, B. A., & Newman, D. (1993). Goal and perceived ability: Impact on student valuing, self-regulation, and persistence. *Contemporary Educational Psychology, 18*, 2–14.

Miller, R. B., & Brickman, S. J. (2004). A model of future-oriented motivation and self-regulation. *Educational Psychology Review, 16*, 9–33.

Miller, R. B., DeBacker, T. K., & Greene, B. A. (1999). Perceived instrumentality and academics: The link to task valuing. *Journal of Instructional Psychology, 26*, 250–261.

Miller, R. B., Greene, B. A., Montalvo, G. P., Ravindran, B., & Nichols, J. D. (1996). Engagement in academic work: The role of learning goals, future consequences, pleasing others and perceived ability. *Contemporary Educational Psychology, 21*, 388–422.

Newman, R. S., & Schwager, M. T. (1993). Students' perceptions of the teacher and classmates in relation to reported help seeking in math class. *Elementary School Journal, 94*, 3–17.

Nolen, S. B. (1988). Reasons for studying: Motivational orientations and study strategies. *Cognition and Instruction, 5*, 269–287.

Osterman, K. F. (2000). Students' need for belonging in the school community. *Review of Educational Research, 70*, 323–367.

Pajares, F., & Miller, D. (1994). Role of self-efficacy and self-concept beliefs in mathematical problem solving: A path analysis. *Journal of Educational Psychology, 86*, 193–203.

Patrick, H., Ryan, A. M., & Kaplan, A. (2007). Early adolescents' perceptions of the classroom social environment, motivational beliefs, and engagement. *Journal of Educational Psychology, 99,* 83–98.

Pintrich, P. R., & DeGroot, E. V. (1990). Motivational and self-regulated learning components of classroom academic performance. *Journal of Educational Psychology, 82,* 33–40.

Pintrich, P. R., & Garcia, T. (1991). Student goal orientation and self-regulation in the college classroom. In M. Maehr & P. R. Pintrich (Eds.), *Advances in motivation and achievement* (Vol. 7, pp. 371–402). Greenwich CT: JAI Press.

Raynor, J. O. (1970). Relationship between achievement-related motives, future orientation, and academic performance. *Journal of Personality and Social Psychology, 15,* 28–33.

Raynor, J. O. (1974). Future orientation in the study of achievement motivation. In J. W. Atkinson & J. O. Raynor (Eds.), *Motivation and achievement* (pp. 121–154). Washington, DC: Winston.

Roeser, R., Midgley, C., & Urdan, T. C. (1996). Perceptions of the school psychological environment and early adolescents' psychological and behavioral functioning in school: The mediating role of goals and belonging. *Journal of Educational Psychology, 88,* 408–422.

Ryan, A. M., & Patrick, H. (2001). The classroom social environment and changes in adolescents' motivation and engagement during middle school. *American Educational Research Journal, 38,* 437–460.

Schraw, G., Horn, C., Thorndike-Christ, T., & Bruning, R. (1995). Academic goal orientations and student classroom achievement. *Contemporary Educational Psychology, 20,* 359–368.

Schunk, D. H. (1989). Self-efficacy and cognitive skill learning. In C. Ames & R. Ames (Eds.), *Research and motivation in education: Vol. 3. Goals and cognitions* (pp. 13–44). San Diego, CA: Academic Press.

Simons, J., DeWitte, S., & Lens, W. (2000). Wanting to have vs. wanting to be: The effect of perceived instrumentality on goal orientation. *British Journal of Psychology, 91,* 335–352.

Skaalvik, E. (1997). Self-enhancing and self-defeating ego orientations: Relations with task and avoidance orientation, achievement, self-perceptions, and anxiety. *Journal of Educational Psychology, 89,* 71–81.

Sletta, O., Valas, H., & Skaalvik, E. (1996). Peer relations, loneliness, and self-perceptions in school-age children. *British Journal of Educational Psychology, 66,* 431–445.

Solomon, D., Battistich, V., Watson, M., Schaps, E., & Lewis C. (2000). A six-district study of educational change: Direct and mediated effects of the Child Development Project. *Social Psychology of Education, 41,* 3–51.

Solomon, D., Watson, M., Battistich, V., Schaps, E., & DeLucci, K. (1996). Creating classrooms that students experience as communities. *American Journal of Community Psychology, 24,* 719–748.

Tinto, V. (1987). *Leaving college: The causes and cures of student attrition.* Chicago: University of Chicago Press.

Trusty, J., & Dooley-Dickey, K. (1993). Alienation from school: An exploratory analysis of elementary and middle school students' perceptions. *Journal of Research and Development in Education, 26,* 233–243.

Turner, J. C., Midgley, C., Meyer, D. K., Gheen, M., Anderman, E. M., Kang, Y., et al. (2002). The classroom environment and students' reports of avoidance strategies in mathematics: A multimethod study. *Journal of Educational Psychology, 94,* 88–106.

Urdan, T. (1997). Achievement goal theory: Past results, future directions. In M. L. Maehr & P. R. Pintrich (Eds.), *Advances in motivation and achievement* (Vol. 10, pp. 99–141). Greenwich, CT: JAI Press.

Urdan, T. (2004). Predictors of academic self-handicapping and achievement: Examining achievement goals, classroom goal structures, and culture. *Journal of Educational Psychology, 96,* 251–264.

Urdan, T., & Midgley, C. (2003). Changes in the perceived classroom goal structure and pattern of adaptive learning during early adolescence. *Contemporary Educational Psychology, 28,* 524–551.

Urdan, T., Midgley, C., & Anderman, E. (1998). The role of classroom goal structure in students' use of self-handicapping strategies. *American Education Research Journal, 35,* 101–122.

Vansteenkiste, M., Simons, J., Lens, W., Soenens, B., Matos, L., & Lacante, M. (2004). Less is sometimes more: Goal content matters. *Journal of Educational Psychology, 96,* 755–764.

Voelkl, K. E. (1996). Measuring student's identification with school. *Educational and Psychological Measurement, 56,* 760–770.

Voelkl, K. E. (1997). Identification with school. *American Journal of Education, 105,* 294–317.

Wentzel, K. R. (1996). Social and academic motivation in middle school: Concurrent and long-term relations to academic effort. *Journal of Early Adolescence, 16,* 390–406.

Wentzel, K. R. (1997). Student motivation in middle school: The role of perceived pedagogical caring. *Journal of Educational Psychology, 89,* 411–419.

Wentzel, K. R. (1998). Social relationships and motivation in middle school: The role of parents, teachers, and peers. *Journal of Educational Psychology, 90,* 202–209.

Wentzel, K. R., & Asher, S. R. (1995). The academic lives of neglected, rejected, popular, and controversial children. *Child Development, 66,* 754–763.

Wigfield, A., & Eccles, J. S. (2002). The development of competence beliefs, expectancies of success, and achievement values from childhood through adolescence. In A. Wigfield & J. S. Eccles (Eds.), *Development of achievement motivation* (pp. 91–120). San Diego, CA: Academic Press.

Wolters, C. A. (2004). Advancing achievement goal theory: Using goal structures and goal orientations to predict students' motivation, cognition, and achievement. *Journal of Educational Psychology, 96*, 236–250.

Wolters, C. A., & Daugherty, S. G. (2007). Goal structure and teachers' sense of efficacy: Their relation and association to teaching experience and academic level. *Journal of Educational Psychology, 99*, 181–193.

Zeldin, A. L., & Pajates, F. (2000). Against the odds: Self-efficacy beliefs of women in mathematical, scientific and technological careers. *American Educational Research Journal, 37*, 215–246.

Zimmerman, B. J., & Bandura. A. (1994). Impact of self-regulatory influences on writing course attainment. *American Educational Research Journal, 31*, 845–862.

2.03

PREDICTIVE DESIGN 1

Exploring the Psychological Predictors of Programming Achievement

Yavuz Erdogan , Emin Aydin, and Tolga Kabaca

ABSTRACT: The main purpose of this study is to explore the predictors of programming achievement. With this aim in mind, the students' success in the programming courses is specified as the dependent variable and creativity, problem solving, general aptitudes, computer attitudes and mathematics achievement are specified as the independent variables. A correlational design was used to explain the relations between dependent and independent variables. The study group consists of 48 high school students in Profilo Anatolia Technical High School, Istanbul. At the end of the study, significant relations were found between the students' programming achievement and their general aptitudes and mathematics achievement. Also, in order to determine the predictors of the students' programming achievement, multiple regression analysis was applied. The findings reveal that only one variable that significantly predicts the students' programming achievement is general aptitude.

There have been many studies in recent years into academic success in computer programming (McNamarah & Pyne, 2004; Byrne & Lyons, 2001; Begum, 2003; Fowler and et al., 2002). Today, industry is keen to accept as many graduates as the academic institutions can produce, and there is an assumption that any bright student can be successful in computer programming. However, experience in the classroom would suggest that this is not true. Students who are proficient in many other subjects sometimes fail to achieve success in programming

(Byrne & Lyons, 2001), because programming is different from other discipline.

The developments of programming languages and methods, and the teaching of them, have up to now hardly been linked to a psychological study of the activity of programming. Psychology must go beyond the procedural aspect of programming; because it is becoming more and more important nowadays due to the variety of applications and the training that programmers receive (Hoc and et al., 1990). Prior research indicates that standardized measures of aptitude (e.g. SAT and ACT scores), prior academic performance (e.g. high school GPA) and effort or motivation explain a significant portion of the variation in student performance (Eskew & Faley, 1981; Hostetler, 1983; Goold & Rimmer, 2000).

Yavuz Erdogan and Emin Aydin, Education Faculty of Marmara University, Istanbul. Tolga Kabaca, Science and Literacy Faculty of Usak University, Usak.

In a review of studies attempting to predict programming achievement done up to 1990, Hostetler and Corman make a specific case for the inclusion of cognitive factors in any study of this kind (Hostetler, 1983; Corman, 1986). They found that some of the demographic, academic, computer exposure or cognitive variables were particularly strong predictors of class performance. According to Taylor and Mounfield (1989) prior experience in programming provides a significant predictor of how students perform in the programming courses. They founded that prior exposure whether at the high school or college level is an important factor to students' success in computer programming.

Also, the link between mathematics ability and programming is widely accepted. Several of the reviewed studies showed that success in Mathematics was a good predictor of success in computer science (Byrne & Lyons, 2001; Fowler and et al., 2002; Werth, 1986; Campbell, 1984; Chmura, 1998). There is a belief that the concepts which a student has to comprehend in order to master mathematics problems are similar to those for programming (Byrne & Lyons, 2001; Werth, 1986).

Besides those there appears to be a number of factors which influence the success in the programming. In general the reviewed research found correlation between computer attitudes and computer programming (Dey & Mand, 1986; Austin, 1987). Also, earlier studies indicated that demographic data impacted on programming success (Byrne & Lyons, 2001; Goold & Rimmer, 2000; Grant, 2003). Five factors were reviewed as potentially predictive to success in programming. They included problem solving ability, motivation, learning style, previous experience, and gender. Even though these variables are helpful in predicting success in computer programming, it appears that they could also predict success in other fields. These findings reveal that programming ability is different from other skills.

Considering all these points, the current study hopes to explore the correlations between students' programming achievement and their creativity, problem solving ability, general aptitudes, computer attitude, and mathematics achievement. With this aim in mind, research questions can be stated as follows;

1. Is there a significant relationship between the students' programming achievement and their creativity, problem solving ability, general aptitudes, computer attitudes and mathematics achievement?
2. Are there any mental factors that significantly predict the students' programming achievement? If so, what are they?

METHODOLOGY

Research Method

In the current study, a correlational design was used to investigate relations between students' programming achievement and their creativity, problem solving ability, general aptitudes, computer attitude, and mathematics achievement.

For the courses, C programming languages was chosen that aims to introduce the students the basic concepts of structured programming: variables, standard functions, subprograms, selection statements, loops, text files, user defined data types, records, pointers, dynamic data structures. Also, to familiarize the student with the C programming language terminology and to create data structures. The courses contains two hours application per week so beside lecturing students will construct their knowledge in laboratories by doing the assignment project to the groups and by doing the regular homework designed for the laboratory.

Participants

The study was conducted in 2005-2006 education year and the sample of this study consisted of 48 students from Profilo Anatolia Technical High School, Istanbul. This school aims particularly to equip the students with computer and educational technologies. The students are capable of computer technologies and programming languages. 25% of the sample was female while 75% of them were male.

Instruments

In this study 5 different measurement tools were used which are programming achievement test, KAI creativity scale, problem solving inventory, general skills test battery, and computer attitude scale. To determine the students' success in mathematics lessons, the first semester grades were obtained from the school administration. These measurement tools are explained below.

Programming Achievement Test (PAT)

A multiple-choice test consisting of 25 questions was developed by the researchers in order to specify the students' success in the programming. The validity and reliability studies of the PAT were carried out again by the researchers. After the item analysis 4 items were removed from the test. At the end of the reliability and validity analysis administered with the remaining 21 questions, the cronbach alfa internal consistency was found to be 0.72.

KAI Creativity Scale

KAI Creativity Scale was developed by (Topaktas, 2001) in order to measure the students' creativity skills contains 33 questions. Students were asked to respond to the statement using a five-point Likert scale ranging from 1 (Strongly Disagree) to 5 (Strongly Agree). The validity and reliability studies were carried out by Topaktas, and the cronbach alfa internal consistency was found to be 0.89.

Problem Solving Inventory (PSI)

This scale was designed by (19) which is a five-point likert scale ranging from 1 (Strongly Disagree) to 5 (Strongly Agree). PSI measures the attitudes of the students about problem solving and consisted of 38 items. 3 items were removed from the scale because their item total-item remainder correlations were insufficient. The latest version of the scale was found to have an internal consistency coefficient of 0.86.

General Skills Test Battery (GSTB)

The original form is in French and it has been adapted to Turkish by (Ozcan, 1985). The test measures analytic thinking, abstract thinking and spatial perception. It's a performance test and can be applied to individuals between 15–17 years of age. The test battery containing 113 items has three different dimensions which are; Letter Series (25 items), Shape Recognition (48 items) and Volume Surface Expansion (40 items) (Oner, 1996).The total score from the three different tests of the battery constitutes the students' general skills. The validity and reliability study of the GSTB was carried out again by the researchers and cronbach alfa coefficient was found 0.85 for Letter Series; 0.94 for Shape Recognition and 0.84 for Volume Surface Expansion.

Computer Attitude Scale (CAS)

Computer attitudes of the students were measured using the Computer Attitudes Scale (Deniz, 1994).This 42-item scale asks participants how frequently they agree with statements such as "Studying with computers is entertaining", "Computers make me angry", and "I believe that computers are beneficial". Participants rated how strongly they agree or disagree with each statement on a five-point scale. Higher scores indicate the greater levels of computer attitudes. There was high internal reliability for this scale; the standardized item alpha was 0.88.

Data Analysis

A bivariate Pearson's correlation was applied between the students' programming achievement and their creativity, problem solving ability, general aptitudes, computer attitude, and mathematics achievement. In order to obtain the most suitable regression equivalent in explaining the students' programming

achievement, multiple regression analysis was used. Multiple regression analysis provides a chance to interpret the total variance of the dependent variable explained by the independent variables and its statistical significance. Programming achievement was included as the dependent variable and other factor as the independent variables. The significance level for all the statistical results in the study was accepted to be 0.05 and all the results were tested two-ways For statistical analysis the software used was SPSS 13.0.

RESULTS

For the data analysis, first, descriptive statistics were presented. Then, the correlations between the students' programming achievement and the other variables were presented. Lastly, results from the multiple regression analysis were stated.

Table 1 shows the descriptive statistics of the measurements. The mean is 66.41 for programming achievement; 119.08 for creativity; 132.04 for problem solving; 52.57 for general aptitudes; 172.68 for computer attitude, and 47.66 for mathematics achievement.

A bivariate Pearson's correlation coefficients were run to determine the degree of relationship between the students' programming achievement and their creativity, problem solving ability, general aptitudes, computer attitude, and mathematics achievement. General aptitudes and mathematics achievement had significant correlations with programming achievement at the .01 level (see Table 2). However, there was no significant correlation between programming achievement and creativity, problem solving ability, and computer attitude.

On the other hand, the strongest correlation score was detected between the students' programming achievement and their general aptitudes ($r = 0.934$; $p < 0.01$). This result indicates that standardized measures of general aptitude scores explain 87.2% of the variation in student performance (r-square$_{effect size}$ = 0.872). This finding reveals that general aptitude is an important factor to students' success in computer programming. The perfect linear correlation between the students' programming achievement and their general aptitudes is presented in Figure 1.

Table 1. Descriptive Statistics

Variables	Mean	SS	Std. Er.
Programming achievement	66.41	13.28	1.44
Creativity	119.08	10.39	1.50
Problem solving	132.04	13.31	1.92
General aptitudes	52.57	19.60	1.82
Computer attitude	172.68	20.68	2.98
Math, achievement	47.66	17.81	2.57

Table 2. The Correlations Among Programming Achievement and Independent Variables

	Programming Achievement	
	r	p
Creativity	0.053	.720
Problem solving	0.072	.626
General aptitudes	0.934	.000
Computer attitude	0.106	.474
Math. achievement	0.447	.001

The second highest correlation was computed between the students' programming achievement and mathematics achievement at the level of 0.01 (r = 0.447; p < 0.01). According to this finding, 19.8% of the variation in students' programming achievement was explained by mathematic scores (r-square$_{effect\ size}$ = 0.198). Mathematics, tries to demonstrate numbers, shapes and the relations between these by analyzing them. In this respect mathematics is a demonstrative discipline. Mathematics does this function of demonstrating through reasoning. Reasoning is the common point between programming and mathematics. This finding supports the belief that the concepts which a student has to comprehend in order to master mathematics problems are similar to those for programming.

In order to identify the predictors of the students' programming achievement, multiple regression analysis was applied. As a result, positive relations were detected between the students' programming achievement and independent variables such as creativity, problem solving, general aptitudes, computer attitude and mathematics achievement (F = 62.845; p < 0.01). Independent variables explain about 88.2% of the total variance of the programming achievement.

The only variable that significantly predict the students' programming achievement is general aptitudes (t = 15.03; p < .01). This result reveals that general aptitudes provide a significant indication of how students perform in the programming courses. The regression

Table 3. The Predictors of Programming Achievement

Variables	B	t	p
Constant	29.82	3.99	.001
Creativity	−0.08	−1.36	.179
Problem solving	0.06	1.43	.161
General aptitudes	0.48	15.03	.000
Computer attitude	−0.24	−0.87	.388
Math. achievement	−0.02	−0.04	.964

R = 0.939, R^2 = 0.882; F = 62.845, p = 0.000

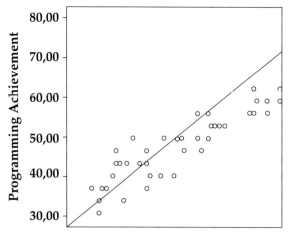

Figure 1. Scatter plot for the programming achievement and general aptitudes.

equation for predicting the students' programming achievement is presented in below:

Programming Achievement = 29.82 + 0.48 general aptitudes + 0.06 problem solving − 0.02 mathematics achievement − 0.24 computer attitude − 0.08 creativity.

DISCUSSIONS

The study which investigates the factors influencing their programming performance reveals some noteworthy findings. For example, there is a significant correlation between programming and non-programming computer performances (r = 0.621; p < 0.01). It is quite probable that students' knowledge about computers makes it easier for them to perform better in programming. This supports finding of the earlier studies (Byrne & Lyons, 2001, Goold & Rimmer, 2000, Taylor & Mounfield, 1989).

Other main factor is the general ability. The analysis of results clearly suggests a very high impact of general ability on programming performance (r = 0.934; p < 0.01). Ability tests can assess skills on cognitive, verbal, spatial and psycho-motor domains including individuals' powers of comprehension, abstract thinking skills and space perceptions (Ozcan, 1985; Oner, 1996).

It is not surprising that students with high general ability scores perform better in tasks involving computer programming, as it is a skill which necessitates high amount of abstraction capacity in the performer.

The results of regression analysis indicates that student' general ability scores are reliable predictors of their programming performances (t = 12.083; p < 0.01) which supported finding of the earlier studies (Austin, 1987).

In this study, it has been revealed that there is a significant correlation between the students' performance in the programming courses and their mathematics achievement at the level of 0.01. (r = 0.447;

$p < 0.01$). These results support the theories and researches to date. Several of the reviewed studies showed that performance in mathematics was a good predictor of performance in computer programming (Byrne & Lyons, 2001; Eskew & Faley, 1981; Campbell, 1984; Konvalina and et al., 1983). There is a belief that the concepts which a student has to comprehend in order to master mathematics problems are similar to those for programming (Werth, 1986). This could be that computing as a subject requires a structure and approach with which students have some experience, and similar cognitive skills used in the study of mathematics. Mathematics aptitude is thus often a pre-requisite for acceptance into computer science programs (Byrne & Lyons, 2001). On the other hand the study has found no correlation between programming achievement and creativity, problem solving, and computer attitude.

There are several limitations of this study. The participants were from a technical high school. Further research could include participants from other institutions like universities. Also, additional researches are needed in order to investigate the other factors that influencing the programming achievement. This study excluded factors such as personal traits, learning styles and demographic factors. These factors could be included in future research.

REFERENCES

McNamarah, S. & Pyne, R. (2004).Teaching a First Level Programming Course: Strategies for Improving Students Performance, *Journal of Art Science & Technology*, 1, 42–49.

Byrne, P. & Lyons, G. (2001). The Effect of Student Attributes on Success in Programming, *Association for Computer Machinery*, 36 (3), 49–52.

Begum, M. (2003). An Ontology for Teaching Programming *Association for Computer Machinery*, 43, 69–182.

Fowler, L., Campbell, V., McGill, D. & Roy, G. (2002). An Innovative Approach to Teaching First Year Programming Supported by Learning Style Investigation, Paper presented at the Australasian Association for Engineering Education, Melbourne.

Hoc, J., Green, T. G., Samurcay, R. & Gilmore, D. J. (1990). *Psychology of Programming*, London : Academic Press.

Eskew, R. K. & Faley, R.H. (1981). Some Determinants of Student's Performance in the First College-Level Financial Accounting Course. *The Accounting Review*. 11 (1), 137–147.

Hostetler, T. R. (1983). Predicting Student Success in an Introductory Programming Course, *ACM SIGCSE Bulletin*, 15 (3), 40–49.

Goold, A. & Rimmer, R. (2000). Factors Affecting Performance in First Year Programming, *ACM CIGCSE Bulletin*, 32, 39–43.

Corman, L, S. (1986). Cognitive Style, Personality Type, and Learning Ability as Factors in Predicting the Beginning Programming Student, *Association for Computer Machinery*, 18, 80–89.

Taylor, H.G. & Mounfield, L. C. (1989). The Effect of High School Computer Science, Gender, and Work on Success in College Computer Science, ACM SIGCSE Bulletin 21. 1, 195–198.

Werth, L. H. (1986). Predicting Student Performance in a Beginning Computer Science Class, In Proceedings of the Seventeenth SIGCSE Technical Symposium on Computer Science Education, Cincinnati, Ohio, United States, 138–143.

Campbell. P. F. & McCabe, G. P. (1984). Predicting the Success of Freshmen in a Computer Science Major, *Communications of the ACM*, 27 (11), 1108–1113.

Chmura, G. A. (1998). What Abilities Are Necessary for Success in Computer Science?, *ACM SIGCSE Bulletin*, 30 (4), 55–58.

Dey, S. & Mand, L. R. (1986). Effects of Mathematics Preparation and Prior Language Exposure on Perceived Performance in Introductory Computer Science Courses, CM SIGCSE Bulletin, 18 (1), 144–148.

Austin, H. S. (1987). Predictors of Pascal Programming Achievement for Community College Students, Proceedings of the eighteenth SIGCSE technical symposium on Computer science education, Missouri, United States, 161–164.

Grant, N. (2003). A Study on Critical Thinking, Cognitive Learning Style, and Gender in Various Information Science Programming Classes, *Association for Computer Machinery*, 42, 96–99.

Ramalingam, V. & LaBelle, D., Wiedenbeck. (2004). S. Self-Efficacy and Mental Models in Learning to Program, The 9th Annual SIGCSE Conference on Innovation and Technology In Computer Science, Leeds, United Kingdom, 171–175.

Topaktas, A. (2001). *Meslek Lisesi Öğrencilerinin Yarauctltk Diizeylerinin Değerlendirilmesi*. Marmara University, Science Institute (Unpublished Thesis), Istanbul.

Kasap, Z. (1997). İlkokul 4. Sinif Öğrencilerinin Sosyo-Ekonomik Düzeye Göre Problem Çözme Başarisi İle Problem Çözme Tutumu Arasindaki İlişki, Marmara University, Social Science Institute (Unpublished Thesis), Istanbul.

Ozcan, A. (1985). *Ülkemiz İçin İsabetli Olabilecek Bir Mesleğe Yöneltme Denemesi*, Publishing of Literature Faculty, Istanbul University, Istanbul.

Oner, N. (1996). *Türkiye'de Kullantlan Psikolojik Testler*, Publishing of Bogazici University, No.584, Istanbul.

Deniz, L. (1994). Bilgisayar Tutum Ölçeği BTÖ-M'nin Geçerlilik, Güvenirlilik, Norm Çalişmasi ve Örnek Bir Uygulama. Marmara University, Social Science Institute (Unpublished Dissertation), Istanbul, 1994.

Konvalina, J., Wileman, S. S. & Stephens, L. J. (1983). Math Proficiency: A key to Success for Computer Science Students, *Communications of the ACM*, 26 (5), 377–382.

2.04

PREDICTIVE DESIGN 2

The Longitudinal Relations of Teacher Expectations to Achievement in the Early School Years

J. Benjamin Hinnant,* Marion O'Brien,* and Sharon R. Ghazarian*

ABSTRACT: There is relatively little research on the role of teacher expectations in the early school years or the importance of teacher expectations as a predictor of future academic achievement. The current study investigated these issues in the reading and mathematic domains for young children. Data from nearly 1,000 children and families at 1st, 3rd, and 5th grades were included. Child sex and social skills emerged as consistent predictors of teacher expectations of reading and, to a lesser extent, math ability. In predicting actual future academic achievement, results showed that teacher expectations were differentially related to achievement in reading and math. There was no evidence that teacher expectations accumulate but some evidence that they remain durable over time for math achievement. In addition, teacher expectations were more strongly related to later achievement for groups of children who might be considered to be at risk.

KEYWORDS: Teacher expectations; teacher perceptions; self-fulfilling prophecy; academic achievement.

The early school years are important building blocks for later academic success. It is during this time that children develop the reading, writing, and mathematics tools essential for later academic work. The trajectories of children's academic success have been shown to be influenced by many factors, including parenting beliefs and behaviors and socioeconomic resources (e.g., Burchinal, Roberts, Zeisel, Hennon, & Hooper, 2006;

* University of North Carolina at Greensboro

  J. Benjamin Hinnant, Marion O'Brien, and Sharon R. Ghazarian, University of North Carolina at Greensboro.

  Sharon R. Ghazarian is now at the School of Medicine, Johns Hopkins University.

  The work reported here was supported in part by the National Institute of Child Health and Human Development Study of Early Child Care through a cooperative agreement (U10). We thank Nayena Blankson for her assistance: the children, families, and teachers who gave so generously of their time: and all the project staff who worked tirelessly to collect the data for this project.

  Correspondence concerning this article should be addressed to J. Benjamin Hinnant, who is now at the Department of Human Development and Family Studies, Auburn University, 206 Spidle Hall, Auburn, AL 36849. E-mail: jbh0020@auburn.edu

Englund, Luckner, Whaley, & Egeland, 2004; Jacobs & Harvey, 2005). During the school years, however, teachers are considered to be a major conduit through which children's academic development is facilitated (Hamre & Pianta, 2005). Thus, the importance of teachers' expectations for children's abilities beyond what can be accounted for by actual achievement is a topic that has received considerable attention from researchers (see Jussim & Harber, 2005, for a recent review). To date, however, relatively little longitudinal research has been conducted in this area. As a result, we know very little about how teacher assessments of ability relate to children's actual performance in the early school years or how teacher assessments early in children's schooling relate to long-term academic achievement.

At the heart of this issue is the idea of the *self-fulfilling prophecy*. As originally defined by Merton (1948), the self-fulfilling prophecy is a situation in which beliefs lead to their fulfillment; a person becomes or exemplifies what it is he or she was believed to be. Frequent evidence for the effect of self-fulfilling prophecies has been found (see Rosenthal & Rubin, 1978, for a meta-analysis of 345 experimental studies on self-fulfilling prophecies). Similar results have been found in nonexperimental studies of teacher expectations (see Jussim & Eccles, 1995, or Jussim & Harber, 2005, for a review). Overall, research consistently indicates that the self-fulfilling prophecy is a real phenomenon, although its statistical effects have been consistently small to moderate (effect sizes generally between .1 and .3; Jussim & Eccles, 1995).

An examination of effects of teacher over- and underestimation of children's academic abilities requires both teacher reports of children's abilities and an objective measure of child performance (usually standardized tests). From these, discrepancy scores can be calculated by regressing teacher perceptions of children's ability on children's actual achievement and using the resulting residual scores as an index of the accuracy of teacher perceptions (Cooper, Findley, & Good, 1982). These residuals, commonly referred to in the literature as teacher expectations, represent the discrepancies between teacher estimates of ability and children's actual achievement. These residuals can be used to predict other factors, such as future academic performance, in order to estimate the effect of the self-fulfilling prophecy. In this report we also refer to these discrepancies as teacher expectations.

It has been hypothesized that the academic outcomes for children may be different when teachers overestimate versus underestimate children's abilities. Indeed, in testing the competing hypotheses of whether teacher over- or underestimations of ability have greater predictive ability to future academic performance. Madon, Jussim, and Eccles (1997) found that teacher overestimations of sixth grade children's aca-

demic ability were more strongly related to future performance than were teacher underestimations of children's actual ability. Alvidrez and Weinstein (1999), on the other hand, found that teacher underestimations of children's abilities at age 4 were more strongly linked to high school GPA than early overestimations. Given the ambiguous evidence for either positive self-fulfilling prophecies (i.e., overestimations) or negative self-fulfilling prophecies (i.e., underestimations) being stronger, we test both possibilities by including an examination of potential nonlinear relations between teacher expectations and child performance.

In this article we explore the extent to which teachers' expectations of children's early academic abilities, particularly in the first crucial years of school, play a role in shaping future academic success over and above children's prior performance on standardized achievement tests. In addition, we examine how child characteristics are linked to teacher expectations and also whether child characteristics moderate the relation between teacher expectations and later child performance. As Jussim, Smith, Madon, and Palumbo (1998) and Jussim and Harber (2005) note, there are relatively few studies that include both measures of teacher perceptions of student ability and objective indices of student achievement. There are none that do so both longitudinally and with a focus on the early school years, although Alvidrez and Weinstein (1999) found that discrepancies between preschool teacher ratings of academic ability and actual achievement were related to students' grades in high school.

It is our primary hypothesis that mismatches between teachers' estimations of children's academic ability and children's actual academic performance, particularly at the time of school entry, are an important factor in children's academic achievement in future years of school. It is our belief that these first years of formal education are formative and that teacher expectations based on factors beyond academic achievement have a particularly strong influence on children's later success. We also examine the potential accumulation of expectancy effects. If underestimations of achievement compound and snowball to have even stronger relations to future performance, then this could clearly become a handicap for children. Extant research is equivocal on this point. Some investigators have found that self-fulfilling prophecies do not accumulate, but rather dissipate over time (Smith, Jussim, & Eccles, 1999; West & Anderson, 1976). However, Raudenbush (1984) found that expectancy effects upon entering a new environment (in this case, high school) were particularly durable and long lasting. The present study allows us to investigate the possibility that teacher expectancy effects may be especially important at the time of school entry and that these effects may accumulate over time or be especially durable.

Prior research has indicated that most teacher assessments of children's academic ability are fairly accurate when compared with children's performance on standardized tests (Brophy, 1983; Doherty & Conolly, 1985; Egan & Archer, 1985; Hoge & Coladarci, 1989; Jussim, 1989; Jussim & Eccles, 1992). Still, some child characteristics may make it more likely that children's abilities will be over- or underestimated by teachers. It is likely that teachers sometimes unwittingly help to create or propagate self-fulfilling prophecies in their students through perceptual biases (Jussim & Eccles, 1992; Jussim et al., 1998). Biases may arise because of social stereotypes (e.g., boys are better at math than girls; children from more advantaged families are smarter) or may be based on experiences with particular children. For example, teachers may view socially competent children as being also academically competent, whereas they perceive troublesome children to be less academically competent than their performance warrants. Several demographic and child factors have been implicated as moderating the relation between teacher expectations and subsequent academic achievement; these include child sex, ethnicity, family socioeconomic status, and social competence. It is particularly important to study these moderators, because stigmatization may result in stronger teacher expectancy effects for some groups. The correlates of teacher expectations have not been studied extensively, but Alvidrez and Weinstein (1999) found 4-year-old children's social skills to be related to teacher overestimations of their academic ability. No evidence has been found for stronger self-fulfilling prophecy effects based on child sex, but effects have been shown to be more robust for African American children and for low-income children, and these moderators were independent of one another (Jussim, Eccles. & Madon, 1996; Madon et al., 1998). For certain groups of children (e.g., low income, racial minority), teacher expectations of academic ability may be more strongly related to academic success; effect sizes much larger than typical (in the range of .4 to .6) have been found with these groups (Jussim et al., 1996).

In this article, we explore the possibility that child sex, ethnicity, family income, and social skills moderate the relation between teacher expectations and children's subsequent academic achievement in the early school years. We anticipate that teacher expectations are more highly related to later academic performance in children from groups perceived to be more at risk: minority children, those from low-income families, and those with poor social skills. In addition, we anticipate teacher expectations to be more highly related to later performance in reading for boys and in math for girls.

This article expands on current research on teacher expectation effects or self-fulfilling prophecies in several important ways. We investigate the child characteristics that are related to teacher expectations at the early school period. It is our hypothesis that teachers overestimate girls' competence in reading and boys' competence in math, underestimate the academic abilities of minority children and those from low-income families, and overestimate the academic abilities of children they perceive as socially competent. Controlling for academic achievement measured prior to school entry, we assess the possibility that teacher expectations may have an influence on subsequent child achievement for years to come (through third and fifth grades). Finally, we investigate the role of child characteristics as moderators in the relation between teacher expectations and later child academic performance, testing the question of whether teacher expectations are more highly related to later child performance for vulnerable children. The data used for these analyses come from the National Institute of Child Health and Human Development (NICHD) Study of Early Child Care and Youth Development, a large national study of more than 1,000 children tracked longitudinally from birth.

METHOD

Overview of Study Design

Children at 10 different geographic sites were followed from birth to fifth grade. From 1 month through the preschool years, children and families were visited at home on six occasions; mothers and children came to the laboratory on four occasions; and the children who were in nonmaternal care were observed in the child care setting. Once children entered school, they were observed in their first, third, and fifth grade classrooms as well as at home; their cognitive skills were assessed in the laboratory; and their teachers completed questionnaires about the children's academic and social functioning, as well as their own education and experience. Further documentation about measures and data collection procedures can be found in the *Manuals of Operation* on the NICHD Study of Early Child Care website (http://secc.rti.org).

Participants

Families were recruited in 1991 through hospital visits to mothers shortly after the birth of a child in 10 locations in the United States: Little Rock, Arkansas; Irvine, California; Lawrence/Topeka, Kansas; Wellesley, Massachusetts; Morganton/Hickory, North Carolina; Philadelphia, Pennsylvania: Pittsburgh, Pennsylvania; Charlottesville, Virginia; Seattle, Washington; and Madison, Wisconsin. During selected 24-hr intervals, all women who gave birth were screened for eligibility and willingness to be contacted again. Of the 8,986 mothers who gave birth during the sampling period, 5,416 (60%) agreed to be telephoned in 2 weeks and met the eligibility requirements (mother over 18, spoke English; mother healthy, baby not multiple birth or released for adoption, live within an hour of research site, neighborhood not too unsafe for teams of researchers to visit) Of that group, a conditionally random sample of 3,015 (56%) was selected to be contacted at 2 weeks; the conditioning assured diversity in terms of family income, maternal education status, and ethnicity. The resulting enrolled sample included 1,364 families with healthy newborns who completed a home interview when the infant was 1 month old. These 1,364 families were very similar to the eligible hospital sample on years of maternal education, percentage in different ethnic groups, and presence of partner in home. The resulting sample was diverse, including 24% ethnic minority children, 11% mothers who had not completed high school, and 14% single-parent mothers.

School observations were carried out for 966 children in first grade, 971 in third grade, and 955 in fifth grade. Because of the nature of this data set, children were not nested within classrooms (i.e., it was highly unusual to have a teacher report on more than one child). Children were included in each analysis reported here if they had complete data on the study variables at each grade; thus, because of missing data on teacher and parent questionnaires, the actual study samples vary with each analysis. At each grade, the participants differed from the children who were recruited but not included in this analysis sample. The participating children were less likely to be members of minority ethnic groups, and the families had significantly ($p < .001$) higher family incomes, as determined by their average income-to-needs ratio between birth and 54 months. Average family income-to-needs ratio for the participants included in the analyses at first grade was 4.01 ($SD = 3.08$); at third grade, 4.36 ($SD = 3.62$); and at fifth grade, 4.61 ($SD = 4.01$). (The income-to-needs ratio is an annually adjusted, per capita index comparing household income to federal estimates of minimally required expenditures for food and shelter. An income-to-needs ratio of 1.0 is the U.S. government definition of poverty, so a ratio of 3.0 represents a per capita income three times the poverty level.) Eighty-three percent of the participating children were European American, non-Hispanic, and 17 percent were members of minority ethnic groups.

MEASURES

Child Characteristics

Demographic characteristics of children and families were collected by mother report. Child sex and ethnicity (scored as White and non-White for analyses) were recorded at 1 month; family income was obtained at each measurement point, and an income-to-needs ratio was calculated in Grades 1, 3, and 5.

To assess teacher-perceived social competence, researchers asked teachers in first, third, and fifth grades to complete the Social Skills Questionnaire from the Social Skills Rating System: Grades K–6 (Gresham & Elliott, 1990). This instrument is composed of 38 items describing child behavior, each rated on a 3-point scale reflecting how often the child exhibited each behavior. Items are grouped into four areas: cooperation (e.g., follows directions), assertion (e.g., makes friends easily), responsibility (e.g., asks permission before using someone else's property), and self-control (controls temper when arguing with other children). The total score used in this report represents the sum of all 38 items, with higher scores reflecting higher levels of perceived social competence (alpha range from .86–.94). The Social Skills Rating System was normed on a diverse, national sample of children and shows high levels of internal consistency (median = .90) and test–retest reliability (.75 to .88) and moderate concurrent and predictive validity to other indices of social competence.

Child Academic Performance

Two measures of children's academic abilities were collected in the spring of the children's first, third, and fifth grade years: teacher report of classroom performance in reading and math and children's scores on standardized measures.

Teacher report. At first, third, and fifth grade, teachers rated children's reading and math ability using the Academic Skills questionnaire adapted for the NICHD Study of Early Child Care from the Early Childhood Longitudinal Study. The Language and Literacy scale deals with skills related to listening, speaking, and early reading and writing and interest in engaging in those activities. The Mathematical Thinking scale deals with the child's ability to perceive, understand, and use skills in solving mathematical problems and interest in math-related activities. Depending on the year of administration, the Language and Literacy scale and the Mathematical Thinking scale had from 10 to 15 items each. Children's performance was rated on a 5-point scale, ranging from 1 (*not yet*) to 5 (*proficient*). Teachers could also respond *not applicable* if the skill had not been introduced in the classroom; these scores were recoded as *not yet* unless they made up more than 60% of the responses, in which case the data were missing (approximately 1% of all questionnaires). The scale was designed to reflect the degree to which a child had acquired and/or chose to demonstrate the targeted skills, knowledge, and behaviors. At each time point, scale scores were computed by averaging across the items making up each scale. Internal consistency was excellent at all time points, ranging from

.94 to .96 for Language and Literacy and from .91 to .94 for Mathematical Thinking.

Standardized assessment. In the spring of the first, third, and fifth grades, children were administered two subtests from the Woodcock-Johnson Psycho-Educational Battery—Revised (Woodcock & Johnson, 1989): Letter-Word Identification, which assesses pre-reading skills in identifying isolated letters and words, and Applied Problems, which measures skill in analyzing and solving practical problems in mathematics. Typically, raw scores are converted to standard scores with a mean of 100 and a standard deviation of 15 (McGrew, Werder, & Woodcock, 1991), but for this study we relied upon W achievement scores, which are transformations of the Rasch raw achievement scores designed to eliminate the need for decimal fractions and negative values. With W scores, "statistical values, such as standard deviations and standard errors of measurement, have the same mathematical meaning at any level and in any area of measurement" (McGrew et al., 1991, p. 52). Thus, for example, a 10-point increase between kindergarten and first grade indicates the same increase in level of success on a subtest as does a 10-point increase between second and third grade.

Teacher Expectancy Score

A discrepancy score between teacher report of child academic performance and children's observed performance on standardized tests was calculated following the work of Jussim and colleagues (e.g., Madon et al., 1997) by regressing teacher perceptions of children's ability on children's Woodcock-Johnson scores for both reading and math in each grade; these residual scores are referred to as teacher expectations. The resulting six residual scores (a reading and a math score at each of three grades) provide an index of the extent to which teacher expectations vary from a child's observed performance. A negative residual score represents teacher underestimation, and a positive residual score represents teacher overestimation; the closer a residual score is to zero, the more accurate the prediction of student achievement (Madon et al., 1997). These residuals were then used to predict achievement in future years of school.

RESULTS

Descriptive statistics and correlations for the teacher expectancy scores and standardized measures of academic achievement in reading and math can be found in Tables 1 and 2. The standardized residuals indicating teacher over- and underestimations of children's academic performance for reading ranged from −4.29 to 2.99 in first grade (median = 0.02), −3.36 to 2.94

in third grade (median = 0.05), and −3.28 to 2.29 in fifth grade (median = 0.12); for math, the ranges were −3.06 to 2.48, −3.14 to 3.10, and −3.04 to 3.34, and the medians were 0.02, 0.09, and 0.02 in Grades 1, 3, and 5, respectively. Teacher expectations are created by regressing teacher ratings of academic ability on objectively measured achievement; they are, in effect, residuals or error, and thus it is not meaningful to correlate them with the variables that were used to create them. All correlations were in expected directions, and, given the large sample size, most were significant. Not surprisingly, children's observed performance on the Woodcock-Johnson reading and math subscales were correlated over time with themselves (see Tables 1 and 2) and with each other within time points (r = .58, .61, and .60 for Grades 1, 3, and 5, respectively). Prior to calculating teacher expectations, we gauged the accuracy of teacher reports of academic ability by correlating them with more objectively measured Woodcock-Johnson scores. Teachers' ratings of academic ability (as reported using the Academic Skills questionnaire) at each grade were highly related to Woodcock-Johnson scores for both reading (r = .64, .67, and .53 for Grades 1, 3, and 5, respectively) and math (r = .54, .57, and .56 for Grades 1, 3, and 5, respectively); teachers tended to estimate children's abilities with a fairly high degree of accuracy.

After calculating teacher expectations, we gauged their relations across domains and over time. Teacher expectancy scores (i.e., teacher discrepancies, inaccuracy, or residuals) in reading and math from first and third grades were highly correlated within the grade (r = .58, .54, and .48 for Grades 1, 3, and 5, respectively), indicating significant overlap in teachers' expectations across academic domains at each time point. Reading expectancy scores were also correlated across grades, but first grade teacher math expectancy scores were not correlated with those from third and fifth grades, indicating that teachers' expectations for reading may have greater continuity over time and from teacher to teacher than do teachers' expectations for math. It is also of note that Woodcock-Johnson measures of academic achievement prior to school entry were positively correlated with later teacher expectations (for all but first grade math expectations); teachers tended to overestimate the abilities of children who had higher preschool academic achievement.

Correlates of Teacher Expectations

Following preliminary examination of the data, two sets of hierarchical regression analyses were conducted. The first set of analyses identified the relations between child characteristics (demographics and social competence) and teacher expectancy scores at first, third, and fifth grade. Regression analyses, controlling for child Woodcock-Johnson performance at

Table 1. Descriptive Statistics and Correlations for Reading Variables

Variable	M (SD)	2	3	4	5	6	7
1. Teacher expectations—reading, G1	—	.24***	.20***	.14***	—	.11***	.13***
2. Teacher expectations—reading, G3		—	.30***	.17***	.11	—	.10
3. Teacher expectations—reading, G5			—	.18***	.14***	.13***	—
4. W-J Letter–Word, 4.5 years	369.36 (21.41)			—	.56***	.51***	.49***
5. W-J Letter–Word, G1	452.59 (23.99)				—	.75***	.67***
6. W-J Letter–Word, G3	493.86 (18.73)					—	.86***
7. W-J Letter–Word, G5	510.12 (17.52)						—

Note: Because the calculation of teacher expectations includes the W-J scores, correlations between the two measures at the same grade are not meaningful; those three cells are left blank in the correlation table. W-J = Woodcock-Johnson Psycho-Educational Battery—Revised; G1 = first grade; G3 = third grade; G5 = fifth grade.
***$p < .001$.

Table 2. Descriptive Statistics and Correlations for Math Variables

Variable	M (SD)	2	3	4	5	6	7
1. Teacher expectations—math, G1		.10	.10	.06	—	.18***	.13***
2. Teacher expectations—math, G3		—	.19***	.18***	.26***	—	.16***
3. Teacher expectations—math, G5			—	.17***	.15***	.15***	—
4. W-J Applied problems, 4.5 years	424.62 (19.27)			—	.60***	.56***	.56***
5. W-J Applied problems, G1	470.05 (15.54)				—	.69***	.69***
6. W-J Applied problems, G3	497.33 (13.19)					—	.78***
7. W-J Applied problems, G5	509.82 (12.85)						—

Note: Because the calculation of teacher expectations includes the W-J scores, correlations between the two measures at the same grade are not meaningful; those three cells are left blank in the correlation table. W-J = Woodcock-Johnson Psycho-Educational Battery—Revised; G1 = first grade; G3 = third grade; G5 = fifth grade.
***$p < .001$.

4.5 years, were run to examine the extent to which child demographics and social competence were related to teacher expectancy scores in reading and math. Results are shown in Tables 3, 4, and 5. In first grade, reading expectancy scores were related to children's earlier performance on the Woodcock-Johnson, indicating actual child performance is a significant predictor of teacher expectations in this domain; however, earlier performance on the Applied Problems subtest of the Woodcock-Johnson was not related to teachers' expectations of math performance. Child social competence was linked to teacher expectations in both reading and math, with more socially competent children being viewed as more academically skilled. The set of demographic factors was not linked to teacher expectancy scores, although child sex was significantly related to teacher expectations of reading ability. Teachers tended to overestimate girls' reading ability and underestimate the reading ability of boys.

The third grade results (Table 4) showed a significant relation between preschool performance on the Woodcock-Johnson and teacher expectations of children's abilities in both reading and math. For reading, there was a significant relation for demographics, attributable to child sex; that is, teachers tended to perceive girls as more academically skilled than their test scores suggested. For both reading and math, there was also a significant relation between child social competence and teacher expectations; again, teachers had more positive perceptions of the academic competence of children they report as socially skilled. A similar pattern was found for reading in fifth grade (Table 5), and the child sex result was similar; girls were perceived as having higher reading ability and boys were perceived as having lower reading ability than their performance indicates. The results for fifth grade teacher math expectancy scores indicated that demographic factors other than child sex were linked to teacher expectations by this age; ethnicity as well as child sex was significantly related to teacher expectancy scores. As with reading, girls were more likely to be perceived as more academically competent than their test scores indicate, whereas children from minority families were perceived as less competent at math. Teacher-rated social competence was again related to teacher expectations of academic skills.

Table 3. Hierarchical Regressions Predicting Teacher Expectations in Children's Reading and Math Abilities in Grade 1

Variable	Reading[a]				Math[b]			
	B	SE	β	ΔR²	B	SE	β	ΔR²
W-J, 4.5 years	0.003	0.002	.068*	.021***	−0.001	0.002	−.023	.004
Demographic characteristics				.006				.002
Child sex	0.160	0.061	.080***		0.027	0.065	.014	
Ethnicity	−0.036	0.087	−.013		0.050	0.095	.018	
Family income/needs, G1	−0.016	0.011	−.049		0.001	0.011	.002	
Child social skills—teacher, G1	0.031	0.002	.427***	.171***	0.022	0.003	.293***	.078***

Note: W-J = Woodcock-Johnson Psycho-Educational Battery—Revised; G1 = Grade 1.
[a]Adjusted R^2 = .192, $F(5, 866)$ = 42.61, $p < .001$. [b]Adjusted R^2 = .079, $F(5, 862)$ = 15.85, $p < .001$.
*$p < .05$. **$p < .01$. ***$p < .001$.

Table 4. Hierarchical Regressions Predicting Teacher Expectations in Children's Reading and Math Abilities in Grade 3

Variable	Reading[a]				Math[b]			
	B	SE	β	ΔR²	B	SE	β	ΔR²
W-J, 4.5 years	0.003	0.002	.068*	.028***	0.005	0.002	.084*	.031***
Demographic characteristics				.018**				.006
Child sex	0.185	0.064	.094***		0.099	0.067	.050	
Ethnicity	0.059	0.089	.022		−0.018	0.097	−.007	
Family income/needs, G3	0.008	0.010	.030		0.011	0.010	.038	
Child social skills—teachers, G3	0.028	0.002	.400***	.150***	0.022	0.002	.311***	.089***

Note: W-J = Woodcock-Johnson Psycho-Educational Battery—Revised; G3 = Grade 3.
[a]Adjusted R^2 = .187, $F(5, 785)$ = 38.26, $p < .001$. [b]Adjusted R^2 = .120, $F(5, 774)$ = 22.26, $p < .001$.
*$p < .05$. **$p < .01$. ***$p < .001$.

Table 5. Hierarchical Regressions Predicting Teacher Expectations in Children's Reading and Math Abilities in Grade 5

Variable	Reading[a]				Math[b]			
	B	SE	β	ΔR²	B	SE	β	ΔR²
W-J, 4.5 years	0.003	0.002	.067*	.038***	0.007	0.002	.140***	.031***
Demographic characteristics				.040***				.013*
Child sex	0.293	0.062	.150***		0.178	0.070	.090*	
Ethnicity	0.037	0.088	.014		−0.242	0.101	−.089*	
Family income/needs G5	0.012	0.009	.049		0.000	0.010	−.001	
Child social skills—teacher G5	0.029	0.002	.426***	.164***	0.014	0.003	.204***	.037***

Note: W-J = Woodcock-Johnson Psycho-Educational Battery—Revised; G5 = Grade 5.
[a]Adjusted R^2 = .237, $F(5, 755)$ = 48.20, $p < .001$. [b]Adjusted R^2 =.072, $F(5, 747)$ = 13.31, $p < .001$.
*$p < .05$. ***$p < .001$.

RELATION OF TEACHER EXPECTATIONS TO LATER CHILD PERFORMANCE

Our second set of analyses predicted later child achievement from earlier teacher expectations. Thus, teacher expectancy scores from Grade 1 were used to predict child observed performance at Grade 3 after accounting for the effects of prior academic performance, demographic characteristics, and social competence: and teacher expectancy scores from both Grade 3 and Grade 1 were used to predict child observed performance at Grade 5. The squared teacher expectancy score was also entered to detect possible curvilinear effects, because some have proposed that teacher underestimates of child ability are more influential than teacher overestimates (Madon et al., 1997). To address the question of whether child characteristics moderate the relation between teacher expectations and later child academic performance, we also included interaction terms in the models. Analyses were conducted separately for reading and math achievement. Results of the regression analyses examining child academic performance are shown in Tables 6 and 7. Different patterns of results were found for reading and math.

Reading

In both third and fifth grades, children's reading performance was linked to demographics and to social competence, but not to teacher expectations from earlier grades. The positive association of income and ethnicity with third and fifth grade reading scores indicates that nonminority children as well as students from higher income families were more likely to demonstrate higher reading achievement in both grades. Additionally, children rated as having higher social skills also performed better on tests of reading competence.

In predicting children's reading performance in third grade we found some evidence supporting previous research findings that teacher expectations may have a stronger relation to later performance specifically for groups of children who may be seen as disadvantaged or marginalized in the classroom (Jussim & Harber, 2005). Analyses of third grade reading performance showed a significant three-way interaction between first grade teacher expectations, child sex,

and child ethnicity (Tables 6 and 7). These interactions indicate that the relation between first grade teacher expectations and children's third grade reading achievement differs on the basis of children's sex and ethnicity. To further explore these findings, we tested the simple slopes in these interactions using procedures outlined by Aiken and West (1991); Bauer and Curran (2005), and Preacher, Curran, and Bauer (2006). First grade teacher expectations were reliably linked to children's third grade reading performance only for minority boys. This relation was positive and marginally significant (β = .19, p = .088), whereas for other groups of children there were no significant links between first grade teacher expectations and third grade reading performance (for White boys, β = .004, p = .92; for White girls, β = .038, p = .42; for minority girls, (β = −.12, p = .21). None of the interactions between teacher expectations and child characteristics were significant in the analysis of fifth grade reading performance.

Math

Results for math performance indicated an effect of earlier teacher expectations over and above the associations with demographic factors and social competence. At third grade, first grade teachers' expectancy scores were significantly associated with child performance, but these findings were tempered by a significant interaction with the income of the child's family. This interaction indicated that the link between first grade teacher expectations and children's third grade math performance depends to some extent on family income.

Table 6. Hierarchical Regressions Predicting Third Grade Reading and Math Achievement

Variable	Reading[a]				Math[b]			
	B	SE	β	ΔR^2	B	SE	β	ΔR^2
W-J, 4.5 years	0.376	0.029	.433***	.260***	0.340	0.022	.492***	.317***
Demographic characteristics				.030***				.039***
Child sex	1.552	2.897	.043		−2.132	1.98	−.083	
Ethnicity	7.021	2.317	.139**		2.099	1.605	.059	
Family income/needs, G1	0.344	0.166	.068*		0.429	0.111	.122***	
Child social skills—teacher, G1	0.212	0.041	.166***	.026***	0.093	0.028	.103**	.012***
G1 Teacher Expectancy score	2.542	2.076	.138	.000	4.575	1.692	.356**	.014***
G1 Teacher Expectancy score squared	−0.543	0.417	−.040	.002	0.554	0.316	.051	.003
Interactions				.011				.009
G1 Teacher Expectancy × Sex	−5.881	2.676	−.232*		−3.179	2.098	−.181	
G1 Teacher Expectancy × Ethnicity	−2.725	2.258	−.133		−3.014	1.792	−.217	
G1 Teacher Expectancy × Income	−0.209	0.180	−.038		−0.258	0.116	−.068*	
G1 Teacher Expectancy × Social Skills	−0.08	0.042	−.062		0.013	0.026	.014	
G1 Teacher Expectancy × Sex × Ethnicity	6.939	2.960	.245*		2.86	2.246	.149	

Note: W-J = Woodcock-Johnson Psycho-Educational Battery—Revised; G1 = Grade 1.
[a]Adjusted R^2 = .318, F (13, 725) = 27.42, p < .001. [b]Adjusted R^2 = .395, F(13, 720) = 36.13, p < .001.
*p < .05. **p < .01. ***p < .001.

Table 7. Hierarchical Regressions Predicting Fifth Grade Reading and Math Achievement

Variable	Reading[a]				Math[b]			
	B	SE	β	ΔR²	B	SE	β	ΔR²
W-J, 4.5 years	0.341	0.030	.413***	.239***	0.283	0.022	.457***	.298***
Demographic characteristics				.044***				.034***
Child sex	−1.109	1.121	−.033		−2.441	0.719	−.108**	
Ethnicity	7.132	1.627	.151***		2.205	1.083	.068*	
Family income/needs, G5	0.431	0.159	.097**		0.268	0.101	.090**	
Child social skills—teacher G5	0.106	0.042	.088*	.007**	0.091	0.027	.113**	.013***
G3 Teacher expectancy score	−0.141	0.600	−.008	.000	0.693	0.390	.060*	.006*
G3 Teacher expectancy score squared	0.218	0.401	.019	.000	−0.345	0.281	−.041	.001
G1 Teacher expectancy score	0.743	0.575	.045	.002	1.012	0.357	.091**	.008**

Note: W-J = Woodcock-Johnson Psycho-Educational Battery—Revised: G1 = Grade 1.
[a]Adjusted R^2 = .284, $F(8, 648)$ = 33.47, $p < .001$. [b]Adjusted R^2 = .351, $F(8, 638)$ = 45.01. $p < .001$.
*$p < .05$. **$p < .01$. ***$p < .001$.

The simple slopes were tested to clarify these findings. We found that for children from families with low and average incomes, teacher expectations were significantly and positively related to later math performance ($β = .20$, $p < .001$; $β = .12$, $p < .01$. respectively), whereas teacher expectations were unrelated to later math performance for high income children ($β = .04$, $p = .38$).

At fifth grade, both first and third grade teachers' expectations predicted child math performance. These associations were linear, as indicated by the lack of significance of the squared expectancy score. Thus, when teachers have a more positive view of children's abilities in math than their test scores suggest is accurate, children tend to perform better in math in future years; when teachers have a more negative view than the child's actual math performance warrants, the children tend to perform less well in future years. These effects, although small in magnitude, appear to be long-lasting: First grade teachers' expectancy scores were still related to child math performance four years later, over and above the third grade teacher's expectations. As with the results for reading, none of the interactions between teacher expectations and child characteristics were significant for fifth grade math performance.

DISCUSSION

This study contributes to research in this area in several important ways: (a) We focus on the early school years and the role of teacher expectations of academic ability during this time; (b) we analyze longitudinal relations between teacher expectations and children's academic performance 2 and 4 years distant (at third and fifth grades); and (c) we differentiate reading and math as discrete domains in which

teacher expectations may have unique roles in the early school years.

Consistent with prior research (e.g., Jussim & Eccles, 1992), we found that teachers' reports of children's academic ability are highly related to objective measures. We also found, however, that teachers' expectations (i.e., inaccuracy) can be predicted. Several child characteristics were consistently significant in predicting teachers' expectations of children's academic abilities. Child sex emerged as a consistent predictor of teacher expectations for reading at all time points, and girls were always more likely to be overestimated. Child sex was related to teacher expectations in math only at fifth grade, and, contrary to our hypothesis, girls were again more likely to be overestimated. Also, children's social skills were significantly and positively related to teacher expectations for both reading and math at all time points. It may be that teachers tend to overestimate the academic competence of children they like and find easy to manage in the classroom. Overall, child characteristics accounted for more variance in teachers' expectations for children's reading ability than for math ability.

Given that prior research has shown that teacher expectancy effects dissipate rather than accumulate over time (Smith et al., 1999), we expected only small main effects for teacher expectations on future academic achievement but larger effects for certain groups of children, particularly those who can be viewed as vulnerable. In terms of main effects of teacher expectations on later child academic performance, our results were mixed. We found no effect of teacher expectations in the reading domain: teacher expectations in first and third grades were unrelated to later child reading performance. It appears that in the early school years, teacher expectations do not accumulate or have very long-lasting impacts in the domain of reading.

In investigating the role of child characteristics as moderators, we found a significant three-way interaction between child sex, ethnicity, and first grade teacher expectations in reading. This interaction accounted for only a small portion of variance in third grade reading performance but was consistent with prior research with older children (e.g., Jussim et al., 1996; Madon et al., 1998), and so it was interpreted. Our analyses indicated that teacher expectations of children's reading abilities were related to later performance for one potentially vulnerable group of children: minority boys. Minority boys had the lowest performance when their abilities were underestimated and the greatest gains when their abilities were overestimated.

In the math domain, we found small but significant main effects for teacher expectations on future math performance over and above that which could be accounted for by prior achievement or child characteristics. First grade teacher expectations of children's math abilities were related to both third and fifth grade math performance, and third grade teacher expectations were marginally related to fifth grade math performance. Moreover, at third grade a significant interaction between first grade teacher expectations and child characteristics was found. For children from low-income families and, to a lesser extent, even average-income families, first grade teacher expectations were related to third grade math performance, whereas the performance of children from high-income families was not linked to earlier teacher expectations.

Our results did not suggest a more important role for teachers' under- versus overestimation of children's abilities. Earlier research has presented mixed findings on this topic (e.g., Alvidrez & Weinstein, 1999; Madon et al., 1997). The present study involved a large number of different teachers and classrooms. It is possible that in some situations teachers communicate positive expectations clearly and invest time and energy in children they perceive to be more able, whereas other teachers may be more likely to communicate negative expectations in a way that discourages children. More detailed observations of the processes by which teachers may convey differential expectations to children are needed to fully understand this process.

Several limitations of the current study must also be noted. In the NICHD study, teacher expectations and child achievement were both measured in the spring of the school year. Thus, we were not able to evaluate the relation of teacher expectations at the beginning of the school year to year-end academic performance, the period of time when teacher misestimations likely have their strongest relation to academic performance. Also, the sample of children in this study

differed from the one originally recruited; it included more children from high-income backgrounds and fewer children from minority families. Given the widespread finding that boys from minority ethnic backgrounds are at particular risk for school failure (Davis, 2005; Tutwiler, 2007), the potential links between teacher expectations for these boys, the boys' beliefs about themselves, and their trajectories of school performance are especially important topics for further study. Another limitation of the present study was that the sample of teachers was almost all female and predominantly White, making it impossible to examine differences in teacher expectations or the outcomes of teacher expectations based on the match or mismatch of gender and ethnic background between teachers and children. It is possible that our measure of reading achievement, the Letter—Word subtest of the Woodcock-Johnson scales, did not capture the complexities of reading performance, especially by third and fifth grades. Additionally, teacher reports of academic ability were based on teachers' comparisons of the participating student to other students in the same class, whereas Woodcock-Johnson achievement scores are normed with a national sample.

A final limitation of the study is that our measures of teacher perceptions of child reading and math ability include an item assessing motivation to participate in reading or math activities along with items assessing ability or skill. Therefore, our index of teacher expectations is not based entirely on perceived ability but also in part on interest and engagement. It is possible that Woodcock-Johnson scores predict teacher-rated ability, and the residual (teacher expectations) is comprised primarily of teacher-rated motivation. This implies that it is possible that teacher-rated motivation is actually accounting for variance in future academic achievement. We acknowledge this possibility but also note that our overall results do not support this interpretation. We found that social skills were a strong predictor of teacher expectations and that teacher expectations had stronger effects for only certain groups of children; we think it unlikely that these results would have emerged if teacher expectations were merely a proxy for teacher-rated motivation.

The present study provided several unique advantages and found evidence for the potential importance of teacher expectations to children's later academic achievement. First, it used a large multisite sample of children and teachers, rather than a limited number of schools or classrooms within a single region. Secondly, it focused on the period of school entry, which can be seen as a time children may be particularly susceptible to teacher influence. Third, it found some evidence that research into teacher expectations should take into consideration differing academic domains. In fact, at least in the math domain, it appears that teacher expectations can have long-lasting effects on children's performance. Fourth, it investigated which child characteristics may moderate the relation between teacher expectations and academic achievement over time.

In conclusion, the evidence presented here indicates that child characteristics, especially child sex and social skills, are related to teachers' expectations of children's academic skills in the early years of school. The relation between teacher expectations and children's later academic performance appears to be complex, in that teacher expectations play a larger role for some groups of children than others. The children whose later performance appears to be most influenced by teacher expectations are those who can be seen as marginalized in the classroom, i.e., children from low-income families and minority boys. These results were especially evident between first and third grade and differed by area of academic achievement. Given the potential importance of children's early school experiences in setting the trajectory for later performance, further research into teacher expectations and misperceptions of children's academic abilities is warranted.

REFERENCES

Aiken, L. S., & West, S. G. (1991). *Multiple regression: Testing and interpreting interactions.* Thousand Oaks, CA: Sage.

Alvidrez, J., & Weinstein, R. S. (1999). Early teacher perceptions and later student academic achievement. *Journal of Educational Psychology, 91,* 731–746.

Bauer, D. J., & Curran, P. J. (2005). Probing interactions in fixed and multilevel regression: Inferential and graphical techniques. *Multivariate Behavioral Research, 40,* 373–400.

Brophy, J. (1983). Research on the self-fulfilling prophecy and teacher expectations. *Journal of Educational Psychology, 76,* 236–247.

Burchinal, M., Roberts. J. E., Zeisel, S. A., Hennon, E. A., & Hooper, S. (2006). Social risk and protective child, parenting, and child care factors in early elementary school years. *Parenting: Science and Practice, 6,* 79–113.

Cooper, H., Findley, M., & Good, T. (1982). Relations between student achievement and various indexes of teacher expectations. *Journal of Educational Psychology, 74,* 577–579.

Davis, J. E. (2005). Early schooling and academic achievement of African American males. In O. S. Fashola (Ed.), *How schools fail African American males: Voices from the field* (pp. 129–150). Thousand Oaks, CA: Corwin Press.

Doherty, J., & Conolly, M. (1985). How accurately can primary school teachers predict the score of their pupils in standardised tests of attainment? A study of some non-cognitive factors that influence specific judgments. *Educational Studies, 11,* 41–46.

Egan, O., & Archer, P. (1985). The accuracy of teachers' ratings of ability: A regression model. *American Educational Research Journal, 22,* 25–34.

Englund, M. M., Luckner. A. E., Whaley. G. J. L., & Egeland, B. (2004). Children's achievement in early elementary school: Longitudinal effects of parental involvement, expectations, and quality of assistance. *Journal of Educational Psychology, 96,* 723–730.

Gresham, F. M., & Elliott, S. N. (1990). *The Social Skills Rating System.* Circle Pines, MN: American Guidance Service.

Hamre, B. K., & Pianta, R. C. (2005). Can instructional and emotional support in the first-grade classroom make a difference for children at risk of school failure? *Child Development, 76,* 949–967.

Hoge, R. D., & Coladarci, T. (1989). Teacher-based judgments of academic achievement: A review of literature. *Review of Educational Research, 59,* 297–313.

Jacobs, N., & Harvey, D. (2005). Do parents make a difference to children's academic achievement? Differences between parents of higher and lower achieving students. *Educational Studies, 31,* 431–448.

Jussim, L. (1989). Teacher expectations: Self-fulfilling prophecies, perceptual biases, and accuracy. *Journal of Personality and Social Psychology, 57,* 469–480.

Jussim, L., & Eccles, J. (1992). Teacher expectations. II: Construction and reflection of student achievement. *Journal of Personality and Social Psychology, 63,* 947–961.

Jussim, L., & Eccles, J. (1995). Naturalistic studies of interpersonal expectancies. *Review of Personality and Social Psychology, 15,* 74–108.

Jussim, L., Eccles, J., & Madon, S. J. (1996). Social perception, social stereotypes, and teacher expectations: Accuracy and the quest for the powerful self-fulfilling prophecy. *Advances in Experimental Social Psychology, 29,* 281–388.

Jussim, L., & Harber, K. D. (2005). Teacher expectations and self-fulfilling prophecies: Knowns and unknowns, resolved and unresolved controversies. *Personality and Social Psychology Review, 9,* 131–155.

Jussim, L., Smith, A., Madon, S., & Palumbo, P. (1998). Teacher expectations. In J. Brophy (Ed.), *Advances in research on teaching* (Vol. 7, pp. 1–48). Stanford, CT: JAI Press.

Madon, S., Jussim, L., & Eccles, J. (1997). In search of the powerful self-fulfilling prophecy. *Journal of Personality and Social Psychology, 72,* 791–809.

Madon, S. J., Jussim, L., Keiper, S., Eccles, J., Smith, A., &. Palumbo, P. (1998). The accuracy and power of sex, social class and ethnic stereotypes: Naturalistic studies in perception. *Personality and Social Psychology Bulletin, 24,* 1304–1318.

McGrew, K. S., Werder, J. K., & Woodcock, R. W. (1991). *WJ-R Technical Manual.* Allen, TX: DLM.

Merton, R. K. (1948). The self-fulfilling prophecy. *Antioch Review, 8,* 193–210.

Preacher, K. J., Curran, P. J., & Bauer, D. J. (2006). Computational tools for probing interaction effects in multiple linear regression, multilevel modeling, and latent curve analysis. *Journal of Educational and Behavioral Statistics, 31,* 437–448.

Raudenbush, S. W. (1984). Magnitude of teacher expectancy effects on pupil IQ as a function of the credibility of expectancy induction: A synthesis of findings from 18 experiments. *Journal of Educational Psychology, 76,* 85–97.

Rosenthal, R., & Rubin, D. B. (1978). Interpersonal expectancy effects: The first 345 studies. *The Behavioral and Brain Sciences, 3,* 377–386.

Smith, A. E., Jussim, L., & Eccles, J. (1999). Do self-fulfilling prophecies accumulate, dissipate, or remain stable over time? *Journal of Personality and Social Psychology, 77,* 548–565.

Tutwiler, S. W. (2007). How schools fail African American boys. In S. Books (Ed.), *Invisible children in the society and its schools* (3rd ed., pp. 141–156). Mahwah, NJ: Erlbaum.

West, C., & Anderson, T. (1976). The question of preponderant causation in teacher expectancy research. *Review of Educational Research, 46,* 613–630.

Woodcock, R. W., & Johnson, M. B. (1989). *Woodcock-Johnson Psycho-Educational Battery-Revised.* Allen, TX: DLM.

2.05

CROSS-SECTIONAL DESIGN

A School-Based Survey of Recurrent Non-Specific Low-Back Pain Prevalence and Consequences in Children

M. A. Jones,[*,†,‖] **G. Stratton,**[†,‡] **T. Reilly,**[§] **and V. B. Unnithan**[¶]

ABSTRACT: The aim of this investigation was to provide evidence of the prevalence and consequences of recurrent low-back pain in children from Northwest England. A cross-sectional survey was conducted involving a standardized questionnaire with established reliability and validity. A cross-sectional sample of 500 boys ($n = 249$) and girls ($n = 251$) aged between 10 and 16 years participated in the study. Average lifetime prevalence of low-back pain was 40.2% [95% confidence interval (CI) = 38.7–41.6]. Most cases of low-back pain were acute episodes that did not lead to disabling consequences. In contrast, 13.1% (95% CI = 12.5–13.7) experienced recurrent low-back pain that led to disabling consequences; 23.1% visited a medical practitioner, 30.8% experienced loss of physical activity/sports and 26.2% had been absent from school because of low-back pain. Recurrent low-back pain was particularly evident during late adolescence where one in five children were cases. The health education implications of low-back pain in children are discussed. It was concluded that low-back pain is a common complaint during childhood, although most cases are acute episodes that represent little health consequence. In contrast, some children experience recurrent low-back pain that can lead to disabling consequences. Future research should focus on recurrent low-back pain cases since they often led to disabling consequences.

INTRODUCTION

It has been recognized that low-back pain is a common phenomenon that affects public health

[*]Sport and Exercise Research Group, Edge Hill College, Ormskirk L39 4QP, UK, [†]REACH Group, [‡]Centre for Physical Education, Sport and Dance and [§]Research Institute for Sport and Exercise Sciences, Liverpool John Moores University, Liverpool L3 2ET, UK and[¶] Exercise Science Department, Syracuse University, Syracuse, NY 13244, USA. [‖]Correspondence to: M. A. Jones, Department of Sport and Physical Education, Edge Hill College, St Helens Road, Ormskirk L39 4QP, UK. E-mail: jonesmi@edgehill.ac.uk

(Maniakis and Gray, 2000). Although a less globally recognized problem, low-back pain has also been described as a public health problem in children (Olsen *et al.*, 1992). Epidemiological evidence indicates that non-specific low-back pain presents during childhood. Estimates of lifetime prevalence for low-back pain in children vary from 13 to 51%, point prevalence ranges from 1 to 33% and prevalence of recurrent low-back pain ranges from 7 to 27% (Salminen *et al.*, 1992; Burton *et al.*, 1996; Leboeuf-Yde and Kyvik, 1998; Harreby *et al.*, 1999; Vikat *et al.*, 2000). The prevalence of pain necessitating medical consultation varies from 8 to 16%, and pain interfering with activities such as school and leisure varies between 7 and 27% (Salminen et al., 1992; Burton et al., 1996; Vikat et al., 2000). The variation in results between investigations may be more related to methodological differences than to population differences (Balague et al., 1999). Investigations have varied in the research design (cross-sectional or longitudinal), method of data collection (questionnaire, interview or examination), and the localization and definition of low-back pain.

Conclusions from existing research indicate that low-back pain is a common complaint during childhood. Furthermore, biannual nationwide surveys in Finland revealed that prevalence of low-back pain in children is on the increase (Vikat et al., 2000). It appears that most of these cases were mild in nature; they can be considered as a natural part of growing and represent little consequence to health (Burton et al., 1996; Salminen et al., 1999). In contrast, some children suffer from recurrent low-back pain. These cases have a more chronic evolution, lead to greater disability and require increased medical attention (Salminen et al., 1992; Harreby et al., 1999). Further research needs to focus on evaluating prevalence and consequences of recurrent low-back pain, since it is this group that is likely to suffer health consequences as a result of the low-back pain. Moreover, recurrent low-back pain during the adolescent years may be a precursor for chronic low-back pain during adulthood (Harreby et al., 1995; Salminen et al., 1995, 1999). The aim of this investigation was to provide evidence of the prevalence and consequences of recurrent low-back pain in children from England.

METHODS

Sample and Design

In total, 538 questionnaires were issued to seven schools in Greater Manchester, Lancashire and Merseyside; a response rate of 93% was recorded. The survey was conducted between September 1998 and November 1998. A cross-sectional sample of 500 boys ($n = 249$) and girls ($n = 251$) participated in the study. Subjects were aged between 10 and 16 years [13.5 (2.0) years] and were distributed across this age range ($n > 66$ in each age group). Verbal assent was obtained and the study was granted ethical approval by The Human Ethics Committee of Liverpool John Moores University.

Low-back Pain Evaluation

Subjects were required to complete a questionnaire to assess for low-back pain history. The questionnaire was designed to identify lifetime prevalence, point prevalence, recurrent prevalence and duration of the low-back pain. Lifetime prevalence was defined as the proportion of the population that had experienced an episode at some point in their lifetime. Point prevalence was defined as the proportion of the population that had been cases within the previous week. Recurrent low-back pain was identified by the question 'do you get back pain regularly'; this question referred to the previous 12 months and was classified by repeated acute episodes. An anatomical drawing was used to identify the localization of the back pain (Department of Health, 1998). The consequences of the low-back pain experience were also examined. Questions were asked relating to absence from school, medical treatment and limitation of activity.

Questionnaire Reliability and Validity

The reliability of the questionnaire was established with a repeated measures study involving 119 children aged 11–16 years (7 days between test and re-test). The criterion validity of the questionnaire was evaluated through comparison with interview. Concordance between repeated measures of the questionnaire, and between the questionnaire and interview was greater than 90%. These findings indicated that a questionnaire approach is both reliable and valid, which concurs with other research concerning the reliability and validity of a questionnaire approach (Staes et al., 1999, 2000).

Analysis

Statistical analysis was conducted using Microsoft Excel 97. Descriptive statistics including means, standard deviations and 95% confidence intervals (CIs) were performed to represent the low-back pain data. Chi-square analysis was used to evaluate the effect of sex and age on lifetime prevalence, point prevalence and recurrent low-back pain. Significance was set at $P < 0.01$.

RESULTS

Low-back Pain Prevalence

The prevalence data are in Table 1. Lifetime prevalence of low-back pain was 40.2%. Chi-square analysis identified a significant difference between age groups ($P < 0.01$); Table 1 indicates that lifetime prevalence increases with advancing chronological age. Point prevalence indicated 15.5% of the children had recently experienced low-back pain. Chi-square analysis revealed no significant age effect for point prevalence. The prevalence of recurrent low-back pain was 13.1%. Chi-square analysis revealed a significant age effect for recurrent low-back pain prevalence ($P < 0.01$); Table 1 indicates that recurrent low-back pain prevalence

Table 1. Lifetime, Point and Recurrent Low-Back Pain Across the Age Groups

Age (years)	Lifetime Prevalence		Point Prevalence		Recurrent Prevalence	
	Boys (%)	Girls (%)	Boys (%)	Girls (%)	Boys (%)	Girls (%)
10.0–10.9	17.6	18.8	5.9	9.4	2.9	3.1
11.0–11.9	21.2	23.7	9.1	10.5	6.1	5.3
12.0–12.9	28.6	33.3	11.4	12.8	8.6	10.3
13.0–13.9	35.9	50.0	12.8	16.7	10.3	16.7
14.0–14.9	50.0	55.9	18.4	20.6	15.8	20.6
15.0–15.9	54.3	57.6	22.9	21.2	20.0	21.2
16.0–16.9	57.1	59.0	22.9	23.1	22.9	20.5
Mean	37.8	42.6	14.8	16.3	12.4	13.9
95% CI	36.4–39.2	41.1–44.1	14.2–15.4	15.8–16.8	11.7–13.0	13.3–14.6

increases with advancing chronological age. No significant sex effect was identified for lifetime, point or recurrent low-back pain prevalence.

Consequences of all Types of Low-Back Pain

Absence from school due to low-back pain was reported to occur in 7.8% (95% CI = 7.3–8.2) of the low-back pain cases. Of the low-back pain cases 6.5% (95% CI = 6.0–7.0) visited a medical practitioner about low-back pain. Girls (8.9%, 95% CI = 8.3–9.5) appeared to be more likely to visit a medical practitioner than boys (3.7%, 95% CI = 3.3–4.1). The low-back pain experiences led to 9.9% (95% CI = 9.6–10.3) of the cases being prevented from taking part in sport or physical activity. The duration of low-back pain experiences revealed most episodes lasted less than 7 days (78.2%); a small proportion of low-back pain episodes lasted more than 1 (19.3%) or 2 (2.5%) weeks.

Recurrent Cases

The consequences of low-back pain were considered separately for those children who reported recurrent low-back pain. Chi-square analysis identified a significant difference in each of the consequences between the recurrent cases of low-back pain and the other cases ($P < 0.01$). The recurrent low-back pain cases were absent from school more often (26.2%), visited a medical practitioner more frequently (23.1%) and were prevented from participating in sports or physical activity more frequently (30.8%) than the other cases (1.5%) because of low-back pain.

DISCUSSION

This investigation aimed to evaluate the prevalence and consequences of low-back pain, with particular emphasis on recurrent low-back pain. An epidemiological school-based survey was carried out. The extent of existing data on low-back pain prevalence in children

is limited with just occurrence or non-occurrence being measured in several investigations (Leboeuf-Yde and Kyvik, 1998; Vikat et al., 2000). Simple occurrence data do not allow health consequences and disease impact to be evaluated (Goodman and McGrath, 1991).

Lifetime and Point Prevalence

Lifetime prevalence of low-back pain was 40.2% and point prevalence 15.5%. These values are similar to previous research that has identified a range of 13–51 and 1–33% for lifetime and point prevalence respectively (Salminen et al., 1992; Burton et al., 1996; Leboeuf-Yde and Kyvik, 1998; Harreby et al., 1999; Vikat et al., 2000). The average lifetime prevalence of low-back pain in children (40.2%) is lower than the 59% reported for British adults (Walsh et al., 1992; Mason, 1994; Leighton and Reilly, 1995). The average point prevalence (15.5%) observed in the sample is actually higher than the 14% reported for British adults (Walsh et al., 1992; Mason, 1994). When comparing the data between children and adults, the different definitions of low-back pain must be considered. Investigations involving adults have specified a 'case' as low-back pain leading to activity limitation, whereas studies involving children have not specified the low-back pain must lead to activity limitation. Only two cases (1.5%) reported consequences from lifetime prevalence of low-back pain in the current study. This finding suggests that a lifetime experience of low-back pain, although common during childhood, represents little health consequence, agreeing with previous research (Burton et al., 1996; Harreby et al., 1999).

Recurrent Low-back Pain

The prevalence of recurrent low-back pain was 13.1%; this figure is in accordance with previous research that has indicated a range from 7 to 27% (Burton et al., 1996; Harreby et al., 1999; Vikat et al., 2000). Comparison across studies is difficult due to different definitions of recurrent low-back pain, specifically the duration over which recurrence is considered. Prevalence of recurrent low-back pain significantly increased with advancing chronological age in the current study. Olsen et al. (Olsen et al., 1992) also found an increase from 6.2% at 10 years to 15.5% at 14 years; these figures are comparable to the current study. The increase of recurrent low-back pain with age indicates a worrying finding. Frequent low-back pain is of much greater consequence both now and in the future (Olsen et al., 1992; Harreby et al., 1999).

Health Implications

Over a quarter of the recurrent low-back pain cases had experienced consequences as a result of their low-back pain, which suggests that recurrent low-back pain represents a potentially serious health problem in this population. This finding agrees with previous research which suggests recurrent low-back pain has a more chronic evolution and leads to greater levels of disability (Salminen et al., 1992; Harreby et al., 1999). Salminen et al. (Salminen et al., 1992) identified 7.8% of children were low-back pain chronics, and experienced recurrent low-back pain and disability. Harreby et al. (Harreby et al., 1999) found that children who reported recurrent or continuous low-back pain utilized increased medical attention and use of analgesics, and experienced reduced quality of life. The economic and public health burden of recurrent low-back pain during childhood is substantial when one considers the young age and potential tracking into adulthood.

Health Education Implications

Research into children's health and health behaviour and the factors that influence them is essential for the development of effective health education and health promotion policy, programmes and practice targeted at young people (Currie et al., 2000). Historically, back health and posture have internationally been important elements of the national curriculum for physical education; by the mid-1980s when heart health became the priority it was largely forgotten (Tinning, 2001). National cross-sectional surveys evaluating the prevalence of back, neck and shoulder pain in Finnish adolescents have identified that the prevalence of low-back pain increased between 1985 to 2001, particularly during the mid-1990s with the trend still continuing (Hakala et al., 2002). It appears from the evidence that there is a strong case to re-introduce the concept of back health into the curriculum or as part of the healthy school initiative.

The WHO has identified the school as an effective setting in which to improve children's health (WHO, 1996). Schools health programmes can simultaneously reduce health problems, increase efficiency of the education system and advance social development. The cause of low-back pain in children appears to be multifactorial, including biological, psychological, social and individual factors (Balague et al., 1999). Given the multifactorial causes of low-back pain, several health education strategies within the school setting have the potential to reduce the incidence of low-back pain. Linking to the WHO healthy schools initiative seems plausible; key areas would be elements of (1) promoting a healthy environment, (2) health education, (3) opportunities for physical education and recreation, and (4) offering programmes for social support.

Currently there is limited research to evaluate the effectiveness of either primary or secondary prevention strategies for low-back pain in children. Plausibly impacting the school environment, including issues such as school chair design and daily load carriage may be an effective strategy. Recent research has suggested that the load carried by school children daily during school-life may impact on low-back pain and is often greater than the legal limits set for adults (Negrini et al., 1999). Health education strategies in school could include advice along the lines of adult back-schools regarding back health and ergonomic advice; preliminary studies have suggested that education about back health may be effective at reducing the incidence of low-back pain in children (Balague et al., 1996; Cardon et al., 2001). Furthermore, the introduction of ergonomic backpacks may be an effective health education strategy (Negrini and Carabolona, 2002). Regarding physical education and recreation, the conditioning of the low-back region and general physical activity of children is considered to be a risk indicator for low-back pain, and so the introduction of specific exercises and increasing opportunity for recreational activities is likely to positively impact on low-back pain. In terms of social support, it has been identified that many pain states, including low-back pain, may be linked to other psychosocial correlates and may be psychosomatic in nature (Vikat et al., 2000).

Limitations

The main limitation of the current study was the cross-sectional nature of the data collected. The variations across chronological age and sex are inferred, and other factors such as environment, heredity and sports participation could intervene. An inherent limitation to all studies of low-back pain is the subjective nature of low-back pain and the need to rely on subject recall. To counteract the effect of this, the reliability and validity of the questionnaire were appraised prior to the study. Moreover, since pain is a subjective phenomenon, personal recall is the only valid way to assess pain (Goodman and McGrath, 1991).

Future Directions

Future research should focus on recurrent cases of low-back pain in children to identify risk indicators for recurrent low-back pain, coping strategies employed to deal with recurrent low-back pain, and the efficacy of a range of primary and secondary prevention strategies. When evaluating primary and secondary prevention strategies, both randomized controlled research designs and action research in community settings are needed to evaluate both the short-term efficacy and long-term effectiveness.

CONCLUSIONS

It was concluded that low-back pain is a common complaint during childhood, although most cases are acute episodes that represent little health consequence. In contrast, some children experience recurrent low-back pain that can lead to disabling consequences. Future research should focus on these recurrent low-back pain cases, since these cases led to disabling consequences.

ACKNOWLEDGEMENTS

The authors would like to acknowledge the support of the REACH (Research into Exercise and Children's Health) group.

REFERENCES

Balague, F., Nordin, M., Dutoit, G. and Waldburger, M. (1996) Primary prevention, education and low back pain among school children. *Bulletin of the Hospital for Joint Diseases*, **55**, 130–134.

Balague, F., Troussier, B. and Salminen, J.J. (1999) Nonspecific low back pain in children and adolescents: risk factors. *European Spine Journal*, **8**, 429–438.

Burton, A.K., Clarke, R.D., McClune, T.D. and Tillotson, K.M. (1996) The natural history of low back pain in adolescents. *Spine*, **21**, 2323–2328.

Cardon, G., Bourdeaudhuij, I.D. and Clercq, D.D. (2001) Generalization of back education principles by elementary school children: evaluation with a practical test and a candid camera observation. *Acta Paediatrica*, **90**, 143–150.

Currie, C., Hurrelmann, K., Settertobulte, W., Smith, R. and Todd, J. (eds) (2000) *Health and Health Behaviour among Young People. WHO Policy Series: Health Policy for Children and Adolescents Issue 1.* WHO, Copenhagen.

Department of Health (1998) The prevalence of back pain in Great Britain in 1998. Available: www.doh.gov.uk/public/backpain.htm (accessed 5 March 2002).

Goodman, J.E. and McGrath, P.J. (1991) The epidemiology of pain in children and adolescents: a review. *Pain*, **46**, 247–264.

Hakala, P., Rimpela, A., Salminen, J.J., Virtanen, S.M. and Rimpela, M. (2002) Back, neck and shoulder pain in Finnish Adolescents: national cross sectional surveys. *British Medical Journal*, **325**, 743–747.

Harreby, M., Neergaard, K., Hesselsoe, G. and Kjer, J. (1995) Are radiological changes in the thoracic and lumbar spine of adolescents risk factors for low back pain in adults? A 25-year prospective cohort study of 640 school children. *Spine*, **20**, 2298–2302.

Harreby, M., Nygaard, B., Jessen, T., Larsen, E., Storr-Paulsen, A., Lindahl, A., Fisker, I. and Laegaard, E. (1999) Risk factors for low back pain in a cohort of 1389 Danish school children: an epidemiologic study. *European Spine Journal*, **8**, 444–450.

Leboeuf-Yde, C. and Kyvik, K.O. (1998) At what age does low back pain become a problem? A study of 24,424 individuals aged 12–41 years. *Spine*, **23**, 228–234.

Leighton, D.J. and Reilly, T. (1995) Epidemiological aspects of back pain: the incidence and prevalence of back pain in nurses compared to the general population. *Occupational Medicine*, **45**, 263–267.

Maniakis, A. and Gray, A. (2000) The economic burden of back pain in the UK. *Pain*, **84**, 95–103.

Mason, V. (1994) *The Prevalence of Back Pain in Great Britain.* HMSO, London.

Negrini, S. and Carabalona, R. (2002) Backpacks on! Schoolchildrens perceptions of load, associations with back pain and factors determining load. *Spine*, **27**, 187–195.

Negrini, S., Carabalona, R. and Sibilla, P. (1999) Backpack as a daily load for schoolchildren. *Lancet*, **354**, 1974.

Olsen, T.L., Anderson, R.L., Dearwater, S.R. Kriska, A.M., Cauley, J.A., Aaron, D.J. and LaPorte, R.E. (1992) The epidemiology of low back pain in an adolescent population. *American Journal of Public Health*, **82**, 606–608.

Salminen, J.J., Pentti, J. and Terho, P. (1992) Low back pain and disability in 14-year-old schoolchildren. *Acta Paediatrica*, **81**, 1035–1039.

Salminen, J.J., Erkintalo-Tertti, M.O. and Paajanen, H.E. (1995) Low back pain in the young: a prospective three-year follow-up study of subjects with and without low back pain. *Spine*, **20**, 2101–2107.

Salminen, J.J., Erkintalo, M.O., Pentti, J., Oksanen, A. and Kormano, M.J. (1999) Recurrent low back pain and early disc degeneration in the young. *Spine*, **24**, 1316–1321.

Staes, F., Stappaerts, K., Vertommen, H., Everaert, D. and Coppieters, M. (1999) Reproducibility of a survey questionnaire for the investigation of low-back problems in adolescents. *Acta Paediatrica*, **88**, 1269–1273.

Staes, F., Stappaerts, K., Vertommen, H., Nuyens, G., Coppieters, M. and Everaert, D. (2000) Comparison of self-administration and face-to-face interview for surveys of low back pain in adolescents. *Acta Paediatrica*, **89**, 1352–1357.

Tinning, R. (2001) Physical education and back health: negotiating instrumental aims and holistic body-work practices. *European Physical Education Review*, **7**, 191–205.

Vikat, A., Rimpela, M., Salminen, J.J., Rimpela, A., Savolainen, A. and Virtanen, S.M. (2000) Neck or shoulder pain and low back pain in Finnish adolescents. *Scandinavian Journal of Public Health*, **28**, 164–173.

Walsh, K., Cruddes, M. and Coggon, D. (1992) Low back pain in eight areas of Britain. *Journal of Epidemiology and Community Health*, **46**, 230–277.

WHO (1996) Promoting Health through Schools: a summary and recommendations of WHO's Expert Committee on Comprehensive School Health Education and Promotion. *WHO Technical Report Series*, **870**, i–vi, 1–93.

2.06

LONGITUDINAL DESIGN

Social Capital, Self-Esteem, and Use of Online Social Network Sites: A Longitudinal Analysis

Charles Steinfield,* Nicole B. Ellison,* and Cliff Lampe*

ABSTRACT: A longitudinal analysis of panel data from users of a popular online social network site, Facebook, investigated the relationship between intensity of Facebook use, measures of psychological well-being, and bridging social capital. Two surveys conducted a year apart at a large U.S. university, complemented with in-depth interviews with 18 Facebook users, provide the study data. Intensity of Facebook use in year one strongly predicted bridging social capital outcomes in year two, even after controlling for measures of self-esteem and satisfaction with life. These latter psychological variables were also strongly associated with social capital outcomes. Self-esteem served to moderate the relationship between Facebook usage intensity and bridging social capital: those with lower self-esteem gained more from their use of Facebook in terms of bridging social capital than higher self-esteem participants. We suggest that Facebook affordances help reduce barriers that lower self-esteem students might experience in forming the kinds of large, heterogeneous networks that are sources of bridging social capital.

KEYWORDS: Facebook; online social networks; social capital; social network sites; emerging adults; self-esteem; life satisfaction; internet use; longitudinal research.

INTRODUCTION

Social network sites constitute an important research area for scholars interested in online technologies and their social impacts, as evinced by recent scholarship in the area (boyd & Ellison, 2007; Donath, 2007; Ellison, Steinfield, & Lampe, 2007; Golder, Wilkinson, & Huberman, 2007; Lampe, Ellison, & Steinfield, 2007; Valkenburg, Peter, & Schouter, 2006). Social network

sites (SNSs) are "web-based services that allow individuals to (1) construct a public or semi-public profile within a bounded system, (2) articulate a list of other users with whom they share a connection, and (3) view and traverse their list of connections and those made by others within the system" (boyd & Ellison, 2007, p. 211). The first social network site was launched in 1997 and currently there are hundreds of SNSs across the globe, supporting a spectrum of practices, interests and users (boyd & Ellison, 2007).

One of the largest social network sites among the U.S. college student population is Facebook, created in February 2004 by Mark Zuckerberg, then a student at

*Department of Telecommunication, Information Studies, and Media, Michigan State University, East Lansing, MI 48824 USA

Harvard University. According to Zuckerberg, "The idea for the website was motivated by a social need at Harvard to be able to identify people in other residential houses" (Moyle, 2004, Dec. 7). Facebook has become very popular among undergraduates, with usage rates upwards of 90% at most campuses (Lampe, Ellison, & Steinfield, 2006; Stutzman, 2006). It has also stimulated much recent research on various aspects of Facebook use, such as the use of Facebook in academic settings (Hewitt & Forte, 2006) and the demographic predictors of Facebook use (Hargittai, 2007). One strand of research focuses on the outcomes of Facebook use.

Among young adults, relationships with peers are important both for generating offline benefits, commonly referred to as social capital, and for psychosocial development. Social capital is an elastic construct used to describe the benefits one receives from one's relationships with other people (Lin, 1999). Ellison et al. (2007) suggest that intense Facebook use is closely related to the formation and maintenance of social capital. In their survey of undergraduates at a large university, Facebook use was found to be associated with distinct measures of social capital, including bridging social capital (which emphasizes the informational benefits of a heterogeneous network of weak ties) and bonding social capital (which emphasizes emotional benefits from strong ties to close friends and family). Moreover, Ellison et al. (2007) found evidence that self-esteem may operate as a moderator of the relationship between social network site use and social capital. That is, young people with lower self-esteem appeared to benefit more from their use of Facebook than those with higher self-esteem. However, with data at only one point in time, it was not possible for Ellison et al. (2007) to establish any time order to the relationships among Facebook use, self-esteem, and social capital.

These findings suggest that more research on the role of social network sites among young adults is needed, since maintaining friendships through SNSs like Facebook may play an important role in psychological development. Arnett (2000) has distinguished the period between ages 18 and 25 as a phase of "emerging adulthood," a liminal period between adolescence and adulthood. Arnett posits that this stage is critical to an individual's adult development because during this time a person builds long term social skills, including those critical for self-dependence, career orientation and relationship maintenance. Other researchers studying the emerging adulthood stage have called for more research on the effect of new media, including social network sites, on adult development and relationships (Brown, 2006). The development and maintenance of friendships during this period has been shown to influence identity formation, well-being and the development of romantic and family relationships over the long term (Connolly,

Furman, & Konarksi, 2000; Montgomery, 2005). Social network sites offer a new set of tools to develop and maintain relationships and are thus of particular importance in emerging adulthood.

The present study contributes to prior work on young adults and their use of social network sites by investigating the relationship between Facebook use and bridging social capital over time, using data from a panel of college students who reported on their use of Facebook at two points a year apart. Based on prior work by Ellison et al. (2007), a particular focus was on whether and to what extent users' self-esteem moderates the relationship between Facebook use and social capital outcomes. We specifically focus on Facebook in this study because of its pervasive use on college campuses across the country and increasingly throughout the world. Indeed, estimates of the proportion of students who have joined Facebook on college campuses in the U.S. range between 85% and 95% (Lampe et al., 2006), making it the most important social network site for this particular cohort of emerging adults.

A longitudinal study is warranted in this area of inquiry for two reasons. First, it can help answer questions regarding the appropriate causal direction of influence among key variables — does greater use of a social network site lead to greater social capital, or do those with more social capital simply have a greater incentive to use social network sites? Second, a longitudinal analysis can help shed light on the development of social capital over time among young people, exploring the possibility that social capital can evolve from relationships that began at an earlier point in time.

Social Capital, Relationships and Internet Use

There are two complementary perspectives on the importance of friendship maintenance, particularly in the U.S. college-aged population. First, relationships help generate social capital (Lin, 1999) and are important components of psychosocial development for emerging adults (Sullivan, 1953). For the college-age populations, sites like Facebook may play a vital role in maintaining relationships that would otherwise be lost as these individuals move from the geographically bounded networks of their hometown. Second, there is also growing evidence that Internet use in general, and social network sites like Facebook in particular, may be associated with a person's sense of self-worth and other measures of psychosocial development, although the positive or negative contributions of Internet use to psychological well-being are hotly debated (Kraut, Patterson, Lundmark, Kiesler, Mukhopadhyay, & Scherlis, 1998; Kraut, Kiesler, Boneva, Cummings, Helgeson, & Crawford, 2002; Shaw & Gant, 2002; Valkenburg et al., 2006).

Relationships and Social Capital

Although social capital is an elastic term with a variety of definitions in multiple fields (Adler & Kwon, 2002), there is general consensus that it refers broadly to the benefits we receive from our social relationships (Lin, 1999). It can be conceived in negative terms, such as when non-group members are excluded from having access to the same benefits as members (Bourdieu & Wacquant, 1992; Helliwell & Putnam, 2004), but is generally perceived to be positive (Adler & Kwon, 2002). It has been linked to such diverse outcomes as career advancement (Burt, 1997), organizational success (Nahapiet & Ghoshal, 1998), and many other positive social outcomes such as better public health and lower crime rates (Adler & Kwon, 2002). Social capital has also been linked to the psychological and physical well-being of young people. In a wide-ranging review, Morrow (1999) found that despite a lack of consistent definition and measurement, prior work suggests that young people with more social capital are more likely to engage in behaviors that lead to better health, academic success, and emotional development.

The ability to form and maintain relationships is a necessary precondition for the accumulation of social capital. For example, Coleman (1988) describes social capital as resources accumulated through the relationships among people. Lin (1999) extends this notion by emphasizing the importance of developing a social network, considering social capital to arise from "investments in social relations with expected returns" (p. 30) and suggests that the benefits arise from the greater "access to and use of resources embedded in social networks" (p. 30). Bourdieu and Wacquant (1992) define social capital as "the sum of the resources, actual or virtual, that accrue to an individual or a group by virtue of possessing a durable network of more or less institutionalized relationships of mutual acquaintance and recognition" (p. 14).

Forms of Social Capital

It is important to distinguish between conceptions of social capital at the individual and relationship level, and conceptions at the community level (Lin, 1999), although we might consider the latter to be an aggregate of the former. For example, community social capital has been viewed as being on the decline in the U.S. for the past several years (Putnam, 2000), a trend associated with increased social disorder, reduced participation in civic activities, and potentially more distrust among community members. On the other hand, greater social capital increases commitment to a community and the ability to mobilize collective actions, among other benefits. At the individual level, social capital allows individuals to capitalize on their connections with others, accruing benefits such as information or support.

Our focus is on individual-level social capital, where research has generally distinguished between two broad types: bonding and bridging social capital (Putnam, 2000). Bonding social capital is found between individuals in tightly-knit, emotionally close relationships, such as family and close friends. Bridging social capital, the focus of the present paper, stems from what network researchers refer to as "weak ties," which are loose connections between individuals who may provide useful information or new perspectives for one another but typically not emotional support (Granovetter, 1983). Access to individuals outside one's close circle provides access to non-redundant information, resulting in benefits such as employment connections (Granovetter, 1973). Although bridging social capital is viewed as an individual-level construct, prior research has conceptualized it in a community context (Putnam, 2000; Williams, 2006). Williams (2006) includes dimensions such as the extent to which people see themselves as part of a broader group and exhibit norms of giving within a broader community in the construct.

Psychological Well-being and Social Capital

Social capital researchers have found that various forms of social capital, including ties with friends and neighbors, are related to indices of psychological well-being, such as self-esteem and satisfaction with life (Bargh, McKenna, & Fitzsimons, 2002; Helliwell & Putnam, 2004). However, most research examining the connections between self-esteem, measures of well-being, and social capital emphasize the importance of family, intimate relationships, and close friends (Bishop & Inderbitzen, 1995; Keefe & Berndt, 1996). There is a need for additional research exploring the potential linkages between psychological well-being and the kinds of weak ties thought to enhance bridging social capital. Constant, Sproull, and Kiesler (1996) argue for such a linkage in their research documenting how people show gains in self-esteem when they provide technical advice to strangers over the Internet.

Internet Use, Relationship Development, and Psychosocial Well-being

In the past decade, a number of studies have explored how Internet use might be related to psychological and social well-being with mixed results (e.g., Kraut et al., 1998; Kraut et al., 2002; McKenna & Bargh, 2000; Nie, 2001; Shaw & Gant, 2002; Valkenburg & Peter, 2007). Kraut et al. (1998) found that heavier Internet use was associated with various measures of loneliness, depression and stress. They argue that this was because weaker ties generated online were replacing stronger offline ties with family and friends. In a follow-up study, Kraut et al. (2002) found that when examined over a longer period of time, Internet use was no longer associated with decreased communication and involvement with family (and the associated measures of loneliness and depression). Indeed, the effects were generally positive. Of particular interest was their finding that measures of introversion and extraversion moderated the outcomes from Internet use, with extraverts more likely to experience benefits from their Internet use than introverts. Other researchers also argue that Internet use has positive impacts on psychological well-being (Bargh & McKenna, 2004; McKenna & Bargh; 2000; Shaw & Gant, 2002). Bargh and McKenna (2004) attribute this to the increases in online interactions, which mitigate any loss in communication with others due to time spent online. In an experiment, Shaw and Gant (2002) found decreases in perceived loneliness and depression as well as increases in perceived social support and self-esteem following engagement in online chat sessions. In related research, Valkenburg and Peter (2007) found that socially anxious adolescents perceived the Internet to be more valuable for intimate self-disclosure than non-socially anxious respondents, leading to more online communication.

Despite the plethora of research on Internet use in general, research examining the complex relationships between psychological well-being and use of online social network services is scarce. In a notable exception, Valkenburg et al. (2006) found that the more people used social network sites, the greater the frequency of interaction with friends, which had positive benefits on respondents' self-esteem and ultimately their reported satisfaction with life.

While considerable research shows that relationships are important elements of social development for young adults, this is also a time of life when relationships are interrupted as people move from one location to another. Entering college, moving between residences, graduating and entering the professional workforce are all events that could disrupt the maintenance of relationships of people in this demographic (Cummings, Lee, & Kraut, 2006). These individuals have an especially urgent need to be able to maintain connections with their previously inhabited networks while still being open to new experiences and relationships in their current geographical context. Hence, we would expect the Internet-based social networking services to play a role in the maintenance of relationships among this population of users.

Social Capital and Use of Social Network Sites

Researchers have started to explore the possibilities social network sites have for building social capi-

tal among users. Resnick (2001), for example, suggests that new forms of social capital and relationship building will occur in social network sites due to the way that technologies like distribution lists, photo directories, and search capabilities support online linkages with others. Donath and boyd (2004) hypothesize that social network sites could increase the number of weak ties a user might be able to maintain because their affordances are well-suited to maintaining these ties cheaply and easily. In particular, bridging social capital might be augmented by social network sites like Friendster or Facebook because they enable users to create and maintain larger, diffuse networks of relationships from which they could potentially draw resources (Donath & boyd, 2004; Resnick, 2001; Wellman, Haase, Witte, & Hampton, 2001). In one of the few attempts to examine the effect of social network site use on social capital among young people, Ellison et al. (2007) surveyed users of Facebook at a large Midwestern University. They assessed levels of bridging and bonding social capital as well as "maintained" social capital, a form of social capital that speaks to one's ability to stay connected with members of a previously inhabited community. They found that intensity of Facebook use was a significant predictor of bridging social capital, even after controlling for a range of demographic, general Internet use, and psychological well-being measures. The mean number of friends reported by these participants was between 150 and 200. This relatively high number of friends suggests that these networks consist of larger, less intimate relationships as opposed to tightly-knit small groups. Moreover, Ellison et al. (2007) found that the relationship between Facebook use and bridging social capital was greater for low self-esteem students than for high self-esteem students, a finding that contradicts the Kraut et al. (2002) "rich get richer" finding that high extraversion subjects gained more from their Internet use than low extraversion subjects. Although introversion/extraversion is not the same variable as self-esteem, such findings suggest that there is value in exploring the extent to which an individual's propensity to form relationships can be influenced in some way by their use of social network sites like Facebook.

Ellison et al. (2007) looked only at cross-sectional relationships between Facebook use and the existence of social capital. Facebook use was strongly associated with the existence of bridging social capital, possibly indicating that young adults were using Facebook to maintain large and heterogeneous networks of friends. However, an equally plausible interpretation is that young adults with a large and heterogeneous network of friends had more motivation to manage this network with a service like Facebook. This would also result in a positive correlation, and a cross-sectional study cannot rule out such an explanation. Moreover, even if Facebook use did influence bridging social capital, it is not clear if such impacts are transient or enduring. Hence, the present study focused on the longitudinal effects of Facebook use.

Summary and Hypotheses

We summarize this review of literature with three broad research questions, and a series of hypotheses that are suggested by prior research.

RQ 1. How does Facebook use among a college population change over time? We make no explicit hypotheses here, but a longitudinal study enables an examination of the extent to which Facebook usage increases or decreases over a year among students, as well as the growth or decline in the size of students' online social network.

RQ 2. What is the directionality of the relationship between Facebook use and development of bridging social capital? Based on earlier work conceptualizing bridging social capital as an outcome of social network site use (Donath & boyd, 2004; Ellison et al., 2007), we hypothesize that:

H1. The more intense the use of Facebook, the greater the perceived bridging social capital.

H2. The direction of influence is from Facebook use to bridging social capital rather than from bridging social capital to Facebook use.

RQ 3. How does an individual's psychological well-being influence the relationship between social capital and social network site use? Based on earlier work relating psychological well-being and self-esteem to social capital (e.g., Bargh et al., 2002; Helliwell & Putnam, 2004), we hypothesize that:

H3. The greater the psychological well-being, the greater the perceived bridging social capital.

In addition, given the earlier findings by Ellison et al. (2007), we propose that:

H4. Psychological well-being will moderate the relationship between Facebook use and bridging social capital.

METHOD

A combination of survey methods and in-depth interviews with a small number of students form the core of the data that were used for this study. To test the relationships over time between Facebook use and social capital, survey data were collected at two points in time a year apart. Respondents were all students at a large Midwestern university. Initially, in April of 2006, a random sample of 800 undergraduate students was sent an email invitation from one of the authors, with a short description of the study, information about confidentiality and an incentive for participation, and a link to the survey. Participants were compensated with a $5 credit to a university-administered

spending account. The survey was hosted on a commercial online survey-hosting site. We focused on undergraduate users and did not include faculty, staff, or graduate students in our sampling frame. A total of 286 students completed the online survey, a response rate of 35.8%. Demographic information about non-responders was not available; therefore we do not know whether a bias existed in regards to survey participation. However, the demographics of our sample compare favorably to the undergraduate population as a whole with a few exceptions. Female, younger, in-state and on-campus students were slightly over-represented in our sample.

In April of 2007, the survey was re-administered to a new random sample of 1987 undergraduate students as well as to 277 respondents from the previous year. The 2007 survey was hosted on the same survey-hosting website as the 2006 version, and compensation was limited to an opportunity to win a $50 raffle. A total of 477 usable surveys from the new random sample were obtained, yielding a 24% response rate. We received 92 completed surveys from the 277 prior respondents (33%) from 2006 who were invited to retake the survey. These 92 respondents comprised our "panel" for investigating the potential over time influences of Facebook use.

As a follow-up to the first year survey, we conducted in-depth interviews with 18 students primarily drawn from the April 2006 sample in order to learn more about the ways in which students used Facebook to maintain existing friendships and make new ones. We asked survey respondents if they were willing to be interviewed about their Facebook use in person, and 176 (62%) said yes. We then wrote to a number of these individuals and from those who responded with availability we were able to schedule 10 women and 6 men for in-depth interviews. To achieve more gender balance, we added two men through referrals from interviewees, resulting in a total of 18 interviews. We were particularly interested in how the affordances of Facebook translated into usage strategies that resulted in the kinds of bridging social capital outcomes found in the first survey. Although we do not report an extensive analysis of our qualitative data in this paper, we include quotations from these interviews to help explicate the survey findings and suggest how Facebook use might be operating to influence social capital outcomes.

Table 1 provides sample descriptive characteristics, revealing that the 92 members of the panel sample did not substantially differ from the random samples in each period on the demographic data we obtained. There were also no demographic differences between the 2006 and 2007 samples, despite the somewhat lower response rate in 2007. However, there was significant growth in Internet and Facebook usage from 2006 to 2007 (discussed in the Results section).

The statistical analyses we report here focus only on the panel sample, exploring how usage of Facebook in year 1 relates to outcomes in year 2.

Measures

In addition to demographic measures noted above, the study relied on four sets of measures drawn from Ellison et al. (2007). Independent measures included general Internet use, Facebook use, and two measures of psychological well-being: self-esteem and satisfaction with life. Our dependent measure is bridging social capital. In general, these variables were assessed in 2007 using the same survey items as in 2006. In a few instances described below, some items were reworded, and we had to do some conversion to allow cross-year comparisons.

Internet Use

In order to investigate the unique effects of social network site use that might be distinct from other uses of the Internet, we included a measure of general Internet use. Internet use was assessed using a measure adapted from LaRose, Lai, Lange, Love, and Wu (2005), which required respondents to indicate how many hours they actively used the Internet each day during a typical week and weekend day. In 2006, respondents selected from a set of options such as 1–2 h (up to a maximum of 10 h), while in 2007, a text box for hours and minutes was provided in order to obtain more exact estimates. The mid-point of the scale was used to estimate actual hours per day for the 2006 data (so 1 h 30 min for the 1–2 h option), and a weighted average of weekend and weekday hours provided a single index of the hours of Internet use per day (see Table 1).

Facebook Use

Respondents were first asked if they were Facebook members, and if they answered yes, were presented with a series of questions related to their Facebook usage. These solicited reports of how many

Table 1. Summary of Descriptive Statistics for Facebook Panel in 2006 and 2007

	2006 Full sample[a] (N = 288)		2006 Panel (N = 92)		2007 Random sample (N = 481)		2007 Panel (N = 92)	
	M/% (N)	SD	M/% (N)	SD	M/% (N)	SD	M/% (N)	SD
Sex								
Male	34% (98)		26% (24)		33% (155)		No change	
Female	66% (188)		74% (68)		67% (312)			
Age	20.1	1.64	20.1	1.36	20.6	2.33	20.99	1.38
Ethnicity								
White	87% (247)		90% (83)		83% (375)		No change	
Non-white	13% (36)		10% (9)		17% (78)			
Year in school[b]	2.55	1.07	2.51	1.04	2.71	1.11	3.34	.89
Home residence								
In-state	91% (259)		91% (83)		92% (428)		No change	
Out-of-state	09% (25)		09% (8)		08% (36)			
Fraternity/sorority member	08% (23)		07% (6)		09% (42)		No change	
Daily hours Internet use[c]	2:56	1:52	2:58	1:52	4:16	4:26	4:04	4:54
Facebook member (%)	94% (268)		98% (90)		94% (440)		No change	
Daily minutes Facebook used[d]	29.48	36.7	32.56	38.96	63.57	53.03	53.76	42.71
Number of Facebook friends[e]	200.62	113.62	223.09	116.36	302.08	217.39	339.26	193.26

[a]*Source:* Ellison et al. (2007).

[b]1 = first year, 2 = sophomore, 3 = junior, 4 = senior.

[c]For comparison purposes, the 2006 data were converted from an ordinal scale by assigning the score of the mid-point of each response category (e.g., 1–2 h = 1 h 30 min). In 2007, Internet use was measured by filling in the value in hours and minutes for weekends and weekdays, and then taking weighted average.

[d]For 2006, minutes of Facebook use were converted from an ordinal scale by assigning the mid-point of each response category, where less than 10 = 5 min, 10–30 = 15, 31–60 = 45, 1–2 h = 90, 2–3 h = 150, more than 3 h = 180 min. In 2007, Facebook minutes were measured by filling in the value in hours and minutes for weekends and weekdays, and then taking weighted average.

[e]To compare 2006 and 2007 friends data, the 2006 number of friends was converted from the original 10 point ordinal scale by assigning the score of the midpoint of each response category: 10 or less = 5, 11–50 = 30, 51–100 = 75, 101–150 = 125, 151–200 = 175, 201–250 = 225, 251–300 = 275, 301–400 = 250, more than 400 = 400. In 2007, respondents simply wrote in their estimated number of Facebook friends. Outliers were capped at 800.

minutes they spent using Facebook each day in the past week and how many total Facebook friends they had. As with Internet usage, an important measurement difference between 2006 and 2007 was that in the earlier survey, respondents selected from a set of response categories for each of these measures, while in 2007 they provided direct estimates (see Table 1 notes). To allow a comparison across years and provide a meaningful estimate of both the average number of minutes per day that respondents used Facebook and the reported number of friends, the 2006 ordinal data were converted to the best approximation possible, replacing each 2006 ordinal value on these two measures with the mid-point of the response category. For example, if a respondent in 2006 estimated that they spent between 31 and 60 min using Facebook per day, this was converted to 45 min; if a respondent in 2006 reported having between 151 and 200 friends, this was converted to an estimate of 175 friends.

Following Ellison et al. (2007), we employed a measure of Facebook use called Facebook Intensity. This scale provides a more robust measure of how Facebook is being used than would simple items assessing frequency or duration of use. The measure includes the number of Facebook friends and the amount of time spent on Facebook on a typical day. It further contains a set of six attitudinal items designed to assess the degree to which the respondent felt emotionally connected to Facebook and the extent to which Facebook was integrated into daily activities. Using a 5-point Likert scale, participants rated the extent to which they agreed or disagreed with the following statements: Facebook is part of my everyday activity; I am proud to tell people I'm on Facebook; Facebook has become part of my daily routine; I feel out of touch when I haven't logged onto Facebook for a while; I feel

I am part of the Facebook community; I would be sorry if Facebook shut down. Because of the much greater ranges of the number of friends and minutes using Facebook, these items were transformed by taking the log of the original response. Responses to the entire set of eight items were then averaged to create a Facebook Intensity scale for each survey year of the panel (see Table 2). There was a significant increase in the intensity of Facebook use from 2006 to 2007 (see Table 2).

Psychological Well-being Measures

As reported in Ellison et al. (2007), self-esteem was measured using seven items from the Rosenberg Self-Esteem Scale (Rosenberg, 1989). Responses were reported on a 5-point Likert scale with a higher score indicating higher self-esteem. As shown in Table 3, the resulting scale was reliable across the two panel years and the mean was unchanged from 2006 to 2007.

Again following Ellison et al. (2007), an amended version of the Satisfaction with Life Scale (SWLS; Diener, Suh, & Oishi, 1997; Pavot & Diener, 1993) was used to measure global cognitive judgments of one's life. We adapted the scale slightly to locate it within the university context so that all respondents would have the same frame of reference. The answers to these questions were reported on a 5-point Likert scale with a higher score indicating greater satisfaction with life at the university. The resulting scale was reliable across the two panel years and the mean was unchanged from 2006 to 2007 (see lower portion of Table 3).

Bridging Social Capital

Our bridging social capital measure was constructed as described by Ellison et al. (2007). It contained five items adapted from Williams' (2006)

Table 2. Summary Statistics for Facebook Intensity in Panel Sample in 2006 and 2007

Individual Items and Scale	2006		2007	
	M	*(SD)*	*M*	*(SD)*
Facebook Intensity[a] (α_{2006}) = .84; α_{2007} = .88) 2007 vs. 2006 $t(87)$ = 4.99, $p < .0001$	2.81	(.72)	3.12	(.72)
Total Facebook friends[b]	223.09	(116.36)	339.26	(193.26)
Minutes per day on Facebook?[b]	32.56	(38.96)	53.76	(42.71)
Facebook is part of my everyday activity	3.29	(1.23)	3.72	(1.25)
I am proud to tell people I'm on Facebook	3.30	(.84)	3.23	(.90)
Facebook has become part of my daily routine	3.11	(1.30)	3.65	(1.25)
I feel out of touch when I haven't logged onto Facebook for a while	2.36	(1.22)	2.84	(1.23)
I feel I am part of the Facebook community	3.39	(1.02)	3.58	(.97)
I would be sorry if Facebook shut down	3.67	(1.07)	3.74	(1.07)

[a]Total friends and Facebook minutes per day were first transformed by taking the log before averaging across items to create the scale due to differing item scale ranges.

[b]For improved comparison, the new estimates of number of friends and time using Facebook were used in place of the ordinal scale values in 2006. See Table 1 for differences in measurement of Facebook friends and minutes per day on Facebook between 2006 and 2007. Other response categories ranged from 1 = strongly disagree to 5 = strongly agree.

Table 3. Summary Statistics for Self-Esteem and Satisfaction with University Life in 2006 and 2007

Individual Items and Scale[a]	2006		2007	
	M	(SD)	M	(SD)
Self-esteem Scale (α_{2006} = .89; α_{2007} = .88) 2007 vs. 2006 t(84) = − .10; ns	4.29	(.55)	4.29	(.52)
I feel that I'm a person of worth, at least on an equal plane with others	4.45	(.60)	4.45	(.59)
I feel that I have a number of good qualities	4.43	(.60)	4.52	(.57)
All in all, I am inclined to feel that I am a failure (reversed)	4.23	(.84)	4.24	(.81)
I am able to do things as well as most other people	4.33	(.56)	4.28	(.55)
I feel I do not have much to be proud of (reversed)	4.30	(.75)	4.30	(.77)
I take a positive attitude toward myself	4.23	(.66)	4.18	(.75)
On the whole, I am satisfied with myself	4.08	(.86)	4.09	(.72)
Satisfaction with university Life Scale				
(α_{2006} = .84; α_{2007} = .89) 2007 vs. 2006 t(84) = .87; ns	3.67	(.67)	3.59	(.75)
In most ways my life at MSU is close to my ideal	3.55	(.93)	3.45	(.93)
The conditions of my life at MSU are excellent	3.68	(.86)	3.61	(.88)
I am satisfied with my life at MSU	3.98	(.71)	3.89	(.84)
So far I have gotten the important things I want at MSU	3.80	(.72)	3.88	(.73)
If I could live my time at MSU over, I would change almost nothing	3.33	(.93)	3.14	(1.04)

[a]Individual items ranged from 1 = strongly disagree to 5 = strongly agree, scales constructed by taking mean of items.

Bridging Social Capital subscale as well as three additional items intended to place outcomes of bridging social capital in the specific university context in order to reduce variance in respondents' answers and to tie it more directly to a salient context. The items used a 5-point Likert scale, with higher scores indicating greater bridging social capital. The scale was reliable across the two panel years and there was no difference across panel years in the scale mean (see Table 4).

RESULTS

The panel design served two broad purposes. First, it helps reveal any changes in Facebook use that might have occurred over the year between data collections. Second, it provides some opportunity to test the direction of causality between our primary independent variable (Facebook Intensity) and dependent variable (Bridging Social Capital).

As shown in Figure 1, participants reported spending significantly more time per day actively using the Internet in 2007 than in 2006, increasing by over an hour per day, t(91) = 2.25, p < .05. Facebook use nearly doubled, increasing by roughly 21 min per day on average, t(84) = 4.30, p < .0001. As one might expect, the number of total friends participants reported having on Facebook also increased, growing by 50% from 223 to 339, t(83) = 9.40, p < .0001. Clearly, in the year that passed Facebook has become an increasingly important part of students' lives by all measures.

Table 4. Summary Statistics for Bridging Social Capital Items Reported in 2006 and in 2007

Individual Items and Scale[a]	2006		2007	
	M	(SD)	M	(SD)
Bridging Social Capital Scale (α_{2006} = .86; α_{2007} = .84) 2007 vs. 2006 t(84) = .14; ns	3.87	(.47)	3.87	(.55)
I feel I am part of the MSU community	3.81	(.74)	3.79	(.91)
I am interested in what goes on at MSU	4.02	(.53)	4.01	(.69)
MSU is a good place to be	4.34	(.75)	4.26	(.79)
I would be willing to contribute money to MSU after graduation	3.38	(.90)	3.40	(1.02)
Interacting with people at MSU makes me want to try new things	3.86	(.62)	3.82	(.75)
Interacting with people at MSU makes me feel like a part of a larger community	3.86	(.67)	3.91	(.77)
I am willing to spend time to support general MSU activities	3.71	(.75)	3.73	(.75)
At MSU, I come into contact with new people all the time	4.13	(.62)	4.09	(.70)
Interacting with people at MSU reminds me that everyone in the world is connected	3.68	(.74)	3.78	(.85)

[a]Source: Ellison et al. (2007). Individual items ranged from 1 = strongly disagree to 5 = strongly agree, scales constructed by taking mean of items.

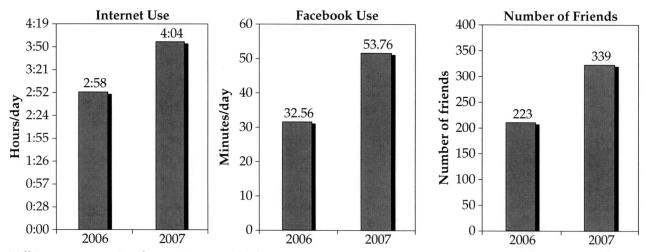

[a]All increases are significant using matched pair *t*-tests: Internet use, $t(91) = 2.25$, $p<.05$; Facebook use, $t(84) = 4.30$, $p<.0001$; number of friends, $t(83) = 9.40$, $p<.0001$.

Figure 1. Growth in Internet use, Facebook use, and the number of friends on Facebook in the panel of Facebook users[a].

In Ellison et al. (2007), a strong association was found between the intensity of Facebook use and a participant's perceived bridging social capital. They theorized that Facebook use helped students turn latent contacts into real connections, often by reducing the barriers that would otherwise prevent such connections from happening. However, as noted above, an equally plausible argument could be made that those with large networks of contacts would have more reason to use Facebook, reversing the causal direction. To address this question, we completed a cross-lagged correlation analysis on our panel. Figure 2 shows the cross-lagged correlations that resulted. Facebook use in time 1 is more strongly associated with bridging social capital in time 2 than the alternative lagged correlation between bridging social capital in time 1 and Facebook use in time 2.

Following Kenny (1979) and Raghunathan, Rosenthal, and Rubin (1996), a modified Pearson-Filon z index (known as the ZPF index) was computed to test the significance of the difference in the lagged correlations. According to these researchers, such a test is appropriate when two variables are measured at two points in time without violating assumptions of synchronicity (i.e., at both time points, the variables are measured at the same time) and stationarity (i.e., that the strength of the relationship between the two variables did not change appreciably across time). The ZPF test is further appropriate for analyzing the difference in non-overlapping (i.e., one variable is not being correlated with two other variables) and non-independent (i.e., the variation across time is within subjects) variables. A significant difference was found ($z = 3.52$, $p < .001$), which lends support to the

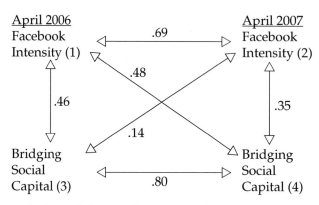

[a]Cross-lagged correlations, difference between r_{14} (.48) and r_{23} (.14) using ZPF analysis (*z* transformed Pearson-Filon statistic), significant ($z = 3.52$, $N = 85$, $p<.001$).

Figure 2. Cross-lagged correlation analysis showing Facebook intensity and bridging social capital relationships across time period 2006-2007[a].

original Ellison et al. (2007) thesis that greater Facebook use leads to increases in bridging social capital.

In order to test the hypothesis that the influence of Facebook use on bridging social capital is moderated by self-esteem, we performed a median split on self-esteem and conducted a cross-lagged correlation analysis on the upper and lower self-esteem sub-samples. The median score for self-esteem was fairly high ($Mdn = 4.29$ on a 5 point scale) and as a result, the difference was not as great as we would have preferred (M for the low self-esteem group = 3.81; M for high self-esteem = 4.70). Nonetheless, the results reveal that the relationship between the lagged intensity of Facebook use and bridging social capital is higher for the lower self-esteem group ($r = .57$) than the high self-esteem group ($r = .43$) (see Fig. 3a and b). This suggests that the interaction effect first reported by Ellison et al. (2007), in which the social capital gains from Facebook use were greater for low self-esteem students than high self-esteem students, remains evident when examining social capital accumulation a year later. Both cross-lagged correlation analyses resulted in significant ZPF scores, strengthening the case that the use of social network sites *precedes* gains in bridging social capital, particularly for lower self-esteem students.

A final set of analyses looked at the extent to which the prior year's use of Facebook predicted participants' estimates of bridging social capital in year 2 after controlling for general Internet use and the measures of psychological well-being. A lagged regression analysis was used to test the predictive power of the lagged version of Facebook Intensity on bridging social capital.

The results confirm the hypothesis that Facebook use leads to greater bridging social capital after controlling for general Internet use and measures of

Table 5. Summary of Regression Analysis Predicting the Amount of Bridging Social Capital in 2007 from Lagged (2006) Independent Variables ($N = 85$)

Independent Variables	Scaled Beta[a]
Intercept	3.86****
Hours of Internet use a day	0.06
Self-esteem	0.24*
Satisfaction with university life	0.44**
Facebook (FB) intensity	0.42****
Self-esteem by FB intensity[b]	−0.46*
	Before interaction term: $F = 10.71$, $p < .0001$, Adj. $R^2 = 32$
	After interaction term: $F = 9.76$, $p < .0001$, Adj. $R^2 = .34$

*$p < .05$. **$p < .01$ ***$p < .001$. ****$p < .0001$.
[a]A scaled beta is similar to a standardized beta in that coefficients are scaled to have a mean of 0 and a range of 2.
[b]The satisfaction with life by Facebook Intensity interaction was not significant, so it is not reported for brevity of presentation.

psychological well-being. As shown in Table 5, general Internet use in 2006 did not exhibit any relationship to bridging social capital in 2007 (scaled beta = .06, *ns*). However, those with higher self-esteem (scaled beta = .24, $p < .05$) and greater satisfaction with life (scaled beta = .44, $p < .01$) at the university in year 1 reported higher bridging social capital in year 2, as expected. Even with these psychological measures in the equation, however, Facebook Intensity in year 1 was a highly significant predictor of bridging social capital in year 2 (scaled beta = .42, $p < .0001$). Moreover, as one would anticipate from the cross-lagged correlation

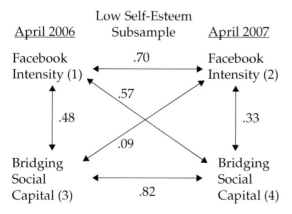

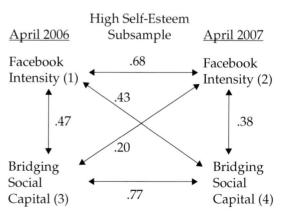

[a]For the low self-esteem sample, difference between r_{14} (.57) and r_{23} (.09) results in $z = 3.53$, $N = 39$, $p<.001$.
[b]For the high self-esteem sample, difference between r_{14} (.43) and r_{23} (.20) results in $z = 1.65$, $N = 46$, $p<.05$.

Figure 3.   Cross-lagged correlation analysis showing Facebook intensity and bridging social capital relationships for both low[a] and high self-esteem[b] sub-samples across time periods 2006–2007.

analysis depicted in Figure 3a and b, there was a significant interaction between Facebook use and self-esteem. The interaction term — the product of Facebook Intensity and self-esteem — was a significant predictor of bridging social capital (scaled beta = – .46, $p < .05$). Figure 4 reveals the nature of this interaction, contrasting the slope of the coefficient for Facebook Intensity as a predictor of bridging social capital for higher self-esteem vs. lower self-esteem students. The graph illustrates the stronger association between Facebook use and social capital for the lower self-esteem students compared to the higher self-esteem students.

Our interviews with Facebook users complement our survey data and help us to make sense of the pattern of findings reported here. These qualitative data support the notion that "Friending" in Facebook served an instrumental purpose, allowing individuals to keep in touch with a wide network of individuals who might be called upon to provide "favors" in the future. For instance, one participant explained,

"I think [Facebook] is very good for networking. . . . it's very good. My high school is very into networking. . . . I guarantee every single person in the high school will make an effort to maintain those Facebook friendships and so that when we're all in our forties, go back to our reunion, and we'll still be able to get in touch with each person we know. You know, 'so and so is a doctor.' And, we wouldn't hesitate to call on them for a favor, just because we went to the same high school. . . ."

Additionally, Facebook provides the technical support needed for social interaction to occur. In addition to the bevy of within-system messaging opportunities ("wall" postings, "pokes," and direct messages between users), the system facilitates face-to-face

communication and communication through other media through the contact information that is often included in users' profiles. In this way, Facebook serves as a ready-made address book, enabling communication outside the system, as expressed by this participant:

"Honestly, I can't remember what I did before Facebook. It sounds really pathetic, but it's just so easy to access information about people. It's not bad information, it's just instead of, 'do you have this person's phone number?' or, 'oh God, where do they live, they live in this dorm but I need the room number,' it's just so easy to just go on there and find it. And if it's not on there at least you could message them, like, 'I need to drop something off at your room, where do you live?' or 'we're in the same class, can we get together and study?'. . . It's just so much easier."

A final quote illustrates the way in which Facebook use interacts with users' self-esteem by helping these lower self-esteem users initiate communication with others while avoiding what might be an awkward phone call or receiving information (about a social event, perhaps) from an acquaintance who would not otherwise contact them:

"Well, the only thing that is really nice about it is, I am in a sorority, and it is very convenient . . . there are so many people in your house, that I don't think you would call all of them. There are people that you are friends with because you see them weekly . . . and you have a common interest, but I probably wouldn't call all of them. So, it is nice to be [on Facebook], and plus it is really easy to figure out what things you have going on, or what you are supposed to be doing . . . . People can send a really quick little message. So, it's convenient. It also breaks the ice for certain people, to talk to them, people that you don't necessarily know really, really well, and you might not want to call them up because a phone call could be awkward, but it's really easy to send them a two sentence message."

DISCUSSION

Previous work on the role that personal relationships play in the self-esteem of young adults has focused on the role of close, intimate relationships (Bishop & Inderbitzen, 1995; Keefe & Berndt, 1996). Even studies of how the Internet is used to maintain relationships have largely focused on these close connections. However, bridging social capital is related to one's ability to develop and maintain weak ties rather than close connections. We find in this study that not only does bridging social capital have a relationship with self-esteem, but that use of an online social network service — Facebook — interacts with self-esteem to influence bridging social capital.

Our results demonstrate that social network sites can help to address the relationship development and

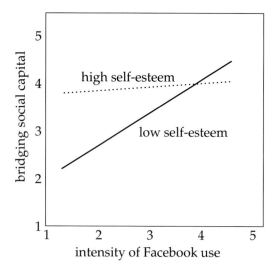

Figure 4. The interaction between self-esteem and Facebook use in predicting bridging social capital using 2006 self-esteem and Facebook use and 2007 bridging social capital.

maintenance needs of young adults at a point in their lives where they are moving away from home and into the university. They face challenges in maintaining former connections while being open to potential friendships with a new set of peers encountered through classes, new living arrangements, and other college activities. Facebook, along with other online social network services, plays a role by facilitating the maintenance of close friendships and the distant relationships that help create bridging social capital. The ability to articulate friends from offline social networks allows a Facebook user to maintain lightweight contact with a broad set of acquaintances (see also Subrahmanyam, Reich, Waechter, & Espinoza, 2008-this issue). Features within the site make it easier for users both to broadcast information about their own activities and to engage in a form of social surveillance wherein they can track the activities of a wide set of Facebook "Friends." More importantly, the site provides both the technical and the social infrastructure for social interaction. For example, the tool provides direct technical support for communication through within-application communication (through wall posts, pokes, messages, etc.) and the inclusion of users' contact information. Additionally, by browsing profiles within the site, users can access identity information about others that might spur face-to-face communication (by serving as a resource for information about others' preferences, personal characteristics, etc.). Learning information about one's "latent ties" (Haythornthwaite, 2005) might lower the barriers to initiating communication, both because potential commonalities are revealed and because crucial information about others, such as relationship status, are provided — thus mitigating fears of rejection.

The way in which Facebook might facilitate communication, especially in initial social interactions, and perhaps mitigate fears of rejection may further explain why lower self-esteem students appear to gain more from their use of Facebook than higher self-esteem students. Lower self-esteem students might face more difficulties than high self-esteem individuals in approaching people in their classes or their dormitories, and hence might not form the casual relationships so essential to bridging social capital. A social network site that makes it easier for lower self-esteem students to engage with others outside of their close personal networks can therefore be expected to have a larger effect for them than for higher self-esteem students.

Our findings regarding bridging social capital also provide a new perspective on Facebook "Friends." Although at first glance, the high number of Facebook friends (mean of 223 in 2006 and 339 in 2007) might suggest a collection of superficial, shallow relationships, the characteristics of this network are precisely what we would expect to see in a network built to support bridging social capital. Facebook networks

appear to be large and thus heterogeneous — a collection of "weak ties" (Granovetter, 1973) well-suited to providing new information. Donath and boyd (2004) suggest that social network sites may better support a large, heterogeneous network, an observation which is supported by data reported here as well as network-level data (Lampe et al., 2007).

Another interesting finding in this work is the increase in the Facebook Intensity (FBI) measure between 2006 and 2007 (Ms = 2.81 and 3.12, respectively). While the mean number of friends reported could be a sign of longevity of participation on the site, the increase in the FBI measure is a more robust indicator of its growing importance to the respondents. We interpret the increase to mean that Facebook has occupied a more central role in supporting the maintenance of social relationships among the undergraduates we studied. While other explanations are possible, we feel that this explanation matches the data presented here.

Returning to the issue of causality, these findings do suggest that Facebook use is related to the generation of bridging social capital in a meaningful way. Particularly, the cross-lagged correlation analysis findings depicted in Figs. 2 and 3 are more consistent with the notion that Facebook leads to gains in bridging social capital than it is with the notion that preexisting social capital levels drive Facebook use. Additionally, the regression analysis (Table 5) demonstrates that even when accounting for other factors, lagged Facebook use relates to increases in bridging social capital. However, since there was no random assignment or experimental control of variables in this study, we recognize that we cannot claim true causality with these results. However, it should be noted that social capital and how it is generated is a notoriously difficult research area to address, and it is unlikely that experimental studies can capture social capital meaningfully outside of game theoretic simulations. Studies like the present one, in which use in-context is studied over time, are an important and appropriate way to address questions of social capital generation and maintenance.

These findings can be summarized in terms of the hypotheses that were proposed. The hypothesis that greater Facebook use would result in greater bridging social capital (H1) was supported. The fact that Facebook use significantly predicted bridging social capital even after controlling for general Internet use supports the notion that there are unique affordances of online social network services, and the relationship to social capital is not an artifact of general Internet activity. Tools like friend lists, wall posting, messaging, and tagging help social network site users maintain distant relationships and weak ties. Moreover, this relationship holds after accounting for the effects of self-esteem and satisfaction with life on bridging social capital. The hypothesis (H2) that the direction of the effect is from Facebook use to bridging social capital and the results of the cross-lagged correlation analysis and lagged regression also support this view. We previously articulated the reasons why this may be true, given the role online social network services like Facebook can play in facilitating lightweight contact with weak ties, social surveillance, and through providing social and technical support for social interaction. The proposal that self-esteem and satisfaction with life would relate to bridging social capital (H3) was indeed supported. However, we were more interested in seeing whether Facebook use accounted for variation in bridging social capital over and above the effects of these psychological variables, and it did. Finally, H4 proposed that self-esteem and satisfaction with life would shape the way that Facebook use affected bridging social capital. This moderating effect holds for self-esteem, but was not supported for satisfaction with life. The interaction effect between self-esteem and Facebook use in predicting bridging social capital as depicted in Fig. 4 is consistent with the interpretation that Facebook use serves to reduce the barriers to interacting with weak ties for those with lower self-esteem. The fact that this held up with a yearlong lag between the independent and dependent measures is noteworthy, and supports the kind of causal interpretation offered.

The study does have important limitations. Only one social network site — Facebook — was examined, limiting generalization of the findings to all such services. This limitation is mitigated by the overwhelming popularity and pervasive use of Facebook on university campuses. Among this population, this is the primary social network site in use. We also only examined users at one university, and there may be differences across institutional settings that we are not able to capture.

CONCLUSION

There are several opportunities for future work in this area. First, the panel of Facebook users should be continued over time, to further explore the relationship between Facebook use and social capital. Additionally, the ability to create applications within Facebook using their open application programming interface (API) offers opportunities for more experimental work related to the generation of social capital. More research should also be done to see if groups other than young adults are receiving the same social capital benefits that we see here.

Emerging adults are using Facebook to maintain large, diffuse networks of friends, with a positive impact on their accumulation of bridging social capital. Although it is tempting to consider these large

networks of acquaintances as shallow, in reality these connections have true potential for generating benefits for Facebook users. Moreover, online social network services appear to offer important affordances, especially for those who otherwise face difficulties in forming and maintaining the large and heterogeneous networks of contacts that are sources of social capital.

REFERENCES

Adler, P., & Kwon, S. (2002). Social capital: Prospects for a new concept. *Academy of Management Review, 27*, 17–40.

Arnett, J. J. (2000). Emerging adulthood: A theory of development from the late teens through the twenties. *American Psychologist, 55*, 469–480.

Bargh, J. A., & McKenna, K. Y. (2004). The Internet and social life. *Annual Review of Psychology, 55*, 573–590.

Bargh, J. A., McKenna, K. Y., & Fitzsimons, G. M. (2002). Can you see the real me? Activation and expression of the "true self" on the Internet. *Journal of Social Issues, 58*, 33–48.

Bishop, J., & Inderbitzen, H. (1995). Peer acceptance and friendship: An investigation of their relation to self-esteem. *The Journal of Early Adolescence, 15*, 476–489.

Bourdieu, P., & Wacquant, L. (1992). *An invitation to reflexive sociology.* Chicago, IL: University of Chicago Press.

boyd, d. m., & Ellison, N. (2007). Social network sites: Definition, history, and scholarship. *Journal of Computer-Mediated Communication, 13*, 210–230.

Brown, J. (2006). Emerging adults in a media-saturated world. In J. Arnett, & J. Tanner (Eds.), *Emerging adults in America: Coming of age in the 21st century* (pp. 279–299). NY: American Psychological Association.

Burt, R. (1997). The contingent value of social capital. *Administrative Science Quarterly, 42*, 339–365.

Coleman, J. S. (1988). Social capital in the creation of human capital. *The American Journal of Sociology, 94*, S95–S120 (Supplement).

Connolly, J., Furman, W., & Konarksi, R. (2000). The roles of peers in the emergence of heterosexual romantic relationships in adolescence. *Child Development, 17*, 1395–1408.

Constant, D., Sproull, L., & Kiesler, S. (1996). The kindness of strangers: The usefulness of electronic weak ties for technical advice. *Organization Science, 7*, 119–135.

Cummings, J., Lee, J., & Kraut, R. (2006). Communication technology and friendship during the transition from high school to college. In R. E. Kraut, M. Brynin, & S. Kiesler (Eds.), *Computers, phones, and the Internet: Domesticating information technology* (pp. 265–278). New York: Oxford University Press.

Diener, E., Suh, E., & Oishi, S. (1997). Recent findings on subjective well-being. *Indian Journal of Clinical Psychology, 24*, 25–41.

Donath, J. (2007). Signals in social supernets. *Journal of Computer-Mediated Communication, 13*, 231–251.

Donath, J. S., & boyd, d. (2004). Public displays of connection. *BT Technology Journal, 22*, 71.

Ellison, N., Steinfield, C., & Lampe, C. (2007). The benefits of Facebook "friends:" Social capital and college students' use of online social network sites. *Journal of Computer-Mediated Communication, 12*, 1143–1168.

Golder, S., Wilkinson, D., & Huberman, B. A. (2007). Rhythms of social interaction: Messaging within a massive online network. In C. Steinfield, B. Pentland, M. Ackerman, & N. Contractor (Eds.), *Proceedings of the third international conference on communities and technologies, Michigan State University* (pp. 41–66). London: Springer.

Granovetter, M. S. (1973). The strength of weak ties. *Amerian Economic Review, 78*, 1360–1480.

Granovetter, M. S. (1983). The strength of weak ties: A network theory revisited. *Sociological Theory, 1*, 201–233.

Hargittai, E. (2007). Whose space? Differences among users and non-users of social network sites. *Journal of Computer-Mediated Communication, 13*, 276–297.

Haythornthwaite, C. (2005). Social networks and Internet connectivity effects. *Information, Communication & Society, 8*, 125–147.

Helliwell, J. F. K., & Putnam, R. D. K. (2004). The social context of well-being. *Philosophical Transactions of the Royal Society B: Biological Sciences, 359*, 1435–1446.

Hewitt, A., & Forte, A. (2006, November). Crossing boundaries: Identity management and student/faculty relationships on the Facebook. Poster presented at the ACM Special Interest Group on Computer-Supported Cooperative Work, Banff, Canada.

Keefe, K., & Berndt, T. (1996). Relations of friendship quality to self-esteem in early adolescence. *The Journal of Early Adolescence, 16*, 110–129.

Kenny, D. A. (1979). *Correlation and causality.* New York: Wiley-Interscience.,

Kraut, R., Kiesler, S., Boneva, B., Cummings, J., Helgeson, V., & Crawford, A. (2002). Internet paradox revisited. *Journal of Social Issues, 58*, 49–74.

Kraut, R., Patterson, M., Lundmark, V., Kiesler, S., Mukhopadhyay, T., & Scherlis. W. (1998). The Internet paradox: A social technology that reduces social involvement and psychological well-being. *American Psychologist, 53*, 1017–1032.

Lampe, C., Ellison, N., & Steinfield, C. (2006, Nov.). A face(book) in the crowd: Social searching vs. social browsing. Paper presented at the ACM Special Interest Group on Computer-Supported Cooperative Work, Banff, Canada.

Lampe, C., Ellison, N., & Steinfield, C. (2007, April). A familiar face(book): Profile elements as signals in an online social network. *Proceedings of the SIGCHI conference on human factors in computing systems. San Jose, CA* (pp. 435–444). New York: ACM.

LaRose, R., Lai, Y. J., Lange, R., Love, B., & Wu, Y. (2005). Sharing or piracy? An exploration of downloading behavior. *Journal of Computer-Mediated Communication, 11*, 1–21.

Lin, N. (1999). Building a network theory of social capital. *Connections, 22*, 28–51.

McKenna, K., & Bargh, J. (2000). Plan 9 from cyberspace: The implications of the Internet for personality and social psychology. *Personality and Social Psychology Review, 4*, 57–75.

Montgomery, M. J. (2005). Psychosocial intimacy and identity: From early adolescence to emerging adulthood. *Journal of Adolescent Research, 20*, 346–374.

Morrow, V. (1999). Conceptualizing social capital in relation to the well-being of children and young people: A critical review. *Sociological Review, 47*, 744–765.

Moyle, K. (2004, Dec. 7). *Internet helps people connect with past friends. University Wire.* Retrieved July 8, 2008, from http://www.dailyevergreen.com/story/10828

Nahapiet, J., & Ghoshal, S. (1998). Social capital, intellectual capital, and the organizational advantage. *The Academy of Management Review, 23*, 242–266.

Nie, N. (2001). Sociability, interpersonal relations, and the Internet: Reconciling conflicting findings. *American Behavioral Scientist, 45*, 420–435.

Pavot, W., & Diener, E. (1993). Review of the Satisfaction with Life Scale. *Psychological Assessment, 5*, 164–172.

Putnam, R. D. (2000). *Bowling alone: The collapse and revival of American community.* New York: Simon & Schuster.

Raghunathan, T. E., Rosenthal, R., & Rubin, D. B. (1996). Comparing correlated but nonoverlapping correlations. *Psychological Methods, 1*, 178–183.

Resnick, P. (2001). Beyond bowling together: Sociotechnical capital. In J. Carroll (Ed.), *HCI in the new millennium* (pp. 647–672). New York: Addison-Wesley.

Rosenberg, M. (1989). *Society and the adolescent self-image (revised ed.).* Middletown, CT:: Wesleyan University Press.

Shaw, B., & Gant, L. (2002). In defense of the Internet: The relationship between Internet communication and depression, loneliness, self-esteem, and perceived social support. *CyberPsychology & Behavior, 5*, 157–171.

Stutzman, F. (2006, Oct.). An evaluation of identity-sharing behavior in social network communities. Paper presented at the International Digital Media Arts Association and the Miami University Center for Interactive Media Studies CODE Conference, Oxford, OH.

Subrahmanyam, K., Reich, S., Waechter, N., & Espinoza, G. (2008). Online and offline social networks: Use of social networking sites by emerging adults. *Journal of Applied Developmental Psychology, 29*, 420–433 (this issue).

Sullivan, H. (1953). *The interpersonal theory of psychiatry*. New York: Norton.

Valkenburg, P. M., & Peter, J. (2007). Preadolescents' and adolescents' online communication and their closeness to friends. *Developmental Psychology, 43*, 267–277.

Valkenburg, P. M., Peter, J., & Schouten, A. P. (2006). Friend networking sites and their relationship to adolescents' well being and social self-esteem. *CyberPsychology and Behavior, 9*, 584–590.

Wellman, B., Haase, A. Q., Witte, J., & Hampton, K. (2001). Does the Internet increase, decrease, or supplement social capital? Social networks, participation and community commitment. *American Behavioral Scientist, 45*, 436–455.

Williams, D. (2006). On and off the 'net': Scales for social capital in an online era. *Journal of Computer-Mediated Communication, 11*, 593–628.

PART III

Qualitative Methods

3.01

SYSTEMATIC DESIGN

Ethnicity, Health and Medical Care: Towards a Critical Realist Analysis of General Practice in the Korean Community in Sydney

Gil-Soo Han and Carmel Davies

ABSTRACT: This paper investigates the use and provision of biomedicine among Korean-Australian men on the basis of interview data from all of the eight Korean-speaking doctors practising in the Korean community in Sydney in 1995. From the viewpoint of these general practitioners, an analysis is made of the processes Korean men go through in adjusting to a new country, being involved in constant hard manual work and long working hours, and explores how they make use of all available resources to stay healthy. The Korean men have fully utilized the 'freely' available medical services under government-subsidized Medicare, bearing in mind that health is a capacity to work under the current environment, although illegal migrants restrained themselves from using it until they obtained legal status. Korean-speaking medical practitioners have been able to provide their fellow Koreans with 'culturally appropriate' health care, with the key factor being the absence of a language barrier. The level of patient satisfaction is high, possibly due to the excellent understanding the doctors have of the social aspects of illnesses, although the doctors do not go beyond curative medicine in their practice. However, the increasing number of Korean-speaking doctors in the small Korean community means that there is competition for patients. Consequently, the medical care is highly entrepreneurial. Referral by Korean doctors to practitioners of Korean herbal medicine is also a notable feature of the health care sector of the Korean community, especially as this offers Korean patients 'satisfactory' health relief for problems that are not easily relieved by doctors in the biomedical system.

KEYWORDS: Medical care; health care utilization; migrant health; general practitioners; critical realism; The Korean community in australia.

INTRODUCTION

Since the 1970s, there has been a large influx of Asian migrants to Australia. These migrants have diverse experiences of urbanization, education and socioeconomic status (Manderson & Mathews 1985, p. 252). However, there is relatively little research available about the use of health care among Asian immigrants in Australia (Savage 1991; Grichting 1994; Chan & Quine 1997; Rice 1999; Hsu-Hage *et al.* 2001). This paper sets out to advance our understanding of medical care among ethnic minority groups, within the context of the political economy of labour and cultural practices, and focuses on the delivery of health care to male Korean migrants in Sydney, from the viewpoint of Korean general practitioners (GPs).

A major shortcoming of most research on the use of health services among immigrants in general is that the use of such services is mainly linked to what is thought of as culturally appropriate health care, on the basis of what may be immediately observable, thus largely neglecting relevant political economic contexts (Heggenhougen 1979; Mathews 1979; Bhopal 1986; Brainard & Zaharlick 1989). This by no means downplays the need for the provision of culturally appropriate health care for a migrant population (Reid *et al.* 2001; Irvine *et al.* 2002). Rather, it is not possible to understand health care without considering its given context and this is a general problem of most research on ethnomedicine (Nichter 1991). Korean men from a non-English-speaking background (NESB) have often experienced underemployment (Han 1999) and this has had a consequent effect on their health (Han & Chesters 2001a, b). When they seek care in a place controlled by the Euro-Australian-dominant market economy, their experiences are distinct from the health care seeking experiences of Euro-Australians. The findings from this unique Korean experience are likely to shed light on how the health care needs of other ethnic minorities could be better addressed.

A critical realist perspective puts health and medicine in a more theoretically fruitful context (Collier 1994; Danermark *et al.* 2002; Han 2002). A basic proposition of critical realism is that an individual agent's behaviour is enabled and constrained by social structure in a particular historical juncture, but the action, in turn, reproduces or transforms the structure (Bhaskar 1989b; Sayer 2000). We argue that a critical realist view considers not only individuals' lived experiences, but also essentially examines the social origins of illness and the allocation of health resources in the context of unhealthy working conditions, the market economy, social relations and social reality (Engels 1968; Doyal 1979; Frankenberg 1980; Waitzkin 1981; Chavez 1986; Scambler 2001).

Following a critical realist view, we intend to investigate GPs' understanding of the common use and provision of biomedical care and its relationship to the practice of medicine as a profession in a disadvantaged immigrant community (Han 1999). To put it differently, this paper aims to show how complex it is for patients to seek, and doctors to provide, economical, effective and professionally rewarding medical care in the context of a NESB migrant community in a European-dominant country with a free market economy.

Under the free market economy, health is referred to as a capacity to work (Han 2000). When a person falls sick, a significant matter which concerns the person is whether s/he can go to work. Work-related stress appears to be the primary cause of some diseases (such as heart disease and cancer), and this often results in high levels of mortality (Goldman *et al.* 2003). People who are supposed to be responsible for their own health have no option but to try all of the available health services. This is not a process of the individual taking an active part in sustaining his/her own health; rather, it is a process of the individual maintaining his/her own health at an optimal level to enable the selling of labour power, which provides the primary source of living (Stellman 1973; Waitzkin 1998).

Korean immigrants make up one of the most recent ethnic groups in Australia and the Australian Bureau of Statistics (ABS) census figures show that, in 2001, there were 38,892 Koreans in Australia (ABS 2002). About 70% reside in the Sydney metropolitan area, while others settled in Melbourne, Brisbane and Perth. The major Korean migration to Australia started in the early 1970s, with the arrival of about 500 Koreans, who had previously fought or worked in the battlefields of the Vietnam War (Han 1994). Most were drawn from low socioeconomic backgrounds in Korea and settled in Australia as over-stayers of their visas until they were approved for permanent resident status through amnesties. They were known as *amnesty migrants*. The majority of Korean immigrants who arrived in Australia in the 1980s were from middle-class backgrounds and they settled as *skilled migrants*; and those who arrived in the 1990s were from the small entrepreneurial class who settled as *business migrants* (Coughlan 1995; Han 1996).

Prior to their arrival in Australia, Korean migrants were well exposed to biomedical/medical care. Nevertheless, they would experience differences between the health services of more than a couple of decades ago in Korea and the health services available in contemporary Australia. For example, Korean health beliefs in the context of Western culture and migrants' health needs, in relation to participation in the labour force, have serious implications for their health care seeking behaviour (Han 1997, 1999, 2001). This paper analyses GPs' views on the health of Koreans and the complex process of providing and seeking effective and satisfactory medical care. This requires consideration of the nature of the interaction between health care providers and consumers who are culturally, linguistically and geographically situated Koreans with diverse socioeconomic backgrounds, in the context of an immigrant community.

METHOD

Study Participants

Data for this paper are largely drawn from eight Korean GPs, and partially from other informants, in the Korean community in Sydney. The paper derives from the first author's (Han) broader project, which involved interviewing 120 Korean men from diverse socioeconomic backgrounds in 1995, and various health practitioners in Sydney. Other aspects of the broader project have been published elsewhere (Han 1999, 2000, 2001; Han & Chesters 2001a, b).

Of all the providers of health care in the Korean community, biomedical doctors were the most reluctant to participate in the broader study, due to situational constraints. The interviewer was, however, able to spend 45 minutes to one hour with each of them without monetary compensation for their time. It was deemed not possible to ask for any more of their time, largely because they were too busy or because patients were waiting in the reception room. On one occasion, a receptionist asked for a 'special' appointment to be made with the doctor. However, the interviewer did not feel comfortable with this idea as the time taken would not be profitable for the doctor.

Data Collection

The first author (Han) had already done some empirical work on a related project in the Sydney Korean community (Han 1994) and had acquired considerable background knowledge related to this study's aims and appropriate research methods. The first author, who did not live in the Sydney area, aimed throughout the study to take a 'native-as-stranger' approach (Minichiello et al. 1990). Informal interviews were often useful as frequently an invitation was given to stay on after the formal interview, to take refreshments with the interviewees.

Ethics approval for research with human subjects was obtained from a university ethics committee. A consent form, either in English or in Korean, was given and the interviewee was asked to sign it. Interviews occurred in a place chosen by the respondents, and this was usually the doctors' consulting rooms. Semi-structured interview schedules were prepared around the health practitioners' views of: (i) health, immigrant life and health care use among Koreans from different socioeconomic backgrounds; (ii) common ailments; (iii) particular difficulties servicing fellow Koreans; (iv) GP referrals to specialists; and (v) the competing nature of doctoring. The interviews with the eight doctors were tape-recorded and then transcribed into a full text report for analysis.

Validation of Data

A previous study of the Korean community (Han 1994) informed many aspects of this study. The comparison of the perspectives provided by the users and providers of health care (Han 1999, 2000, 2001; Han & Chesters 2001a, b) has been an important basis for cross-checking the data so that the validity has been increased (Minichiello et al. 1990). The cross-checking has also served as a stimulus for comparing and contrasting. For example, discrepancies between the views from the users and providers are observed rather than merely being regarded as 'distorted' or inaccurate (Silverman 1985). The findings from the doctors' interviews presented in this paper are remarkably in common with those of the users, despite the fact that the literature suggests there is a risk in relying on the memory and perspective of privileged medical practitioners (McKeown 1979). Nonetheless, the doctors' views will be critically analysed according to the critical realist perspective, in an attempt to understand their actions, within the constraints of a given social structure.

Grounded Theory and Data Analysis

A constant use of *inductive* and *deductive* thinking and *verification* has been a major principle in the process of analysing (coding) data from informants and respondents, which makes theory *grounded in data* (Strauss & Corbin 1998). The three specific steps used to analyse the data are as follows. Firstly, open coding was used. This involved breaking down and analysing words, phrases, sentences and paragraphs and developing their properties and dimensions. The purpose was to identify concepts, events and incidents. They were grouped to form a category(ies), which is a classification of concepts. Secondly, axial coding was used which involved making connections between major categories or between a category and its sub-categories by examining under what conditions and context an event occurred and by examining the consequences of any action/interaction that was taken. The final stage of coding was selective coding. This was the process of selecting the core category (i.e. the central phenomenon under investigation: health care use and provision) and systematically relating (or integrating) it to other categories (Strauss & Corbin 1990, p. 111).

The following methodological issues have been considered in preparing interview schedules: (i) what fundamentally consists of the characteristics of the relations between Korean immigrants' involvement in 'migrant work', illness and the provision of medical care?; and (ii) what properties must exist for health professionals to demonstrate a high degree of medical entrepreneurship, both at the level of health professionals and in the context of the Korean ethnic community? This is a specifically critical realist inquiry to seek influential or relevant qualities beyond what is immediately given or observable (Sayer 1992; Danermark *et al.* 2002). From a critical realist perspective, social reality has ontological depth and consists of domains of actual, empirical and real—that is, *actual* phenomena of the use and provision of medicine in the Korean community may have produced perceived (*empirical*) views which can be further explained by relevant structural or *real* underpinning factors.

Since critical realism has guided the analysis of the findings, we have endeavoured to establish the links between what individual agents had to say and how their views could be best put in the given context of social structure. A realistic picture of agents' health seeking behaviour would not be merely based upon their experiences, but upon critical analysis of the experiences in the pre-existing given context which enables and restrains the experiences. This is indeed a way to overcome methodological individualism (Bhaskar 1989a). The names used in this paper are fictitious.

FINDINGS AND DISCUSSION

When Koreans fall sick or are unable to work due to health reasons, the first institutional help they look for is from medical doctors (GPs) in the Korean community. All the doctors in the community charge fees to the government by bulkbilling.[1] Coming from a developing country where medical services are not as easily accessible as in Australia, the Korean attitude towards visiting medical doctors in the first instance is: 'The service is free so there is nothing to lose.'

By 1995, there were eight Korean-speaking biomedical doctors practising in the Korean community (*Sydney Korean Telephone Directory* 1989–1994; *Chugan Saenghwal Chôngbo* 1995, 14 July). Six were trained in Australia, and two were trained in Korea and registered in Australia after completing a required course. All of the six Australian-trained medical doctors (five male and one female) are the children of amnesty migrants. (We refer to the only female doctor as a male in order to preserve confidentiality.)

Overall Differences in Illnesses Experienced by the Two Migrant Groups

Just as Koreans in Sydney often categorize themselves as amnesty, skilled or business migrants, the medical doctors mentioned the health condition of Koreans with reference to these three categories. The doctors' broad and deep understanding of their fellow Koreans might have been possible because their clients are predominantly Korean-Australians. While the views of the doctors were remarkably consistent with those of the users, the doctors' views enriched the

information ascertained from previous studies (Han 1999, 2000, 2001; Han & Chesters 2001a, b). Similarly, we found it particularly interesting and informative to hear Dr Son's observations regarding the health and level of satisfaction of immigrant life comparing 'two groups': (i) amnesty, and (ii) skilled and business migrants (Han & Davies 2000):

> There're two groups. The first group is not well educated . . . Although they've been doing heavy manual work, their wage is higher than that earned by labourers in Korea . . . they enjoy egalitarianism that they wouldn't have enjoyed in Korea. They're a group of happy people. The second group is well educated or rich who had a respected status in Korea . . . They aren't happy and some of them have returned to Korea. Now, talking about the illness, the first group . . . tend to suffer frequently from physical illnesses such as arthritis, gastroenteric disorders, digestive problems . . . The second group has more problems with mental problems such as sleeplessness, palpitations, hypertension. (Dr Son Chae-young)

These views are highly analytical, representing the lived experiences of Korean migrants and illuminating the generative mechanisms that explain the social origins of health and illness of Koreans (Scambler 2001). With reference to business migrants, the doctors found that they frequently suffered from the consequences of business activities in Korea, which involved heavy drinking with little rest:

> Business migrants rarely suffer from muscular problems. However, many . . . seem to have problems with the stomach or liver, often related to heavy drinking for the sake of their business [in Korea]. (Dr Ha P'ilkwang)

This view is consistent with the interview data from business migrants (Han 1996). Status anxiety and frustration with immigrant life seemed to bother business migrants significantly:

> *Is there a special problem suffered by Korean business migrants?*
> Mental illness is common such as depression, overanxiety and *hwappyông* [the illness caused by an extremely high degree of frustration for various reasons]. I find it hard to suggest any advice because they're much older than me. I don't think there's any solution. But I try and listen to them. (Dr Yi Chi-su)

Common and Other Ailments

Talking about common diseases among Koreans in Sydney, the medical doctors generally agreed that the most common ailments were stomach-related

---

[1]The doctor sends a single bill containing a number of services directly to the Commonwealth government which pays the doctor by a single cheque (Russell & Schofield 1986).

problems, muscular pain and depression (*Hanho T'aimjŭ* 1996, p. 29). Stomach-related disease has been one of the most common illnesses in Korea, too, partly because many Korean foods are salty and hot (Sawyers 1992). However, Koreans in Sydney are increasingly picking up problems more frequently found in the West, such as high blood pressure, obesity and cholesterol-related diseases. Like most doctors, Korean doctors in Sydney did not fail to blame individual habits and culture for the illnesses of Koreans:

> As soon as Koreans enter Australia, their diet changes rapidly. They start to eat lots of red meat that they couldn't frequently eat in Korea. This sudden change of diet causes heart disease or a stroke or paralysis. As they say, you're what you eat. (Dr Kim Hyo-jun)

> *Is there any connection between work and illness among Koreans?*
> Maybe a bit. The important thing is life pattern, that is, how to control food habit and stress. Cigarettes, drinking, hot and salty food are the major problems for ill health. (Dr Ha P'il-kwang)

In their search for the reasons of ill health, doctors tend to overstate what people eat. However, all of the eight doctors saw a connection between the illnesses of Koreans in Sydney and their stressful immigrant life and work involvement (Brunner & Marmot 1999):

> Many Koreans have been involved in cleaning work. They have trouble with shoulders and backaches.... Holding two or three jobs, they don't have regular meal times. Irregular meal times, over-eating when hungry, and tiredness exacerbate already existing conditions, such as tuberculosis or liver-related disease. (Dr Ha P'il-kwang)

The Strong Connection between Work, Stress and Illness among Korean Men in Sydney

Clearly, the doctors were aware of many hardships the majority of Koreans suffered as they were reminded of their own fathers who had to leave their homeland to support their families; they entered Australia without knowing what was going to happen to their future and worked hard, often doing two or three jobs at a time (Han 1999). Although only about 50% of Koreans in Sydney reside in dwellings they *own* or *are purchasing*, Koreans tend to be 'workaholic' in order to establish a better life for themselves as quickly as they can (i.e. owning a home, a good car and accumulating a large bank balance) (Coughlan 1995):

> *Is there any connection between work and illness among Koreans?*
> Gastroenteric trouble is common ... The more stress patients have, the more frequent are instances of gastroenteric trouble ... Lack of qualifications has led many Koreans to work in factories or to do cleaning

> ... Shop owners work seven days a week ... They have difficulties speaking English. They aren't used to Australian culture. (Dr Min Han-sik)

> Most Koreans work too long ... More than twelve hours every day. It's just too hard. Drinking and smoking are ways for them to overcome the stress from work. They don't take a holiday. However, these are the things I can't mention to my patients. (Dr Min Han-sik)

Another factor impacting on Koreans' health is the short time taken to have their meals:

> Apart from eating salty and hot food, eating fast and irregular meal times also contribute to stomach-related diseases. Korean immigrant life is often not balanced. They work much too hard, rest little and eat fast. All these cause bad health conditions. (Dr Kim Hyo-jun)

The migrants of NESB work hard in occupations that are often not commensurate with their qualifications and experiences, and their hard work often has an adverse effect on their health (Morrissey & Jakubowicz 1980; Scambler 2002). Their relatively good health status at the time of immigration deteriorates rapidly. There are some illnesses which are frequently suffered by Korean immigrants because of their involvement in 'immigrant work':

> Koreans suffer frequently from gastroenteric disorders. They've some common health problems, such as the illnesses resulting from psychological stress and heavy manual work, and repetitive strain injuries of those working in factories, depression, and anxiety. (Dr Yi Chi-su)

A large number of Korean men are self-employed in small businesses. Although some of them predominantly deal with Korean customers, others are serving non-Koreans as well. When they are not able to communicate easily with their customers, this leads to depression, which also tends to cause stomach-related and other illnesses (Drs Kim and Son). While it is true that doctors consider the social aspects of illness, some health problems, such as mental depression and stress-related problems, are easily medicalized. Dr Min To-jin mentioned that if a person is suffering stress, the immune system would not function properly, and this can lead to other diverse illnesses. As Frankenberg (1980, p. 200) argued:

> In all class divided society, but especially in an advanced capitalist society, making social conflicts is too threatening. Sickness is therefore pushed back through psychological illness to biological disease. The social processes paradoxically operate in order to individualize.

The doctors seem to be conscious of the social roots of ill health, but they are used to helping the clients primarily with biological and medical knowledge. Dr Yi Chi-su maintained that in dealing with fellow Koreans in Sydney, a good understanding of their psychological problems (caused by their hard immigrant life) can be the key to successful treatment of their illnesses. Dr Han Sang-sik said that as many as 40% of his patients would be categorized as mental health patients, while the rest have more common problems, such as flu, muscular pain, high blood pressure and diabetes. He pointed out that 'the common problems' are also frequently found among non-Koreans. Although mental illness cannot be understood separately from physical illness, Dr Han's comment indicated the level of depression or frustration suffered by Korean immigrants (cf. Song 1996, p. 9).

Solutions to Ill Health of Korean Immigrants

Any kind of serious health problem is often known as *imin ppyông* or 'immigrant disease' among Koreans in Sydney. In answering the question, from a journalist, as to a possible solution to many stress-related health problems of Koreans in Sydney, Dr Kim Du-min said that there are many cases of illness for which doctors cannot offer a solution and went on to say, jokingly, that winning a million dollars in Lotto could fix many of the problems. He is only too well aware of how Korean immigrants have to live under the restraints of the given social structure:

> It's crucial to take up only a moderate amount of work. However, the majority have no alternative. The continuing struggle to lead an everyday life as an immigrant is inescapable. It's especially so if they want to support their family and offer their children tertiary education (Dr Kim Du-min cited in *Hanho T'aimjŭ 1996*).

Although Dr Kim realizes that his fellow migrants face situational constraints and a competitive market economy, and knows there are limits to his assistance, he feels that something should be done. Yet, he thinks that bringing about change in the workplace is beyond the responsibility of medical personnel (cf. Waitzkin 1984, p. 343). Any involvement in such reforms would not be desired by him or his professional organization. This political economy or critical realist insight into the underlying reasons for ill health clearly indicates the social origins of illness or the significance of preventative health policies. Yet, the current modes of addressing illness seem predominantly based upon curative medicine or individual approaches such as cognitive behavioural therapy rather than paying equal attention to individual and structural approaches.

Difficulties in Serving Fellow Koreans: 'Self-Diagnosis' and Demand for Antibiotics

As the doctors are dealing with Korean patients, they have to provide extra services or approach the patients with attitudes that are appropriate in a Korean cultural context. There are certain expectations that clients have of the doctor–patient relationship, and this is true for clients of both Korean and Australian backgrounds. Part of the difficulty in servicing Koreans is that they continue to have the same expectations of health care as they had when in their home country. In Korea, when people catch influenza many want an injection of antibiotics as a quick solution and many doctors are willing to offer injections as often as the patient demands.[2] This is what Koreans in Sydney are requesting of fellow Korean doctors, and this trend concerns the doctors. Although most Korean patients are well informed of Australian medical practice, those Koreans who were used to Korean medical practice prior to their immigration to Australia, seemed to demand 'Korean care' in their dealings with their fellow Korean doctors. Korean patients' self-diagnosis often puts the doctors in a difficult situation. Koreans would not demand 'Korean care' or disclose self-diagnosis in their consultation with Euro-Australian doctors:

> When their diagnosis is incorrect, it's hard to prescribe the right medication . . . On behalf of them, I often make appointments for further diagnosis and have worked as an interpreter for them . . . Most patients were used to . . . injections and overmedication in Korea and they want to receive similar treatments here . . . Some even tell me, 'Just an injection will fix me nicely.' It's hard to change such an attitude. (Dr Ha P'il-kwang)

Dr Ha seems too well aware of the difficulties facing his patients when consulting specialists. Dr Min Han-sik has a more accommodating attitude towards self-diagnosis among Koreans:

> We can't blame Koreans for self-diagnosis because the medical system in Korea makes patients seek out medicine from pharmacists . . . That's why people go to a chemist, looking for medicine for the flu and to buy antibiotics. The Australian medical system is different. Some people with flu still ask for an injection or antibiotics. I explain to them they don't need antibiotics. Most of them understand, but some don't. If I think a patient will eventually get antibiotics and there's no adverse consequence, I prescribe them. (Dr Min Han-sik)

Any doctor would like to avoid lengthy arguments over antibiotics or the development of an

---

[2]Resistance to Penicillin has increased in most countries. In the case of Australia, it increased from 1% in 1989 to 6.4% in 1995 and 15% in 1997. At the 20th International Congress of Chemotherapy in Sydney in July 1997, it was reported that the highest rate of resistance to Penicillin was observed in Korea, recording 80% resistance (Foreshew 1997, p. 3).

uncomfortable doctor–patient relationship when taking into consideration the small number of people in the Korean community.

Dr Yi Chi-su's attitude towards self-diagnosis was even more understanding:

> Self-diagnosis shows their interest in the issue of health . . . However, self-prescription of medication can be a problem . . . I provide service on the basis of an equal relationship between the doctor and the patient. I . . . realize that a patient's diagnosis is often correct. I'm more comfortable with Korean patients than with others.

> *Your kind attitude seems to attract many patients. I was told you're well prepared to listen to your patients.*
> The doctor–patient relationship is just like a husband and wife relationship in many ways. Every doctor is different. Some patients may not like my style. My patients complain of long waiting times. (Dr Yi Chi-su)

Dr Yi Chi-su was the most popular doctor in the Korean community at the time of data collection in 1995. Whenever the interviewer visited the clinic, at least six or seven patients were in the waiting room. Yi said that the minimum waiting time in his clinic was two hours. Of all the medical doctors in the community, he appeared to be the one who found most difficulty in making time for an interview for this study.

In Korea, it is common that patients often self-diagnose before they see a pharmacist or doctor. They would rarely try to present their diagnosis to doctors although they would do it more explicitly to pharmacists. If patients tried to do this in Korea, they would be reprimanded by doctors:

> Some patients take a long time before consulting a doctor . . . those people are often too stubborn to listen to me. Doctors in Korea will deal harshly with such patients . . . Some of my patients make up their minds by analyzing my attitudes towards them instead of what I say. One way to solve the problem is to tell them, 'The problem can develop into a serious complaint if not looked into' . . . When I deal with older patients as if I were older than them, they listen to me. This reflects the doctor–patient relationship in Korea. (Dr Ha P'il-kwang)

From the viewpoint of Korean patients, they are in a much better position to express or demand what they want by consulting Korean doctors rather than non-Korean doctors, as they feel they have an advantage in being fellow Koreans. This does not seem to be easily ignored by Korean doctors, either:

> *It's often mentioned that Korean doctors sometimes prescribe a stronger medication than usual because Korean patients want a quick fix?*
> That's probably not true. It may be possible that Korean doctors tend to provide Korean patients with

more injection services than they would for Australian patients. (Dr Ha P'il-kwang)

According to Dr Kim Du-min (*Hanho T'aimjŭ 1996*), only a limited amount of injection, for example, a narcotic pain-killer, is allocated to each GP and it can be used only for necessary cases. Korean doctors often have a difficult time explaining this regulation to their patients. Nonetheless, many patients said that Korean doctors tend to overuse injections as a way of maintaining their customers. Although it is certainly not true that Korean doctors voluntarily offer unnecessary injections, it seems safe to say that the use of injections in the Korean community is more common than it is in the broader Australian community. It must be difficult for the doctors to practise best medicine for the sake of both their profession and patients and simultaneously make their private practice financially sustainable in a competitive environment (Alubo 1990). Medical practitioners in Australia have recently argued that the current bulkbilling rate under subsidized Medicare is not able to sustain the private practice of most GPs (cf. Caldwell *et al.* 2004; Jones *et al.* 2004; Swerissen 2004). The common practice of bulk-billing by GPs in the city seems to create an unintentionally competitive environment, especially in an ethnic community with a small number of GPs.

Referral to Specialists: Dumping Patients onto Others

Although a few Korean doctors were undergoing training to be specialists, and a British trained Korean eye specialist served the 'Australian' public, no Korean was practising as a specialist in the community at the time of data collection (Han 2001). When a Korean GP refers a patient to a specialist, the referral letter is written in detail, especially if the patient is not to be accompanied by a Korean doctor. The receptionist at the Korean doctor's clinic then arranges the appointment for the patient.

Euro-Australian GPs refer their patients to specialists if it is required. Korean doctors do the same. However, Dr Yi Chi-su argues that Korean doctors in Sydney tend to have a more responsible attitude than their Euro-Australian counterparts in that Korean doctors would do their best before they referred a patient to a specialist. In contrast, there also seems to be a tendency for Korean doctors, when feeling the limits to their curative capacities, to think that a referral might take away their burden. Unfortunately, the referral system in Australia may be thought of, by some GPs, as a way of escaping trouble. The Korean doctors have little choice but to adapt to the Australian health system that existed before their entrance to medical school (cf. Collier 1994). Whether or not Korean doctors are more committed to their fellow patients could not be ascertained in this study.

It is interesting to note that Korean medical doctors practise referral to another kind of health practitioner, the *hanbang* doctor (Han 2001). The *hanbang* doctor is usually trained in a fully fledged university department for six years in Korea and provides Korean indigenized herbal medicine and acupuncture that originated in China. This referral does not involve writing a letter, unlike a referral to a specialist. There are many problems that biomedical doctors simply cannot cure, no matter how hard they try. The most frequent problems that patients present with are a restless feeling and weakness 'without' reason. It is recommended to these patients to take a course of restorative medicine from a Korean herbal doctor. Korean doctors have no hesitation in telling patients who have problems with joints or backache to resort to acupuncture. In fact, a significant proportion of Korean doctors and their families in Sydney regularly use *hanbang* tonic medicine (*poyak*).

Thus, when chronic fatigue cannot easily be detected, GPs tend to refer their patients to what is known as 'under-developed' medicine, which is available in the Korean community (Frankenberg 1980). The medical doctors' understanding of herbal medicine and their referral to herbal doctors tend to prevent competition between the two groups. Korean medical doctors' referral is partly based on their trust in *hanbang* doctors, and while there appears to be little sense of competition between the two types of doctor in the Korean community, it has been increasing rapidly in Korea. This does not imply that there is a cooperative relationship between biomedical and *hanbang* doctors in the Korean community. The biomedical doctors' position is still dominant. The unintended side of such referrals is that they could be used as a way of dumping patients onto others. Fatigue cannot be diagnosed anyway, unless all the social origins of the patient's illness are considered.

Hanbang medicine has long been rooted in the history of medicine in Korea and is well received in the Korean community (Han 1997, 2000, 2001). Dr Ha says that he referred some patients to *hanbang* doctors because the patients did not want to take pharmaceutical medicine or go through a surgical operation:

When they are tired they often seek *hanbang*. There's no biomedicine for the symptom. The tiredness results from their frustrated and stressful immigrant life. Unlike Koreans in Korea, Koreans in Sydney don't know how to overcome stress. Social clubs like alumni associations have a positive influence on the health of Koreans. (Dr Ha P'il-kwang)

If medical doctors find nothing wrong with a patient, no medication can be prescribed. Let's take fatigue as

an example. A comprehensive medical check-up wouldn't detect any problem. Then, medical doctors would say that nothing is wrong and nothing can be done. However, *hanbang* can strengthen the health of the patient. Still, it may be best to consult a GP first so that the patient makes sure that no serious disease develops. (Dr Min Han-sik)

The doctors practising scientific medicine seemed prepared enough to refer their patients to herbal doctors who are trying hard to build up their practice on evidence-based medicine. Yet, the biomedical doctors wish to continue to enjoy the dominant status of biomedicine. Some medical social scientists such as Frankenberg (1980, p. 199) have pointed out that when no disease is detected, a doctor collects a fee when appropriate and recommends that the patient visit other professionals such as herbal doctors. This is how biomedical doctors utilize other health professionals or so-called 'under-developed' medicine. The doctors tend to be reluctant to acknowledge the limits to their own capabilities since their profession is backed up strongly by science. There is another kind of referral, that is, Korean GPs 'referring patients to themselves'. Whilst more than 3,000 Australian GPs are practising acupuncture, two Korean doctors are doing so. To enquire further on the issue of alternative medicine use, the interviewer asked:

What do you think of hanbang medicine or acupuncture? They're effective for some purposes. I practise acupuncture myself. I learned it through a course. Most [pharmaceutical] medicines for rheumatism cause inflammation in the stomach. Elderly people can't use the medicine because of their weak stomach. When patients come with backache, shoulder ache or rheumatism, acupunctural therapy is effective. (Dr Ha P'il-kwang)

Some patients go to Dr Min and Dr Ha who practise acupuncture as well. The important reason Korean patients go to them for acupunctural therapy, instead of going to other Korean acupuncturists, is that bulk-billing is available, whereas *hanbang* acupuncturists charge upfront. Dr Ha is not sure whether his patients come to him because of his qualifications in both acupuncture and biomedicine. Korean GPs have a trust in Korean herbal medicine and acupuncture, but with some reservations:

What do you think of hanbang, tonic medicine and acupuncture? It'd be best to consult a biomedical doctor in the first place . . . It could be dangerous to rush to other than medical doctors. For example, a cancer victim may seek various therapies from other than medical doctors for a period. By the time the patient goes to a medical doctor, it's too late . . . I'm not arguing their diagnosis is quackery. I've tried *hanbang* herb medicine and I'm currently taking it. (Dr Min Han-sik)

Doctoring as a Business: 'Time and Money Rather than a Holistic Approach'

The Sydney Korean telephone directory lists all the providers of health services and other businesses in the Korean community. In the 1995 directory, only five medical doctors were listed with the names of the clinics, addresses and phone numbers. It costs nothing to be listed. In addition, all five doctors have inserted an extra quarter or half a page, which costs $200 – $500. As the longest practising doctor in the Korean community was not listed in any of the two parts, the interviewer asked him what happened:

> No doctors are supposed to advertise their clinic. Doctoring isn't a business. If doctors are found to have advertised, they'll be in trouble . . . After all, I'm the first practitioner in the community and every Korean knows me. Why should I bother advertising? It'll make little difference . . . The members of the Korean Doctors' Association in Sydney agreed not to do 'too much advertising', although a new clinic can for six months. (Dr Kim Hyo-jun)

Korean ethnic newspapers are used for the advertisements. The two magazines published weekly, the *Kyomin Chaptchi* (*Korean Ethnic Magazine in Sydney*) and the *Chugan Saenghwal Chôngbo* (*Weekly Korean Life Review*) list the recent phone numbers of businesses and include medical doctors. Similar to the annual directory of the Korean community, the two magazines do not charge for the listings. However, we learned that two Korean doctors who were trained in Korea and registered in Australia, advertised their practice for much longer than six months when they opened their clinics. Advertising may make little difference to the doctors who have worked in the community for a few years. However, they are seriously concerned about whether or not they are already known to their potential clients. The prospect of financial reward seems to be one of the most important reasons why they were encouraged to enter medical school, and these rewards are well achieved, after due training. When Korean doctors complain of the common practice of 'not having a family doctor', their concern over the size of their patient lists becomes obvious:

> Australian patients are faithful in terms of sticking to their own home doctor. Koreans aren't always so. I had some patients who've been coming to me for a long time. However, once they experience a slight discomfort, they'll quickly turn to other Korean doctors. It's understandable that newcomers may shop around until they find somebody they like, but the business of shopping around continues even after they have settled as migrants for years. (Dr A)

On a slightly different matter, Dorothea Sich (1978, p. 31) a German doctor who worked in a Korean teaching hospital, noticed that Korean patients in general were 'not as compliant as' her German and American patients. A possible explanation may be that the concept of 'personal or home doctor' is only a recent one, but it is still not common in Korea, and patients there have access to specialists in the first place, according to their need. However, a group of privileged people have had their personal doctors since biomedicine was introduced to Korea. During the fieldwork for this study, a new clinic was opened. Many patients had the attitude of 'Let's go and see what he is like!' In this respect, Koreans would not worry too much about compliance with their doctor's opinion or developing a doctor–patient relationship. There seems to be a tendency that the less popular a doctor is, the more concerned he is about the doctor–patient relationship. After interviewing a number of Koreans using biomedical services, the interviewer learned that whether or not a doctor is popular is not always relevant to the personality or capacity of the doctor. One of the informants talked of an episode which was widely shared by many Koreans:

> Dr B used to be popular in the community. His clinic was always packed with patients. He's a capable doctor. Unfortunately, one of his close family members was involved in an incident of broken *kye* group [a Korean traditional method to help each member to save a large sum of money]. The matter had nothing to do with him. Many of his patients suddenly became reluctant to consult him. The Korean community is so small that anything can affect everything. (Lee Mi-yŏn, informant)

Dr B said, 'A patient may have been with me for years. A slight dissatisfaction about me would easily lead the patient to quit coming to me.' We are unsure as to whether or not Koreans are more likely to 'shop around' for their doctors than non-Koreans do. The contemporary tendency is to encourage patients to seek a second opinion and doctors are wary that the status of the medical profession has undergone a change (Lupton 1997; Coburn & Willis 2000). One of the more popular doctors said that Korean patients' shopping-around tendency is desirable because it indicates that they are taking their own health seriously. This leads the doctors to make consistent efforts to maintain a certain number of patients:

> I've learned a holistic approach towards every illness. A balanced understanding of the physical and mental health of the patient is critical in treating illness. However, in reality, the application of such an approach isn't practical for two reasons: time and money. (Dr Han Sang-sik)

He might have meant that, considering the aspiration for a certain level of monetary reward, he can only offer 'limited' services in a given time. No matter how well-intended the doctor may be, no doctor seemed to go beyond 'the normal entrepreneurial medicine'. Yi Su-jin, an ethnic liaison officer for women's health, felt unpopular among doctors in the community because she often encouraged Korean women to utilize community health services (or the new public health) (Baum 1998) before rushing to the doctor.

Competition for More Patients: 'Criticizing Each Other' and Restraining an Authoritarian Attitude as a Method to Attract More Patients

Koreans think that Korean doctors are kind. Korean doctors think that doctors in Korea are authoritarian and that Koreans in Sydney suffered from this authoritarianism prior to their immigration. If a doctor is known to be bossy, patients share the view about the doctor with their relatives and friends. In small Korean communities, where members have frequent contact through social clubs and church meetings, it is not too long before the 'known-to-be bossy' doctor comes to worry about his reputation. As such incidents happen in the community, a particular doctor was known to be trying to develop a more considerate and understanding attitude towards his patients, at the time of data collection. Unlike in Korea, in Sydney, Korean patients disclose part of their self-diagnosis to their doctors. Living in a less authoritarian society, Korean patients seem much more prepared to put forward self-diagnosis to the doctor. The patients not only want their opinions considered in the doctor's diagnosis, but also the doctor wants to hear from the patients.

A physiotherapist in the Korean community observed that the way in which Korean doctors in Sydney deal with patients' self-diagnoses is somewhere between Korean and Australian ways, that is, not as rejecting as Korean doctors and not as accommodating as Australian doctors. Although, whether or not Australian doctors are patient and take notice of what the patient says is open to debate. It is worth noting that the friendly attitude of Korean doctors towards their patients does not imply that the doctors have given up their professional authority. It means rather, that their authoritarian attitude is more restrained or unexercised because of the different social setting (Bhaskar 1989b; Collier 1994; Sayer 2000). The tension over the issue of authoritarianism may surface because the general attitudes of both Korean doctors and patients are still 'more Korea-oriented' in the short history of Korean migration to Australia.

Dr Kim Du-min expresses concern over the competition among Korean doctors, saying, 'Fellow doctors, being over-conscious of the number of their clients, engage in unnecessary competition and criticism of each other. These should be avoided' (cited in Sin 1996, p. 17).

Korean doctors do not work at night. No patient will have been given night contact numbers. This leaves the doctors' commitment to their patients ambiguous to a degree, although no Korean would argue that Korean doctors have less concern over the health of Koreans. Dr Yi Chi-su, who was the busiest doctor in the community in 1995, indicates that his patients took it for granted that they should go to a 24 hour medical centre or hospital emergency unit during the night or on Sundays. As a consequence, emergency health care would be stretched to the limit:

> If your patient falls sick over the weekend, what can be done? Two possibilities. One is to go to a 24 hour medical centre and the other an emergency care room at the hospital. Practising a solo service, I'm working 58 hours from Monday to Saturday. If I work at night as well, I would get terribly tired. If I become stressful, it would adversely affect the patients. . . . If I had any concerned patient I would ring the patient. I wouldn't give my home number. If I work in association with other doctors, I'd be able to attend emergency care once a week. (Dr Min Han-sik)

A solo service may break the continuity of service provided for a patient whereas a doctor working as a member of a medical practice can refer a patient to his/her colleague. Yet, there was only one Korean doctor working as a member of a collaborative medical team. As many Korean students have undertaken medical degrees at universities, doctoring in the Korean community could become much more competitive in the future, which may adversely affect the patients' use of medical care.

CONCLUSION

Korean biomedical doctors generally agree that fellow Koreans suffer from *work*-related ill health. This view is consistent with that which Korean immigrants have expressed (Han 2000; Han & Chesters 2001a, b). Korean doctors are undoubtedly able to provide their fellow Koreans with culturally appropriate medical care, which may not be easily achieved by non-Korean doctors. There seems to be a mutual benefit of both professional and customer satisfaction. The use of state-subsidized medical care, since the introduction of Medibank by the Australian Labor government in 1972 and Medicare in 1984, has intensified among the amnesty migrants on obtaining permanent residency, and among the skilled and business migrants soon after their arrival in Australia. Their limited access to medical care or relatively lower quality service prior to emigration has been an influential factor in the ways in which Koreans seek health care in Australia. The different health care systems in Australia and Korea also caused confusion for Koreans in using medical care. However, as the doctors in this study recognized, the heavy involvement in manual *work*, long work hours and the stressful immigrant life have been the most influential factors affecting health care use among Korean men in Sydney. Consequently, the ill health of Koreans has led to a boom in health services in the community. While the population of the Korean community in Sydney stays relatively small, more Korean-speaking medical practitioners are opening their clinics in the community. Medical care may become even more entrepreneurial in the future and this may adversely affect patients' health care seeking behaviour and its outcome. Doctors' entrepreneurial medicine as a way of practising their profession is also exacerbated by the contemporary economic climate that encourages 'fee-for-service' or individual rather than social responsibility for health and illness. That is, the change in the broad context of health and medical care exerts limits on the choices of health care that individual patients are constantly encouraged to use, especially in the supposedly postmodern era (Archer & Tritter 2000).

A large number of Koreans, including biomedical and *hanbang* doctors, have migrated to North America, Canada and Australia where they have demonstrated remarkably similar patterns in terms of their under-employment, long work hours and heavy involvement in manual work. Also importantly, 'medical entrepreneurship' has been prominent in Korea during its rapid industrialization over the last few decades. This medical entrepreneurship has been 'translated' in Korean communities together with the flux of Koreans moving overseas (Shin & Chang 1988; Miller 1990; Han 1997, 2000; Cho 2000).

At theoretical and methodological levels, this paper has demonstrated the complex links between individual behaviour and observable surface phenomena (agent) and the given social and economic climate (structure) from a critical realist perspective.

When Korean patients demand 'Korean care' and Korean doctors are accommodating it in Australia to some degree, medical care provision becomes complex. That is, the provision of, and access to health care in an ethnic community are both enabled and restrained by the given socioeconomic climate to which members of the migrant community are exposed. As a consequence, we are observing a unique aspect of the phenomenon of medical care provision as well as similarities within the broader Australian community. A critical realist perspective is an alternative to the approach that is preoccupied by either 'agent-related' or 'structure-related' factors, and consequently offers a fuller picture of reality. The application of critical realism in analysing health status and health care provision/use is still at an early stage (Porter 1993; Scambler 2001, 2002; Han 2002). Undoubtedly, a fuller understanding of the intricate relations between health status and health care provision/use and the broader social context encompassing the market economy remains an important task. Moreover, globalization and the culture of individuals being increasingly better informed than in the past are likely to contribute significantly to the improvement of people's health outcomes irrespective of their class, gender and race.

REFERENCES

ABS (2002) *Census of Population and Housing*, ABS, Canberra.

Alubo, S. O. (1990) 'Doctoring as business: a study of entrepreneurial medicine in Nigeria', *Medical Anthropology*, vol. 12, pp. 305–324.

Archer, M. S. & Tritter, J. Q. (eds) (2000) *Rational Choice Theory: Resisting Colonization*, Routledge, London and New York.

Baum, F. (1998) *The New Public Health: An Australian Perspective*, Oxford University Press, Melbourne.

Bhaskar, R. (1989a) *The Possibility of Naturalism*, 2nd edn, Harvester Wheatsheaf, Hemel Hempstead.

Bhaskar, R. (1989b) *Reclaiming Reality: A Critical Introduction to Contemporary Philosophy*, Verso, London.

Bhopal, R. S. (1986) 'The inter-relationship of folk, traditional and western medicine within an Asian community in Britain', *Social Science & Medicine*, vol. 22, pp. 99–105.

Brainard, J. & Zaharlick, A. (1989) 'Changing health beliefs and behaviors of resettled Laotian refugees: ethnic variation in adaptation', *Social Science & Medicine*, vol. 29, no. 7, pp. 845–852.

Brunner, E. & Marmot, M. (1999) 'Social organization, stress, and health', in *Social Determinants of Health*, eds M. Marmot & R. Wilkinson, Oxford University Press, Oxford, pp. 17–43.

Caldwell, T. M., Jorm, A. F., Knox, S., Braddock, D., Dear, K. B. & Britt, H. (2004) 'General practice encounters for psychological problems in rural, remote and metropolitan areas in Australia', *Australian and New Zealand Journal of Psychiatry*, vol. 38, no. 10, pp. 774–780.

Chan, Y. F. & Quine, S. (1997) 'Utilisation of Australian health care services by ethnic Chinese', *Australian Health Review*, vol. 20, no. 1, pp. 64–77.

Chavez, L. R. (1986) 'Mexican immigration and health care: a political economy perspective', *Human Organization*, vol. 45, no. 4, pp. 344–352.

Cho, B.-H. (2000) 'The politics of herbal drugs in Korea', *Social Science & Medicine*, vol. 51, pp. 505–509.

Chugan Saenghwal Chŏngbo[*Weekly Korean Life Review*] (1995) 14 July.

Coburn, D. & Willis, E. (2000) 'The medical profession: power, knowledge and autonomy', in *The Handbook of Social Studies in Health and Medicine*, eds G. L. Albrecht, R. Fitzpatrick & S. C. Scrimshaw, Sage, Thousand Oaks, CA, pp. 377–393.

Collier, A. (1994) *Critical Realism: An Introduction to Roy Bhaskar's Philosophy*, Verso, London.

Coughlan, J. E. (1995) 'Korean immigrants in Australia: the characteristics of recent Korean-born immigrants to Australia and a socio-demographic and economic profile of the Korean-born community from the 1991 Census', *Korea Observer*, vol. 26, no. 3, pp. 379–417.

Danermark, B., Ekström, M., Jakobsen, L. & Karlsson, J. Ch. (2002) *Explaining Society: Critical Realism in Social Sciences*, Routledge, London.

Doyal, L. (1979) *The Political Economy of Health*, Pluto Press, London.

Engels, F. (1968) *The Condition of the Working Class in England in 1844*, Stanford University Press, Stanford, CA.

Foreshew, J. (1997) 'Penicillin suffers in superbug fight', *The Australian*, 2 July, p. 3.

Frankenberg, R. (1980) 'Medical anthropology and development: a theoretical perspective', *Social Science & Medicine*, vol. 14b, pp. 197–207.

Goldman, R., Hunt, M. K., Allen, J. D., Hauser, S., Emmons, K., Maeda, M. & Sorensen, G. (2003) 'The life history interview method: applications to intervention development', *Health Education & Behavior*, vol. 30, no. 5, pp. 564–581.

Grichting, W. L. (1994) 'Health and health care of immigrant Australia', *Migrant Health Bulletin*, no. 1, pp. 23–42.

Han, G.-S. (1994) *Social Sources of Church Growth: Korean Churches in the Homeland and Overseas*, University Press of America, Lanham, MD, New York and London.

Han, G.-S. (1996) 'Korean business migrants in Australia', *Asian Migrant*, vol. 9, no. 3, pp. 80–85.

Han, G.-S. (1997) 'The rise of Western medicine and revival of traditional medicine in Korea: a brief history', *Korean Studies*, vol. 21, pp. 96–121.

Han, G.-S. (1999) 'Immigrant life and work involvement: Korean men in Australia', *Journal of Intercultural Studies*, vol. 20, no. 1, pp. 5–29.

Han, G.-S. (2000) *Health and Medicine under Capitalism: Korean Immigrants in Australia*, Associated University Presses, London.

Han, G.-S. (2001) 'The provision of hanbang herbal medicine in the Korean community in Australia: entrepreneurial or caring for fellow Koreans', *Australian Health Review*, vol. 24, no. 4, pp. 146–155.

Han, G.-S. (2002) 'The myth of medical pluralism: a critical realist perspective', *Sociological Research Online*, vol. 6, no. 4, pp. U92–U112.

Han, G.-S. & Chesters, J. (2001a) '"Chasing money" and "damaged health": Korean men in Australia, Part I, amnesty migrants', *Australian Journal of Primary Health*, vol. 7, no. 1, pp. 39–45.

Han, G.-S. & Chesters, J. (2001b) '"Chasing money" and "damaged health": Korean men in Australia, Part II, skilled and business migrants', *Australian Journal of Primary Health*, vol. 7, no. 2, pp. 9–14.

Han, G.-S. & Davies, C. (2000) 'Koreans in Australia—illegal, skilled and business migrants: who settled better and why?', *Journal of Australian Studies*, vol. 7, no. 1, pp. 55–72.

Hanho T'aimjŭ (1996) T'ukppyôl int'ôbyu: Kimhyônshin wônjanggwa [Special interview with Dr Kim Hyoun-sin], *Hanho T'aimjŭ* [*Hanho Times*], 19 January, p. 29.

Heggenhougen, H. K. (1979) 'Why does traditional medicine persist?', *Bulletin of the Public Health Society*, vol. 13, pp. 60–64.

Hsu-Hage, B. H.-H., Tang, K. C., Li, R. J., Lin, V., Chow, T. & Thien, F. (2001) 'A qualitative investigation into the use of health services among Melbourne Chinese', *Australian Journal of Primary Health*, vol. 7, no. 3, pp. 38–44.

Irvine, R., McPhee, J. & Kerridge, I. H. (2002) 'The challenge of cultural and ethical pluralism to medical practice', *Medical Journal of Australia*, vol. 176, no. 4, pp. 175–176.

Jones, G., Savage, E. & Hall, J. (2004) 'Pricing of general practice in Australia: some recent proposals to reform Medicare', *Journal of Health Services Research & Policy*, vol. 9, suppl. 2, pp. 63–68.

Lupton, D. (1997) 'Doctors on the medical profession', *Sociology of Health & Illness*, vol. 19, no. 4, pp. 480–497.

Manderson, L. & Mathews, M. (1985) 'Care and conflict: Vietnamese medical beliefs and the Australian health care system', in *Immigration and Ethnicity in the 1980s*, eds I. Burnley, S. Encel & G. McCall, Longman Cheshire, Melbourne, pp. 248–260.

Mathews, M. (1979) *Vietnamese Food Customs in Pregnancy and Lactation*, BSc (Med.) Thesis, University of Sydney.

McKeown, T. (1979) *The Role of Medicine: Dream, Mirage or Nemesis?*, Basil Blackwell, Oxford.

Miller, J. K. (1990) 'Use of traditional Korean health care by Korean immigrants to the United States', *Sociology & Social Research*, vol. 75, no. 1, pp. 38–48.

Minichiello, V., Aroni, R., Timewell, E. & Alexander, L. (1990) *In-depth Interviewing: Researching People*, Longman Cheshire, South Melbourne.

Morrissey, M. & Jakubowicz, A. (1980) *Migrants and Occupational Health: A Report*, Social Welfare Research Centre Reports and Proceedings, No. 3, University of New South Wales, Sydney.

Nichter, M. (1991) 'Ethnomedicine: diverse trends, common linkages: commentary', *Medical Anthropology*, vol. 13, pp. 137–171.

Porter, S. (1993) 'Critical realist ethnography: the case of racism and professionalism in a medical setting', *Sociology*, vol. 27, no. 4, pp. 591 609.

Reid, G., Crofts, N. & Beyer, L. (2001) 'Drug treatment services for ethnic communities in Victoria, Australia: an examination of cultural and institutional barriers', *Ethnicity & Health*, vol. 6, no. 1, pp. 13–26.

Rice, P. L. (ed.) (1999) *Living in a New Country: Understanding Migrants' Health*, Ausmed, Melbourne.

Russell, C. & Schofield, T. (1986) *Where it Hurts: An Introduction to Sociology for Health Workers*, Allen & Unwin, Sydney.

Savage, A. (1991) *Traditional Beliefs and Practices which may Affect the Health of Lebanese Muslim, Vietnamese, and Ethnic Chinese Women from Vietnam: Literature Review*, University of Melbourne & La Trobe University, Melbourne.

Sawyers, J. (1992) 'Gastric cancer in the Korean-American: cultural implications', *Oncology Nursing Forum*, vol. 19, no. 4, pp. 619–623.

Sayer, A. (1992) *Method in Social Science: A Realist Approach*, Routledge, London.

Sayer, A. (2000) *Realism and Social Science*, Sage, London.

Scambler, G. (2001) 'Critical realism, sociology and health inequalities: social class as a generative mechanism and its media of enactment', *Journal of Critical Realism*, vol. 4, no. 1, pp. 35–42.

Scambler, G. (2002) *Health and Social Change: A Critical Theory*, Open University Press, Buckingham.

Shin, E.-H. & Chang, K.-S. (1988) 'Peripherization of immigrant professionals: Korean physicians in the United States', *International Migration Review*, vol. 22, no. 4, pp. 609–626.

Sich, D. (1978) 'Some aspects of traditional medicine and illness behavior in Korea', *Korea Journal*, vol. 18, no. 3, pp. 30–35.

Silverman, D. (1985) *Qualitative Methodology and Sociology*, Gower, Aldershot, Hants.

Sin, A.-Y. (1996) Imin Ŏgil: Dr Kim Hyŏ n-sin [An interview with Dr Kim Hyŏn-sin], *Tong-A Ilbo*, 25 April, p. 17.

Song, C.-B. (1996) Sŭt'uresŭ chilhwan kyop'o mana kŏktchŏngi apsŏmnida [Concerned about the increasing number of fellow Koreans suffering from stress related diseases], *Wikŭ T'op*, 7 June, p. 9.

Stellman, J. M. (1973) *Work is Dangerous to Your Health: A Handbook of Health Hazards in the Workplace and What You Can Do About Them*, Vintage Books, New York.

Strauss, A. L. & Corbin, J. (1990) *Basics of Qualitative Research: Grounded Theory Procedures and Techniques*, Sage, Newbury Park, CA.

Strauss, A. L. & Corbin, J. (1998) *Basics of Qualitative Research: Techniques and Procedures for Developing Grounded Theory*, Sage, Thousand Oaks, CA.

Swerissen, H. (2004) 'Australian primary care policy in 2004: two tiers or one for Medicare?', *Australian and New Zealand Health Policy*, vol. 1, no. 1, p. 2.

Sydney Korean Telephone Directory (1989–1994) Sydney Korean Society, Sydney.

Waitzkin, H. (1981) 'The social origins of illness: a neglected history', *International Journal of Health Services*, vol. 11, pp. 77–103.

Waitzkin, H. (1984) 'The micropolitics of medicine: a contextual analysis', *International Journal of Health Services*, vol. 14, pp. 339–378.

Waitzkin, H. (1998) 'Is our work dangerous? Should it be?', *Journal of Health & Social Behaviour*, vol. 39, pp. 7–17.

3.02

EMERGING DESIGN

Relationships and Their Potential for Change Developed in Difficult Type 1 Diabetes

Vibeke Zoffmann* and Marit Kirkevold†

ABSTRACT: Few researchers have explored how relationships between patients and providers might change problem solving in clinical practice. The authors used grounded theory to study dyads of 11 people with diabetes and poor glycemic control, and 8 nurses interacting in diabetes teams. Relational Potential for Change was identified as a core category that involved three types of relationships. Professionals mostly shifted between less effective relationships characterized by I-you-distant provider dominance and I-you-blurred sympathy. Although rarely seen, a third relationship, I-you-sorted mutuality proved more effective than the others in exploiting the Relational Potential for Change. The three types of relationship differed in (a) scope of problem solving, (b) the roles assigned to the patient and the professionals, (c) use of difficult feelings and different points of view, and (d) quality of knowledge achieved as the basis for problem solving and decision making. The authors discuss implications for practice and further research.

KEYWORDS: Relationship; diabetes; problem solving; change; grounded theory.

Patient–provider relationships might play a neglected role in chronic care. In difficult diabetes care, failed problem solving over several years provides a good reason for studying patient–provider relationships and their influence on the effectiveness of problem solving. The extent to which these relationships influence how much a given potential for change in the patient's situation is exploited in problem solving also deserves study.

Previously, researchers have approached patient–provider relationships mostly from a theoretical perspective without knowing if the ideals presented were workable or of true value in clinical practice. Recent research, moreover, has questioned some of these

*Vibeke Zoffmann, RN, MPH, PhD, is an assistant professor at The University Hospitals' Centre for Nursing and Care Research (UCSF), Copenhagen, Denmark.

†Marit Kirkevold, RN, EdD, is a professor in the Department of Nursing Science, University of Aarhus, Denmark, and a professor at the Institute of Nursing Science, University of Oslo, Norway.

ideals in relationships. Egalitarian relationships between patients and professionals have, for instance, been questioned by Thorne (1999), who warned against a tendency to adopt equality uncritically as an incontestable and overarching truth and overlook its limitations. Earlier, Roter (1987) concluded that neither authoritarian guidance nor independent decision making should be recommended as the best alternatives for an optimal client–provider relationship; rather, a relationship based on mutuality, partnership, and the active participation of both clients and providers should be promoted.

Research has shown that providers find diabetes more difficult to manage than other chronic conditions because it is more complex and its successful management relies to a greater extent on lifestyle change, which is outside provider control (Larme & Pugh, 1998). Important differences have been found between practitioners' and patients' goals, evaluations, and strategies, with patients being rooted in a lifeworld perspective, whereas the professionals were rooted in a clinical context (Hunt, Arar, & Larme, 1998).

An acknowledgement of the value of empowerment seems to be widespread in policy for diabetes care (European Diabetes Policy Group, 1998, 1999), and positive health outcomes have been documented as a result of autonomy support and empowerment (R. M. Anderson, 1995; R. M. Anderson, et al., 1995; Williams, & Deci, 1998). Qualitative studies of diabetes patients' experiences of empowerment in clinical practice have concluded, however, that professionals' proclaimed intention of using empowerment was seldom perceived by patients. Even patients with good glycemic control rarely experienced that professionals were interested in listening to their opinion concerning their health problems (Hernandez, 1995; Paterson, 2001). Similar inconsistencies in physicians' attitude toward patients were found by Loewe et al. (Loewe, Schwartzman, Freeman, Quinn, & Zuckerman, 1998). Although physicians discussed the importance of negotiating with patients, several physicians told stories that portrayed the doctor as an adversary or authority figure. Research thus shows that the intention to use empowerment in clinical practice seems frequently to fail.

In view of this, our knowledge of relationships in clinical practice requires an empirical and critical foundation. In the current study, we have aimed at developing a theory that interprets patient–provider relationships as a framework for acknowledging and exploiting the relational potential for change in difficult diabetes care. The theory was developed in the initial phase of a research program conducted at a Danish university hospital between 1996 and 2004 (Zoffmann, 2004; Zoffmann & Kirkevold, 2005; Zoffmann & Lauritzen, 2006).

METHOD

In the study, we used grounded theory method comprising a symbolic interactionist perspective (Lomborg & Kirkevold, 2003) and a constant comparative method (Glaser, 1978, 1992; Glaser & Strauss, 1967; Strauss & Corbin, 1998).

Patients and nurses from an inpatient unit or day clinic at a Danish university hospital were invited to participate. Inclusion criteria for patients were (a) age at least 18 years, (b) diagnosed with diabetes for at least 1 year, and (c) admitted because of poor glycemic control (HbAlc ≥ 8.0%). Nurses were included if they were familiar with traditional diabetes care and had more than 1 year of experience in a specialized diabetes unit. The dyads were formed based on the assignment of nurses to patients in the units, taking the needs of ordinary clinical practice into account. The researchers did not interfere with this process in any way.

The first patient included possessed a high level of resources for the self-management of diabetes (highly educated, knowledgeable about diabetes, good family relations, well occupied) and yet still had poor metabolic control. We identified these resources by listening to a conversation between the nurse and the patient at admittance and by reading the patient's medical records. The patient was highly critical of the approach to care adopted by health care professionals. Following the principles of theoretical sampling, we used this case to generate a hypothesis that interactions between professionals and patients who displayed an imbalance between poorly regulated diabetes, on one hand, and high levels of self-management resources, on the other, would reveal how the potential for change in relationships was perhaps being used inappropriately. To investigate and compare the processes related to this discrepancy, subsequent patients were theoretically sampled to ensure a variation in levels of self-management resources. The assessment of self-management resources was based on information in the patients' medical records. Further investigation during data collection verified or modified this first impression and led to the sample included in this study.

As the primary sources, two patient–nurse conversations were taped from each dyad, one at the beginning and one at the end of the hospital stay. These documented what was discussed, planned, accomplished, and evaluated. In addition, each nurse was asked to tape a discussion with a doctor, dietician, or another nurse from the team that she considered to be important in assessing the patient's situation. These latter conversations revealed observations, feelings, concerns, and ideas exchanged internally in the diabetes team when patients were not present. In each case, all three conversations were listened to before semistructured interviews were conducted, first with the patients after discharge and then with the nurse. These interviews revealed the experiences, considerations, and feelings of both parties with regard to the hospital stay. Finally, an interview with the patient half a year later revealed how he or she assessed the outcome of the hospital stay, taking into consideration the changes accomplished or still unaccomplished in daily life with the illness.

The reason for focusing primarily on nurse–patient interactions was our belief that nurses bear the main responsibility in the team for helping patients to live with their diabetes. Interactions between patients and other professionals, such as physicians and dieticians, were, however, investigated indirectly through the participation of these professionals in the taped conversations with nurses and because they were referred to by patients and nurses in interviews and conversations.

Data were concurrently analyzed by the first author supported by the Qualitative Media Analyzer (a computer program providing simultaneous access during coding to the original auditory details of the data and connected transcriptions and notes). The inductive process of applying constant comparative analysis, as recommended in grounded theory (Glaser, 1978, 1992; Glaser & Strauss, 1967), was performed in four steps. First, we performed initial open coding on each conversation or interview soon after it had taken place. Through a combination of listening and writing notes, we discovered in vivo codes, providing ideas for the tentative advancement of more abstract codes. Second, a critical comparison focused on the most solid categories, which were now supported by transcriptions of the coded data. We used this to specify the content and further the advancement of lasting categories and subcategories. Step 2 ended when saturation was achieved and ideas for tentative links between categories appeared to emerge. During the third step, we performed comparison across data sources to explore and confirm links between concepts and thus pattern out theoretical ideas and connections. These initial theoretical constituents were compared in the fourth step, which continued throughout the process of writing, to connect them into larger constituents for further theory building. At each step, we returned to former steps to test fit, work, relevance, and modifiability (Glaser & Strauss, 1967).

For instance, when sudden shifts in the nurses' approach to patients occurred at the same time as patients expressed criticism of the health care system or expressed difficult feelings related to diabetes, we were alerted to the two most commonly used relationships—I-you-distant provider dominance and I-you-blurred sympathy—and the changes between them. Continued comparison revealed distinctions between I-you-blurred sympathy and a third type of relationship: I-you-sorted mutuality. To clarify the content differences between the three relationships, we organized them into a matrix (Table 1). The content of each relationship revealed the varying characteristics of the I-you-borders between patients and professionals. Finally, continued comparison helped us identify a core category, Relational Potential for Change, which we identified as a possibility common to all three types of relationship but acknowledged and exploited to different extents in each.

Threats to validity were considered at several levels. We acknowledged Glaser's (1978) contention that a researcher's assumptions can be helpful in developing alertness or sensitivity to what is going on but can also prevent him or her from discovering a new theoretical formulation through emergence. To increase critical awareness of our assumptions and benefit from them to sharpen the focus of the study, we expressed our ideas on vital issues in mutual decision making prior to the study. In addition, a pilot study convinced us that individual interviews with patients and nurses were not enough. To know what was going on in problem solving, we had to know what actually happened during patient–provider conversations, so conversations were recorded at strategic times at the start and end of the hospital stay to provide a reliable impression of the care delivered. We also acknowledged the fact that the interaction would not be fully understood if the considerations behind what each party said were not known. We therefore compared the patient–nurse interactions we observed with the way in which both parties independently referred to the interaction: the nurse in a conversation with a colleague and in an interview and the patient in two interviews at different times.

Being aware that the character of a conversation might change because patients and professionals might be distracted by a researcher's presence, we chose to ask permission for the interaction between patient and nurse to be audiotaped without the researcher's being present. The aim was to capture a reliable image of the usual care in daily practice by asking nurses to "do as usual." If they wanted to be especially competent, it was suggested that they be "especially competent in doing as usual."

Informed consent was obtained from all participants, who were assured that their statements would be handled anonymously and confidentially. The protocol was prepared in accordance with the Helsinki declaration (World Medical Association, 1989) and approved by the ethics committee of Aarhus County.

Table 1. Matrix Showing Relationship and Distinctions Between Them

	I-You-Distant Provider Dominance	I-You-Blurred Sympathy	I-You-Sorted Mutuality
Scope of problem solving	Implicitly decided by professionals and comprising biomedical problems or problems typical for the patient group	Diffuse and nondelimited; professionals focus on similarities between patients and themselves as a means of establishing or maintaining contact	Explicitly specified, comprising what the two parties assess as being currently important and difficult for the patient
Roles assigned the patient and professionals	Professionals are in charge, expected to be sole investigators finding solutions to the problems; patients are expected to follow the professionals' suggestions; patients are bored while professionals are busy	Problem solving recedes into the background; professionals are emotionally involved and aim to establish and maintain contact with patients; good contact tends to become a goal instead of a means and fails if the parties are too different	Both the patient and the professionals are in control; patients are seen as the "owners" of the problem and the final problem solvers; professionals support and challenge patients
Use of difficult feelings and differences in experiences and points of view	Differences in experience and points of view are seldom detailed or even discovered; patients and professionals ignore each other's ideas in problem solving; difficult feelings are considered to be ill-timed and to disturb problem solving; if patients perceive important difficulties being ignored, they resist professionals' suggestions; if professionals are irritated, they show reluctance or discuss their feelings with colleagues	Difficult feelings and differences in patients' and professionals' experiences and points of view are expressed but diminished and blurred as they create tension, which is apparently difficult to tolerate; blurring the difficulties and differences in experiences and points of view means reduced use of their potential; the relationship tends to end in stagnation, conformity, and coziness	The parties express difficult feelings and exchange different points of view; they overcome the tension by discussing and exploring the sources; this gives them access to a potential for change implied in difficult feelings and different points of view
Quality of knowledge achieved as the basis of problem solving and decision making	Knowledge is delimited to areas found important by professionals; physical aspects are predominant; professionals' hypotheses of difficulties perceived by patients in living with diabetes remain unverified; patients' unexpected reactions to the illness are unknown	Professionals tend to overestimate similarities between the patients and themselves; they rely on impressions instead of verifying their hypotheses of patients' reactions to illness; the true character of problems is blurred, creating a risk of pseudounderstanding	The patients' insight into their difficulties in living with diabetes is supported and challenged; patients' and professionals' hypotheses of each other's points of view are verified through mutuality; together they cocreate a person-specific knowledge of the patient's lived difficulties as the basis for decision making and problem solving

FINDINGS

Eleven patients and 8 nurses were invited and agreed to participate. Eight of the patients were aged 18 to 42 years and had had type 1 diabetes for 2 to 25 years (median 9). Three were aged 49 to 63 years and had been diagnosed with type 2 diabetes 1 to 4 years earlier. All patients (7 female and 4 male) with HbAlc 8.4 to 18.0 had attended individual or group-based diabetes education as conventionally offered by the hospital. With regard to levels of self-management resources, 7 patients were judged to be at a high and 4 patients at a low level. Eight nurses with 1 to 17 years of experience in diabetes care (median 4) participated as "contact nurses" responsible for care of the patients.

Five of the nurses were responsible for the care of 1 patient each, whereas 3 of the nurses cared for 2 patients.

Three kinds of relationships were identified and labels according to the characteristics of the I-you boundaries during problem solving: (a) I-you-distant provider dominance, (b) I-you-blurred sympathy, and (c) I-you-sorted mutuality (Table 1). Relational Potential for Change was identified as a core category, because it was a possibility common to all of the relationships. Accessing this potential, however, meant tackling difficult feelings and different points of view, which could create tension in the relationship. This process was managed differently in each of the relationships (Figure 1), and as a result, the extent to which the relational potential for change was exploited varied.

The potential for change was almost unacknowledged in I-you-distant provider dominance relationship

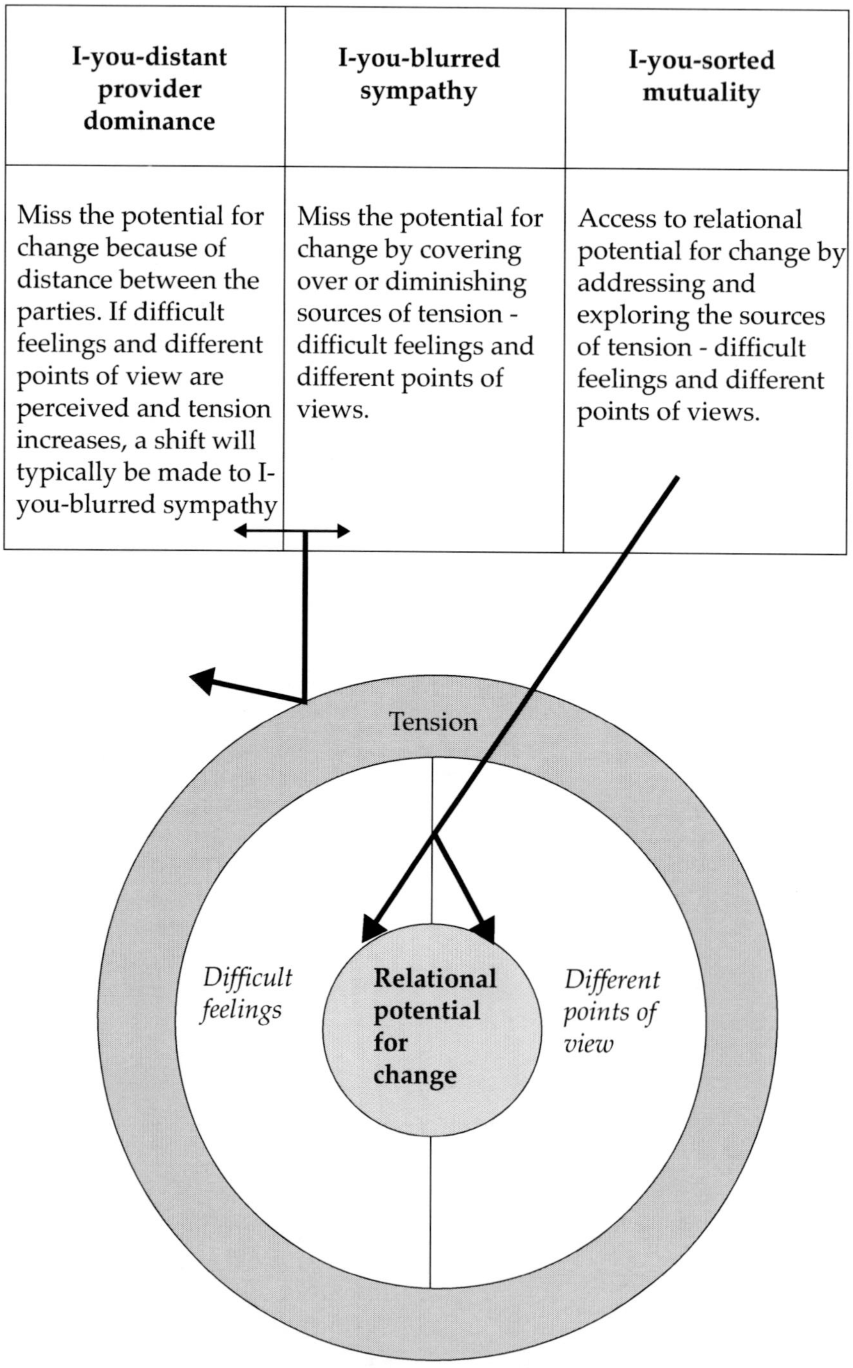

I-you-distant provider dominance	I-you-blurred sympathy	I-you-sorted mutuality
Miss the potential for change because of distance between the parties. If difficult feelings and different points of view are perceived and tension increases, a shift will typically be made to I-you-blurred sympathy	Miss the potential for change by covering over or diminishing sources of tension - difficult feelings and different points of views.	Access to relational potential for change by addressing and exploring the sources of tension - difficult feelings and different points of views.

Figure 1. Relational potential for change and its connections with the three relationships.

and was obscured in I-you-blurred sympathy. It was fully acknowledged and exploited only in the I-you-sorted mutuality relationship. The boundary between professionals in each relationship appeared to be defined by a combination of factors: (a) scope of problem solving, (b) roles assigned the patient and the professionals, (c) use of difficult feelings and different points of view, and (d) quality of knowledge achieved as the basis for problem solving and decision making (Table 1). In the following paragraphs, we will detail the three types of relationship and the way in which they access and use Relational Potential for Change.

I-You-Distant Provider Dominance

I-you-distant provider dominance appeared to be the typical framework for patient–provider interaction. It was implicitly based on the provider perspective and a narrow range of biomedical or typical problems, and an unquestioned distance appeared to exist between patients and professionals. The professionals were in charge and were expected to assess the nature and relevance of problems and be the sole investigators for finding solutions to them. Once problems had been investigated and solutions found, patients were expected to follow professional suggestions.

Although professionals could be nice and friendly, patients perceived the narrow scope of their focus as a lack of interest in and knowledge about the patient as a person. This was expressed by a 55-year-old woman with type 2 diabetes:

> So, you know, I think they flick through the pages in that thing [the journal]. It seemed a bit like it was just something they had to get over and done with.

Another patient, a 29-year-old man, strongly regretted that his worries about late complications were not an issue in conversations with professionals. He felt that the disease-oriented perspective actually failed to treat him as a person:

> They measure some values, and then they adjust the medication . . . so that the results look better. If I was sitting here as a person, then we would not have to go through all this talk about results. Then we would also talk about how the person was doing: "How is your family coping with your diabetes? What are your thoughts about the late complications?" Now I have had laser treatment on my eyes. "What thoughts have you had about that?"

A perception that the difficulties of daily life with diabetes were not considered as being relevant tended to reduce patients' expectations and use of professionals. A 43-year-old woman with type 1 diabetes, for instance, referred to a situation in which she was interrupted by a doctor asking for her blood sugar results while she was talking about difficulties at work. She expressed her reduced expectations this way:

> They can come up with some good ideas. Suggest that I might take that much insulin. But I can't use them for much else.

A general feature of this type of relationship was that patients were not assigned an active role in problem solving and decision making. Some patients perceived this as a lack of interest in their experience and as being connected with their poor regulation. They felt they had been labeled as incompetent in managing diabetes, as was expressed by a 32-year-old woman who had been living with type 1 diabetes for 23 years:

> Well they don't want to know. . . . It is like being put in a box that says: this is a diabetic who can't manage (laughs), and then they don't want to know about your experience because you can't do it right anyway—so it is the wrong experience.

Patients tended to react to this lack of involvement by developing resistance to professionals, expressed in the form of anger by the patient above:

> It is the same with all hospitals. Very few listen to the patients' experience. It is not just me saying that. This goes for everybody in my ward. And we are cross about it, especially when we have had diabetes for many years.

As I-you-distant provider dominance relationships focused on diabetes-specific matters in a general and often physical way, difficult feelings and different points of view were not openly addressed or revealed but, rather, were kept at a distance. Nevertheless, these differing points of view remained, and difficult feelings in the form of frustration and irritation were expressed by professionals as a consequence of failed problem solving and by patients because they felt they had not been heard. These feelings appeared to be transformed into patient resistance or despondency and professional pressure or reluctance. A 54-year-old woman with type 1 diabetes, for instance, reacted with resistance because she was reprimanded at a diabetes clinic for not taking her insulin properly and told by a doctor to take it without any adjustments. Although she knew it would turn out badly, she deliberately did as she had been told as a way of resisting pressure from the doctor.

> Last time I was told to tighten up and keep control and take my insulin as prescribed. This meant that I felt rather awful for three months—It fluctuated between too high and too low. I suffered a lot then. Yes, I had much too much [insulin].

"Doing as you are told" was seen as a patient response to professional pressure and a form of resistance apparently used to show that professionals' decisions were wrong.

For professionals, feelings related to the persistent failure of problem solving appeared to manifest themselves as reluctance about patients, as was noticed by the nurse caring for an 18-year-old man with type 1 diabetes who had been frequently admitted with no result.

> I believe that many in here have got him stuck in their throats. He has been here so many times. It is the same every time. He is a problem here instead of being a possibility. It has something to do with our point of view and it is that point of view that shines through because we see the problem. It is a huge big problem that walks through the door when he arrives—Well it is.

When feelings that were considered ill-timed in I-you-distant provider dominance relationships were transformed into patient resistance and professional reluctance, as seen above, this could even deadlock problem solving by making difficulties personal and directing energy away from problem solving.

In I-you-distant provider dominance, nurses tended to ask questions that were not real questions, as the nurses already had the "correct" answers to these questions. The questions and answers comprised rules or general knowledge about diabetes and its best treatment, and the purpose of asking these questions appeared to be to test whether patients also knew the answers and, if not, to teach them. This happened several times in one dyad during the first conversation. When the nurse found out that the patient appeared to be satisfied with too high a level of blood glucose after meals, she wanted to test whether the patient knew what was recommended and thus asked, "What did they say yesterday?" (during diabetes education). When the patient was not quite sure, the nurse repeated the correct answer and then explained the risk of late complications as a consequence of too high a level of blood glucose.

Patients thus experienced that the recommendations of professionals were based on fixed rules rather than knowledge about their specific situation and the experiences they had. When patients experienced that professionals made decisions without asking for their opinion, they could also resist by refusing to comply. This occurred when a 29-year-old patient with type 1 diabetes was being put on new medication. During interviews, the patient said that at the time, he was nervous, because he was about to have his eyes laser treated. The nurse was present during the discussion about medication and recalled the decision as follows:

> I remember . . . he wasn't asked if he was happy with this. I believe the doctor took it for granted . . . well this was how it should be . . . and there was something about writing notes. He [the patient] didn't really have the opportunity to say no . . . so unfortunately he wasn't involved in the decision there.

The patient would have preferred to have the new medication postponed for a couple of weeks, expecting that difficulties in distinguishing between the side effects of the new medicine and symptoms resulting from fluctuations in blood sugar would require his full attention. A lack of knowledge about this patient's attitude toward the medication meant that implementation of the decision was delayed; resenting the way in which the medication above was prescribed, the patient did not take it for months.

I-you-distant provider dominance was the typical relationship observed and relied exclusively on the potential of professionals. Even this potential was, however, inadequately used because of patient resistance and professional reluctance. Neither patients nor professionals discovered or accessed a relational potential for change. Yet, despite the fact that difficult feelings and different points of view were kept at a distance, professionals could not entirely avoid becoming aware of them. The typical reaction to this awareness appeared to be sudden shifts to an I-you-blurred sympathy relationship.

I-You-Blurred Sympathy

I-you-blurred sympathy relationships appeared to be established spontaneously when professionals became aware during problem solving of difficult feelings and different points of view, which apparently caused tension they found difficult to tolerate. A conspicuous feature of this relationship was the identification of similarities between patients and professionals, which professionals appeared to use spontaneously in an attempt to neutralize the tension. For example, a shift to I-you-blurred sympathy was seen in one dyad when the patient, a young man of 18, told the nurse that he had been "playing" with the idea of suicide:

> *Patient:* It is bloody hard. Then I can feel really unhappy. Then you do something stupid and think of something stupid and such like.
>
> *Nurse:* But we all do that. I do it when I lose my head, right? Do some things which I realise afterwards are completely stupid, right?

After the nurse's reply, they at once stopped talking about the patient's serious thoughts. By signaling that the difficulty had been recognized and that she had thought of and even experienced it, the nurse somehow removed the energy from the experience. The tension that had been created by the patient's sharing this confidence was thereby dissipated.

Professionals were thus emotionally involved and sensitive to different points of view and difficult feelings but tended to minimize the tension by accentuating similarities to their experience. In other words, they tended to overestimate the shared experience between patients and them by inferring an illusory degree of similarity based on a few actual ones. This tendency appeared to blur not only the true difficulties perceived by patients but also the boundaries between patient and professional. This was apparent several times in the study, as in this instance, when a younger nurse discovered that she had assumed too many similarities:

> Once her daughter arrived and then, I think, I must have looked completely baffled because she was a big girl of sixteen and I had all the time felt as if we were very much on the same wavelength, in age as in everything else.

When similarities and agreement were nurtured, the patient and the professional appeared to feel comfortable in each other's company. The aim of maintaining contact appeared to become a goal instead of a means. Often contact was established quickly, with the two parties' feeling that they were on the same wavelength. Both patients and professionals settled for contentment and the relationship seemed satisfactory to the patient, the professional, and outsiders. However, if the two parties were too different, it was not possible to establish contact. This was noticed by the nurse in a dyad with a 32-year-old woman with type 1 diabetes:

> There wasn't much of a relationship between the patient and me. . . . We were two different types who clashed, or more rightly did not clash.

All in all, the scope of the I-you-blurred relationship appeared to be unfocused and diffuse, with indistinct roles assigned to patients and professionals. When differences and disagreement were diminished or covered over like this, tensions between patients and professionals would be invalidated and the potential for change in the relationship reduced. That a relationship characterized by I-you-blurred sympathy did not influence the patient's situation was apparent in the following statement made by a 29-year-old man with type 1 diabetes at an interview 5 months after discharge from hospital. The patient said,

> She [the nurse] could talk to me about many things. We have really talked about many different things, but in relation to my treatment it hasn't made any difference. In my own way of approaching the illness and coping with the fact that I've got this illness, nothing has happened.

In I-you-blurred sympathy relationships, professionals did not actively seek out differences and the specifics of each patient's situation and instead only looked for what was expected based on their world of ideas. As a result, they did not obtain any unexpected knowledge. The nurse in the following example made assumptions in her questions that showed

that she expected the patient's everyday life to resemble what she knew from her own life. Her questions, therefore, did not invite the patient to present anything that differed from her assumptions:

> *Nurse:* Do you have children yourself?
>
> *Patient:* Yes, I've got two small boys.
>
> *Nurse:* And your days are very much alike I imagine, when you've got children and such.
>
> *Patient:* Yeah . . . well there is a lot . . . it does go very much by a certain rhythm I suppose. But . . .
>
> *Nurse:* Yes I know that so very well myself. It's not just like that . . . You get up and, um you also eat at the ordinary times.
>
> *Patient:* Yes . . .
>
> *Nurse:* Well, it has to be like that.

Professional understanding of a patient's situation could, to an extent, become a kind of pseudounderstanding if elements from the professionals' world got mixed up with a general understanding of the patient's situation. Then, the boundaries between the two parties became blurred, and professionals unknowingly risked assessing the patient's possibilities based on their own values and situation. This was evident in the dyad above, in which the nurse assessed the patient's opportunities for exercising every day based on her own situation:

> *Nurse:* He . . . knew very well that he didn't get as much [exercise] as he really should, but he did have two small children and found it difficult to get out, and things like that. Yes, but I understood him very well because I've got small children myself. I know how difficult fitting it in is—if he wanted to attend classes of some kind. It is almost impossible, or at least very difficult.

When professionals relied on unverified hypotheses about person-specific difficulties, they were at risk of basing problem solving on pseudounderstanding. Unclear decisions seemed to be made, and the relationship faced the pitfall of ending in stagnation, conformity, and "coziness," which impeded professionals in helping patients to actively achieve a positive change. The professionals' use of sympathy to compensate for and balance the weaknesses of I-you-distant provider dominance thus appeared to be a rather unsuccessful way of "patching up" its negative consequences.

I-You-Sorted Mutuality

As an exception, a third form of relationship, I-you-sorted mutuality, was established in two dyads. This kind of relationship appeared to be initiated when one of the parties explicitly identified a clear problem in a specific patient's response to diabetes. Thus, "poor memory" because of painter's syndrome was a problem stated by the patient in one dyad and "not yet having accepted diabetes" was suggested as being a problem by the nurse in another. Instead of being covered up or diminished, feelings related to these problematic responses were exchanged and explored in this type of relationship. In addition, both sides showed their disagreement during the conversation.

In the first of the abovementioned dyads, the patient's poor memory was addressed effectively, as the patient and nurse exchanged different points of view and ideas about how to solve problems related to having a poor memory while changing from tablets to insulin treatment.

In the second of the abovementioned dyads, I-you-sorted mutuality appeared to be further developed during a conversation between the doctor and the patient (a 43-year-old woman with type 1 diabetes), which was witnessed by the nurse one day during ward rounds. The patient commented on the conversation, saying that it had given her "something to think about," whereas the nurse described it as "what benefited the patient most during the entire admission."

The doctor suggested that "blaming diabetes for everything" was one of the patient's responses to diabetes and thereby suggested that she should reconsider this response. The conversation was recounted in the words of the nurse, as follows:

She was just sitting there, crying and crying. She couldn't cope even if she did what we said. She couldn't cope with work. She couldn't, she couldn't, she couldn't. . . . Then he simply got angry with her: Now he did not want to hear any more about what she couldn't do. That was a lot of nonsense. There was only one thing wrong with her, and that was that she blamed everything on her diabetes.

Here, the doctor gave vent to his feelings by getting irritated—"he had had enough"—and he expressed his thoughts about "blaming it . . . for everything" as a way of telling the patient that she had attributed too much negative value to her diabetes. At first, the patient responded that "he was not the one who had diabetes." Yet the nurse made some important comments on this conversation, which revealed that she was aware that a relationship with certain qualities had been established. Although they had shown their disagreement during the conversation, she emphasized, "All three of us could laugh about it afterwards." By adding, "I did not have to go in and pick up the pieces afterwards," she accentuated the fact that typical ways of compensating for tensions had not been necessary in this relationship.

Being given "something to think about" apparently assigned the patient an active role in reappraising her position on diabetes; something that, according to the nurse, appeared to take place when the patient was alone: "Nothing much was said about it after-

wards. The patient needed time to 'digest' it." "She came back a few days later and said that she had thought about it and realized it was true."

The patient's comments on the conversation in a later interview showed that she valued the doctor's approach, which she described as follows:

I have also experienced something else there, that doctor, I experienced him differently. He saw me more like a whole person, not just the diabetes. It gives you something to think about. Because he said, "Now don't blame everything on the diabetes. Other things have happened in your life. You have started a new job and such like, right?" and this gave me something to think about because I have known deep down that this was part of it. [That it] had something to do with me feeling absolutely awful.

This patient was evidently able to cope with and profit from the direct way in which the doctor expressed his assumptions about her reaction to diabetes. This is also clear from a fact emphasized by the nurse, that "the patient asked afterwards to see this doctor every time in the out-patient clinic."

Difficult feelings and different points of view between the two parties were not just revealed. They also appeared to be addressed as important information about what needed to be explored and were thus constructively used to develop a reasoned response to difficulties in the patients' way of living with diabetes. The patients' insight into their difficulties in living with diabetes was, in addition, valued and challenged by professionals. The final judgment, however, appeared to be made by patients with the professionals functioning as guides. When assumed difficulties were mutually explored and verified, person-specific knowledge appeared to be cocreated by both parties working together. This kind of concrete knowledge seemed to represent a potential for change that could easily be exploited in decision making and problem solving.

DISCUSSION

These three types of relationship with their core category of Relational Potential for Change were important findings. They revealed the nature of patient–provider relationships in clinical practice and the differences between them, which, in turn, explained different ways of acknowledging and exploiting the relational potential for change of difficult feelings and different points of view. Shifts between relationships were explained as a consequence of professional responses to perceived tensions, and this was identified as an integral part of Relational Potential for Change. The frequent shifts from I-you distant provider dominance to I-you-blurred sympathy relationships by blurring or covering over the sources of tension was an unexpected finding of importance to practice. On the basis of our findings, we can conclusively connect I-you-distant provider dominance and I-you-blurred sympathy relationships, and the shifts between them, with failed problem solving in clinical practice. In contrast we can connect I-you-sorted mutuality with successful problem solving, as this relationship is clearly better for accessing the potential for change of exploring difficult feelings and different points of view. In the following discussion, we will further develop our conclusions and discuss why this last type of relationship is quite rarely established despite its advantages over the two other relationships.

Our findings suggest that relationships can be seen as frameworks made up of more or less conscious choices and expectations in terms of what would and could take place in approaching the difficulties of living with diabetes. The frameworks set overall principles for the "rules of the game," which were decisive for how patients and professionals exploited their potential. I-you-distant provider dominance advocated the principle of paternalism, valuing the potential of professionals at the expense of patients. I-you-blurred sympathy advocated the principle of equality, covering over the power difference between patient and professionals and, at the same time, neutralizing the potential of both parties. I-you-sorted mutuality advocated the principle of autonomy, allowing the potential of both patients and professionals to be used autonomously in a process that supported the patient in taking on the role of final problem solver. The relationships revealed patterns that patients and professionals appeared to fall into as a framework for meeting each other's different explanatory models (Kleinman, 1980).

The finding that I-you-distant provider dominance was the typical relationship confirmed frequent critical findings that a compliance paradigm (R. M. Anderson & Funnell, 2000b; Glasgow & Anderson, 1999; Hernandez, 1995; Mullen, 1997) was the normal starting point for nurses as much as for others. It is worth noting that nurses contributed to a narrow biomedical approach in the scope of problem solving by focusing on preconceived, typical problems instead of being open to the range of difficulties experienced by different patients. These findings are in line with Stubblefield's conclusion in a study based on interviewing nurses about their practices (Stubblefield & Mutha, 2002). Despite the fact that according to another study (Clark & Hampson, 2003), nurses have a stronger belief in the need for patient autonomy in diabetes self-management than other team members, this belief appears not to influence the relationships they establish with patients. These relationships can,

accordingly, be interpreted as lived paradigms, the existence of which passes unnoticed; actual practice might vary significantly from professionals' stated paradigm without professionals' discovering this inconsistency. Relationships might also play a role and explain the inconsistencies between professionals' explicit intentions and their behavior found in other studies (Freeman & Loewe, 2000; Paterson, 2001).

The reason that professionals in I-you-distant provider dominance relationships appeared to be rather disempowered in spite of the potential of their professional competence can be explained by patient resistance (in itself a form of power). The strength of this patient resistance was seen in our study from the fact that professional power frequently had to give way in the face of resistance, as has also been shown in reactance research (Fogarty, 1997; Meddaugh, 1990). The observed causes of this resistance were professional paternalism and a narrow focus on the medical disease, which can easily be perceived by patients as pure healthism, "the belief or cultural value that health is more important than all other rewards or satisfactions" (Nutbeam, 1986, p. 119; see also Zoffmann & Kirkevold, 2005).

The patients' perception that in this relationship, professionals did not bother to listen to them raised the question of whether professionals regarded the experience of patients with poor glycemic control as the wrong experience, which did not need to be taken into account. According to Blumer (1969), however, insight into patients' experience will always be of value, as it gives access to the basis on which patients construct their acts, regardless of whether they are successful or unsuccessful:

> The fact that the human act is self-directed or built up means in no sense, that the actor necessarily exercises excellence in its construction. Indeed, he may do a very poor job in constructing his act. He may fail to note things of which he should be aware, he may misinterpret things that he notes, he may exercise poor judgment, he may be faulty in mapping out prospective lines of conduct, and he may be halfhearted in contending with recalcitrant dispositions. Such deficiencies in the construction of his acts do not belie the fact that his acts are still constructed by him out of what he takes into account. (p. 64)

Blumer's (1969) point that patients' acts are self-constructed from the things they take into account means that the basic principle of I-you-distant provider dominance (compliance with professional expectations) can be regarded as questionable. Moreover, our findings illustrated the potentially negative consequences of patients' complying with professionals against their own conviction. This supports the point made by Thorne (1990) that noncompliance in chronic illness can at times even be regarded as constructive.

Although I-you-distant provider dominance relationships appeared to keep difficult feelings and different points of view between the parties at a distance, it became increasingly clear during analysis that this was possible only to an extent. For example, facing the tension arising from patient resistance made it difficult for professionals to maintain I-you-distant provider dominance. Covering over or exploring the sources of tension appeared to be two opposite ways of reducing the uncomfortable feeling it was causing. As concluded by Smith and Hart (1994), perceiving patient anger might pose a great threat to self and imply a risk of disconnecting with the angry patient. Our study indicates that professionals felt uncomfortable when tension arose and appeared to be aware of the danger of disconnecting with patients. This might explain the frequent shifts to I-you blurred sympathy. We do not interpret the fact that I-you-blurred sympathy seemed to be the nurses' preferred way of managing tension as being the result of thorough professional consideration. We see it, rather, as a spontaneous and human mechanism probably legitimized by support for equality as an overall moral principle, as mentioned previously.

The negative consequences of I-you-blurred sympathy in the form of neutralizing the potential of patients and professionals make it relevant to consider ways of handling power differences in relationships. Although some authors, such as Stang (1998), have proposed strategies for equalizing power differences between patients and professionals, the philosopher Løgstrup (1997) has argued that power differences in relationships are inevitable and should not be avoided. Instead, he stresses that an ethical demand exists for the more powerful party to use his or her power to the best advantage of the other. In line with this, Thorne (1999) has criticized a notion in nursing that always understands power as oppressive, with the consequence that nurses are reluctant to use their power in practice, education, and research. She has asked for awareness of the limitations of equality and, furthermore, has pointed to the possibility of using power with instead of power over the patient.

The tendency to overestimate similarities and avoid seeing differences in a sympathetic relationship appears to remove nurses' readiness to express their professional judgment of good and bad choices. This might imply a move toward consumerism (Roter & Hall, 1996), which regards patients as always being right and tends to avoid the use of professional potential. This emphasizes the importance of recalling Løgstrup's (1997) comment that the ethical demand is silent and is therefore not necessarily identical to the desire expressed by patients:

> If it were merely a matter of fulfilling the other person's expectations and granting his or her wishes,

our association would mean nothing less than—irresponsibly—making oneself the tool of the other person. Our mutual relations would no longer present any challenge but would consist merely in reciprocal flattery. (p. 21)

I-you-blurred sympathy tended to please patients. Clinical research, however, has shown that patients appreciate true awareness and do not necessarily find it important to be pleased by professionals. Paterson (2001) found that the very few professionals who actually practiced empowerment were not necessarily perceived as being "warm and tender" (p. 577). Patients more often perceived them as being "willing to really hear" (p. 577) them. Neither the distance between patient and professional boundaries in I-you-distant provider dominance nor the blurred boundaries in I-you-blurred sympathy relationships apparently allowed patients and professionals to discover and exploit their potential. The effect of blurred borders in I-you-blurred sympathy corresponds with a study that connects boundary confusion with projection and transference (Briant & Freshwater, 1998). Our conclusions support the authors of this study when they argue that nurses should be responsible for "holding" the boundaries and recommend mutuality instead of equality as an appropriate position for doing this.

In I-you-sorted mutuality, professionals took responsibility for holding the boundaries and managed tension by exploring its sources. This appeared to provide a framework for sorting out questions such as Who is the owner of the problem? Who is the owner of specific points of view? and Who is the owner of a specific difficult feeling? Successful problem solving in this type of relationship can be explained by the fact that professionals supported patients in their change process and worked on the basis of shared knowledge about problems and the patients' current considerations in constructing the acts to solve these problems. This basis was in contrast to the superficial "pseudounderstanding," which was a risk in I-you-blurred sympathy and which even diabetes patients with good glycemic control have perceived in relationships with their diabetes educators (Hernandez, 1996). Empowerment has already shown the benefits of letting patients explore instead of conceal their difficult feelings (R. M. Anderson & Funnell, 2000a). Our study highlights the additional potential for change in exploring different points of view. This supports Helman's (1985) suggestion that clinicians' knowledge of a patient's explanatory model might have a predictive value in determining future clinician–patient communication and patient compliance and satisfaction. Professionals in our study, however, did not generally have such knowledge, and we recognize the conclusion of Cohen et al. (Cohen, Tripp-Reimer, Smith, Sorofman, & Lively, 1994) that patients revealed greater access to and awareness of professionals' explanatory models than vice versa. The fact that I-you-sorted mutuality, despite its obvious advantages, was seen in only 2 out of 11 dyads in our study gives reason to consider the conditions needed to establish this relationship. One key condition was seen in 2 dyads when either the patient or the professional made a clear and explicit statement about current difficulties in the patient's life with diabetes. These statements appeared to pave the way for assigning active roles to both patient and professional in problem solving, as suggested in studies about relational responsibility (McNamee & Gergen, 1999). Few professionals, however, appeared to have the courage to approach conflicts openly, and they did not generally feel comfortable expressing their assumptions directly to patients. Indeed, the direct way in which the doctor in one of the dyads expressed his assumptions about the patient's difficulties with the disease could frighten some patients and have the opposite effect of that intended.

The three types of relationship with their core category of Relational Potential for Change provided insights into the content of relationships between patients and professionals in clinical practice and the way they approach the relational potential for change. We recommend that health care providers use the differences between these relationships in a critical analysis of their relationships with patients. Our findings also highlight the necessity to develop alternative ways of establishing I-you-sorted mutuality and inviting the expression of difficult feelings in a non-threatening way in change processes. Further research must comprise intervention studies on the importance and effect of establishing I-you-sorted relationships between patients and professionals in difficult problem solving.

REFERENCES

Anderson, R. M. (1995). Patient empowerment and the traditional medical model: A case of irreconcilable differences? *Diabetes Care, 18,* 412–415.

Anderson, R. M., & Funnell, M. (2000a). *The art of empowerment: Stories and strategies for diabetes educators.* Alexandria, VA: ADA.

Anderson, R. M., & Funnell, M. M. (2000b). Compliance and adherence are dysfunctional concepts in diabetes care. *Diabetes Educator, 26,* 597–604.

Anderson, R. M., Funnell, M. M., Butler, P. M., Arnold, M. S., Fitzgerald, J. T., & Feste, C. C. (1995). Patient empowerment: Results of a randomized controlled trial. *Diabetes Care, 18,* 943–949.

Blumer, H. (1969). *Symbolic interactionism.* Berkeley: University of California Press.

Briant, S., & Freshwater, D. (1998). Exploring mutuality within the nurse-patient relationship. *British Journal of Nursing, 7,* 204–211.

Clark, M., & Hampson, S. E. (2003). Comparison of patients' and healthcare professionals' beliefs about and attitudes towards type 2 diabetes. *Diabetic Medicine, 20,* 152–154.

Cohen, M. Z., Tripp-Reimer, T., Smith, C., Sorofman, B., & Lively, S. (1994). Explanatory models of diabetes: Patient practitioner variation. *Social Science & Medicine, 38,* 59–66.

European Diabetes Policy Group, I.D.F. (1998). A desktop guide to type 1 (insulin-dependent) diabetes mellitus. *Experimental and Clinical Endocrinology and Diabetes, 106,* 240–269.

European Diabetes Policy Group, I.D.F. (1999). A desktop guide to type 2 diabetes mellitus. *Diabetic Medicine, 16,* 716–730.

Fogarty, J. (1997). Reactance theory and patient noncompliance. *Social Science & Medicine, 45,* 1277–1288.

Freeman, J., & Loewe, R. (2000). Barriers to communication about diabetes mellitus: Patients' and physicians' different view of the disease. *Journal of Family Practice, 49,* 507–512.

Glaser, B. (1978). *Theoretical sensitivity.* San Francisco: University of California Press.

Glaser, B. G. (1992). *Basics of grounded theory analysis.* Mill Valley, CA: Sociology Press.

Glaser, B. G., & Strauss, A. (1967). *The discovery of grounded theory: Strategies for qualitative research.* New York: Aldine de Gruyter.

Glasgow, R. E., & Anderson, R. M. (1999). In diabetes care, moving from compliance to adherence is not enough. *Diabetes Care, 22,* 2090–2092.

Helman, C. G. (1985). Communication in primary care: The role of patient and practitioner explanatory models. *Social Science & Medicine, 20,* 923–931.

Hernandez, C. A. (1995). The experience of living with insulin-dependent diabetes: Lessons for the diabetes educator. *Diabetes Educator, 21,* 33–37.

Hernandez, C. A. (1996). Integration: The experience of living with insulin dependent (type 1) diabetes mellitus. *Canadian Journal of Nursing Research, 28,* 37–56.

Hunt, L. M., Arar, N. H., & Larme, A. C. (1998). Contrasting patient and practitioner perspectives in type 2 diabetes management. *Western Journal of Nursing Research, 20,* 656–676.

Kleinman, A. (1980). *Patients and healers in the context of culture.* Los Angeles: University of California Press.

Larme, A. C., & Pugh, J. A. (1998). Attitudes of primary care providers toward diabetes: Barriers to guideline implementation. *Diabetes Care, 21,* 1391–1396.

Loewe, R., Schwartzman. J., Freeman, J., Quinn, L., & Zuckerman, S. (1998). Doctor talk and diabetes: Towards an analysis of the clinical construction of chronic illness. *Social Science & Medicine, 47*, 1267–1276.

Løgstrup, K. E. (1997). *The ethical demand*. Notre Dame, IN: University of Notre Dame Press.

Lomborg, K., & Kirkevold, M. (2003). Truth and validity in grounded theory: A reconsidered realist interpretation of the criteria: Fit, work, relevance and modifiability. *Nursing Philosophy, 4*, 189–200.

McNamee, S., & Gergen, K. J. (1999). An invitation to relational responsibility. In S. McNamee & K. J. Gergen (Eds.), *Relational responsibility* (pp. 3–28). Thousand Oaks, CA: Sage.

Meddaugh, D. I. (1990). Reactance: Understanding aggressive behavior in long-term care. *Journal of Psychosocial Nursing and Mental Health Services, 28*, 28–33.

Mullen, P. D. (1997). Compliance becomes concordance. *British Medical Journal, 314*, 691–692.

Nutbeam, D. (1986). Health promotion glossary. *Health Promotion, 1*, 113–127.

Paterson, B. (2001). Myth of empowerment in chronic illness. *Journal of Advanced Nursing, 34*, 574–581.

Roter, D. (1987). An exploration of health education's responsibility for a partnership model of client-provider relations. *Patient Education and Counseling, 9*, 25–31.

Roter, D. L., & Hall, J. A. (1996). Patient-provider communication. In K. Glanz, F. M. Lewis, & B. K. Rimer (Eds.), *Health behaviour and health education* (2nd ed., pp. 206–226). San Francisco: Jossey-Bass.

Smith, M. E., & Hart, G. (1994). Nurses' responses to patient anger: From disconnecting to connecting. *Journal of Advanced Nursing, 20*, 643–651.

Stang, I. (1998). *Makt och bemyndigelse: Om å ta pasient-og brukerudvikling på alvor*. Oslo, Norway: Universitetsforlaget.

Strauss, A., & Corbin, J. (1998). Grounded theory methodology. In N. K. Denzin & Y. S. Lincoln (Eds.), *Strategies of qualitative inquiry* (pp. 158–183). Thousand Oaks, CA: Sage.

Stubblefield, C., & Mutha, S. (2002). Provider-patient roles in chronic disease management. *Journal of Allied Health, 31*, 87–92.

Thome, S. E. (1990). Constructive noncompliance in chronic illness. *Holistic Nursing Practice, 5*, 62–69.

Thorne, S. E. (1999). Are egalitarian relationships a desirable ideal in nursing? *Western Journal of Nursing Research, 21*, 16–29.

Williams, G. C., Freedman, Z. R., & Deci, E. L. (1998). Supporting autonomy to motivate patients with diabetes for glucose control. *Diabetes Care, 21*, 1644–1652.

World Medical Association. (1989). *The World Medical Association declaration of Helsinki*. Retrieved December 2, 2004, from http://www.fda.gov/oc/health/helsinki89.html

Zoffmann, V. (2004). *Guided self-determination: A life skills approach developed in difficult type 1 diabetes*. Aarhus, Denmark: University of Aarhus, Department of Nursing Science.

Zoffmann, V., & Kirkevold, M. (2005). Life versus disease in difficult diabetes care: Conflicting perspectives disempower patients and professionals in problem solving. *Qualitative Health Research, 15*, 750–765.

Zoffmann, V., & Lauritzen, T. (2006). Guided self-determination improves life skills with type 1 diabetes and A1C in randomized controlled trial. *Patient Education and Counseling, 64*(1–3), 78–86.

3.03

CONSTRUCTIVIST DESIGN

Understanding Patterns of Commitment

Student Motivation for Community Service Involvement

Susan R. Jones and Kathleen E. Hill

Increased interest in and attention to community service in both high schools and colleges suggests the importance of understanding *why* students participate in community service activities. The literature clearly supplies evidence for high-school students' interest and participation in community service. Data on high-school seniors from the 1970s through the 1990s suggest that 22–24% of seniors report consistent service involvement (Youniss, McLellan, & Yates, 1999). Results from a recent survey conducted by The National Center for Education Statistics of the U.S. Department of Education report that 83% of all public high schools had students involved in school sponsored community service activities and 46% offered service-learning opportunities in the classroom (Westat & Chapman, 1999). Findings from the 2000 survey of first-year college students report that just over 81% of students had performed volunteer work in the past year. However, only 22.7% of students indicated that it was important to participate in a community action program, and 30.9% indicated they

valued becoming a community leader (Higher Education Research Institute, 2001).

While research suggests that participation in community service in high school predisposes students to continue their involvement in college (Astin & Sax, 1998; Astin, Sax, & Avalos, 1999; Berger & Milem, 2002; Vogelgesang & Astin, 2000), only 23.8% of first-year students in the 2000 survey sample indicated that the chances were very good that they would participate in volunteer or community service work (Higher Education Research Institute, 2001). These data raise questions about why high-school students are volunteering, the motives high-school and college students provide for involvement, and the relationship between high-school community service and college participation.

Using Selznick's (1992) theory of social participation, which distinguishes between core (connected to identity, motivated by values, and more consistent in nature) and segmental (connected to extrinsic factors, motivated by personal interests, and sporadic) participation, findings from a study on a national sample of high-school students suggested that student interests and personal goals, values, and normative environments

Susan R. Jones is assistant professor and Kathleen E. Hill is a doctoral candidate at The Ohio State University.

influence high school-seniors' participation in community service (Marks & Kuss, 2001). Further, in a study that followed these same students into their college years, the extent to which these students persevered as participants in community service after high school appears to be related to patterns established in high school as well as whether or not students have internalized their reasons for participation (Marks & Jones, in press). This investigation builds upon the work of Marks & Kuss, and Marks and Jones by using a constructivist approach to understand student perceptions of their patterns of participation from high school to college. An earlier study conducted by Serow (1991) demonstrated that qualitative methodologies resulted in far greater depth of understanding of the phenomenon of motivations for community service than "requiring them [students] to choose among prepackaged responses" (p. 552).

Although some research suggests that patterns identified in high school are typically carried over into college (Astin, Sax, & Avalos, 1999; Berger & Milem, 2002; Marks & Jones, in press), little is known about changes in motivations from high school to college or the meaning students attribute to their motivations. Several studies have focused on college student motivation for involvement in community service activities. Typically, reasons have been organized into the categories of altruistic, egoistic, and obligatory (Berger & Milem, 2002; Fitch, 1987; Marotta & Nashman, 1998; Serow, 1991; Winniford, Carpenter, & Grider, 1997). In one study when asked why they were involved, 80% of student respondents cited personal satisfaction from helping others, 56% gave as a reason a perceived requirement through a course or organization, and 54% indicated a sense of responsibility to correct social and community problems (Serow, 1991). Berger and Milem concluded that understanding students' motivations to serve is related to producing positive outcomes associated with community service as well as increasing the numbers of students involved in such activities.

A few studies have connected motivation to participate in community service to the identity development process for both high-school and college students (Rhoads, 1997; Youniss & Yates, 1997). In both studies, community service contributed to the process of the development of a sense of self and social responsibility. Involvement in community service engaged students in developing greater knowledge of self through meaningful work with others, which resulted in the development of both a personal and collective identity (Rhoads, 1997; Youniss & Yates, 1997). Further, Youniss and Yates found that high-school student interest in continuing community service depended upon factors such as the level of reflective thinking and family and peer influences on volunteering. They concluded, "High school commitment cannot be linked simply to adult behavior without taking account of such communities that encourage and shape the direction individuals take in their identity development" (Youniss & Yates, 1997, p. 115).

Baxter Magolda (2000, 2001), in her work on the development of self-authorship, described a process in which young adults move from external, formulaic definitions of self to an internal foundation of identity that integrates relationships with others. She speculated that well-designed service-learning programs provide the opportunities for the development of self-authorship in students. Applying the work of Baxter Magolda to Selznick's (1992) theory of social participation suggests the possibility that core (internally motivated by values) or segmental (externally motivated by personal interests) participation may be influenced by where students are in the identity process.

The purpose of this study was to uncover the meaning students make of their participation in and motivations for community service and to develop an understanding of students' perceptions of their own patterns of participation in community service. In particular, the relationship between high-school involvement and college participation was explored. The guiding research questions for this study were: What are students' reasons for participation in community service in high school? What are students' reasons for participation in community service (or not) in college? How do students explain and understand the relationship between high-school and college involvement? To what do students attribute differences/changes in their motivations as well as experiences?

METHODOLOGY

The exploratory focus of this study led to a constructivist approach to the design. A constructivist approach "assumes a relativist ontology (there are multiple realities), a subjectivist epistemology (knower and respondent cocreate understandings), and a naturalistic (in the natural world) set of methodological procedures" (Denzin & Lincoln, 2000, p. 21). This approach was well-suited to the study because the aim of our inquiry was understanding students' construction of meaning and their perceptions about their own patterns of participation. A constructivist approach requires a close relationship between researchers and participants to elicit from students their own stories told in their own words (Charmaz, 2000). As the qualitative counterpart to the quantitative study examining patterns of participation (Marks & Jones, in press), the design emphasized the construction of an emic understanding of this phenomenon and data generated from the words and perspectives of the students to tell their stories with precision and appropriate depth. All decisions regarding methods for this study were anchored in a constructivist approach to the design (Charmaz, 2000; Crotty, 1998).

Procedures

Sampling. Purposeful sampling (Patton, 1990), or sampling for information-rich cases, was used in this study for both the identification of college and university participants and then for the selection of student participants at each institution. Letters of invitation were sent to all Directors of Community Service programs at Ohio Campus Compact schools (*n* = 39). The Ohio Campus Compact is a consortium of Ohio colleges and universities established to support the development of social responsibility and citizenship initiatives on member campuses. We bounded the sample by Ohio Campus Compact institutions because these schools represented a diverse array of institutions and presumably, by virtue of their membership in Ohio Campus Compact, a stated commitment to providing opportunities for public and community service to students. Directors were informed about the purpose of the study and asked to serve as gatekeepers by nominating four students for participation. We also asked directors to send us materials about their campus that provided data about community service programs and campus culture. Eleven directors responded that they were interested in participating.

Because of our interest in information-rich cases (Patton, 1990) we narrowed the group of participating institutions to six campuses. Criteria for sampling included institutional diversity (i.e., size, classification, rural/urban, commuter/residential), variety in reporting line and institutional structure for community service programs, and variety in student composition. These criteria led to a final sample of six institutions—3 urban, 3 rural; 3 large (over 15,000 students), 3 small (under 3,000 students); 3 private, 3 public; 2 liberal arts, 1 Catholic, 2 research, and 1 state university.

The next stage of sampling involved the recommendation by the directors at each of the six participating institutions for student participants in the study. Each director was asked to nominate four students, all of whom had participated in community service in high school, two of the four who had continued their involvement in college, and two who had discontinued service in college. For the purposes of this study, we broadly defined community service as any form of service (curricular or co-curricular) performed in an off-campus community context and for which payment was not received. Additional criteria for participant selection included year in school and a demographic profile that mirrored the general student population at that institution. This strategy resulted in a sample of 12 students participating in community service in

college and 12 who had discontinued their high-school participation in college; 9 males and 15 females; ranging in age from 18–25 years and over 50% of junior or senior class status; 17 white, 5 African American, 1 Asian Indian, and 1 Philippino American; and a diverse array of academic majors including English, history, political science, biology, art, and physical therapy. Thus, the total sample consisted of 24 students (4 from each of 6 participating institutions) who agreed to participate in on-campus interviews for the study (see Appendix for complete list of participants). Students were contacted by letter with a formal invitation to participate, information about the nature of the study, and a request for scheduling an on-campus interview. Follow-up email messages facilitated the communication and scheduling process.

In-depth Interviews

The primary strategy for data collection was in-depth, semistructured interviewing (Patton, 1990) on the campuses of each student. The interview protocol was developed and piloted with undergraduate students at the home institution of the researchers. Adjustments to the nature and order of questions were made based upon the piloting of the interview protocol. Questions focused on the nature of community service involvement in high school and college, the reasons students attributed to their participation, and the meaning they attached to community service.

One interview with each student was conducted. The two researchers conducted all interviews. Interviews generally lasted from 45 to 90 minutes. All interviews were audiotaped and transcribed verbatim. All except three interviews were conducted on the campus of each student in a room designated by the director of community service programs. Due to scheduling or last minute conflicts, three interviews were conducted on the telephone.

Document Review and Campus Visits

In addition to in-depth interviews with each of the students, we were interested in understanding the campus context in which students' decisions about community service participation were enacted (Janesick, 2000; Jones, 2002). To this end, we examined materials sent to us from the directors of community service programs. These included campus admissions materials, office brochures and organizational charts, student newspapers, and strategic planning documents. We also viewed web sites for each of the institutions. We were interested in how institutional commitment and support for community service is evidenced in campus publications as well as assessing institutional culture and campus norms for service. During our campus visits, we toured the campus, visited the community service programs offices, and spent time talking with each director. We used the insights gleaned from reviewing these materials and touring campuses as a context for understanding students' experiences. Both researchers made notes in an analytic journal to record observations and insights from these activities.

Trustworthiness

Several strategies were utilized to assure the trustworthiness of findings. Both researchers independently read and coded all the data. Meetings to compare notes and discuss the results of analysis followed this process. A detailed narrative serving as a summary of findings was sent to all participants for member checking (Lincoln & Guba, 1985). And last, an inquiry auditor (Lincoln & Guba, 1985) read all the transcripts and reviewed the analytic and interpretive work of the researchers.

Data Analysis

All data were analyzed using the constant comparative method characteristic of grounded theory methodology (Glaser & Strauss, 1967; Strauss & Corbin, 1990). As a constructivist study, the analytic process moved from more concrete codes to abstract themes and categories that are reflective of the meaning participants attach to their experiences, rather than the generation of objective truth (Charmaz, 2000). This required data analysis to proceed not as a linear process of concrete to abstract, but in a more cyclical manner by constantly returning to the data with new questions and ideas until a narrative emerged that described the essence of experience for study participants. In constructivist ground theory, this essence of experience is described as the core story (Charmaz, 2000; Strauss & Corbin, 1990).

FINDINGS

Core Story: External and Internal Influences on Participation and Commitment

Because all the participants in this study were involved in community service in high school, the core story describes a process of meaning-making about the role of service in their lives and the relationship between participation and commitment. For those for whom community service was consistent, the process mirrored a movement away from external influences on participation and an emerging commitment. For those participants who discontinued their community service once in college, service was motivated largely by external factors, requiring little investment of them, making fewer claims on their sense of self, and resulting in

limited commitment. Participant understandings of service then were mediated by whether or not service was more internally or externally motivated and, hence, how service was integrated with an evolving sense of self.

High-school involvement was almost always motivated by external factors, such as the influence of family and friends or a school requirement. Participants, even when it was required, enjoyed community service because it made them feel good about themselves and enabled them to spend time with their friends and family. With the exception of those whose service was connected to their churches or religious beliefs, there was little evidence that participants thought much about why they were engaged in service. This was particularly true when service was required rather than voluntary.

As participants made the transition to college, new environments, the opportunity to make decisions on their own, and the identity development process complicated the process of meaning-making. For some participants, community service was relegated to a lower priority as they negotiated a new collegiate environment. For others, now out from under the influence of parents, teachers, or a requirement, interests took them in different directions, among which community service was not included. And for a few others, community service was evolving into an important part of their identities. They had developed a passion for a social issue, a more active stance toward social change, and an emerging commitment to social responsibility. Regardless of the path taken in terms of continued participation in community service, all participants were engaged in a process of meaning-making that involved reflecting on their identities and their place in the world. For some, community service contributed to this process, and for others it did not. The themes that form the core story and findings are elucidated below.

Influences in the High School Years: Supports and Barriers to Participation

Family Role Models

Family members' encouragement heavily influenced participation in community service in high school. Active parents, aunts, and grandparents who modeled the importance of involvement in the community introduced community service to participants. David reported, "My parents got us involved, . . . and that gave me the role model to get involved." Emily spoke of her aunt with whom she spent a lot of time growing up and "she would always try to involve me in everything she did. She was big on volunteering." Robert learned early on from his mother about caring for others. Growing up in "the projects," he watched his mother give their food to neighbors who had less than they did. Robert noted, "My mom, if it were not for her community involvement, I would not be as involved as I am. She is a strong advocate for the poor. She fights for the poor . . . and pushed me to get involved." Several participants grew up on farms and learned an ethos of service that required everyone to do their part in completing chores and taking care of families and neighbors. However, despite encouragement and role modeling from family members, many of these participants did not always think about what they were doing as community service. Instead, it was simply "something my family does" and yet, had become what was perceived as an important "family tradition."

Religious Foundations

Church commitments and religious beliefs also influenced participation in high school. Several participants were active in youth ministry, leading retreats and teaching religious education classes, which they perceived as community service. Brad, commenting on his involvement in community service, articulated, "My youth ministers and people involved in church, . . . they were the ones that pushed me a lot." Similarly, Carol noted that it was her director of religious education at her church who "really is the one who got me coming to things and got me involved and really active." Rob recalled growing up in a family guided by a set of religious principles that "taught that the ideal is that it is better to give to those less fortunate. So even going Sunday and putting my twenty-five cents into the jar every time, that was probably a beginning."

Socializing with Peers

Friends played a big role in high-school participation in service. Essentially, if friends were involved in service, then these students were more likely to participate. Service became the vehicle for fun and spending time with friends. Friends also influenced involvement in school clubs and organizations that required service. While involvement in school clubs or organizations like National Honor Society or Key Club introduced participants to service, that was not usually the primary motivation for joining the organization—it was more about being around friends and the social benefits of meeting new people. Ann emphasized that she only participated in service if she was part of a group in which "we had to fulfill requirements that way."

Required Service: Mixed Blessing

Many participants noted that required service in high school produced increased numbers of students involved in community service, presumably accomplishing some good. However, almost without exception, students noted that required service quickly took on a negative connotation for themselves as well as their friends. They were clear: as soon as they met the requirement, they were moving on to other activities. Participants' comments on required service ran along two paths. The first was, if community service is required, it is not community service. And the second was, because service was required, they only thought about meeting the requirement and not why they were performing service.

Michael articulated, "If someone's telling you that you have to go do community service, . . . I would tend not to see that as community service." In his view the "desire has to come from within." Another participant likened required community service to a "sentence" which carried a terrific negative stigma. Alternatively, Emily noted that she and her friends enjoyed their community service "because we weren't required to do it." Speaking about her high-school requirement, R. noted "A lot of people either found it difficult or, not exactly bad to do, but more difficult to find the time to do it." When service was required, several students emphasized, "once the requirement is met, the service will end."

A prevalent theme with regard to required service was that because the emphasis was on the requirement, students never had to think about what they were doing. Grace viewed her required service as "just another homework assignment." As a result of the requirement, she was "turned off to participating in college." Likewise, R. articulated, "I never really thought about 'what does [service] do for me?' other than the fact that it was on the resume, but because it was also a requirement, I never had to think 'what if we didn't have this requirement?'" Destiny participated in high school because she was told to, but suggested, "If I knew what I was doing, what the reason was, and I knew the person or the organization it was helping, . . . maybe that would make me feel better about doing it" [community service].

High-school Environments

Community service was highly visible at Catholic high schools. Carol proudly recited her Catholic high-school motto "Omnibus Caritas"—in all things charity. Brad knew that the priests at his school were interested in graduating strong moral leaders and therefore exposed students to social issues through community service. Many schools took an approach to community service through blood drive or food can competitions. By and large, however, students commented that at best, community service was one of many activities that were important at their high school (sports often being the most important) and, more often, was not encouraged or visible in the classroom or as an extracurricular activity. A few students commented positively on teachers who took the time to explain the importance of community service, inspired students to get involved, and connected service to larger social issues. For example, Kathy noted, "In my classes, I had really great teachers, really wonderful enlightened people who challenged me, 'Why do you think that's wrong? Go out and find out.'"

Several participants talked about engaging in service, whether required or not, because teachers told them it would build their resumes and help them with their applications for scholarships and college. They were also aware that engaging in community service increased popularity among their peers and garnered them recognition and notoriety from important school and city officials. Erica unabashedly emphasized that her high-school community service included working on the mayoral campaign because "I just wanted to know the Mayor. I wanted to be cool with the Mayor!"

High School Constructions of Self and Service

External Motivations

These factors identified (i.e., family and friends, required service, the high-school environment) influenced students' constructions of self and service in their high-school years. For most of the participants, they were involved in community service in high school because it was fun. In addition, participants commented on the good feeling they got about themselves through helping others—several referred to service as a "big ego boost." Bob referred to this as the "warm, gushy feeling" he received when engaged in service. Participants felt good about what they were accomplishing through service as well as enjoyed the appreciation and recognition they received for their involvement. As Carol indicated:

> We did it because we felt good after we did it, and we helped so many people; . . . just to see the responses from people and how grateful and how it really affected them even it if was something small, . . . just to see appreciation and gratitude and the smiles on their faces and the thanks in their eyes. That was one of the things that motivated me to keep doing it [community service].

For the most part, reasons for involvement in service were more external than internal. Service existed outside the individual and was motivated more by external factors such as friends, family, requirements, and recognition. Service was understood by many as "anything done for which you are not paid." Most students recognized that service also involved helping others out, but thought of it more as a nice thing to do, rather than as contributing to larger societal concerns.

Internal Motivations

For those participants who were more consistently involved in direct service in high school and attended a high school that supported active involvement in community service, service was an eye-opening experience that caused reflection on their own backgrounds, responsibilities, and potential for improving life for others. As Carol recalled, "I think it [service] made me grow as a person and I know it really changed me. . . . It exposed me to other people and populations, other socioeconomic statuses, and it really opened my eyes and broadened my scope." Similarly, Casey reflected, "I think basically it [service] is good, makes me feel good, and I think I had a sense that it helped people. I don't know if I had a sense of how much it helped people yet; . . . I think in high school I just kind of sensed that it was a good thing to do. It was right, . . . and it helped me grow as a person." Kathy left high school with the idea that she was committed to community activism rather than community service, which she perceived as "too rah rah. . . . I don't think community service is the way to solve everything. I think community activism is. If you change the problems at the root, then you don't have to serve." As these students approached college they brought with them some initial understandings of personal responsibility for social problems, interest in working toward a greater good beyond individual interest, and a growing commitment to the role of community service in their lives.

Influences in College: Supports and Barriers to Participation

Transition to College and a New Community

The transition from high school to college was a big one for nearly all the participants and, in many cases, of a magnitude for which they were unprepared. Those involved in community service, as well as those not involved, commented on this transition in terms of learning to manage their time, establish priorities, and find their way around a new environment. Several commented on the rigor of the academic program compared to high school and the need to actually study in college. Ann commented, "It is hard to organize your time because you have so much more work." Similarly, Mary noted, "Your whole first year all you are doing is learning how to set your priorities." Nearly every student not currently involved in community service in college mentioned time and setting priorities as a deterrent to their continued participation in service. In addition, every participant, with the exception of two, was balancing significant employment obligations, with more than half working over 11 hours a week.

An awareness of the need to manage the transition to college caused some participants to put community service "on hold" until they figured out college life. Of the twelve students currently not participating in community service in college, all articulated that involvement in community service was not possible in the earlier years of their college experience. However, those who had been consistently involved in high school spoke positively about resuming their community service participation in college once they got settled. Dwight referred to this as "getting back into the community service loop" because he had "gotten out of the habit" in college.

Part of the transition for students involved getting to know a new community—both the college environment as well as the neighborhoods in which community service typically took place. Several participants at larger schools talked about the "bureaucracy" of big institutions and trying to navigate these places—both in terms of survival as well as learning where community service opportunities might be found. R. emphasized: "My first quarter, I didn't do any service. It was me versus the school!" Similarly, Destiny emphasized that on her mind were questions like, "How am I going to adjust?. . . I had too many other worries to think about community service, . . . making sure I was ready, because I couldn't turn around and go home." Victoria noted, "At such a big campus, bureaucracy is always there."

Participants also commented on the difficulty of getting around a new town or city and figuring out where community service opportunities might be found. In high school, because she knew the area, Emily would "just get in my car and go" to community service agencies. But in college she indicated she couldn't easily volunteer because she didn't "know the places around here very well." Students attending college in urban areas also discussed fear in venturing out into unfamiliar neighborhoods. April mentioned that she was "scared" to go into the city. Brad mentioned this also, but then went on to say that his unfamiliarity was perhaps a positive thing, because he did not carry the stereotypes others had about going into "bad neighborhoods in the city."

Role of Peers in Participation

As in high school, friends and peers were mentioned by many participants as influencing participation. However, this was more prevalent from those not participating in college than from those who were involved. Those not currently involved in service speculated that had their friends been involved in community service, then the likelihood of their involvement would have increased. In addition, encouragement from other students makes a difference; as Rob mentioned, "I don't know a whole lot of the people who

are involved, especially the upperclassmen. And I think if I knew some of them, saw them on a regular basis, and they said, 'hey, you should come to this,' kind of reinforcing that it was available, that would help." Those students who were consistently involved in college talked about volunteering with friends as fun, but also that this peer group shared values and social concerns.

Institutional Influences on Participation

The visibility and accessibility of community service programs influenced participation. Students at the smaller institutions were much more aware of community service opportunities than those at large institutions. At the liberal arts institutions, students spoke about the wide range of activities in which involvement was possible. In addition, these students talked about "all-campus" events with a community service or social issue focus. So while not all students chose to take advantage of community service opportunities, these students knew they were available and were also more likely to be involved in other activities. Many of the students attending smaller institutions commented that at their college, "it is easy to get involved." This was not the case for students from large universities.

Students from larger institutions consistently mentioned that it was hard to find the community service opportunities on campus. Several students noted that they knew there was a great need in the community for student volunteers, but that they did not observe strong support on campus for such efforts. Casey commented "I think there are a lot of opportunities in the community, but I don't see really strong support for it here." Likewise, Mark reflected, "Well, it is such a big university. I think there are a lot of people who do put a lot of emphasis on community service, but I don't know if the University as one voice has been like, 'service is important.'" Fraternities and sororities provided opportunities for sporadic involvement for some students at both small and large institutions, although service was not the primary reason for joining and was often constructed as a requirement of membership.

Community service received some visibility at institutions where scholarships are given for community service work. Students all commented on the irony of "providing payment for service" and their perception that scholarship recipients were only performing service to maintain their scholarships rather than for the good their volunteering might do. Michael commented, "They'll do their 30 hours and won't serve again." The paradox of this kind of institutional "support" for community service is that, according to these participants, it produces negative outcomes. R. was a recipient of such a scholarship and acknowledged, "I honestly believe that the scholarship, for a lot of college students, is a struggle with mandatory service. It is hard to see the focus of the service when they tack a number to it, rather than linking it to quality for the server or the served."

Programmatic Support for Participation

Specific programs and activities were mentioned by students as having a big influence on their involvement in community service. Several students mentioned activities fairs at the beginning of the school year as a time when community service opportunities were visible. In most cases, students recalled picking up printed materials but usually did not follow up on opportunities. They indicated that had there been some follow-up and help in getting them directly involved, they might have been more likely to get involved. Students from several campuses talked about orientation programs that included community service components. One institution took a select group of students to Washington, D.C., for several days of community service. This program included both direct service as well as visits to Capitol Hill to learn about public policy implications. This made a big impact on students' thinking about service in general as well as their own involvement. Kathy referred to her trip to DC as "the most amazing experience ever, . . . it just totally opened my eyes and made me reaffirm how I want to go about living my life and how I want to continue community activism for as long as I live."

Alternative Spring Break programs were also mentioned as "life changing" learning opportunities. Michael described his week in Appalachia as "the most incredible week of my life." Carol spoke of a broadened perspective from her spring break trip to New York City where she received "a taste of what it was like to work with the homeless, what it was like to be immersed in these situations and just kind of help out." Both of these programs included small groups of students who received training to prepare them for their experiences and on-site reflection with the faculty and staff who traveled with the students. These were the most structured community service opportunities we heard about from students and also, not coincidently, the experiences about which the students spoke with the greatest enthusiasm and insight in relation to their interest in and commitment to community service.

College Constructions of Self and Service

External Influences

Only three students made clear that they had absolutely no interest in community service in college and their high-school participation was entirely externally driven. They had participated in high school as a resume builder for college applications and because it was required. They indicated that they had reaped the intended benefits of service in high school and saw no need to get involved in college. Erica conveyed this poignantly in her discussion of community service connected to college scholarship applications, "I tried to get involved in everything so I could reap the benefits. . . . I'm now going to college, . . . so I really don't see it as beneficial anymore because I already got what I was striving for."

Further, those college students who were no longer involved in community service described themselves as the "typical apathetic, lazy, and uncaring college student." Jen boldly declared, "Hey, I am lazy. I like to sit around. . . . I think students in general are lazy; . . . I mean, in concept, the whole community service thing is a nice thing, but I am too lazy to get out and do it." Dwight commented, "I am probably at the point where I just want to relax and not do nearly as much as I did during high school." Christy commented more generally that "some kids here, this is typical wherever you are, they haven't grown up enough not to be self-centered, they're just not willing to go out of their way to help somebody else. It's easier to just sit at home and watch T.V. and call your friends." Thus, for these students, community service has no relationship to how they see themselves, nor did their high-school participation, motivated by external factors, produce any fertile ground for commitments to grow.

Internal Influences

Those who continued their community service involvement in college offered reasons for continuing with community service that reflected a movement in the direction of greater focus on others, rather than solely on the benefit it was bringing to them. Brad conveyed that in the past he had been "blinded by being the center of attention, more so than how I was actually helping people." Laura explained:

> Right now, my main reason for doing community service is so I can give back to people who may be less fortunate than I am and to show them that there are "normal" people out in the world who do care. . . . I have learned that wherever you go, there will always be people facing the same problems, and these people are just like myself and others, but they have bigger obstacles to overcome on their journey through life.

Several participants connected to their own past personal experiences as recipients of services or feeling marginalized and hence felt a strong sense of responsibility to give back to the community. Rachel emphasized several times in our conversation, "I remember what it felt like when I needed help." Bob recalled, "My mother was 18 when she had me, . . . a young mother and two kids, . . . no where to go, . . . going from welfare to working, so I just think helping people was a good feeling because people did that for me."

Several students directly connected service with self. David commented on the reciprocal nature of service and self in observing, "whatever I do gets reflected back really quickly." And Victoria reflected, "I like being known for what I am passionate about." Casey commented on the potential of community service, "It's a way to grow and learn yourself . . . and understand what other people go through. I think it is very important to put yourself in other people's shoes and see from their perspective. People would be much better to one another if they did that, and I think community service helps." However, as R. pointed out, in order for service to be connected with self, "you have to get yourself immersed in it." Mary reiterated, "You only know it is important if you are a part of it." Those who continued their service began to see who they were (and who they wanted to become) and community service as connected and interrelated.

Evolving Understanding of Service

A couple of students talked about the importance of linking community service to social change or community activism. Because voting is frequently identified as a measure of civic engagement, we asked students whether or not they had voted in the recent election. Of note, 75% of those currently participating in community service voted, while fewer than half of those not participating had voted. Politically active as president of the college Democrats on campus, Robert emphasized that through his work in the community and his life experiences, he learned the importance of taking a stand and speaking up. He declared, "I have a passion for individual rights, whether it is civil rights, gay rights, student rights. I believe in social change because without those elements, nothing can change. You must be out there in the forefront to effect change. It begins with you and starts with you." These participants in college were developing commitments to social issues through connecting a sense of self with their involvement in community service.

DISCUSSION

Based upon our conversations with all of the participants, patterns of participation in community service are mediated by involvement influences and motivations in high school, the role of peers, and by how closely community service is connected to an emerging sense of self. For the most part, patterns of participation begun in high school carried over into college. For those who were involved more sporadically in high school, primarily for external reasons

such as meeting a requirement, service involvement was discontinued in college. For those for whom service was more consistent in high school and motivated by family and school encouragement, service took on more personal motivations and altruistic interests, and thus the likelihood was greater that involvement would be continued in college. Further, early personal experiences that cultivated empathy also influenced continued participation in community service and an ethos of caring for others. In addition, if teachers or family members took the time to explain the reasons for community service or introduced the larger social context in which service is provided, then service took on a more meaningful role and encouraged a developing commitment in college.

The Importance of Service as Personally Meaningful

This ingredient, service as personally meaningful, seemed to be the foundation of the participation and commitment process from high school to college. Those who continued their service after high school were those who were also involved in voluntary service, were more likely to have been involved in direct service in the community, and who had teachers who helped explain why community service was important. Continued involvement in community service provided a unique opportunity to reflect on one's identity and what is important in one's life. Beginning in high school and then further developed in college, participation in service introduced participants to others who might or might not share the same life experiences and to a diverse array of complex social issues. Continued community service provided the impetus for students to think through their responsibility for making life better for others whose lives had been impacted by conditions such as poverty, sickness, and unemployment. Service influenced how they see the world and their place in it. It brought clarity about the self that perhaps few other life experiences had afforded, especially in the context of education. Initial commitments to integrating service into a sense of self were made. Many of the participants were quite passionate about their community service work and articulated a commitment to continued action.

For community service to be meaningful, a relationship between the service and evolving constructions of self was present. The research in this area suggests patterns in identity development that revolve around the processes of individuation and differentiation, separation and connection, or agency and communion (Baxter Magolda, 2000; Belenky, Clinchy, Goldberger, & Tarule, 1986; Erikson, 1968; Perry, 1970). Our research suggests that patterns of participation in community service may mirror patterns of identity development in moving from external definitions to an internal authority. Baxter

Magolda (2000) speculated, "Connection to others in service contexts can create dissonance with perspectives adopted from external sources" and "offers the opportunity to acquire an internal sense of self and to struggle with the relationship of agency and communion" (p. 154). Our findings support the idea that how individuals integrate service with self and make sense of their community service experiences may be influenced by where they are in the identity development and self-authorship process. These findings are also consistent with the research of Rhoads (1997), who explored students' evolving sense of self through community service work.

Intersection of Identity Dimensions and Community Service Participation

The results of this study also suggest the significance of looking at the intersections of identity dimensions such as race, gender, social class, and religion when exploring student constructions of community service and their experiences with service. For example, several of the African American students, although classified as non-participants in community service, were really quite involved in their communities. However, giving back to the community is so much a part of how they see themselves and their cultural heritage that it was impossible for them to pull out that one aspect of who they are and hold it up for scrutiny. Several of the men in the study engaged in service through what they described as more competitive than relational ways. They mentioned blood drive and food can competitions or earning points for their fraternities through service involvement. However, with increased involvement in service, a voice of care entered into their dialogue, reflecting an interest in learning how to care with others (Noddings, 1984; Rhoads, 1997). Students with strong religious beliefs or faith traditions engaged more readily in community service because they perceived service as the morally right thing to do. While community service on college campuses is frequently the activity of white, middle-class students (O'Grady, 2000), this is not always the case—and will become less so if community service is encouraged and supported for a greater diversity of students. Our research suggests that how students understand, construct, and engage in community service is influenced by the socially constructed identities they bring to the experience.

A number of the community service participants spoke persuasively and eloquently about their personal connections to service because of their own experiences as recipients of service or experiences with being marginalized as, for example, "the only Asian American in my school." This is consistent with the findings of a study on the factors that influence individuals to lead lives of commitment to the common good (Parks Daloz, Keen, Keen, & Daloz Parks, 1996). While over half of those studied by Parks Daloz et al. reported experiencing marginality, these individuals were also "able to transform the pain of their marginality into a deepened capacity for compassion and a strength of identity and purpose" (Parks Daloz et al., p. 73). In our study, community service both enabled this transformation among participants who had experienced marginality, as well as created the conditions for others to experience marginality, perhaps for the first time, and thus, cultivate empathy and compassion for those whose life circumstances they did not share.

Patterns of Participation: The Relationship Between High School and College

The connections between high-school and college participation in community service uncovered in this study are consistent with previous research (Astin, Sax, & Avalos, 1999; Berger & Milem, 2002; Marks & Jones, in press). In other words, those who are consistently involved in high school will likely continue participation in college, with a deepening commitment to service and greater understanding of the motivations beyond themselves for engaging in service. High-school experiences with community service that resulted in continued participation were most often voluntary, encouraged by family or friends, and made meaningful by teachers or others who helped explain why community service was important.

Conversely, those who are sporadically involved in high school, motivated by external factors, are unlikely to sustain participation in college, given their perceptions of required service, the demands of adjusting to college, and the absence of peer encouragement. Required service in high school led many participants to drop service as soon as it was no longer required. For these students, service was constructed as an obligation, with little thought given to the meaning of the service itself. During the high-school years, this negative perception of service was somewhat attenuated by viewing participation as an opportunity to spend time with friends.

Implications

The results of this study provide policy implications for requiring community service. The participants in this study were adamant about the negative, albeit unintended, consequences of requiring community service. Policies requiring service, crafted with the best of intentions, became a deterrent to continued involvement and any development of commitment to civic and social responsibility. Requiring service led to a singular focus on simply meeting the requirement with little consideration of the purpose of the service. Further, "community" service constituted everything from sweeping the floors of the high school to raking a neighbor's yard—not typically the work that produces the intended benefits of social and civic responsibility. This suggests that if the quality of required service were high (i.e., students performing meaningful service), the negative outcomes may be reduced. However, as typically constructed, required service in high school led many of the participants to drop community service as soon as it was no longer required. To increase the likelihood of continued service after required high-school service, students' involvement in voluntary and direct service could be encouraged, with opportunities provided for understanding why community service is important.

The results also suggest implications for practice. If colleges and universities are interested in accomplishing the positive outcomes associated with community service, then active, intentional steps must be taken. College faculty and administrators can enhance the likelihood of community service involvement by making opportunities visible and easily accessible as well as helping students negotiate demands on time. If colleges and universities are interested in engaging greater numbers of students in meaningful community service, attention must be focused not only on those who will most likely continue, but also on those most likely to "get out of the habit" when transitioning from high school to college. Those students who have been consistent participants in service in high school will most likely seek out these opportunities at college. However, more sporadic participators, most often for externally motivated reasons, will need extra encouragement from peers, administrators, and faculty to make initial connections for involvement.

Very few participants talked about either service-learning courses or structured reflection opportunities. It seemed clear that when someone helped students make sense of why they were doing what they were doing, it was more meaningful to them and their commitments deepened. Students who had participated in more intense community service activities (i.e., Alternative Spring Break programs) were much more articulate about the meaning and significance of their work. This is consistent with the research of Eyler and Giles (1999), who found that the quality of the service work makes a difference to producing positive outcomes. Community service programs then would be well served to design and implement activities that are consistent with the research on the principles of high quality service (Eyler & Giles, 1999).

Further research on patterns of participation would continue to add depth and breadth to an understanding of the connections between community service participation, commitment, and identity development. Continued study of the relationship between community service and self-authorship is needed. The results of this study suggest the importance of research exploring the intersections between dimensions such as race, social class, gender, and religion on the constructions of self and service. In addition, this study only touched upon the influence of campus cultures and normative environments in relation to community service participation. While students commented on their perceptions of the college environment, more detailed assessments of campus culture would create a picture of those institutional environments that promote community service involvement. Further, additional research examining the relationship between student age and the developmental influences on participation and commitment is warranted. Because of the variability in age of participants in this study, it was inappropriate to speculate on a possible relationship.

Results released from the 2001 Freshmen Survey indicate that 82.6% of first-year students reported performing volunteer work in their senior year of high school. However, only 24% indicated that chances are very good that they will participate in community service in college (Bartlett, 2002). The results of our research provide an explanation for this apparent discontinuity in patterns of participation. If the majority of high-school students are involved in community service because it is required, in a sporadic fashion, and with limited explanations for the purposes of their participation, then most students will discontinue their community service in college, because it is not perceived as important or personally meaningful. Participation in community service will more likely grow into commitment if it is direct, of high quality, and integrated into an evolving sense of self. With encouragement from friends and a nudge from university faculty and student affairs educators, the possibilities of developing internal motivations for service and for connecting service to students' sense of self could be realized. More intentional efforts, in both high school and college, to engage students in meaningful community service will not only increase the likelihood of students sustaining the participation begun in high school, but also developing internal motivations to serve and then to develop the commitment required for active citizenship. In fact, several students articulated that society's success depended upon students' abilities to understand their commitments to the communities in which they live. Kathy made sense of her community service experiences this way: "I think I have the means, the capability, and the intelligence to affect social change, so I have to do it; . . . there's no way I can just sit and watch things happen."

Appendix. Patterns of Commitment in Community Service

Name	HS Type	Service in HS	College Type	Service in College	Age	Vote?
			Participants in College*			
1.Brad	Catholic	Sporadic**	Catholic	Sporadic	19	No
2. Laura	Public	Consistent	Catholic	Consistent	20	Yes
3. Bob	Public	Consistent	Liberal Arts	Consistent	22	Yes
4. Mary	Catholic	Consistent-required & vol.	Liberal Arts	Sporadic	19	Yes
5. Robert	Public	Consistent	State	Consistent	25	Yes
6. Carol	Catholic	Consistent	State	Consistent	22	Yes
7. Michael	Public	Sporadic	Research	Consistent	23	Yes
8. R.	Catholic	Consistent-required & vol.	Research	Consistent	19	No
9. Casey	Public	Sporadic	Research	Sporadic	22	Yes
10. Victoria	Catholic	Consistent	Research	Consistent	21	No
11. David	Public	Consistent	Liberal Arts	Consistent	20	Yes
12. Kathy	Public	Sporadic-required & vol.	Liberal Arts	Consistent	18	Yes
			Non-Participants in College*			
1. April	Public	Consistent	Catholic	—	19	Yes
2. Grace	Public	Consistent-required	Catholic	—	18	No
3. Ann	Public	Sporadic-required	Liberal Arts	—	19	Yes
4. Dwight	Public	Sporadic	Liberal Arts	—	??	??
5. Erica	Public	Consistent	State	—	23	Yes
6. Christy	Public	Sporadic	State	—	20	No
7. Destiny	Catholic	Consistent-required & vol.	Research	—	20	No
8. Rachel	Public	Consistent	Research	—	19	No
9. Jen	Public	Sporadic	Research	—	19	No
10. Mark	Private-Christian	Sporadic	Research	—	24	Yes
11. Rob	Public	Consistent	Liberal Arts	—	19	Yes
12. Emily	Public	Sporadic	Liberal Arts	—	21	No

*Names are pseudonyms and/or chosen by participants.

**Sporadic and consistent were identified by the participants as the terms that best describe their participation in high school and college.

REFERENCES

Astin, A., & Sax, L. (1998). How undergraduates are affected by service participation. *Journal of College Student Development, 39* (3), 251–263.

Astin, A., Sax, L., & Avalos, J. (1999). Long-term effects of volunteerism during the undergraduate years. *Review of Higher Education, 22*(2), 187–202.

Bartlett, T. (2002, February 1). Freshmen pay, mentally and physically, as they adjust to life in college. *Chronicle of Higher Education*, p. A35.

Baxter Magolda, M. B. (2000). Interpersonal maturity: Integrating agency and communion. *Journal of College Student Development, 41*(2), 141–156.

Baxter Magolda, M. B. (2001). *Making their own way: Narratives for transforming higher education to promote self-development.* Sterling, VA: Stylus Publishing.

Belenky, M., Clinchy, B., Goldberger, N., & Tarule, J. (1986). *Women's ways of knowing: The development of self, voice, and mind.* New York: Basic Books.

Berger, J. B., & Milem, J. F. (2002). The impact of community service involvement on three measures of undergraduate self-concept. *NASPA Journal, 40*(1), 85–103.

Charmaz, K. (2000). Grounded theory: Objectivist and constructivist methods. In N. K. Denzin & Y. S. Lincoln (Eds.), *Handbook of qualitative research* (2nd ed., pp. 509–536). Thousand Oaks, CA: Sage.

Crotty, M. (1998). *The foundations of social research.* Thousand Oaks, CA: Sage.

Denzin, N. K., & Lincoln, Y. S. (2000). Introduction: The discipline and practice of qualitative research. In N. K. Denzin & Y. S. Lincoln (Eds.), *Handbook of qualitative research* (2nd ed., pp. 1–28). Thousand Oaks, CA: Sage.

Erikson, E. (1968). *Identity, youth, and crisis.* New York: Norton.

Eyler, J., & Giles, D. E., Jr. (1999). *Where's the learning in service learning?* San Francisco: Jossey-Bass.

Fitch, R. T. (1987). Characteristics and motivations of college students volunteering for community service. *Journal of College Student Development, 28*(5), 424–431.

Glaser, B., & Strauss, A. (1967). *The discovery of grounded theory: Strategies for qualitative research.* Chicago: Aldine.

Higher Education Research Institute. (2001). *The American freshman: National norms for fall 2000.* Los Angeles: University of California at Los Angeles.

Janesick, V. J. (2000). The choreography of qualitative research designs: Minuets, improvisations, and crystallization. In N. K. Denzin & Y. S. Lincoln (Eds.), *Handbook of qualitative research* (2nd ed., pp. 379–399). Thousand Oaks, CA: Sage.

Jones, S. R. (2002). (Re-)Writing the word: Methodological strategies and issue in qualitative research. *Journal of College Student Development, 43*(4), 460–473.

Lincoln, Y. S., & Guba, E. (1985). *Naturalistic inquiry.* Thousand Oaks, CA: Sage.

Marks, H. M., & Jones, S. R. (in press). Community service in the transition: Shifts and continuities in participation from high school to college. *Journal of Higher Education.*

Marks, H. M., & Kuss, P. (2001). Socialization for citizenship through community service: Disparities in participation among U. S. high school students. *Sociological Focus, 34*(3), 377–398.

Marotta, S., & Nashman, H. (1998). The generation X college student and their motivation for community service. *College Student Affairs Journal, 17,* 18–31.

Noddings, N. (1984). *Caring: A feminine approach to ethics and moral education.* Berkeley: University of California Press.

O'Grady, C. R. (2000). *Integrating service learning and multicultural education in colleges and universities.* Mahwah, NJ: Lawrence Erlbaum Associates.

Parks Daloz, L. A., Keen, C. H., Keen, J. P., & Daloz Parks, S. (1996). *Common fire: Leading lives of commitment in a complex world.* Boston: Beacon Press.

Patton, M. Q. (1990). *Qualitative evaluation and research methods* (2nd ed.). Newbury Park, CA: Sage.

Perry, W. G. (1970). *Forms of intellectual and ethical development in the college years: A scheme.* Troy, MO: Holt, Rinehart, & Winston.

Rhoads, R. (1997). *Community service and higher learning: Explorations of the caring self.* Albany, NY: State University of New York Press.

Selznick, P. (1992). *The moral commonwealth: Social theory and the promise of community.* Berkeley: University of California Press.

Serow, R. (1991). Students and voluntarism: Looking into the motives of community service participants. *American Educational Research Journal, 28*(3), 543–556.

Strauss, A.,& Corbin, J. (1990). *Basics of qualitative research: Grounded theory procedures and techniques.* Newbury Park, CA: Sage.

Vogelgesang, L. J., & Astin, A. W. (2000). Comparing the effects of community service and service-learning. *Michigan Journal of Community Service Learning, 7,* 25–34.

Westat, R. S., & Chapman, C. (1999). *Service-learning and community service in K-12 Public Schools.* Washington, DC: U.S. Department of Education.

Winniford, J. C., Carpenter, D. S., & Grider, C. (1997). Motivations of college student volunteers: A review. *NASPA Journal, 34*(2), 134–146.

Youniss, J., McLellan, J. A., & Yates, M. (1999). Religion, community service, and identity in American youth. *Journal of Adolescence, 22,* 243–253.

Youniss, J., & Yates, M. (1997). *Community service and social responsibility in youth.* Chicago: The University of Chicago Press.

3.04

REALIST DESIGN

The Dignity of Job-Seeking Men
Boundary Work among Immigrant Day Laborers

Gretchen Purser*

ABSTRACT: Drawing on interviews and comparative ethnographic fieldwork in two day labor hiring sites (a street corner labor market and a "regulated" day labor worker center), this article examines the discourses through which Latino immigrant day laborers make sense of, and find dignity within, their ongoing quest for work. My findings reveal a clear pattern of "boundary work" along the center/street divide, wherein each group of day laborers asserts its dignity and masculinity by repudiating what they construe to be the feminine submission exemplified by the other group. I argue that gender both shapes and is shaped through the articulation of these moral boundaries and show how workers' struggle to attain dignity—in this case, via strategies of social differentiation and distinction—can act against the formation of a collective identity.

KEYWORDS: Day labor; immigrants; work; masculinity; symbolic boundaries.

Immigrant day laborers, known as *jornaleros* or *esquineros* in Spanish, have sparked considerable controversy in cities across the country.[1] Now estimated to total well over 100,000 nationwide, these poor, predominantly undocumented men are a ubiquitous presence on urban street corners, a visible indicator of labor market casualization, flawed immigration policy, and the state's failure to enforce even minimal regulation at the bottom of the labor market. While residents and merchants express concern over "quality of life" issues in "besieged" neighborhoods, worker and immigrant rights advocates raise concerns about the men's vulnerability to abuse at the hands of their drive-by employers. An increasingly common, if contentious, local policy response has been to establish an alternative to curbside hiring in the form of quasi-regulated—but nonetheless informal—day labor worker centers, where labor-starved employers are encouraged to hire work-hungry job seekers (Esbenshade 2000; Fine 2006). More

* University of California, Berkeley

Gretchen Purser is completing her doctorate in sociology at the University of California, Berkeley. Her research interests lie at the intersection of changing employment relations, urban poverty, and the labor market experiences of the formerly incarcerated. Her dissertation is a workplace ethnography of the formal day labor industry in Oakland and Baltimore.

[1] *Jornalero*, or "day laborer," denotes the occupation's peculiar dimension of time, whereas *esquinero*, or "street corner man," denotes its peculiar dimension of space.

than doubling in number since the year 2000, there are now 63 such centers throughout the nation run by community organizations, city government agencies, or church groups (Valenzuela et al. 2006). Viewed by many scholars as "the most promising policy intervention to restore the floor under the day labor market" (Theodore, Valenzuela, and Melendez 2006, 408), these day labor centers now coexist, in numerous communities, with curbside hiring sites.

While we know a good deal about the ways in which this informal labor market operates (see Valenzuela 2003), we know very little about the cultural meanings day laborers assign to their work and the role these might play in shaping where and how they go about the relentless task of searching for it. Taking as its starting point Everett C. Hughes' (1994, 61) proposition to study "the social and social-psychological arrangements by which men make their work tolerable, or even glorious," this article explores the discourses through which these most marginalized of workers, perched precariously on the fringes of the labor market, conceive of self-worth.

Drawing on interviews and ethnographic data gathered at two day labor hiring sites—a street corner labor market (International Avenue) and a "regulated" day labor program (the Bay Area Worker's Center [BAWC])—I find that immigrant day laborers engage in a process of "boundary work" (Lamont 2000), wherein they draw on gendered imagery to distance themselves from each other and reaffirm their masculinity.[2] Whereas job seekers on the street construct the men who go to the center as lazy and dependent (evoking the specter of the "welfare queen"), the men at the center view those on the street as engaged in a desperate act of selling their bodies (evoking the specter of the "prostitute"). By repudiating what they view as the feminine submission exemplified by the other group, members of each group constitute themselves as engaged in an appropriately masculine, dignified pursuit of work. These findings reveal how the everyday "struggle to achieve dignity and attain some measure of meaning at work" (Hodson 2001, 4) can act against the formation of a collective identity, with important implications for research on, and organizing efforts among, immigrant day laborers.

LITERATURE REVIEW

The existing literature on the informal day labor market predominantly employs survey methods to document the scope of the phenomenon, the demographic characteristics of the workforce, and the characteristic pay and working conditions of this market (Theodore, Valenzuela, and Meléndez 2006; Valenzuela 1999, 2003; Valenzuela et al. 2006). Scholars using an ethnographic

approach have analyzed the social organization underpinning this informal trade (Malpica 2002) as well as the social needs men fulfill through their presence on the corner (Turnovsky 2006). Given the nearly exclusive focus on grasping the basic contours of how this market is organized, there are no qualitatively detailed studies addressing day laborers' subjective experiences. We thus know very little about how day laborers perceive, make sense of, and cope with the precarious labor market in which they take part.

A notable exception is the work by Walter, Bourgois, and Loinaz (2004), which broaches these questions by exploring the "embodied social suffering" of immigrant day laborers who face injury, illness, or disability. The authors highlight the central role played by gender in shaping the social and psychological experience of injury. They argue that "cultural constructions of patriarchical masculinity among undocumented Latino day laborers organize their sense of self-worth and define their experience of poverty and social marginalization" (2004, 1160). Successfully crafting a male, hardworking identity, the authors suggest, "becomes a bulwark for maintaining self esteem" in the face of poverty, insecurity, and social marginalization (2004, 1162). Overlooked in this analysis, however, are the specific practices and discourses through which immigrant day laborers constitute this masculine, hardworking "self."

This article investigates these everyday practices and discourses, revealing a consistent pattern of "boundary work" through which immigrant day laborers distinguish themselves from other immigrant day laborers. This article thus not only contributes to the empirical literature on the pertinent topic of day labor, but also contributes to the literature on symbolic boundaries, defined as the "conceptual distinctions made by social actors to categorize objects, people and practices" (Lamont and Mólnar 2002, 168). In *The Dignity of Working Men*, Michèle Lamont (2000) draws on interviews with working class men in France and the United States to reveal that moral standards, as opposed to economic status, are the key principles of their evaluations of worth and perceptions of social hierarchy. Lamont's influential work has focused scholarly attention on morality as an "alternative measuring stick" by which individuals of low social and economic status judge themselves vis-à-vis others (2000, 147). However, her work fails to address how gender shapes, and is—in turn—shaped through, the repeated articulation of these moral boundaries. Lamont's consideration of gender appears to be only indirect, in so far as it is part of a broad "cultural repertoire" that influences moral standards. As scholars

---

[2] All proper names of individuals, places, and organizations are pseudonyms to ensure anonymity.

have noted, there was no "serious attempt at understanding how the term *men* in her book title and in the lives of her subjects functions to shape the very identities and social processes she sets out to explore" (Raissiguier 2002; see also Carr 2001).

Paying critical attention to the gendered dimensions of worker's discourses, I argue that men's struggle for self-worth—the positioning of oneself as privileged on a symbolic hierarchy—cannot be divorced from the "struggle over masculinity" (Connell 1995). My comparative data reveal that the cultural construction of moral boundaries goes hand-in-hand with the cultural construction of gender: both involve the identification and repudiation of a contextually dependent "other." I highlight men's assertion of moral boundaries through the invocation of gender, but in so doing reveal what Leslie Salzinger (2003, 25) has theorized as the "basic emptiness" of gendered categories, their extraordinary "malleability and variability." While soliciting work from the curbside is constructed as "masculine" by one set of actors, it is viewed as "feminine" by another. What both groups of day laborers share in common is a compulsion to frame their job-seeking practices as dignified and appropriately masculine via internecine strategies of social distinction and differentiation.

I begin by describing the two fieldwork settings, a street-corner-based labor market and a day labor worker center. I then describe my research methodology. Next, I turn to my two case studies, highlighting the discourses through which each group of day laborers conceives of self-worth. Finally, I conclude by drawing out the implications of these findings for scholarship on both day labor and symbolic boundaries.

RESEARCH METHODOLOGY

Day Labor Hiring Sites

As a major traffic thoroughfare with on and off ramps to two of the region's major freeways, International Avenue cuts through the residential, commercial, and cultural heart of the city's Latino immigrant community.

As an epicenter of battles over gentrification, the historically working-class neighborhood bisected by International Avenue is now a curious mixture of urban chic and urban blight: homeless sidewalk vendors hawk their wares outside high fashion boutiques, *taquerías* and *pupuserías* hug either side of trendy upscale restaurants, old run-down apartment buildings and single room occupancy hotels stand shoulder-to-shoulder with new luxury loft condominiums.

Yet what is most striking about International Avenue is that it moonlights as a modern day, drive-through "shape-up," an informal day labor hiring site

where employers come to handpick and hire immigrant day laborers.[3] From six in the morning until as late as six in the evening, hundreds of men eager for work line the side of the street, occupying every street corner for more than a half-mile span. The job seekers are dressed similarly in comfortable clothes: sweatshirts layered over button-down cotton or flannel shirts over white t-shirts, jeans or carpenter paints, tennis shoes or work boots, and baseball caps. Many of the men wear clothes splattered with paint, a detail which on this street serves as a mark of distinction, a status symbol of sorts, signifying jobs completed and a willingness to work (Parker 1994, 65; Valenzuela 2003).

The majority of these job seekers are homeless.[4] Some spend their nights sleeping in alleyways, nearby parks, or under the freeway. Others opt for a bed in one of several homeless shelters scattered throughout the city. Still others are lucky enough to find shelter in a car or to team up with a half dozen other immigrant men and cram into a studio or one-bedroom apartment. These men live in a sea of material deprivation, albeit one with ebbs and flows depending on the season, the economy and, as one man resolutely pointed out to me, *"por suerte"* [sheer luck].[5]

Action on the street is frenzied and unpredictable. There seem to be no rules governing this open-air market, no institutionalized mechanisms for either distributing work in a "fair" or organized manner or ensuring that employers respect workers' rights or pay a minimum wage. As is typical of all casual labor markets, there is a chronic labor surplus, making the competitive tension on the street quite palpable. Given this stiff competition, individual workers try to maximize their

---

[3] The term *shape-up* refers to the traditional hiring system along the waterfront. As depicted in the 1954 award-winning film, *On the Waterfront*, starring Marlon Brando and directed by Elia Kazan, longshoremen seeking jobs "shaped-up" each morning at the docks and waited for a hiring foreman to blow his whistle and pick out the men for that day's work. Variously described as inefficient, archaic, brutal, degrading, a spawning place for crime, and a system that promotes chronic unemployment among longshoremen, the "shape-up" hiring system persisted on the New York docks until 1953 (Larrowe 1976). Shape-up is now sometimes used to refer to informal day labor hiring sites.

[4] This is in glaring contrast to Valenzuela's findings on the population of immigrant day laborers in Los Angeles, only 6 percent of whom are believed to be homeless (Valenzuela 1999). While Valenzuela's report compared the situation of day laborers in southern California to that of day laborers in "other industrialized countries," my research indicates that the situation in southern California cannot be taken as indicative of the United States as a whole. These divergent findings beg further analysis of the way in which the lived experience of homelessness shapes the day labor market and day laborers' subjective understandings of their work.

[5] Just like the Algerian subproletariat studied by Bourdieu (2000, 221), immigrant day laborers, who "liv[e] at the mercy of what each day brings," highlight what happens when life is turned into what they perceive to be a "game of chance."

chances of attaining work by appearing the cleanest, strongest, and most assertive. "It's all about how you look, how you carry yourself," explained Efraín, a 25-year-old from Guatemala, as he flexed his youthful muscles in a purposefully exaggerated display of strength. Like Efraín, several day laborers point to some aspect of masculine "bodily capital" (Wacquant 1995) —build or appearance—as key to finding work in this informal casual labor market.[6] Dozens of men stand right on the curb, even several feet into the street, their right arms extended outward, similar to a gesture made by a hitchhiker. When a car or truck slows down, even if it is merely to obey traffic lights, workers on the corner rush over to the vehicle and begin a scene they will repeat dozens, even hundreds of times that day. Men huddle around the vehicle, each trying to be noticed by raising their hands higher in the air, similar to eager students who know the answer but can hardly wait to be called on. Usually this scene lasts but a minute, not unlike a fast-food pick-up at a drive-through window. Even as the truck pulls away with the chosen few tucked inside, a few men still scurry along, pleading with the employer through the side window to add just one more to the day's work crew.

The presence of these curbside job seekers, on International Avenue as well as similar street corners throughout the country, has sparked considerable controversy. The Bay Area Worker's Center (BAWC) was established over a decade ago by city officials as a practical—albeit contentious—response to ongoing complaints and concerns about day laborers from residents, merchants, and immigrant rights advocates. Located nearly a mile away from the hiring site along International Avenue, the nonprofit BAWC was thus founded to serve as an alternative to the street corner labor market.

The BAWC is a hybrid organization, serving as many as five loosely integrated functions. First, it operates as a labor market intermediary, an organization that brokers the relationship between job seekers and employers. The BAWC not only *facilitates* the meeting of supply and demand, advertising "energetic and dependable" workers to employers, but also *regulates* it by establishing collectively agreed-on rules to monitor and oversee the hiring of day laborers. These rules aim to curb labor exploitation as well as allocate jobs in such a way so as to abolish competition. To that end, the center requires both workers and employers to register, heightening accountability in an otherwise informal and often anonymous exchange, and pay the established minimum wage, which was $10 per hour at the time I conducted this research. Unlike the lottery system that is used in some day labor worker centers, the BAWC distributes work on a rotational basis according to a formal list that job seekers sign each time they come to the center in search of work. They

are dropped to the bottom of the list if they go out on a job for five hours or more, break a rule and are suspended from the program, or fail to sign the list two days in a row.

The second function of the worker center is service delivery. BAWC staff members view service delivery as a key component of the center's mission to provide day laborers with what they advertise as a "dignified gathering place" to meet potential employers and provide the necessary support for laborers to achieve economic independence. Thus, the BAWC offers restroom facilities, free food, clothing distribution, shelter referrals, and educational, social, medical, and legal services. Through the BAWC, job seekers have access to ESL classes, job training workshops, a physical and mental health clinic, and legal representation to recover unpaid wages.

Worker organizing constitutes the third function of the BAWC. To this end, staff work doggedly to promote a sense of collective empowerment among day laborers, encouraging them to take a leadership role in setting the policies and priorities of the center. The BAWC thus provides the space and resources for day laborers to meet on a weekly basis to collectively grapple with the challenges they face. They also do "outreach" to the day laborers on International Avenue: informing them of their rights and distributing booklets to encourage them to write down the days and hours they work, along with information on the employer, so as to make it easier to recover unpaid wages, if need be.[7] The fourth function served by BAWC is advocacy. The staff and leadership of the BAWC play an active role in both educating the wider public about day labor and advocating on behalf of the poor and immigrant communities, particularly at the local level, but also at the state and federal levels.

Finally, the BAWC functions as a day shelter of sorts, offering a relatively quiet and safe space where people can pass the time. When describing this function of the BAWC, a staff member described it as a "community drop-in center or homeless campsite."

Housed in a run-down trailer, the BAWC attracts anywhere between 50 to 100 men daily, only a handful

---

[6] During the Great Depression, in what became known as the Bronx Slave Market, African American women from Harlem would line up on street corners and wait for White, primarily Jewish, women to pick them up for a day's work as domestic helpers. Similar to the purported importance of masculine bodily capital among contemporary immigrant day laborers, "Black women [in the Bronx Slave Market] with the most calloused knees would be hired first," seeing as that "worn knees indicated that the women were accustomed to scrubbing floors" (Sullivan 2001).

[7] National survey data suggests that immigrant day laborers are regularly denied payment for their work. Almost half of all day laborers in the sample experienced at least one instance of wage theft in the 2 months prior to being surveyed (Valenzuela et al. 2006).

of whom will succeed in finding work. With a few exceptions, all are Latino immigrant men, roughly identical to the men on the street in terms of demographic, living arrangement, and economic status.[8] They arrive as early as six in the morning, sign up on the list, and wait for an indeterminate length of time, sitting on the cement or on a few scattered folding chairs that are strewn throughout the parking lot. On a typical day, several people can be seen sleeping below the trailer, curled up in tattered blankets, venturing out now and again for a trip to the port-a-potty or in search of food. Others chat and tell jokes with friends, pick up stones and toss them into the metal waste can, or discretely sell cigarettes for 25 cents apiece. Next to the trailer, enclosed by a chain-link fence, is a soccer field owned and operated by the city's park district. Lacking the extraneous funds needed to pay the fee to use it, many of the day laborers peer longingly at the empty field, mere spectators of an image which confronts them as a symbol of exclusion.

Data Collection and Analysis

The data for this study were gathered over a period of five months in 2001. The data collection involved ethnographic fieldwork and interviews with individual day laborers. I spent 2 to 3 days per week in *each* field site throughout the period of research, sometimes combining visits to both sites in the course of a single day. My role in each site, however, varied.

I began my fieldwork on the street as an observant pedestrian. After gaining some familiarity with the faces and features of the street, I approached the men on the corner, explained that I was a student studying day labor, and asked if I could hang around and watch as they sought work. Most field notes were drawn from the vantage point of one of two street corners on opposite ends of the more than half-mile span where men seek work. To integrate myself into the life of the BAWC, I combined my role as researcher with that of volunteer. This was advantageous in that it enabled me to participate in a wide variety of the center's activities, including, but not limited to, canvassing city neighborhoods with flyers promoting the center, answering phone calls, attending meetings and public hearings on day labor, filling out job-intake forms, accompanying participants to homeless shelters and other social service establishments, and gathering food from the food bank. Despite these various activities, I spent the majority of my time at the center hanging around, casually talking with the job seekers and jotting down notes, which I used to jumpstart the more elaborate field notes that I typed in the evenings. Although all were aware of my status as researcher from the university, it is nonetheless probable that many workers in this site associated me with the center's staff.

I conducted a total of 22 in-depth, loosely structured interviews with day laborers, 10 of whom regularly sought work out of the center and 12 of whom regularly sought work on the street. I asked a series of open-ended questions that focused on the objective and subjective dimensions of the men's work experiences and job-searching strategies. Substantial attention was devoted to understanding how the men made sense of their precarious position on the margins of the labor market. Respondents ranged in age from 18 to 52. All were male immigrants from Latin America, with roughly two-thirds (n = 15) from Mexico and the remaining third (n = 7) from Central America (Guatemala, Honduras, El Salvador, and Nicaragua). At the time of the interviews, respondents had been living in the United States for as long as 16 years to as little as 2 months, with an average length of 3 years. Since most respondents spoke little or no English, all but two of the interviews were conducted in Spanish. Four of the 22 interviews were tape recorded and later transcribed and translated. For those men who expressed discomfort with the recorder, I took detailed notes during and again after each interview. I used an inductive approach to data analysis, coding my field notes and interviews by theme (Glaser and Strauss 1967).

The fact that day laborers spend much—often all—of their day *waiting* facilitated my ability to attain in-depth interviews in two ways. First, many of the men I approached with a request for a one-on-one interview were eager to find ways of passing the time and were, thus, quite willing to talk with me. Second, although the majority of interviews lasted about an hour, many others carried on informally for several hours. While most of the interviews were conducted at the sites where my respondents waited for work, providing me with ample opportunity to watch their expectations ebb and flow each time a job prospect arose, eight of the interviews took place during walks around the neighborhood or over coffee or lunch at a nearby corner store or cafe.

There are two identifiable methodological limitations of this study, both of which stem from the particularities of this informal, casual labor market. First, my sample undoubtedly reflects a selection bias, given that the day laborers I interviewed and most often observed were those who, on that particular day, had been unsuccessful in their attempt to find work. Valenzuela (2003, 329) also makes note of this methodological challenge and suggests the need for rigorous sampling frameworks that account for "fluid or

---

[8] Given that it is a publicly supported center, the homogeneity of the job seekers is remarkable. During the course of my research, I saw five non-Latinos come through the center: two women (one White, one Black) and three men (two White, one Black).

impossible to identify universe populations." Second, given the unpredictable nature of this labor market and the fact that it is what one of my respondents referred to as a "rolling" (*rolando*) population—meaning that you do not necessarily see the same people everyday—my relations with several of the men were fleeting, one-time encounters, as opposed to the durable relations in the field that ethnographic research uniquely makes possible. For a discussion of similar dynamics in the study of panhandlers, see Lankenau (1999, 293).

Research Findings

For both groups of intermittently employed men, *how* they search for work is seen to be a measure of their character, a mark of their masculinity, and an indicator of their moral worth. Both groups see their own pursuit of work as dignified and, to varying degrees, state that they would feel "shame" to find themselves in the other's shoes, using gendered language and imagery to distinguish and distance themselves from the other. On the one hand, the day laborers on the street corner emphasize their perceived autonomy, skill, assertiveness, and work ethic, and differentiate themselves from those at the center whom they view as dependent, deferential, incompetent, and lazy. The day laborers at the center, on the other hand, differentiate themselves from those on the corner whom they see as desperate and self-compromising.

View from the Corner

Toward the end of our conversation, as we sipped down the last few drops of our coffee, Margarito handed me his business card. Simple and to-the-point, the card listed his name, cellular phone number, and the occupational title "handyman." When I asked him to describe how he felt about searching for work on the street, he explained:

> The work is hard and you never know what you're going to get, but I can come and go when I want and I can negotiate the pay. The truth is that I have autonomy. If a guy comes by here looking for someone to work for $6 an hour, I can say "never." I'm a hard worker and know I can earn more than that. So, if you're ambitious, a little creative, and you work hard, it's really good on the corner because you can start building up clients who come back for you regularly. I have five clients now.

Although Margarito, who is originally from Guatemala and has been in the United States for 8 years, was the only day laborer who used the term "client" to refer to his drive-by employers, his emphasis on autonomy and negotiation was something that I heard over and over again throughout the course of my research.[9] While nearly all of the day laborers said

that they were looking for a steady job that pays well, they nonetheless perceived International Avenue to be paved with economic opportunity. The street corner labor market offers to those with "ambition," "creativity," and undoubtedly patience, the prospect—however illusory and improbable—of steady employment.

This *perceived* autonomy—exemplified by Margarito's stylized self-presentation as a freelance entrepreneur (Valenzuela 2001)—is one basis on which the men on the street assess their self-worth and construct a sense of dignity (Duneier 1999; Gowan 2000; Hodson 2001). However, both autonomy and the ability to negotiate the pay and responsibilities of the job are constrained by material necessity. Thus, this portrayal of themselves as free and autonomous individuals engaged in an entrepreneurial activity is repeatedly contradicted by their actions. Because of the stiff competition on the street as well as the paucity and unpredictability of jobs, several of the men stated that, rather than coming and going as they please, they frequently stand out on the street for more than 12 hours at a time, hesitating to go to the nearest public bathroom out of fear that they may miss their one and only opportunity to get work that day, not to mention their one and only chance to achieve the illusive goal of a stable job. As much as they highlighted their ability to negotiate wages, the men I interviewed also noted that they are frequently bargained down from the wage that they had desired by one of their aggressive curbside competitors.

Other men drew on the "fleeting" nature of day labor work and the incessant, unpredictable rotation of jobs to highlight the breadth and superiority of their skills (Davis 1959). In this respect, they renounced widespread depictions of themselves as unskilled laborers, scavenging for crumbs at the bottom of the labor market. They asserted a sense of dignity in their ability to *"hacer todo"* (do everything), regardless of their lack of formal training and credentials. As Eduardo, a 31-year-old from Veracruz, Mexico, explained:

> Sometimes the employers pull up here and ask me if I know how to, for example, drywall. I say, "Look, *patron*, I'm a dry waller, a construction worker, a carpenter, a window installer, a landscaper, a mover, a roofer, a plumber, a painter. I can do everything." On the corner, I've had jobs of all types. Each day is something different. I know people look at me standing out

---

[9] In his analysis of the structure and informal organization of the street corner labor market, Malpica (2002) argues that two different hiring practices take place on the corner. *Esquineros* can either be hired by "regular" employers, with whom they have made previous arrangements, or "unclaimed" employers. Malpica argues that "deference at the corner is granted to those employed by 'regular' employers."

here and think I'm a miserable guy, but I know . . . and God knows . . . I have more skills than them. I can do everything. [In a resolute tone] I tell the boss "hire me" and if he is not happy with my work, he does not have to pay me.

This emphasis on skills was echoed in the statements made by a small group of a half-dozen day laborers who attended a meeting organized by the staff of the Bay Area Worker's Center to combat the increasing prevalence of police harassment on International Avenue. After discussing the possibility of creating (unofficial) photo identification cards for the day laborers on the street in an attempt to curb police harassment, one of the staff members proposed that each worker's occupational specialty or profession be printed on the IDs. Muffled sounds of frustration instantly filled the small, stuffy room in the basement of the Catholic church, and a man who had been perched on a table in the corner stood up and announced that he did not support such a proposal since he considered himself to have "diverse specialties" and took pride in the fact that he was "not only a painter." Several other workers reiterated this assertion; one shouted emphatically that he had "hands of magic." In the end, they agreed to the catch-all title of "trabajadores de la Avenida Internacional" (workers of International Avenue) over more limiting occupational affiliations.

Other men prided themselves on their assertiveness, emphasizing a set of skills more typical of a hustler (Duneier 1999; Venkatesh 2002; Wacquant 1998). Thirty-eight year old Milo, from Mexico City, drew an analogy between his job-searching strategy on the corner and the skills required by a salesman:

Here on the street you have to be aggressive, very aggressive . . . and I am a good talker. I see a truck pulled over on the corner and a lot of guys standing around it and I go up to the employer and ask him directly: "How much are you paying? Ten? Well, I'll take nine." [He motions with his finger, hand up in the air, as if making a bid at an auction.] When the employer sees that he often picks me because he can see that I am very sharp. I take pride in the work I do. After five years of this, I am like a specialist in salesmanship (soy cómo especialista del arte de vender). And that has helped me in all different areas of my life. [Laughing] See, I am a really good salesman.

Still other men pointed to their daily and highly visible quest for work as evidence of their unparalleled work ethic, entailing perseverance, discipline, and moral fortitude. Jorge, a 51-year-old man from Michoacán, Mexico, who had recently quit a $5 per-hour dishwashing job at a bakery and now finds himself working on the corner, exclaimed in a tone of righteous indignation:

We are the most hardworking people in this country. Each and every day, we are standing here on the corner, from early in the morning until late at night, looking for work. Who else has so much patience, so much dedication? We are not here to amuse ourselves, but to work, to take care of our families. I don't understand the White people who yell at us from the windows of their cars. They should reward us for our hard work, our sacrifices. We don't want to bother anyone, we just want to work.

While the day laborers who line the street fashion themselves as autonomous, skilled, assertive, and hard-working, they tend to evaluate those who search for work through the center as dependent, incompetent, deferential, and lazy, a set of attributes that collectively evoke the specter of the "welfare queen." By casting those at the center in this pejorative female-identified role, the day laborers on the street constitute themselves as engaged in an appropriately masculine, and dignified, pursuit of work.

With its rotational distribution of jobs, the BAWC takes away individual day laborers' competitive advantage with respect to securing employment. Thus, for the men on the street, those who use the center provide a foil against which they cast themselves as assertive, competent, and hard-working. As Milo, the self-proclaimed "specialist in salesmanship," stated with regard to the people who seek work through the BAWC:

Some of them may be there physically, standing around, but they're not there [pointing to his head] mentally, understand? They are not ready to work. They are just there to sit around and maybe make a little money for their beer or their drugs so they can go home, get high, and watch soccer, understand? They are not there to work. They are not there to take care of their families.

Milo draws a clear-cut distinction between those who merely work for survival or to feed addictions and those who, like himself, are both physically and mentally "ready to work" to fulfill their masculine role as breadwinners. Pointing out that "they're not there mentally" and that "they are not there to work," Milo constructs the center's participants as lazy and incompetent.

Carlos, a spunky 22-year-old from El Salvador who sports a shiny silver tooth and a black and white bandana tied tightly around his head, had similarly depreciatory things to say about the program and its participants:

I first came down here [to International Avenue] with a Salvadoran guy I met my first day in the city over on Main Street [location of one of the most frequently used homeless shelters in the city]. We have been coming here now for six months . . . One time, I went to the center, just to check it out, nothing more, but it's much better to work in the street because the process at the program is slow, very slow. I don't need help, I just need a job. The people there [at the center] go to get food, coffee, and tickets for clothes; they don't really want to work. I'd prefer one thousand times more to work than to receive a damn ticket for clothes! . . . I'm a man and I have to work!

With its provision of services—albeit extremely meager ones—the worker center is construed by men like Carlos to be a form of welfare, a place one goes for "help" as opposed to a place one goes for a job. By explicitly distinguishing and distancing himself from the center's participants, whom he deems dependent, deferential, and emasculated, Carlos reaffirms his own sense of autonomy, self-sufficiency and manhood: "I'm a man and I have to work!" These statements echo the dominant American discourse on "dependency"—that the poor who receive "hand-outs" are morally and psychologically degraded—a discourse that has, over the years, become increasingly pejorative, individualized, and feminized (Fraser and Gordon 1994; Gans 1995; Katz 1990).

Carlos's derision of the program and its participants was echoed by Felipe, a witty and bespectacled 50-year-old man from Mexico City. Felipe has been working on International Avenue as a day laborer for 14 years. He is the self-proclaimed "founder" of the corner where we first met, the first to have broken off from the original corner in front of the construction supply store, setting into motion the rapid outward expansion of the informal day labor hiring zone such that today it spans more than a half mile in length. As for the center, Felipe exclaimed in English: "Oh, I don't trust them! Too much corruption. They give out cookies and coffee and say 'we're gonna help you' [in an effeminate voice and mocking tone]. Besides, they're too slow." A little later in the conversation, Felipe asserted, still in reference as to why it is better to look for work on the street than at the center: "A man has to be willing to take risks."

Hector, a 31-year-old man from Aguascalientes, Mexico, also drew an explicit comparison between the men on the street and the men at the center, echoing the assessments made by others on the corner:

> [The center] is full of lazy people with problems. Here on the street are all of the healthy, strong, and hard-working men. I would be ashamed or embarrassed to be picked up by an employer at the program because it is filthy and the guys are all just sitting around, looking tired and hopeless . . . They are fucking weaklings.

Milo, Carlos, Felipe, and Hector share a similar assessment of the men who go to the program: they "do not really want to work." They draw on particular characteristics of the center's operations and use gendered imagery to make moral judgments of those who use it as their job-searching strategy. Despite the

program's stated mission to provide day laborers with a *dignified* gathering place to meet potential employers, many men on the street interpret the passive waiting that occurs at the center (because of its bureaucratic, rotational distribution of jobs) as well as the provision of services (English classes, clothing, food, legal aid, medical clinic) to be indicators of participants' dependency, deference, incompetence, and faltering work ethic. "Real workers" and "real men," they assert simultaneously through these acts of repudiation, look for work in the street.

What is particularly revealing in these discourses of self worth is the degree to which they are premised on the logic of making a "virtue of necessity" (Bourdieu 1977, 46). The men on the street corner turn the uncertainty that is endemic to this casual labor market into the masculine virtue of risk-taking. They interpret the lack of stable and enduring relations to employers as a virtue of autonomy. They turn the competitive tension on the street into the basis for assertiveness. And they interpret their public quest for work (the street corner as open-air labor market) as a stage on which to enact and display their work ethic. As De Genova (2006, 250) argued in his ethnographic study of Latino migrant laborers, these findings reveal the complicity between the men's "compulsions of masculinity" and their "own exploitation."

View from the Center

"I don't want to beg for work," Hugo tells me, as we sit on the concrete in the parking lot of the Bay Area Worker's Center. Hugo is number 27 on the list today (out of 62) and as he waits, he is weighing his options, considering whether he should "throw in the towel," as they say, and try his chances out on the street. He has been coming to the center for a little over two months and tells me that he has been out on six jobs in that time, only one of which lasted for longer than a day. "There are not many options," Hugo readily admits, looking down at his worn and calloused hands. [Being on the street] "makes me feel sick and dirty. Here at the center we are all treated the same, with dignity. There is no begging, no desperate chase." Clemente, a short Oaxacan man with a fondness for boxing who sits near us in a folding metal chair, chimes in: "In this place, we get work in a dignified manner. We sign the list and wait until our turn."

Compared with the men on the corner, the men at the BAWC spent considerably less time talking about their self-conception as workers. I did not hear the type of boastful claims of superiority pertaining to skill, autonomy, and work ethic that were so common on the street. Unlike the men on the corner, who were battling their vilified status in the eyes of residents, business owners, and politicians alike, the men at the BAWC seemed to feel less of a need to prove their status on the symbolically profitable side of the working/nonworking divide. As Rachel Sherman (2005, 133) argued in her comparative study of interactive service workers in luxury hotels, organizational factors "both enable and limit workers' interpretations of themselves and others." In this case, the practices and rhetoric provided by the BAWC played a key role in shaping the day laborers' evaluations of self and other. As a worker center, staff members legitimated participants' claims to a worker status. Each job seeker at the center was given a photo identification card and invited to be an active participant in weekly meetings of the "workers' committee." Staff consistently made reference to them as not only hard-working men, but as bearers of rights, worthy of respect. Not surprisingly, then, much of the day laborers' discourse of self-worth focused on being a member of this community. Again and again, men at the center told me that they came there because of the camaraderie and companionship it offered. Gustavo told me that he comes to the center each and every day, even when he already has a job and even during the two-week period when he was suspended from the center for having yelled at another worker: "It is like my family," he explained. "I have become accustomed to coming here and when I don't come, I feel sad."

Nonetheless, the men did engage in the same kind of "boundary work" vis-à-vis the day laborers along International Avenue. And here, too, they drew on gendered imagery to distinguish themselves from the day laborers on the street corner and to reaffirm the notion that searching for work through the center is not only more dignified, but more appropriately masculine.

At the time of our interview, Marco had been a regular participant in the BAWC for a little over two years. At 20, he is one of the youngest men at the center. He lives with his uncle and four other men, all from his hometown of Tijuana, Mexico, in a one-bedroom apartment located less than a mile from the center. He rides a lowrider bike and can often be found "popping wheelies" and performing other tricks in the BAWC parking lot, much to the amusement, and sometimes annoyance, of the other men waiting for work. During a walk around a nearby park one afternoon, Marco launched into an analysis of what distinguished the men at the program from those on the street:

> The street is not a place for a man to look for honest work. It took me one week to figure that out before I said "that's enough." I saw guys being picked up for all kinds of things . . . sexual favors [laughing nervously]. I will not stand on the street corner to be bought by other men.

Marco reaffirms his own masculinity and dignified pursuit of "honest work," by distinguishing and distancing himself from what he considers to be the sexual depravity of the day laborers on the street. Marco explicitly contrasts the mediated search for work through the BAWC to the unmediated search for work on the street corner, where men are "bought by other men." The gendered imagery of prostitution is central to how Marco describes the differences and symbolic hierarchy between the men at the BAWC and the men on the street corners.[10]

Clemente used a similarly gendered discourse to distinguish between the two job-searching practices and, hence, the two day labor populations:

> On the corner, when a truck pulls up, the driver looks you up and down. He measures how strong you look from the outside. It's like [in English] "Miss America." He only sees your body. And those guys seem to love the attention. I think it's better here [the BAWC]. Here, everyone is serious and hardworking.

Clemente uses the metaphor of a beauty contest to make sense of the practice of searching for work on the corner, reproducing the folk theory that employers' selection process is based on the physical appearance and stature of job seekers. In doing so, he attributes highly gendered meanings to each job-searching strategy: if standing on the corner is constituted as feminine submission to, and homoerotic tension under, the objectifying gaze of other men, then waiting at the center is constituted as appropriately masculine, a place for "serious and hardworking" men. For both Marco and Clemente, dignity is asserted and masculinity is affirmed through the repudiation of the act of displaying or selling one's body on the street corner.

Although presented here as the interpretations of individual day laborers in the context of one-on-one interviews, these cultural meanings do appear to circulate among the group as a whole and in the midst of dynamic group activity. For instance, on my first day in the field, I attended a meeting of the "worker's committee" at the BAWC, which all of the center's participants were encouraged to attend. In the midst of reporting on some of the recent outreach work being done along International Avenue to advertise the program and its services, one of the BAWC staff members, aware of the lack of affiliation and identification between the two groups of day laborers, stated that "the street and the center are the same thing, the same cause." The comment elicited a handful of muffled

---

[10] Let me point out that although this discourse of prostitution was a key means through which the day laborers at the center differentiated and distanced themselves from the day laborers on the street, I did not over the course of this study gather any evidence that men on International Avenue were being hired for prostitution. For further discussion on this topic, however, see Gonzalez-Lopez (2005).

snickers, followed by one brazen man's whistling and catcalling, followed by an eruption of group laughter. At the time, I did not know what to make of the occurrence, chalking it up to some kind of inside joke. But, as I began to recognize a clear pattern of "boundary work," the significance of this event became all the more apparent, revealing the widespread recognition of the gendered meanings BAWC participants ascribe to the curbside quest for employment.

Even when they do not refer to explicitly gendered imagery, the men at the BAWC evaluate searching for work on the corner as somehow "less than human." Luís came to the United States 3 years ago from Honduras. After spending some time working as a day laborer in both Phoenix and Seattle, Luís now lives in a homeless shelter and regularly seeks work through the BAWC.

> The program doesn't really serve its purpose because there is not sufficient work. I have not had a job in, like, eight days. It's hard. It's very hard. In the street, there are more options, but it's degrading to go around chasing after cars like a dog like that. Here it is more peaceful and I feel like a man treated with respect.

Like Hugo, presented at the beginning of this section, who sees the men on the corner as "begging" for work, Luís contrasts his job searching strategy to the desperate act of "chasing after cars like a dog."

Byron, a 36-year-old man from Guatemala, told me that he had spent ten years working the corner before joining the worker center. Over lunch at a nearby Mexican restaurant, he carefully drew a picture of a deformed-looking rabbit in my field notebook and explained that the guys on the street are like "crazy rabbits" [*conejos locos*] when it comes to trying to find work. By contrasting their job searching strategy through the BAWC to the desperate, animalistic chase on the street, all three of these men place control at the core of their construction of self worth.

DISCUSSION

Studies of the burgeoning informal day labor market have overwhelmingly focused on the demographic characteristics of the workforce and the basic organization and working conditions of this distinctive trade, overlooking the question of how day laborers make sense of their daily pursuit of work while asserting and defending their dignity. Drawing on interview and comparative ethnographic fieldwork in a worker center and a street corner hiring site, this article reveals a clear pattern of "boundary work," wherein participants in each site construct a set of moral boundaries via identification and repudiation of what they interpret to be the feminine submission exemplified by the day laborers in the other site. The

day laborers on the street tended to contrast themselves to the purported dependency, deference, incompetence, and faltering work ethic of the men at the program. The day laborers at the program tended to contrast themselves to the purported sexual depravity and desperation of the men on the street. The same activity that is construed as appropriately masculine and dignified by one group is invoked as emblematic of feminine submission by the other, thus revealing the tremendous "malleability and variability of gendered categories" (Salzinger 2003, 25). These findings suggest the need for further attention to the mutually constitutive process whereby gender and moral boundaries are constituted.

I do not mean to suggest in this article that the cultural meanings day laborers ascribe to the street and the center determine which of the two sites they go to in search of work. Given the profound dearth of work opportunities in either site, I would argue that the men go wherever they believe they will have the best chance of securing work. This calculation of chance, however, may very well relate to the cultural meanings I have discussed throughout this article (e.g., If day laborers view the center as a place one goes to get handouts, they will likely calculate the chances of obtaining work through the center as quite marginal). What I am suggesting is that these cultural meanings are the vehicle through which the men constitute their daily quest for work as dignified. The repeated identification and repudiation of the alternative job-seeking strategy (soliciting work from a street corner or participating in a worker center) reveals just how limited their choices for obtaining work are and yet, how important it is to their senses of self-worth to feel that they are making a choice, constrained as it might be.

These contextually specific moral boundaries illustrate the way in which the quest for dignity can lead workers to be complicit with their own exploitation and thwart the emergence of the sense of commonality and feelings of solidarity that are needed to collectively organize day laborers. The findings present a challenge to the successful operation of nonprofit day labor centers established by community organizations and city governments in metropolitan areas throughout the nation, for they reveal how the creation of a regulated and service-providing day labor worker center can have the perverse effect of serving as the perfect foil against which the curbside day laborers define themselves. I would thus echo Valenzuela's (2003, 326) claim that we do not know enough about the real and, particularly, *perceived* benefits of regulated informal hiring sites to the workers themselves. Developing effective organizing strategies among day laborers requires that we further examine the cultural meanings day laborers attach to their work as part of their creative pursuit of dignity.

Two important questions about symbolic boundaries are raised, but not answered, by this article. The first concerns the durability and malleability of these symbolic boundaries, particularly in light of fluid social boundaries. All of the men I interviewed at the BAWC had at one time or another sought work along International Avenue. Some of them still do, either on occasion or as a routine strategy for maximizing their chances of obtaining work. These are thus not rigidly separate and easily distinguishable groups. But the fluidity between the hiring sites does raise the question of how these men rationalize their participation in an activity that they have deemed to be both morally faltering and "feminine." To what extent do the cultural meanings the men have elaborated about the street as participants of the BAWC shape their behavior when they clamor for work on the street corner? To what extent are these cultural meanings durable, if simply in their effect?

Second, this article raises the question of whether the moral boundaries drawn by and between groups or individuals in contexts of social and economic marginalization are more apt to explicitly invoke gender than are those drawn by groups or individuals vis-à-vis those above or below them on the socioeconomic hierarchy. Along these lines, we might ask whether gender is invoked in the strategies of differentiation and distinction between the panhandlers and the magazine vendors on Sixth Avenue studied by Duneier (1999, 83), both of whom assert that they have "too much pride to engage in each other's activity." The point here is not to diminish the overall centrality of gender to understanding how individuals construct moral boundaries, but rather to question whether the prominence of gendered imagery in the assertion of moral boundaries stems from the fact that the men in this case have few other recourses for establishing self-worth, other than through explicit repudiation of that which they construe as feminine.

REFERENCES

Bourdieu, Pierre. 1977. *Outline of a theory of practice.* New York: Cambridge University Press.

——. 2000. *Pascalian meditations.* Stanford, CA: Stanford University Press.

Carr, Patrick J. 2001. Review of *The dignity of working men: Morality and the boundaries of race, class and immigration,* by Michèle Lamont. *American Journal of Sociology* 107:503–5.

Connell, R. W. 2005/1995. *Masculinities,* 2nd ed. Berkeley: University of California Press.

Davis, Fred. 1959. The cabdriver and his fare: Facets of a fleeting relationship. *American Journal of Sociology* 65:158–65.

De Genova, Nicholas. 2006. The everyday civil war: Migrant working men, within and against capital. *Ethnography* 7:243–67.

Duneier, Mitchell. 1999. *Sidewalk.* New York: Farrar, Straus & Giroux.

Esbenshade, Jill. 2000. The "crisis" over day labor: The politics of visibility and public space. *WorkingUSA* 3:27–70.

Fine, Janice. 2006. *Worker centers: Organizing communities at the edge of the dream.* Ithaca: ILR.

Fraser, Nancy, & Linda Gordon. 1994. A genealogy of *dependency*: Tracing a keyword of the U.S. welfare state. *Signs: Journal of Women in Culture & Society* 19:309–36.

Gans, Herbert J. 1995. *The war against the poor: The underclass and antipoverty policy.* New York: Basic Books.

Glaser, Barney, and Anselm Strauss. 1967. *A discovery of grounded theory: Strategies for qualitative research.* Hawthorne, NY: Aldine.

González-López, Gloria. 2005. *Erotic journeys: Mexican immigrants and their sex lives.* Berkeley, CA: University of California Press.

Gowan, Teresa. 2000. Excavating "globalization" from street level: Homeless men recycle their pasts. In *Global ethnography: Forces, connections and imaginations in the postmodern world,* ed. Michael Burawoy, Joseph Blum, Sheba George, Zsuzsa Gilli, Millie Thayer, Teresa Gowan, Lynne Haney, Maren Klawiter, Steve Lopez, and Sean Riain., 74–105. Berkeley: University of California Press.

Hodson, Randy. 2001. *Dignity at work.* New York: Cambridge University Press.

Hughes, Everett C. 1994. *On work, race and the sociological imagination.* Chicago: University of Chicago Press.

Katz, Michael B. 1990. *The undeserving poor: From the war on poverty to the war on welfare.* New York: Pantheon.

Lamont, Michèle. 2000. *The dignity of working men: Morality and the boundaries of race, class and immigration.* Cambridge, MA: Harvard University Press.

Lamont, Michèle, and Virág Molnár. 2002. The study of boundaries in the social sciences. *Annual Review of Sociology* 28:167–95.

Lankenau, Stephen E. 1999. Stronger than dirt: Public humiliation and status enhancement among panhandlers. *Journal of Contemporary Ethnography* 28:288–318.

Larrowe, Charles P. 1976. *Shape-up and hiring hall: A comparison of hiring methods and labor relations on the New York & Seattle waterfronts.* Westport, CT: Greenwood.

Malpica, Daniel Melero. 2002. Making a living in the streets of Los Angeles: An ethnographic study of day laborers. *Migraciones Internacionales* 1:124–48.

Parker, Robert E. 1994. *Flesh peddlers and warm bodies: The temporary help industry and its workers.* New Brunswick, NJ: Rutgers University Press.

Raissiguier, Catherine. 2002. Review of *The dignity of working men: Morality and the boundaries of race, class and immigration,* by Michèle Lamont. *Gender & Society* 16:136–7.

Salzinger, Leslie. 2003. *Genders in production: Making workers in Mexico's global factories.* Berkeley: University of California Press.

Sherman, Rachel. 2005. Producing the superior self: Strategic comparison and symbolic boundaries among luxury hotel workers. *Ethnography* 6:131–58.

Sullivan, C. J. 2001. Bronx stroll: The slave market. *New York Press*, February, 14–20.

Theodore, Nik, Abel Valenzuela Jr., and Edwin Meléndez. 2006. *La esquina* (the corner): Day laborers on the margins of New York's formal economy. *Working USA* 9:407–23.

Turnovsky, Carolyn Pinedo. 2006. *A la parada*: The social practices of men on a street corner. *Social Text* 24:55–72.

Valenzuela Jr., Abel. 1999. Day laborers in Southern California: Preliminary findings from the day labor survey. Center for the Study of Urban Poverty, University of California, Los Angeles.

——. 2001. Day laborers as Entrepreneurs? *Journal of Ethnic and Migration Studies* 27:335–52.

——. 2003. Day labor work. *Annual Review of Sociology* 29:307–33.

Valenzuela Jr., Abel, Nik Theodore, Edwin Melendez, and Ana Luz Gonzalez. 2006. On the corner: Day labor in the United States. Working paper, Center for the Study of Urban Poverty, UCLA, and Community Development Research Center, New School University.

Venkatesh, Sudhir. 2002. Doin' the hustle: Constructing the ethnographer in the American ghetto. *Ethnography* 3:91–111.

Wacquant, Loïc. 1995. Pugs at work: Bodily capital and bodily labor among professional boxers. *Body & Society* 1:65–93.

——. 1998. Inside the zone: The social art of the hustler in the Black American ghetto. *Theory, Culture and Society* 15:1–36.

Walter, Nicholas, Philippe Bourgois, and H. Margarita Loinaz. 2004. Masculinity and undocumented labor migration: Injured day laborers in San Francisco. *Social Science & Medicine* 59:1159–68.

3.05

CRITICAL DESIGN

Harms and Benefits: Collecting Ethnicity Data in a Clinical Context

Colleen Varcoe,* Annette J. Browne,* Sabrina Wong,* and Victoria L. Smye*

ABSTRACT: Although ethnicity data are collected in most countries at the population level, it has become more common to collect such data in healthcare settings, partially in response to growing health and social inequities worldwide. However, the implications of doing so have not been studied. This two-year study was designed to critically examine the implications of collecting ethnicity data in healthcare settings. Using a critical ethnographic approach, we interviewed 104 patients, community and healthcare leaders, and healthcare workers within diverse clinical contexts in a large city in Western Canada in 2006–2007. This paper presents an interpretive thematic analysis, using an ethical lens, of the harms and benefits associated with the process of data collection in a clinical context. While most leaders and healthcare workers and some patients envisioned potential benefits associated with *having* ethnicity data, these benefits were seen as largely contingent upon action being taken to ameliorate inequities. Overwhelmingly, however, leaders from ethno-cultural communities and patients of diverse identities anticipated potential harm arising both from having ethnicity data and the process of collection. The analysis illustrates that in today's sociopolitical context, collecting ethnicity data in clinical contexts may engender considerable harm, particularly for racialized, vulnerable patients. If ethnicity data are currently collected at the population level, evidence of benefit is required before proceeding to collect these data at the point of care.

KEYWORDS: Canada; Race/ethnicity; data collection; Ethics; inequity; health disparities; Discrimination.

INTRODUCTION

Interest in collecting data regarding ethnicity has grown in recent years, partially in response to growing social and health inequities worldwide. In many countries, ethnicity data are routinely collected at the population level through self-report surveys such as the National Health Interview Survey in the United States (National Center for Health Statistics, 2008). In healthcare settings, collecting data on patients' ethnicity has become routine in places such as the United Kingdom, United States, and New Zealand. The main rationale is to enable identification of and provide a basis for rectifying inequities in order to achieve more

*School of Nursing, University of British Columbia, 2211 Wesbrook Mall, Vancouver, BC, Canada V6T 2B5

equitable and culturally competent care (see for example, King et al., 2008; New Zealand Ministry of Health, 2004; Sheth et al., 1997; Smedley, Stith, & Nelson, 2002). Ethnicity data are typically collected as part of administrative data, or at the point of care, that is, when people seek care at physicians' offices, hospitals or community health centers.

Unlike other countries, in Canada, information on ethnicity is generally *not* collected in healthcare contexts (Rummens, 2003). Exceptions occur in certain agencies that seek information for their own records, particularly to identify First Nations people (one group of Aboriginal people in Canada) to whom specific policies may apply. No federal, provincial, or other governmental mandates require healthcare institutions or agencies to collect data on ethnicity. Therefore, most Canadian research on ethnicity and health uses large population-based surveys as sources of ethnicity data. However, the meaningfulness of Canadian ethnicity data has been much debated (Bourhis, 2003; Jedwab, 2003; Rummens, 2003) with an increasing proportion of the population identifying "Canadian" as their ethnicity on census data, reflecting the extent to which ethnicity and identity are fluid constructs shaped by individual and sociopolitical contexts (Thomas, 2005).

Statistics Canada (2006) acknowledges ethnicity as an ambiguous concept because it can encompass multiple different aspects such as "race," country of origin or ancestry, identity, language and religion, changing from context to context as a result of new immigration flows and the development of new identities. In healthcare contexts (as in other sectors of society), ethnicity is often conflated with "race", contributing to a narrow and erroneous categorical conceptualization of ethnicity. For example, in the USA, ethnicity is used interchangeably with race, contributing to the mistaken assumption that these are biological and/or genetic rather than social categories (Krieger, 2004). The notion that race is a valid, biological, meaningful, *a priori* category persists despite the decades of scientific evidence from population genetics, social epidemiology, anthropology and sociology that calls race into question as an essential and meaningful set of biological categories (Krieger, 1999a; United Nations, 1952). This is not to deny the significance of ethnicity or race as social categories, and the effects of racial discrimination or ethnic stereotyping on health or access to healthcare. Problematic, however, is the way ethnicity — as a multifaceted concept — has been constructed narrowly for the purposes of data collection and analysis in health research.

Despite these limitations of categorization, healthcare organizations in some parts of Canada are increasingly focused on collecting ethnicity data as a way of monitoring which groups are accessing services and potentially reducing access inequities and making services more culturally relevant. This was the case in one Western province, where a Health Authority (a regional body responsible for healthcare delivery) planned to collect ethnicity data at clinical points of contact. Prior to implementation, representatives of the Health Authority joined with university researchers to examine critically the implications of collecting ethnicity data in clinical contexts. As one aspect of our analysis, we used an ethical lens to consider the potential harms and benefits. The purpose of this paper is to report that analysis.

BACKGROUND TO THE STUDY

Over the past two decades researchers have made compelling calls to examine variables such as ethnicity, race, and socioeconomic status that underlie persistent inequities (see, for example, Bhopal, 2001; Krieger, 1999b; New Zealand Ministry of Health, 2004; Sheth et al., 1997; Smedley et al., 2002; Williams, 2002; Wu & Schimmele, 2005). Within a research context, these and other authors argue that progress or setbacks in addressing racial and ethnic inequalities in health cannot be monitored without population-level racial and ethnic data (Krieger, 2000; Krieger et al., 2005). Although some take this position while cautioning that collecting race and ethnicity data is a "double edged sword" (Krieger, 2004), others argue for elimination of racial and ethnic categories in data collection, as classifying people by race and ethnicity tacitly reinforces racial and ethnic divisions in society (Bhopal, 1998; Kaplan & Bennett, 2003).

Beyond the research context, there has been a trend toward collecting ethnicity data within healthcare agencies and institutions. For example, in the USA where ethnicity data have been collected for decades, the Institute of Medicine (IOM), Physicians for Human Rights, and The Commonwealth Fund support the collection of standardized data on race, ethnicity, and primary language of patients within healthcare organizations (Hasnain-Wynia & Baker, 2006; Hasnain-Wynia, Pierce, & Pittman, 2004; King et al., 2008; Perot & Youdelman, 2001; Physicians for Human Rights, 2003; Smedley et al., 2002). This has been suggested primarily a) to identify and mitigate existing health disparities by facilitating the provision of culturally and linguistically appropriate healthcare, and b) to promote quality healthcare for all population groups by contributing to better information databases (New Zealand Ministry of Health, 2004; Sheth et al., 1997; Smedley et al., 2002). According to the IOM, "a critical barrier to eliminating disparities and improving the quality of patient care is the frequent lack of even the most basic data on race, ethnicity or primary language of patients within healthcare organizations" (Hasnain-Wynia et al., 2004, p. v). The assumption is that providing equitable, quality care requires race and ethnicity data, but to date research has not shown that knowledge about health inequities leads to better healthcare services at the individual level. Indeed in the UK, Aspinall (2000) found that little use was made of ethnicity data collected in healthcare settings. Aspinall and Anionwu (2002) reported that although the ethnic identities of patients were obtained for an annual total in England of over 11 million admissions, the information has only been used to produce indices of quality, not to improve the quality of care provided. The possible reasons for such failure include that the contribution of racism and causes of inequities is complex, encompassing structural inequities and institutional racism (Bhopal, 2007) and that additional resources required to address such inequities may not be prioritized in the context of global healthcare reforms that have emphasized cost cutting.

Given growing interest in ethnicity data in healthcare contexts and interest in collecting such data, the general public and patients have been surveyed regarding their attitudes toward ethnicity data collection. Quan, Wong, Johnson, and Ghali (2006) found that of 2799 respondents to a telephone survey randomly selected from those with listed phone numbers in a Western Canadian city, 84.8% felt comfortable about recording their ethnicity in hospital charts. This finding did not vary by ethnicity, however, 73% of the sample identified as "white" and there was a 45% non-response rate. In the United Kingdom, Pringle and Rothera (1996) found that 72% of patients thought that general practitioners "definitely" or "possibly" should record ethnicity, but the response rate was 56% and the ethnic identity of respondents was not published. In the United States, Baker et al. (2005) found that of 220 patients in a general internal medical setting about 80% somewhat or strongly agreed that healthcare providers should collect information on patients' race/ethnicity. However, 28% had significant discomfort reporting their own race/ethnicity, and 58% (including three quarters of the African American participants) were somewhat or very concerned the information could be used to discriminate against patients. Although these surveys provide a glimpse into the complexities involved, to date, the possible harms and benefits of collecting ethnicity data at the point of care have received little attention and have not been examined in Canada.

Collecting ethnicity data in a clinical context, particularly in Canada where such data have not been collected previously, has different features than collecting data in the context of vital statistics data, a national survey or census, or in other population-based research contexts. In healthcare contexts, eth-

nicity tends to be conceptualized very narrowly, and is often used as synonymous with "race" (Anderson & Kirkham, 1998; Bhopal, 2001; Ford & Kelly, 2005; Gerrish, 2000). This is problematic in terms of data collection, given the ambiguity of the concept. Further, research provides mounting evidence of ethnic and racial discrimination and structural racism in healthcare (e.g. Anderson & Kirkham, 1998; Balsa, McGuire, & Meredith, 2005; Bhopal, 2007; Bourassa, McKay-McNabb, & Hampton, 2004; Henry & Tator, 2006). Thus, the implications of collecting ethnicity data within such contexts are not known.

RESEARCH METHODS

In order to explore the implications of collecting ethnicity data in healthcare settings, we employed a critical ethnographic design and collected data in four modes in a large Western Canadian city: (a) in-depth interviews with 10 decision-makers and policy leaders affiliated with several health authorities and policy research units; (b) three focus groups of community leaders ($n = 18$) from a range of ethno-cultural groups who served on committees of the Health Authority to represent patients' perspectives concerning healthcare planning; (c) semi-structured interviews with patients ($n = 60$) seeking health services in either a sub-acute area (an area designed to respond to patients triaged as stable and non-urgent) of a large urban Emergency Department (ED), or a community health center (CHC); (d) interviews with 16 healthcare workers who were involved in either administering an ethnic identity question in healthcare agencies, or whose agencies were considering doing so as part of intake data. Data were collected between February 2006 and August 2007.

Ethical approval was obtained from the University Research Ethics Board. Patients were recruited in the waiting room of the ED or CHC. They were approached initially by a unit clerk. If interested, they were directed to a trained research assistant who explained the study fully and, if consent was obtained, conducted the interview. All other participants were recruited by word of mouth through our research partners in the Health Authority. Interviews focused on their thoughts regarding people being asked to identify their ethnicity in healthcare settings, past experiences with being asked, the benefits that might be gained from such information and their possible concerns. Interviews were audio-recorded and transcribed. Field notes recorded appearance, non-verbal behaviour and tones of voice during interviews.

The policy decision-makers/leaders included those responsible for patient information systems, Aboriginal health and "diversity" portfolios in the Health Authorities and those associated with policy research units dealing with health disparities. The focus group participants included: (a) Focus Group #1 — community leaders who self-identified as "visible minorities", primarily as East Indian or Chinese people. In Canada, visible minorities are defined in racializing terms as "persons who are. . .non-Caucasian in race or non-white in Colour. . .Aboriginal persons are not considered to be members of visible minority groups" (Statistics Canada, 2006); (b) Focus Group #2A and B — two groups of community leaders who self-identified as Aboriginal, the term used to refer generally to the indigenous inhabitants of Canada including First Nations, Métis and Inuit peoples (Royal Commission on Aboriginal Peoples, 1996, p. xii). This included both status and non-status people, with "status" denoting those people registered with the federal government's Indian Registry.

The patients we interviewed included 22 people who self-identified as members of an Aboriginal group, and 17 who identified as English-speaking Euro-Canadians. The remaining 21 patients self-identified as members of various other ethno-cultural groups. These included people who would be defined as visible minorities having immigrated or descended from immigrants from places such as India, Taiwan, South America, Turkey, and people who would not be so defined who were recent immigrants from places such as Eastern Europe.

An interpretive thematic analysis was conducted. Each transcript and associated field notes were read to get a sense of the whole and then coded thematically. Themes were compared across interviews and revised. We used a qualitative software package (NVivo™) to manage data and organize preliminary coding. This paper presents our analysis of the data using an ethical lens as our theoretical perspective.

AN ETHICAL LENS

Ethics are concerned with values and morality. However, as feminist and contextual ethicists (e.g. Sherwin, 1992; Walker, 2001) argue, ethics "is fundamentally, a discourse about morality and power" (Walker, 2001, p. 4). An ethical lens that considers power was useful because of our interest in critical inquiry and need to scrutinize ideological assumptions within our own analysis and the practices under study. Inherent in the quest to understand the implications of collecting ethnicity data was the desire to optimize the benefits and avoid harm. Such questions are ethical questions. Further, the research addresses contexts of power and the social positions of patients within existing power structures — patients are to be asked certain questions within social structures and organizational systems in which power differentials operate with par-

ticular effects. Patients coming for healthcare are often vulnerable due to illness, disability and social positioning within the healthcare system. These vulnerabilities are compounded by racializing and marginalizing practices in healthcare. Finally, the implications of collecting ethnicity data are of considerable moral concern because they involve categorization, racializing and in some cases, discriminatory processes. While discrimination may simply mean 'to distinguish between', as Lippert-Rasmussen argues "discrimination is bad, when it is, because it *harms* people" [emphasis added] (2006, p. 167). Thus, an ethical analysis of the approaches to asking about ethnicity must address the extent to which the practices involved (which may include *not* collecting such data) may harm people.

The concept of harm is central to ethics. However, what is meant by harm varies. Within biomedical ethics the caveat "First, do no harm" — for example as articulated within the mid-range principles proposed Beauchamp and Childress (2001) — is interpreted primarily to mean that one should not cause harm to others in the course of delivering healthcare. The emphasis is on physical harm caused by individual providers in the process of giving care to individual clients (Pauly, 2008). However, within bioethics, rarely are wider contexts and *preventing* harm considered or seen as a priority. Through the principle of autonomy, individual liberty is stressed and freedom of choice implicitly understood as the mechanism by which individuals protect their interests and mitigate harm, a perspective that overlooks power dynamics. For example, some proponents of ethnicity data collection argue that harm is mitigated because individual patients have the choice whether or not to answer an ethnicity question. Such understanding does not account for the pressures and vulnerabilities patients may experience when seeking care and how such pressures may affect their capacity to exercise choice. Thus, in concert with trends within procedural justice research, as Sandefur (2008) argues, an important approach to inequality and access to justice come from research that explores people's subjective evaluations of their experiences.

From a broader theoretical perspective, harm can be understood as the consequence of a wide range of circumstances or actions beyond those of particular individuals. Feminist philosophers such as Young (1990) draw attention to the harms associated with belonging to certain groups and experiencing certain conditions. To consider the implications of collecting ethnicity data, analysis of possible harms associated with being assigned to or being seen as belonging to particular ethnic groups is required. Thus, we understood harm to refer to damage that might ensue from a wide range of social structures and practices, while focusing on practices related to collecting ethnicity data.

FINDINGS

The findings of this study surface tensions between good intended by collecting and using ethnicity data, and the harms that may be incurred through the process of collecting and using data.

POSSIBLE BENEFITS AND GOOD INTENTIONS

I'm assuming they would use that information for good purposes (Patient #44)

A range of possible benefits of ethnicity data were imagined. Policy decision-makers/leaders and healthcare workers generally were more positive than community leaders and patients, and focused upon the potential uses of *having* ethnicity data (rather than on the processes used to obtain that data) to better understand patterns among groups. The advantages fell into three overlapping areas that participants appeared to see as being causally linked: a) the advantage of being able to map the ethnicity of the patient populations (determining who is accessing care), b) the possibility of identifying barriers to care based on ethnicity, and c) the opportunity to make care better and more equitable, primarily by better tailoring services to meet the needs of diverse ethno-cultural groups. Decision-makers articulated these benefits most clearly:

> "The main reason for collecting ethnicity data or any kind of ethnic coding is to identify and therefore be able to develop strategies to address health disparities" Decision-maker #10
>
> "If we can't measure disparities in either their health status, access to services, types of treatment prescribed, health outcomes, it is an invisible problem" Decision-maker #6

Albeit to a lesser extent, some community leaders and several patients identified similar potential benefits for groups. Some patients supposed that ethnicity data might be used to ameliorate health disparities and racism and made assumptions similar to those made by policy decision-makers/leaders that data collection would lead to action. For example, Patient #1, who was Canadian-born, referred to himself as "black", and identified as "Canadian", thought the collection of such data could hypothetically convey to people in healthcare *"that racism is being watched and monitored, and they will be held accountable for any wrongful action . . ."* Some patients expressed a sense of faith in healthcare as an essentially equitable system, and therefore saw the collection of ethnicity data as innocuous. As Patient #44, who identified as Euro-Canadian, said *"Well, because we live in Canada and we're such a mixed culture. . .everybody is kind of equal so I don't think anyone specifically is being targeted for anything [in*

healthcare]". Further, patients often expressed implicit trust that data would be used for a good purpose, and that if it was being requested, it must be necessary. Patient #50, who identified as Pilipino said *"I would readily give away where I'm from if that would help the medical team resolve the problem"*. Patient #31 who identified as Aboriginal (Nuxalk and Métis) offered: *"I mean, if they have a panel of all different ethnics [referring to leaders in healthcare], sure, let them [use the data]"*.

Patients did not emphasize benefits and only occasionally suggested benefits for groups, instead focusing on the effects on particular individuals being asked. They generally associated possible advantages with knowing a person's country of origin, primary language, or presumed genetic makeup, and connected that knowledge with some anticipated benefit in terms of better clinical care for that person. For example, Patient #2 who identified as a German-American Canadian said *"if you come from a poorer country. . .you hear people from Africa, their water supply is pretty bad over there, so. . .it could have an effect on health, so. . .I think the doctor needs to know. . . for better treatment, right?"*

The primary benefit identified by both patients and decision-makers was that having ethnicity data might ensure that clinical care would take into account risk factors associated with health problems that they, sometimes erroneously, thought were biologically or genetically linked. Reflecting popularized discourses in Canadian society (and other countries) that conflate ethnicity with biological/genetic notions of race, ethnicity was understood as a means through which to identify biologically based risk factors.

> . . .for instance Asians are more prone to liver cancer, Japanese have very high instances of stomach cancer . . . Focus Group #1
>
> "There are certain groups in the population that might be prone to certain diseases based on your ethnicity, so I guess it goes back to genetics" Patient #1 (Canadian)
>
> "The only need for that information would be genetic, and you know, derivatives of perhaps your genotype that would be susceptible. . ." Patient #18 (Métis)
>
> "Your roots, like they could look back into your family history and get you the proper healthcare" Patient #20 (Euro-Canadian)

Participants' assumptions mirrored popularized, though erroneous, assumptions about the genetic basis of disease patterns, and often conflated the notion of family history as an easily identifiable risk factor, with presumed genetic relatedness among ethno-cultural groups. Participants thought that knowing ethnicity might explain why people have trouble taking their prescribed medications, or could help with identifying what people eat. Several thought there would be advantages to collecting ethnicity data if the person did not speak English. However, as we continue to discuss, ethnicity as a single variable collected at the point of care is unlikely to yield this type of information, which could be better obtained by directly asking about family history, languages spoken or diet preferences.

Perceptions of benefits (and harms) were related to participants' own identities, social and historical locations, and experiences. For example, Patient #31 related a positive healthcare experience that she associated with the physician knowing about her ethnicity.

> I had a couple of doctors that did know native background and he asked me where I was from and automatically he knew what kind of [pause] he asked me these questions, like there's heart disease and arthritis, and there's a kind of blood type we get in this area. . .and I have one of them. And he seemed to understand more. . .and right away I got the help I needed instead of doing all the run around.

Those who self-identified as 'white', Euro-Canadian or Caucasian, tended to see no benefit to reporting ethnicity for themselves. Patient #36 thought there was no benefit *"because I am part of the mainstream"*. Patient #44 said *"For me specifically it probably won't benefit me that much because I was born and raised in Canada, and so I am quite fluent in English. . ."* If they imagined benefits, then they associated the benefits with people who have immigrated to Canada, are not fluent in English or could be classified as visible minorities. Similarly, they did not tend to see potential harms as applying to themselves. For example, Patient #35 said, *"I am a Canadian white guy, so it doesn't bother me at all"*.

HARMS AND CONCERNS

"What do you mean, what am I? I'm here to get treatment, is what I am, right?" Patient #21

At the same time as suggestions were offered regarding the potential benefits, primarily of *having* ethnicity data and serving groups better, the overwhelming response to the idea of the *process of asking* about ethnicity was deep concern. Patients and community leaders raised these concerns emphatically. Because we conducted patient interviews in an Emergency unit and a community healthcare center, patients were ideally positioned to consider data collection in a clinical context. In contrast to asking about the experience more theoretically in surveys, patients in waiting rooms could imagine the experience more directly. As when considering benefits, participants identified harms by drawing on their own identities, experiences, social positions, and experiences of discrimination.

Across focus group and patient participants, the harms anticipated included being judged on the basis of assumptions and stereotypes, and the possibility of receiving poorer care based on such judgements. While some benefits were associated with groups, participants anticipated harmful effects primarily for individuals. Participants expressed their concerns in relation to groups they thought likely to be vulnerable to the effects of inequities and racialization, such as Aboriginal people and visible minorities. Many were concerned that ethnicity data could influence healthcare staff to reinforce stereotypes that link certain health behaviours to particular groups — for example, the commonly-held stereotype in Canada that links Aboriginal people to alcoholism (Furniss, 1999). Many who self-identified as 'white', Euro-Canadian or Caucasian expressed concern, not for themselves, but for those they saw as targets of negative judgement. Patient #36 said

> "just imagine if you had a physician or a nurse that didn't like Aboriginal people or didn't like Indo Canadians or didn't like new immigrants. . .I worked a lot with Aboriginal people, so the issue for them is, can the data be used against them?"

Implicit was that healthcare and social inequities are prevalent. Adding questions related to one's ethnocultural background was viewed as a process that would fuel anxieties about ongoing inequities, and how inequities could manifest in healthcare contexts because of negative perceptions or assumptions that some staff may have toward particular groups. Several patients said that they would not answer ethnicity questions. Patient #26, who identified as "Canadian" and appeared Caucasian, said *"[If] I thought they were going to treat me differently, I'd probably lie to them"*. Patient #7 who identified as "Ismaili" said *"It depends who is working behind the desk and what kind of attitude [they have]. . .I think a lot of people are just racist. . .They've got the wrong people working behind the desk often"*.

Of great concern was the extent to which those who identified as members of a visible minority or as Aboriginal expressed concern for themselves. When asked their thoughts regarding ethnicity being collected as part of routine patient information at the point of care, many expressed anxiety, fear and anger. Patients who would be identified as "visible minorities" said:

> I feel extremely highly discriminated towards by asking such a question. Patient #48
> I'd be [offended] if this was asked of me. It's just another means to divide. Patient #21
> Because its, its, its not a good question, its not a good question at all, it doesn't relate to my health, this sort of question, it makes me really angry. Patient #41

Concerns extended beyond the stress of being asked to fear that such questions both signalled and could lead to further discrimination and poorer care. Patient #21, explained

. . . being a black man. . . I have a tendency to be kind of squeamish about any type of questions. . . and my first thought when you ask me that coming into an emergency. . . if I was kind of bleeding and everything else and they asked me well where am I from, okay, I might assume that they're thinking well this is an African, you know, they're paranoid of getting AIDS or something else.

Participants who identified as Aboriginal expressed similar concerns.

I would feel insulted, offended, marginalized, targeted. I would wonder how this is going to affect my treatment, I would wonder how this would affect nurses', doctors' behaviour towards me. My first response would probably be "what difference does it make?" So I would be on the offensive. I feel that almost, even as you asked the question, like how would I feel? I feel something rise up in me, to just really. . . and it makes me angry, immediately. And that's just in this room. I can't even imagine how I would feel if I was hurt or if I was bringing in my husband who is dead or dying or whatever, and then to be asked if I was, what are you? I think I'd probably go through [pause] I wouldn't be able to behave properly, probably. Focus Group #2B

Each participant who identified as Aboriginal described the effects of discrimination on his or her health. For example, Patient #31 described how the stereotypical idea that Aboriginal people sell their pain medications not only can create problems for pain management, but also may create or exacerbate the problem of street sale of prescription drugs:

A lot of us have arthritis, and. . .are being put down from Tylenol 3's to Tylenol 2's, then to regular Tylenol because [doctors] don't want to hand it out, they think we are selling them. In other words we have to go out and buy our medications off the street sometimes.

The idea that "Aboriginality" could be interpreted as a risk factor for health or social problems was identified by several participants — and echoed Smylie's (2005) concerns about the risks of pathologizing "Aboriginality" itself as a risk factor in healthcare contexts.

Importantly, patients and focus group members were concerned that inequities played out along the intersecting axes of class, culture, race and ethnicity. Patient #1 who referred to himself as "black", and identified as Canadian, explained

. . . If they respect you more because you're rich . . . they'll treat you with more respect. . .that's why, about ethnicity, um, about your race rather, . . .I would feel right away, I mean being classified as being prejudged and people would treat me accordingly.

Most participants who identified as Aboriginal discussed these intersections to some extent. For exam-

ple, Patient #31 spoke at length regarding her different experiences of accessing care depending on how she was dressed. She explained how her family carefully planned their appearances when accessing healthcare, arguing that class assumptions were at least as powerful as those based on ethnicity. Similarly, Patient #56 described how his treatment differed when he was able to shower in contrast to when he was living on the street and unable to do so. These concerns reflect anxieties that Aboriginal people have expressed in other studies about the need to transform one's appearance when seeking healthcare as a means of gaining legitimacy and credibility as a medical subject (e.g. Tang & Browne, 2008).

Patients, focus group participants and some healthcare leaders identified concerns based on harmful discrimination that they had either experienced directly or witnessed — both within healthcare and wider social interactions. For example, in Focus Group #2A, one woman associated her daughter being treated rudely and her own experience of having her pain ignored with being identified as Aboriginal. Participants drew upon experiences of racial and class discrimination, most often as race, ethnicity and class intersected. Patient #13, who identified as Métis, recounted observing how a man was treated in Emergency.

He was bleeding all over the place and they just ignored him. You could see he needed more treatment. . . he was the one that needed the help the most and he was the last one they seen. . . he looked like a bum off the street so. . .they put the high class first, like, the ones that look you know, well off.

His experiences fuelled his concern that indigent patients likely would be treated differentially regardless of need — which fed his worry about how he might be treated on the basis of his perceived socioeconomic status and ethnicity. Similarly, an admitting clerk responsible for collecting ethnicity data had considerable caution about doing so because of numerous personal experiences such as the following;

my brother had a head injury. . . slipped on the ice and he and my brother had been hunting and they went back to a cabin and were sharing a bottle of wine with people and there was alcohol on his breath and they medivaced [him] from the hunting area and they treated him like another drunk Indian because of the fact that he was acting violently and he's not a violent person, my brother was begging them, "this is not my brother['s normal behaviour] and there's something wrong. . ." and it was the head injury. . . it took twenty-four hours for them to [transport] him to Vancouver. Healthcare Worker #3

Patients and focus group participants frequently linked their concerns about being asked their ethnicity to questions about how the information might be used — and for what aims. Thus, in addition to anticipating harm to individuals, and in contrast to the explicit trust expressed by some, many participants of all identities questioned the usefulness of ethnicity data, including how and whether such data might be used beneficially. Patient #24 who identified as 'white' said *"[I'm] concerned, well, yeah, curious as to why. . .what's the data being used for. . . ?"* Similarly, participants in Focus Group #1 expressed caution.

> I guess it really depends on the context within which you do ask. Is it for the purpose of diagnosing? So if you're Chinese you might have some idea of your diagnosis. Whereas if you were asked at a walk-in [clinic] or emergency and you are asked what ethnicity you are, it's like, well, "what difference does it make? I'm here because I need help!"

Patient #32 who identified as "First Nations" said

> I'm just afraid that they might put a, our ethnicity [as] more vulnerable to diseases which I don't think is true, right, and I'm afraid they might put more onto that and . . . it will be used against us sometime in the future. . .

Similarly, Patient #6, who identified her ethnicity as Roman Catholic (and whose first language was Portuguese), said

> Particularly in the future if the Health Authority or the federal government started asking people for their ethnic origin, because it separates the people based on color of skin or where they're from, then we can't call ourselves a society. Just can't.

Participants expressed overall caution about collecting ethnicity data. For example, Patient #11 identified as Iranian-Canadian, and although he had "no difficulty" sharing his ethnicity and expressed trust in healthcare providers, he said:

> I hope in a naive manner that everybody who comes in or works in a hospital, all the physicians, would have the best interest of the patient in mind . . . and not all the time that would be true so it's a really sensitive issue and should be really scrutinized before being implemented.

DISCUSSION

In contrast to perceptions of Canada as egalitarian and equitable, and despite universal healthcare, health and healthcare inequities are significant and persistent, and experiences of racialization and discrimination routinely shape peoples' access to and utilization of services (e.g. Anderson & Kirkham, 1998). This exploratory study sheds light on the complexity of issues at play in Canadian healthcare settings in relation to asking people to identify their ethnicity at the point of care. More research is needed to more fully

understand the complex range of issues involved, particularly as patients receiving care in other healthcare locations may have different views than the participants in this study. However, these findings provide evidence for why there can be distress generated in the process of self-categorization of ethnicity and widespread inaccuracy of data within clinical contexts. Through the analysis it became evident that the collection of ethnicity data represented a racializing process for many patients, with potentially harmful effects.

Discrimination is used in relation to ethnicity, culture, and race in two senses: "*racialism*, which is the not necessarily objectionable view that the human race is divided into different, biologically real races, and *racism*, which is the objectionable view that this supposedly biologically real division involves a hierarchy of value" (Lippert-Rasmussen, 2006, p. 168). The collection of ethnicity data presumably involves a well-intentioned implementation of racialism that is inevitably perpetuated because of the conflation of race and ethnicity. However, the findings from this study suggest that it is not possible to implement collection of ethnicity data at the point of care (on the basis of racialism) without invoking anxieties about racism and racist classifications — particularly among people who have experienced racialization and healthcare inequities. Despite the ethically-motivated intentions of Health Authorities in Canada to redress health and healthcare inequities by collecting ethnicity data at the point of care, current levels of inequities, and their disproportionate effects on particular groups of people, preclude any "neat" separation of racialism and racialization.

The findings highlight that concerns about harm must be taken seriously. These harms are not simply perceptions and the harms of racializing processes are not limited to the psychological effects of discrimination. Rather, as Stuber, Meyer, and Link (2008) recently argued, discrimination is thought to be health harming through various pathways including a) the direct effects of stress arising from interactions that are *perceived* to be discriminatory, b) denial of access to resources, c) internalization of stigma and discrimination, and d) vigilance in anticipation of negative treatment leading to stress and impaired social interactions between marginalized and non-marginalized persons. Discriminatory assumptions can have significant effects on a range of decisions and the allocation of healthcare resources (King et al., 2008; van Ryn & Fu, 2003). For example, in the United Kingdom, Balsa et al. (2005) found that racialized assumptions made by physicians even before observing any particular signal from the patient, and communication problems between "white" physicians and minority patients affected diagnostic decisions to the point that these effects could account for "racial" or ethnic group differences in the diagnosis of hypertension and diabetes. Further, the collection of such data may contribute to reluctance by some to access care. For example, in the US, Baker et al. (2005) found that 18.5% of African Americans and 26.3% of Hispanics said they would be less likely to go to a hospital or clinic that collected information about race and ethnicity, suggesting such connections should be further explored.

While aggressive action to address health inequities is urgent, given available population and research evidence of inequities and lack of evidence of action based on clinically collected ethnicity data, it is questionable whether individual level ethnicity data collected in a Health Authority — as an isolated variable of interest — are necessary to increasing equitable care. Our results suggest that collecting ethnicity data in a clinical context is not a neutral process. The potential harms to individuals are considerable and include harms that may directly contribute to exacerbating inequities and serve as barriers to healthcare access. Such practices must be evaluated in the context of increasing politics of fear, racial profiling and growing inequities and alternatives sought. These concerns lead us to recommend that, in the current climate of healthcare, evidence is required regarding the benefits of collecting ethnicity at the point of care before the widespread adoption of such action. This study clearly supports Pringle and Rothera's (1996) similar conclusion in the United Kingdom regarding general practice — clearer evidence of benefit is required before asking about ethnicity can be recommended. If, despite these concerns, healthcare organizations in Canada pursue collection of ethnicity data in clinical contexts, then care should be taken to mitigate harms at individual and group levels. Collection methods should be considered carefully. Given evidence of preferences for computer-based, or paper and pencil responses to screening for violence (e.g. MacMillan et al., 2006), these alternatives should be evaluated. For face-to-face data collection, strategies to mitigate harm, including extensive training of data collectors, will be required. Even when protocols regarding ethnicity data collection call for self-identification, admitting clerks often "assign" ethnicity based on appearances (Gomez, Kelsey, Glaser, Lee, & Sidney, 2005; Hasnain-Wynia & Baker, 2006). Reasons for collecting ethnicity data should be clearly articulated by healthcare organizations and communicated to both care providers and patients, and commitment to action related to those reasons made and enacted.

Most importantly, perceived discrimination and the issues underlying such discrimination in healthcare settings must be taken seriously and addressed at the system level. The assumption should be challenged that providing equitable, quality care in the clinical context requires the collection of race and ethnicity data (particularly at the point of care), and strategies for providing equitable care should be pursued actively. Indeed, actions to address structural inequities should be taken immediately at healthcare levels and beyond (Smedley, 2008; Smedley, Rich, & Erb, 2005).

ACKNOWLEDGEMENTS

The research reported in this study was funded by the Michael Smith Foundation for Health Research.

The authors would like to acknowledge the important contributions of the people we interviewed, and Dr. Koushambhi Basu Kahn, Ms. Laurel Jebamani and Ms. Tej Sandhu for their assistance in data collection and analysis. We would also like to acknowledge the leadership provided by the co-investigators on our research team: Dr. Betty Calam, Department of Family Practice, Faculty of Medicine; Ms. Nadine Caplette, Vancouver Coastal Health (until April 2008); Mr. Ron Peters, Vancouver Coastal Health; Ms. Elizabeth Stanger, Vancouver Coastal Health.

REFERENCES

Anderson, J., & Kirkham, S. R. (1998). Constructing nation: the gendering and racializing of the Canadian healthcare system. In V. Strong-Boag, S. Grace, A. Eisenberg, & J. Anderson (Eds.), *Painting the maple: Essays on race, gender, and the construction of Canada* (pp. 242–261). Vancouver, BC: University of British Columbia Press.

Aspinall, P., & Anionwu, E. (2002). The role of ethnic monitoring in mainstreaming race equality and the modernization of the NHS: a neglected agenda? *Critical Public Health, 12*(1), 1–15.

Aspinall, P. J. (2000). The mandatory collection of data on ethnic group of inpatients: experience of NHS trusts in England in the first reporting years. *Public Health, 114*(4), 254–259.

Baker, D. W., Cameron, K. A., Feinglass, J., Georgas, P., Foster, S., Pierce, D., et al. (2005). Patients' attitudes toward healthcare providers collecting information about their race and ethnicity. *Journal of General Internal Medicine, 20*(10), 895–900.

Balsa, A. I., McGuire, T. G., & Meredith, L. S. (2005). Testing for statistical discrimination in health care. *Health Services Research, 40*(1), 227–251.

Beauchamp, T. L., & Childress, J. F. (2001). *Principles of biomedical ethics.* New York: Oxford University Press.

Bhopal, R. (1998). Spectre of racism in health and healthcare: lessons from history and the United

States. *British Medical Journal, 316*(7149), 1970–1974.

Bhopal, R. (2001). Ethnicity and race as epidemiological variables: centrality of purpose and context. In H. Macbeth, & P. Shetty (Eds.), *Health and ethnicity* (pp. 21–40). London: Taylor & Francis.

Bhopal, R. (2007). Racism in health and healthcare in Europe: reality or mirage? *European Journal of Public Health, 17*(3), 238–241.

Bourassa, C., McKay-McNabb, K., & Hampton, M. R. (2004). Racism, sexism, and colonialism: the impact on the health of Aboriginal women in Canada. *Canadian Woman Studies, 24*(1), 23–29.

Bourhis, R. Y. (2003). Measuring ethnocultural diversity using the Canadian census. *Canadian Ethnic Studies, 35*(1), 9–33.

Ford, M. E., & Kelly, P. A. (2005). Conceptualizing and categorizing race and ethnicity in health services research. *Health Services Research, 40*(5), 1658–1675.

Furniss, E. (1999). *The burden of history: Colonialism and the frontier myth in a rural Canadian community.* Vancouver, BC, Canada: University of British Columbia Press.

Gerrish, K. (2000). Researching ethnic diversity in the British NHS: methodological and practical concerns. *Journal of Advanced Nursing, 31*(4), 918–925.

Gomez, S., Kelsey, J., Glaser, S., Lee, M., & Sidney, S. (2005). Inconsistencies between self-reported ethnicity and ethnicity recorded in a health maintenance organization. *Annals of Epidemiology, 15*(1), 71–79.

Hasnain-Wynia, R., & Baker, D. W. (2006). Obtaining data on patient race, ethnicity, and primary language in healthcare organizations: current challenges and proposed solutions. *Health Services Research, 41*, 1501–1518.

Hasnain-Wynia, R., Pierce, D., & Pittman, M. (2004). *Who, when, and how: The current state of race, ethnicity, and primary language data collection in hospitals.* New York: The Commonwealth Fund.

Henry, F., & Tator, C. (2006). *The colour of democracy: Racism in Canadian society.* Toronto, ON: Nelson.

Jedwab, J. (2003). Coming to our census: the need for continued inquiry into Canadian's ethnic. *Canadian Ethnic Studies, 35*(1), 33–51.

Kaplan, J. B., & Bennett, T. (2003). Use of race and ethnicity in biomedical publication. *JAMA: Journal of the American Medical Association, 289*(20), 2709–2716.

King, R. K., Green, A. R., Tan-McGrory, A., Donahue, E. J., Kimbrough-Sugick, J., & Betancourt, J. R. (2008). A plan for action: key perspectives from the racial/ethnic disparities strategy forum. *Milbank Quarterly, 86*(2), 241–272.

Krieger, N. (1999a). Embodying inequality: a review of concepts, measures, and methods for studying health consequences of discrimination. *International Journal of Health Services, 29*(2), 295–352.

Krieger, N. (1999b). "Whiting out" white privilege will not advance the study of how racism harms health. *American Journal of Public Health, 89*(5), 782–783.

Krieger, N. (2000). Refiguring "race": epidemiology, racialized biology, and biological expressions of race relations. *International Journal of Health Services, 30*(1), 211–216.

Krieger, N. (2004). Data, "race," and politics: a commentary on the epidemiological significance of California's proposition 54. *Journal of Epidemiology and Community Health, 58*(8), 632–633.

Krieger, N., Chen, J. T., Waterman, P. D., Rehkopf, D. H., & Subramanian, S. V. (2005). Painting a truer picture of US socioeconomic and racial/ethnic health inequalities: The Public Health Disparities Geocoding Project. *American Journal of Public health, 95*(2), 312–323.

Lippert-Rasmussen, K. (2006). The badness of discrimination. *Ethical Theory & Moral Practice, 9*(2), 167–185.

MacMillan, H. L., Wathen, C. N., Jamieson, E., Boyle, M., McNutt, L.-A., Worster, A., et al. (2006). Approaches to screening for intimate partner violence in healthcare settings. *JAMA: Journal of the American Medical Association, 296*(5), 530–536.

National Center for Health Statistics. (2008). National health interview survey 1957–2007.

New Zealand Ministry of Health. (2004). *Ethnicity data protocols for the health and disability sector.* (p. 32). Wellington, New Zealand: New Zealand Ministry of Health.

Pauly, B. (2008). Harm reduction through a social justice lens. *International Journal of Drug Policy, 19*(1), 4–10.

Perot, T., & Youdelman, M. (2001). *Racial, ethnic, and primary language data collection in the healthcare system: An assessment of federal policies and practices.* (p. 40). New York: The Commonwealth Fund.

Physicians for Human Rights. (2003). *The right to equal treatment A report by the panel on racial and ethnic disparities in medical care by Physicians for Human Rights.* Washington, DC: Physicians for Human Rights.

Pringle, M., & Rothera, I. (1996). Practicality of recording patient ethnicity in general practice: descriptive intervention study and attitude survey. *BMJ: British Medical Journal, 312*(7038), 1080–1082.

Quan, H., Wong, A., Johnson, D., & Ghali, W. (2006). The public endorses collection of ethnicity information in hospital: implications for routine data capture in Canadian health systems. *Healthcare Policy, 1*(3), 55–64.

Royal Commission on Aboriginal Peoples. (1996). *Report of the Royal Commission on Aboriginal Peoples.* Ottawa: Canada Communications Group-Publishing.

Rummens, J. A. (2003). Ethnic ancestry, culture, identity, and health: using ethnic origin data from the 2001 Canadian census. *Canadian Ethnic Studies, 35*(1), 84–110.

van Ryn, M., & Fu, S. S. (2003). Racial/ethnic bias and health. Paved with good intentions: do public health and human service providers contribute to racial/ethnic disparities in health? *American Journal of Public Health, 93*(2), 248–255.

Sandefur, R. L. (2008). Access to civil justice and race, class, and gender inequality. *Annual Review of Sociology, 34*(1), 339–358.

Sherwin, S. (1992). Feminist and medical ethics: two different approaches to contextual ethics. In H. Bequaret Holmes, & L. Purdy (Eds.), *Feminist perspectives in medical ethics* (pp. 17–31). Indianapolis: Indiana University.

Sheth, T., Nargundkar, M., Chagani, K., Anand, S., Nair, C., & Yusuf, S. (1997). Classifying ethnicity utilizing the Canadian mortality database. *Ethnicity & Health, 2*(4), 287–295.

Smedley, B. D. (2008). Moving beyond access: achieving equity in state healthcare reform. *Health Affairs (Project Hope), 27*(2), 447–455.

Smedley, B. D., Rich, R. F., & Erb, C. T. (2005). Racial and ethnic healthcare disparities: the role of personal choice vs. structural inequality. In R. F. Rich, & C. T. Erb (Eds.), *Consumer choice: Social welfare and health policy — Policy studies review annual* (pp. 83–98). New Brunswick, N.J. and London: Transaction.

Institute of Medicine Committee on Understanding and Eliminating Racial and Ethnic Disparities in Healthcare. In Smedley, B. D., Stith, A. Y., & Nelson, A. R. (Eds.), *Unequal treatment: Confronting racial and ethnic disparities in healthcare.* Washington, D.C.: Institute of Medicine National Academies Press.

Smylie, J. (2005). The ethics of research involving Canada's Aboriginal populations. *Canadian Medical Association Journal, 172*(8), 977.

Statistics Canada. (2006). *Definitions, data sources and methods.* Ottawa: Statistics Canada.

Stuber, J., Meyer, I., & Link, B. (2008). Stigma, prejudice, discrimination and health. *Social Science & Medicine, 67*(3), 351–357.

Tang, S. Y., & Browne, A. J. (2008). 'Race' matters: racialization and egalitarian discourses involving aboriginal people. *Ethnicity & Health, 13*(2), 1–19.

Thomas, D. (2005). I am Canadian. *Canadian Social Trend* 1–7.

United Nations. (1952). *The race question in modern science: The results of an inquiry — The concept of race.* Paris: United Nations.

Walker, M. U. (2001). Seeing power in morality: a proposal for feminist naturalism in ethics. In P. DesAutels, & J. Waugh (Eds.), *Feminists doing ethics.* Oxford, London: Rowman & Littlefield.

Williams, D. R. (2002). Racial/ethnic variations in women's health: the social embeddedness of health. *American Journal of Public Health, 92*(4), 588–597.

Wu, Z., & Schimmele, C. M. (2005). Racial/ethnic variation in functional and self-reported health. *American Journal of Public Health, 95*(4), 710–716.

Young, I. M. (1990). *Justice and the politics of difference.* Princeton, NJ: Princeton University Press.

3.06

CASE STUDY DESIGN

Men Do Matter

Ethnographic Insights on the Socially Supportive Role of the African American Uncle in the Lives of Inner-City African American Male Youth

Joseph B. Richardson Jr.*

ABSTRACT: This article examines the role of the African American uncle as a vital yet over-looked form of social support and social capital in the lives of adolescent African American male sons living in single-female-headed households. Research rarely examines the affective roles and functions of men in Black families; moreover, poor urban Black male youth are typically portrayed as a monolithic and homogeneous group who lack positive relationships with their biological fathers. The absence of these relationships has been correlated to numerous social problems for Black male youth—specifically, delinquency and violent behavior. Although much of the work on African American fatherhood has focused on the role of the biological father (and, to some extent, the stepfather), minimal attention has been given to men within extended familial networks and their impact on successful adolescent development among young African American males.

KEYWORDS: Families; youth development; fathers; African American; delinquency.

My older brother Tommy comes and gets my sons all the time, and he takes them out to the Pocono Mountains or wherever they really want to go with him. He lets them stay with him all the time, just about every weekend. And my brother, Timothy, he just got released from prison. He's the one that stays here with me because he is on parole. Timothy takes [my sons] out to the movies or dinner all the time. Timothy gets them whatever they want, but I have to tell him all the time,

"Don't be giving them everything they want, because when you're gone I ain't going to be giving it to them. You know?" [laughs] But I'm really lucky, I guess, that I got my three brothers to help me take care of my sons. I don't know what I would do without them.

—Rhonda Brown (age 40, mother of sample member Clyde, age 13)[1]

*University of Maryland at College Park

[1]All names (persons, communities, schools, and otherwise) are pseudonyms.

This article examines the role of nonbiological fathers—specifically, the African American uncle—as a vital yet often overlooked source of social support and social capital in lives of African American male youth. Despite a significant body of literature on the role of the African American grandmother as an almost heroic figure in poor inner-city families—in many instances, serving as the primary caregiver and surrogate mother for her grandchildren (Pearson, Hunter, Ensminger, & Kellam, 1990)—few studies have examined the socially supportive role of men in extended familial networks (i.e., grandfathers, uncles, cousins; Jarrett, Roy, & Burton, 2002). Research on the African American grandmother suggests that in the absence of the biological father, many poor single-female-headed households often rely on the additional social support and parenting provided by grandmothers (Pearson et al., 1990).

Extensive data on the inner-city African American family suggest that this collective of women are often left with the task of raising young African American males alone, without the assistance of biological fathers. However, the extensive research on the role of women in extended familial networks has left an unaddressed gap in the research on the African American family—specifically, the role of men in extended familial networks as surrogate fathers and primary caregivers to single-female-headed households. To date, there are no qualitative research studies that examine the role of nonbiological African American fathers within family networks—namely, the role of the African American uncle as a primary source of social support and social capital to single-female-headed households and male youth. Data from a recent qualitative research study[2] on social capital in the lives of at-risk African American male youth reveals that single-female-headed households often rely on their biological brothers, brothers-in-law, and older male extended family members (i.e., grandfathers and cousins) to serve as father figures for their adolescent boys in the absence of biological fathers.

As such, this article explores the role of these men as fathers in poor inner-city African American families and their successful parenting practices and strategies in preventing delinquency and violent behavior and fostering successful adolescent development among at-risk male youth (Jarrett, 1997a, 1997b). Although the literature on African American fatherhood and young African American males has primarily examined the relationship between biological fathers and their sons, the majority of the research on African American fatherhood has relatively ignored the relationship between older male extended family members and male youth. The unique relationship that uncles have with their nephews as male role models and, in many instances, as surrogate fathers has been virtually absent from

literature on African American fatherhood. Thus, this article focuses on the relationships between men in extended familial networks (uncles) and (a) single-female-headed households and (b) at-risk male youth. This analysis highlights the significant functions of these relationships, such as trustworthiness, social obligations and expectations, reciprocity, information channels, and the social norms that men within these relationships provide to single-female-headed households and at-risk youth to foster prosocial youth behavior and successful adolescent male development. All these factors are significant determinants of social capital that in turn influence youth behavior and their decision-making processes to engage in violence (Rose & Clear, 1998; Wilkinson, 2003).

This article uses data from a 4-year ethnographic adolescent life-course study of social capital and serious violence among a small group of 15 early-adolescent African American males and their families, living in a predominately poor African American community in New York City. These 15 case studies were drawn from a larger ethnographic research study on the social context of adolescent violence in schools and communities conducted by the Vera Institute of Justice from 1997 to 2001. For the purposes of this article, 3 case studies are used for the discussion. They were selected from the 15 case studies because they provide compelling contextual narratives and ethnographic data on the role of the African American uncle as a surrogate father.

THE AFRICAN AMERICAN UNCLE AND CONTEMPORARY TELEVISION: A VISUAL SOCIOLOGY ON AFRICAN AMERICAN FAMILIES AND FATHERHOOD

In light of the dearth of qualitative research on the relationship between the African American uncle and his nephews as a more nuanced and overlooked form of African American fatherhood, pop culture and (ironically) not sociological research appears to be the sociological harbinger in this area of research. Consequently, the analysis of this relationship begins in a most unusual place: African American–themed television sitcoms and films that have done a more-than-adequate qualitative exploration of this aspect of African American fatherhood. Surprisingly, contemporary media on African American families has devoted much more attention than that of the sociological field to identifying and highlighting the vital, socially supportive role that uncles play in the African American

---

[2]This was my own research study conducted in Central Harlem from 1997 to 2000; the data collected from this study was used as the basis for this article.

family and in the lives of African American children. Over the course of the past two decades, television and film have been at the forefront of sociological research on the African American uncle, shedding much-needed light on the role of the African American uncle as a primary caregiver and surrogate father figure in African American families. Popular sitcoms and films with predominately African American cast, such as the *Fresh Prince of Bel-Air* (1990–1996), the *Bernie Mac Show* (2001–2006), and a more recent film *ATL* (2006), all have highlighted the role of the African American men in extended familial networks as primary caregivers and surrogate fathers within African American families. In each of these sitcoms and films, African American uncles have served as primary caregivers for the children of their biological sisters, often filling the role of surrogate father for their nephews and nieces when the biological fathers were not present. Although these sitcoms and films provide great humor and compelling storylines, the sociological diamond in the rough within these stories is the valuable role of African American men in extended familial networks who function as fathers and primary caregivers in African American families.

Similar to the socially supportive role of the African American grandmother as the second line of maternal defense in the African American family is the role of the African American uncle as the primary caregiver and father for African American boys when the biological father is not present. However, when discussing and examining family-based social capital within African American families, researchers often fail to acknowledge African American men within extended families as important sources of family-based social capital (Burton & Snyder, 1998).

PATERNAL INVOLVEMENT AND FAMILY-BASED SOCIAL CAPITAL

Much of the earlier work on social capital (Coleman, 1990) analyzed its production for the benefit of children by examining the absence or presence of two parents within families. Single-parent households where men were absent were often perceived as socially deficient models of social capital, unable to produce the wealth of such capital, which would prevent negative outcomes for children, such as dropping out of school or engaging in delinquency (Coleman, 1990). However, few studies of social capital have actually addressed how it is produced within families, regardless of their structure. How social capital is produced within poor African American families is a question that has been answered more by assumption than by examination, although some work is beginning to emerge (Furstenberg, 2001).

Much of the discussion on the relationship between social capital and fatherhood within African American families has focused on the presence or absence of the biological father or stepfather. Almost no work has been done on the collaborative parenting relationships that men in extended familial and fictive kinship networks engage in with single mothers. The majority of research on fathers and social capital has been confined to analyzing the added value of a father's presence in generating social capital. However, Furstenberg (2001) notes,

> We could ask what effect if any additional parent (grandmother, uncle, or much older sibling) offers when he or she reinforces the values and regulations of a single parent. Thus, fathers may or may not be distinctive in their ability to help generate social capital in the family.

The discussion of fathers as a significant form of family-based social capital is critically important in the discourse on African American families and fatherhood. If we have only begun to scratch the proverbial surface on the role of fathers in generating social capital, it is safe to say that the exploration is virtually non-existent on the role of African American men within extended familial and fictive kinship networks as surrogate fathers. Family researchers have generally assumed that fatherhood within African American families does not often go beyond the scope of the biological father or stepfather. Furthermore, what transpires within African American families to generate larger or lesser amounts of social capital for children is unclear—specifically for at-risk adolescent African American males. Part of the explanation may reside in the failure of scholars to intimately examine the role of men in the extended kin and family systems, beyond the immediate household. Indeed, over the past two decades, one of the most significant areas of research in the Black family literature has concerned the role and functioning of the extended family as an informal support network (Taylor, Chatters, Tucker, & Lewis, 1990). Similar to the structure of immigrant families, which use a broader range of kinship ties for social support and social capital, kinships systems within African American families go well beyond the immediate household, utilizing the social support of grandparents, aunts, uncles, cousins, in-laws, and godparents. Yet, few studies have qualitatively documented support exchanges among African American men in extended familial networks, such as cousins and in-laws, not to mention relationships between in-laws, divorce and remarriage chains, and more distal sets of kin.

With the increased discourse on social capital in African American communities and families, African American fatherhood, and its influence on youth development—particularly, educational success and resisting participation in juvenile delinquency and serious violent behavior—researchers must begin to address the role of fatherhood beyond its traditional and myopic view, defined as a biological parent or stepparent (Salem, Zimmerman, & Notaro, 1998). Fatherhood should be defined by its function, not by its list of usual suspects who have been traditionally defined as fathers (i.e., biological and stepfathers). Consequently, research is sorely needed on how fatherhood is defined and mediated in African American families and what role men in extended family and fictive kinship networks play in creating mechanisms that foster positive life outcomes, monitor and regulate youth behavior, sustain informal social controls, and provide emotional and psychological support for at-risk male youth. This is critically important when examining how systems of social support are produced and accessed within poor single-female-headed households. Much of this discussion focuses on the collective parenting relationships between siblings (single mothers and their biological brothers) in the creation of social capital for the benefit of children. It is vitally important to give attention to not only these relationships but how certain factors play (e.g., mutual obligation, trustworthiness, expectations, effective norms and sanctions) in the role of the African American uncle as a surrogate father in these families. But it is more important to explore how the African American uncle actively engages in the collective familial body to monitor and regulate youth behavior. The African American uncle is often a primary participant in the collective and unified body of familial solidarity in the parenting process of at-risk African American male youth.

AN ETHNOGRAPHIC APPROACH TO SUCCESSFUL ADOLESCENT DEVELOPMENT AND THE ROLE OF AFRICAN AMERICAN UNCLE

This article is framed by data collected from a longitudinal ethnographic research study that examined the social context of adolescent violence for 15 early-adolescent African American males. The research methodology for the study involved in-depth life-history interviews and ethnographic participant observations with 15 young men and their single mothers over a period of 4 years. The use of ethnography provided thick and rich contextual data that could not be achieved through quantitative analysis. Although quantitative studies can identify the relationship between variables, they cannot fully explicate the range of parenting processes that transpire in real families. However, qualitative research using in-depth

interviews and participant observations is particularly suitable for exploring the interaction between individuals and their social environment. Qualitative inquiry highlights the contextual nature of social life; it explores subjective perceptions and meanings; and it identifies social processes and dynamics. Qualitative studies can describe everyday family life in poor African American neighborhoods, and it can present accounts of how parents and adolescents feel about their lives and their worlds and how they cope with poverty and create strategies for dealing with it. Qualitative studies—particularly, ethnographic research—can explain in great detail the nuances of African American family life and the parental activities and behaviors that may account for youth outcomes (Burton, Allison, & Obeidallah 1996; Jarrett, 1995).

THE STUDY

The ethnographic data used for this article were collected over a 4-year period in Soulville, a predominately African American community in New York City. According to New York City Police Department crime statistics, during the period of this study, Soulville ranked in the top five communities in New York City in homicides, robberies, and assaults. Soulville also ranked first in New York City in per-capita rates of tuberculosis infections, infant mortality, and children suffering from asthma. During the period of this study, the Soulville community experienced an emerging violent youth gang crisis, as notorious West Coast–based youth gangs—namely, the Bloods and the Crips—formed in the Soulville community and actively recruited Soulville African American male youth from local schools, neighborhood playgrounds, and street corners. Soulville Junior High—a local school from which the young men for this study were selected for the sample group—was the most violent junior high school among the four that served the Soulville community. A significant proportion of young men who attended Soulville Junior High were members of the Bloods and the Crips. One young man was a member of the Crips; another was a member of the Bloods; and a third belonged to the Valley, a local youth gang based in a notoriously violent local housing project. Consequently, several of the young men in the sample had numerous contacts with the criminal justice system. For those reasons, the young men in this group have been classified as *at risk*.

Life history interviews were conducted every year with the sample members and their parents—all of whom were single mothers. When possible, men within extended family networks were also interviewed. When men did participate in life history interviews, the majority were not the biological fathers, stepfathers, or boyfriends of the single mothers; they were often their older biological brothers or brothers-in-law.

African American male youth were selected for this study because they disproportionately represent offenders and victims of violent crimes in poor urban areas. They are also the most vulnerable population of youth; that is, they are most likely to be victims of early violent deaths via gun-related homicides. Deaths of adolescents attributed to firearm-related injuries are disproportionately concentrated among non-Whites—especially, African American teenagers and young adults (Wilkinson, 2003). Young African American males are also almost 5 times more likely to die from firearm-related injuries than from natural causes. According to data published by the Centers for Disease Control and Prevention, homicide is the most common cause of death among African American male youth (48 deaths per 100,000 persons). Since 1988, the firearm-related death rate among African American male teenagers (15–19 years) exceeded the death rate attributed to natural causes or any other cause (Wilkinson, 2003). More than 29% of African American males are likely to go to prison at some point in their lives, compared to 4% of White males. In New York City, where this study was conducted, almost 50% of African American males do not graduate high school and are not employed. Several criminological studies have noted that poor urban communities with high proportions of single-female-headed households often have high rates of juvenile delinquency and youth violence because the absence of adult males restricts the number of adult males to supervise young men in the community. These dire statistics, combined with the reality that several members of this sample study were active participants in violent local youth gangs, unequivocally defined this vulnerable population of youth at risk.

The research study began at the start of the sample group's 7th-grade year (or at approximately age 12, which typically marks the onset of delinquent behavior), and it ended at the end of its 10th-grade year (age 16, which marks the peak of delinquency). To intimately explore the social context of violence and adolescent development for these 15 young men, the method used for this study was longitudinal and ethnographic. Each sample member represented a life-course case study of early to midadolescence.

Participant observations were conducted daily across a multiple social settings: at Soulville Junior High, around the local Soulville community, and within households. Although this study centered on contextualizing adolescent violence in the Soulville community among African American male youth, one of the unexpected findings was the emergence of the African American uncle as a protective resource and surrogate father in the lives of African American male youth.

In the annual life-history interviews conducted with the single mothers of these young men, many were quite candid and insightful about the valuable role that their brothers played in the collaborative-parenting process. Throughout the study, the young men in the sample and their mothers emphasized the importance of men in extended familial networks who served as surrogate fathers. During the annual life-history interviews with the young men in the sample, the question was posed, "Who are the most important adults in your life and why?" Several of the young men consistently responded that their uncles were the most important male adults in their lives. When the single mothers were asked to identify who they relied on for assistance in the parenting process, many cited their brothers as valuable resources in providing additional adult supervision. In the analysis of the data following the completion of the study, it became clear that the consistent theme of uncles as a valued commodity in the parenting process warranted considerable attention. However, given that much of the analysis on the role of the African American uncle as surrogate father occurred following the completion of the study, the sampling of uncles/surrogate fathers was not attempted in all cases. As such, the following qualitative analysis is based on three case studies, taken from the larger sample of 15 cases.

In these three cases studies, the young men in the sample and their mothers were able to clearly identify and explain the socially supportive role that uncles filled as surrogate fathers. In some instances, the uncles themselves articulated their roles as surrogate fathers. Although uncles played a valuable role in the lives of African American male youth among the five remaining cases, for the purposes of this article, these three case studies are presented that best highlight that role.

CASE STUDY: CLYDE

In many instances, uncles were primary decision makers within single-female-headed households. Like the Black inner-city grandmother so often discussed as a primary caregiver within African American families, these men often served similar roles. In this case study, Rhonda Brown, age 36, a young single mother of three African American boys—Clyde (age 13) and his younger brothers, Barry (age 10) and Terry (age 6)—utilized her three older brothers and an older male cousin as a collective group of surrogate fathers for her three boys. Taylor et al. (1990) note that "having an available pool of relatives, frequent interaction with family members and close familial relationships were predictors for receiving support from extended family." Single mothers such as Rhonda relied on the men within her extended familial networks for social support. Here she discusses her perspective on why her brothers played a significant role in the successful adolescent development of her children:

> I think for all young men, really, they need somebody older in their life. It could be a brother, an uncle, a cousin, anybody. They just need to find a man that is going to show them the right way to go, someone that they can put their trust into—fortunately, for me, those men are my brothers.

Rhonda's son Clyde echoed these sentiments in an interview. In fact, African American male youth in this study often looked to older men within their extended families for advice, ranging from how to negotiate the street to how to navigate intimate relationships with the opposite sex. Male youth often recognized the void that uncles filled in their lives in the absence of their biological fathers. The following excerpt was taken from a life history interview question that asked, "Who do you rely on for advice or social support?"

> I could go to my mother with my problems, but any boy would rather talk to their uncle or father about a problem or whatever . . . like getting into beef [dispute on the street] or like girls or whatever. There are just certain things you can't talk to your mom about that you can talk to your uncle about. My uncles understand me better because I'm a boy. (Clyde)

Rhonda enlisted the social support of her three brothers and an older male cousin (referred to as an uncle) to collectively engage in raising her three boys. All four men served as surrogate fathers throughout Clyde's adolescence. During the first year of this study, two of Clyde's uncles, Tyrone (age 40) and Timothy (age 43), were incarcerated, whereas a third uncle, Tommy, worked as a bus driver for Greyhound. Tommy resided in the Pocono Mountains in Pennsylvania, about a 90-min drive from Soulville. Every weekend, Tommy would arrange with Rhonda to pick up Clyde and his two younger brothers after school, where they would begin the drive from Soulville to his home for what Tommy and Rhonda referred to as "a weekend retreat." Rhonda and her brother Tommy agreed that taking Clyde to his home, in such a rural setting, provided a necessary social, psychological, and emotional escape from the violent and volatile world of Soulville. Tommy's home was utilized as a temporary "safe haven" from the streets of Soulville. Qualitative studies on the African American family have provided insight on how some poor families create strategies that provide stability for their children in light of neighborhood social disorganization. Some families are able to construct social worlds that limit the impact of the dangers in which their children's lives are embedded (Jarrett, 1997a, 1997b).

Rhonda's older brother, Timothy, was released from prison during the second year of the study and was subsequently paroled to Rhonda's home. It was during his parole that Timothy became instrumental in serving as a surrogate father to Clyde and his two younger brothers, especially after Rhonda resumed permanent employment at the post office. Timothy checked Clyde's homework daily and monitored his studies. He also attended all open school nights and Parent—Teacher Association meetings at Clyde's school, Soulville Junior High. These social behaviors are often defined as significant measures of social capital. Rose and Clear (2002) also acknowledge that upon reentry into communities and families following periods of lengthy incarceration, African American men often serve as vital forms of social capital. A growing body of research demonstrates the importance of these men in the collective-parenting process. When these men are removed from familial networks via incarceration, their absence often disrupts the collective-parenting process that occurs within many poor African American families (Jarrett, 1997a, 1997b; Rose & Clear, 2002). Consequently, the reentry of ex-offenders into supportive familial networks often facilitates successful transitions into families and communities following incarceration.

Clyde's older cousin Rocky (age 38) also served as a surrogate father and actively engaged in the parenting process. Although Rocky was Clyde's older cousin, the family referred to him as an uncle. This kind of fictive relationship is an adaptive role present in many poor African American families (Jarrett, 1997a, 1997b, 1999). When Timothy and Tommy were not actively engaged in monitoring and supervising Clyde's activities, Uncle Rocky, who was recently discharged from the army, played an integral role in mentoring and parenting Clyde. In addition, although Tyrone was incarcerated, he remained active in Clyde's life as well, providing him with sound advice about life and why he should acquire a solid education and employment—namely, so that he would never end up in prison.

Within Clyde's family, uncles provided sound advice on the code of the streets (Anderson, 1999). How to survive and negotiate the streets of Soulville was passed intergenerationally from uncles to their nephews. In this interview, Rocky provides keen insights on the code of the streets and how he taught the code to his nephew Clyde. The following interview was conducted with Rocky while he was at Rhonda's home taking care of her three sons while Rhonda worked a double shift at the post office.

> As far as the streets go, I tell [Clyde] that he's going to have to know how to handle himself out there on the streets. I tell him that the police will stop you for anything. So whatever they ask you just say, "Yes, sir" or "No, sir." You have to act like you're giving them respect, so they know you're not disrespecting them . . . 'cause today, man, you can't even move when the [New York

City Police Department] stop you—you can't even dig in your pockets, 'cause they think all young Black men are carrying guns, but that's not really true. I also tell Clyde how he don't need to be in a gang. I don't even know why people join a gang today anyway, but we got a lot of gangs around here now. I tell Clyde, "We got a big family." You know what I'm saying? He's got uncles, a father, and cousins, so I tell him, "Anything you have a problem with, you can come to us." He's got a lot of role models in his life to look up to. So I don't even see being in a gang in his picture because he knows we would check him on that. I tell him if he has any problems, they can always be handled. He always has me to talk to.

Rocky also monitored Clyde's activities while Clyde was on the streets, thus providing an informal source of social control. Although the neighborhood of Soulville was for the most part socially disorganized, men such as Rocky provided informal social controls that in many respects fostered a form of community policing regarding the activities of Soulville youth. Rose and Clear (1998) note that "social capital is the essence of social control for it is the very force collectives draw upon to enforce order." In this interview, Rocky discusses how he monitored Clyde's behavior on the streets of Soulville:

INTERVIEWER: So do you ever run into Clyde on the streets?
ROCKY: Yeah, most definitely. Sometimes when I walk on the avenue, I will see him. I will call him over, and we will stop and talk. The first question I ask him is "Where are you going?" Then I ask, "What time are you going home?" Then I get on the phone and call his mother, and I tell her, "Look, Rhonda, what do you want me to do with him? Do you want me to send him home or what?" Most of the time, she's like, "As long as he's with you, he can stay out." I'm like, "Okay," because I don't feel cool unless I know everything is all right.

In many respects, Rocky served as the family's eyes and ears for Clyde while he ventured out on the often-volatile streets of Soulville. Jarrett's research (1999) on successful parenting in high-risk neighborhoods suggests that community-bridging parents protect their adolescents from negative neighborhood influences by closely supervising their time, space, and friendships.

Rose and Clear (1998) argue that individual and familial networks are often disrupted by incarceration, which in turn disrupts communities:

It is logical to assume that the loss of criminal males benefits the communities simply because they are seen as residents who are committing crime. When criminals are gone, communities are safer. But if some offenders occupy roles within networks that form the basis for informal social control, their removal is not solely a positive act, but also imposes losses on those networks and their capacity for strengthening families and community life. (p. 458)

Clyde's case study touches on the unintended consequences of incarceration and the added social support that men contribute to their families once they are released from prison.

Timothy immediately assumed the role of primary caregiver and surrogate father once he was released from prison and paroled to his sister's home. One could also assume that once Tyrone was released from prison (he was incarcerated at the time of the study), he too would serve as a primary source of social capital within Clyde's familial network, especially when considering that he had been doing so while incarcerated.

In neighborhoods deficient of social capital, where young men are often left on the streets unsupervised and unmonitored, the presence of older men serves as a deterrent to involvement in serious violent behavior (Anderson, 1999). The collective efficacy displayed by these men in parenting their nephew in many respects refutes popular public opinion about the absence of positive father figures in the lives of at-risk African American male youth and single-female-headed households.

The common assumption is that poor African American communities, disproportionately populated by single-female-headed households, often lack the social capital to encourage children toward completion of their education, discourage them from engaging in delinquency and crime, and sanction them appropriately in informal and intimate relationships. Clearly, however, even in homes absent biological fathers, other male figures often serve in socially supportive roles to these households and children. We need much more information and research about these networks that are so fundamental to the social networks and social control of at-risk African American male youth. More important, we must learn more about the role of men in extended familial networks in poor African American families and their impact on the behaviors of at-risk African American male youth.

CASE STUDY: JALEN

My uncle Rich used to be in jail. My other uncle, Ronald, was in jail, too, and my other uncle, Dickie, is in jail now, and so is my father. Two of my cousins, Mark and Tucker, are locked up, too. My family got a long record. If people in my neighborhood or the police know you're a Smith [family's last name], they'll be like, "Oh, I know you're going to jail." That's why I don't like being a Smith. I really want to change my last name. You know, I want to change it for emergency situations like, say, for instance, someone gets robbed around here and accuses me of it. If they know I'm a Smith, then they'll think I probably had a pretty good chance of doing it. I mean, my family just has a bad reputation around here. . . . If I had one wish, I just wish I could change my name.

—Jalen Smith (age 13)

Jalen had witnessed firsthand the destruction that awaited African American men, young and old, on the streets of Soulville. Jalen needed to look no further than the men in his family to understand the devastating impact of those streets and the fatal blows they delivered to the lives of men in his family. The majority of men in Jalen's family had extensive criminal histories and had experienced some form of incarceration during their lives. Jalen's father, George Smith, was a career criminal and was in and out of prison for the majority of Jalen's life. The majority of Jalen's paternal uncles and male cousins were either serving prison sentences or had recently been released from prison. Two of his maternal uncles died on the streets of Soulville. His mother's oldest brother, James, died from a heroin overdose. Her youngest brother, William, was murdered in Soulville, severely beaten by a man with a baseball bat.

The number of men in Jalen's family-based social network who were lost to the criminal justice system significantly reduced the opportunity for them to monitor and supervise Jalen's social activities. Furthermore, the loss of such men to the criminal justice system is symbolic of the enormous aggregate loss of men in the Soulville community who could provide informal social control and social support (Rose & Clear, 1998, 2002).

When this study began, Jalen had few men in his familial network who were able to offer social support or engage in the collective-parenting process. Jalen resided in a household headed by his mother, Valerie Smith, and his paternal grandmother, Grace Moe. Grace Moe was Jalen's primary caregiver and parent. She was the central authority figure, disciplinarian, and decision maker in the Smith household. During much of Jalen's life, he lived with his grandmother in a two-bedroom apartment in a low-income housing tenement. His mother lived several floors below, in the same building, with Jalen's two younger brothers. Several months following the initiation of this study, Valerie's brother Richard (age 36) was released from prison. "Big Rich," as he was called by his family and neighbors, was a former drug enforcer in the Soulville community. He was well respected and feared by many of the residents of Soulville. In a situation similar to that of Clyde's uncle Timothy, when Richard returned to Soulville from prison, he was paroled to his mother's home (Grace Moe's). Upon reentry into this familial setting, Richard immediately assumed the role of Jalen's surrogate father.

Jalen was an avid basketball player who spent most of his leisure time playing in organized youth basketball leagues. These leagues provided valuable community-based social capital that steered Jalen away from violence and crime. The coaches in these leagues often served as role models and mentors to young men. Few fathers of the young men in the basketball leagues attended the games or engaged in the league activities (i.e., serving as coaches or chaperones). This was often a reflection of the few men in the community who were actively involved in the lives of their sons. Such lack of involvement and social interaction between older and younger men in Soulville left a deficit in community- and family-based social capital, which in turn resulted in fewer forms of informal social controls.

However, Big Rich attended all of Jalen's games, and he often served as a team chaperone when the team traveled to basketball tournaments outside of Soulville. Jarrett (1999) notes that "a commonly used monitoring strategy among poor African American families is chaperonage, or the accompaniment of children in the neighborhood by a parent, family friend or sibling." Through his chaperonage, Rich developed close social ties with the coaches in the basketball leagues. He was also highly respected by men in the local neighborhood and was regarded as a neighborhood celebrity of sorts. His reputation in Soulville served as a protective family feature for Jalen.

> INTERVIEWER: So do you think Big Rich gets a lot of respect in the neighborhood?
> JALEN: Yeah, in my neighborhood and all around, really. Every time we walk around here, he stops to talk to someone, like on every block—like at least two people on every block.
> INTERVIEWER: Do you think he's like a celebrity around here?
> JALEN: Yeah!
> INTERVIEWER: So how do feel about that?
> JALEN: It's cool because when I'm with him, people be like, "Oh, that's Rich's nephew," so they look out for me because of him. So now I'm cool with, like, almost everybody around here.

Richard's constant involvement in monitoring Jalen's activities, as well as his expansive social networks in the community, provided Jalen with additional community-based social capital. Unlike many boys in Soulville, who relied on their crew or gang for "backup" in street disputes, Jalen admitted that he would rely first on an adult—specifically, Richard. In the youth culture of Soulville, adolescents did not readily admit to relying on their parents or family members for assistance in a dispute, but Jalen bucked that pattern. Young men typically relied on their peers for assistance in street disputes, but Jalen relied on Richard.

By the end of Jalen's last season of junior high school basketball, he was heavily recruited by numerous high school basketball programs. During this process, Jalen's older cousin Steven, whom the family referred to as "Uncle Steven," assumed the role of Jalen's informal guardian. Steven, a track coach and gym teacher at Eisenhower High (a basketball powerhouse in New York City), had extensive experience working with college basketball recruiters and scouts, who often used desperate measures to recruit young naïve men such as Jalen into their basketball programs. Confident that Steven would steer Jalen in the right direction, the Smith family decided that Steven should informally serve as Jalen's guardian during his last year of junior high school. Ultimately, the family decided that it would be best if Jalen attended Eisenhower High, where Steven could closely monitor his progress. Over Jalen's adolescent life course, Steven would eventually assume the role of a father figure and mentor in Jalen's life.

Steven played an instrumental role as a father figure, mentor, coach, confidante, and friend. Steven had an extensive history of working in the Soulville community with at-risk children. Consequently, he was adeptly skilled in preparing Jalen for all the pitfalls that many young men in Soulville encounter. Steven also provided Jalen with temporary escapes from Soulville, utilizing community-bridging strategies (Jarrett, 1995), such as trips to visit college campuses, to assist Jalen in exposing him to a world outside of Soulville. This array of strategies, which the family created, minimized the exposure to the neighborhood dangers prevalent in the Soulville community. As the track coach for Eisenhower High, Steven encouraged Jalen to join the track team. As a result, not only would Jalen eventually break two longstanding high school track records, but he would also rank third in the city in the triple jump. In an interview with Jalen's mother, Valerie, she acknowledges the importance of Steven in Jalen's life:

> I don't know what I would do without Steven, especially with things like basketball and track, because I don't know too much about those things, so I'm happy he's here for him. If Steven takes him to play ball or wants to talk to him about condoms, sex, the streets, whatever, I let Steven do whatever he wants with him. Steven tells me that Jalen is a pretty good basketball player. He calls and tells me that Jalen has broken all kinds of school records. See, Jalen won't tell me these things, maybe because I am a woman and his mother—he does not think I would understand. He's a weird kid. He's the most nonchalant kid I ever met. Nothing fazes him. He broke a 19-year-old and a 10-year-old school record and didn't even tell me. Steven told me that at one of his games, college scouts were watching him. Steven always tells me, "Don't let them scout him too early, because you don't know

who's who." I told Steven if I get a call or mail from the colleges, I will contact him first because he knows more about this scouting stuff than I do. Steven calls Jalen all the time—they'll be on the phone for hours at a time. I'm glad it's a male figure in my family that can talk to him like that, even though Darryl [her boyfriend] talks to him, but Darryl's really not a talker, so I'm glad Steven is here for him.

In this case study, two uncles actively participated in collectively parenting Jalen. Uncle Rich served as Jalen's eyes and ears on the street, thereby providing supervision on the street. This form of parental supervision was similar to the role that Rocky played in Clyde's life. Rich protected Jalen from the streets of Soulville but also used his street respect and contacts to provide Jalen with safety (Borgois, 1995). In Jalen's family network, Uncle Steven was a crucial source of family-based social capital. He understood how to negotiate and work social institutions, both informal and formal. Steven served as a representative and liaison between Jalen and the college scouts who aimed to recruit him for his basketball talents. Steven was also Jalen's high school basketball and track coach, another important form of social support and informal social control. This collective of surrogate fathers ultimately led Jalen to a successful collegiate basketball career.

CASE STUDY: COREY

The final case study highlights an extraordinary relationship where an uncle assumed permanent guardianship of his nephew. Corey (age 12) lived with his mother and older brother in a renovated tenement building on the south side of Soulville. Corey's father, Curtis Townsend, spent the majority of Corey's childhood going in and out of prison before he was murdered, when Corey was 10 years old. There were few organized recreational youth centers in his southside neighborhood and fewer older male mentors. Although this area was much safer than his former neighborhood in northern Soulville, it lacked the community-based social capital that seemed to be abundant in both the central and the northern neighborhoods of Soulville. Consequently, the majority of the social institutions that provided positive community-based social capital for young men in his community were located more than 20 blocks from Corey's home. In this excerpt from an interview with Corey, he explains the absence of community-based social capital in his neighborhood:

INTERVIEWER: How do you like living in this neighborhood?

COREY: My neighborhood is boring—its dull and dead. There's nothing to do around here unless we make something to do, like chase kids and beat them up or something like that.

During the first year of the study, Corey's older brother, Darnell, spent a year in prison for robbery. Darnell was a high school dropout. In this excerpt from an interview with Corey, 1 week before his graduation from Soulville Junior High, he discusses why he so desperately wants to be successful in life:

> People always tell me, "Don't be like your older brother, because he gets into a lot of trouble." I don't want to be like him, with no life and no job. I want to have a future 'cause I was realizing that everybody was looking forward to me doing good in school because my brother dropped out. I wanted to make my family proud. So I stopped hanging out with my friends—I left them alone. That's why they're getting left back, getting in trouble and stuff like that and I'm graduating. I left them alone and had to do what I had to do. I'm just solo now. I'm just by myself because you can't trust people. People are backstabbers. They don't want you to get ahead.

Although Tina Jackson (Corey's mother, age 39) invested much of her time creating positive pathways for her younger son (Corey), her older son (Darnell, age 19) spent the majority of his time getting into trouble, hanging out on the streets of Soulville. As Darnell moved further into a life of crime, Tina focused more of her efforts and energies on keeping Corey from following the same, self-destructive trajectory.

> INTERVIEWER: As Corey gets older, do you have any serious concerns about him?
> TINA: Definitely, especially about being with the right people and going in the right direction. His brother Darnell is getting into a lot of trouble, being with the wrong crowd. He's 19, and I'm about to kick him out the house because he's not doing anything with his life but hanging with the wrong people, you know, the "do-nothing crowd." So you can understand by seeing that, I don't want Corey with the wrong crowd and especially not to hang out on the corners around here. All of my family is so spread out, so we are basically down here alone and it's rough down here. The ghetto is a rough place for a young Black man. There are a lot of policemen doing dirty things to young Black boys around here. They're just looking for young boys to harass and lock up, like they did my older son. He was arrested for a mistaken identity for a robbery and had to go to jail for a year. That was the most terrible and miserable thing I've ever been through. I don't want that to happen to either one of my boys again. That's why I will always send Corey to some type of after-school activity, something to keep his mind busy because it's rough out here.

Corey's mother relied heavily on the advice and support of her family—particularly, her brother Melvin—to assist her with rearing her two boys. The Jackson family—Tina's mother-in-law, Eldoise

Townsend (age 60); Tina's brother Melvin (age 44), who resided in Dallas; and her sister Janice (age 37)—collectively engaged in resolving family problems and disputes. They also shared a consensus on the rules, rituals, and values that they instilled in Corey. When families act as a united body and make choices that reflect a solidarity and mutuality of interests, they are generally more successful in mobilizing social capital for their children. A system that is high in social capital is one in which its members believe that they are indebted or obligated to respond to the needs of other family members (Furstenberg, 2001).

As Corey moved through his early adolescence (a period often marked by the onset of delinquent behavior), he spent much of his time floating among various peer groups, trying on different hats of social identity, but never finding one group that provided the right social fit. Early in his seventh-grade year, Corey flirted with the social identity of a "thug," forming a relationship with Sly, a chronic and serious violent offender and a member of two violent Soulville youth gangs. Their primary activity together was getting into trouble and into fights, in and around the public housing projects where Sly lived. It was during Corey's brief relationship with Sly that he was involved in two violent altercations. After the completion of the first year of the study, Corey discontinued his relationship with Sly. He later formed a relationship with several basketball players who attended his junior high school. Jalen was a member of this new peer group. Corey, who was an above-average basketball player, did not play in quite as many leagues as Jalen. Basketball, like many other activities in Corey's life, was treated as a fleeting hobby. As Corey approached his first year in high school, he enrolled at Browning High School, one of the worst-performing high schools in the city. Browning also had a notorious reputation for serious violent youth gangs and violence. During the third year of this study, Browning was the site of a school shooting where an African American male student was murdered.

Although Corey's uncle Melvin had been consistently involved in Corey's life, it was at this juncture in Corey's adolescent development that Melvin decided to assume permanent parental guardianship of Corey, subsequently moving Corey to his home in Dallas, Texas. When monitoring strategies such as intensive supervision and chaperonage become ineffective, some community-bridging parents resort to extreme measures, referred by some researchers as *exile*—that is, geographically separating teens from their biological parents to promote conventional development (Jarrett, 1999). As a former resident of Soulville for much of his adolescence and young adulthood, Melvin intimately knew the many pitfalls that young African American males faced in Soulville that often impeded and undermined their successful adolescent development. Melvin was a Soulville success story. He had climbed out of poverty to become a corporate executive for a *Fortune* 500 company, and he was now living in an affluent middle-class African American enclave in a suburb of Dallas. In light of Melvin's stable middle-class status, Corey's mother was initially hesitant about Corey's relocation.

> My brother wants Corey to come and live with him, now that he's getting ready to go to high school. He wants to keep Corey down in Texas because he believes that it will be better for him. I'm contemplating letting him go because it's nice down there and it's more of a country environment and Corey likes it down there. He gets to go fishing and ride bikes and all kinds of stuff. But my brother, he is so serious about him coming down there. He wants to make Corey a Texas person. He doesn't want him to be in Soulville anymore. I think my brother wants Corey to change his whole lifestyle and make him live down there. But I told brother, "Let Corey make his own decision." I don't want my brother to force Corey to stay there, but my brother keeps pushing it and pushing it, calling here every day asking, "When are you sending Corey down to stay with me?" But as a mother, I'm not sure if I want him to go.

Eventually, Melvin and Corey's mother collectively decided that it would be best if Corey relocated to Dallas. Corey attended a high school in Dallas that emphasized academic excellence and had a wealth of resources—a school in stark contrast to the resource-deprived and gang-controlled Browning High School, in New York. While in Dallas, Corey became a solid B student and joined the school's basketball team. Throughout his high school career, Corey stayed completely clear of violence or delinquency. By the completion of the study, Tina embraced the role of her brother as a surrogate father for her son:

> I'm happy that I sent him to Texas with my brother. My brother has been like the father Corey never had. I won't lie—I miss Corey, but I figure what's good for him is good for me, too. I want the best for him. I think he has a better chance down there to achieve his goals. There's a better school system there, and from what I saw, the teachers put more time into the kids—they seem to care a little bit more. That just seems to be the way of the South, you know—people are more caring and sensitive. If he would have stayed here, I really don't know what the situation might have been, but I would have tried as much as possible to keep him out of those situations, but it would have been rough. More importantly, he really likes being with my brother. It's a more easygoing type of environment, you know, country like. I am glad that my brother convinced me to let him go.

In Soulville, parents often sought safe havens for their children. In Clyde's case, his mother sent him to

stay with his uncle Tommy in the Pocono Mountains on the weekends; similarly, Corey's family utilized Uncle Melvin's home in Dallas as a safe haven as well. A community-bridging pattern with supportive adult networks offers parents the ability to provide broader opportunities for their children by tapping into extended and often socioeconomically diverse kinship networks (Jarrett, 1995). Social networks that provide additional adults furnish young people with additional care, concern, and resources (Aschenbrenner, 1975; Jarrett, 1992; Jeffers, 1967; Martin & Martin, 1978; Valentine, 1968; Williams, 1978).

African American men within poor families and communities have faced the brunt of the most extreme forms of this social, economic, and political marginalization. The social and economic marginalization of African American men has been correlated to high rates of incarceration and the loss of social capital in urban communities and families. Rose and Clear (2002) have extensively documented that men within immediate and extended familial networks are significant sources of social capital and collective efficacy for poor African American families. When these men are removed from communities and families via incarceration, there are significant collateral consequences. One consequence is that fewer men are available to engage in the collective-parenting process and supervision of at-risk African American male youth. For men who have been incarcerated, the implications of successful reentry into African American families are integral to criminal justice and family policy initiatives. In other words, an unintended finding in this research on at-risk African American male youth is the successful reintegration of adult African American men into familial networks following incarceration that strengthened familial based social capital, enhanced the collective parenting process in families, and prevented delinquent and violent behavior among young African American males. As these men integrated back into urban families and assumed socially supportive roles for their sisters' children, in several instances they resisted engaging in future criminal activities because they had become highly valued commodities within these families as surrogate fathers and, often, primary caregivers. But more important, the presence of African American uncles in the lives of at-risk African American male youth fosters positive adolescent development, successful transitions into young adulthood, and the informal social controls that keep delinquency and youth violence in check. If the role of the African American grandmother serves as a first line of defense for many poor single-mother households, then the data produced from this study may lead to the African American uncle's assuming the second line of defense in the collective-parenting process of African American male youth.

Although it is impossible to make generalizations about the highly valued role of men in extended family and fictive kinship networks within African American families through the analyses of three ethnographic case studies, this data may provide an alternative perspective and approach in understanding the various forms of African American fatherhood. To date, much of the sociological research on the African American family continues to approach this multifaceted familial unit through a Westernized perspective and analysis. Furstenberg and Kaplan (2004) acknowledge in their work on social capital and the family that "we know relatively little about the operation of the broader kinship systems in the West." These ethnocentric approaches have done little to enhance or increase our knowledge of African American families and the role that male extended family members play in providing social support to children.

The strengthening of families via the role of fathers has significant implications for future social work research, practice, and policy on fatherhood in the African American community. This article discusses the importance of expanding how we define *fatherhood*—specifically, the male extended family and fictive kinship ties, which have been traditionally utilized within poor African American families to build social capital for the successful development of at-risk children. As scholars, we have failed in many respects to explore the complexity of these relationships and the social structures that exist within poor African American families, particularly among men. Consequently, as we continue policy discussions on how to strengthen poor African American families and reconnect disconnected adult males and disadvantaged African American male youth to mainstream opportunities (Edelman, Holzer, & Offner, 2006), we need to ask, how are we defining the function and role of fatherhood? More important, how can family and social welfare systems and institutions support alternative forms of fatherhood that will foster the social development of at-risk youth?

With so much effort being directed toward bolstering the involvement of the biological father in the African American family and the lives of his children, few policy or programmatic efforts have been created to encourage a broader range of fatherhood involvement that extends beyond the biological father. The strengthening of families must begin to move away from the traditional family structure (i.e., mother, father, and children) and toward a new cultural and social adaptation of how families and, more important, how fathers are defined in the 21st century. These cultural and social adaptations of fatherhood encompass a multitude of social structures and relationships. Recent reports and studies indicate that almost 70% of African American children are born to single

women (e.g., African American Healthy Marriage Initiative; U.S. Department of Health and Human Services, Administration for Children and Families, 2005). Mincy (2006) notes—in his seminal work on young Black men (Black Males Left Behind)—that only 39% of Black children under the age of 18 live with both parents, compared with 77% of White children and 65% of Hispanic children. Furthermore, in 2001, among less-educated Black men who were fathers, 10% lived with their children (Mincy, 2006). Consequently, the issue of family composition severely affects Black families and children. These data reveal the serious problems faced by poor young Black men as they fulfill their roles as fathers. Ideally, this work will lead to broader definitions and characterizations of fatherhood, ones not strictly defined by tradition but more so the functions carried out by men who fulfill these roles in the absence of biological fathers. Therefore, the discourse on public policy and fatherhood must begin to reflect new policies and programs (e.g., welfare programs, employment/prisoner reentry, faith-based initiatives) that support those who assume the role of father within poor Black families (Mincy, 2006).

During the period that this article was written, there were more than 300 homicides in Philadelphia, with the majority of the victims and perpetrators being young African American males between the ages of 16 and 24. The majority of both the victims and the perpetrators came from poor single-female households. Despite an urgent national call within poor urban areas to engage more fathers in the lives of at-risk African American male youth, the social policy and practice discourse has been minimal at best regarding how to engage men who serve as surrogate fathers to at-risk youth (i.e., men in extended family networks, fictive kin, and neighborhood mentors). In October 2007, Philadelphia police commissioner Sylvester Johnson and civic community organizer/developer Kenny Gamble initiated a program entitled A Call for Action, which called for 10,000 African American men to take back their communities and families, to stem the rising tide of Black male violence and homicide (Clark, 2007). Policy makers, city officials, community residents, families, and Black men in the city of Philadelphia have engaged in a hotly contested debate over the feasibility of a call for 10,000 African American men to save their communities and families. If men do matter in the lives of at-risk African American youth, what could we possibly learn from this model of surrogate fatherhood? How could this emerging theory of fatherhood affect how we develop and frame social policy? As criminologists and sociologists of the family, we need to do a much better job of collecting data on the role that nonbiological fathers have in preventing delinquency and youth violence. We must also broaden our analyses of what void these men fulfill as fathers in the lives of at-risk youth in the absence of their biological fathers. One limitation of this study is that the analysis of the African American uncle and of surrogate fatherhood occurred after the completion of the study. Questions were not designed to elicit responses on the role that men in extended familial networks play in the lives of at-risk youth.

Future studies on the impact of surrogate fatherhood in the lives of at-risk African American male youth could compare young men and single mothers who have identified and utilized male extended family members or fictive kin as surrogate fathers, compared to a control group of at-risk African American male youth and single mothers who have not. This kind of comparative study may shed much-needed light on men in extended familial and kinship networks (i.e., uncles, grandfathers, cousins, godfathers) and the role they play as surrogate fathers in the successful social development of African American male inner-city youth.

Within this small sample of 15 case studies, those young men who identified extended family members and fictive kin as surrogate fathers fared much better in resisting crime and delinquency than did those young men from single-female-headed households who lacked a surrogate father relationship. Because the analyses of this emergent finding did not occur until after the completion of the study, the sampling of uncles/surrogate fathers was not attempted in all cases. However, future research studies on the relationship between poor single-female-headed African American households, African American male youth, adolescent development, and crime should examine the role of men in extended familial and fictive kinship networks who function as fathers.

Future research on at-risk adolescent male development and the role of fathers should expand beyond the scope of blood ties and so explore the role of men within the social networks of youth and single-female-headed households who have nonblood ties, such as mentors, coaches, and neighbors. More research must also be conducted that examines how low-income single mothers generate, accumulate, and manage family-based social capital for the benefit of their children. Furstenberg and Kaplan (2004) note,

> How social capital is produced within families is a question that has been more assumed than examined by researchers. All too little ethnographic work exists on the ways parents create family worlds: rules, rituals, and routines that regulate children's everyday behaviors and impart a sense of what is normal. Yet, we know relatively little about the broader kinship system in the West.

Unfortunately, as scholars on the African American family and youth development, we must acknowledge that in many respects Hollywood has done a much better job uncovering and unveiling this relationship on the socially supportive role of the African American uncle as surrogate father in the lives of African American children. This myopic and narrow view of what defines African American fatherhood has perpetuated a sociological myth—namely, that the absence of biological fathers in poor African American families implies that children (specifically, at-risk African American males) lack a heterogeneous pool of socially supportive men who are able to fill the fatherhood void. These three case studies are not intended to make broad, generalized assumptions on the socially significant role of the African American uncle in the lives of single-female-headed households and at-risk adolescent African American males; rather, they are to illustrate that this relationship warrants serious attention by family researchers and social policy makers. It is interesting that a wealth of research has been done on African American women in extended familial and fictive kinship networks as surrogate mothers—particularly, the role of the African American grandmother and aunt as primary caregiver (Anderson, 1996); yet, few studies have examined the role of men in extended familial and fictive kinship networks as surrogate fathers. In light of the plethora of literature and studies that suggest that the presence of a father in the lives of at-risk African American male youth reduces the propensity to engage in delinquency, violence, and crime, it is highly problematic that the analysis of the relationship between fatherhood and youth crime has not revealed alternative forms of fatherhood.

This new and unique pathway to parenting African American males deserves continued exploration. Redefining social practices and policies that support new pathways to parenting at-risk African American males may be crucial in reducing crime, delinquency, and violence among at-risk youth. Until we further explore the multiple and often complex forms of fatherhood within African American families and their impact on the social development of African American male youth, we will continue to take our cues on the heterogeneity of African American fatherhood from Hollywood.

REFERENCES

Anderson, E. (1996). The Black inner-city grandmother: Transition of a heroic type? In T. R. Swartz & K. M. Weigert (Eds.), *America's working poor* (pp. 9–43). South Bend, IN: University of Notre Dame Press.

Anderson, E. (1999). *Code of the street: Decency, violence, and the moral life of the inner city*. New York: Norton.

Aschenbrenner, J. (1975). *Lifelines: Black families in Chicago.* New York: Holt, Rinehart & Winston.

Bourgois, P. (1995). *In search of respect: Selling crack in el barrio.* Cambridge, UK: Cambridge University Press.

Burton, L., Allison, K., & Obeidallah, D. (1996). Ethnographic perspectives on social context and adolescent development among inner-city African-American teens. In R. Jessor, A. Colby, & R. Shweder (Eds.), *Essays on ethnography and human development* (pp. 395–418). Chicago: University of Chicago Press.

Burton, L., & Jarrett, R. L. (2000). In the mix, yet on the margins: The place of families in urban neighborhood and child development research. *Journal of Marriage and the Family, 62,* 1114–1135.

Burton, L., & Snyder, A. (1998). The invisible man revisited: Comments on the life course, history and men's roles in American families. In A. Booth & A. C. Crouter (Eds.), *Men in families* (pp. 31–40). Mahwah, NJ: Lawrence Erlbaum.

Clark, V. (2007, October 23). 10,000 reasons to declare their appeal to success. *Philadelphia Inquirer.*

Coleman, J. (1990). *Foundations of social theory.* Cambridge, MA: Harvard University Press.

Edelman, P., Holzer, H., & Offner, P. (2006). *Reconnecting disadvantaged young men.* Washington, DC: Urban Institute Press.

Furstenberg, F. (2001). Managing to make it: Afterthoughts. *Journal of Family Issues, 22*(2), 150–162.

Furstenberg, F., & Kaplan, S. (2004). Social capital and the family. In J. Scott, J. Treas & M. Richards (Eds.), *The Blackwell companion to the sociology of families* (pp. 218–232). Malden, MA: Blackwell.

Jarrett, R. L. (1992). A family case study: An examination of the underclass debate. In J. Gilgun, K. Daly, & G. Handel (Eds.), *Qualitative methods in family research* (pp. 172–197). Newbury Park, CA: Sage.

Jarrett, R. L. (1995). Growing up poor: The family experiences of socially mobile youth in low-income African-American neighborhoods. *Journal of Adolescent Research, 10,* 111–135.

Jarrett, R. L. (1997a). African-American family and parenting strategies in impoverished neighborhoods. *Qualitative Sociology, 20*(2), 275–288.

Jarrett, R. L. (1997b). Resilience among low-income African-American Youth: An ethnographic Perspective. *Ethos, 25*(2), 218–229.

Jarrett, R. L. (1999). Successful parenting in high-risk neighborhoods. *The Future of Children, 9*(2), 45–50.

Jarrett, R. L., Roy, K., & Burton, L. (2002). Fathers in the "hood": Insights from qualitative research on low-income African-American men. In C. Tamis LeMonda & N. Cabrera (Eds.), *Handbook on fatherhood involvement: Multidisciplinary perspectives* (pp. 211–248). Mahwah, NJ: Lawrence Erlbaum.

Jeffers, C. (1967). *Living poor: A participant observer study of choices and priorities.* Ann Arbor, MI: Ann Arbor Publishers.

Martin, E., & Martin, J. (1978). *The Black extended family.* Chicago: University of Chicago Press.

Mincy, R. (2006). *Black males left behind.* Washington, DC: Urban Institute Press.

Pearson, J., Hunter, A., Ensimger, M., & Kellam, S. (1990). Black grandmothers in multigenerational households: Diversity in family structure and parenting involvement in the Woodlawn community. *Child Development, 61,* 434–442.

Rose, D., & Clear, T. (1998). Incarceration, social capital and crime: Implications for social disorganization theory. *Criminology, 36,* 441–479.

Rose, D., & Clear, T. (2002, January). *Incarceration, reentry and social capital: Social networks in the balance.* Paper for the "From Prison to Home" conference, Washington, DC.

Salem, D., Zimmerman, M., & Notaro, P. (1998). Effects of family structure, family process, and father involvement on psychosocial outcomes among African-American adolescents. *Family Relations, 47,* 331–341.

Taylor, R., Chatters, L., Tucker, M., & Lewis, E. (1990). Developments in research on Black families: A decade review. *Journal of Marriage and the Family, 52,* 993–1014.

U.S. Department of Health and Human Services, Administration for Children and Families. (2005, May). *Summary report: Framing the future a fatherhood and healthy marriage forum.* Paper presented at "Framing the Future: A Fatherhood and Healthy Marriage Forum," Rome, GA.

Valentine, C. (1968). *Culture and poverty.* Chicago. University of Chicago Press.

Wilkinson, D. (2003). *Guns, violence, and identity among African-American and Latino youth.* New York: LFB.

Williams, M. (1978). Childhood in an urban black ghetto: Two life histories. *Umoja, 2,* 169–182.

Wilson, W. J. (1987). *The truly disadvantaged: The inner-city, the under class and public policy.* Chicago: University of Chicago Press.

3.07

NARRATIVE DESIGN

Autobiographical Memories of Early Language and Literacy Development

Judith C. Lapadat*

ABSTRACT: The aim of this study was to apply a narrative, autobiographical approach to inquiry into the acquisition of language and literacy. This article reports the results of a qualitative analysis of nine women's written recollections of their early language and literacy development, as rooted in family, cultural, school, and community experiences and contexts, and the meanings they give to these memories. In these narratives recounted by adults about their childhood experiences, the stories are weighted with their own interpretations, and the events selected for retelling are ones that, on reflection and in the light of subsequent experience, they have come to see as formative in their lives. Key themes that participants discussed relate to the centrality of the family, their self-descriptions as avid readers, their negative perceptions of school, and their perceptions about the role of culture. Two contributions of this study are that it methodologically complements traditional observational approaches to language acquisition research, and that voices from underrepresented communities are heard. (*Language Development, Literacy, Adult Learning, Narrative Analysis, Autobiographical Approach, Qualitative Research*)

Memory seems to be the main place where culture exists, and it is also the locus of interaction between the reality of the individual and the reality outside the individual. Thus, memories are both intensely personal and also reflective of a culture at a given time and place. (Teski & Climo, 1995, p. 2)

The development of language occurs across multiple contexts throughout one's life. However, as of yet, there has been relatively little research on language development across the lifespan. Furthermore, most research on language and literacy development has employed empirical, often descriptive methodologies that overwhelmingly emphasize the researcher's theoretical stance, problem-formulation, and interpretations, rather than seeking the narratives, points of view, and interpretations of participants. The wider purpose of my research is to investigate the ongoing language and literacy development of educated adults as contextualized by their early experiences. I am interested in the stories people tell about their lives, and the ways in which they interpret these stories. In this paper, I present a study that is part of this program of research. It is a qualitative analysis of nine women's written recollections of their early language and literacy development, as rooted in family, cultural, school, and community experiences and contexts, and the meanings they give to these memories.

*University of Northern British Columbia, Canada

THEORETICAL FRAMEWORK

Constructivists describe knowledge as cognitively and socially constructed by learners, in context (Bruner, 1996; Edwards & Mercer, 1987; Hicks, 1996; Lemke, 1989). Knowledge construction is mediated by language, and, simultaneously, reciprocally influences language meanings (Bloome & Bailey, 1992; Giles & Coupland, 1991; Lapadat, 1995; Mercer, 1993). That is to say, the structures and functions of language interact with cognition as individual learners develop and elaborate their cognitive schemas; the body of social and cultural knowledge is both shaped and transmitted through discourse; and both cognitive and social meanings, in turn, influence language interaction in the moment as well as language change over time. Constructivist viewpoints assume diversity of participants, content, processes, and outcomes (Delpit, 1990; Lapadat, 2000a). The views and interpretations of research participants, the teachers and learners themselves, are seen as essential to understanding the nature of knowledge and learning processes (Eisner, 1999; Kirsch, 1993). Yet much of the basic theoretical work of tracing language and literacy development across the lifespan from childhood through adulthood remains to be done (Haswell, 1991; Obler, 2001; Yussen & Smith, 1993).

Much recent research examines language acquisition and emergent literacy by observing practices in the home (Haden, Reese, & Fivush, 1996; Purcell-Gates, 1995; Snow & Ninio, 1986). Similarly, children's continuing language development throughout the school years; the types of reading, writing, and discourse that promote both literacy and learning in the broader sense; and the relationships between language and culture are the focus of many studies (McCabe, 1997; Pappas, Kiefer, & Levstik, 1999; Wells, 1986, 1990). Typically, such studies are empirical, observational, and descriptive. Those few that have been longitudinal have emphasized prediction, such as by posing questions about the relationships between early language or literacy measures and later language, literacy, or academic achievement measures (Haden et al., 1996; Wells, 1986).

Few studies have been reflective and retrospective in design, seeking to elicit participants' narratives of their experiences of developing language and literacy, or examining the interpretations individuals give to their own experiences (but see Purcell-Gates, 1995; Thomas & Maybin, 1998). Yet retrospective designs have a great deal to contribute to our understanding of language and literacy development. Observational studies are, by design, limited to selectively recorded behavioral events. The researcher decides which events to observe, and evaluates and interprets what is seen. It is difficult to balance these data with the observed participants' perspectives as language and literacy emerge at a young age when children have not yet reached a stage of sufficient metacognitive and metalinguistic awareness to produce reflective narratives or to evaluate and express the meanings that their language experiences hold for them. They can, however, contribute such reflections retrospectively. Retrospective narratives relate what the participant (rather than the interviewer or researcher) thinks is important (Ritchie, 1995). Ritchie points out another strength of retrospective data: "the passage of time enables people to make sense out of earlier events in their lives. Actions take on new significance depending on their later consequences" (1995, p. 13).

Narrative approaches, using a variety of methodologies for eliciting oral or written accounts of experiences or more lengthy life histories, are being used across disciplines in the social sciences (Lieblich, Tuval-Mashiach, & Zilber, 1998; Muchmore, 1999; Portelli, 2001). Wengraf, Chamberlayne, and Bornat (2002) have described the biographical turn as a paradigm shift within the social sciences. The new, changed knowledge culture values subjective, lived experience, putting "the subject center stage with the authority that comes with ownership of a scarce and unique resource: the personal account" (Wengraf et al., 2002, p. 254). The implications for social science research processes and outcomes have been "democratizing, reflexive, critical, and emancipatory. . . . Opportunities to reveal, revise, and reclaim the past have led to individual life changes as well as collective challenges to established accounts and dominant narratives" (Wengraf et al., 2002, p. 254).

Connelly and Clandinin (1990) say that "humans are storytelling organisms who, individually and socially, lead storied lives. The study of narrative, therefore, is the study of the ways humans experience the world" (p. 2). They offer the following definition: "education is the construction and reconstruction of personal and social stories" (p. 2).

A number of researchers have pointed to the value of biography and autobiography for eliciting participants' notions of self (Bateson, 1989; Cooper, 1991; Stoddart, 2001; Teski & Climo, 1995). Such researchers argue that, through voicing and interpreting the identity themes that thread their stories, individuals will be empowered to deeply understand their own life, and perhaps make changes to alter its course (Cooper, 1991; Coyle, 1998; Helle, 1991; Witherelle, 1991), or even the wider course of how history unfolds or is perceived (Errante, 2000; Rosenwald & Ochberg, 1992). For example, Cooper (1991) writes:

> A notebook, a diary, or a journal is a form of narrative as well as a form of research, a way to tell our own story, a way to learn who we have been, who we are, and who we are becoming. We literally become teachers and researchers in our own lives, empowering ourselves in the process. (p. 98)

Perhaps for this reason, a number of recent studies employ narrative methods to investigate adult learning, in both formal (Ball, 1998; Brody, Witherell, Donald, & Lundblad, 1991; Cohen, 1996) and informal (Banister, 1999; Bateson, 1989) educational contexts.

The aim of the present study was to apply a narrative, autobiographical approach to inquiry into the acquisition of language and literacy. The study of adults' memories of their own language and literacy learning complements earlier observational data, and adds the unique advantage of hearing the stories in the learners' own voices. As these are narratives constructed by adults about their childhood experiences, the stories are weighted with their own interpretations, and the events selected for retelling are ones that, on reflection and in the light of subsequent experience, they have come to see as formative in their lives (see Cooper, 1991; Errante, 2000; Rosenwald & Ochberg, 1992; Teski & Climo, 1995 on selection of memories for retelling). Educated adults who have had occasion to think deeply about the nature of language and learning may be particularly able to contribute insights about their personal experiences. Finally, looking backward to the past rather than extrapolating forward developmentally provides another perspective on assumptions about relationships between educational success and factors such as class, family status, literacy practices, and school experiences.

METHOD

Participants

Participants included nine women at a Canadian university enrolled in a graduate Education seminar in Language Development that I taught. They ranged in age from 24 to 48 years. Two were fourth year Psychology students taking the course out of interest and the others were graduate Education students for whom this was a required course. Three participants had limited professional experience, while the rest had five or more years. Their professional experiences were diverse, including speech-language pathology, and elementary, secondary, and college teaching, with specializations in learning assistance, French immersion, teaching English as a second language, adult basic education, Aboriginal education, and high school geography. Two spoke English as a second language (their first languages being Korean and German respectively), while one was raised in a bilingual English/French household, and another was exposed to Gaelic along with English in early childhood. Alice[1] acquired French as a second language and is fluent in it. Lisa has lived and worked in Aboriginal communities throughout her adult life. All nine have spent all or most of their lives in Canada, growing up in rural

areas, towns, or small cities, with the exception of one who grew up in a large urban center. Five have children, and one has grandchildren.

Data

As a course assignment, students kept a journal in which they made regular entries over the semester reflecting on their own personal history of language and literacy development. Although the assignment was required, participation in this study was voluntary. This analysis focuses on journal data written over the first half of the semester, in which participants reflected on their memories of learning language and literacy from the preschool years through to the end of adolescence. Their task was to recall personally significant events, situations, and people that made a difference to their learning, as well as ways in which their learning and use of language made a difference to their life.

Students were provided with the following examples of questions they might pose for themselves:

> How did my particular development of, use of, or struggles with language make a difference to who I was as a child? What interested me and fueled my language and literacy learning, and what impeded me? What were my preferred strategies for learning and using language? Whom did I observe or interact with that made a difference to my language learning, and how? What are some "aha!" moments when I had a sudden insight into the nature of language? What were my choices of literacy materials and ways of interacting with them? How did I see myself as a speaker, listener, writer, or reader? (course handout)

The students were instructed to formulate their thoughts in prose rather than in point-form, to structure entries around particular topics they set for themselves, to avoid holding tightly to a chronological sequence, to discuss specific examples, and to link their observations to readings and discussion topics in class. My pedagogical purpose in assigning this journal writing was the belief, informed by constructivist theory, that by eliciting personal memories of the experience of language and literacy acquisition, students would reach a deeper, more coherent, and more meaningful understanding of language and literacy than they would by only reading and discussing the theories and research of others. Such deep understandings are key to transformation of teaching practices (see Neilsen, 1998).

Approach to Analysis

An inductive thematic analysis (Miles & Huberman, 1994) was conducted to discover themes

---

[1] All participant names used in this article are pseudonyms.

and patterns within each participant's journal, as well as themes commonly mentioned across participants. After reading through all the journals twice, I identified five preliminary categories that reflected topics discussed by all or most of the participants. Throughout the coding process, I reorganized and added to these categories, which resulted in nine categories in all: (a) family and home, (b) peers and friends, (c) school and teachers, (d) books and becoming literate, (e) oral traditions and experiences, (f) culture and languages, (g) community and wider environment, (h) perceptions of self, and (i) major life events or traumas.

Coding involved several steps. I began with a careful reading paired with margin coding (Miles & Huberman, 1994) of idea units (Lincoln & Guba, 1985), or key ideas. The next step involved sorting these identified phrases or close paraphrases into the initial five thematic categories, re-labeling, reorganizing, and adding categories on an ongoing basis until all of the journals had been coded. I used a version of poetic transcription (Glesne, 1997, 1999) in order to retain the narrative structure in a way that was both coherent and succinct, while also representing how the writer had foregrounded or backgrounded particular elements of an episode (also see Boyatzis, 1998; Lapadat, 2000b; Lapadat & Lindsay, 1999; McCabe, 1997). This approach also enabled me to avoid premature labeling. Episodes were multiply coded as appropriate. For example, a description of bedtime stories would be coded under both "family and home" and "books and becoming literate."

The following is an example from Emily's journal of how a word-for-word segment was abbreviated using poetic transcription, with the poetic segment first, followed by the verbatim one (coded as "school and teachers"):

Poetic:
I moved to another community with my parents in grade 1
I did not do well in school that year
my memory was affected
one time I couldn't do the test the teacher put on the board
I couldn't remember the teacher ever having taught the lesson
it was very frightening to not know what to do
I could no longer read (Emily dc, p.3)

Verbatim:
[Two paragraphs describing the family's move and placing it in time]
My mother has told me that I did not do well in school that year. She said I became very silent, yet before we moved from my grandparents I was always jabbering away. She also said my memory was affected. Story books I could read before the move, I could no longer read. I do remember one incident in class when the teacher had a test on the board I had to put the words to, two and too in the correct sentences and I couldn't remember the teacher ever having taught the lesson. To this day I remember how frightening this was for me when I didn't have a sweet clue as to what to do.

This extract was multiply coded. The poetic transcription segment coded under "major life events or traumas" includes different elements from the word-for-word journal entry, and foregrounds/backgrounds phrases differently than in the above example.[2] Where exact wording was judged essential, verbatim quotes were incorporated into the poetic transcripts.

Following this descriptive coding, I identified central issues or patterns for each individual and added these pattern codes into the coding, signifying them using capital letters. (Often, these were explicitly pointed out by the writers.) Then I wrote a brief profile for each participant summarizing central themes and patterns. The next step was a review of all the coded files and profiles across participants to look for commonalities as well as differences. Conceptual mapping (Miles & Huberman, 1994) was helpful in this process. Finally, I returned a draft write-up of the thematic analysis to the participants for suggestions and approval.[3]

Although my aim was to be minimally intrusive in the students' recounting, the stories and interpretations are, necessarily, collaborative constructions (Portelli, 2001). Initially, I was aware of three ways in which I contributed to the stories that were told and their interpretations. First, as the course instructor, I selected the readings for the course, guided the class discussions, and designed the journal assignment and its guiding questions. Second, I served as the audience for their journal writing, thus influencing what they chose to tell or not tell, and how they framed it. Third, as the researcher, I read, coded, analyzed, and interpreted the broader themes emerging across the nine journals. Later, during the process of analysis, I became aware of a fourth way in which I colluded in constructing the stories, via holding insider status.

RESULTS

The thematic analysis yielded for each participant a record of ideas and anecdotes pertaining to the nine

---

[2] I have chosen a brief text segment to illustrate the transcription approach here. However, most of the time, poetic transcription considerably abbreviated the word-for-word journal entry, while retaining the key ideas. A detailed coding protocol is available from the author on request.

[3] Feedback from participants regarding the draft analysis was highly positive. Several participants thanked me for putting their stories and insights into writing for dissemination, or commented on the greater sense of community they felt with the other students on reading the analysis. One participant identified wording that was not accurate and I revised it according to her clarification.

common themes on language and literacy development, as well as interpretive patterns within and across participants. Across all nine women, most had more to say about family and home than any other topic. The role of school and teachers, and the topic of books and becoming literate also were discussed a great deal by most participants. Several also wrote at length about their self perceptions. Other topics were addressed at length by particular individuals but not by everyone.

Community

Although most of the women wrote only a little about their communities or childhood environments, there were some interesting similarities in their experiences. Eight of the women spent all or most of their childhood growing up in a single community. The exception to this was Sigrid, whose family moved around a lot.

Aside from Sigrid, and Judy (who lived in a city), all of the women spent their childhood in rural areas or in small communities far from an urban center. Doris attended a one-room school enrolling 10–12 students, and Alice's rural school had 2 grades per classroom. Most of the women grew up in the same Canadian province, in various "frontier towns" with less than 50 years of history. Several mentioned that television did not come to their community until later in their childhood, and there was only one anecdote about the influence of TV across all the journals. However, many of the women recalled listening to radio programs and records, reading and writing (individually or with family members or peers), and fantasy play as frequent and favored pastimes.

Although I had not anticipated it, as the researcher I felt like an "insider." This was partly due to my closeness in age to several of the women and shared gender, but also because I too grew up in the same province as most of them in a small town just down the road from Rita's, Lee's, and Tina's hometowns. I have visited most of these women's hometowns, and, as an adult, I have lived in Tina's and Judy's childhood communities. Thus, as Errante (2000) describes, I was situated in the stories told, my subjectivity influenced by my own memories of those times and towns, as the memories they recounted "intersected with another running narrative: my own" (p. 24).

The three women who described their communities at greater length were Lisa, Rita, and Emily. Lisa described the "kids' culture" she was involved in by being part of the neighborhood gang of mixed ages and genders. It was up to children to fill their own time, and they did so by forming clubs, acting out Lone Ranger episodes, playing games like kick the can, hiking around the hills, and writing newsletters.

Rita described first learning English by playing with the "street kids." She described her resource-based town as attracting many immigrants to work in the plant:

[MULTICULTURAL CONTEXT]
at work at the plant
    there were a lot of immigrants
    particularly from Portugal, Italy, Greece
    they wanted to make money and go back home
these are the children I grew up with
there were so many immigrants that I associated with
    that people with funny speech
    didn't stand out
English, whatever the form
had to be our common language (Rita, p. 15)

In contrast, Emily grew up in a cohesive, homogeneous rural community in the Canadian Maritimes which had been settled many generations ago by Scottish and Irish immigrants. The close-knit community included many multigenerational families. Emily described her grandparents as speaking Gaelic with their friends, and told how her grandfather passed along the Scottish oral traditions to her through singing ballads, reciting poetry, and telling stories about ancestors and history. Similar traditions were reflected across the community and in the school, such as in the school poetry and speech clubs. Other examples of the cultural traditions of the community can be seen in the forms of address:

many of the families had been there for generations
    Scottish or Irish heritage
    mostly last names beginning with Mc or Mac
    lots of relatives around the area
we learned not to address adults as Mr. or Mrs.
    it didn't provide our parents with enough
    information

[QUOTE #2 Living in our area there were three Duncan MacLeans all related in some way but from different branches of the family. One Duncan was elderly so he was referred to as Old Duncan. The other Duncan MacLean lived on Gander Road so he was referred to as Duncan from Gander. The other Duncan had a pond in the back of his home. Therefore he was referred to as Duncan from the pond. I would tell my parents I'm going to visit Duncan on the pond even though I was visiting his daughter and we were not going near the pond.] (Emily, p. 6)

Similarly, Emily describes the expectation of giving a family history when introducing oneself:

we introduced ourselves by providing a family history
[QUOTE #3 If I was introducing myself to an adult who didn't know me I would say "I'm Emily Burns from Earl of Piper." Earl was the name of my father and we lived beside Piper's Beach. Therefore I would not be confused with Uncle Terry's or Uncle Nevin's

brood. . . . If my father's name was not enough I would tell them my grandfather's. Eventually we would get to the right branch.]
relating family history was part of the 'getting to know you' process (Emily, p. 7)

Learning the pragmatic language rules and appropriate discourse styles depended on the being aware of the norms in the particular community.

Family and Home

Three of the women described their parents as "educated"—Alice, who described her parents' British private school education as a primary formative factor for her, and Rita and Judy, who both mentioned that, as immigrants, their parents did not have the opportunity to work in their professions in Canada. Judy wrote: "we were very poor when we first came to Canada." Thus, another commonality across several participants was growing up in a working class community and/or family.

Five of the participants, Alice, Emily, Judy, Lisa, and Rita, described their families as strongly valuing education. Judy wrote:

[FAMILY PLACED HIGH VALUE ON EDUCATION]
in grade 1, my mother would always ask me if I did my homework
    I always told her that I did not have any
    she did not believe me
        in Korea, students are assigned homework from a very early age
        after regular school is over, they must go to a ha-kwan
        an additional school
        it teaches them art, singing, dancing, math
my mother always pushed me to excel in school
my mother told me if I studied hard
    everyone would want to be my friend (Judy, p. 1)

However, Judy felt pressured to achieve, and when her marks dropped in junior high school, she dropped out of school. She reflected that:

[ACHIEVEMENT]
I was always at the top of my class

but whenever I didn't do well in school I would cry
I could never measure up to my sisters
I tried really hard to do well
I usually did better than most people in my class
but I was never the smartest person (Judy, p. 11)

If family pressure to excel might have been a factor in Judy's dropping out, the high value the family placed on education helped her succeed in her return to school the following year:

when I returned to school after dropping out in grade 9
my mother got me the best tutors in the city (Judy, p. 3)

Like Judy, Lisa rebelled against school as an adolescent, but for different reasons. She describes her mother and older brother as great influences on her language and literacy development, and credits them with her very successful years in elementary school. However, the loss of these two people changed her view of school:

[TRAUMATIC LOSS OF MENTORS]
when I was 12, my mother died
    and my brother moved away to college
I lost the 2 people who made learning important to me
    from grade 7 on I rejected learning
    I was extremely rebellious (Lisa, p. 7)

All of the participants reported many literate activities in their home, and Alice, Emily, Lisa, Rita, and Sigrid also described having many opportunities for extended conversations with older family members. On the topic of early literacy, all except Sigrid said they had many books and were read to from a young age. Alice, Emily, and Rita said they could already read on beginning school (Rita in German), and all except Lee describe themselves as learning to read rapidly and excelling in Language Arts. Lisa and Judy were in the "top language group" and often were chosen to help other students, Sigrid was often selected to read to the class because she was considered a good reader, and Tina was placed in "enrichment" classes.

Seven of the participants named particular people who were influential in their language and literacy development, and all of these primary influences were family members. Doris, Rita, and Sigrid pointed to their father as most significant, and Alice and Judy named both parents. Emily's primary influence was her grandfather (she lived with her grandparents in her early childhood), and Lisa's mother and older brother were central influences. As secondary influences, three of the nine mentioned mothers, three mentioned siblings, and three mentioned same-aged peers. Two mentioned aunts, two mentioned same-aged extended family members, and two mentioned teachers. One mentioned a grandmother, and another a teenaged babysitter.

That fathers were mentioned in a primary role more than mothers is surprising, given the strong emphasis given to the role of mothers' input language in the research literature. The relative absence of mention of teachers as mentors also seems striking. Lisa commented that, as a teacher herself, she would like to hope that some of her students remember her as important to their learning, but added: "I have no recollection of a supportive classroom teacher." Although she mentioned one high school English teacher who encouraged her, she said: "he never taught me in a classroom; he took me under his wing on his own time."

A final observation about participants' families is that not all spent their childhood in nuclear family structures. Alice's parents separated and her father remarried. Lisa's mother died when she was 12. Sigrid wrote that: "my natural mother left us when I was 7 or 8 years old and I have only a few memories of her." Emily was left with her grandparents as baby when a new sibling with medical problems was born and her parents moved to a city to obtain medical care. She describes herself as very happy in this home filled with members of her extended family, and traumatized when her parents reclaimed her at age 6:

> my parents moved back to the Island
>   I was frightened that they took me away with them
> this time in my life seems like a black hole
> my mother has told me
>   I did not do well in school that year
>   I became very silent
>   my memory was affected
>   I could no longer read
>   I became unresponsive
>   I lost weight and became ill
>   I regressed academically and socially
>   I withdrew into a world of my own
> we moved back to my old neighbourhood the next year
>   two doors away from my grandparents
>   my parents moved for my benefit
> from that time on I had a foot in both houses
>   during the day and evening I lived with my family
>   after my bath I went to bed at my grandparents'
> (Emily, p. 8)

It is clear that for these nine women, their families were extremely important influences on their language and literacy development, and their attitudes toward learning. Furthermore, their families varied in structure and typical practices, although all were literate households.

Books and Becoming Literate

All of the women except Lee described themselves as avid readers. For example, Tina said she always had her nose in a book, and Emily, Rita, and Sigrid said they read everything they could get their hands on. Several described their joy at discovering the public or school library. Several described developing a love of reading, reciting, or writing poetry (Doris, Emily, Judy, and Rita), or of listening to and singing songs (Alice, Doris, Emily, Lee, and Sigrid). Many listed favorite books or series at various points in their childhood, recounted details from stories, and commented on seeking out these same books as adults to introduce to their own children.

In fact, both Emily and Sigrid described spending too much time reading. Emily wrote:

> my life was filled with books
>   I read anything I could get my hands on
> my mother scolded me for spending too much time reading

and not enough time playing outside with other children
unhealthy to spend too much time in someone else's world (Emily, p. 4)

Similarly, Sigrid wrote of the great satisfaction she found in reading. However, she reflected that the amount of reading she did also might have impeded her in learning to use language socially:

[QUOTE: I often chose to read when other kids went off looking for someone to play with. As stated earlier, I counted books among my best friends. . . . Relating to my peers, beyond a small core of close friends, was a painful process with which I generally felt unsuccessful. I didn't feel like I fit in, and I was often at a loss over how to join into or maintain a conversation with them. It was easier to hide in the library or at home with the security of my books than to venture into social situations where I didn't know what was expected of me.] (Sigrid, p. 10)

In contrast to the others, Lee developed a self-perception of herself as a poor reader, due to school activities that emphasized social comparison of skills. These included a test of alphabet knowledge in kindergarten, round robin reading in grade 1, and timing the students' rate of silent reading in grade 6. She wrote:

[SELF-PERCEPTION AS POOR READER]
I began to see myself as a poor reader
    at some point in the early elementary years
while I always demonstrated strong comprehension skills
    I struggled with oral reading
when reading out loud in front of others
    I stammered
    struggled over words
    this was a great source of embarrassment to me
I would dread being asked to read out loud
my teacher in grade 6 had us count the rate at which we read
    when silent reading
most of my friends could read much faster than me
    this contributed further to my self-perception as a poor reader
    and further embarrassment
I rarely read for pleasure
I focused my attention away from reading
I went to lengths to avoid it whenever possible
(Lee, p. 5)

Lee describes this self-perception as arising "despite my perfectly adequate exposure to literature" as a preschooler, and enjoying being read to, and being able to "'read' many Dr. Seuss books by memory" before starting school. The consequence for her was that she avoided reading unless required, and then she would select books "by the width of the spine."

Five of the women, Alice, Doris, Judy, Lee, and Lisa, wrote that, during their school years, they saw themselves as writers or future writers. Judy and Lisa, in particular, explained that they found writing to be a route to understanding and self-expression. Judy preferred to write poetry and to keep a diary. Lisa described writing to help the healing process: "I learned to write my thoughts down, then burn the pages." She also discovered journalism as a means for social action. Alice, on the other hand, commented:

> I have often dreamed of being a writer
>> but there is so much more to it than loving to read or speak or write
>> there is such a skill to making the printed word come alive (Alice, p. 6)

In contrast, Sigrid described herself as successful with school writing tasks that involved recounting the words or replicating the story structures of others, but far less comfortable with tasks such as journal writing that required her to record her original thoughts in her own voice.

In summary, most of these women described their predisposition to read a lot for pleasure as a personal inclination that arose naturally out of their experiences with literacy in the home as small children, supplemented by their early and positive introduction to literacy in primary school. Other than this, school itself was not attributed as having a causal role in their love of reading, although several mentioned particular activities at school, such as making books (Lee), going into "the reading house," (Judy), the English Literature 12 course (Rita), or grammar lessons (Lee, Rita) that extended their writing skills or their interests in literature.

School and Teachers

All of the participants wrote a considerable amount about their experiences in school. Most of them began school with strong oral language skills, and well prepared for literacy. Most of them also described themselves as excelling at school during the elementary years, and in certain subject areas in high school. They recounted anecdotes of being singled out for awards, or having their work displayed, or being chosen to help peers who were less successful. Several wrote about positive memories of particular instructional activities or subject areas that they enjoyed. Yet, only Emily wrote that she liked school. Furthermore, when all the remarks about school are compiled across the nine participants, it is clear that the tone is overwhelmingly negative.

Some of the remarks centered on the topic of boredom. Alice wrote that knowing how to read on entering school resulted in her not being sufficiently challenged:

[QUOTE #1: I learned to read at a very early age and was reading fluently when I started school. This was not a real advantage to me though, because I was

often bored. I attended a small rural school with two grades to a class and a very traditional teacher who had to keep things manageable so I was made to sit in the reading circle and follow along as my classmates stumbled to master "See Lucia.'" and "See Buttons." I remember getting into trouble for not attending to the person reading because I was reading ahead to the pages which had three or four lines of text!] (Alice, p. 3)

Eventually, Alice's teacher began sending Alice and another student to the library during reading lessons. Alice discovered a way to cope with the lack of challenge by developing a friendly rivalry with this student:

> we kept each other going all through elementary school
> I worked to beat him in everything and vice versa
> we both excelled (Alice, p. 30)

On the topic of boredom, Lisa wrote:

> [SCHOOL AS A NEGATIVE FACTOR]
> I don't remember any significant moments at school
>> that helped me improve my language ability
> the boring parts
>> tracing letters for hours in my McLean's writing book
>> seem to have taken up most of the school day (Lisa, p. 4)

She explained that boredom was one of the reasons she skipped out often in high school. Similarly, Judy mentioned boredom as a precursor to her dropping out in grade 9. In contrast, Emily wrote that she never was bored in school.

Although Alice used competition with a school peer in a positive way, Judy, Lee, and Sigrid wrote at length about the competitive atmosphere at school and its emphasis on social comparison, and how these had a negative impact on them. The themes of competition and pressure to achieve run throughout Judy's entries, and she relates these to feelings of being different or less capable. Lee, as described previously, came to see herself as a poor reader, which had an impact on her learning and life choices.

Sigrid wrote that she was "shy and self conscious" at school, in contrast with being "confident and at ease in my conversations" with siblings, friends, and kids in the neighborhood—even "downright bossy." She described hating to have attention drawn to herself at school, such as the "embarrassment" and "agony" caused her because of her "unusual name." She recalled:

[QUOTE: Throughout school, I was nervous speaking in front of the class and didn't like to give answers to questions. I stuttered and I got "tongue-tied", especially when I had time to rehearse what I might have to say. I was sure that the other kids would laugh at me if I stuttered, or worse, would think I was showing off if I got the answer to a question right. Many times I wanted to respond to the teacher, but was too afraid to speak out voluntarily. I didn't mind reading out loud, but I think that was because I was really good at it, and the words that I was saying weren't my own. That made oral reading safe, unlike having to speak my own mind.] (Sigrid, p. 7)

She offered the insight that "the pressure of fitting in socially" at school was a large source of her distress.

Doris recorded how upset she was at being singled out by a teacher for extra help with her "terrible handwriting." However, when her handwriting improved after many of these sessions, she began to take pride in her handwriting and came to appreciate that teacher.

All nine of the women wrote about events at school that led them to feel mistrustful, inadequate, or bad about themselves. One particularly dramatic example is the following from Lisa:

[POWER OF LANGUAGE TO MANIPULATE]
I learned about the manipulation of language
in grade 7
the message was, don't trust people in authority
[QUOTE #1: One aspect of the manipulation of language came to me unexpectedly, and the message, don't trust people in authority, has stayed with me to this day! . . . One afternoon in grade 7, I skipped out with a group of friends and went to a bush party. The next day, the vice-principal called me in and said that he knew where we had been because everyone else had told him, so he just wanted me to confirm the story. I told him the whole thing. Later, when I found out that he had lied to me, and that no one else had said anything, I was devastated. I was a novice at this kind of thing, but the fact that someone that I had expected to always tell the truth, a grown up with authority, had actually lied to get something he wanted changed my life.] (Lisa, p. 4)

Other negative factors mentioned included being made to do instructional activities not at an appropriate level (Alice, Lee), and being insufficiently prepared for university (Judy, Rita). In addition, as an Asian and a speaker of English as a second language, Judy experienced miscommunication, differences in discourse expectations, and racism at school that she found very frustrating and upsetting.

Culture and Languages

Neither the notion of culture nor the impact of speaking languages additional to English were mentioned at all by Lee, Lisa, or Sigrid, all of whom portrayed themselves as mainstream English-speaking Canadians. Tina, Doris, Emily, and Alice each wrote some entries about languages and culture. Tina briefly described a best friend who came to Canada from India, and how she taught her friend English and her friend taught her some Hindi. She mentions that this initiated her great interest in learning other languages and was a factor in her choice to study both French and German in high school. In Doris's family, her father's first language was French:

my father's first language is French and his second language is English
my mother's first language is English
we spoke English at home
my father often spoke to us in French
    we always answered in English
my siblings and I speak terrible French
insufficient exposure to acquire the language
but we have faultless accents like native speakers
(Doris, p. 3)

Despite her father's efforts, Doris learned only the majority language of her community.

As described previously, Emily's cultural background with its strong oral traditions was a highly important factor for her growing up in a long-established community with a Scottish and Irish heritage. This also held true for Alice, who wrote about her strong sense of her British heritage, and the associations this had for her with a having good education, the value of education, the importance of literacy, the value of studying other languages (French and Latin), and the learning of formal rules of politeness in the form of both pragmatic language skills and socially appropriate behavior. For example, Alice wrote:

I credit my parents for my affinity for languages
    and my ability to speak, write, and read well
my parents were educated in private schools in Britain
    so they have a prodigious background
        in history, literature, language, overall knowledge (Alice, p. 1)

She observed that many of her peers came to school less well prepared for literacy, or not having been taught "the niceties and social protocols" and therefore embarrassing themselves "by their gauche speech behaviours."

For Rita and Judy, who both learned English as a second language, the topic of culture and languages was the predominant theme in their journals. Rita's family moved to Canada from Germany when she was four, and although she learned some English from "the street kids," had to work hard to learn English in school. However, because her family lived in a multicultural, multilingual community of immigrants, she did not stand out as "different," as many of her peers also were learning English. She described thinking first in German then translating into English, although at some point she switched to thinking first in English. She wrote:

once we started school
    the English came quite quickly
I don't know at which point I switched over to English
    as my main language of communication
    I know I did
    because my mother had to struggle
    to keep up with me
German was still the main language at home
    by the time I was in mid-elementary
I went between the two languages quite easily
(Rita, p. 14)

German was used in Rita's home in both spoken and written forms throughout her childhood. As she learned English and received formal instruction in it at school, the German vocabulary did not keep pace, and written German began to seem difficult and hard to decipher. Nevertheless, she described herself as a mixture of both cultures and languages and said that, today, although she has lost some of her German, she still finds that she can communicate quickly and easily with German people when she is around them.

Judy's family moved to Canada from South Korea two years before she was born. She said that "by the time I was 3, I knew I was to speak Korean at home and English with the neighbourhood kids." However, when she entered kindergarten, she struggled with English, and was pulled out to work with a teacher of English as a second language.

I did not have the same command of the English language as the other kids
    when I entered kindergarten at age 5
I thought I understood English and spoke it perfectly
    but my lack of knowledge of English was apparent
    a girl in my class asked the teacher why I talked so funny (Judy, p. 8)

Not only was the language strange, but also there were cultural and discourse differences.

at school
    we were allowed to express our thoughts
    tell the teacher why we were angry or sad
at home
    a child is taught to obey their parents
    and not to express emotions (Judy, p. 8)

Judy wrote about several occasions of miscommunication at school, and her puzzlement and frustration at not being understood. As she began to switch to predominantly speaking English, the experience of not being understood was repeated, this time at home, as her mother often did not understand the English. Judy wrote:

my mother was fearful that her children would lose their ability to speak Korean
    she encouraged us to use our mother tongue at home

my older sisters were ashamed to speak Korean
we became more comfortable speaking English
    as we spent more time at school and less at home
    soon English became the main language of communication
    my parents spoke to us in Korean
    we would answer back in English
I soon lost my ability to speak my native tongue
    at the end of grade 1
I remember thinking to myself that I no longer sounded like my dad
    around the same time I was losing my Korean
    I was reading actively
by grade 3 I had forgotten most of my Korean (Judy, p. 9)

So, in contrast to Rita, Judy rapidly lost her ability to speak her first language. However, unlike Rita, she described always standing out as "different," as well as incidents of overt racism:

[EXPERIENCE OF RACISM]
my sisters and I were the only Asians in the school
    I remember coming home crying
        because someone would not play with me
        or someone had called me a racist name
    a lot of kids made fun of me
        because I couldn't say certain words (Judy, p. 9)

Several different patterns and responses are apparent in the participants' writing on this topic. Doris and Judy, whose heritage language was not spoken in the surrounding community or was seen as a source of difference and reason for unkind treatment by peers, avoided or quickly discarded their language other than English. Rita, however, who grew up in a community where speaking English as a second language was the norm, was able to learn the English language and Canadian ways while also retaining her German language and culture. Alice, rather than trying to erase her cultural difference saw it as an advantage over her peers. Emily acquired the cultural traditions and linguistic values of her homogeneous community. However, it was only upon leaving her community as an adult that she acquired the distance and experience within another cultural context (mainstream Canadian) to enable her to reflect on her community's unique subculture.

In contrast, participants like Lee and Sigrid, who have remained within their childhood language and culture, did not acquire an alternative perspective from which to view the characteristics of their own cultural experience, and thus culture is implicit and unexamined within their journals. The participants who had to negotiate two languages or cultures, although describing experiences that were often difficult and frustrating, present in their journals elaborated and explicit perspectives on the formative role of languages and culture.

Summary

When asked to keep a journal reflecting on their language and literacy development from birth to the end of high school, the nine women participating in this study wrote about many topics. For example, Emily wrote at length about oral traditions, community, and extended family. Both Judy and Lisa wrote about rebellion and resistance, and writing as a route to understanding. Sigrid, Judy and Lee reflected on their self-perceptions as language users and the insidious consequences of social comparison at school. Rita and Judy wrote about the challenges they faced learning English as a second language. All of the participants discussed family, school, and their experiences of becoming literate. Many also wrote about languages and culture, peers, community, threats to their self-perceptions, and affirming events or people in their lives.

CONCLUSIONS AND IMPLICATIONS

This study differs from most studies of language and literacy development in that it employed a retrospective approach. The participants, well-educated Canadian women mostly employed as teachers, composed autobiographical reflective narratives about their childhood experiences of language and literacy development. Some of the findings, such as the importance of a positive and early introduction to literacy in the home, affirm the results of much observational research. Other results of this study represent surprising counterpoints with implications for research and educational practice.

An important contribution of this study is that it presents voices that have been largely absent from language acquisition research—those of small-town Canadians who grew up in the 1950's, 60's, and 70's. As such a background is typical of the demographics of many currently practicing teachers in Canada, it is important to have an insight into their understandings, experiences, and values relating to language and literacy. The particulars described by these women–stable working-class communities, the "frontier-like" nature of their small towns, the absence of television as a major influence, and the role of "kids' culture"—also are important in the narratives. Stories have the power to shift the reader from stereotypic and bipolar us-other thinking. Although there are certain commonalities and intersections in the narratives, it is the complexity and uniqueness of each of the nine different stories that I especially value. Wengraf et al. (2002) remark, "we make our own histories but not under conditions of our own choosing" (p. 251).

Memories have the capacity to shift forward and back through time in the telling, and to sort, value, and re-present what the participant deems meaningful (Portelli, 2001; Ritchie, 1995), unlike observational and prospective studies which are blind to the future, and interpretatively constrained by the researcher's theoretical and methodological frames. These rich individual narratives defy simple generalizations. They remind us, as researchers, about the limitations inherent in observational and other empirical research approaches, and might inspire the design of more open-ended and multi-perspective studies, or lead us to be more cautious about prescribing practice based on generalizations.

An important finding that triangulates with much extant research on language development and emergent literacy is that these nine participants identified aspects of their family and home environment as the predominant factors in their language and literacy development. All came from literate households, although these were more diverse in structure than the traditional two-parent home that typically has been studied. Most of the women reported having the opportunity for extended talk with an older family member. A surprise, given the focus of the extant research literature on language development, was the extent to which these women pointed to their fathers as a primary influential figure in their language or literacy development, and saw their mothers in a secondary role. Also surprising was the relative absence of mention of teachers as mentors. Further research is needed to determine how typical these perceptions are among educated adults, and also to discover why teachers were not seen as mentors.

A consistency across these educated women was that most described themselves as avid readers, and they seemed to see this as a personal inclination arising from their positive experiences of early literacy in the home and supported in kindergarten and grade one, rather than as something arising out of subsequent formal instruction at school. This result emphasizes the importance of positive experiences of emergent literacy if children are to develop a love of reading. These participants who loved reading persisted in doing a great deal of reading regardless of their subsequent experiences at home or school.

Although most of the women wrote a considerable amount about their experiences at school, to a large extent these recollections had a negative tone. They spoke of boredom, negative experiences of social comparison, anxiety about how they were perceived or treated by schoolmates, and events that led them to feel mistrustful or inadequate. This is particularly surprising in that these women had excelled at school, been recognized for their achievements, and gone on to complete university degrees. Also, as most of them chose to become teachers, I would have expected that their recollections about school would have emphasized the positive. This worrisome finding calls out for further efforts to improve schools to make them more welcoming places for students, and to provide learning opportunities that acknowledge and honor the diversity among all students (see Stoddart, 2001).

A final, important observation relates to the theme of culture and multiple languages. Three participants who portrayed themselves as "mainstream Canadian" did not write about culture at all in their journals. In contrast, those whose parents had recently immigrated and thus were brought up in two cultures, fore fronted culture and language-culture connections. These participants tended to see culture as overarching, and family and school as experiential subcomponents of culture. As well, those who were brought up in a distinct subculture, exposed to two languages in the home, or who had formed a close relationship with someone from another language and culture, reflected on cultural issues. Perry (2001) has examined "the processes by which white identities are constructed as 'cultureless' among white youth" (p. 57). She argues that by claiming to have no culture, whites assert racial superiority, as 'no culture' implies conforming to the (rational) norm, whereas having a culture marks one as (less developmentally advanced) 'other.' In this study, such a strong claim is not warranted. Nevertheless, culture seemed invisible to those participants whose experiences were limited to "the mainstream," whereas others engaged in integrating, seeking out, or living within two cultures had more opportunities to become "culture-aware" or "culture-rich." This supports the move toward recognizing, encouraging, and celebrating diversity in our schools as a fundamental way of enriching education for all of our students. It also supports the need for critical study of contemporary North American culture in schools as a way of making culture visible, not just a marker of 'otherness.'

In conclusion, examination of educated adults' autobiographical memories of language and literacy development shows promise for revealing insights about these processes that have not been available through the commonly used observational and descriptive approaches. Further work of this type is needed to shed light on the methodological issues involved, such as the shifting nature of memory depending on the purpose or audience at hand (Errante, 2000; Grumet, 1991; Teski & Climo, 1995), the subjective role of the researcher (Banister, 1999; Errante, 2000), and ways of avoiding the temptation to privilege one perspective and instead incorporating multiple possible interpretations (Errante, 2000; Grumet, 1991; Lieblich et al., 1998; Rosenberg, Rosenberg, & Farrell, 1992). Autobiographical reflec-

tive writing also warrants further examination as an instructional practice that may enhance personal and professional transformation.

AUTHOR NOTE

This article extends a paper presented at the annual meeting of the American Educational Research Association, Montreal, QC, April, 1999. That earlier conference paper is available in the ERIC database under the title "Family, Culture, School and Community: Reflections on Language and Literacy Development" (ERIC Document Reproduction Service No. ED 431 325). I wish to thank Maria Franquiz for her helpful comments on that earlier paper, and my research assistant, Jennifer Little, for assisting with typing and transcription.

REFERENCES

Ball, A. F. (1998). The value of recounting narratives: Memorable learning experiences in the lives of inner-city students and teachers. *Narrative Inquiry, 8*(1), 151–180.

Banister, E. M. (1999). Evolving reflexivity: Negotiating meaning of women's midlife experience. *Qualitative Inquiry, 5*(1), 3–23.

Bateson, M. C. (1989). *Composing a life*. New York: Penguin.

Bloome, D., & Bailey, F. M. (1992). Studying language and literacy through events, particularity, and intertextuality. In R. Beech, J. L. Green, M. L. Kamil, & T. Shanahan (Eds.), *Multidisciplinary perspectives on literacy research* (pp. 181–210). Urbana, IL: National Council of Teachers of English.

Boyatzis, R. E. (1998). *Transforming qualitative information: Thematic analysis and code development*. Thousand Oaks, CA: Sage.

Brody, C. M., Witherell, C., Donald, K., & Lundblad, R. (1991). Story and voice in the education of professionals. In C. Witherell & N. Noddings (Eds.), *Stories lives tell: Narrative and dialogue in education* (pp. 257–278). New York: Teachers College Press.

Bruner, J. (1996). *The culture of education*. Cambridge, MA: Harvard University Press.

Cohen, J. B. (1996). Rewriting our lives: Meaning-making in an adult learning community. *Journal of Narrative and Life History, 6*(2), 145–156.

Connelly, F. M., & Clandinin, D. J. (1990). Stories of experience and narrative inquiry. *Educational Researcher, 19*(5), 2–14.

Cooper, J. E. (1991). Telling our own stories: The reading and writing of journals or diaries. In C. Witherell & N. Noddings (Eds.), *Stories lives tell:*

Narrative and dialogue in education (pp. 96–112). New York: Teachers College Press.

Coyle, S. (1998). Dancing with the chameleon. In A. Banks & S. P. Banks (Eds.), *Fiction and social research: By ice or fire* (pp. 147–164). Walnut Creek, CA: Altamira Press.

Delpit, L. D. (1990). Language diversity and learning. In S. Hynds & D. L. Rubin (Eds.), *Perspectives on talk and learning* (pp. 247–266). Urbana, IL: National Council of Teachers of English.

Edwards, D., & Mercer, N. (1987). *Common knowledge: The development of understanding in the classroom.* London: Methuen.

Eisner, E. (1999, February). *Concerns, dilemmas, and possibilities for qualitative research in the next millennium.* Plenary Session presented at the Advances in Qualitative Research Methods conference, Edmonton, AB, Canada.

Errante, A. (2000). But sometimes you're not part of the story: Oral histories and ways of remembering and telling. *Educational Researcher, 29*(2), 16–27.

Giles, H., & Coupland, N. (1991). *Language: Contexts and consequences.* Buckingham, UK: Open University Press.

Glesne, C. (1997). That rare feeling: Re-presenting research through poetic transcription. *Qualitative Inquiry, 3,* 202–221.

Glesne, C. (1999). *Becoming qualitative researchers: An introduction* (2nd ed.). New York: Longman.

Grumet, M. R. (1991). The politics of personal knowledge. In C. Witherell & N. Noddings (Eds.), *Stories lives tell: Narrative and dialogue in education* (pp. 67–77). New York: Teachers College Press.

Haden, C. A., Reese, E., & Fivush, R. (1996). Mothers' extratextual comments during storybook reading: Stylistic differences over time and across texts. *Discourse Processes, 21,* 135–169.

Haswell, R. H. (1991). *Gaining ground in college writing: Tales of development and interpretation.* Dallas, TX: Southern Methodist University Press.

Helle, A. P. (1991). Reading women's autobiographies: A map of reconstructed knowing. In C. Witherell & N. Noddings (Eds.), *Stories lives tell: Narrative and dialogue in education* (pp. 48–66). New York: Teachers College Press.

Hicks, D. (Ed.) (1996). *Discourse, learning, and schooling.* New York: Cambridge University Press.

Kirsch, G. E. (1993). *Women writing the academy: Audience, authority, and transformation.* Carbondale, IL: Southern Illinois University Press.

Lapadat, J. C. (1995). *Learning language and learning literacy: Construction of meaning through discourse.* Smith Research Center, Bloomington, IN: ERIC Clearinghouse on Reading, English, and Communication Skills. (ERIC Document Reproduction Service No. ED 371 422).

Lapadat, J. C. (2000a). Construction of science knowledge: Scaffolding conceptual change through discourse. *Journal of Classroom Interaction, 35*(2), 1–14.

Lapadat, J. C. (2000b). Problematizing transcription: Purpose, paradigm and quality. *International Journal of Social Research Methodology: Theory & Practice, 3,* 203–219.

Lapadat, J. C., & Lindsay, A. C. (1999). Transcription in research and practice: From standardization of technique to interpretive positionings. *Qualitative Inquiry, 5,* 64–86.

Lemke, J. L. (1989). Social semiotics: A new model for literacy education. In D. Bloome (Ed.), *Classrooms and literacy* (pp. 289–309). Norwood, NJ: Ablex.

Lieblich, A., Tuval-Mashiach, R., & Zilber, T. (1998). *Narrative research: Reading, analysis, and interpretation.* Thousand Oaks, CA: Sage.

Lincoln, Y. S. (1995). Emerging criteria for quality in qualitative and interpretive research. *Qualitative Inquiry, 1,* 275–289.

Lincoln, Y. S., & Guba, E. G. (1985). *Naturalistic inquiry.* Newbury Park, CA: Sage. McCabe, A. (1997). Cultural background and storytelling: A review and implications for schooling. *The Elementary School Journal, 97,* 453–473.

Mercer, N. (1993). Culture, context, and the construction of knowledge in the classroom. In P. Light & G. Butterworth (Eds.), *Context and cognition: Ways of learning and knowing* (pp. 28–46). Hillsdale, NJ: Lawrence Erlbaum.

Miles, M. B., & Huberman, A. M. (1994). *Qualitative data analysis: An expanded sourcebook* (2nd ed.). Thousand Oaks, CA: Sage.

Muchmore, J. A. (1999, April). *Toward an understanding of life history research.* Paper presented at the annual meeting of the American Educational Research Association, Montreal, QC, Canada.

Neilsen, L. (1998). *Knowing her place: Research literacies and feminist occasions.* San Francisco: Caddo Gap Press.

Obler, L. K. (2001). Developments in the adult years. In J. B. Gleason (Ed.), *The development of language* (5th ed., pp. 455–488). Boston: Allyn & Bacon.

Pappas, C. C., Kiefer, B. Z., & Levstik, L. S. (1999). *An integrated language perspective in the elementary school: An action approach* (3rd ed.). New York: Addison Wesley Longman.

Perry, P. (2001). White means never having to say you're ethnic: White youth and the construction of "cultureless" identities. *Journal of Contemporary Ethnography, 30*(1), 56–91.

Portelli, A. (2001). *The death of Luigi Trastulli and other stories: Form and meaning in oral history.* New York: State University of New York Press.

Purcell-Gates, V. (1995). *Other people's words: The cycle of low literacy.* Cambridge, MA: Harvard University Press.

Rosenberg, S. D., Rosenberg, H. J., & Farrell, M. P. (1992). In the name of the father. In G. C. Rosenwald & R. L. Ochberg (Eds.), *Storied lives: The cultural politics of self-understanding* (pp. 41–59). New Haven: Yale University Press.

Rosenwald, G. C., & Ochberg, R. L. (1992). Introduction: Life stories, cultural politics, and self-understanding. In G. C. Rosenwald & R. L. Ochberg (Eds.), *Storied lives: The cultural politics of self-understanding* (pp. 1–18). New Haven: Yale University Press.

Ritchie, D. A. (1995). *Doing oral history.* New York: Twayne.

Snow, C. E., & Ninio, A. (1986). The contracts of literacy: What children learn from learning to read books. In W. H. Teale & E. Sulzby (Eds.), *Emergent literacy: Writing and reading* (pp. 116–138). Norwood, NJ: Ablex.

Stoddart, K. (2001). People like us: Memories of marginality in high school and university. *Qualitative inquiry, 7,* 171–191.

Teski, M. C., & Climo, J. J. (1995). Introduction. In M. C. Teski & J. J. Climo (Eds.), *The labyrinth of memory: Ethnographic journeys* (pp. 1–10). Westport, CT: Bergin & Garvey.

Thomas, K., & Maybin, J. (1998). Investigating language practices in a multilingual London community. In A. Egan-Robertson & D. Bloome (Eds.), *Students as researchers of culture and language in their own communities* (pp. 143–166). Cresskill, NJ: Hampton Press.

Wells, G. (1986). *The meaning makers: Children learning language and using language to learn.* Portsmouth, NH: Heinemann.

Wells, G. (1990). Talk about text: Where literacy is learned and taught. *Curriculum Inquiry, 20,* 369–405.

Wengraf, T., Chamberlayne, P., & Bornat, J. (2002). A biographical turn in the social sciences? A British-European view. *Cultural Studies ↔ Critical Methodologies, 2,* 245–269.

Witherell, C. (1991). The self in narrative: A journey into paradox. In C. Witherell & N. Noddings (Eds.), *Stories lives tell: Narrative and dialogue in education* (pp. 83–95). New York: Teachers College Press.

Yussen, S. R., & Smith, M. C. (Eds.). (1993). *Reading across the life span.* New York: Springer-Verlag.

PART IV
Mixed Methods

4.01

CONVERGENCE DESIGN

How Do Linguistically Diverse Students Fare in Full- and Half-Day Kindergarten? Examining Academic Achievement, Instructional Quality, and Attendance

Kendra M. Hall-Kenyon,[*] Gary E. Bingham,[†] and Byran B. Korth[‡]

Research Findings: This study investigated the effects of full- and half-day kindergarten programs on classroom instructional quality and children's academic achievement. Considerations were given for how the length of the school day, language status (English language learner [ELL] and non-ELL), and children's attendance patterns influenced achievement. Quantitative and qualitative data were collected concurrently and were interpreted to note the convergence (or lack thereof) of the findings. Quantitative results revealed no difference in the quality of instruction being offered in full- and half-day classrooms. Additionally, full-day kindergarten positively impacted children's academic achievement in literacy but not in mathematics, regardless of children's language status. In regard to language development, ELL children benefited more from full-day kindergarten than did their English-speaking peers, whereas all (ELL and non-ELL) children enrolled in full-day kindergarten made greater language gains when they missed fewer than 10 school days. *Practice or Policy*: Findings from this study have significant policy and practice implications related to the overall quality, availability, and cultural and developmental appropriateness of kindergarten programming in the United States.

Recent education reform initiatives place increasing pressure on schools to demonstrate child growth and achievement in the areas of literacy and mathematics.

Given previous research suggesting that children's achievement trajectories are often set during their first few years in school (Alexander & Entwisle, 1988; Snow, Burns, & Griffin, 1998), many school districts have turned to early childhood programs to help improve children's developmental outcomes before or at the beginning of formal schooling (Bowman, Donovan, & Burns, 2001; Snow et al., 1998). Most notably, one of the most popular ways that school

[*]Department of Teacher Education, Brigham Young University
[†]Department of Early Childhood Education, Georgia State University
[‡]Department of Teacher Education, Brigham Young University

districts have tried to meet the diverse academic needs of young children has been the adoption of full-day kindergarten programs (Lee, Burkam, Ready, Honigman, & Meisels, 2006; National Center for Education Statistics, 2000).

AVAILABILITY OF FULL-DAY KINDERGARTEN: CURRENT U.S. TRENDS

Full-day kindergarten programs have grown in prevalence in the last 20 years. Patterns of access to full-day kindergarten show that more than half of U.S. public schools offer full-day programs (Lee et al., 2006), with a higher percentage in private settings (Kauerz, 2005). Access also appears to be far less prevalent in the western United States and, in general, is more common among schools with high percentages of minority children and children who live in poverty (Lee et al., 2006; National Center for Educational Statistics, 2004). In fact, full-day programs are frequently targeted toward minority children, particularly those with second language status, as a way to ameliorate the "learning curve" often associated with the first years of formal schooling (Vecchiotti, 2003). Hence, in many cases, the lengthening of the school day is seen as a compensatory program for children at risk for early school failure and is designed to lessen the performance gap between non-minority and minority students that is still present in public schools (Lee et al., 2006; National Center for Education Statistics, 2004; Vecchiotti, 2003).

BENEFITS OF FULL-DAY PROGRAMS

Research examining the efficacy of full-day and half-day kindergarten experiences on children's academic outcomes has demonstrated that children in full-day settings fare better on measures of vocabulary, literacy, and math achievement (Baskett, Bryant, White, & Rhoads, 2005; Cryan, Sheehan, Wiechel, & Bandy-Hedden, 1992; Puleo, 1988; Yan & Lin, 2005). For example, in a representative sample of kindergarten children in the United States, Lee and colleagues (2006) found that children in full-day programs outperformed children in half-day programs in the areas of literacy and mathematics. Moreover, such gains persisted even when the researchers took into account the structural, social, and academic features of the children and schools (i.e., location, rural/urban, school socioeconomic background). These findings are typical in both large- and small-scale studies.

Positive effects of full-day kindergarten programs on children's development are also found in areas outside the cognitive realm. For example,

Elicker and Mathur (1997) found that children who attended full-day programs were rated as having slightly more positive affect and better work habit scores than children attending half-day programs. Cryan and colleagues (1992) found similar results, with children in full-day programs being rated as having more positive classroom behaviors (i.e., independent learning, classroom involvement, working well with peers) as well as fewer negative behaviors (i.e., failure, anxiety, withdrawn behavior). In addition to positive findings in the realm of social skills, children who attend full-day kindergarten are less likely to be retained than their peers who attend half-day kindergarten programs (Cryan et al., 1992; Gullo, 2000).

Although the positive effects of full-day kindergarten are encouraging, questions still exist regarding its effectiveness for children who are second language learners. Are their gains equal or greater to those of their English-only peers? Unfortunately, to date, few research studies examining the impact of full-day and half-day programs on young children's development have considered how children from diverse ethnic or linguistic backgrounds fare in such settings. For example, in their study of children in full-day, alternative-day, and half-day programs in Ohio, Cryan and colleagues (1992) considered the role that child characteristics may play in moderating the effect that length of day has on children's literacy and math achievement. Child characteristics that they accounted for included the child's age at kindergarten entry, the child's gender, and previous preschool experience. They failed to examine how children's ethnic group or language status related to achievement. Similarly, in a more recent study examining the effect of length of day on children's academic achievement over time, Gullo (2000) failed to examine whether or not children's ethnic or linguistic backgrounds related to variation in their academic performance in full-day and half-day programs. Such oversights are problematic given the number of full-day programs that are targeted at children with second language status (National Center for Education Statistics, 2004; Vecchiotti, 2003) and given recent research suggesting that children from diverse backgrounds may experience the effects of full-day experiences differently than those in half-day (Lee et al., 2006). Clearly, additional research is needed to examine how different kindergarten experiences impact children from diverse backgrounds.

BEYOND LENGTH OF DAY: INSTRUCTIONAL QUALITY AND ATTENDANCE PATTERNS

Although many researchers have suggested that children in full-day programs make greater academic gains than their peers in half-day programs, few have examined whether these effects are simply a result of lengthening the school day or whether they have to do with other important variables such as instructional quality and children's attendance patterns. Simply, lengthening the school day may not facilitate changes in the type and quality of instruction for young children. Thus, a child's participation in a full-day kindergarten program, depending upon the quality, may or may not improve his or her kindergarten experience or better prepare the child for the increasing demands of later schooling. Similarly, little attention has been given to children's attendance patterns in both types of programs (full- and half-day) and the impact that attendance may have on children's academic performance.

Instructional Quality

Research has suggested that kindergarten is a "highly variable experience" (Pianta, La Paro, Payne, Cox, & Bradley, 2002, p. 236) with a wide range of variability in terms of curriculum, instruction, and environment. However, there is one area of agreement which is the importance of instructional quality and its potential impact on child outcomes (Early & Winton, 2001; National Association for the Education of Young Children, 2005a, 2005b, 2006). Even with this agreement, researchers and policymakers still need to come to a clearer determination of the indicators of instructional methods and quality that will most likely ensure that all children receive a high-quality kindergarten experience regardless of length of day. Most recently, Pianta and colleagues have suggested characteristics of social climate, management of time and activities, and instructional support (La Paro, Pianta, & Stuhlman, 2004; Pianta, 2003; Pianta et al., 2002) as critical indicators of instructional quality. For example, in early childhood classrooms where children manifest positive outcomes, teachers engage in high levels of "confirming feedback" (Meyer, Wardrop, Hastings, & Linn, 1993, p. 159), are familiar with children's academic needs, and show sensitivity toward individual children. Teachers in quality early childhood settings use proactive approaches to discipline and promote children's success through appropriate questioning and feedback, scaffolding, and other approaches to instructional support (Rimm-Kaufman, La Paro, Downer, & Pianta, 2005).

In reference to full- and half-day kindergarten, previous research has shown that teachers in full-day classrooms may approach instruction differently (e.g., type of instruction—small vs. large group, amount of formal instruction) than those in half-day programs (Elicker & Mathur, 1997; Lee et al., 2006). Despite these few studies examining the amount and type of instruction that occurs in full-day and half-day programs, little research has examined the differences in the overall quality of instruction. For example, it is unclear whether or not levels of productivity and engagement differ among full- and half-day programs or whether or not teachers in full-day programs offer more in-depth feedback as a result of the increased amount of time available for instructional activities. Additional research is needed to examine the nature of instruction that is occurring in full-day and half-day kindergarten programs, including the particular variables that ensure high-quality instruction in kindergarten, regardless of the length of the day.

Attendance Patterns

In addition to instructional quality, there is some interest in the relationship between children's participation in a full- or half-day program and their attendance patterns. This is an important policy issue because kindergarten is not mandated in many parts of the United States (Vecchiotti, 2003), and therefore not all children are expected to attend. Although few studies have examined the impact of full- and half-day kindergarten programs on children's attendance patterns (e.g., Gullo, 2000), initial evidence suggests that children in full-day programs attend more days than children in half-day settings. Thus, when talking about the impact of length of day (i.e., full-day) on children's development, one should also consider the number of days children actually attend kindergarten. For example, some argue that the additional time in kindergarten is what impacts children's academic achievement. Although this may be true, it may not be necessary to move to a full-day program to increase a child's time in kindergarten. Simply requiring children to attend kindergarten, even in a half-day program, may positively impact children's development. These are questions that, to date, have not been addressed and yet have significant policy ramifications and implications for funding. This is especially true in states where many are still debating the importance of early childhood programming and making critical decisions about how to move forward with the implementation of full-day kindergarten.

PURPOSE

The purpose of this study was twofold: to examine (a) the effects of full-day kindergarten programming on instructional quality; and (b) the impact of the length of day (full- vs. half-day), language status (English language learner [ELL] vs. non-ELL), and attendance (fewer than 10 absences vs. 10 or more absences) on children's academic achievement. Qualitative data were collected to further understand which factors, as perceived by teachers and administrators, influence instructional quality and academic achievement.

In the state of Utah, where this study took place, children have little, if any, access to full-day kindergarten programs. Similarly, Utah does not provide state-funded pre-kindergarten programming for young children and does not mandate kindergarten (Kauerz, 2005). As a result, children are not required to attend kindergarten, and kindergarten experiences are not funded in the same manner as other grades (Vecchiotti, 2003). However, in recent years the governor's office has proposed legislation that would dramatically increase the availability of full-day kindergarten programs for children who are at risk for school failure (Utah Legislature, 2007). This political climate, similar to that found in other western states, requires local studies that further validate the value of full-day kindergarten. These studies, even when they mimic national findings, may be more compelling for local leaders and policymakers. Furthermore, these policies have important implications for children and families, making it especially critical to examine local opinions and experiences of stakeholders from multiple perspectives. The perceptions of these stakeholders are especially critical in promoting greater understanding and compelling evidence for policies that will promote early childhood programs that are beneficial to all children, regardless of their language status. Furthermore, the results from this study may have implications for other areas in which educators are advocating for policy changes and additional funds to promote quality early childhood programming for all children.

METHOD

Given the social and political context, the current literature on full- and half-day kindergarten, and the

importance of instructional quality, the major foci of this study were to examine (a) instructional quality, (b) children's academic achievement (with particular concentration on linguistically diverse students and children's attendance patterns), and (c) teachers' and administrators' perceptions of full- and half-day kindergarten.

Participants

The study was conducted at two schools located in the same school district. The treatment school volunteered to participate in the district's pilot full-day kindergarten program and was one of the first public schools to implement full-day kindergarten in the state of Utah. The control school was selected because it offered a half-day kindergarten program and was, of the other schools in the district, the most similar to the treatment school in terms of demographics. At the time of data collection, the treatment school had 622 students enrolled, with 112 kindergarten students. Sixty-three percent ($n = 390$) of the total student population were classified as ELLs, with 69% ($n = 77$) of the 112 kindergarten students classified as ELLs. The control school had a total student population of 470, with 80 kindergarten students. Twenty-six percent of the total student population ($n = 123$) and 26% of the kindergartners ($n = 21$) in the control school were classified as ELLs. See Table 1 for a description of school and kindergarten classroom demographics.

A total of eight kindergarten classrooms were used—four full-day classrooms (four teachers with four full-day sessions) and four half-day classrooms (two teachers with two morning and two afternoon sessions). The four kindergarten classrooms from the treatment school were in their first year of implementing a full-day kindergarten pilot program. The pilot program had approved funding for a 3-year period.

Table 1. Demographics of Schools and Kindergarten Classrooms

Variable	Treatment		Control	
	School	Kindergarten	School	Kindergarten
Total enrollment, n	622	112	470	80
Students classified as ELL/LEP, % (n)	63 (390)	69 (77)	26 (123)	26 (21)
Ethnicity, % (n)				
White	21 (130)	23 (26)	56 (261)	45 (36)
Hispanic	74 (459)	71 (79)	35 (166)	44 (35)
Black	1 (8)	< 1 (1)	2 (9)	< 1 (2)
Native American	3 (18)	4 (4)	3 (13)	1 (4)
Asian	< 1 (1)	< 1 (1)	1 (4)	< 1 (2)
Polynesian	< 1 (3)	< 1 (1)	1 (6)	0 (0)
Other	< 1 (3)	0 (0)	2 (11)	< 1 (1)
Students receiving free or reduced lunch, % (n)	90 (562)	91 (102)	74 (346)	55 (44)

Note: ELL = English language learner; LEP = limited English proficient.

Children in these classrooms were living within the school boundaries when the school decided to implement a full-day program. If parents did not wish for their children to attend a full-day program, they were allowed to move their children to another neighborhood school where their children could attend a half-day program. The school administrators indicated that during this particular school year none of the parents chose to move their children, although they did have a few requests for special placement from parents of children who did not live within the school boundaries so that their children could attend full-day kindergarten. The four control classrooms were implementing a half-day kindergarten program as usual. There was no option for these children to attend a full-day program.

At the beginning of the year, 118 (64 treatment, 54 control) children in the eight classes received parental consent to participate in the study. Over the course of the school year, 22 children (7 treatment, 15 control; 8 ELL, 14 non-ELL across both treatment and control) moved away and were no longer part of the study. All analyses were conducted with the 96 children (57 treatment, 39 control; 52 ELL, 44 non-ELL) who attended school for the full year in their respective classrooms. The 52 ELL students who participated in this study all spoke Spanish as their primary language. See Table 2 for a description of student participant demographics.

Design

Concurrent triangulation strategy, a mixed method model, was used as the study design (Creswell, 2003). The quantitative and qualitative data were collected concurrently and were interpreted to note the convergence (or lack thereof) of the findings. It is often ideal that the quantitative and qualitative data have equal priority; however, it is more common that greater priority is given to one or the other (Creswell, 2003). In the current study, greater priority was given to the quantitative data, and the qualitative data were used to further explain and give depth to the quantitative findings.

Table 2. Student Participant Demographics

Variable	Full-Day	Half-Day
Language status, *n*		
ELL	39	13
Non-ELL	18	26
Gender, *n*		
Female	24	21
Male	33	18
Age (years), *M (SD)*	5.5 (0.32)	5.6 (0.26)

Note: ELL = English language learner.

Measures

Both quantitative and qualitative measures were used to examine different aspects of this study. Quantitative measures were used to examine instructional quality and academic achievement (math and literacy). Qualitative data were used to examine teacher and administrator perceptions of full- and half-day programs.

Instructional Quality

To date, many of the studies of full- and half-day kindergarten have not considered the importance of instructional quality. However, early childhood programming, regardless of length of day, is dependent upon quality environments and instruction (Fromberg, 1986; Herman, 1984; Naron, 1981). As such, instructional quality for each of the eight classrooms was assessed using the Classroom Assessment Scoring System (CLASS; La Paro et al., 2004). The CLASS is an observational instrument designed to assess instructional quality in preschool through third-grade classrooms and is based on the interactions of teachers and students in the classroom, not on the presence of materials, the physical environment, or the use of a specific curriculum. The CLASS measures classroom instructional quality based on three domains. The first domain is socioemotional climate and includes the constructs of *positive climate*, *negative climate*, and *teacher sensitivity*. The second domain is classroom management and includes the constructs of *regard for students' perspectives*, *behavior management*, and *productivity*. The third domain is instructional support and includes the constructs of *concept development*, *instructional learning formats*, *quality feedback*, and *student engagement*.

Before using the CLASS, all users must be trained by a certified CLASS trainer and meet reliability criteria, which involves watching and coding six video segments with at least 80% reliability. All three of the authors participated in the CLASS training and met the reliability criteria (80% or better). In addition to this training, the authors also established inter-rater reliability, for the specific purpose of this study, by conducting the first four observations in pairs. A comparison of the independently scored observations indicated a high level of reliability (97%) among all three raters.

All procedures for using the CLASS, as laid out by the certified CLASS trainer, were followed during each of the observations. A CLASS observation involves a 30-min cycle that includes a 20-min observation of both structured and unstructured classroom activities, making notes regarding the 10 CLASS constructs, and paying particular attention to the teacher's instructional behaviors and interactions. This is followed by a 10-min coding segment in which the observer scores each construct on a scale of 1 to 7 (1, 2 = *low frequency*; 3, 4, 5 = *mid frequency*; 6, 7 = *high frequency*). It is recommended that a minimum of four segments be obtained per classroom to establish one observation. During data collection, each of the eight classrooms was observed three times throughout the year (beginning, middle, and end of the school year). Each observation session was composed of a series of four to five 30-min observation segments (which included a 10-min scoring segment), for a total of twelve to fifteen 20-min observation segments for each teacher across the course of the school year. Observations took place during both the morning and afternoon.

Academic Achievement

Children's academic achievement was assessed at the beginning and end of the school year using the following measures: the Peabody Picture Vocabulary Test—III (PPVT-III; Dunn & Dunn, 1997), the Phonological Awareness Literacy Screening (PALS-K: Rhyming, Alphabet Knowledge, Letter Sounds, Spelling, and Word Recognition; Invernizzi, Sullivan, & Meier, 2001), and the Roswell–Chall Auditory Blending Test (Roswell & Chall, 1997). In addition to these literacy measures, the Applied Problems subtest of the Woodcock–Johnson III (Woodcock, McGrew, & Mather, 2001) was administered to assess general math achievement.

Teacher and Administrator Perceptions

Teacher/administrator perceptions of full- and half-day kindergarten were collected during a semi-structured interview at the end of the school year. Interviews were conducted with each of the four full-day kindergarten teachers and their Title I facilitator and principal, and the two half-day kindergarten teachers and their principal. Several questions were asked during the interviews that focused on (a) perceptions of full- and half-day kindergarten (What are the benefits of full-day kindergarten? What are the benefits of half-day kindergarten?), (b) opinions about the success of their kindergarten program during the year in which the study was conducted (What do you feel were your greatest successes this year?), and (c) views of the children's (ELL and non-ELL) academic progress during the school year (How has full-day [or half-day] kindergarten helped your students? What impact has full-day [or half-day] kindergarten had on (1) ELL students' literacy skills, (2) overall academic achievement?).

Data Analysis

Quantitative data were analyzed to determine the impact of full-day kindergarten (length of day) on instructional quality and academic achievement (literacy and math). Analyses also examined the impact of language status (ELL vs. non-ELL) and attendance (fewer than 10 absences vs. 10 or more absences) on academic achievement. Qualitative data were analyzed to determine teacher/administrator perceptions of full- and half-day kindergarten and their beliefs about the impact of full-day kindergarten on ELL and non-ELL students' academic performance. Data were analyzed separately, and then results were interpreted to identify areas of convergence (Creswell, 2003).

Quantitative Analyses

Quantitative analyses (univariate and multivariate analyses) were conducted on CLASS observation data and child academic achievement data (PPVT-III, PALS-K, Woodcock–Johnson III, Roswell–Chall Auditory Blending Test). Each of the analyses is described in more detail below.

Classroom instructional quality was analyzed using a multivariate analysis of variance (MANOVA). The independent variable was length of day (full- and half-day), and the dependent variables were the three subscales of the CLASS Observation: Socio-Emotional Climate, Management, and Instructional Support (La Paro et al., 2004).

Child academic achievement data were analyzed using both multivariate and univariate analyses. It should also be noted that child achievement data were analyzed on the child level (rather than the classroom level) using gain scores. Data were analyzed on the child level because there was not a significant difference among any of the eight classrooms in instructional quality as measured by the CLASS (see "Results"). This allowed us to assume that children in either group, regardless of their classroom, were receiving comparable instruction. Gain scores were used because analyses for child academic achievement pretest data revealed that the two groups (full- and half-day) were not equal at the outset of the study (Rachor & Cizek, 1996). A MANOVA on children's pretest scores for the subtests of the PALS-K showed that children in the half-day program outperformed children in the full-day program on Rhyming, Alphabet Knowledge, and Spelling Subtests. There was no difference between the two groups on the Letter Sounds and Word Recognition subtests. Other univariate analyses of variance (ANOVAs) on the PPVT-III, the Roswell–Chall Auditory Blending Test, and the Woodcock–Johnson III revealed that children in half-day programs scored significantly higher on the PPVT-III and Woodcock–Johnson III at the pretest. There was no difference on the Roswell–Chall Auditory Blending Test. The differences on the PPVT-III (half-day > full-day) may have been, in large measure, related to the larger number of ELL students in the full-day program. In other words, there were fewer ELL children in the half-day program, and thus their scores were, on average, higher on the PPVT-III than those of the children in the full-day program. See Table 3 for mean scores and standard deviations on pretest measures.

Two MANOVAs were conducted using the PALS-K gain scores as the dependent variables. The subtests on the PALS-K were separated for the analyses to examine the development of early skills (rhyming and letter naming) separate from that of more advanced skills (letter sounds, spelling, and word recognition). The first MANOVA included length of day (full- and half-day), language status (ELL and non-ELL), and attendance (fewer than 10 absences and 10 or more absences) as the independent variables and gain scores (posttest scores minus pretest scores) for the Rhyming and Alphabet Knowledge subtests of the PALS-K (Invernizzi et al., 2001) as the dependent variables. The second MANOVA included the same independent variables—length of day (full- and half-day), language status (ELL and non-ELL), and attendance (fewer than 10 absences and 10 or more absences)—and gain scores (posttest scores minus pretest scores) for the Letter Sounds, Spelling, and Word Recognition subtests of the PALS-K (Invernizzi et al., 2001). Three univariate ANOVAs were conducted with length of day (full- and half-day), language status (ELL and non-ELL), and attendance (fewer than 10 absences and 10 or more absences) as the independent variables and with the following dependent variables: (a) gain scores (posttest minus pretest) for the PPVT-III (Dunn & Dunn, 1997), (b) gain scores (posttest minus pretest) for the Roswell–Chall Auditory Blending Test (Roswell & Chall, 1997), and (c) gain scores (posttest minus pretest) for the Applied Problems subtest of the Woodcock–Johnson III (Woodcock et al., 2001).

Qualitative Analysis

Teachers and administrators from both schools were interviewed at the end of the school year using the same interview protocol. Interview transcriptions were analyzed inductively by two of the three authors. The two authors independently read all of the interview transcriptions and coded each separate idea generated by the teachers and administrators into categories. The two authors then collapsed the categories into meaningful groups or themes. The authors then met and worked to consensus on the common themes/categories (Bogdan & Biklen, 1998). Six categories emerged from the data: academic progress, curriculum, discipline, relationships, parental support, and logistics.

In terms of *academic progress*, full-day teachers commented that a full-day program allowed them to see more progress in their students, especially ELL students. Several teachers and administrators indicated that the additional time in school would help children be more prepared for the academic demands of school. In contrast, the half-day teachers expressed the concern of a full-day program having too much focus on academics.

In comments related to *curriculum*, full-day teachers acknowledged the ability to address and organize curriculum in a more meaningful and age-appropriate manner. That is, the curriculum could be addressed at a more in-depth and comprehensive level. Half-day teachers again expressed the concern of full-day programs overemphasizing academics and not allowing sufficient time to play.

Discipline was a common theme addressed by both full-day and half-day teachers. Both indicated that the longer day may result in a greater number of behavior problems. Full-day teachers also felt that through proactive planning, such discipline problems could be decreased. The half-day teachers were less optimistic in terms of overcoming these difficulties.

Table 3. Mean (*SD*) Scores on Pretest Measures for Full- and Half-Day Students

Measure	Full-Day	Half-Day	F
PALS-K			
Rhyming	4.75 (3.02)	9.67 (0.577)	7.59*
Alphabet Knowledge	8.75 (8.92)	23.00 (1.00)	7.34*
Letter Sounds	4.50 (7.21)	12.67 (10.12)	3.06
Spelling	2.05 (4.03)	15.00 (5.19)	25.13***
Word Recognition	5.60 (8.06)	3.33 (1.52)	0.23
Roswell–Chall Auditory Blending Test	3.59 (7.23)	5.21 (7.65)	1.09
PPVT-III	43.26 (39.31)	90.69 (15.49)	47.58***
Woodcock–Johnson III	11.56 (4.72)	15.53 (4.29)	16.69***

Note: PALS-K = Phonological Awareness Literacy Screening; PPVT-III = Peabody Picture Vocabulary Test–III.
*$p < .05$. ***$p < .001$.

The development of *relationships* was another common theme. Because there was more time to interact one-on-one with the students, full-day teachers felt they were able to get to know them better, which allowed them to make better decisions regarding the students' developmental needs. A few of the full-day teachers also commented that a full-day program also allowed them more time to establish a stronger collaborative relationship with the other kindergarten teachers. Half-day teachers commented that a half-day program allowed children more time to make friends at home or out of the context of school. Full-day teachers did not make reference to children's friendships in or out of school.

Both full- and half-day teachers addressed the issue of *parental support* and the negative impact the lack of parental support had on students' success and development. Both groups of teachers also expressed the concern that parents would use a full-day program as a "babysitting service" and not provide the necessary level of parental support and involvement. However, the full-day teachers also commented that a full-day program could, in some ways, help make up for a deficit in parental support. In addition, full-day teachers reported opportunities to develop better relationships with the children's parents because they had half the number of children compared to half-day teachers, who taught two sessions of kindergarten.

The interviews with the school administrators primarily focused on the *logistics* of implementing and coordinating a full-day program. Logistical concerns involved both financial and physical facilities as well as the day-to-day impact. These included the issue of servicing fewer children in a full-day program, and the lack of physical space. The day-to-day logistics, such as lunch time, also presented some concern as administrators reflected on the difficulties associated with helping young children become familiar with lunchroom routines and procedures (e.g., remembering the child's identification code, cleanliness, safety/supervision). Finally, administrators brought up staffing concerns, that is, the difficulty of having to hire additional teachers when there is already a shortage of qualified candidates.

All of the six categories offered interesting insights into teachers' and administrators' beliefs about full-day kindergarten. However, three of the six categories (i.e., academic progress, curriculum, and parental support) further illuminated the quantitative findings and are used here in the interpretation of the study results.

RESULTS

Instructional Quality—CLASS Observations

In terms of classroom instruction, multivariate analysis (MANOVA) was used to analyze CLASS data (socio-emotional climate, management, and instructional support (La Paro et al., 2004). Results indicated that there was also no difference between full- and half-day classrooms in terms of instructional quality as measured by the CLASS (Wilks' $\Lambda = .93$), $F(3, 6) = 1.59$, $p = .20$. See Table 4 for mean scores and standard deviations on CLASS observations for full- and half-day classrooms.

These results indicated that simply lengthening the day did not automatically result in higher instructional quality. In fact, these data suggested that these two full- and half-day programs had similar instructional quality. The CLASS scores (see Table 4) further demonstrated that both the full- and half-day teachers provided a generally warm classroom climate (5.41 and 5.18 on a 7-point scale) with moderate levels of management and instructional support (4.25–4.82 on a 7-point scale).

Several of the teachers' comments from the interviews that had been categorized as *curriculum* corroborated the results of the MANOVA, suggesting that there was no difference in instructional quality between the two groups (full- and half-day). Teachers in both full- and half-day programs indicated that full-day programs offer additional time to "go more in-depth" or to "spend more time with hands-on things . . . [to] enhance science units . . . and the arts." However, they also indicated that there is still much to do to include more "student-directed, in-depth exploration" in their instruction. In essence, both groups of teachers expressed the fact that more time in the school day could provide an opportunity for deeper, more meaningful instruction. However, it seems that there are several difficulties associated with these ideals. For example, teachers in full-day programs indicated that it was difficult to keep high levels of productivity throughout the entire day: "In the morning we do our big literacy [push], and math games and all of our centers . . . We tried to mellow it out a little bit more in the afternoon." It should also be noted that the teachers were in the first year of implementing full-day kindergarten and were still facing some of the difficulties associated with making the necessary instruc-

Table 4. Mean (*SD*) Scores on CLASS Observations for Full- and Half-Day Classrooms

CLASS Observation	Full-Day	Half-Day	F
Socio-Emotional Climate	5.41 (0.50)	5.18 (0.57)	3.04
Management	4.82 (0.81)	4.77 (0.83)	0.05
Instructional Support	4.44 (0.87)	4.25 (0.65)	0.88

Note: CLASS = Classroom Assessment Scoring System.

tional and procedural shifts. In sum, it appears that the kindergarten teachers participating in this study were still grappling with the best methods and procedures for creating high-quality kindergarten experiences for all children.

Academic Performance: Literacy and Mathematics

The first MANOVA on children's gain scores for the Rhyming and Alphabet Knowledge subtests of the PALS-K revealed a main effect for length of day (full- and half-day), with children in full-day programs making greater gains than their peers in half-day programs (Wilks' Λ = .792), $F(2, 87)$ = 11.41, p = .000. Follow-up univariate analysis showed that children in full-day kindergarten programs made significantly greater gains when compared to children attending half-day programs on both of the measures: Rhyming, $F(1, 88)$ = 7.88, p = .006; and Alphabet Knowledge, $F(1, 88)$ = 20.17, p = .000. There was also a main effect for language status (Wilks' Λ = .935), $F(2, 87)$ = 3.02, p = .054, with ELL students making greater gains than non-ELL students. Follow-up univariate analysis showed that children who were ELLs made significantly greater gains on Alphabet Knowledge, $F(1, 88)$ = 6.06, p = .016. There was no difference on Rhyming, $F(1, 88)$ = 0.73, p = .394. There was no main effect for attendance (Wilks' Λ = .981), $F(2, 87)$ = 0.83, p = .441. There were no significant interactions: Length of Day × Language Status (Wilks' Λ = .988), $F(2, 87)$ = 0.51, p = .603; Length of Day × Attendance (Wilks' Λ = .964), $F(2, 87)$ = 1.64, p = .200; Language Status × Attendance (Wilks' Λ = .992), $F(2, 87)$ = 0.34, p = .713; Length of Day × Language Status × Attendance (Wilks' Λ = .981), $F(2, 87)$ = 0.83, p = .441. See Table 5 for mean gain scores and standard deviations on the Rhyming and Alphabet Knowledge subtests of the PALS-K (Length of Day, Language Status, and Attendance).

The second MANOVA on children's gain scores for the Letter Sounds, Spelling, and Word Recognition subtests of the PALS-K revealed a main effect for length of day, with children in full-day programs making greater gains than their peers in half-day programs (Wilks' Λ = .682), $F(3, 86)$ = 13.37, p = .000. Follow-up univariate analysis showed that children in full-day kindergarten programs made significantly greater gains when compared to children attending half-day programs on all of the measures: Letter Sounds, $F(1, 88)$ = 27.70, p = .000; Spelling, $F(1, 88)$ = 31.90, p = .000; and Word Recognition, $F(1, 88)$ = 6.20, p = .015. There were no main effects for language status (Wilks' Λ = .959), $F(3, 86)$ = 1.23, p = .302; or attendance (Wilks' Λ = .978), $F(3, 86)$ = 0.69, p = .592. There were also no significant interactions: Length of Day × Language Status (Wilks' Λ = .981), $F(3, 86)$ = 0.55, p = .651; Length of Day × Attendance (Wilks' Λ = .993), $F(3, 86)$ = 0.21, p = .889; Language Status × Attendance (Wilks' Λ = .923), $F(3, 86)$ = 2.39, p = .074; Length of Day × Language Status × Attendance (Wilks' Λ = .993), $F(3, 86)$ = 0.19, p = .902. See Table 6 for mean gain scores and standard deviations on the Letter Sounds, Spelling, and Word Recognition subtests of the PALS-K (Length of Day, Language Status, and Attendance).

Three univariate ANOVAs were conducted for the PPVT-III, the Roswell–Chall Auditory Blending Test, and the Woodcock–Johnson III Applied Problems subtest. Results for the Roswell–Chall Auditory Blending Test indicated that the children who attended full-day kindergarten made significantly greater gains than the children who attended half-day kindergarten, $F(1, 88)$ = 14.09, p = .000. There was no difference between ELL and non-ELL students, $F(1, 88)$ = 0.416, p = .521; and no difference between children who were absent fewer than 10 days and those who were absent 10 or more days, $F(1, 88)$ = 1.35, p = .249. There were no significant interactions: Length of Day × Language Status, $F(1, 88)$ = 0.11, p = .739; Length of Day × Attendance, $F(1, 88)$ = 0.000, p = .983; Language Status × Attendance, $F(1, 88)$ = 0.002, p = .962; and Length of Day × Language Status × Attendance, $F(1, 88)$ = 0.54, p = .466.

Results for the PPVT-III indicated that there was a main effect for length of day, language status, and

Table 5. Mean (*SD*) Gain Scores and Standard Deviations on Rhyming and Alphabet Knowledge Subtests (PALS-K) for Length of Day, Language Status, and Attendance

Measure	Length of Day			Language Status			Attendance		
	Full Day	Half Day	F	ELL	Non-ELL	F	Fewer Than 10 Absences	10 or More Absences	F
Rhyming	3.71 (3.03)	1.58 (2.20)	7.88***	3.44 (2.99)	2.16 (2.69)	0.733	3.66 (2.76)	2.22 (2.89)	1.11
Alphabet Knowledge	17.92 (7.80)	8.95 (7.82)	20.18***	17.82 (8.08)	10.09 (8.13)	6.06**	15.42 (9.34)	13.39 (8.61)	0.201*

Note: PALS-K = Phonological Awareness Literacy Screening; ELL = English language learner.
* p < .05. ** p < .01. *** p < .001.

Table 6. Mean (*SD*) Gain Scores and Standard Deviations on Letter Sounds, Spelling, and Word Recognition Subtests (PALS-K) for Length of Day, Language Status, and Attendance

Measure	Length of Day			Language Status			Attendance		
	Full Day	Half Day	F	ELL	Non-ELL	F	Fewer Than 10 Absences	10 or More Absences	F
Letter Sounds	20.46 (5.79)	12.28 (6.87)	27.70***	18.51 (7.26)	15.50 (7.33)	0.012	18.73 (7.04)	15.88 (7.52)	0.522
Spelling	14.31 (5.56)	6.28 (5.89)	31.90***	12.67 (5.93)	9.13 (7.54)	0.085	12.88 (5.51)	9.63 (7.58)	1.66
Word Recognition	16.05 (15.03)	9.33 (10.59)	6.20*	12.01 (12.35)	14.86 (15.24)	3.14	15.19 (11.94)	12.73 (17.83)	0.677

Note: PALS-K = Phonological Awareness Literacy Screening; ELL = English language learner.
* $p < .05$. *** $p < \sum.001$.

attendance. More specifically, children who attended full-day kindergarten made significantly greater gains than children who attended half-day kindergarten, $F(1, 88) = 42.17$, $p = .000$; ELL students made greater gains than non-ELL students, $F(1, 88) = 6.29$, $p = .014$; and children who had fewer than 10 absences outgained children with 10 or more absences, $F(1, 88) = 4.43$, $p = .038$. There were also two significant interactions: Length of Day × Language Status, $F(1, 88) = 6.32$, $p = .014$; and Length of Day × Attendance, $F(1, 88) = 5.43$, $p = .022$. See Figures 1 and 2 for an illustration of the interaction effect for PPVT-III gain scores (Length of Day × Language Status and Length of Day × Attendance, respectively).

The Woodcock–Johnson III Applied Problems subtest gain scores indicated that there was no significant difference between the two groups (full and half-day), $F(1, 88) = 1.02$, $p = .316$; no significant difference for language status, $F(1, 88) = 0.984$, $p = .324$; and no significant difference for attendance, $F(1, 88) = 0.001$, $p = .974$.; and no interactions: Length of Day × Language Status, $F(1, 88) = 0.456$, $p = .501$; Length of Day × Attendance, $F(1, 88) = 2.14$, $p = .147$; Language Status × Attendance, $F(1, 88) = 0.389$, $p = .534$; Length of Day × Language Status × Attendance, $F(1, 88) = 1.66$, $p = .201$. See Table 7 for mean gain scores and standard

deviations for the Roswell–Chall Auditory Blending Test, the PPVT-III, and the Woodcock–Johnson III Applied Problems subtest (Length of Day, Language Status, and Attendance).

In terms of academic achievement, it is clear that the children who participated in full-day kindergarten outgained their peers in the half-day program on most of the academic measures. There were also two significant interaction effects (Length of Day × Language Status and Length of Day × Attendance) for the PPVT-III, suggesting that ELL students in the full-day program made greater gains in oral language (receptive vocabulary) than (a) their non-ELL peers who also attended full-day kindergarten as well as (b) the ELL and non-ELL students who attended the half-day program. In regard to absences, ELL students who had fewer absences made greater gains in oral language (receptive vocabulary) than their peers who missed more days of kindergarten in either full- or half-day programs.

Teacher interviews corroborated the quantitative findings, as they further suggested that *academic progress* was one of the most significant factors related to full-day kindergarten. All of the full-day kindergarten teachers made reference to the specific emphasis on literacy during full-day kindergarten: "The

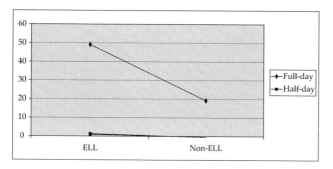

Figure 1. Interaction effect for Peabody Picture Vocabulary Test–III gain scores (Length of Day × Language Status). ELL = English language learner.

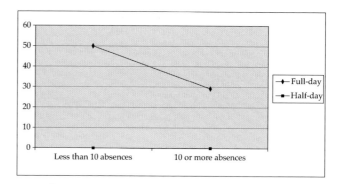

Figure 2. Interaction effect for Peabody Picture Vocabulary Test–III gain scores (Length of Day × Attendance).

Table 7.   Mean (*SD*) Gain Scores and Standard Deviations for Roswell–Chall Auditory Blending Test, PPVT-III, and Woodcock–Johnson III Applied Problems Subtest (Length of Day, Language Status, and Attendance)

Measure	Length of Day			Language Status			Attendance		
	Full-Day	Half-Day	F	ELL	Non-ELL	F	Fewer Than 10 Absences	10 or More Absences	F
Roswell–Chall Auditory Blending Test	19.14 (11.20)	8.69 (8.65)	14.09***	17.21 (11.66)	12.56 (10.62)	0.416	17.81 (10.93)	12.63 (11.38)	1.34
PPVT-III	39.91 (32.73)	0.051 (10.67)	42.17***	37.27 (32.20)	7.70 (25.24)	6.29**	34.69 (35.59)	15.19 (27.54)	4.43*
Woodcock–Johnson III Applied Problems	5.54 (3.33)	4.44 (4.99)	1.02	5.65 (3.18)	4.43 (4.93)	0.984	5.21 (3.59)	5.00 (4.49)	0.001

Note: PPVT-III = Peabody Picture Vocabulary Test–III; ELL = English language learner.
* *p* < .05. ** *p* < .01. *** *p* < .001.

entire morning was spent focusing on reading and phonics skills . . ." Other comments were related to full-day teachers' overall confidence in the children's literacy progress: "I think every one of my students can tell you all the ABCs and all the sounds. I've taught kindergarten for five years and I think this is the first year I can say that about every student." Similarly, another full-day teacher reported that "most of [the children] are ready for first grade . . . only a few are still struggling . . . the rest of the class knows the letters and sounds and how to put words together." Half-day teachers also expressed success related to literacy achievement; however, their comments expressed much less optimism: "A good majority of them are reading although they're not reading on level." Half-day teachers also did not emphasize the amount of time, when compared to other areas of the curriculum, they spent teaching literacy. Thus, we see a qualitative difference in the time teachers reported spending teaching literacy and their overall feelings related to children's literacy achievement.

In terms of math achievement, there was an over-all absence of comments from the teachers, both full- and half-day, related to mathematics instruction and/or student achievement. One full-day teacher made reference to her desire to adjust her instruction next year to emphasize mathematics: "I want to figure out a block in the morning when I can do math." Another full-day teacher indicated that they spent time in the morning focusing on literacy and mathematics. The half-day teachers made no specific reference to

instruction or achievement in mathematics. The sheer absence of teacher comments suggests one possible explanation for the fact that children's mathematics achievement did not differ when comparing full- and half-day programs. It is perhaps the emphasis on literacy, and the limited use of the afternoon, that leaves full-day teachers with little time to focus on other areas of the curriculum, such as mathematics.

Teachers made several comments specifically related to ELL students and their academic progress. The majority of these comments were related to the idea that full-day kindergarten gives children "a lot more time to learn English" and/or "time to play with English." This confirmed the interaction effect that was found for the PPVT-III. That is, ELL students in full-day kindergarten had significantly higher scores on the PPVT-III, a measure of oral language. The only reference to ELL students by the half-day teachers was a reference to the difficulties associated with adapting instruction to meet the unique needs of ELL students in a short school day. In sum, the full-day teachers emphasized the opportunities for children to hear and use English, and half-day teachers indicated the difficulties associated with meeting the needs of children who come from linguistically diverse backgrounds.

Overall, teachers emphasized a focus on academic progress for both ELL and non-ELL students. Although this set of responses confirmed the quantitative findings, it is also important to note a few of the teachers' comments related to their concern that there is an overemphasis on academics in kindergarten at the expense of other areas (i.e., social, emotional, physical). These comments were primarily made by the half-day teachers, although nearly all of the teachers made reference to making kindergarten a place where teachers can focus on the development of the whole child and not just academics.

Although *absences* was not a category that emerged from the qualitative data, it is interesting to note that the number of days children were absent was only a concern for the half-day teachers. The full-day kindergarten teachers made no reference to children's attendance patterns. In contrast, the half-day teachers referred to absences as one of the "biggest hindrances to progress." It is clear from both the quantitative and qualitative data that children in half-day programs were more frequently absent compared to their peers in full-day programs.

DISCUSSION

Research examining the efficacy of full- and half-day kindergarten experiences on children's academic outcomes demonstrates that children in full-day settings fare better on measures of language, literacy, and math achievement (Baskett et al., 2005; Cryan et al., 1992; Puleo, 1988; Yan & Lin, 2005). Despite such research, and the prevalence of programs targeted toward linguistically and economically diverse populations, relatively little attention has been given to the impact that these programs have on second language learners. Given such limitations, the current research study contributes to the research literature on full- and half-day kindergarten in a number of important ways.

First, we found that, regardless of child language status, full-day kindergarten positively impacted children's literacy performance on measures of rhyming, alphabet knowledge, letter sound associations, spelling, word recognition, blending, and oral language (receptive vocabulary). This benefit was clearly recognized by teachers implementing full-day programs. For example, full-day kindergarten teachers articulated how having more time with the children improved their ability to delve "deeply" into the literacy curriculum and also contributed positively to their excitement and confidence in children's literacy knowledge and development. Although the teachers in half-day settings also commented on children's developing literacy skills, they expressed less confidence in their students' skills and greater concern about how many children were still considered below grade level. For the full-day teachers, the lengthening of the school day appeared to help them focus their instruction more on meeting the individual needs of children (in literacy)

and allowed them to spend more time on curriculum that they valued.

In addition, it is interesting to note that, although ELL students did not appear to benefit more from full-day kindergarten in regard to overall literacy development than their non-ELL peers or the ELL students in the half-day setting, they did appear to benefit more in the area of language development (receptive vocabulary). This is perhaps not surprising given that ELL children in full-day settings potentially had more experience than ELL children in half-day settings hearing and speaking English. In fact, full-day teachers commented on how the full-day program benefited their ELL students by allowing them more time to learn and play with English. This language exposure was clearly evident in children's gains in oral language skills. In contrast, half-day teachers did not emphasize the impact that their curriculum was having on ELL students' language growth. Rather, teachers commented on the difficulty they experienced in adapting instruction to meet their children's diverse language needs. Such views appear to reflect the limited time that half-day kindergarten teachers felt they had to meet the needs of ELL students and may also reflect their general frustrations with the challenge of meeting the needs of linguistically diverse children within the time constraints of a half-day kindergarten program (approximately 3.5 hr).

Our finding that children in full-day settings are significantly advantaged in regard to literacy growth over their peers in half-day settings is supported by previous research (Baskett et al., 2005; Cryan et al., 1992; Yan & Lin, 2005). Unlike previous research, however, we considered what impact such programs have on both ELL and non-ELL children's literacy, and language skills. What is particularly interesting about our results is that both ELL and non-ELL children in full-day programs benefited more significantly in regard to literacy skills than their peers in half-day settings, and ELL children in full-day settings experienced significantly larger gains in oral language development than all other children. These findings are important because of research demonstrating the way that full-day programs are being used in many schools as a compensatory program aimed at increasing minority children's academic achievement, particularly those with diverse language backgrounds. The positive literacy gains experienced by students suggest that teachers in the full-day program are finding success in teaching reading skills to all children regardless of their language background.

Despite literacy and language gains, there was no difference between children in full- and half-day settings on math achievement. In fact, children's scores, regardless of program, on the math measure employed for this study, evidenced little growth. One reason for this finding may be explained through teachers' statements regarding the limited focus in their curriculum on math skills. For example, teachers in full-day settings acknowledged that did not feel as successful in math instruction and primarily focused on math concepts in the afternoon when children were more tired. In contrast, half-day teachers did not make any comments regarding their teaching of, or their children's development of, math knowledge. Our findings suggest that teachers were not attuned or focused in their teaching toward helping their children acquire math skills. Although previous research has documented positive effects for full-day kindergarten programs on children's development of math knowledge (Cryan et al., 1992; Yan & Lin, 2005), our findings suggest that children in full-day programs did not outgain their half-day peers. This is most likely an indication of the instructional focus of schools or teachers on the need to guarantee that all children begin first-grade reading "at grade level." Such a conjecture is supported by teachers' comments about the need to focus on literacy skills as well as a general consensus in the field of education about the extreme importance of helping children develop the necessary reading and writing foundation before first grade (Alexander & Entwisle, 1988; Snow et al., 1998). One concern raised by this finding is that in order to meet accountability pressures, teachers may be ignoring large portions of the curriculum that are important to promoting the development of the whole child (Bowman et al., 2001).

Second, our data contribute to the larger literature on the effects of full-day kindergarten programs on children's academic achievement by focusing on the impact that children's attendance patterns have on achievement. Surprisingly, we found few relationships between children's attendance patterns in kindergarten and their achievement, with one exception. Students who missed fewer than 10 days of school in full-day programs performed significantly better on oral language development than children in full-day programs who missed more than 10 days. It appears that children who had more absences from full-day kindergarten also missed out on important language experiences. Our finding appears to complement research examining the impact of early childhood environments on ELL children's language development (Swanson, Saez, & Gerber, 2006) and to speak to the importance of kindergarten classrooms as a place where young children have significant opportunities to hear and participate with peers and teachers in language experiences (Bowman et al., 2001; Lesaux, Rupp, & Siegel, 2007). What is odd about our finding is that we did not find that attendance patterns impacted literacy or math gains. Given the policy implications that are associated with attendance in

kindergarten programs, additional research should continue to examine this association and explore the impact of attendance on outcomes.

One criticism of previous kindergarten research is that few studies have considered the differences between full- and half-day programs in terms of instructional quality. Given previous research documenting the impact of early childhood experiences on children's growth and development (Bowman et al., 2001; Burchinal & Cryer, 2003; Burchinal, Peisner-Feinberg, Pianta, & Howes, 2002; Burchinal et al., 2000), examining the instructional quality of kindergarten environments appears tantamount in understanding whether the effects of full- and half-day programs are a result of a lengthening of the school day or a result of positive improvements to instruction. In this study, full-day and half-day settings did not differ on measures of instructional quality. This finding suggests that it was the length of time that children spent in full-day settings that positively contributed to their literacy development. Hence, for these full-day kindergarten teachers, the positive effects seen on children's early literacy skills appear to be a result of having more time to instruct children in early literacy skills, not a result of an overall improvement in the quality of instruction compared with half-day programs. Teacher interviews suggested that teachers in full-day programs felt that the extra time in kindergarten allowed them to delve deeper into the curriculum and help students attain important literacy skills. In contrast, the half-day teachers expressed concern that the overemphasis on academics took away from a more developmentally appropriate approach to instruction and was not congruent with their views of quality kindergarten instruction.

This finding may be viewed as being at odds with other studies that have examined instruction in full- and half-day settings. For example, Elicker and Mathur (1997) found that children in full-day kindergarten programs tend to spend more time in child-directed, individual work and free-play activities than children in half-day settings. Although documenting how children spend their time in full-and half-day settings is important, our measurement of instructional quality related less to time spent in activities and more to the teachers' management style, emotional climate, and instructional support. In other words, one reason we may have found no difference between half- and full-day settings relates to how it was measured. As the CLASS is an observational instrument that rates instruction, it may not be finely tuned enough to capture variation in instructional formats (i.e., time spent in different types of activities, such as child-directed vs. teacher-directed formats). It is possible that distinct differences existed between full- and half-day teachers but that we failed to capture those with the CLASS observation.

Although it is possible that the CLASS failed to document ways in which the full- and half-day classrooms differed as a result of the measure, an alternative explanation for finding no difference between full- and half-day programs may be a result of teachers simply using the full-day setting to participate in "more of the same" types of instruction. This explanation seems quite possible, particularly when one considers that teachers were implementing full-day kindergarten for the first time. Full-day kindergarten teachers' articulation regarding their curriculum focus appears to support this assertion. For example, teachers' comments suggested that they were grateful for the extra time that the lengthening of the school day gave them to teach literacy skills and gave them more time go in-depth and be more comprehensive with their curriculum. Despite such comments, teachers failed to articulate how the lengthening of the school day allowed them to dramatically change or improve the quality or nature of their instruction. For example, the full-day allowed teachers more time to help children build a strong literacy foundation, as evidenced by their comments about their literacy curriculum and children's literacy scores, but they did not seem to use the time to focus on other areas of development or learning. This assertion also appears to be supported by the evidence that children's math scores did not differ by program.

Finally, with regard to instructional quality, it should be noted that the quality of all of the kindergarten classrooms was certainly adequate by CLASS standards, but not necessarily high (Pianta & La Paro, 2003). Rather, our findings, which echo the results of recent national research studies (i.e., National Institute of Child Health and Human Development, 2002; Pianta et al., 2002) suggest that many early childhood classrooms are often high in emotional support but may lack intentionality of teaching. In other words, most early childhood classrooms provide happy, comfortable learning environments but lack instruction that is sufficiently systematic and/or explicit. Pianta and La Paro suggested that improving the quality of such "academically passive" classrooms should be the main priority of policymakers and other educational stakeholders (p. 28). We echo this suggestion by contending that examining the quality of early childhood classrooms (regardless of the length of day) is a much-needed educational priority, particularly in light of the fact that such programs are often targeted toward linguistically diverse children, and, to date, our understanding of how these children fare in such settings is still limited (Tabors & Snow, 2001). In fact, examinations of teacher interviews revealed that, beyond giving them more time to focus on literacy

skills, teachers had very little to say about how the length of the school day helped their instruction become more culturally or developmentally responsive to children's diverse needs.

Limitations

Although the demographics demonstrated a diverse sample, the sample size of this study was small, which limited the researchers in evaluating interactions and effect sizes. In connection with the sample size, there was also a sizable attrition rate among students, especially in the half-day program. These limitations affect the generalizability of the findings. Additionally, teachers in full-day programs were in their first year of implementation, which may have influenced their instruction and overall feelings about their full-day kindergarten programs. However, this may also add to the value of the study, as policymakers need to carefully consider the support teachers and administrators will need as they begin full-day kindergarten programs to ensure immediate success, particularly as it pertains to instructional quality and ELL students' academic achievement.

Policy and Practice

The prevalence of full-day kindergarten programs has greatly increased during the past 20 years, with new programs being increasingly targeted toward minority children who live in poverty and who are diverse language learners (Lee et al., 2006; Vecchiotti, 2003). In the current study, teachers and administrators viewed the full-day kindergarten program as a way to level the playing field for second language learners by providing them with the language and literacy experiences to help lessen the performance gap between ELL and non-ELL children. Although calls to view kindergarten as an important public policy opportunity are not new (Vecchiotti, 2003), the growing prevalence of kindergarten programs being used as early intervention environments, in part to meet the accountability pressures of the No Child Left Behind legislation, is unexplored. Furthermore, additional research related to the relationship between instructional quality and children's academic achievement, regardless of language status, is needed to make informed policy and practice recommendations.

Ultimately, we must improve the quality of kindergarten programs for all children while remaining aware of the critical need to address the quality and appropriateness of programs that are being provided as early intervention services for ELL students. Given that teachers in this study who implemented full-day kindergarten did not talk about how they were making their instruction culturally responsive to diverse learners, beyond discussions of how it allows children extra time to experience English and strengthen their literacy skills, the need for additional professional development opportunities for teachers in these programs appears great. Because kindergarten is not currently mandated in the majority of U.S. states (Vecchiotti, 2003), there is more variability in children's attendance patterns for kindergarten than for upper elementary grades. This not only has funding implications, but also, as the findings from this study suggest, may impact children's academic achievement—particularly in relation to language development. We do, however, make this recommendation cautiously, as we cannot have our whole focus in kindergarten on children's academic development. Rather, as others in the field suggest (National Association for the Education of Young Children, 2005a, 2005b, 2006), we advocate for kindergarten programs that espouse curriculum that meets the cultural and developmental needs of all children in U.S. schools by promoting the development of the whole child—particularly the social and emotional development. Because previous research documents the importance of these skills to children's later development (see Raver, 2002, for a review), we must continue to work to create kindergarten programs (both full- and half-day) that meet the needs of all children and that are not focused solely on academics. In sum, this requires adequate funding, well-prepared teachers, culturally sensitive pedagogy, and additional time with children.

Future Research

Although the findings from this study are encouraging, the limitations mentioned above raise questions regarding the effectiveness of full-day kindergarten on children's developmental outcomes, particularly those of children with second language backgrounds. In addition, more research is needed to determine the long-term effects of full-day kindergarten on children's academic achievement. This requires longitudinal studies that track children's progress as they move into the primary grades. This research should pay particular attention to the contribution that such programs have on linguistically and economically diverse children's development after the termination of such programs. In addition, more research is needed to examine how teachers in full-day classrooms are spending instructional time and how they may or may not be adapting pedagogy to meet the needs of diverse learners. To date, very few studies have examined how teachers plan and implement curriculum in full-day kindergarten settings and how their choices impact children's academic and social development, particularly for children who are learning a second language. Finally, given the concerns of the teachers in this sample regarding the academic demands of full-

day settings on young learners, additional research is needed to compare full-day programs with one another to determine which components of a full-day program lead to positive outcomes in children's development of social skills and academics. Such studies would allow educators and policymakers to better understand the components that are most important to children's overall growth and help them make appropriate decisions about developing and funding high-quality kindergarten programs.

REFERENCES

Alexander, K. L., & Entwisle, D. R. (1988). Achievement in the first two years of school: Patterns and processes. *Monographs for the Society for Research in Child Development, 53*(Serial No. 218).

Baskett, R., Bryant, K., White, W., & Rhoads, K. (2005). Half-day to full-day kindergarten: An analysis of education change scores and demonstration of an educational research collaboration. *Early Child Development and Care, 175*, 419–430.

Bogdan, R. C., & Biklen, S. K. (1998). *Qualitative research in education: An introduction to theory and methods* (3rd ed.). Boston: Allyn & Bacon.

Bowman, B., Donovan, M. S., & Burns, M. S. (Eds.). (2001). *Eager to learn: Educating our preschoolers.* Washington, DC: National Academy Press.

Burchinal, M. R., & Cryer, D. (2003). Diversity, child care quality, and developmental outcomes. *Early Childhood Research Quarterly, 18*, 401–426.

Burchinal, M. R., Peisner-Feinberg, E., Pianta, R., & Howes, D. (2002). Development of academic skills from preschool through second grade: Family and classroom predictors of development. *Journal of School Psychology, 40*, 415–436.

Burchinal, M. R., Roberts, J. E., Riggins, R., Jr., Zeisel, S. A., Neebe, E., & Bryant, D. (2000). Relating quality of center-based child care to early cognitive and language development longitudinally. *Child Development, 71*, 339–357.

Creswell, J. W. (2003). *Research design: Qualitative, quantitative, and mixed method approaches* (2nd ed.). Thousand Oaks, CA: Sage.

Cryan, J. R., Sheehan, R., Wiechel, J., & Bandy-Hedden, I. G. (1992). Success outcomes of full-day kindergarten: More positive behavior and increased achievement in the years after. *Early Childhood Research Quarterly, 7*, 187–203.

Dunn, L. M., & Dunn, L. M. (1997). *Peabody Picture Vocabulary Test—III.* Circle Pines, MN: American Guidance Service.

Early, D. M., & Winton, P. J. (2001). Preparing the workforce: Early childhood teacher preparation at 2-and 4-year institutions of higher education. *Early Childhood Research Quarterly, 16*, 285–306.

Elicker, J., & Mathur, S. (1997). What do they do all day? Comprehensive evaluation of a full day kindergarten. *Early Childhood Research Quarterly, 12*, 459–480.

Fromberg, D. (1986). *The full-day kindergarten.* New York: Teachers College Press.

Gullo, D. F. (2000). The long term educational effects of half-day vs. full-day kindergarten. *Early Child Development and Care, 160*, 17–24.

Herman, B. (1984). *The case for the all-day kindergarten.* Bloomington, IN: Phi Delta Kappa.

Invernizzi, M., Sullivan, A., & Meier, J. (2001). *PALS-K phonological awareness literacy screening.* Charlottesville: University of Virginia.

Kauerz, K. (2005). *Full-day kindergarten: A study of state policies in the United States.* Denver, CO: Education Commission of the States.

La Paro, K. M., Pianta, R. C., & Stuhlman, M. (2004). The Classroom Assessment Scoring System: Findings from the pre-kindergarten year. *Elementary School Journal, 104*, 409–426.

Lee, V. E., Burkam, D. T., Ready, D. D., Honigman, J., & Meisels, S. J. (2006). Full-day versus half-day kindergarten: In which program do children learn more? *American Journal of Education, 112*, 163–208.

Lesaux, N. K., Rupp, A. A., & Siegel, L. S. (2007). Growth in reading skills of children from diverse linguistic backgrounds: Findings from a 5-year longitudinal study. *Journal of Educational Psychology, 99*, 821–834.

Meyer, L. A., Wardrop, J. L., Hastings, C. N., & Linn, R. L. (1993). Effects of ability and settings on kindergarteners' reading performance. *Journal of Educational Research, 86*, 142–160.

Naron, N. K. (1981). The need for full-day kindergarten. *Educational Leadership, 38*, 306–309.

National Association for the Education of Young Children. (2005a). *NAEYC early childhood program standards and accreditation criteria: The mark of quality in early childhood education.* Washington, DC: Author.

National Association for the Education of Young Children. (2005b). *Teachers: A guide to the NAEYC early childhood program standards and related accreditation criteria.* Washington, DC: Author.

National Association for the Education of Young Children. (2006). *Educational qualifications of program administrators and teaching staff: Building better futures for children and the profession.* Retrieved November 20, 2007, from www.journal.naeyc.org/btj/200703/btjprofdev.asp

National Center for Education Statistics. (2000). *Early Childhood Longitudinal Study: ECLS-K base year data files and electronic codebook.* Washington, DC: U.S. Department of Education.

National Center for Education Statistics. (2004). *Full-day and half-day kindergarten in the United States: Findings from the Early Childhood Longitudinal Study Kindergarten class of 1998–99* (NCES Report No. 2004–078). Washington, DC: U.S. Department of Education.

National Institute of Child Health and Human Development, Early Child Care Research Network. (2002). The relation of global first-grade classroom environment to structural classroom features and teacher and student behaviors. *Elementary School Journal, 102*, 367–387.

Pianta, R. C. (2003). *Experiences in P–3 classrooms: The implications of observational research for redesigning early childhood education.* New York: Foundation for Child Development.

Pianta, R. C., & La Paro, K. M. (2003). Improving early school success. *Educational Leadership, 60*(7), 24–29.

Pianta, R. C., La Paro, K. M., Payne, C., Cox, M. J., & Bradley, R. (2002). The relation of kindergarten classroom environment to teacher, family and school characteristics and child outcomes. *Elementary School Journal, 102*, 225–238.

Puleo, V. T. (1988). A review and critique of research on full-day kindergarten. *Elementary School Journal, 88*, 427–439.

Rachor, R. E., & Cizek, G. J. (1996, April). *Reliability of raw gain, residual gain, and estimated true gain scores: A simulation study.* Paper presented at the annual meeting of the American Educational Research Association, New York, NY.

Raver, C. C. (2002). Emotions matter: Making the case for the role of young children's emotional development for early school readiness. *Social Policy Report: Giving Child and Youth Development Away, 16*(3), 1–20.

Rimm-Kaufman, S. E., La Paro, K. M., Downer, J. T., & Pianta, R. C. (2005). The contributions of classroom setting and quality of instruction to children's behavior in kindergarten classrooms. *Elementary School Journal, 105*, 377–394.

Roswell, F., & Chall, J. (1997). *Roswell–Chall Auditory Blending Test.* New York: Essay Press.

Snow, C. E., Burns, M. S., & Griffin, P. (1998). *Preventing reading difficulties in young children.* New York: National Academy Press.

Swanson, H. L., Saez, L., & Gerber, M. (2006). Growth in literacy and cognition in bilingual children at risk or not at risk for reading disabilities. *Journal of Educational Psychology, 98*, 247–264.

Tabors, P., & Snow, C. (2001). Young bilingual children and early literacy development. In

S. Neuman & D. Dickinson (Eds.), *Handbook of early literacy research* (pp. 159–179). New York: Guilford Press.

Utah Legislature. (2007). *Extended day kindergarten legislation.* Retrieved September 2007 from le.utah. gov/~2007/htmdoc/sbillhtm/SB0049.htm

Vecchiotti, S. (2003). Kindergarten: An overlooked educational policy priority. *Social Policy Report: Giving Child and Youth Development Away, 17*(2), 1–20.

Woodcock, R. M., McGrew, K. S., & Mather, N. (2001). *Woodcock Johnson III: Tests of achievement.* New York: Riverside.

Yan, W., & Lin, Q. (2005). Effect of class size and length of day on kindergarteners' academic achievement: Findings from Early Childhood Longitudinal Survey. *Early Education and Development, 16,* 49–67

4.02

DATA TRANSFORMATION DESIGN

An Empirically Derived Taxonomy of Factors Affecting Physicians' Willingness to Disclose Medical Errors

Lauris C. Kaldjian, MD, PhD,[*, †] Elizabeth W. Jones, MHSA,[*, ‡] Gary E. Rosenthal, MD,[*,‡] Toni Tripp-Reimer, PhD, RN,[‡,§] and Stephen L. Hillis, PhD[*,‡]

BACKGROUND: Physician disclosure of medical errors to institutions, patients, and colleagues is important for patient safety, patient care, and professional education. However, the variables that may facilitate or impede disclosure are diverse and lack conceptual organization.

OBJECTIVE: To develop an empirically derived, comprehensive taxonomy of factors that affects voluntary disclosure of errors by physicians.

DESIGN: A mixed-methods study using qualitative data collection (structured literature search and exploratory focus groups), quantitative data transformation (sorting and hierarchical cluster analysis), and validation procedures (confirmatory focus groups and expert review).

RESULTS: Full-text review of 316 articles identified 91 impeding or facilitating factors affecting physicians' willingness to disclose errors. Exploratory focus groups identified an additional 27 factors. Sorting and hierarchical cluster analysis organized factors into 8 domains. Confirmatory focus groups and expert review relocated 6 factors, removed 2 factors, and modified 4 domain names. The final taxonomy contained 4 domains of facilitating factors (responsibility to patient, responsibility to self, responsibility to profession, responsibility to community), and 4 domains of impeding factors (attitudinal barriers, uncertainties, helplessness, fears and anxieties).

* Division of General Internal Medicine, Department of Internal Medicine, University of Iowa Carver College of Medicine, Iowa City, IA, USA;† Program in Biomedical Ethics and Medical Humanities, University of Iowa Carver College of Medicine, Iowa City, IA, USA;‡ Center for Research in the Implementation of Innovative Strategies in Practice, Iowa City VA Medical Center, Iowa City, IA, USA;§ University of Iowa College of Nursing, Iowa City, IA, USA.

Dr. Kaldjian is supported by funding from the Robert Wood Johnson Foundation's Generalist Physician Faculty Scholars Program (grant # 45446). We are grateful to Dr. Paul Haidet for his review of an earlier version of this manuscript, to 2 expert ethicists, and to the many focus group participants. The views expressed in this article are those of the authors and do not necessarily represent the views of the Department of Veterans Affairs.

None of the authors have any conflicts of interest to declare. Some of the data from this study were presented at the Society of General Internal Medicine's 27th Annual Meeting, Chicago, May 15, 2004 and have been published as an abstract (J Gen Intern Med. 2004;19(S1):177).

CONCLUSIONS: A taxonomy of facilitating and impeding factors provides a conceptual framework for a complex field of variables that affects physicians' willingness to disclose errors to institutions, patients, and colleagues. This taxonomy can be used to guide the design of studies to measure the impact of different factors on disclosure, to assist in the design of error-reporting systems, and to inform educational interventions to promote the disclosure of errors to patients.

KEYWORDS: Medical errors; error reporting; patient safety; disclosure; medical ethics.

The disclosure of medical errors is a vital part of ongoing efforts to improve patient safety and the quality of care.[1–10] Disclosure of medical error through direct communication with patients and their families is also an integral part of patient care,[11–14] and candor about errors between colleagues is essential to professional learning.[15–18] However, there are diverse and potent factors that impede a physician's willingness to disclose errors to institutions, patients, and colleagues.[5, 6, 12, 16, 19–25] Recommendations to address these impediments by changing professional culture[7,8,25–29] are accompanied by sobering descriptions of the tension between the transparency promoted by the patient safety movement and the silence induced by the malpractice system.[30,31] The number and variety of variables affecting a decision to disclose an error pose serious challenges for those trying to design systems and promote practices that increase disclosure. Because of this complexity, there is a need to define and organize the various influences on error disclosure, both to enhance multifaceted, disclosure-promoting interventions and to aid evaluation and interpretation of the results of such interventions. To address this need, we used qualitative and quantitative methodologies to develop an empirically based, comprehensive taxonomy of factors that may impede or facilitate the voluntary disclosure of errors by physicians.

METHODS

We used a sequence of methodologies to collect qualitative data (structured literature search and exploratory focus groups), perform quantitative data transformation (sorting and hierarchical cluster analysis), and validate our results (confirmatory focus groups and expert review) (Figure. 1). We considered "disclosure" to include admitting errors to patients, discussing them with colleagues, and reporting them to health care institutions. We used the term "factor" to denote a variety of variables (attitudes, emotions, desires, beliefs, circumstances) that may impede or facilitate disclosure. This project was approved by the University of Iowa Institutional Review Board.

Literature Review

We performed a MEDLINE search of English-language articles published between January 1975

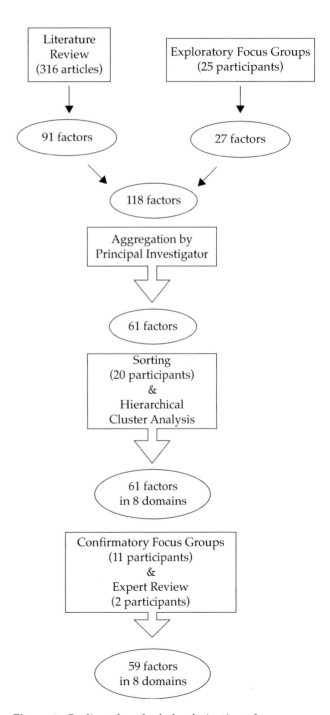

Figure 1. Outline of methods for derivation of taxonomy.

and March 2003. The Medical Subject Heading terms and key words that we used are reported elsewhere.[32] To be included in the review, articles had to (1) have an identifiable first author, (2) address the clinical experience of physicians, and (3) discuss error disclosure or reporting. We selected articles with identifiable first authors in order to be able to abstract data by unique first authors as well as by article, a design that allowed us to quantify results of the literature review by calculating the citation frequency of individual factors that facilitate or impede disclosure.[32] We selected articles that addressed the experience of physicians because of their unique professional, legal, and institutional status. All types of articles (empirical studies, reviews, editorial/commentaries, letters, personal narratives, interviews) were reviewed so long as they met the inclusion criteria.

Two investigators (E.W.J. and L.C.K.) screened 4,382 articles by titles. One investigator (E.W.J.) reviewed the entire content of 606 articles and identified 316 articles that satisfied the inclusion criteria; the second investigator (L.C.K.) was consulted whenever there was uncertainty about an article's satisfaction of the inclusion criteria. Bibliographies of included articles were screened for additional articles.

After analyzing 10 articles for factors related to disclosure, 2 investigators created a provisional list of factors that facilitate or impede disclosure to form a data-abstraction template; this template was then tested on another 10 articles and expanded. One investigator (E.W.J.) reviewed the remainder of the articles and consulted with the second investigator (L.C.K.) when uncertain about factor categorization or when a new factor was identified for inclusion in the data-abstraction template. Labels for facilitating and impeding factors were derived through an iterative process. Factors were first named using the language of the articles in which they were found. As more articles were reviewed, labels were modified to reflect similar concepts phrased variously by different authors. This iterative process of naming served to synthesize the linguistic heterogeneity of the literature reviewed.

The second investigator (L.C.K.) reviewed 64 randomly selected articles (20% of sample) to assess the interrater reliability of facilitating and impeding factors. To assess intrarater reliability of the sample, the first investigator (E.W.J.) repeated the data abstraction from these 64 articles after a hiatus of 11 weeks.

Exploratory Focus Groups

We conducted 5 focus groups, segregated by training level, to discuss factors related to physician self-disclosure of medical errors to institutions, patients, and colleagues. We identified convenience samples of fourth-year medical students, resident physicians (internal medicine, family medicine, pediatrics), community attending physicians (general internal medicine), and university attending physicians (general internal medicine, family medicine, general pediatrics) (Table 1). Two of the investigators attended each focus group, 1 serving as moderator (L.C.K.) and 1 as assistant (E.W.J.). The moderator adhered to a formal question route (Appendix A) based on the literature review. A physician-investigator served as moderator to enhance the perceived credibility of the focus groups among participants who are professionals. We recognized that a moderator's identity can influence participant discussion, but based on focus group literature[33,34] we concluded that the benefits of professional credibility outweighed the risks of undue influence. Sessions lasted 90 minutes and were audio-taped; audiotapes were transcribed verbatim.

We designed an anonymous exit questionnaire to assess participant perceptions about the influence of peers and the moderator. All participants either *disagreed or strongly disagreed* with the following 2 statements: (1) "The presence of my peers made it hard for me to say what I really thought"; or (2) "The presence of the moderator made it hard for me to say what I really thought." All participants either *agreed or strongly agreed* with the following 3 statements: (1) "The moderator made me feel comfortable enough to speak my mind during the discussion," (2) "The duration of the

Table 1. Participant Demographics for Exploratory Focus Groups

	n	Age (Mean)	Years Since Medical School Graduation (Mean)	Female (%)	Ever Reported an Error to an Institution (%)	Ever Disclosed a Mistake to a Patient (%)
Fourth-year medical students	7	26	−1	71	0	29
First-year residents	6	31	1	33	33	100
Third-year residents	3	28	5	67	67	67
Attending physicians (community)	3	44	19	0	33	100
Attending physicians (university)	6	42	17	33	33	100

focus group provided me enough time to say what I wanted to say," and (3) "Overall, I was able to say what I really thought about the issues we discussed."

Transcripts were coded for content independently by 2 investigators (E.W.J. and L.C.K.) using the list of factors generated from the literature review and analyzed for new factors or new wording of previously identified factors. Discrepancies were resolved by consensus between the 2 investigators.

Combination and Aggregation of Factors

The factors identified from the focus groups were combined with the factors from the literature review. To increase the feasibility of the next step (pile sorting), 1 investigator (L.C.K.) reviewed all the factors and aggregated into mini-groups those factors that appeared directly related. The factors and factor mini-groups were printed on index cards for the sorting task; cards containing factor mini-groups listed each factor within the mini-group.

Pile Sorting and Hierarchical Cluster Analysis

The pile-sorting task[35] involved 9 attending physicians (general internal medicine and family medicine, 7 men and 2 women), 5 resident physicians (internal medicine and family medicine, 2 men and 3 women), and 6 fourth-year medical students (3 men and 3 women), who had not participated in the exploratory focus groups. Participants were given index cards with 1 factor or factor mini-group on each card (ordered alphabetically) and instructed to sort the index cards into 5 to 10 groups by placing together cards that were most related. Participants sorted the cards at their convenience.

The pile-sorting results were entered into a database for hierarchical cluster analysis[36] using the CLUSTER procedure in SAS to construct clustering schemes derived from the number of participants who placed a given pair of factors together in a group. This organized the factors according to participants' assessment of the conceptual proximity of each pair of factors. For each pair of factors, we computed a "distance" score, defined as 20 (the total number of participants) minus the number of participants who placed the 2 factors in the same group. Thus, the distance score for a pair of factors was an integer between 0 and 20, with 20 indicating no relatedness and 0 indicating maximum relatedness.

Four types of hierarchical cluster analysis were performed: single linkage, complete linkage, average linkage, and Ward's minimum variance method. Ward's method performed the best because it resulted in unique solutions and higher R^2 values and lower semipartial R^2 values for a given cluster size.[37]

Validation: Confirmatory Focus Groups and Expert Review

Eleven of the sorting task participants (3 students, 2 resident physicians, 6 attending physicians) accepted invitations to participate in 1 of 3 focus groups to validate the initial cluster scheme. Focus groups were segregated by training level and moderated by the principal investigator (L.C.K.). Each cluster was individually projected onto a screen. Participants identified items that did not appear to belong in a given cluster. Consensus was required to dismiss or relocate an item to another cluster. Participants were also asked to suggest words that best summarized the factors in each cluster. At the final session involving attending physicians, participants affirmed or rebutted (by consensus) changes that were suggested by the other 2 confirmatory focus groups. Final cluster titles were suggested by the moderator and modified by consensus.

The resulting taxonomy was independently reviewed by 2 expert ethicists, each a full professor with a PhD in ethics. Our choice of experts in ethics who had no particular background in patient safety or error disclosure allowed us to engage conceptual expertise that was unlikely to be accompanied by formal preconceptions about errors or disclosure.

Final Labeling of Factors

To enhance the taxonomy's comprehensibility, we made 3 final adjustments. To express the meaning of factor labels more fully, we added words to factor labels to flesh out the original meaning of a given factor (e.g., "integrity" was changed to "desire to maintain one's integrity"). We reviewed the content of the factor mini-groups (see Appendix B) and, where appropriate, used words from other factors within a given mini-group to modify or expand the final label for that mini-group. In order to condense factors within a domain, we combined some related factors using the conjunction "or."

RESULTS

Literature Review

Three hundred and sixteen articles, representing 254 unique first authors, were included (109 reviews, 74 editorials/commentaries, 69 empirical studies, 42 letters, 18 personal narratives, 4 interviews). Content analysis of the articles identified 91 factors (53 impeding and 38 facilitating), as shown in Appendix B. Reliability testing showed that the majority of the most commonly cited factors were reproducibly identifiable within and between investigators (K statistics for the 10 most commonly cited facilitating and impeding factors ranged between 0.47 and 0.96).

The literature review identified 91 factors (53 impeding and 38 facilitating), as shown in Appendix B. The 10 most frequently cited facilitating factors were as follows: accountability, honesty, restitution, trust, reduce malpractice risk, consolation, fiduciary relationship, truth-telling, avoid "cover up," and informed consent. The 10 most frequently cited impeding factors were as follows: professional repercussions, legal liability, blame, lack of confidentiality, negative patient/family reaction, humiliation, perfectionism, guilt, lack of anonymity, and absence of a supportive forum for disclosure. The 3 most common contexts for error disclosure were as follows: (1) reporting errors to institutions to improve patient safety; (2) discussion of errors among physicians to enhance learning; and (3) informing patients about errors as part of patient care. Statistical analyses (32) showed that the most commonly cited facilitating factors, except for accountability, were more frequently mentioned in articles focusing on disclosing errors to patients, as opposed to institutions or colleagues ($P < .001$). By contrast, impeding factors showed no consistent differences in the frequency of citation based on the context of disclosure.

Exploratory Focus Groups

Content analysis of focus group transcripts produced 27 new factors (see Appendix B) and resulted in the rewording of some previously identified factors based on focus group vernacular. These new factors tended to focus on the actual experience of disclosing an error—particularly to patients. Participants noted emotional responses to errors such as "that sinking feeling," the desire to explain the circumstances surrounding an error, and practical difficulties such as lack of time to explain errors to patients. Issues specific to the training environment were also prominent, such as lack of support from supervising physicians, competition with peers, and fear of looking foolish in front of junior colleagues.

Final Taxonomy, with Selected Annotations from Exploratory Focus Groups

The 27 factors identified from the focus groups were combined with the 91 factors from the literature review for a total of 118 facilitating and impeding factors. All the factors were reviewed by 1 of the investigators (L.C.K.) and those factors that appeared directly related were aggregated into mini-groups, as shown in Appendix B, reducing the number of factors and factor mini-groups to 61. In the pile-sorting task, participants placed the 61 factors and factor mini-groups into an average of 7 piles. In the hierarchical cluster analysis, plots of cluster statistics did not reveal a definitive jump in the values that would suggest an

obvious cluster solution. Using Ward's method, we reviewed printouts of 5 different clustering solutions (factors clustered into 5, 6, 7, 8, and 9 clusters) and determined that the 8-cluster solution ($R^2 = .586$) was the most satisfactory in terms of clinical interpretation; this solution established the number of domains for the taxonomy as well as the initial contents of the 8 domains. As a result of the confirmatory focus groups, 4 items were relocated, 1 item was deemed redundant and dismissed, and 1 item ("restitution") could not be categorized due to competing interpretations that resisted consensus. Two expert ethicists found the taxonomy to be comprehensive and recommended changes to the first 4 domain names to increase descriptive clarity and movement of 2 items from 1 domain to another. The final taxonomy comprised of 4 domains of facilitating factors (Figure. 2) and 4 domains of impeding factors (Figure. 3).

Responsibility to patient focuses on the physician's fundamental respect for the patient as a person, through open communication and ongoing care. The core of this domain was suggested by a student who said "It boils down to just how you view other people. Do you view them as worthy of knowing?" An intern spoke similarly "That's really the focus of what we're doing here: patient care . . . it comes down to what's happened with this particular patient."

Responsibility to Patient	Responsibility to Profession
Desire to communicate honestly with patients or explain the circumstances of an error	Desire to share lessons learned from errors
Desire to show respect for patients or treat patients fairly	Desire to serve as a role model in disclosing errors or breaking bad news
Desire to facilitate further medical care for harmed patients	Desire to strengthen inter-professional relationships and build inter-professional trust
	Desire to change professional culture by accepting medicine's imperfections and lessen the focus on managing malpractice risks
Responsibility to Self	**Responsibility to Community**
Desire to be accountable for one's actions	Desire to enhance the health of future patients
Sense of duty as a physician	Desire to sustain patients trust in the medical profession
Desire to be courageous or altruistic	Desire to foster physician-patient relationships that can absorb the shock of error
Desire to maintain one's integrity	
Desire to treat others as one would like to be treated	Desire to help patients be more realistic about medicine's imperfections
Desire to empathize and apologize	Desire to help patients understand the complex causes of errors
Desire to alleviate guilt or pursue forgiveness	
Willingness to accept one's fallibility and limitations, and to be vulnerable	
Desire to follow one's conscience or 'do the right thing'	
Desire to follow one's religious/spiritual beliefs	

Figure 2. Factors that facilitate physician disclosure of medical errors.

Attitudinal Barriers	Helplessness
Perpetuating perfectionism, and blaming and humiliating those involved with errors	Lacking control of what happens to information once it is disclosed
Perpetuating silence about errors, denying errors, or believing others don't need to know about one's errors	Lacking confidentiality or immunity after disclosure
Being arrogant and proud	Lacking institutional and collegial support after disclosure or a professional forum for discussion
Placing self-interests before patient-interests	Believing error reporting systems penalize those who are honest
Allowing competition with peers to inhibit disclosure	Lacking feedback after reporting errors or a sense of ownership in the quality improvement process
Believing disclosure is an optional act of heroism	Lacking time to disclose errors
Doubting the benefits of disclosure	Feeling helpless about errors because one cannot control enough of the system of care

Uncertainties	Fears and Anxieties
Being uncertain about how to disclose	Fearing legal or financial liability
Being uncertain about which errors should be disclosed	Fearing professional discipline, loss of reputation, loss of position, or loss of advancement
Being uncertain about the cause of an adverse event	Fearing patient's or family's anger, anxiety, loss of confidence, or termination of physician-patient relationship
Disagreeing with a supervisor or trainee about whether an error occurred	Fearing the need to admit actual negligence
	Fearing the need to disclose an error that cannot be corrected
	Fearing the possibility of looking foolish in front of junior colleagues or trainees
	Fearing negative publicity
	Fearing the possibility of 'fallout' on colleagues
	Feeling a sense of personal failure, loss of self-esteem, or threat to one's's identity as a healer

Figure 3. Factors that impede physician disclosure of medical errors.

Responsibility to self focuses on personal and professional values that derive from the physician's character, commitments, and desire for integrity. An intern stressed the importance of "being accountable for our errors and not being a weasel or arrogant or denying that we ever make errors." A faculty physician acknowledged the need for courage "If you don't have the guts to say, "I screwed up" to a patient, you're in the wrong business." A resident commented that "in order to receive forgiveness you have to admit to your wrong," and another expressed the need to "make amends" with a harmed patient in order to move forward. Participants saw the need to accept fallibility and to be willing to be vulnerable. Such willingness, a student observed, will drive "a lot of your desire to report to anybody because you are going to be vulnerable when you say "I made a mistake." Some participants articulated spiritual or religious motivations, such as the student who said: "I should be motivated by love and also I'm ultimately responsible to God for my actions . . . whether I'm deceptive with patients or whether I tell them the truth about what's going on."

Responsibility to profession focuses on the physician's desire to improve the medical profession

through sharing lessons learned, modeling disclosure skills, fostering a culture of disclosure, and providing support to colleagues who are involved with errors. A faculty physician described the need for role modeling in discussing and disclosing errors "If I as a faculty member can't express my own fallibility . . . how can the learner learn?" A resident said "When people have come out and told the patient, have taken responsibility—it's usually based on just a need to do the right thing and the need to be a good role model for those who are training under you." A student spoke of the need for support "There's a catharsis in being able to say to your colleagues, 'This is what happened' and then to be able to hear, 'I made that same mistake, I've been there, I know how you feel, this is what I did to correct it.'"

Responsibility to community focuses on the physician's desire to improve the quality of care for all patients, to enhance society's trust in physicians and the medical profession, and to educate the community about medicine's complexities and imperfections. One student's remark about reporting errors to improve systems of care was representative "Your one case may not seem to make a difference, but if there are trends at a certain hospital or in a certain area of the country, this is how we get demographic information, this is how we improve our care . . . and there are public health implications of reporting, if you feel there's a duty to improve for the greater good."

Attitudinal barriers focus on a range of attitudes that may hamper disclosure. Perfectionism was a persistent theme in the focus groups. An intern explained "Even though I know it's not logical for me to think that doctors aren't going to make errors, I hold doctors to that standard, that we're going to be perfect and we're not going to make errors." Participants also drew a connection between silence about errors and the competitive nature of medical training.

A student observed:

[As a student] you're competing within your class, competing with yourself, and trying to reach the academic goals that you want. As a resident you're competing to attain that certain fellowship position. You don't get points for making mistakes; in fact, you get points taken away. It's like the SATs. So admitting to mistakes doesn't exactly help your career. . . . It's the inherent competition within our career that kind of fuels a lot of people who want to put their mistakes under the carpet and just show off their achievements and try to put themselves in the best light possible.

Uncertainties focus on doubts about how to disclose errors, which ones to disclose, what constitutes an error, and disagreements between clinicians about whether an error occurred. A student expressed the struggle to discern the difference between a complication and an error:

There's a risk that you're going to cause a pneumothorax when you do a thoracentesis. . . . But if I am the one that causes that pneumothorax, is it because I was an idiot? Do I say, "You know, I collapsed your lung, I'm really sorry, I made a mistake" or do I just present it as, "It's one of the risks, you signed informed consent." I really struggle with how you even define some of the errors.

A faculty physician described the difficulty of determining whether an error is significant enough to disclose "At what level does the error become big enough that now something needs to be done about it?" A resident spoke of conflicting views between supervisors and trainees "Medicine is vague enough sometimes that even though I feel [an error occurred], there's no higher power for me to appeal to if the higher power within my group feels that the right thing was done."

Helplessness focuses on dissatisfactions with the process, context, follow-up, and outcome of error disclosure, as well as not having the power necessary to improve the system of care. A student complained of not knowing what will "happen with what you [report], the path [the information] is going to take, and who's going to be reading it," suggesting that reported errors may be "going down a black hole" and may result in "retributions that come back to you." An intern described discussion forums at a prior institution that were demoralizing:

Morbidity & mortality conferences were just brutal. We wouldn't go, we wanted nothing to do with them. The students would actually sometimes go to see the residents they didn't like just get toasted.

Participants were disappointed by lack of feedback after reporting errors. A resident complained "So far as I know, [the report] goes to some dead space out there and it's vaporized. . . ."

Fears and anxieties focus on a range of potential negative consequences of error disclosure. Participants spoke about profound personal struggles related to their identities as healers. An intern said "[Patients are] coming in here, they're sort of putting their life in my hands, and they're trusting me and I've violated this trust." Another intern remarked "Disclosing to the patient makes you admit to yourself that—what's that first tenet of our oath, "First do no harm?"—well, we did harm." A faculty physician opined "I'm delivering bad news to the patient about something, but I'm also delivering bad news about myself because I have been the cause of that bad news." A resident articulated the difficulty of apologizing for negligence:

Saying "I'm sorry" has got to be some of the toughest words in any language and we, as physicians, take a lot of pride in the fact that we're pretty smart and capable people. . . . To make a mistake that acknowl-

edges my own [fallibility] is in a way saying that I'm not as good as I could be. . . . If it is something like you forgot to deflate the catheter that ends in the patient dying, that's a pretty, pretty serious outcome. Like, if you're flying a jet and you drop the bomb on the wrong person. Those things live in your memory forever. . . .

A resident feared the loss of reputation: "There's the fear of other people saying, 'Boy, he dropped the ball, he screwed up, he's not really a good doctor, he really doesn't know what he's doing.' You don't want people pointing fingers at you. It's enough to be pointing fingers at yourself, but you don't want other people to say 'he doesn't belong among us.'"

DISCUSSION

This taxonomy defines and organizes the complex motivational context surrounding the decision to disclose a medical error, clarifying the host of factors—positive and negative, personal and environmental—that may influence this uniquely challenging process. The taxonomy's *impeding* factors describe variables that need to be addressed to enhance the likelihood that policies and procedures instituted to increase disclosure will succeed. The *facilitating* factors describe variables that may help promote error disclosure by encouraging clinicians to connect their personal and professional values with the goals of improving the quality of care, respecting patients through candid communication, and enhancing professional learning.

Amidst current discussions about ways to encourage or mandate error disclosure to institutions or patients, this taxonomy helps define the motivations and concerns that surround the discretionary role of the individual clinician. Although a systems emphasis is necessary to understand the causes of medical errors and the systems-related factors that inhibit their disclosure, the taxonomy reminds us how intrinsically challenging disclosure is for individuals. Policies to increase disclosure need to be informed by the concrete experience of clinicians and the systems within which they operate.

The 2 sides of this taxonomy stress the need to focus both on the factors that impede disclosure *and* on those that facilitate it. Facilitating factors represent substantial motivational resources that physicians can rely upon in the face of potent fears and anxieties. It is important to explore how these resources may counteract internal threats to a physician's identity as a healer and perceived external threats from aggrieved patients (39% of whom may support punishment for error-committing physicians[38]) or their attorneys (as candor with patients about errors may not result in fewer lawsuits.[30,31])

The development of our taxonomy had limitations. Regarding the literature review: initial screening of articles by titles may have excluded some relevant articles; only 1 investigator analyzed most of the selected articles for content; and although 69 articles were empirically based, the majority of articles represented authors' personal assessments rather than systematically collected data from physicians. Regarding the focus groups, physician participants were generalists; however, only 27 of the factors were identified through focus groups, compared with 91 factors identified from the structured literature review (which was not limited to generalist disciplines), suggesting that the content of our taxonomy should be generalizable. Using a physician-investigator as a moderator may have influenced the content of the discussions, and the risk of social desirability bias is always present. Lastly, our taxonomy was not designed to identify the relative importance of different facilitating or impeding factors, and for the sake of clarity and simplicity, we have listed the factors without explicating the potentially numerous and complex interactions among them.

Our taxonomy suggests several directions for educational and institutional change. First, educators and leaders should acknowledge and address the *diversity* of facilitating and impeding factors that affect disclosure. Second, the taxonomy should help clinicians view disclosure holistically, that is, as a unified process of information sharing oriented toward patient safety (disclosure to institutions), professional learning (disclosure to colleagues), and direct clinical care (disclosure to patients). Third, the individual's role in reporting and discussing errors should complement the systems orientation of the patient safety movement. Fourth, error disclosure should be included in the teaching of medical ethics and professionalism, as has already been recommended.[39] Fifth, innovations to enhance error disclosure should consistently address both sides of the equation: impeding factors should be removed and facilitating factors should be promoted.

Our work suggests a number of research questions for the future. Which facilitating and impeding factors have the greatest influence on disclosure? Does the influence of specific factors vary by level of training and speciality? Does the influence of specific factors vary according to the context of disclosure (to institutions, colleagues, or patients)? How does professional environment affect attitudes toward disclosure? Do current training practices support or discourage disclosure? Future research will need to ascertain whether educational and institutional interventions actually reduce the influence of impeding factors or enhance the influence of facilitating factors.

This taxonomy provides a comprehensive framework of the diverse factors that may affect a physician's willingness to disclose medical errors to institutions, patients, and colleagues. It advances our understanding of this complex subject by articulating and organizing the wide range of facilitating and impeding factors that are cited in the literature and described by physicians. Although hospitals and leaders increasingly endorse the importance of disclosing errors, there is evidence to suggest that such endorsements may not be reflected in practice.[40,41] To advance the transition from institutional ideals to individual practice, it is important to acknowledge and engage the factors that influence disclosure. To this end, our taxonomy should be useful to policy makers, health care administrators, and educational leaders who are endeavoring to increase disclosure through better error-reporting systems, more candid dialogue with affected patients, and enhanced professional forums to promote learning.

REFERENCES

1. Kohn LT, Corrigan JM, Donaldson MS. To Err is Human: Building a Safer Health System. Washington, DC: *National Academy Press*; 2000.
2. Weingart SN, Wilson RM, Bibberd RW, Harrison B. Epidemiology of medical error. *BMJ*. 2000;320:774–7.
3. Leape LL. Error in medicine. *JAMA*. 1994;272:1851–7.
4. Leape LL, Woods DD, Hatlie MJ, Kizer KW, Schroeder SA, Lundberg GD. Promoting patient safety by preventing medical error. *JAMA*. 1998;280:1444–7.
5. Reason J. Human error: models and management. *BMJ*. 2000;320: 768–70.
6. Altman DE, Clancy C, Blendon RJ. Improving patient safety—five years after the IOM report. *N Engl J Med*. 2004;351:2041–3.
7. Leape LL. Reporting of adverse events. *N Engl J Med*. 2002;347: 1633–8.
8. Flynn E, Jackson JA, Lindgren K, Moore C, Poniatowski L, Youngberg B. Shining the Light on Errors: How Open Should We Be? Oak Brook, IL: *University Health System Consortium*; 2002.
9. Weissman JS, Annas CL, Epstein AM, et al. Error reporting and disclosure systems: views from hospital leaders. *JAMA*. 2005;293:1359–66.
10. Aspden P, Corrigan JM, Wolcott J, Erickson SM. Patient Safety: Achieving a New Standard for Care. Washington, DC: *National Academy Press*; 2004:237.
11. Baylis F. Errors in medicine: nurturing truthfulness. *J Clin Ethics*. 1997;8:336–40.
12. Rosner F, Berger JT, Kark P, Potash J, Bennett AJ. Disclosure and prevention of medical errors. *Arch Intern Med*. 2000;160:2089–92.

13. Council on ethical and judicial affairs. Code of Medical Ethics. Chicago, IL: *American Medical Association*; 1998–1999:141–2.

14. Gallagher TH, Waterman AD, Ebers AG, Faser VJ, Levinson W. Patients' and physicians' attitudes regarding the disclosure of medical errors. *JAMA*. 2003;289:1001–7.

15. McIntyre N, Popper K. The critical attitude in medicine: the need for a new ethics. *BMJ*. 1983;287:1919–23.

16. Wu AW, Folkman S, McPhee SJ, Lo B. Do house officers learn from their mistakes? *JAMA*. 1991;265:2089–94.

17. Orlander JD, Barber TW, Fincke BG. The morbidity and mortality conference: the delicate nature of learning from error. *Acad Med*. 2002;77:1001–6.

18. Pierluissi E, Fischer MA, Campbell AR, Landefeld CS. Discussion of medical errors in morbidity and mortality conferences. *JAMA*. 2003;290:2838–42.

19. Kaldjian LC. Disclosing our own medical errors: are three good reasons enough? *Johns Hopkins Adv Stud Med*. 2003;3:51–2.

20. Finkelstein D, Wu AW, Holtzman NA, Smith MK. When a physician harms a patient by medical error: ethical, legal, and risk-management considerations. *J Clin Ethics*. 1997;8:330–5.

21. Greely HT. Do physicians have a duty to disclose mistakes? *West J Med*. 1999;171:82–3.

22. Sexton JB, Thomas EJ, Helmreich RL. Error, stress, and teamwork in medicine and aviation: cross-sectional surveys. *BMJ*. 2000;320: 745–9.

23. Wu AW, Cavanaugh TA, McPhee SJ, Lo B, Micco GP. To tell the truth: ethical and practical issues in disclosing medical mistakes to patients. *J Gen Intern Med*. 1997;12:770–5.

24. Kapp MB. Legal anxieties and medical mistakes: barriers and pretexts. *J Gen Intern Med*. 1997;12:787–8.

25. Brennan TA. The Institute of medicine report on medical errors—could it do harm? *N Engl J Med*. 2000;342:1123–5.

26. Berwick DM. Not again! preventing errors lies in redesign—not exhortation. *BMJ*. 2001;322:247–8.

27. Studdert DM, Brennan TA. No-fault compensation for medical injuries: the prospect of error prevention. *JAMA*. 2001;286:217–23.

28. Cohen MR. Why error reporting systems should be voluntary. *BMJ*. 2000;320:728–9.

29. Schoenbaum SC, Bovbjerg RR. Malpractice reform must include steps to prevent medical injury. *Ann Intern Med*. 2004;140:51–3.

30. Studdert DM, Mello MM, Brennan TA. Medical malpractice. *N Engl J Med*. 2004;350:283–92.

31. Kachalia A, Shojania KG, Hofer TP, Piotrowski M, Saint S. Does full disclosure of medical errors affect malpractice liability? *Jt Comm J Qual Safety*. 2003;29:503–11.

32. Kaldjian LC, Jones EW, Rosenthal GE. Facilitating and impeding factors for physicians' error disclosure: a structured literature review. *Jt Comm J Qual Patient Safety*. 2006;32:188–98.

33. Krueger RA. Moderating Focus Groups (Focus Group Kit, Vol. 4). Thousand Oaks, CA: *Sage Publications*; 1998:37–40.

34. Krueger RA, Casey MA. Focus Groups. 3rd edn. Thousand Oaks, CA: *Sage Publications*; 2000:97–101.

35. Weller SC, Romney AK. Systematic Data Collection. Newbury Park, CA: *Sage Publications*: 1988:20–31.

36. Everitt B. Cluster Analysis. London: *Heinemann*; 1974.

37. Sharma S. Applied Multivariate Techniques. New York: *Wiley*; 1996:185–236.

38. Mazor KM, Simon SR, Yood RA, et al. Health plan members' views about disclosure of medical errors. *Ann Intern Med*. 2004;140: 409–18.

39. Medical professionalism in the new millennium: a physician charter. *Ann Intern Med*. 2002;136:243–6.

40. Leape LL, Berwick DM. Five years after *To Err is Human*: what have we learned? *JAMA*. 2005;293:2384–90.

41. Gallagher TH, Lucas MH. Should we disclose harmful medical errors to patients? If so, how? *J Clin Outcomes Manage*. 2005;12:253–9.

4.03

VALIDATING QUANTITATIVE DATA DESIGN

Transition Services for Incarcerated Youth: A Mixed Methods Evaluation Study*

Laura S. Abrams[†], Sarah K.S. Shannon[‡], and Cindy Sangalang[§]

ABSTRACT: Despite a considerable overlap between child welfare and juvenile justice populations, the child welfare literature contains sparse information about transition and reentry programs for incarcerated youth. Using mixed methods, this paper explores the benefits and limitations of a six-week transitional living program for incarcerated youth offenders. Logistic regression analysis found that only age at arrest and number of prior offenses predicted the odds of recidivism at one-year post-release. Youth who participated in the transitional living program and dual status youth (those involved in both child welfare and juvenile justice systems) were slightly more likely to recidivate, but these differences were not statistically significant. Qualitative interviews with youth and staff revealed that both groups viewed the transitional living program as having many benefits, particularly independent living skills training. However, follow-up with youth in the community lacked sufficient intensity to handle the types of challenges that emerged. Implications for future research and transition programming with vulnerable youth are discussed.

KEYWORDS: Transition services; High risk youth; Juvenile justice; Mixed methods; Independent living skills.

INTRODUCTION

The past several years have witnessed increased interest in transition and reentry services for incarcerated youth (Mears & Travis, 2004). Nearly 100,000 juvenile offenders are released annually from out-of-home correctional or custodial facilities (Snyder, 2004); and according to meta-analyses, at least 45% of released youth offenders will be arrested for another crime in the weeks, months, or few years following their release (Lipsey, 1999; Wilson, Lipsey, & Soydan, 2003). High recidivism rates and other poor outcomes for formerly incarcerated youth prompt some scholars to question the value of intensive correctional rehabilitation programs without adequate transition or reentry services (Author, 2006; Steinberg, Chung, & Little, 2004).

*The authors wish to thank Bridget Freisthler, Duncan Lindsey, and the anonymous reviewers of Children and Youth Services Review for their assistance with this manuscript.

[†]*University of California, Los Angeles, United States.*
[‡]*University of Minnesota, Twin Cities, United States.*
[§]*University of California, Los Angeles, United States.*

The child welfare literature has not widely considered youth reentry services, yet there are several reasons to attend to this evolving field of study. First, although data are scarce, existing evidence shows significant overlap between the child welfare and juvenile justice populations. For example, Jonson-Reid and Barth (2000) found that 19% of youth incarcerated in California Youth Authority facilities had child abuse cases investigated after age six, which they consider a "conservative" estimate of the total number of dependent youth who are incarcerated as juveniles. Moreover, longitudinal studies demonstrate that both child maltreatment and child welfare system involvement are significant risk factors for future involvement in juvenile or adult penal systems (English, Widom, & Brandford, 2001; Widom 1989, 2003).

There are also many parallels between the issues of youth reentry and the transition to independence from foster care (Snyder, 2004). Research finds similar, distressing outcomes for youth who transition to adulthood from either the child welfare or juvenile justice systems. For example, Cook, Fleischman, and Grimes' (1991) study of youth aging out of foster care found that two to four years after discharge, only 54% completed high school or obtained a GED, 30% received some form of public assistance, and 25% spent at least one night homeless. Another longitudinal study of youth exiting foster care highlighted high rates of mental health services use and highly unstable employment patterns (Courtney, Piliavin, Grogan-Kaylor, & Nesmith, 2001). The youth reentry population faces very similar risks as former foster youth. Bullis and Yovanoff's (2002) longitudinal study of over 500 released juvenile offenders in Oregon found that at one-year post-release only 31% were engaged in either work *or* school. It is also estimated that one out of every five youth in the juvenile justice system has serious mental health problems (Cocozza & Skowyra, 2000).

Despite considerable overlap in child welfare and juvenile justice populations and documentation of similar transition challenges, there is little published research in the child welfare literature that investigates transition or reentry services for incarcerated youth. The purpose of this paper is to describe and evaluate a transitional living program designed to prepare incarcerated youth for community reentry through gradual freedoms and life skills training in the context of a six-week transition cottage. In this exploratory evaluation study, the authors use mixed methods to understand the benefits and limitations of the transitional living program model and its potential to reduce the risk of recidivism and other troubling outcomes for vulnerable youth involved in one or more public systems of care.

LITERATURE REVIEW

Transition Services for Incarcerated Youth

Research documents multiple and interrelated challenges for formerly incarcerated youth in the arenas of employment, educational attainment, mental health, substance abuse, and housing (Altschuler & Brash, 2004). In response, juvenile justice scholars suggest that youth who are reentering their communities from correctional settings need specific supports to successfully reintegrate into society, requiring more than just surveillance-oriented probation services. These transition strategies should help youth to practice and maintain pro-social behaviors and skills learned in secure confinement and to continue to infuse structure and goal-setting into their home lives (Altschuler & Brash, 2004; Spencer & Jones-Walker, 2004). Juvenile justice experts also suggest that transition services should be targeted to individual needs with a wide array of interventions and linkages with social networks, and that youth should receive supervision that gradually tapers off in intensity (Altschuler & Armstrong, 2001).

The most extensive recent research on juvenile reentry program models has focused on the Office of Juvenile Justice and Delinquency Prevention (OJJDP) initiated Intensive Aftercare Program (IAP). The IAP model emphasizes individualized treatment during the incarceration phase, a structured, distinct transition phase, supportive community resources in aftercare and varying degrees of surveillance in the community, depending on offenders' level of risk. The IAP is considered to be distinct from other models based on its structured transition period and an emphasis on reentry throughout all phases of correctional confinement (Altschuler & Armstrong, 2001).

In 1987, OJJDP established a research program to design, test, and disseminate information on the comprehensive IAP model for serious juvenile offenders. Initial process evaluations showed promising effects of several demonstration projects (Altschuler & Armstrong, 2002, September). However, two recent outcome evaluations found no statistically significant effects of the IAP program on recidivism between control and treatment groups. Frederick and Roy's (2003, June) evaluation of New York's IAP program found no reduction in post-release rates of arrest, but did find a reduction in violent recidivism, particularly in the first six months post-release. More recently, the National Council on Crime and Delinquency's evaluation of three IAP sites in the cities of Denver, Las Vegas, and Norfolk, Virginia examined a range of outcomes using experimental designs. Across the three program sites, the study found no differences between IAP and controls on measures of recidivism (arrest or conviction) and no differences in the severity of these offenses (Wiebush, Wagner, McNulty, Wang, & Le, 2005). However, the authors did find an impact on intermediate indicators of success, such as lower numbers of misconduct reports during incarceration and decreased length of institutionalization for IAP program participants. Moreover, qualitative interviews conducted as part of this comprehensive evaluation found that facility staff believed peer and family influences to be the key determinants of reentry outcomes for youth. Staff reported that while the institutions provided services to address these concerns, they were the hardest areas to influence (Wiebush et al., 2005).

Overall, Wiebush et al. (2005) caution against dismissing the IAP as a viable model for transition and reentry services, arguing that attention should be given to intervention fidelity. They also assert that greater financial and technical assistance may improve IAP outcomes. Similarly, Frederick and Roy (2003, June) question whether difficulties in faithful implementation of IAP led to their findings of mostly null effects. In sum, although the IAP is hailed as a premiere transition and reentry model, lessons drawn from program demonstrations lack evidence of success in reducing recidivism. It is also unclear *why* a program with such intensive transition preparation has not produced discernable or quantifiable results.

Dual Status Youth and Transitions

A growing body of research centers on youth who are involved in both the child welfare and juvenile justice systems, otherwise known as "dual status" or "crossover" youth (Dunlap, 2006; Ryan, 2006). While the precise number of dual status youth is difficult to measure, research documents that maltreatment and dependency are significant risk factors for delinquency and juvenile incarceration (Ryan & Testa, 2005; Widom, 2003). Foster care status and aging out of the child welfare system are also risk factors for criminal involvement. For example, Courtney et al. (2001) found that 18% of youth transitioning out of out-of-home care had been arrested at least once within twelve to eighteen months. In a different study comparing a sample of youth transitioning from out-of-home care with a nationally representative sample of youth, Cusick and Courtney (2007) found that the proportion of offenses committed by transitioning youth was double that of the national sample.

Although the various points of connection and overlap between child welfare and juvenile justice system involvement are established, very little research has examined the outcomes of incarceration or correctional treatment programs for dual status youth. In the one recidivism study that we were able to locate involving youth in the child welfare system, Ryan (2006) found that a "Positive Peer Culture" model was less effective in reducing recidivism for dependent youth compared to their non-dependent peers. Other studies with dual status youth focus more on pathways through these two systems. For example, in one study examining pre-adjudication detention decision among youth in New York City, youth with prior involvement in foster care were 10% more likely to be detained than those with no history of foster care (Conger & Ross, 2001). Freundlich and Morris' (2004) qualitative research found that dependent youth within the juvenile justice system reported to have inadequate legal representation and harsher punishments for less severe offenses than their non-dependent counterparts.

Some of the challenges related to understanding criminal trajectories of youth in the child welfare system stems from their involvement in complex and sometimes competing public bureaucracies. However, greater awareness of the concerns and negative outcomes associated with concurrent child dependency and delinquency statuses has resulted in recent federal and state policies supporting coordinated responses to dual status youth. The 2002 amendment of the Juvenile Justice and Delinquency Prevention Act included provisions that encouraged program development targeted toward dual system youth in order to reduce re-offending. Furthermore, the revised Child Abuse Prevention and Treatment Act of 2003 required states to report the number of cases that are transferred from child welfare to the state juvenile justice system (Dunlap, 2006). Even with greater policy attention, outcome data for these dual status youth as they transition to adulthood is difficult to locate. This gap may be partly attributed to the lack of clarity regarding the accountability for youth in both systems. Policies regarding the jurisdiction of crossover youth vary widely from state to state. For example, while some states allow for concurrent supervision dependency—delinquency cases, other states require that child welfare supervision ceases once a youth enters custody of delinquency court (Herz, Krinksy, & Ryan, 2006). In sum, little information exists regarding potentially different transition needs for dual status youth in juvenile corrections. Given the current state of knowledge in this arena, exploratory and descriptive research concerning the dual status population is warranted.

Study Aims

Given the scarcity of information on how specialized services can facilitate successful transitions for youth reentering their communities from correctional placements, particularly in the child welfare literature, the goal of this study is to describe and evaluate preliminary outcomes from an IAP-modeled program involving a six-week case-coordinated transitional living program. Mixed methods will be used to illustrate the benefits and limitations of this model in preparing youth for community reentry. The following specific aims will be addressed:

1. To examine recidivism outcomes for youth participants in a transitional living program at one-year post-release;
2. To explore child protective services involvement as a risk factor for recidivism at one-year post-release; and
3. To compare youth and staff perspectives on the strengths and limitations of the transitional living program in preparing youth for community reentry.

METHOD

Setting and Study Design

This study took place at a public correctional institution for felony-level juvenile offenders in a large urban area of the upper Midwest.[1] The facility houses youth offenders for periods of 9–12 months and offers both correctional (i.e. punitive, rules-driven) and rehabilitation-oriented (i.e. therapeutic) programming. As part of their rehabilitation, offenders are required to attend daily process groups and participate in cognitive-behavioral programming, substance abuse treatment, vocational rehabilitation, and other specialized therapeutic programs, such as anger management. Cognitive-behavioral techniques are stressed at all levels of the program. Youth are housed in cottages and primarily sorted by age, gender, and level of risk, with the exception of one cottage designated specifically for male sex offenders.

In 2002, the institution implemented a transitional living program (TLP)—a six-week intensive program that focuses on independent living skills—as part of their comprehensive IAP redesign. In this specific transition program, youth spend the night in the TLP cottage but are released into the community during the day to attend work or school and gradually spend increased time over the weekends in their home settings. Case managers work very closely with the youth to build their daily schedules and their plans for release. Only males are able to participate in the TLP intervention due to restrictions on mixed-gender housing.

A mixed methods design was used to conduct this exploratory evaluation study. The two primary methods included a quantitative analysis of recidivism outcomes for graduates of the TLP cottage in 2003 and qualitative interviews with TLP youth participants and program staff from 2004–2005. There are many ways to balance mixed methods, and no standard prescription (Padgett, 1998). In this study, the methods were implemented simultaneously and we used the quali-

tative component to understand and interpret the quantitative findings in more depth and with additional context.

Quantitative Analysis of Existing Records

Sample

The sample for the quantitative component consisted of 83 offenders who were released from the correctional facility between January 1, 2003–December 31, 2003. This sample was a full population census of exiting offenders for the first year that the TLP was implemented. Of these 83 offenders, 46 males completed the TLP, and an additional 15 males and 22 females completed the treatment program but did not participate in the TLP. Some male offenders were excluded from the TLP due to administrative mandates (such as early release or transfers) or space limitations, rather than any systematic criteria. A court order from a county juvenile superior court judge was used as blanket permission to examine the de-identified quantitative data.

Data Sources

Archival data were retrieved from two primary sources: 1) the state administrative data system for juvenile and adult offenders; and 2) official client case records. The state data was imported into an SPSS spread sheet with case number, and those case numbers were then matched to youths' records. The researchers then created fields for additional variables of interest extracted from the case records and added them to the existing state data.

Variables retrieved from the state administrative data included basic demographic information (age, gender, etc.), number of prior arrests, new substantiated crimes up to one-year post-release, and participation in the TLP. Variables retrieved from the intake forms included history of child welfare system involvement, family structure, substance abuse, and additional comprehensive descriptors of each case.

Independent Variables

The primary independent variable is participation in the six-week TLP cottage. This variable was measured as "yes" or "no" and was extracted the administrative data set. Child welfare system involvement (what we subsequently label CPS) is another key independent variable of interest. This variable is coded as "yes" if the client intake forms

---

[1]The names of the facility, the program, and all the participants and staff are masked in this paper for confidentiality.

indicated past or current dependency status in the public child welfare system. The authors recognize the compromised validity of combining past and current dependency status into one variable. However the records that were available to the researchers did not clearly indicate these distinctions.

Dependent Variable

The dependent variable for this analysis is recidivism at one-year post-release. There are many ways to operationalize recidivism (i.e. self-report, court referrals, etc.), and all have their benefits and limitations. For this study, recidivism is defined as any *substantiated* felony, misdemeanor, or status offense charge in either the juvenile or adult system within the year following their release from the program. The limitations of this variable are that we did not have access to out of state crime data, which may have reduced recidivism rates only slightly.

Control Variables

Control variables retrieved from the administrative database included number of prior arrests, race, and age at admission to program. Prior studies establish that younger youth, those with more prior arrests, and youth of color are more likely to recidivate (Brent & Tollett, 1999; Heilbrun et al., 2000; Myner, Santman, Cappellety, & Perlmutter, 1998; Niarhos & Routh, 1992). Offense history is the most consistent predictor of recidivism across studies (Cottle, Lee, & Heilbrun, 2001).

Juvenile justice research handles investigations of racial differences in processes and outcomes in diverse ways. The body of recent research on "disproportionate minority confinement" (DMC), shows that youth of color more generally, and African American youth in particular, are disproportionately over-represented at all stages of juvenile justice processing. Here youth "of color" are lumped into one category, despite noted limitations (Pope, Lovell, & Hsia, 2002). Some recidivism research breaks down racial categories into African American, Hispanic, and White (Heilbrun et al., 2000; Myner et al., 1998); or African American, White, and "Other" (Cottle et al., 2001). Other studies, even with larger samples, simply use "White" and "Persons of Color" (Brent & Tollet, 1999) or "White" and "Black" (Schwalbe, Fraser, Day, & Cooley, 2006). In our study, race will be collapsed into two categories: "White" and "Youth of Color" due to the low numbers of youth comprising racial categories other than White or African American (see Table 1). Although dichotomizing race is not the most meaningful way to operationalize this category in light of the diversity among youth of color, for a small sample, it is the best way to preserve statistical power.

Analysis

Descriptive statistics were initially computed using SPSS to understand the basic demographics of the aggregate sample (i.e. age, gender, race, CPS status) and the recidivism rates at one-year post-release. Next, bivariate tests (*t*-tests and chi-square) were used to assess any systematic differences between TLP and non-TLP male participants and to explore possible correlates of recidivism at one-year post-release. The data were then transferred from SPSS to STATA. Using STATA, step-wise logistic regression models were run to understand the unique influence of the independent and control variables on recidivism rates at one-year post-release, beginning with control variables and subsequently adding the two independent variables. Finally, several interaction terms were explored for significance, resulting in the addition of one interaction term to the final model.

Qualitative Interviews

Sample

The sample for the qualitative component of the study included 10 youth TLP participants, interviewed repeatedly over a six-month period, and one-time interviews with five TLP staff. For youth under age 18, parental consent was required for their participation. Youth who were 18 or over consented to their own participation. All of the youth referred to the TLP cottage during the first six months of the study period ($n = 25$) were approached to participate in this component of the project. In all, 12 youth volunteered, and the required consent forms were obtained for 10 of those participants. All of these participants completed at least two interviews with an average of 3 interviews per participant.

The staff sample was also selected by convenience. All of the TLP staff (case managers and supervisors; $n = 8$) were invited to participate in an interview. Of this group, five staff consented to the interview and completed the process.

Data Collection

Interviews with youth were semi-structured. The initial interview took place during the youth's stay in the TLP cottage and subsequent interviews were continued for a variable period of time (4–6 months) upon their return to the community. The main purpose of the interview series was to understand their transition process and the role of the TLP cottage in preparing them for this transition. These interviews were taped with a digital recording device and took place either at the TLP cottage in a private room, at the youths' homes, or in public locations such as coffee shops or libraries. Follow-up interviews with three of the youth took place in correctional facilities following subsequent placements. The researchers (including the primary author, the second author, and another graduate student) had a list of topics to cover at each interview but were not required to follow any specific order. Youth were also asked to elaborate in areas where rich or pertinent information emerged.

Interviews with staff occurred after the youth interview component of the project was completed. These interviews were more structured than the youth set, in that all of the staff members who were interviewed were asked the same open-ended questions in a standard order. Questions were geared to gather staff perspectives on the important components of transition, the benefits and limitations of the TLP, and their views on the challenges of youths' post-release environments. Interviews with staff were completed in the correctional facility in a confidential meeting space.

Analysis

Digitally taped interviews were transcribed verbatim by a professional transcriber and imported into the QSR NVIVO software program. Analysis techniques followed Miles and Huberman's (1984) four stage process for qualitative data analysis, including: 1) data organization, 2) data management, 3) data reduction, and 4) interpretation/conclusion drawing. The authors first read the transcripts and marked areas where the respondents discussed their perceptions of program strengths and weaknesses and their views on successful transitions, including definitions of this term and their perceptions of TLP components that promoted successful transitions. These larger categories were then broken down into subcategories through codes that were derived inductively from the transcripts. When all the data were coded, the authors created summary displays, including codes and key passages, for each

participant. To facilitate data interpretation, findings were displayed in the aggregate and tables were created to reflect differences between youth and staff perceptions. When all of the visual displays were completed, the authors returned to the original data to check the assumptions they were making and to confirm the coding. Once these assumptions and codes were checked, the authors were able to draw several interpretations and comparisons between youth and staff perceptions of program strengths and limitations.

RESULTS

Quantitative Analysis

For the quantitative analysis, we first present descriptive statistics concerning the 2003 cohort, followed by recidivism outcomes, and then logistic regression models predicting recidivism for males who exited the facility in 2003.

Descriptive Statistics

Table 1 presents descriptive statistics for the exiting 2003 cohort as a whole ($n = 83$) and two subgroups: males who participated in the TLP in 2003 ($n = 46$) and males who did not participate in the TLP ($n = 15$) but who also completed the correctional program. Key independent and control variables are included in this table, including average age at admission, gender, race, number of prior arrests, and child welfare system involvement (CPS).

As Table 1 indicates, the average age at admission for the 2003 cohort was nearly 16 years old. While females comprised 27% of the overall sample, they did not participate in the TLP intervention. For this reason, we confine the subsequent analyses of outcomes to the TLP male ($n = 46$) and non-TLP male ($n = 15$)

Table 1. Sample Demographics

Variable	2003 cohort ($n = 83$)	TLP 2003 ($n = 46$)	Non-TLP males 2003 ($n = 15$)
Mean age	15.9	15.6	16.4
Sex			
Male	73%	100%	100%
Female	27%		
Race			
White	18 (22%)	11 (24%)	5 (33%)
African American	41 (49%)	25 (54%)	6 (40%)
Native American	13 (16%)	7 (15%)	0
Asian	7 (8%)	2 (4%)	3 (20%)
Native Hawaiian or Pacific Islander	4 (5%)	1 (2%)	1 (7%)
Mean prior arrests	11.6	12	10.4
CPS involvement			
No CPS	73%	63%	67%
CPS	27%	20%	20%

sub-groups. The TLP sample was similar to the over-all 2003 cohort in terms of race and number of prior arrests. In the overall sample, nearly 27% had prior or current dependency status in the child welfare system, and the proportions of CPS cases were equivalent among TLP males and non-TLP males (at 20%).

As stated earlier, the young men who did not participate in the TLP cottage were excluded from participation based on arbitrary administrative obstacles and space limitations. Table 1 shows that the non-TLP male group was slightly older (16.4 vs. 15.6 years), had slightly more White members (33% vs. 24%) and had slightly fewer prior arrests (mean of 10 vs. 12). Independent samples t-tests for the continuous variables, age at admission and prior arrests, and chi-square tests for the dichotomous variables, race and CPS involvement, indicated that none of these differences between TLP males and non-TLP males were statistically significant.

Recidivism Outcomes

Table 2 presents basic recidivism outcomes in terms of new convictions for the 2003 sample. As a baseline consideration to be interpreted with caution, we first looked at outcomes from an evaluation of recidivism data conducted at the same facility in 2000 (Krmpotich, 2002), before the implementation of the TLP cottage. Although we did not have direct access to the raw 2000 data, the information provided by the County for in the 2000 study allows us to examine some general indicators of recidivism outcomes. In 2000, the reconviction rate at one-year post-release, *not* including status offenses, was 34% overall (including both males and females). For the 2003 exiting cohort, the overall reconviction rate remained the same, at 33%. Overall, these descriptive statistics show that the rates of reconviction were very similar from 2000 and 2003 despite the advent of the transition program.

The next question we posed was, did the TLP intervention influence recidivism rates for 2003 participants? Table 2 displays the 2003 exiting cohort data concerning recidivism including all types of substantiated charges (felonies, misdemeanors, and status offenses) in juvenile or adult court. Without controlling for risks, TLP males appeared to have higher

reconviction rates than the 2003 cohort as a whole, and particularly more than non-TLP males. For the TLP group, the overall reconviction rate was 48%; and for non-TLP males, was 27%. TLP participants also had a higher rate of felony convictions than the 2003 cohort as a whole and the non-TLP males (20% vs. 12% and 7%, respectively). Thus, not only did TLP males have a higher recidivism rates, they also committed proportionately more felony-level offenses than either the overall cohort or the non-TLP males.

Not reflected in Table 2, dual status youth (both males and females) had slightly higher recidivism rates at one-year post-release than corrections-only youth in this sample (42% vs. 38%), and among the TLP males ($n = 46$), rates of recidivism for dual status youth were higher, at 55%, vs. 45%. However, these differences were not statistically significant.

Logistic Regression Analyses

To examine predictors of recidivism for the males only, we performed a step-wise logistic regression analysis. Although our dataset, excluding the females, includes a small number of cases ($n = 61$), one rule of thumb suggests that a minimum of 60 cases for five independent variables is acceptable (Eliason, 2003). Thus, we limited the number of independent and control variables in the models to maximize the statistical power of the sample. As noted earlier, the covariates we selected (age, prior arrests, and race) are substantiated in the juvenile justice literature as key predictors of recidivism.

Table 3 provides the estimated coefficients for the step-wise logistic analysis of the male-only 2003 cohort. For the variables that showed statistical significance, we calculated percentage change estimates. Step 1 includes the control variables of age at admission, race, and number of prior arrests. In this model, only age at admission and prior arrests were statistically significant in predicting recidivism at one-year post-release. In terms of age, a one-year increase in age reduces the odds of recidivism by 43%. However, each additional prior arrest increases the odds of recidivism by 14%.

In Step 2, we added the TLP variable. Age at admission becomes marginally significant ($p \le .10$) and prior arrests remain the only significant variable in this model

Table 2. Recidivism Outcomes at One-Year Post-Release

| Group | Recidivism Rate | Offense Level | | | |
		Felony	Gross Misdemeanor	Misdemeanor	Status
2003 cohort	40%	12%	12%	8%	7%
TLP 2003	48%	20%	9%	11%	9%
Non-TLP Males 2003	27%	7%	13%	7%	0%

Table 3. Estimated Coefficients and Percentage Change of Step-Wise Logistic Regression Models Predicting Recidivism — 2003 Male Cohort

Variable	Coefficient	Percentage Change
Step 1		
Age	−.5611668**	−43%
Race	.3518597	
Prior arrests	.1334482**	14%
Step 2		
Age	−.5280604*	−41%
Race	.2985828	
Prior arrests	.1342481**	14%
TLP	.557428	
Step 3		
Age	−.6142266*	−46%
Race	.2476768	
Prior arrests	.0803422	
TLP	.0032341	
CPS	.0032341	
Step 4		
Age	.9284794	
Race	.066621	
Prior arrests	3.007976**	1900%
TLP	.6349762	
CPS involvement	−.0499064	
Age * prior arrests	−.1878301**	

Note: $N = 61$; ** $p < .05$, * $p < .10$.

at a similar rate to Model 1. TLP participation is not significant, although the coefficient indicates that TLP participation increases the odds of recidivism. Step 3 adds the CPS variable, which is also not significant. However, including CPS involvement eliminates prior arrests as a significant variable. Age at admission remains marginally significant at ($p \leq 10$).

Step 4 includes an interaction term for age at admission and prior arrests. The interaction term is significant, indicating that the effect of age on recidivism is dependent on the number of prior arrests. Once this interaction is controlled for, the number of prior arrests emerges as the only significant independent variable affecting recidivism. Its effect is substantial. In this sample, for each increase in prior arrests, the odds of reconviction are 20 times greater (percentage change of 1900%).

Overall, the logistic regression analysis suggests that neither of the two independent variables significantly predicted recidivism outcomes. Rather, risk factors such as younger age, and particularly number of prior arrests, significantly increased the odds of being reconvicted for a crime within one-year post-release. The qualitative data detailed in the next section provides the context to further interpret these quantitative findings of null effects.

Qualitative Analysis

Perceptions of TLP Effectiveness

The TLP provides practice in independent living skills within the context of structure, supervision, and case management driven daily planning. When asked to describe the benefits of the TLP, both youth and staff emphasized the practical skills component of the program. For example, the youth appreciated the opportunity to develop very specific skills such as completing job applications, riding the bus, or learning how to set and follow through with a daily schedule. Nick, a young person who was confined for nearly three years because of his committing offense (criminal sexual conduct), described: "I learned I can do things on my own without needing someone else to give me a ride or be there to help me. So I can do things on my own, and I can make friends" (Interview, 8/9/04). In addition to these pragmatic independent living skills, TLP staff also perceived the program as successful in facilitating the development of trusting and supportive relationships with adults. Some of the youth also suggested that the relationships with TLP case managers were highly beneficial, describing the staff as "comforting", "on my level" and "interactive". However, as expected in an involuntary correctional program, views of the staff were varied and some youth resented staff's position of power and authority over them.

In addition to practical and social skills, both youth and staff discussed the strong benefits of cognitive skills that are taught in the general program and reinforced during the youths' six-week TLP stay. Examples of these cognitive skills, as explained by youth participants, included "thinking before reacting", "learning to control impulses", and "constructive problem solving". For example, George, an 18-year-old father and former methamphetamine addict, stated:

> So I mean, more so now, I think a lot more before I react. . . . Cause I mean, I learned a lot about myself, about the people that I've hurt. There are a lot of kids who don't take the program seriously, and I think I took the program seriously to the best of my benefit (Interview, 7/17/04).

For the most part, staff also believed that the cognitive skills reinforced in the TLP cottage would help the youth to deal effectively with life situations and challenges on the outs. One staff member said, ". . .the guys, for six weeks, get to simulate what they're going to get out of the program and what they're going to do" (Interview, 5/12/2005). This quote illustrates the shared perception that the transition program provided the opportunity for youth to practice these cognitive skills in the context of real-life situations and interactions.

Skills Used on the "Outs" and Experienced Challenges

The youth who were interviewed in their post-release environments were asked to describe the skills learned in the cottage or the TLP that they were able to use in the community. The primary skill empha sized fell under the general theme of "refusal skills", with "practical skills" constituting a secondary theme. The significance of these refusal skills is directly linked with the challenges that youth experienced in the community. While youth described an array of challenges ranging from job disappointments to conflicts with their girlfriends, by far the primary thematic content of these challenges revolved around "old friends and influences". Under this category, the youth sample described struggling to navigate reintegration into their old networks, family, peer, and gang, without resorting to old behaviors, such as substance use or criminal activity. Ace, a 16-year-old father who was re-incarcerated shortly after his release, described his own cycle of negative influence that revolved around his old friends and influences:

> I mean them (my old friends) are the only people I know, y'know what I mean, so boredom too, like if I get bored, I would stay home a lot, but if I didn't have work or anything, I'd just shoot over to my old neighborhood and walk by myself and then I see the old associates, so I go over there and start talking and y'know what I'm saying, we just more than talking and then just start hanging out again, and that was hard (Interview, 10/14/2004).

Like Ace, many of the youth were returned to their old environments and peer groups that, by and large, hadn't changed during their incarceration. To cope with these situations, they employed a number of strategies, including the refusal skills that they had learned in the correctional program. For example, Buddy, an 18-year-old African immigrant provided a good example of his refusal skills in practice:

> If I'm with them <my friends> and there's a fight gonna happen right there, I will fight. I'm not gonna stop if somebody's hitting my cousin, I'm just standing right here and they jumpin' him. But if I'm in the house and they call me and they say yeah, we got to go to a fight right now, I'd say know, y'all go do your thing (Interview, 3/24/ 2005).

In this quote, Buddy describes his ability to selectively involve himself with old friends—yet to remove himself from a potentially dangerous situation. Other youth also employed refusal skills to minimize potential negative impact with drugs and alcohol, or with gang affiliated friends and family members.[2]

Staff perceptions of the major challenges of transition were largely similar to those that the youth actually described, as they also emphasized the potential criminal trappings of old friends, influences,

peer groups and gangs. One staff explained that he used to attribute reentry failure to family dysfunction, but later realized that, ". . . every kid that I've had fail it was always with some guy they used to run around with you know almost 95% of the time it was the first couple of weeks" (Interview, 05/03/2005).

In addition to the challenges of old friends and influences, the youth also faced disappointments and challenges in finding jobs, enrolling in school, securing stable housing, or other logistical matters. These gaps in their reentry plans were commonplace. Ace, the youth respondent who was re-incarcerated shortly after his release, described his rapid cycle of job loss, issues with transportation, and housing instability that led to his self-described return to criminal activity. He stated:

> Like I'd do anything to support [my daughter]. I mean, that's kind of how I got my <new> charge. I was selling drugs to make more money than I was making . . .? (Interview, 11/24/04).

In this sample, these practical challenges were intensified for youth, like Ace, who had unstable living situations or who did not return to homes with caring adults or older family members. Blue, for example, left the facility at age 18 with vague plans of independent living and a strained relationship with his family of origin. Prior to his incarceration, he had resided with his grandfather on and off because of difficulties between he and his mother. Blue never successfully completed the TLP cottage and ended up hiding out with a drug dealer friend because, according to him, his living situation with his older brother had deteriorated. Within a few weeks of leaving TLP and without fulfilling the terms of his court order, he received a court order to serve another four to six months at the same facility.

Responsibility for Change

One interesting angle to interpret these transition challenges is to examine youth and staff beliefs about what it takes to 'change' a criminal trajectory during the critical the reentry period. Overwhelmingly, the major theme expressed among the youth was that change is individual and largely "mental", in that offenders can change their course by focusing on their goals and sticking to their plan. This theme resonates well with the refusal skills that the youth also valued and practiced. For example, when asked about how much the program had helped him, Ace replied, "It's all up to the person. I mean, people can talk to you, they can tell you need to do this and this in the program . . . but it's really up to you" (Interview, 6/28/04). Another take on the theme of individual responsibility for change was expressed in terms of dealing with

---

[2]This topic of old friends and influences is detailed in another paper recently published by the first author (Abrams, 2007).

the consequences of your own actions. Caleb, a 15-year-old resident of a foster group home, suggested:

> Cause that's the life <gang> that I chose. It's natural. If you gonna be a gang banger and you gonna be a thug, getting shot at and getting shot, and going to jail, that's part of what you becoming, so when it happens [you are arrested] you can't be mad if you chose to do it (Interview, 6/23/04).

This individual responsibility philosophy was highly congruent with the cognitive focus of the treatment they had learned and was also very much supported by staff, who talked about the "individual" ingredients for change such as "self-discipline, intelligence, confidence, and cognitive ability". However, the staff, even more than the youth, also recognized that change does not occur in a vacuum, and expressed the need for external supports that facilitate and promote success in transition, such as social support, housing, food, and solid families. One staff member worried that foster children have fewer social supports, and perhaps then less reason to exercise their ability to "do well" on the outs. He stated,

> They <the youth> gotta have reason to want to get out of here. . . a focus at the end to see it worth it something to go home to something to which a lot of these guys don't even have. We've got enough guys that go to foster care, and they just gotta have something at the end to make it worth it. If they feel hopeless at the end they are not going to get much out of it all (Interview 5/12/2005).

The staff framed successful transition as both individual and environmental, and also believed in interconnectedness of these ingredients.

TLP Gaps and Weaknesses

Youth and staff expressed fairly disparate perceptions of the program's major weaknesses. In reflecting on the TLP several months after release, most of the youth respondents (with a couple of notable exceptions) felt that, all things considered, the cottage was an inefficient use of or "waste" of their time. One youth expressed frustration with the life skills training stating:

> We ain't kids and all that. They think they ain't dealing with kids, man. You know, and to be honest with you, I don't need a library card. . . Its like they send you out into the community but they send you out to jump through hoops (Interview, 5/1/05).

While not all the youth who were interviewed concurred with the waste of time opinion, overall, regard for the TLP cottage and the skills learned tended to wane as time went on in their release.

Directly contrasting the youth findings, staff expressed frustration concerning the *insufficient* amount of time afforded to the program to provide adequate preparation for transition. For example, several staff members emphasized the need for more gradual transition due the discrepancies in experiences within the institution vs. the community environment. One case manager described:

> I just don't think that [the staff] are given an opportunity to really get into what's going on with the kids. Whether that's the kid's fault because they're not disclosing or the system's fault for making people so busy with paperwork, they can't really get into stuff (Interview, 5/06/2005).

So while youth felt that the six weeks was too long for this program, the staff believed it not to be nearly enough time to help youth to prepare for the realities of reentry.

However, one key point of agreement between youth and staff was that youth did not receive necessary follow-up or aftercare services upon their release. For example, youth reported needing help in three key areas that the transition program targets—jobs, schooling, and housing—but did not necessarily know where to seek help. According to the program supervisor, TLP case managers were ideally supposed to maintain contact with released youth twice a month for two months. However, when asked about participating in aftercare, the youth did not sense a strong aftercare presence and felt "cut off" after they left the facility. C.J., a 16-year-old offender, stated:

> I don't like to build relationships like that <with staff> where you live with someone for almost a year and then it's just like. . . you're done! You're on your own (Interview, 4/2/05).

With one notable exception where a case manager made significant attempts to keep in touch with his caseload during aftercare, staff mainly corroborated the youths' view concerning the lack of aftercare continuity. They advocated for longer periods of follow-up with the youth, a more gradual transition, and stronger linkages with social services, education, and pro-social activities in the community.

DISCUSSION

Common wisdom would suggest that an intensive transitional living program for incarcerated youth would help to increase the odds of a successful community reentry. As other scholars argue, the skills learned in a correctional facility will do little unless they are highly relevant to real-life settings and situations and continue to be reinforced in the community (Abrams, 2006; Steinberg et al., 2004). Using a sole quantitative indicator of post release success, this study found that participation in a six-week transitional living program did not make a significant difference in recidivism outcomes at one-year post-release, and in this case, the TLP participants were slightly more likely to be reconvicted of offenses than non-program participants. This finding echoes other studies of the IAP model that find recidivism rates essentially unaffected by programs that teach youth to adjust to gradual independence through transitional living programs and follow-up care (Frederick & Roy, 2003, June; Wiebush et al., 2005). The factors that did drive recidivism rates in this study, age at admission and number of prior arrests, were unrelated to program participation. These risk factors support other literature on recidivism risks with larger samples (Brent & Tollett, 1999; Heilbrun et al., 2000; Myner et al., 1998; Niarhos & Routh, 1992.) Additionally, while dual status youth had slightly higher recidivism rates than corrections-only youth within the TLP sample in particular, this variable did not emerge as a significant risk factor in either bivariate or multivariate significance tests.

The qualitative component of this study provides the context to understand the benefits and limitations of a transitional living program for incarcerated youth. Despite unchanged recidivism rates, both youth program participants and staff found the TLP to be highly beneficial in several ways. Youth reported gaining specific practical skills that support independence, especially with goals related to vocation and education. Youth and staff also believed that the opportunity to develop positive relationships with adults and to reinforce cognitive-based refusal skills in a supportive setting helped youth to better navigate the challenges of reentry.

While youth largely bought into the individual, cognitive-based philosophy of the correctional program and the TLP reinforcements, they experienced many challenges related to transition that tested the efficacy of their program lessons. These challenges revolved around associations with old friends and influences and also with practical and logistical gaps in their reentry plans. Although youth found they were able to use the mental preparation they received in many situations, elements of their largely unchanged community environments still tested their resolve to stay away from crime. For some of the youth who we followed longitudinally in the community, re-incarceration happened quickly following their release.

So what might explain some of the gaps between perceptions of the TLP benefits (by youth and staff) and its measured effects? As discovered by the qualitative data, the main issue in this particular case was found in the lack of continued ties between the transition program and aftercare. Although the facility had adopted the IAP model which involves some degree of aftercare, both youth and staff agreed that strong aftercare links did not exist, and according to the staff, the duration of the TLP intervention did not appear

to permit for relationships and skills gained to be sustained for long periods of time. Although the youth nearly universally confronted changes in their reentry plans, they didn't know who to turn to for help with these complications. It seems that in the cottage–transition program–aftercare continuum, the third part of this sequence was the least apparent. This finding provides insight into the null effects on recidivism in this study and other studies of similar programs and indicates the need to develop much stronger aftercare and follow-up components. Follow-up and aftercare services may be especially important for the unique needs of dual status youth with a history of interrupted relationships or placement instability.

IMPLICATIONS

This study is non-experimental, and thus is limited in terms of understanding whether or not participation in the TLP actually made a difference in terms of recidivism rates. A small sample from one program year does not give a full picture of how the TLP fared after two or three post-implementation. Moreover, other indicators of transition success, such as school entry or job readiness, or were not explored. The quantitative data were mostly reliable. However, the child welfare involvement (CPS) variable was extracted from records, rather than from the state administrative data, and we were unable to separate past and current dependency status. For these reasons, we might not have captured the significance of this variable on recidivism outcomes. Finally, our dichotomized race variable might have missed differences between racial sub-groups.

Despite these limitations, this mixed methods study provides an interesting snapshot of this particular program and several ideas about how to strengthen transition and reentry programs for youth who are exiting residential care. One key point raised by this study is the significant challenges that youth face in regard to their refusal/cognitive skills, and also in regard to unexpected gaps or failures in their reentry plans. This finding speaks to the limitations of programs that operate primarily at the individual cognitive level as well as the need for ongoing case management and aftercare to build on both treatment and transition services. Aftercare can play a significant role in modeling positive relationships and reinforcing skills in the context of real-life situations, interactions, and relationships. In addition, extended programming can help youth to problem solve problems that come up in regard to school, work, or stable housing. Youth in this study clearly struggled to retain their skills learned in a correctional context far removed from everyday challenges experienced in unchanged environments. Providing offenders with continued support in translating skills to real-world settings may be the next challenge for juvenile justice and community-based programs for the reentry population.

In terms of how to best target reentry services, the quantitative data in this study show that accounting for TLP participation, younger youth and those with more prior arrests were at higher risk of recidivism. While this finding is not surprising, it does indicate that youth with these specific risk factors may need even more supervision and/or supports upon their reentry into the community. For dual status youth, their risks for poor outcomes may be even higher due to instability in family structure and living situation. It is important that child welfare researchers and practitioners maintain awareness of the possibly unique transition challenges of the dual status population. More research is needed in regard to dual status youth in general—including how many dual status youth exist, their specific needs, and their outcomes in relation to corrections-only youth. Moreover, the qualitative portion of this study found that both youth and staff attributed increased transition stress and disruption to the absence of a stable adult. This variable should be explored for both its independent and interaction effects with dependency status.

Finally, providing insight into the needs of youth who transition in and out of any public system of care, these study findings reinforce the vulnerability of these youths to negative outcomes and to disappointments and challenges that impede their progress toward independence. These youth appear to need a great deal of guidance and formal supports to make healthy transitions between institutions and communities, and to reach independence as young adults and for some, as fathers. The growing body of research on transition age youth (Osgood, Foster, Flanagan, & Ruth, 2005) notes many similarities and overlaps between youth who are incarcerated, involved in the child welfare system, and who are homeless. It is incumbent upon child welfare researchers to pay close attention to these linkages between populations, as well as notice programmatic innovations in juvenile justice or other systems of care that may aid vulnerable youths' adaptation to adulthood and independence more generally.

CONCLUSION

Although researchers are finding that transitional living programs for incarcerated youth are making little dent in the main outcome goal of reduced recidivism, future research should also examine other indicators of transition success, such as educational or vocational engagement. These intermediate outcomes may provide more insight into factors lead to subsequent incarceration. Moreover, future empirical study is needed to test the idea that stronger aftercare programs will produce more positive results. Our qualitative data suggest that aftercare may be the missing link in meeting the needs of these youths, yet rigorous testing of this hypothesis does not exist. As decades of research on foster care show, abrupt transitions to independence for youth upon reaching age of exit produces detrimental outcomes. Transferring this knowledge to a similar population, it is incumbent upon those concerned with the welfare of children to better understand and attend to the needs and environmental obstacles experienced by the youth reentry population.

REFERENCES

Altschuler, D. M., & Armstrong, T. (2001). Reintegrating high-risk juvenile offenders into communities: Experiences and prospects. *Corrections Management Quarterly, 5*(3), 72–88.

Altschuler, D. M., & Armstrong, T. (2002, September). Juvenile corrections and continuity of care in community context: The evidence and promising directions. *Federal Probation,* 72–77.

Altschuler, D. M., & Brash, R. (2004). Adolescent and teenage offenders confronting the challenges and opportunities of reentry. *Youth Violence and Juvenile Justice, 2*(1), 72–87.

Abrams, L. S. (2006). Listening to juvenile offenders: Can residential treatment prevent recidivism? *Child and Adolescent Social Work Journal, 23*(1), 61–85.

Abrams, L. S. (2007). From corrections to community: Youth offenders' perceptions of the challenges of transition. *Journal of Offender Rehabilitation, 44*(2/3), 31–53.

Brent, B. B., & Tollett, C. L. (1999). A study of recidivism of serious and persistent offenders among adolescents. *Journal of Criminal Justice, 27*(2), 111–126.

Bullis, M., & Yovanoff, P. (2002). Those who do not return: Correlates of the work and school engagement of formerly incarcerated youth who remain in the community. *Journal of Emotional and Behavioral Disorders, 10*(2), 66–79.

Cocozza, J. J., & Skowyra, K. R. (2000). Youth with mental health disorders: Issues and emerging responses. *Office of Juvenile Justice and Delinquency Prevention Journal, 7*(1), 3–13 Retrieved on September 11, 2007 from: http://www.ncmhjj.com/resource_kit/pdfs/Overview/Readings/YouthMHDis.pdf

Conger, D., & Ross, T. (2001). *Reducing the foster care bias in juvenile detention decisions: The impact of project confirm.* New York: Vera Institute of Justice.

Cook, R., Fleischman, E., & Grimes, V. (1991). *A national evaluation of Title IV-E foster care independent living programs for youth in foster care: phase 2, final report, Vol. 1.* Rockville, MD: Westat.

Cottle, C. C., Lee, R. J., & Heilbrun, K. (2001). The prediction of criminal recidivism in juveniles: A meta-analysis. *Criminal Justice and Behavior, 28*(3), 367–394.

Courtney, M. E., Piliavin, I., Grogan-Kaylor, A., & Nesmith, A. (2001). Foster youth transitions to adulthood: A longitudinal view of youth leaving care. *Child Welfare, 80*(6), 685–717.

Cusick, G. R., & Courtney, M. E. (2007). Offending during late adolescence: How do youth aging out of care compare with their peers? Chapin Hall Center for Children: issue brief #111. Retrieved on June 18, 2007 from. http://www.chapinhall.org/article_abstract.aspx?ar=1443

Dunlap, B. (2006). Dependents who become delinquents: Implementing dual jurisdiction in California under Assembly Bill 129. *Whittier journal of child and family advocacy.* Retrieved on June 20, 2007 from: http://www.perspectivesonyouth.org/Pages-Nonsubmit/WhittierJournal-Summer-Fall-2006.htm

Eliason, S. R. (2003). *Maximum likelihood estimation: logic and practice.* Newbury Park, CA: Sage.

English, D. J., Widom, C. S., & Brandford, C. (2002). *Childhood victimization and delinquency, adult criminality, and violent criminal behavior.* Washington, DC: National Institute of Justice.

Frederick, B., & Roy, D. (2003, June). *Recidivism among youth released from the Youth Leadership Academy to the City Challenge Intensive Aftercare Program.* Washington, DC: Office of Juvenile Justice and Delinquency Prevention.

Freundlich, M., & Morris, L. (2004). *Youth involvement in the child welfare and juvenile justice systems: A case of double jeopardy?* Washington, D.C.: Child Welfare League of America.

Heilbrun, K., Brock, W., Waite, D., Lanier, A., Schmid, M., Witte, G., et al. (2000). Risk factors for juvenile criminal recidivism: The post-release community adjustment of juvenile offenders. *Criminal Justice and Behavior, 27*(3), 275–291.

Herz, D. C., Krinsky, M., & Ryan, J. P. (2006). Improving system responses to crossover youth: The role of research and practice partnerships. *The Link: Connecting Juvenile Justice and Child Welfare, 5*(1), 1–9.

Jonson-Reid, M., & Barth, R. (2000). From maltreatment report to juvenile incarceration: The role of child welfare services. *Child Abuse and Neglect, 24,* 505–520.

Krmpotich, S. A. (2002). *2000 cohort study.* Minneapolis, MN: Department of Community Corrections.

Lipsey, M. W. (1999). Can intervention rehabilitate serious delinquents? *Annals of the American Academy of Political and Social Science, 564,* 142–166.

Mears, D. P., & Travis, J. (2004). Youth development and reentry. *Youth Violence and Juvenile Justice, 2*(1), 3–20.

Miles, M. B., & Huberman, A. M. (1984). *Qualitative data analysis: a sourcebook of new methods.* Beverly Hills, CA: Sage.

Myner, J., Santman, J., Cappelletty, G. G., & Perlmutter, B. F. (1998). Variables related to recidivism among juvenile offenders. *International Journal of Offender Therapy, 42*(1), 65–80.

Niarhos, F. J., & Routh, D. K. (1992). The role of clinical assessment in the juvenile court: Predictors of juvenile dispositions and recidivism. *Journal of Clinical Child Psychology, 21,* 151–159.

Osgood, D. W., Foster, E. M., Flanagan, C., & Ruth, G. R. (Eds.). (2005). *On your own without a net: the transition to adulthood for vulnerable populations* Chicago: University of Chicago.

Padgett, D. K. (1998). *Qualitative methods in social work research: challenges and rewards.* Thousand Oaks, CA: Sage.

Pope, C., Lovell, R., & Hsia, H. M. (2002). *Disproportionate minority confinement: a review of the research literature from 1989 through 2001.* Retrieved on September 11, 2007 from: http://ojjdp.ncjrs.org/dmc/pdf/dmc89_01.pdf

Ryan, J. P. (2006). Dependent youth in juvenile justice: Do positive peer culture programs work for victims of child maltreatment? *Research on Social Work Practice, 16*(5), 511–519.

Ryan, J. P., & Testa, M. F. (2005). Child maltreatment and juvenile delinquency: Investigating the role of placement and placement instability. *Children and Youth Services Review, 27*(3), 227–249.

Schwalbe, C. S., Fraser, M. W., Day, S. H., & Cooley, V. (2006). Classifying juvenile offenders according to risk of recidivism: Predictive validity, race/ethnicity, and gender. *Criminal Justice and Behavior, 33*(3), 305–324.

Snyder, H. N. (2004). An empirical portrait of the youth reentry population. *Youth Violence and Juvenile Justice, 2*(1), 39–55.

Spencer, M. B., & Jones-Walker, C. (2004). Interventions and services offered to former juvenile offenders reentering their communities: An analysis of program effectiveness. *Youth Violence and Juvenile Justice, 2*(1), 88–97.

Steinberg, L., Chung, H. L., & Little, M. (2004). Reentry of young offenders from the justice system: A developmental perspective. *Youth Violence and Juvenile Justice, 2*(1), 21–38.

Wiebush, R. G., Wagner, D., McNulty, B., Wang, Y., & Le, T. (2005). *Implementation and outcome evaluation of the Intensive Aftercare Program: final report.* Washington, DC: National Council on Crime and Delinquency.

Widom, C. S. (1989). Child abuse, neglect, and violent criminal behavior. *Criminology, 27,* 251–271.

Widom, C. S. (2003). Understanding child maltreatment and juvenile delinquency: The research. In J. Wilig, C. S. Widom, & J. Tuell (Eds.), *Understanding child maltreatment and juvenile delinquency: from research to effective program, practice, and systematic solutions* (pp. 1–10). Washington, DC: CWLA Press.

Wilson, S., Lipsey, M., & Soydan, H. (2003). Are mainstream programs for juvenile delinquency less effective with minority youth than majority youth? A meta-analysis of outcomes research. *Research on Social Work Practice, 13,* 3–26.

4.04

MULTILEVEL DESIGN

A Qualitative Evaluation of an Employee Counselling Service from the Perspective of Client, Counsellor and Organization

M. S. Elliott* and D. I. Williams*

ABSTRACT: An evaluation of a Fire Brigade counselling service examined the viewpoints of all three stakeholders (clients, counsellors and organization), using a multi-method approach using interviews, questionnaires and staff records. All parties expressed satisfaction with the provision, but noted the need for better communication and marketing. The counselling service was demonstrated to be needed and effective in both human and fiscal terms.

INTRODUCTION

Stress in the workplace is widely accepted as having repercussions not only for the health and safety of the individual (Peterson, 1994), but also for the organization through increased absenteeism and reduced productivity (Schabracq et al., 1996). Workplace counselling is one strategy for ameliorating the adverse effects of stress with the expectation that it not only meets the needs of the individual employee but also demonstrates its efficacy through financial savings (Berridge et al., 1997). Findings are presented here of a 2-year, in depth, evaluation of an employee counselling service which provided time limited counselling for the entire staff of the Northern Ireland Fire Brigade (NIFB).

Emergency service personnel may experience any of the three types of occupational stress stemming from the organization, external pressures of life and the operational factors inherent in emergency work (Hodgkinson, 1990; McLeod and Cooper, 1992); no more so than in Northern Ireland. Firefighters are at risk of Post Traumatic Stress Disorder (PTSD) (Bryant and Harvey, 1996; Elliott and Smith, 1993; Mitchell, 1992; Moran and Briton, 1994), and it has been claimed that the acute stress experienced by firefighters can 'induce heart attacks and strokes . . . at an inordinate rate' (Lewis, 1994, p. 58). Stress levels in control rooms are rising (Hoffman, 1996), and organizational demands placed on Fire Service staff in the UK are increasing within the context of constant staffing levels (Meldrum, in Hoffman, 1996).

Counselling Provision in the NIFB

The Service is a relatively small concern staffed by two part-time counsellors, one male and one female. Though the Service offers up to four free counselling

*University of Hull, Hull, UK

sessions, individual flexibility and prudence is exercised in individual cases. In practice an average of 10.23 sessions are conducted with each client, a reflection that almost 75% of presenting problems were the psychological sequel to trauma. Aspects of organizational life (interpersonal conflict—task overload—organizational change) formed the next most frequent source of presentation, while non-work issues (including matrimonial disharmony and ill health) encompased about 5% of problems. Counsellors are external to the organization, the format considered most acceptable to this occupational group. Clement-Green (1992) is sure that a wholly internal counselling system would not be effective within the fire service, where it would be perceived as insecure on the grounds of distrust by a workforce skeptical about confidentiality and concerned about loss of face (Tucker, 1990).

Rationale for Study

Evaluation of employee counselling has concentrated on outcomes from the viewpoint of either employee or employer. The present study attempts to examine the process seeking a holistic understanding of the provision. In particular it was guided by a recognition of the needs of all three parties to the deal: the client, the counsellor and the organization. Each of these perspectives is examined separately. Methodology was guided both by appropriateness-to-context (Shapiro, 1973) and utility. The qualitative approach adopted allowed research to be fused with clinical practice (Rennie, 1994). In accordance with the practice of counselling itself data collection was sensitive to emotional issues and information was gathered with empathy and understanding, the inquiry being flexible enough to 'follow' the data (Elliott and Williams, 2001).

Workplace counselling comprises a triune relationship (Orme, 1997). This study sought to assess the degree of congruence across the aims and expectations of all three parties—the client, counsellor and organization; in particular to examine whether the NIFB counselling service meets the needs of all three stakeholders thereby resulting in a win-win-win outcome (Orme, 1997). Or would Greenwood's (1997) description of workplace counselling as a potential breeding ground for friction be confirmed?

METHODS

Client Data

Twenty-one former clients were contacted by letter asking if they would take part in the study. All agreed to do so. Semi-structured interviews were carried out with each of them. The form of the interviews followed the client's path from before counselling to the present. Participants were interviewed between 6 and 20 months post-termination of counselling.

Counsellor Data

a. The relevant counsellor completed an 'encounter questionnaire' with respect to each of the clients interviewed in the study. The counsellor was asked for an evaluative trace through counselling for each client concentrating on five key areas; conceptualization, process and outcome, impact on the organization, professional issues and personal issues raised by the work.

b. An intense in-depth study of the counsellor perspective was conducted through a series of four linked interviews with one of the counsellors.

Organizational Data

a. Semi-structured interviews were held with ten 'key players' including the Chief Fire Officer, Occupational Physician, Welfare Officer, Human Resource Director and representatives of different ranks.

b. To assess awareness of the counselling provision within the Brigade 150 questionnaires were circulated to a stratified sample of all staff.

c. To assess the 'bottom-line' benefit the sickness records of the client group were scrutinized.

RESULTS

Our contention is that the contextual appreciation of the study, the multi-method approach and the depth and width of the evaluation detail produced provides a type of outcome beyond the reach of traditional research methods.

The Client Perspective

Interview data was transcribed, themes and subcategories were then identified (the system being independently validated by a second observer) and particular responses allocated to themes (with this classification also being independently checked), and frequency of occurrence recorded. Analysis was made less problematic by an overriding consensus amongst the 21 participants in identifying issues and in the certainty with which views were expressed. Results are presented here in the stages through entry to termination of counselling.

Employee to Client

Emerging from the interviews was a higher order concept of transformation; an individual journey embedded within the larger client experience, a metamorphosis between being 'there' (before counselling) to being 'here' (after counselling). For many this change was difficult, for some fortuitous and for many laced with relief.

Just over half the client group had no knowledge of the counselling service prereferral, while the remainder only had vague information. Discomfort, rather than service awareness, was the initial point of referral for many, while in severe cases a consultation with the Occupational Physician prompted them to see a counsellor—'It was . . . during a medical that I actually broke down. When [the Doctor] asked I admitted it, and he referred me to counselling. It was lucky I went to see the Doctor that day'. Stigma was for most the initial bar to using the provision.

For each member of the entire group the initial telephone call to their counsellor was a moment of appraisal, offering them the opportunity to evaluate whether counselling was for them. The conversation was more than an introductory chat. Clients admitted to judging the counsellor's personality and competence at this time. The evaluation, when positive, 'She sounded a friendly and warm person' served as further motivation. A blend of perceived humanness coupled with an immediate therapeutic dividend (reduced anxiety, gaining reassurance, information and clarity as to what was offered) led clients to conclude at the point of first contact that the counsellor was probably competent and that counselling was a route worth following. The transformation to client status, for some, brought fears over confidentiality, feelings of stigma and embarrassment, and puzzlement as to the mechanics of counselling. For those who had overcome their fear of stigma there was anxiety that counselling would be ineffective, making the effort not worthwhile.

In anticipation of counselling client's spoke of the need for symptom relief and improved functioning in their domestic and working lives: 'I needed so much for that damn mood to go. It just hung around me. I wanted this to change'; 'I wanted to get rid of the awful images and thoughts—to stop getting anxious, and to enjoy life free from stress . . . to be my old relaxed self again'.

Client in Counselling

There was a high degree of unanimity amongst the client group as to the active ingredients of counselling that they deemed to be important—namely counsellor characteristics and counsellor interventions. Clients appreciated: listening skills and approachability; the feeling that they were the focus—and valued; the active participation of the counsellor. Insights gained were particularly appreciated: 'He made what was only dimly apparent very apparent, and that was most helpful'; 'The educational part of counselling was the strongest part'; 'counselling threw light on it all, and it clicked. Once I understood how it all worked things moved quickly for me'. A positive factor for many were homework assignments, and in particular the use of 'thought diaries'. Challenging was seen by some as the lever that opened doors, but for others a confrontational style was unsettling—at least at the outset. The product of counselling was generally held to be a renewed feeling of being in control. Such empowerment stimulated progress and resulted in stability.

Importantly, and impressively, the clients detailed evaluation of their experience of counselling was substantially at one with the specific views expressed by their counsellor in the 'encounter questionnaire'.

Consequences of Counselling

All 21 participants were emphatic in stating that counselling helped them. For many the progress made was significant: 'the anxiety just dropped off', 'my depression lifted'; 'I ended up not needing antidepressants'; 'and I haven't had any panic attacks since counselling ended'. Clients were able very specifically to identify areas of change including: cognitive and behavioural shifts ('helped me to turn my thinking around'; 'helped me to stop hiding'); improved personal relationships ('really counselling reunited my family. My wife and kids smile again'; enhanced ability to cope and work ('my work load is now being dealt with more quickly'; 'counselling got me back to work').

The vast majority of participants pointed to positive dividends for the NIFB in terms of improved work performance, work attitude and working relationships. Several identified the 'chain of change' in the workplace; symptom relief and elevated enthusiasm made for better relationships at work. As one previously irritable, anxious and socially withdrawn firefighter, who returned to work after counselling, explained 'I was likeable again. They needed me back the way I was'. Without counselling several clients said that 'I would not have had a job', 'I would have never got back to work again'.

Counselling/NIFB Interface

Clients acknowledged that the NIFB organization had an impact on their counselling experiences. They perceived, and responded to, a powerful cultural hint to keep hidden from view their suffering from stress and visits to the counsellor: 'I didn't want to ruin my image and fall below those (emotional) standards and maybe lose my position. Many men would have felt the same as me, no doubt'. The organizational culture seemed also to stimulate self-denial: 'The culture undermines your ability to even admit stress to yourself, let alone to others at work. This then affects your ability to use the counselling service'. Stress was seen by many as a personal weakness: 'How can you prove you are better . . . they'll always think you could crack up at any time'. It is of little surprise, therefore, that clients were relieved to learn of the counselling services external locus. Their concerns were of management control and fragile confidentiality: 'I would've had great reservations about using an internal service. You can't open up if you believe it's all going to be reported all over the Brigade'.

Clients typically said that they had participated in the study in the 'hope that it will help others'. There was a belief that stress should be legitimized and the counselling service actively promoted—with strong and consistent management support. One suggestion was that the counsellors should be introduced in person to the workforce.

The Counsellor Perspective

Transcripts of interviews were analysed thematically in the same way as the client interviews.

The counsellor explained that she held crystalline and firm practice needs engendered by her training, but that the NIFB context created uncertainties. While her responsibility was to the client there were also assumed responsibilities to the organization: 'While my goal is most obviously client oriented, I'm well aware that there is a organizational attachment. The organization is a client too'. But she had not pushed for the issue to be addressed. She wanted a closer link with the organization, but was apprehensive about treading on toes. She realized that greater integration of the service would depend on improved channels of communication between the counsellor and her employer. She felt on the periphery of the organization, and thus vulnerable as she was unclear of her role and of organizational expectations. This created moments of conflict: 'I'm not really sure if I'm permitted, from the organization's perspective to be here simply for the client first, organization second'. So while confident of her work with clients the counsellor was less clear about impact on the organization or of achieving organizational aims—she said she worked on the 'no news is good news' principle.

The Organizational Perspective

The vast majority of those interviewed put the welfare of employees as the primary objective of the counselling service. Some placed firm emphasis on what one man called 'an organizational impact'. Certainly there were hoped for benefits for the employer, but expectations were realistic as one person said: 'Counselling should lead to a reduction in absenteeism and retirements, but it's hard to expect it to be totally responsible for such an organizational result'.

In evaluating the service, responses could be categorized in terms of core counselling function and context. The organizational perspective as reflected in the views of all 10 'key players' was most positive in terms of the effectiveness of counselling. They cited examples from their own staff and other wider feedback. There was less satisfaction with the way the service operated. Concern was expressed about service/counsellor contact-ability, service to host feedback/communication and the cultural constraints surrounding admission of stress and counselling take up rate. There was spontaneous support for this evaluation. Participants looked for information on the efficiency of the service and the value of the investment, and hoped the study would provide a platform to relaunch a (better) service.

Awareness Questionnaire

There was a 47% return rate on the questionnaire. Some 40% of respondents did not know the service existed; almost all those that were aware were uniformed staff. Knowledge had been obtained from: (1) post-critical incident information (23%); (2) in-house lecture/seminar (16%); (3) Brigade circular (14%); and (4) employee grapevine (14%). There are four referral points for the service; no one knew of all four. Of those aware of the service only 20% knew that it was available to all personnel; the majority thought it was open only to operational staff or those exposed to trauma. The most frequently cited deterrent to using the service was fears over confidentiality. Eighty per cent of those aware of the service said they drew comfort from knowing that it existed.

Analysis of Absence

Days of absence for the 21 clients interviewed showed a striking reduction from pre to post-counselling. The average reduction over a 3 month period was 66% (mean reduction from 15 to 5 days), and for 6 months either side of counselling was 65% (mean reduction from 23 to 8 days). Caution has to be exercized in extrapolating from this data. But the figures suggest a saving of £2000 for each employee counselled. Based on a service utilization rate of 1.2% this would correspond to savings of £50 000 per annum. The lack of a control group does not allow firm conclusions to be drawn here, but changes are consistent with previous findings (Cooper, 1996) and are of a magnitude that cannot be ignored.

CONCLUSION

A win-win-win result was found for the three stakeholder groups. Clients were well satisfied with the service, Counsellors received confirmation that their perceptions were mirrored by clients and the Organization noted the benefit of the service and that this could be demonstrated in financial terms. The like-mindedness between parties was gratifying, but needs to be built upon. In particular there is a need to refine and formalize the NIFB/Counselling Service relationship, reposition the service closer to the NIFB, improve communication systems, market the service more comprehensively and train managers in how and when to refer.

In both human and financial terms the counselling service in the NIFB has been shown to be both effective and needed.

REFERENCES

Berridge, J., Cooper, C.L. & Highley-Marchington, C. (1997) *Employee assistance programmes and workplace counselling.* Chichester: Wiley.

Bryant, R.A. & Harvey, A.G. (1996) Post-traumatic stress reactions in volunteer firefighters. *Journal of Traumatic Stress, 9,* 51–62.

Clement-Green, M. (1992) An examination of the need for a system of stress and trauma counselling in the Fire Service, unpublished report.

Cooper, C.L. (1996) *Handbook of stress, medicine and health.* Boca Raton, FL: CRC Press Inc.

Elliott, D. & Smith, D. (1993) Coping with the sharp end: recruitment and selection in the Fire Service. *Disaster Managment, 5.*

Elliott, M.S. & Williams, D.I. (2001) Paradoxes of Qualitative Methods. *Counselling & psychotherapy research, 1*(3), 181–183.

Greenwood, A. (1997) Stress and the EAP Counsellor. In M. Carroll and M. Walton (eds) *Handbook of counselling in organizations* (pp. 260–272). London: Sage.

Hodgkinson, P. (1990) Stress and the firefighter. *Fire Prevention,* 235 December 22–23.

Hoffman, S. (1996) Increasing demands on firefighters are causing stress. *Fire International 96 Review, 21/24.*

Lewis, K.W. (1994) Stress in the fire service: a matter of life and death. *Firehouse,* October, 58–60.

McLeod, J. & Cooper, D. (1992) A study of stress and support in the Staffordshire Fire and Rescue Service, unpublished report.

Mitchell, J. (1992) Protecting your people from critical incident stress. *Fire Chief,* May, 61–64.

Moran, C.C. & Briton, N.R. (1994) Emergency work experience and reactions to traumatic incidents. *Journal of Traumatic Stress, 7,* 575–585.

Orme, G. (1997) On being a chameleon—A freelance Workplace Counsellor's perspective. In M. Carroll and M. Walton (eds) *Handbook of counselling in organizations* (pp. 57–73). London: Sage.

Peterson, C.L. (1994) Work factors and stress: a critical review. *International Journal of Health Services, 24,* 495–519.

Rennie, D.L. (1994) Clients' deference in psychotherapy. *Journal of Counselling Psychology, 41,* 427–437.

Schabracq, M.J., Winnubst, J.A.M. & Cooper, C.L. (1996) *Handbook of work and health psychology.* Chichester: John Wiley.

Shapiro, E. (1973) Educational evaluation: rethinking the criteria of competence. *School Review, 81,* 523–549.

Tucker, W.R. (1990) An analysis of the need for and design of a planned process to deal with stress and trauma during and after major incidents, unpublished report.

4.05

EXPERIMENTAL DESIGN

Cognitive Tools for Scaffolding Students Defining an Ill-Structured Problem

Janet Mannheimer Zydney*

ABSTRACT: This study assessed the effect of cognitive tools on scaffolding students defining an ill-structured problem. Seventy-nine 10th-grade students used the *Pollution Solution* software to study an environmental problem. A quasi-experimental, mixed-method design was used. One class received the organization tool, a second class received the higher-order thinking tool, a third class received both tools, and a control group received neither tool. The organization tool group obtained a moderate understanding of the problem, which was significantly higher than the control group. Students who received the organization tool also asked significantly more problem-related questions than the other groups. The higher-order thinking tool prompted students to ask significantly more questions than the other groups. The combination tool group did not perform as well as expected. This study raised some questions about whether combining tools will add the effects of these individual tools.

Most problems in everyday life are ill-structured and emerge organically out of a natural situation; however, students are not taught to solve these types of problems in school (Jonassen, 2003). Students are taught well-structured problems (e.g., story problems), where the problems are perfectly set up for them (Rowell, Gustafson, & Guilbert, 1999). These problems have a defined initial state, clear goals, and a finite number of operators to obtain the final solu-

tion (Chi & Glaser, 1985). Researchers have found that solving ill-structured problems requires a different set of skills than solving well-structured problems (e.g., Shin, Jonassen, & McGee, 2003). Jonassen hypothesized that students have difficulty solving ill-structured problems because they are not taught how to represent or define these types of problems. He argued that "problem representation is the key to problem solving" (Jonassen, 2003, p. 364). This issue was exemplified in the study by Rowell et al. These researchers asked practicing engineers what the most difficult aspect of their job was, and many responded that defining the problem was the most challenging for them because they did not learn this skill in school.

---

*New York University
Janet Mannheimer Zydney is now at the Department of Teacher Education at the University of Cincinnati.

Although researchers have begun to theorize strategies for helping students with defining problems, little has been done to empirically validate these concepts. Given this need, this study focused on the activities during problem representation, the early stages of problem solving. The purpose of this study was to investigate whether computer-based tools could help students define a complex problem. In order to do this, a learning environment called *Pollution Solution* was developed specifically for this research. The *Pollution Solution* software presented students with a complex environmental problem that could be solved in many different ways and provided different types of tools to help students investigate and eventually solve the problem.

THEORETICAL BACKGROUND

Problem Representation of Ill-Structured Problems

Solving a problem involves two components: the representation process and the solution process (Voss & Post, 1988). "The *representation* of a problem consists essentially of the solver's interpretation or understanding of the problem" (Chi & Glaser, 1985, p. 232). Problem representation is an important step in solving ill-structured problems because these types of problems have one or more aspects of the problem that are not clearly defined (Chi & Glaser, 1985). Moreover, the information needed to solve these problems is not completely provided to the learner. During this initial stage of problem solving, the learner interprets the problem, makes connections between the problem and knowledge of the domain, defines its goals and scope, identifies the causes of the problem, examines divergent perspectives, and hypothesizes different solutions (Chi & Glaser, 1985; Rowell et al., 1999).

Problem representation places both cognitive and metacognitive demands on the learner (Ge & Land, 2004). The cognitive demands require that learners have both domain-specific and structural knowledge. Domain knowledge is helpful for learners to determine relevant versus irrelevant information and to fill in information that may be missing from the problem definition. Structural knowledge is helpful for learners to organize information (Ge & Land, 2004) and to represent and interpret new information in the problem (Bransford, Brown, & Cocking, 2000). The metacognitive requirements in representing problems involves thinking about how much is known about the problem, related prior knowledge, and what aspects still need to be learned (Ge & Land, 2004). Metacognitive functions enable learners to create a plan for solving the problem.

The way the problem is presented can influence the approach students take in the problem-solving process (Jonassen, 2003). When problems are presented in a well-defined way, students typically solve the problem by identifying the correct formula, plugging the data from the problem into the formula, and solving for the unknown. Students, who are novice problem solvers, often focus on the surface features of a problem rather than trying to develop a conceptual understanding of the problem, as expert problem solvers do (Chi, Glaser, & Farr, 1988). In order to develop a conceptual understanding of the problem, Jonassen argues that students need to learn to represent problems in multiple ways. "When students try to understand a problem in only one way, especially when that way conveys no conceptual information about the problem, they do not understand the underlying systems in which they are working" (Jonassen, 2003, p. 364).

One method to preserve the complexity of the problem is to present the problem through multiple perspectives, themes, schemas, or analogies, as recommended in the cognitive flexibility theory (CFT) (Spiro, Coulson, Feltovich, & Anderson, 1988). Presenting problems to students through different means may encourage them to represent the problem in multiple ways. CFT was developed to address the issues of learners developing misconceptions about ill-structured domains as a result of instruction being presented in overly simplistic ways. Research has shown that CFT environments can improve students' conceptual understanding (Fitzgerald, Wilson, & Semrau, 1997; Jacobson & Archodidou, 2000), a critical element of problem representation; however, further testing is needed to validate whether CFT can be used to help students define problems in an ill-structured domain.

Researchers have studied various aspects of students representing problems. For example, students can define a given problem through questioning (Chin, Brown, & Bruce, 2002; Czarnik & Hickey, 1997; Dori & Herscovitz, 1999; King, 1991; Olsher & Dreyfus, 1999). Asking questions can help students determine what is unknown about the problem. Past research on questioning has focused on the nature of questions asked during an activity (e.g., Chin et al., 2002; Keys, 1998; Olsher & Dreyfus, 1999) or the changes in students' questions from the beginning to end of instruction (e.g., Czarnik & Hickey, 1997; Dori & Herscovitz, 1999). Researchers have found that students who are more familiar with a problem ask a greater number of questions (Dori & Herscovitz, 1999) and their questions become more specific with increased expertise (Czarnik & Hickey, 1997). Moreover, students with increased expertise in a problem have been found to ask more questions related to the problem domain (Czarnik & Hickey, 1997) and its solution (Dori & Herscovitz,

1999). Closely linked to students' questioning is their underlying knowledge about the problem because in order "to ask a question, one must know enough to know what is not known" (Miyake & Norman, 1979, p. 357). Thus, several researchers have investigated students' knowledge or conceptual understanding of the problem in addition to their questions (Dori & Herscovitz, 1999; Olsher & Dreyfus, 1999).

Researchers have also assessed how students formulate hypotheses to define a problem (Hoover, 1994; Hoover & Feldhusen, 1990). Formulating good hypotheses requires that students go beyond simply asking questions. "To create a hypothesis, subjects should have some expectation or inferred understanding beyond the given material; hypotheses thus imply the asker is active in constructing a knowledge structure" (Miyake & Norman, 1979, p. 363). Researchers have examined the number and quality of hypotheses generated by students in connection with problem-representation activities (Bennett & Rock, 1995; Hoover, 1994; Hoover & Feldhusen, 1990). These studies found a relationship between questioning and hypothesis formulation and students' fluency or flow of ideas (Bennett & Rock, 1995; Hoover, 1994; Hoover & Feldhusen, 1990). Given this established relationship found in the literature, it may be important to control for this factor in studies involving problem representation.

Cognitive Tools as Scaffolding for Ill-Structured Problem-Solving

Students often need some support or scaffolding to succeed with open-ended, complex, problem-solving environments (Liu, Bera, Corliss, Svinicki, & Beth, 2004). Scaffolding in these environments can help learners achieve goals beyond their ability level (Wood, Bruner, & Ross, 1976). Although the original concept of scaffolding was concerned with the support provided by a more experienced person (see Palincsar, 1986), more recently researchers have been studying scaffolding provided through cognitive tools. "Cognitive tools are any technologies that engage and facilitate specific cognitive activities" (Jonassen, 2003, p. 372). These tools are designed to help learners with cognitive tasks, such as problem solving, critical thinking, and higher-order learning (Jonassen & Reeves, 1996). Examples of these tools range from low-tech tools such as hand-drawn concept maps to high-tech tools such as computer-based simulations (Jonassen & Reeves, 1996).

Researchers have suggested a wide range of cognitive tools along the technology spectrum that can be utilized for scaffolding students with problem representation (Ge & Land, 2003, 2004; Jonassen, 2003). One low-tech tool that has been found to scaffold students with representing ill-structured problems are question prompts, which were provided either on a static course Web page or in paper format (Ge & Land, 2003). Ge and Land (2003) found that the question prompts helped students organize their thoughts, break down the problem, and make connections between different parts of the problem. The questions also served a metacognitive function in helping students recognize what information they needed to know. One limitation of this study was that some students failed to take advantage of the question prompts provided to them. To address this issue, Ge and Land (2004) recommend for future research to make the question prompts more technologically advanced by embedding them within the computer application, requiring students to use them. On the higher end of the technological continuum, sophisticated simulations may help students externalize their mental representations of the problem space (Jonassen, 2003); however, more empirical research is needed to determine whether these types of computer-based tools are effective within this area.

Although there is little research to validate whether computer-based cognitive tools can help students with representing ill-defined problems, there has been a great deal of research on computer-based tools to help students with problem solving. Since representing the problem is the first phase of problem solving, it is logical to assume that some tools used to scaffold problem solving will be helpful during the representation phase. Research that supports this notion has found that computer-based tools that assist with cognitive processing and share cognitive load are used more often during earlier stages of problem solving (Liu & Bera, 2005). Examples of these tools include databases that provide a well-organized knowledge structure and notebooks and bookmarks that help students collect and organize information (Liu & Bera, 2005). Researchers have hypothesized that the tools needed to scaffold problem representation are ones that support both the cognitive and metacognitive requirements of this activity (Ge & Land, 2004). Two categories of computer-based cognitive tools that emerged from the problem-solving literature that may be helpful in serving these functions can be classified as organization and higher-order thinking tools.[1]

Organization Tools

Organization tools "help learners to interpret, connect, and organize the represented information meaningfully" (Iiyoshi & Hannafin, 1998, p. 3). These

---

[1] Organization and higher-order thinking tools are my interpretation of these broad categories; thus, this nomenclature is not necessarily used by the authors.

tools can help learners with the structural knowledge needed to interpret the problem (Ge & Land, 2004). Organization tools can be found in many forms, including templates, concept maps, or categorizing tools. The common design feature of these tools is providing a structural component for organizing information. For example, electronic templates provide a structure into which students can add information; concept maps allow students to visually organize information into categories; and categorizing tools enable students to organize information by dragging and dropping it into different groupings or sections.

Assisting learners with organizing knowledge can help improve their conceptual understanding by integrating new problem information into their conceptual framework (Jonassen, 2003). For example, Saye and Brush (2002) found qualitative evidence that storyboard templates were helpful to students in conceptualizing their presentations. Other researchers have found evidence that templates can help students develop scientific explanations (Land & Zembal-Saul, 2003; Sandoval & Reiser, 2004). However, Land and Zembal-Saul found that these templates were more effective for students with high prior knowledge. Concept maps have been found to improve students' ability to categorize data and make connections between hypotheses and data (Toth, Suthers, & Lesgold, 2002). Finally, a categorizing tool, which allowed students to organize evidence for comparing different theories, was found to improve students' understanding of different perspectives (Bell, 2004). Some studies found organization tools to not be effective because they were not used very much by the students (Brush & Saye, 2001; Oliver & Hannafin, 2000).

Higher-Order Thinking Tools

Higher-order thinking tools are designed to help facilitate processing of content at a deeper level. This higher-level thinking allows problem solvers to recognize what they do not know about the problem (Winn & Snyder, 1996). They help learners "reflect on how much they already know about a problem domain, relate various problem aspects to their prior knowledge, and select goals" (Ge & Land, 2004, p. 11). They also help learners "monitor knowledge construction process as well as their knowledge status" (Iiyoshi & Hannafin, 1998, p. 3). Higher-order thinking tools can be found in different forms, such as electronic journals, prompts, or sentence starters. The design feature shared by the tools in this category is a means for reflection during problem solving. For example, an electronic journal provides an open space for students to write their thoughts; prompts or sentence starters give students a few words to help them begin writing their ideas and reflections.

Some studies found that higher-order thinking tools in the form of question prompts improve students' knowledge integration (Davis, 2003; Davis & Linn, 2000). Other research has shown that reflection can prompt students with high background knowledge to develop more sophisticated scientific explanations (Land & Zembal-Saul, 2003). Similarly, Wolf and Brush (2000) found that this type of tool, used in combination with other tools, improved students' reports. Some studies did not find this type of tool to be effective; however, the tools used in these applications were not required (Brush & Saye, 2001; Oliver & Hannafin, 2000).

Combined Tools

A number of studies examined combinations of organization and higher-order thinking tools (Brush & Saye, 2001; Davis & Linn, 2000; Ge & Land, 2003; Iiyoshi & Hannafin, 1998; Land & Zembal-Saul, 2003; Oliver & Hannafin, 2000; Wolf & Brush, 2000). Combined organization and higher-order thinking tools were found to improve students' knowledge integration (Davis & Linn, 2000; Wolf & Brush, 2000) and problem solving (Ge & Land, 2003). However, it is difficult to know whether the combined scaffolding was necessary or if one tool attributed to most of the students' improvement. Researchers have found that as students became more familiar with multiple tools they are better able to optimize the use of multiple tools (Iiyoshi &Hannafin, 1998; Liu & Bera, 2005). Similarly, Land and Zembal-Saul found that students with high prior knowledge were better able to take advantage of combined scaffolds. More research is needed to analyze the effects of multiple tools on students' performance in these types of environments.

FRAMEWORK FOR THE DESIGN OF THE STUDY

This study advances a continuing line of research on how cognitive tools in a multimedia program can scaffold students in representing an ill-defined problem. This section of the article will describe the conceptual framework and design of the learning environment used in this research, summarize results from a study conducted during the previous year, and explain the purpose of the present study.

Conceptual Framework and Learning Environment

In order to support students in defining problems, I developed a learning environment called *Pollution Solution* specifically for this research. In this environment, the students take on the role of an intern for an environmental consulting firm. They are given a client who explains the symptoms of his company's legal problem involving air pollution. The students must construct the problem and come up with recommendations for a solution. During their research, students hear multiple perspectives on this problem from various experts in the environmental field. The students must grapple with these different perspectives in developing their solution.

The complex, ill-structured problem presented within *Pollution Solution* is designed based on principles from the cognitive flexibility theory (CFT) and situated learning theory. Based on CFT, this learning environment presents students with multiple perspectives on the problem, offers a variety of cases, highlights the relationships between different disciplines, and provides students with the opportunity to integrate knowledge (Jacobson & Spiro, 1995). Situated learning theory complements CFT by drawing on cases from the real world that are inevitably richer and more complex than ones that are fabricated (Li & Jonassen, 1996).

As a result of formative evaluations with teachers and students over a 3-year period, I observed the need to add instructional supports or scaffolding elements to *Pollution Solution*. Through this iterative design-and-development process, I conceptualized a new instructional model called the scaffolded flexibility model (SFM) (Zydney, 2005). This model expands on CFT by presenting the instructional cases in an authentic context and including layers of scaffolding. This scaffolding is designed to support learners in several ways: (a) improving their cognitive processes; (b) providing guidance through modeling and coaching; and (c) assisting with time management. Multiple levels of support are provided by distributing the scaffolding across different cognitive tools within the learning environment (Puntambekar & Kolodner, 2005). As students progress through this learning environment, the scaffolding fades. During the introduction, the timing and access to the tools is completely controlled by the system. Later on, in the problem-solving environment, the learners are given more control over the use of these tools. For a more detailed explanation of the SFM model, see Zydney (2005).

The scaffolding within the *Pollution Solution* software was provided to students through a virtual office, which included filing cabinets, research notebook, and reference manuals as well as a phone, e-mail, and notepad. For example, students received help with time management through e-mails that provided deadlines for deliverables. They obtained coaching through simulated telephone calls from their supervisor who offered helpful advice and tips, and they received modeling of problem solving through video of experts in the field. A research notebook provided students with the ability to take notes and organize

their research. Within the research notebook, an organization tool called the research plan template was designed to help students conceptually organize information about the problem by providing headings and focusing questions. Another tool called a status report was designed as a higher-order thinking tool. The goal of this tool was to help students reflect on the problem and uncover gaps in their knowledge. Different versions of the software were developed with different tools available in order to isolate the effectiveness of these tools on students' understanding of the complexity of the problem.

Summary of Findings from an Earlier Study

During the previous year, I conducted a similar study to the present study (Zydney, 2005). This earlier study used the same *Pollution Solution* learning environment to investigate which cognitive tool most effectively helped students to define a complex, ill-structured problem. The sample for this study was 60 8th-grade students from four earth science classes, all taught by one teacher, in a New York City public school. The classes were randomly assigned to one of four treatment conditions, which received varying types of scaffolding tools.

The findings from the first study indicated that the organization tool was most effective in helping students understand the problem, develop hypotheses, and ask more specific questions inside the problem domain (Zydney, 2005). The higher-order thinking tool was most effective at prompting students to ask more questions (Zydney, 2003) and helping students grasp the multiple perspectives of the problem (Zydney, 2005). However, using a combination of tools was not as effective as using these tools individually.

Based on the results of the first study, some enhancements were made for the present study. First, a speculation for the reason why the combined tools were not as effective as expected was that this group had less time to complete one of the graded assignments. To correct for this problem in the present study, the timing of the tasks was changed so that all groups received the same amount of time to complete graded assignments. Second, it was difficult to analyze the student-generated questions because students' reasoning for asking the questions was unclear. For this present study, the question-generation activity was enhanced to prompt students for an explanation of why their questions were important to solving the problem. Finally, observations indicated that students were not taking the question assessment as seriously as the work they did on the computer. To remedy this issue, this assessment was changed from a paper-based activity to an evaluation embedded within the software program.

Purpose of the Present Study

This present study investigated the effectiveness of different types of cognitive tools in an SFM environment for helping students define a complex problem. In order to determine this, different treatment conditions of the learning environment were developed with varying types of tools to support the learners. The research question was: What is the effect of cognitive tools in scaffolding students defining an ill-structured problem, as measured by: (a) students' problem understanding; (b) ability to generate questions; and (c) their ability to formulate hypotheses on how to solve the problem?

Based on this research question, the following were the expected outcomes for the different treatment conditions:

Organization Tool

The organization tool was expected to help learners with the structural knowledge needed to improve their ability to understand the problem, ask more specific questions relevant to the problem, and formulate hypotheses of higher quality. These expectations grew out of the underlying theory of how the organization tool is designed to work within an SFM learning environment. The organization tool used a template design with headings and question prompts to help learners make connections and organize information meaningfully, thereby improving their understanding of the problem. Increased knowledge of the problem should enable learners to ask more specific questions that are problem oriented (Czarnik & Hickey, 1997). Moreover, greater problem understanding should lead to improved ability to develop hypotheses for solving the problem (Miyake & Norman, 1979).

Higher-Order Thinking Tool

The higher-order thinking tool was expected to help students generate more questions and hypotheses. This tool is designed to help learners with the metacognitive strategies needed to "monitor knowledge construction process as well as their knowledge status" (Iiyoshi & Hannafin, 1998, p. 3). In assisting learners to reflect on the problem, this tool is designed to help learners think about what they need to learn about the problem, thereby prompting them to ask more questions. In addition, by helping learners think about different perspectives on the solution to the problem, this tool should encourage them to ask more solution-oriented questions and develop alternative hypotheses.

Combined Tools

The combination of organization and higher-order thinking tools was expected to help students excel across all measures. Based on the SFM model, one would expect that combining these tools would combine their effect and would produce outcomes that were the same or better than those obtained with the tools separately. Thus, students who received the combined tools should have a solid understanding of the problem, ask many questions that are very specific and related to the problem, and formulate many hypotheses of a high quality.

METHOD

In order to test the effect of different types of cognitive tools, a quasi-experimental design with intact classes was used. This study used mixed methods with the quantitative methods as the dominant paradigm (Johnson & Onwuegbuzie, 2004). The quantitative and qualitative data were collected concurrently. The quantitative data were obtained through computer-based assessments, and the qualitative data were captured through classroom observations.

Participants and Setting

This study took place in a typical classroom in a public high school in New York City. This school had a very diverse student body, representative of a large urban center along both cultural and socio-economic lines. The small school created an intimate setting in which the students became quite close to one another, and, as a result, each class developed its own distinct personality. These unique, unquantifiable characteristics may have affected the results and, thus, will be described in further detail in the Discussion section.

Seventy-nine students, ranging from 15 to 16 years of age, gave their consent to be included in the sample for this study. These students were taking 10th-grade biology, and it had been 2 years since they had studied environmental science. They were using the *Pollution Solution* software as a review of this material for the NY State Regents exam on the living environment. Thus, although they had prior knowledge of the environmental science content covered in the software, it had been a long time ago. In addition, the students were not familiar with the specific problem scenario presented in the software.

These students were divided into four classes that were all taught by the same teacher. This teacher received her undergraduate education in biology and psychology and her master's in educational technology; thus, she was very comfortable using technology in her classroom. Prior to implementation, she received a demonstration of the software and a training manual that provided detail descriptions of the daily classroom activities. In addition, the teacher received on-site technical support each day to troubleshoot any problems that occurred.

All classes were taught in the same classroom at different times of the day. These classes were on a rotating schedule to account for students' changes of behavior between morning and afternoon. The class periods ranged from 50 minutes to 1 hour and 20 minutes in order to accommodate differences in schedules of specialty teachers. At the end of each day, we documented at what point each class was in the study. During the study, the classroom was configured in a team setting. Teams of four students sat together at two lab tables pushed together to form a square; altogether there were six table groupings. Each student worked on his or her own laptop computer but participated in team as well as full-class discussions throughout the study. Around the room hung chart paper capturing the major concepts covered during the project. There was an LCD projector that the teacher and I used to show the introductory videos and demonstrate certain tools in the software.

Treatment

Over a 3-week period, the classroom was transformed into an environmental consulting firm. The students, through the use of *Pollution Solution*, became interns for this fictitious firm and were given a client, a utility company, who had just been sued for violating the Clean Air Act. The project began with a virtual interview (through a digital video clip) with the vice president of the utility company who explained the symptoms of the problems to the students. In this scenario, the teacher and I played the role of internship supervisors to assist the interns in defining and eventually recommending solutions to their client. The treatment was the first 6 days of this project during which time the students defined the complex problem. They wrote qualitative descriptions of the problem and formulated investigative questions and hypotheses about how to solve the problem.

The classes were randomly assigned to one of four conditions of the treatment. Although intact classes were used in this study for logistical reasons, students were randomly assigned to these classes to the extent possible by the school at the beginning of the academic year. All students in the same classroom received the same condition. Each condition utilized a slightly different version of the software. All versions included the same introduction to the problem, offered the same references for students to use in their research, and provided the same directions for writing the research plan. However, the treatments varied in whether the organization or higher-order thinking tools were available. Table 1 shows the cognitive tools associated with each treatment condition. The control group (C) provided students with directions to write the research

Table 1. Cognitive Tools for Each Treatment Condition

Treatment Condition	Cognitive Tool	Description
C (control)	None	Research plan w/o template[a] No status report
O	Organization	Research plan template[b] No status report
H	Higher-order thinking	Research plan w/o template[a] Status report[c]
OH (combination)	Organization and Higher-order thinking	Research plan template[b] Status report[c]

[a]See Figure 1 for the research plan without template.
[b]See Figure 2 for the research plan template.
[c]See Figure 3 for the status report.

plan (see Figure 1). * Another group received the organization (O) tool. The organization tool was in the form of a research plan template, which provided headings and question prompts designed to help students organize their research (see Figure 2). A third group received the higher-order thinking tool (H). The higher-order thinking tool was in the form of a status report, which gave the students reflective question prompts to help them process the content more deeply (see Figure 3). The last group received a combination of the organization and higher-order thinking tools (OH) and included the research plan template and the status report.

Measures

The measures used as covariates were fluency and computer-treatment time, and the dependent measures were students' problem understanding and their ability to formulate questions and hypotheses. All dependent measures were assessed through rubrics, which were created based on categories that emerged as important from the research literature. An earth science teacher, with expertise in assessing these areas, reviewed these rubrics to confirm their validity. Two evaluators rated each of the dependent measures independently and then came together again to discuss discrepancies. These evaluators were not affiliated with the *Pollution Solution* project. One evaluator was another science teacher at the school where the study was conducted, and the other evaluator was a graduate student in educational technology with a strong science background. The evaluators were blind to the treatment condition the students

---

*Figure 1, 2, and 3 omitted for this edition.

had used. Inter-rater reliabilities are reported in the sections describing each variable.

Fluency

Fluency was measured by the Topics Test (reliability = .81) (Ekstrom, French, & Harman, 1992). For this Topics Test, students were given a word or phrase and needed to generate as many ideas as possible that were related to it. The reliability of this instrument was retested for this study (α = .86).

Computer-Treatment Time

The computer-treatment time was the total time students spent using *Pollution Solution*. A log file recorded the start and stop time of each student's session, and the duration of time was computed. The computer-treatment time was the sum of the session times. In some cases, the end time of one of the sessions in the log file was not recorded because students' computers crashed at some point during the week. The end time for these sessions was estimated as the last recorded time in the log file.

Problem Understanding

The students were asked to write a research plan that included a qualitative description of the problem that they were trying to solve. In order to demonstrate a strong understanding of the problem, students needed to describe several factors in their research plans, such as the cause of the acid rain problem, regulations of the Clean Air Act, the lawsuit against the company, the company's economic issues, their public relations problems, and the decision faced by the company. Students received 1 point for each factor and up to 1 extra point for mentioning a factor not specified in the evaluation rubric. Students could receive up to 7 points for their problem understanding. A high problem understanding score would be greater than 5 points, a moderate understanding score would be between 2 and 5 points, and a low understanding score would be less than 2 points. The inter-rater reliability was .81.

Question Generation

After writing the research plan, students generated investigative questions about what they needed to know in order to understand the problem and their reasons for asking these questions. The students' questions were evaluated for their frequency, type, and specificity.

Question frequency. Question frequency was computed by adding the number of questions asked by each student.

Question type. Students' questions were categorized into subject oriented, problem oriented, solution oriented, or unclear. These different categories were ordinal in nature and indicated an increased level of expertise in problem understanding. Subject-oriented questions were ones dealing with the general subjects related to the problem (e.g., economics, environmental science, law, or engineering), such as "What is the Clean Air Act?" Problem-oriented questions dealt with factors connected with the client's objectives and goals. These factors included the political and legal considerations of the problem, environmental factors, economic aspects, ethical issues, or the public relations problem. An example of a problem-oriented question was the following: "What is the standard sulfur dioxide emission level according to the EPA?" Solution-oriented questions asked about the different alternative solutions to the problem. "How much can solar powered energy cost?" was an example of a solution-oriented question. The number of questions for each type was computed, and the percentages of each question type was calculated based on the total number of questions generated. The raters agreed on 94.6% of these ratings.

Question specificity. Students' questions were also coded for level of specificity. Unclear question were statements that were ambiguous or contained misconceptions. General questions dealt with general content knowledge, such as "What are some clean air technologies?" Specific questions elicited data needed to develop a solution to the problem. For example, "How much do clean air technologies cost?" was rated as a specific question. However, specific questions required further questions to get to a more precise answer. In the previous question, the student would need to ask how the different types of clean air technologies work. Very specific questions also elicited data but were at the most detailed level. For example, students could propose a very specific question dealing with this same topic, such as "What would be the exact cost and sellable value (of the byproduct) of the sulfur dioxide recovery system?"

Unclear questions, general questions, specific questions, and very specific questions were coded 0, 1, 2, 3, respectively. To compute a student's mean question-specificity score, the number of questions in each category was multiplied by its value. The sum of these weighted scores was then divided by the student's total number of questions. For example, one unclear question, five general questions, two specific questions, and two very specific questions would result in a mean question-specificity score of 1.5. The inter-rater reliability was .91.

Hypothesis Formulation

The students were also asked to write about their hypotheses for possible solutions in their research

plans. The hypotheses were evaluated for their frequency and quality.

Hypothesis frequency. The total number of hypotheses
was computed. The inter-rater reliability was .88.

Hypothesis quality. The quality of the hypotheses was
assessed by the following criteria: definition, relevancy,
feasibility, rationale, originality, and consideration of
more than one perspective. Each criterion was worth 1
point; thus, a student could receive a hypothesis-quality
score, ranging from 0 to 6, for each hypothesis. In order
to compute a student's mean hypothesis-quality score,
each hypothesis was multiplied by its quality score, and
the sum of these weighted scores was divided by the
student's total number of hypotheses. The mean
hypothesis-quality scores ranged from 0 to 5 points. The
inter-rater reliability was .85.

Controls

Potential factors that might affect the results of the
study were collected. These factors included students'
number of absences during the study, amount of time
worked at home, level of discussion outside of class,
and amount of technical problems/loss of work. This
data were analyzed to determine if any of these factors were inconsistent across the classes. None of these
factors were found to affect the results of the study.

Procedures

During six class periods, the students participated
in the study. During the first session, the students were
introduced to the project and completed the fluency
test. During the second session, the class met (through
digital video clips) their supervisor and their client,
who explained the acid rain problem faced by the company. During the third session, the class discussed
what information they needed and saw a brief
demonstration on how to find information within the
Pollution Solution learning environment. During the
fourth session, the students independently researched
and took notes about the problem. At the end of the
day, the students with the higher-order thinking tool
and the combination tool completed their status
reports, and the organization tool and control groups
continued their research. Over the next 2 days, the students wrote their research plans. After completing
their research plans, the students completed a questioning assessment. For this assessment, the students
had 15 minutes to generate as many questions as they
could think of that would help them to solve the problem and explain their reasoning for asking each question. After this assessment, the students answered a
few survey questions to determine if they were absent,
worked at home, lost any data during the study, or discussed their work outside of class.

Data Analysis

Quantitative Analysis

To determine whether the classes were equivalent for student fluency and computer-treatment
time, one-way ANOVAs were performed on these
measures with cognitive tool type as the between-
subjects factor. To determine the effectiveness of the
cognitive tool on the dependent measures,
ANCOVAs were computed with cognitive tool type
as the between-subjects factor and computer-treatment time and fluency as potential covariates. The
purpose of including covariates in the model was to
make the statistical test more powerful by increasing
its sensitivity. A correlation analysis between the
dependent measures and covariates was used to confirm the choice of covariates (Tabachnick & Fidell,
2001). With the exception of question frequency, the
fluency measure was dropped as a covariate because
it was not found to correlate with the dependent
measures.[2] When ANCOVAs found statistically significant F-results, pairwise comparisons, with adjustment for multiple comparisons set to Bonferonni,
were used to determine which means were different
from one another. An α level of .05 was used to judge
significance for all analyses.

The assumptions of normality, linearity, homogeneity of variance, homogeneity of regression slopes,
and equality of covariance matrices were tested for all
these analyses. The results of this testing was satisfactory unless noted otherwise.

Qualitative Analysis

Field notes carefully described the classroom
activity during the study, and special notes were made
of any differences between the classes. I played the role
of both the participant and observer (Merriam, 2001).
Observing the classrooms provided me with an
"insider" perspective on the students' use of the multimedia learning environment (Merriam, 2001).
Although a certain level of objectivity was most likely
sacrificed in order to obtain this perspective, these
observations added a level of richness to the data collected.

To analyze these field notes, qualitative differences among the classes were coded. For example,
if one class had a deeper discussion on a topic than
the other classes, this difference was noted and coded
by level of discussion. Or, if one class had more

---

[2] The question frequency measure was the most similar in nature
to the fluency measure as they were both timed activities where students generated either ideas or questions.

misbehavior than the other classes on a given day, this difference was noted and coded by behavior type. These qualitative differences were organized in a chart along with the quantitative findings in order to see whether the statistical differences found could be explained by the qualitative differences among the classes. The qualitative descriptions are reported in the discussion of the quantitative findings in order to contextualize the results (Creswell, 2003). The teacher reviewed the qualitative descriptions of the classes and the activities to ensure accuracy of the account.

RESULTS

Individual Differences

The one-way ANOVA analyses revealed that there was no significant difference for students' fluency or computer-treatment time. Thus, prior to the treatment, the classes were found to be equivalent across the test for fluency ($F(3, 74) = 0.62$, $p = .61$, $\eta_p^2 = .02$) and in the amount of time students spent using the computer ($F(3, 74) = 1.51$, $p = .22$, $\eta_p^2 = .06$).

Effect of Cognitive Tools on Students' Performance

Students' ability to grasp the complexity of the problem was measured by their problem understanding, question generation (frequency, type, and specificity), and hypothesis formulation (frequency and quality). With the exception of question type (where computing an average of a type was not meaningful), the descriptive statistics for the different measures for the various treatment conditions are provided in Table 2.

Problem Understanding

Students' problem understanding varied significantly for different treatments ($F(3, 74) = 3.58$, $p = .02$, $\eta_p^2 = .13$). Pairwise comparisons revealed that students who used the organization tool had a significantly higher problem understanding than the control group ($p = .02$). No significant difference between the other pairs was found. Figure 4 illustrates the differences in problem understanding scores for the different conditions.

Question Generation

Question frequency. Each student generated up to 10 questions/explanations. The number of questions generated by the students was found to be significantly different ($F(3, 72) = 4.77$, $p < .01$, $\eta_p^2 = .17$) for the different conditions.[3] Pair-wise comparisons revealed

Table 2. Means and Standard Deviations for the Dependent Measures for Different Treatment Conditions

Dependent Measure	Condition	N	Mean	Standard Deviation
Problem Understanding	C	21	1.38	0.82
	O	20	2.40	1.32
	H	18	1.57	0.80
	OH	20	1.78	1.01
Question Frequency	C	20	4.20	1.94
	O	20	4.25	1.21
	H	18	5.24	2.05
	OH	20	4.25	1.67
Question Specificity	C	21	1.48	0.43
	O	20	1.59	0.54
	H	18	1.42	0.52
	OH	20	1.69	0.43
Hypothesis Frequency	C	21	1.67	0.94
	O	20	1.50	0.95
	H	18	1.64	1.20
	OH	20	1.70	0.77
Hypothesis Quality	C	21	2.76	1.26
	O	20	3.11	1.46
	H	18	2.62	1.42
	OH	20	3.19	1.05

Note: C = Control; O = Organization; H = Higher-Order Thinking; OH = Combined Organization and Higher-Order Thinking.

that students who used the higher-order thinking tool asked significantly more questions than the control group ($p < .01$), the organization tool group ($p = .03$), and the combined tool group ($p = .02$).

Question type. Students' questions were judged for whether they were subject oriented, problem oriented, solution oriented, or unclear. Since these data violated the normality assumptions of the ANCOVA, a nonparametric equivalent for an ANCOVA was computed. The nonparametric ANCOVA works similarly to a parametric ANCOVA, except it allows one to use nonnormal data that must be at least ordinal. It uses a rank-based method, and it ranks all variables including the covariates (Bathke & Brunner, 2003). The type of cognitive tool did not have a significant effect on the percentage of unclear questions ($A = 2.48$, $df = 3$, $p = .46$),[4] subject-oriented questions ($A = 2.18$, $df = 3$,

---

[3] One case was identified as a multivariate outlier. After examining this case more closely, it was discovered that this student had technical problems, resulting in loss of time on the computer and some data loss; thus, this case was eliminated for this analysis.

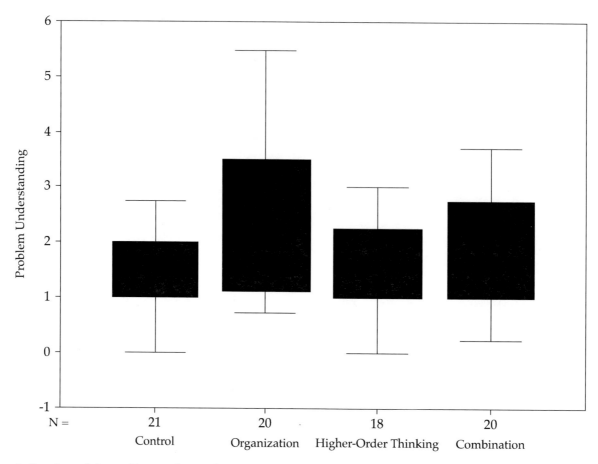

Figure 4. Boxplots of the problem understanding score for different treatment conditions.

$p = .53$), problem-oriented questions ($A = 2.25$, $df = 3$, $p = .51$), or solution-oriented questions ($A = 3.56$, $df = 3$, $p = .30$).

Figure 5 shows how the mean percentage of questions in each type differed among the treatment conditions. Although not significant, students who used the organization tool and the combined tools tended to ask a higher percentage of problem-oriented questions; whereas, the students who used the higher-order thinking tool and the control group tended to ask a higher percentage of solution-oriented questions. Given these opposing trends of the problem-oriented and solution-oriented questions, planned comparisons were employed. The treatments were regrouped into groups that included the organization tool (i.e., the organization tool and the combined tools) and groups that did not include the organization tool (i.e., the control group and the higher-order thinking tool). Then, a Mann Whitney U analysis was computed to compare the differences between the percentage of problem-oriented and solution-oriented questions for treatments with and without the organization tool. This analysis revealed that there were significantly more ($U = 536$, $Z = -2.10$, $p = .04$) problem-oriented questions for

treatments with the organization tool than without the organization tool. In addition, there were significantly more ($U = 530$, $Z = -2.19$, $p = .03$) solution-oriented questions for treatments without the organization tool than with the organization tool.[5]

Question specificity. No significant treatment effect was found for question specificity ($F(3, 74) = 0.79$, $p = .31$, $\eta_p^2 = .03$).

Hypothesis Formulation

Students' ability to formulate hypotheses was measured by both frequency and quality of the hypotheses generated.

Hypothesis frequency. The students formulated between zero and four hypotheses. The number of

---

[4] A is the value of the statistic, ats_k, from a nonparametric ANCOVA; A is analogous to the F in the parametric ANCOVA.

[5] Percentages were used for the measure of question type to eliminate the influence of question frequency. A correlation was performed to confirm that question type did not correlate with question frequency. Thus, the group differences in question frequency did not influence the results of this analysis.

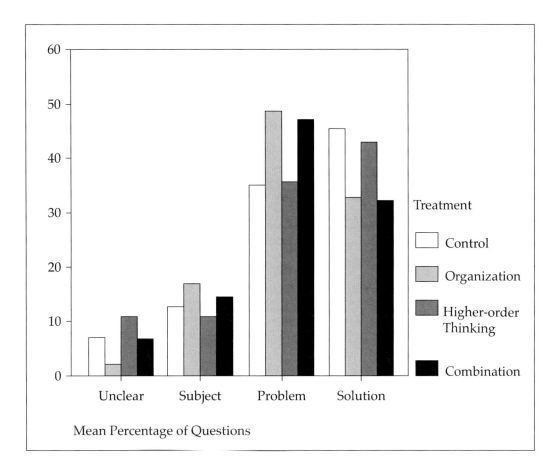

Figure 5. Mean percentage of questions in each question type for different conditions.

hypotheses was not found to be significantly different among the treatment conditions ($F(3, 73) = 0.37$, $p = .77$, $\eta_p^2 = .02$).

Hypothesis quality. The ANCOVA analysis did not reveal a significant treatment effect for hypothesis quality ($F(3, 74) = 0.51$, $p = .68$, $\eta_p^2 = .02$).

Summary of Findings

The ANCOVA analyses showed that the students' problem understanding and question frequency were significantly different among the four treatment conditions. Some covariates had a moderating effect on the main effect of cognitive tool. A summary of the major findings is provided in Table 3.

DISCUSSION

This study found that organization and higher-order thinking tools had varying effects on different aspects of students defining ill-structured problems. In order to contextualize the findings, qualitative descriptions of each class are reported at the beginning of each section.

Table 3. Summary of Major Findings

Variable	F	p	η_p^2
Problem Understanding			
Cognitive tool	3.58	.02	.13
Time	4.18	.05	.05
Question Frequency			
Cognitive tool	4.77	< .01	.17
Time	10.94	< .01	.13
Fluency	17.33	< .01	.19
Question Specificity			
Cognitive tool	0.79	ns	ns
Time	0.62	ns	ns
Hypothesis Frequency			
Cognitive tool	0.37	ns	ns
Time	8.91	< 0.1	.11
Hypothesis Quality			
Cognitive tool	0.51	ns	ns
Time	3.07	.08	.04

Note: Question type reported separately because it used a nonparametric analysis.

Organization Tool

During the study, the class, who received the organization tool, appeared engaged and fairly well behaved. There were a handful of extremely bright students in the class who required extra challenges to maintain their interest level and contributed to a competitive atmosphere in the classroom. While observing the class, there was some concern that the few top students as well as the class's competitive nature might skew the results, making this class perform better than expected; however, these concerns were not brought to fruition. It turned out that this class was much more heterogeneous in nature than observations originally indicated. The teacher mentioned that there were a few English language learners in the class, and she also suspected that a couple of students may have had learning disabilities that were not officially classified.

Students who were given the organization tool were found to have a significantly higher understanding of the problem than the control group. This result was also found in the first study on *Pollution Solution* (Zydney, 2005). However, even with the use of the organization tool, the students in the present study only achieved a moderate understanding of the problem. The problem-understanding scores were, on the whole, lower in this study than in the first study. A possible explanation for this is that the students in the first study had much more prior knowledge on the subject from which to draw upon because they had been immersed in studying similar environmental topics throughout the year. On the other hand, students in this present study had been taught this material 2 years earlier and likely had forgotten some of the concepts covered. This may indicate that the organization tool is more powerful when students have a greater knowledge base with which to make connections to the new information presented. This finding is in line with earlier research which found that students with higher prior knowledge make better use of scaffolds (Land & Zembal-Saul, 2003). Future research may examine approaches to enhance scaffolding use for students with low prior knowledge.

The students who used the organization scaffold also asked significantly more questions related to the problem (as opposed to the solution) compared to the other groups. In observing the students, I noted that they were naturally inclined to rush to find a solution. It is likely that the organization tool helped students focus on the problem, increasing their problem understanding, and, in doing so, helped them to ask more questions related to the problem. On the other hand, the organization tool did not significantly help students ask more specific questions or formulate better hypotheses. One explanation for this may be that students need to go beyond a certain threshold of understanding to be able to do these tasks. For example, in the first study, the students who used the organization tool asked significantly more specific questions than the other groups (Zydney, 2005). This may be because the students in the first study had higher problem understanding scores than the students in the present study.

The findings from the present study confirmed the results of previous studies that found that organization tools helped improve students' conceptual understanding (Bell, 2004; Land & Zembal-Saul, 2003; Sandoval & Reiser, 2004; Saye & Brush, 2002). These findings did not support the results from previous studies that found these tools to be ineffective (Brush & Saye, 2001; Oliver & Hannafin, 2000). This may be due to the fact the organization tool used in the present study was a required element of the software; whereas, the previous studies did not require the use of these scaffolds. This is in line with the recommendation by Ge and Land (2004) to embed the scaffolds in the application so that students are required to use them.

Higher-Order Thinking Tool

The class who used the higher-order thinking tool was a heterogeneous mix of students, ranging from some who performed well academically to others who had to overcome various learning difficulties, including a few English language learners, a handful of students classified as having learning disabilities, and a couple of students who the teacher suspected may have had behavioral disorders but were not officially classified. While generally well behaved, hardworking, and focused, there was a handful of "smart alecks" in the class who sometimes gave the teacher a hard time. This classroom was typically noisier than the class that received the organization tool. Since it often took this class a little while to settle in, there was some concern that they may have had less time on the computer than the other groups. However, analyses revealed that all classes had statistically equivalent amounts of time on the computers.

The students who received the higher-order thinking tool asked significantly more questions than the other groups. This result was also found to be true for the first study on *Pollution Solution* (Zydney, 2003). When this group was combined with the control group, the two groups together asked significantly more questions related to the solution than the groups with the organization tool. However, the students who used the higher-order thinking tool tended to ask a lower percentage of solution-oriented questions than the control group. Thus, it may not have been the higher-order thinking tool that prompted students to think more about the solution, but a natural inclination for students to rush to the end of the problem.

This finding is in line with earlier research which found "that some students jumped right to the solution process without first trying to interpret the problem" (Ge & Land, 2004, p. 11). One speculation is that it may be the lack of the organization tool that caused students to lose focus on the problem they were trying to solve, allowing them to concentrate more on the solution. However, without a strong understanding of the problem, they often chose ineffective solutions to the problem. For example, after the study ended, many students in their final presentations picked solutions that might have been effective solutions elsewhere but not for this specific situation. Many students recommended using solar energy, but it turned out that the fictitious company in *Pollution Solution* was located in one of the cloudiest cities in the United States; therefore, solar panels would not be a viable solution for this particular case.

The higher-order thinking tool was not found to influence the number of hypotheses generated by the students about possible solutions to the problem. This unexpected result may have been due to the different nature of the hypothesis-formulation and question-generation activities. The students formulated hypotheses within the context of writing their research plans, which they did over the course of several days. It is possible that the students eliminated some of their initial ideas as they did more research on the problem. On the other hand, the question-generation activity was a timed 15-minute period where students were asked to write down as many questions that they could generate. This explanation is supported by the fact that fluency did not significantly correlate with the hypothesis-formulation measures. One possibility for eliminating this discrepancy in future studies is to make the processes for generating hypotheses and questions more similar.

The findings from this present study are consistent with previous research, which found that higher-order thinking tools in the form of question prompts improved students' recognition of what information they need to learn (Ge & Land, 2003). The present research conflicted with previous studies that showed that this tool was either not used or not used effectively (Brush & Saye, 2001; Oliver & Hannafin, 2000). As mentioned previously, the tool in this present study may have been more effective than these previous studies because it was a required element of the software. However, the present research did not find that the higher-order thinking tool by itself could support the level of knowledge integration seen in previous studies (Davis, 2003; Davis & Linn, 2000). These results may have improved if a different higher-order thinking tool had been selected. For example, researchers have found that not all kinds of higher-order thinking tools are equally effective in helping students (Davis, 2003; Davis & Linn, 2000). Davis found that generically

worded prompts were more effective than prompts with more specific directions. For future studies, researchers have suggested several ways to improve the effect of the higher-order-thinking tools, including changing the wording (Davis, 2003), altering the timing/location (Davis, 2003), and providing more time to use the tool (Brush & Saye, 2001).

Combined (Organization and Higher-Order Thinking) Tools

The students who received the combined organization and higher-order thinking tools consisted of many bright students, who, although excited about the project, had difficulty focusing at times. This was a rambunctious group of students and the noise-level frequently became quite loud. These students often "called out" answers rather than being "called on" by their teacher and often had to be disciplined for their behavior, especially their lateness. The teacher mentioned that there were a number of students who were classified as having behavioral disorders. Unfortunately, the behavioral issues in this class may have contributed to why they did not do as well as originally expected.

The combined tools did not have a statistically significant effect on students' performance. This discrepancy between expected and actual results may have been caused by the fact that the students had less time for researching because they were required to use both tools. Another possible explanation is a confusion caused by the similar formats of the organization and higher-order thinking tools. In the classes that received the higher-order thinking tools, several students had difficulty discerning the difference between the status report (i.e., the higher ordering thinking tool) and the research plan (i.e., the organization tool) and asked, "Didn't we already do this activity?" Since this confusion took place early on in the study, it is possible that it caused them to not perform as well with activities in the beginning, but once this confusion dissipated, they were able to do better on some of the later tasks. It is also plausible that it takes time for students to become comfortable using multiple tools. Researchers have found that students become more proficient at using multiple tools as they become more familiar with them (Iiyoshi & Hannafin, 1998; Liu & Bera, 2005).

The results from this study raised some questions about whether combining tools will add the effects of these individual tools. This was also found to be the case in the first study on *Pollution Solution* (Zydney, 2005). However, it is difficult to determine whether this was the situation with other studies because the design of these studies was not set up to assess this question. For example, many studies used in-depth qualitative case studies to examine the use of computer-based tools (Iiyoshi & Hannafin, 1998; Land & Zembal-Saul, 2003; Oliver & Hannafin, 2000). Other studies used quantitative methods to test the effect of the combined tools, but did not isolate the effects of the individual tools (Brush & Saye, 2001; Wolf & Brush, 2000). Other researchers tested each individual tool separately but did not test these tools in combination or tested the effects of the combined tools compared to only one of the individual tools (Davis & Linn, 2000). From these designs, it is difficult to ascertain whether the combined tools were necessary or if one tool attributed to most of the students' achievement. Thus, more research is needed to answer the question of whether combining individual cognitive tools has an additive effect.

Control Group

The control group consisted of mostly strong academic students who were highly motivated and eager to learn. This class displayed a strong sense of team, had good class participation, and was extremely well behaved. The students in this class were also very attentive and focused during the project. Some were so engaged in the program that they were actually observed talking to the people in the videos as if they were physically present in the situation. This class had a few more students classified as learning disabled than the other classes and, as a result, had extra resource teachers on hand. The teacher made a special point of mentioning how well her students with learning disabilities were doing with the software. One student, in particular, who never wrote more than a paragraph, was capturing pages of research in the software. In addition to the extra resources, at one point during the study, this class asked to review material from a previous class before moving on to the next activity.

Despite this additional assistance and review, this class did not perform as well as the other classes across the various measured outcomes. These results were not unexpected because this group did not receive either the organization or higher-order thinking tool. It is important to note that this group was statistically equivalent to the other groups on the fluency test and historically performed academically as well as the other classes. The findings from this study also confirmed the results found for the control group in the first study (Zydney, 2005).

CONCLUSION

This study found that different types of cognitive tools in an SFM learning environment scaffold different aspects of defining a problem. Students who used the organization tool obtained a moderate understanding of the problem, which was significantly higher

than the control group. Moreover, students who received treatment conditions with the organization tool asked significantly more problem-oriented questions. In contrast to the organization tool group, the higher-order thinking tool group asked significantly more questions than the other groups. Students who used the combined tools did not do as well as expected. More research is needed on the effect of using multiple tools within a multimedia environment on students' performance.

Despite the limitations of this study, such as the restricted sample size, the use of intact classes, and the technical challenges faced in implementing the study, it is encouraging that many of the findings from this study confirmed the results of the first study (Zydney, 2005), which was done at a different school in a different grade with a different teacher. Although greater management would have been possible in a controlled lab setting, the complexity of an authentic classroom setting added to the richness of the data and hopefully increased the applicability of these results to other classrooms. The present study provides some evidence that similar types of tools traditionally studied in problem-solving environments can be effectively used during problem representation. It also supports the idea that CFT environments with appropriate scaffolding may be used to help students develop a conceptual understanding of problems. These results may be helpful for educators and instructional designers in selecting appropriate tools in learning environments that assist students in defining complex problems.

ACKNOWLEDGMENTS

I would like to acknowledge the invaluable contributions of my dissertation chairperson Jan L. Plass, and the thoughtful commentary and advice from my committee members W. Michael Reed and Richard C. Richardson. I greatly appreciate Francine Shuchat Shaw for her constructive feedback on the design of *Pollution Solution*. I would also like to thank Marc Scott, Robert Norman, and Arne Bathke for their statistical advice. In addition, this study would not have been possible without the contribution and involvement of Annie Chien. I am also extremely grateful for the generosity of time and expertise from Allison Godshall, Megan Roberts, and Jennifer Yamron. Finally, I greatly appreciate the students who participated in this study.

REFERENCES

Bathke, A., & Brunner, E. (2003). A nonparametric alternative to analysis of covariance. In M. G.

Akritas & D. N. Politis (Eds.), *Recent advances and trends in nonparametric statistics* (pp. 109–120). Amsterdam: Elsevier.

Bell, P. (2004). Argument construction and collaborative debate. In M. C. Linn, E. A. Davis, & P. Bell (Eds.), *Internet environments for science education* (pp. 115–143). Mahwah, NJ: Lawrence Erlbaum Associates.

Bennett, R. E., & Rock, D. A. (1995). Generalizability, validity, and examinee perceptions of a computer-delivered formulating-hypotheses test. *Journal of Educational Measurement, 32,* 19–36.

Bransford, J. D., Brown, A. L., & Cocking, R. R. (Eds.). (2000). *How people learn: Brain, mind, experience, and school.* Washington, DC: National Academy Press.

Brush, T., & Saye, J. (2001). The use of embedded scaffolds with hypermedia-supported student-centered learning. *Journal of Educational Multimedia and Hypermedia, 10,* 333–356.

Chi, M. T. H., & Glaser, R. (1985). Problem-solving ability. In R. J. Sternberg (Ed.), *Human abilities: An information-processing approach* (pp. 227–250). New York: W. H. Freeman and Company.

Chi, M. T. H., Glaser, R., & Farr, M. J. (1988). *The nature of expertise.* Hillsdale, NJ: Lawrence Erlbaum Associates.

Chin, C., Brown, D. E., & Bruce, B. C. (2002). Student-generated questions: A meaningful aspect of learning in science. *International Journal of Science Education, 24,* 521–549.

Creswell, J. W. (2003). *Research design: Qualitative, quantitative, and mixed method approaches* (2nd ed.). Thousand Oaks, CA: Sage Publications.

Czarnik, J. C., & Hickey, D. T. (1997, April). *Problem generation in the mission to Mars curriculum.* Paper presented at the annual meeting of the American Educational Research Association, Chicago, Illinois.

Davis, E. A. (2003). Prompting middle school science students for productive reflection: Generic and directed prompts. *The Journal of the Learning Sciences, 12,* 91–142.

Davis, E. A., & Linn, M. C. (2000). Scaffolding students' knowledge integration: Prompts for reflection in KIE. *International Journal of Science Education, 22,* 819–837.

Dori, Y. J., & Herscovitz, O. (1999). Question-posing capability as an alternative evaluation method: Analysis of an environmental case study. *Journal of Research in Science Teaching, 36,* 411–430.

Ekstrom, R. B., French, J. W., & Harman, H. H. (with Derman, D). (1992). *Manual for kit of factor-referenced cognitive tests 1976* (Office of Naval Research Contract N00014-71-0117). Princeton, NJ: Educational Testing Services.

Fitzgerald, G. E., Wilson B., & Semrau, L. (1997). An interactive multimedia program to enhance teacher problem-solving skills based on cognitive flexibility theory: Design and outcomes. *Journal of Educational Multimedia and Hypermedia, 6,* 47–76.

Ge, X., & Land, S. M. (2003). Scaffolding students' problem-solving processes in an ill-structured task using question prompts and peer interactions. *Educational Technology Research and Development, 51,* 21–38.

Ge, X., & Land, S. M. (2004). A conceptual framework for scaffolding ill-structured problem-solving processes using question prompts and peer interactions. *Educational Technology Research and Development, 52,* 5–22.

Hoover, S. M. (1994). Scientific problem finding in gifted fifth-grade students. *Roeper Review, 16,* 156–159. Retrieved October 10, 2002 from Academic Search Elite database.

Hoover, S. M., & Feldhusen, J. F. (1990). The scientific hypothesis formulation ability of gifted ninth-grade students. *Journal of Educational Psychology, 82,* 838–848.

Iiyoshi, T., & Hannafin, M. J. (1998, April). *Cognitive tools for open-ended learning environments: Theoretical and implementation perspectives.* Paper presented at the annual meeting of the American Educational Research Association, San Diego, California.

Jacobson, M. J., & Archodidou, A. (2000). The design of hypermedia tools for learning: Fostering conceptual change and transfer of complex scientific knowledge. *The Journal of the Learning Sciences, 9*(2), 145–199.

Jacobson, M. J., & Spiro, R. J. (1995). Hypertext learning environments, cognitive flexibility, and the transfer of complex knowledge: An empirical investigation. *Journal of Educational Computing Research, 12,* 301–333.

Johnson, R. B., & Onwuegbuzie, A. (2004). Mixed methods research: A research paradigm whose time has come. *Educational Researcher, 33*(7), 14–26.

Jonassen, D. H. (2003). Using cognitive tools to represent problems. *Journal of Research on Technology in Education, 35,* 362–382.

Jonassen, D. H., & Reeves, T. C. (1996). Learning *with* technology: Using computers as cognitive tools. In D. H. Jonassen (Ed.), *Handbook of research for educational communications and technology* (pp. 693–719). New York: Simon & Schuster Macmillan.

Keys, C. W. (1998). A study of grade six students generating questions and plans for open-ended science investigations. *Research in Science Education, 28,* 301–316.

King, A. (1991). Effects of training in strategic questioning on children's problem-solving performance. *Journal of Educational Psychology, 83,* 307–317.

Land, S. M., & Zembal-Saul, C. (2003). Scaffolding reflection and articulation of scientific explanations in a data-rich, project-based learning environment: An investigation of progress port-folio. *Educational Technology Research and Development, 51,* 65–84.

Li, T., & Jonassen, D. (1996). The effect of lesson structures on prediction and inference. *Proceedings of Selected Research and Development Presentations at the 1996 National Convention of the Association for Educational Communications and Technology, Indianapolis, Indiana, 18,* 423–429.

Liu, M., & Bera, S. (2005). An analysis of cognitive tool use patterns in hypermedia learning environment. *Educational Technology Research and Development, 53,* 5–21.

Liu, M., Bera, S., Corliss, S. B., Svinicki, M. D., & Beth, A. D. (2004). Understanding the connection between cognitive tool use and cognitive processes as used by sixth graders in a problem-based hypermedia learning environment. *Journal of Educational Computing Research, 31,* 309–334.

Merriam, S. B. (2001). *Qualitative research and case study applications in education* (2nd ed.). San Francisco, CA: Jossey-Bass.

Miyake, N., & Norman, D. A. (1979). To ask a question, one must know enough to know what is not known. *Journal of Verbal Learning and Verbal Behavior, 18,* 357–364.

Oliver, K., & Hannafin, M. J. (2000). Student management of Web-based hypermedia resources during open-ended problem solving. *The Journal of Educational Research, 94,* 75–92.

Olsher, G., & Dreyfus, A. (1999). Biotechnologies as a context for enhancing junior high-school students' ability to ask meaningful questions about abstract biological processes. *International Journal of Science Education, 21,* 137–153.

Palincsar, A. S. (1986). The role of dialogue in providing scaffolded instruction. *Educational Psychologist, 21,* 73–98.

Puntambekar, S., & Kolodner, J. L. (2005). Toward implementing distributed scaffolding: Helping students learn science from design. *Journal of Research in Science Teaching, 42,* 185–217.

Rowell. P. M., Gustafson, B. J., & Guilbert, S. M. (1999). Engineers in elementary classrooms: Perceptions of learning to solve technological problems. *Research in Science & Technological Education, 17,* 109–118. Retrieved January 25, 2001, from ProQuest database.

Sandoval, W. A., & Reiser, B. J. (2004). Explanation-driven inquiry: Integrating conceptual and epistemic scaffolds for scientific inquiry. *Science Education, 88,* 345–372.

Saye, J. W., & Brush, T. (2002). Scaffolding critical reasoning about. history and social issues in multimedia-supported learning environments. *Educational Technology Research and Development, 50,* 77–96.

Shin, N., Jonassen, D. H., & McGee, S. (2003). Predictors of well-structured and ill-structured problem solving in an astronomy simulation. *Journal of Research in Science Teaching, 40,* 6–33.

Spiro, R. J., Coulson, R. L., Feltovich, P. J., & Anderson, D. K. (1988). *Cognitive flexibility theory: Advanced knowledge acquisition in ill-structured domains* (Tech. Rep. No. 441). Champaign, IL: University of Illinois at Urbana-Champaign.

Tabachnick, B. G., & Fidell, L. S. (2001). *Using multivariate statistics* (4th ed.). Needham, MA: Allyn & Bacon.

Toth, E. E., Suthers, D. D., & Lesgold, A. M. (2002). "Mapping to know": The effects of representational guidance and reflective assessment on scientific inquiry. *Science Education, 86,* 264–286.

Voss, J. F., & Post, T. A. (1988). On the solving of ill-structured problems. In M. T. H. Chi, R. Glaser, & M. J. Farr (Eds.), *The nature of expertise* (pp. 261–285). Hillsdale, NJ: Lawrence Erlbaum Associates.

Winn, W., & Snyder, D. (1996). Cognitive perspectives in psychology. In D. H. Jonassen (Ed.), *Handbook of research for educational communications and technology* (pp. 112–142). New York: Simon & Schuster Macmillan.

Wolf, S. E., & Brush, T. (2000, October). Using the big six information skills as a metacognitive scaffold to solve information based problems. *Proceedings of Selected Research and Development Papers Presented at the National Convention of the Association for Educational Communications and Technology, Denver, Colorado,* 471–481.

Wood, D., Bruner, J. S., & Ross, G. (1976). The role of tutoring in problem solving. *Journal of Child Psychology, Psychiatry, & Applied Disciplines, 17,* 89–100.

Zydney, J. M. (2003). [The effect of different types of scaffolding in a multimedia program on students' problem finding]. Unpublished raw data.

Zydney, J. M. (2005). Eighth-grade students defining complex problems. *Journal of Educational Multimedia and Hypermedia, 14,* 61–90.

4.06

CORRELATIONAL DESIGN

Schizophrenia and the Motivation for Smoking

Cheryl Forchuk, PhD, RN, Ross Norman, PhD, Ashok Malla, MBBS, MRC Psych, FRCP(C), DPM, Mary-Lou Martin, PhD(C), RN, Terry McLean, MA,RN, Stephen Cheng, BA, RN, Kristine Diaz, MEd, RN, Elizabeth McIntosh, BA, RN, Ann Rickwood, BA, RN, CPMH(C), Sandra Vos, MscN, RN, and Cynthia Gibney, MscN, RN

PROBLEM: People with mental illness are twice as likely to smoke than people without a mental illness.

METHODS: Data were collected through interviews with individuals who smoke and have been diagnosed with schizophrenia (N = 100). The research design included a descriptive, correlational design that described and examined the relationships among psychiatric symptoms, medication side effects, and reasons for smoking; and a qualitative analysis of the subjective experience of smoking.

FINDINGS: A positive relationship was found between the age of onset of smoking and the onset of schizophrenia. Subjects reported they smoked primarily for sedative effects and control of negative symptoms of schizophrenia. Subjects also reported smoking related to addiction. Most indicated they would like to quit smoking or at least cut down on the number of cigarettes.

CONCLUSIONS: Among people with schizophrenia, the motivation to smoke is related to their schizophrenia.

SEARCH TERMS: Motivation, qualitative research, quantitative research, schizophrenia, smoking.

Cheryl Forchuk, PhD, RN, is Associate Professor, University of Western Ontario, and Scientist, Lawson Health Science Research Centre, London, ON. Ross Norman, PhD, is a Psychologist, Program for Early Prevention of Psychosis (PEPP), London Health Sciences Centre, London, ON. Ashok Malla, MBBS, MRC Psych, FRCP(C), DPM, is a Psychiatrist/Professor, Department of Psychiatry, London Health Sciences Centre/University of Western Ontario, London, ON. Mary-Lou Martin, PhD(C), RN, is a Clinical Nurse Specialist/Associate Professor, St. Joseph's Mountain Health Care, McMaster University, Hamilton, ON. Terry McClean, MA, RN, is a Clinical Leader, PEPP. Stephen Cheng, BA, RN, is a Mental Health Therapist, Urgent Consultation Services, London Health Sciences Centre. Kristine Diaz, MEd, RN, is Program Manager, London Mental Health Crisis Service, London, ON. Elizabeth Mcintosh, BA, RN', is Nurse Case Manager, PEPP. Ann Rickwood, BA, RN, CPMH(C), is Case Manager, School Health Services, Community Care Access Centre, St. Thomas, ON. Sandra Vos, MscN, RN, is Interim Director, Housing and Mental Health: Community University Research Alliance, London, ON. Cynthia Gibney, MscN, RN, is Coordinator of Medical Services, Canadian Blood Services, London, ON, Canada.

Lasser et al. (2000) found in a nationally representative U.S. sample that individuals with a mental illness are approximately twice as likely to smoke than are people without a mental illness. Individuals with schizophrenia tend to smoke. Studies over two decades have consistently found that between 74% and 90% of those with schizophrenia smoke (Benowitz, 1999; de Leon, 1996; Glynn & Sussman, 1990; Goff, Henderson, & Amico, 1992; Hughes, Hatsukami, Mitchell, & Dahlgren, 1986; Kramer, 2000; O'Farrell, Connors, & Upper, 1984). Smoking rates of individuals with schizophrenia are higher than for the general public (Glassman, 1993; Lasser et al.; Lyon, 1999), and higher than for other individuals with psychiatric problems (de Leon; Lyon), Although there has been some speculation about why this is so, very little is understood from the perspective of the person with schizophrenia who smokes. Understanding the issue of motivation is critical to assisting these people to quit smoking. De Leon reported that individuals with schizophrenia had great difficulty in quitting smoking, and only 8% were successful compared with 45% of the general U.S. population. The high incidence of smoking and difficulty in quitting smoking places a vulnerable population at high risk for other physical problems.

Smoking as a Health Concern

The single most important cause of cancer is smoking (Austoker, Sanders, & Fowler, 1994). Lung cancer alone remains the leading cause of cancer deaths (Statistics Canada, 2001).

A much higher risk of cancer is associated with smoking cigarettes than with other forms of tobacco. Risk of developing lung cancer is associated, with duration of smoking and number of cigarettes smoked. Therefore, the more cigarettes smoked over a longer period of time, the higher the risk an individual faces for developing lung cancer. Individuals who smoke 10 cigarettes a day reduce their life expectancy by an average of 2 to 3 years. Individuals who smoke 20 cigarettes a day reduce their life expectancy by 5 to 7 years, and those choosing to smoke 40 cigarettes a day are reducing their life expectancy by 8 to 10 years. Risk of cancer can be reduced by quitting smoking. After 10 years, a person who quit smoking may be at the same risk for cancer as someone who is a lifelong nonsmoker (Austoker et al., 1994).

Smoking and Schizophrenia

Previous authors have suggested that the reason for the high prevalence of smoking among people diagnosed with schizophrenia is that there may be unique motivators for smoking (Benowitz, 1999; Desai, Seabolt, & Jann, 2001; Farnam, 1999; Forchuk, Norman, Malla,

Vos, & Martin, 1997; Glassman, 1993; Lohr & Flynn, 1992; McEvoy & Brown, 1999). Lohr and Flynn conducted a literature review related to schizophrenia and smoking. They concluded that psychological aspects of smoking in schizophrenia may lead to an increased rate of smoking. These psychological effects included the use of tobacco as a stimulant, a coping mechanism to deal with stress, an aid to concentration, and a facilitator of relaxation. In a later review of the literature, Forchuk and colleagues suggested that the possible effect of nicotine on positive and negative symptoms of schizophrenia, and the potential of nicotine reducing the side effects of antipsychotic medication, may explain the high prevalence rate.

There is some evidence to suggest there may be a biological motivation to smoke related to symptom reduction. Dalack, Healy, and Meador-Woodruff (1998) found that nicotine may mediate some symptoms of schizophrenia. Symptoms of schizophrenia are typically classified as positive (e.g., hallucinations, delusions) and negative (e.g., lack of energy, lack of motivation). The positive symptoms tend to be more responsive than the negative symptoms to medication. Therefore, relief from negative symptoms may be a powerful motivation for smoking. The pathophysiology of negative symptoms remains uncertain. It is hypothesized, however, that negative symptoms are related to reduced activity in the prefrontal cortex. This hypofrontality may be related to increased dopamine activity in nigrostriatal and mesolimbic systems (DeLisi et al., 1985; Weinberger, Berman, & Illowsky, 1988). Correlational human and, animal studies have suggested that nicotine promotes the release of dopamine, especially from the dopamine terminals in the striatum (Dalack et al.) or possibly the mesolimbic system (Benowitz, 1999). This release of dopamine could, theoretically, reduce the negative symptoms.

Desai et al. (2001), in a review of current literature, found that pharmacokinetic and pharmacodynamic properties of many commonly used psychotropic drugs are affected by smoking, suggesting a biological basis for a possible role of nicotine in influencing drug metabolism and reducing side effects of antipsychotic medications. Nicotine may reduce the bioavailability of the medication and therefore reduce effectiveness as well as side effects (Desai et al.; Farnam, 1999). Nicotine also may reduce side effects through modulation of dopamine activity. To support these findings, there is some evidence linking smoking to a reduction in parkinsonian tremors related to use of neuroleptics, and there is also a reduced incidence of Parkinson's disease among smokers (Gorell, Rybicki, Johnson, & Peterson, 1999).

Despite these speculations about unique motivation, only two studies were found that directly asked clients with schizophrenia why they smoked. In a sample of 36 outpatients diagnosed with a serious mental illness, Van Dongen (1999) found the major motivators were habit and routine (58%), socialization (58%), relaxation (42%), and addiction (33%). Similarly, in a study of 59 individuals diagnosed with schizophrenia, Glynn and Sussman (1990) reported motivators as relaxation (80%), habit (67%), and to settle nerves (52%). No studies were found that directly tested the hypotheses regarding unique motivation by asking specific questions related to effect on schizophrenic symptoms or medication side effects.

In summary, the literature on smoking and schizophrenia suggests little is known about why so many people with schizophrenia smoke. The role of dopamine in both schizophrenia and nicotine use suggests there may be biological connections, but the literature remains speculative.

General Motivation for Smoking

Many studies have examined reasons for smoking (e.g., Best & Hakstian, 1978; Ikard, Green, & Horn, 1969; Leventhal & Avis, 1976; Russell, Petro, & Patel, 1974; Tate, Pomerleau, & Pomerleau, 1994; Tomkins, 1966; Van Dongen, 1999). The instruments used have varied in the specific questions asked, the underlying model of smoking used to generate the measures, and whether the measures focus on situations in which smoking occurs or on the results of smoking. Despite these differences, a remarkable degree of consistency in the principal reasons for smoking has emerged from multivaried analyses of responses in these studies (e.g., Tate, Schmitz, & Stanton, 1991). The labels given as the primary reasons for smoking vary, but the underlying themes are common. Tate et al. (1994) suggest a terminology to understand smoking motivation: (a) automatic and habit; (b) sedative and anxiety reduction; (c) addictive and to reduce craving; (d) stimulation to increase level of alertness and/or energy; (e) sociability to facilitate getting on with people in social situations; (f) indulgence, sometimes referred to as pleasure, relaxation, or taste factor; and (g) sensorimotor manipulation and the pleasure associated with the handling of a tobacco product.

The importance of assessing these separate dimensions of motives for smoking is supported not just by the consistency with which they emerge from factor analytic studies, but also by studies showing that smokers who differ in the reasons they describe for their smoking behavior also show differences in their response to relevant experimental manipulations (Leventhal & Avis, 1976; Ikard & Tomkins, 1973). It usually is assumed that at least some of the reasons for smoking are mediated by the pharmacological effects of smoking, particularly those related to nicotine (Benowitz, 1999; Dalack et al., 1998; Desai et al., 2001; Farnam, 1999). Higher-order factor analysis suggests

there may well be two basic dimensions underlying the above list of motives, which correspond to a distinction between pharmacological and nonpharmacological reasons for smoking (Russell et al., 1974; Tate et al., 1994). The pharmacological dimension appears likely to include the automatic, addiction, stimulation, and sedation motives; and the nonpharmacological dimension includes sociability, indulgence, and sensorimotor manipulation. Additional studies support the construct validity of this distinction between the pharmacological and nonpharmacological dimensions of smoking motivation (Niavra, Goldstein, Ward, & Abrams, 1989; Russell et al.; Tate et al; West, Hajek, & Belcher, 1986; West & Russell, 1985), although there is evidence from some of these studies that the indulgence motive may involve a pharmacological mediator.

Study Hypothesis and Objectives

It was hypothesized that individuals with schizophrenia would be motivated to smoke for relief of psychiatric symptoms and to relieve antipsychotic medication side effects.

The research objectives included;

- To identify and describe issues related to starting smoking, including when smoking was initiated, and the relationship to the development of schizophrenia
- To identify and describe issues related to smoking maintenance, including perceived effects of smoking, and the perceived relationship of smoking behavior to medication side effects, and symptoms of schizophrenia
- To identify and describe issues related to smoking cessation.

METHODS

Research Design

The research design included two components to examine smoking and schizophrenia: (a) a descriptive, correlational design that described and examined the relationships between psychiatric symptoms, medication side effects, and reasons for smoking; and (b) a content analysis of open-ended questions related to the subjective experience of smoking.

Data were collected through a single interview with individuals who have been diagnosed with schizophrenia for a minimum of 1 year and who smoke.

Instruments

Motivation for Smoking

To assess motives for smoking, the motivators identified earlier by Tate et al. (1994) were adopted, and three additional motivators were added. These motivators included control of positive symptoms of schizophrenia, control of negative symptoms of schizophrenia, and control of side effects of antipsychotic medication. Each motivator corresponded to three items on the questionnaire. The additional motivators were further responded to by rating amount of symptom change on a 4-point scale (1 = little symptom change to 4 = a severe symptom change).

A search of the literature reveals no questions that have been used to identify motives for smoking based on their influence on symptoms of schizophrenia or side effects of medications. Investigators in this application have been involved in extensive research concerning the measurement of symptomatology related to schizophrenia and movement problems associated with schizophrenia and its treatment (Malla, Norman, Aguilar, Carnahan, & Cortese, 1995; Malla, Norman, Williamson, Cortese, & Diaz, 1993; Norman & Malla, 1991, 1994). We developed an additional nine questions designed to assess the possibility that participants smoke because of the impact of smoking on positive symptoms, negative symptoms, or side effects of medication.

Severity of Illness

Severity of Illness was measured with the Positive and Negative Syndrome Scale (PANSS) (Kay, Fiszbein, & Opler, 1987; Kay, Opler, & Lindenmayer, 1988, 1989). The scale contains 30 items, each with a 7-point severity scale. It contains scores for positive syndrome, negative syndrome, and general psychopathology. Interrater consistency within one rating point varies between 69% and 94% among the various subscales and a Pearson r of .84 across raters for the composite index (Kay et al., 1988). Interclass correlations ranged between .54 and .93 (Bell, Millstone, Beam-Goblet, Lysaker, & Cicchetti, 1992). For this study, the Cronbach's alphas were .84 for the positive syndrome scale, .87 for the negative syndrome scale, and .84 for the general psychopathology scale.

Demographic Information

Demographic data related to general information such as age, gender, and socioeconomic status. Questions related to schizophrenia also were asked, such as age of onset of illness, first hospital admission, length of most recent hospital admission, and medication history (Table 1). Questions related to smoking included age at initiation of smoking and current number of cigarettes smoked.

Open-ended Questions

Open-ended questions were asked related to perceived benefits and drawbacks of smoking, motivation for smoking, and thoughts on quitting smoking.

Procedure

Participants were selected randomly by staff members at the various study settings. After informed consent was obtained, the interviewer and participant agreed on a meeting place. Participants received an honorarium of $5 for their participation. The interview took approximately 1 hour. All data were collected through interview format, which included the questionnaires and open-ended questions.

Setting and Participants

One hundred participants from Southern Ontario, Canada, were interviewed for this study. Half of the participants were from acute care psychiatric (general hospital) settings, while the other half was from tertiary care (provincial hospital) psychiatric settings. Participants included both inpatients and clients in the community. Participants were 72% male and 28% female. The average length of exposure to antipsychotic and anticholinergics was 10.7 years (SD = 9.73) and ranged from 0 to 45 years. At the time of the interview, 96.8% of participants were taking antipsychotic medication, and 37.6% were taking antiparkinson medication. The employment status of participants diagnosed with schizophrenia is shown in Table 2. The table includes data of 83 of the participants who reported their employment status.

Smoking Behavior

Participants smoked 4 to 60 cigarettes per day, with a mean of 23.3 and standard deviation of 10 cigarettes. The average age participants started smoking was 17.48, with a standard deviation of 7.24. Participants averaged 18.77 years of smoking. A moderate relationship ($r = .26$, $p < .05$) existed between the

Table 1. Demographic Profile of Participants Diagnosed With Schizophrenia

	Range	M	SD
Age (years)	17–65	36.2	10.9
Onset of psychiatric illness (years)	0–44	14.7	10.0
Time since diagnosis (years)	0–44	12.3	9.6
Previous hospitalization (years)	0–30	3.7	6.2
Length of 1st admission (years)	0–21	.69	2.8
Total # of psychiatric admissions	0–45	7.6	8.9
Average length of exposure to antipsychotic and anticholinergics	0–45	10.7	9.7

Table 2. Employment Status of Participants Diagnosed With Schizophrenia (*n* = 83)

	Male		Female	
	Number	%	Number	%
Unemployed	27	75	9	25
Public assistance	19	76	6	24
Part-time employment	5	100		0
Full-time employment	5	56	4	44
Volunteers	1	20	4	80
Students	3	100		0
Total	60		23	

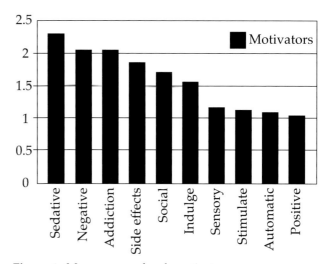

Figure 1. Mean scores of each motivator.

age participants started smoking and the onset of schizophrenic symptoms.

FINDINGS

Participants' responses, summarized in Figure 1, illustrate that participants reported their strongest motivations to be relief from negative symptoms and medication side effects. The strongest motivators were:

- Sedative effect (*M* = 2.32, *SD* = .87)
- Control of negative symptoms (*M* = 2.10, *SD* = 1.05)
- Addiction (*M* = 2.09, *SD* = 1.00)
- Control of side effects (*M* = 1.85, *SD* = .92)

These results indicate the motivators specific to schizophrenia are important to the participants.

PANSS Scores

The PANSS was used to determine severity of illness. Subjects were scored by the interviewer on positive syndrome, negative syndrome, and general psychopathology subscales of the PANSS. Means and standard deviations by subscale are summarized in Table 3.

Correlations Regarding Motivation for Smoking and Demographic Data

The greater total length of time spent in hospital was related to a greater likelihood of smoking due to addiction (*r* = .22, *p* < .05). As well, the younger the

age of onset of smoking was related to smoking as an automatic behavior (*r* = .27, *p* < .01) and control of positive symptoms (*r* = .21, *p* < .05).

Correlations With Symptom Severity and Demographic Data

Symptom severity was not related to the age of onset of psychiatric illness or the age when subjects started smoking. Greater symptom severity, however, was related to length of illness, total length of time spent in hospital, total number of admissions to hospital, and age.

Correlations With Symptom Severity and Motivation

Both addiction (*r* = .30, *p* < .01) and automatic behavior (*r* = .33, *p* < .01) motives were positively related to higher severity of positive symptom scores. In addition, addiction (*r* = .22, *p* < .05), automatic behavior (*r* = .31, *p* < .01), and increased sociability (*r* = .22, *p* < .05) motives were positively related to greater general psychopathy.

Qualitative Questions

When participants were asked what else was happening in their lives at the time they began smoking, 49.4% reported stressors at home or school, whereas

Table 3. Scores by Subscale on the PANSS

	Possible Range of Scores on Scale	Actual Minimum	Actual Minimum	*M*	*SD*
Positive syndrome subscale	7–49	7	35	17.10	7.38
Negative syndrome subscale	7–49	7	38	19.43	8.06
General psychopathology scale	16–112	16	68	36.54	11.46

37.9% reported remembering nothing notable was happening. However, 11.5% of participants indicated the start of their illness occurring when they started smoking.

When the participants were asked why they think they started smoking, 41.5% stated because their friends smoked and 25.6% indicated to look older. Also, 20.7% of the participants reported they started smoking because it was something to do, while 17% stated it helped them relax. When participants were asked why they thought they smoke now, 41% said because they are addicted. Other reasons given were to help them relax (20%), because of enjoyment (15%), to pass the time (12%), and that smoking is a crutch (8%).

When participants were asked what they thought the benefits of smoking were, 50.5% indicated that smoking relaxes them. However, 36.8% stated there are no benefits accrued from smoking. Another 8.4% stated that smoking was beneficial to pass the time, and 4.2% stated they smoked for the enjoyment.

When participants were asked if they would like to quit smoking, 40% indicated they did want to quit, while 12% stated they "wanted to quit," but then qualified the response in some way, such as they do not want to quit immediately. Another 6% of reported "No," they did not want to quit, and an additional 6% stated "No," but qualified the response. Furthermore, 33% of the participants indicated they did not want to quit but would like to cut down, and 3% could not answer.

Participants were asked for suggestions about what they think should be included in a program to help others quit, and 25.3% reported they would include distractions, walks, and other diversions. Another 16% indicated they would include group meetings, 9.3% indicated they would make food and drink available, and 13.3% recommended a combination of the above suggestions as being helpful for a program to help others quit smoking. Other suggestions included things such as going cold turkey (1.3%), reducing the number of cigarettes (2.7%), scaring people with statistics, (5.3%), staying away from people who smoke (1.3%), emphasizing self-esteem (1.3%), hypnotism (1.3%), supplying nicotine gum (5.7%), treating schizophrenia first (1.3%), and charting smoking patterns (1.3%).

DISCUSSION

In general, tobacco use poses a significant health risk. This risk is greater in the schizophrenic population, which has a much higher smoking rate than the general public. Each year, tobacco causes 3.5 million deaths worldwide (World Health Organization [WHO], 1999). By the year 2030 the number is expected to rise to 10 million annually (Jha & Chaloupka, 2000). Successful long-term cessation rates will depend on the implementation of educational programs and supportive resources for smokers who want to quit (WHO). Findings from this study provide insight into reasons why individuals with schizophrenia begin and continue to smoke throughout their adult lives. Nurses need to be aware of the unique motivation for smoking for this population in order to implement appropriate cessation programs. Suggestions from participants could be used to create meaningful smoking cessation programs for the schizophrenic population.

This study has provided a beginning understanding of the relationship between smoking and schizophrenia. A relationship was found between the age of onset of smoking and the onset of schizophrenia. Participants reported that they smoked primarily for the sedative effects and the control of negative symptoms. In the qualitative component of the study, participants reported smoking due to addiction. Although there are only two similar studies reported in the literature, the findings are consistent. Van Dongen (1999) reported the following themes in the subjects' responses: habit and routine, socialization, relaxation, and addiction. Glynn and Sussman (1990) reported relaxation, habit, and to settle nerves as reasons for smoking.

Many of the participants in this study indicated they would like to quit smoking, or at least cut down on their number of cigarettes. This is consistent with Glynn and Sussman (1990). The 59 participants in that study also described reasons they wanted to quit smoking, such as health concerns (47%), dislike of addiction (39%), and desire to save money (37%). Participants in the current study were able to make concrete suggestions for smoking-cessation programs when asked for their input. It is interesting that the most common suggested strategy was use of distraction. This is quite different from alternate relaxation techniques that are the focus of many available smoking-cessation programs.

Advanced clinical nurses, must consider the effect nicotine has on their patients while counseling them to quit smoking. Traditional activities (e.g., increasing relaxation techniques, removing rituals associated with cigarettes, or partaking in expensive alternative therapies) may not be feasible for this population. Because smoking increases energy levels and decreases feelings of depression, stimulation, such as exercise and distraction, needs to replace the perceived benefits of smoking. Other strategies to deal with feelings of depression also must be planned. Counseling, support, and careful assessment of tobacco replacement products are interventions particularly important to the psychiatric population.

Careful monitoring of medication is essential in patients who are hospitalized for stabilization. If there are restrictive smoking policies in place, the sudden drop in number of cigarettes smoked will increase the bioavailability of their medications, which may not reflect their usual situation. Education becomes important to help patients understand the interrelationship between nicotine and antipsychotics, such as clozapine (Coombs & Advokat, 2000) or haloperidol (Farnam, 1999).

CONCLUSION

This study provides support for the hypothesis that the reason so many people with schizophrenia smoke is related to the effects, of smoking on their illness experience. Participants reported that smoking assists with the negative effects of schizophrenia, as well as reducing medication side effects. Nurses working with clients who have schizophrenia and who smoke need to be aware of the interrelationships of these two issues.

ACKNOWLEDGMENTS

Department of Psychiatry, Faculty of Medicine, University of Western Ontario, Seed Fund.

REFERENCES

Austoker, J., Sanders, D., & Fowler, G. (1994). Cancer prevention in primary care: Smoking and cancer Smoking cessation. *British Medical Journal, 308,* 1478–1482.

Bell, M., Millstone, R., Beam-Goblet, J., Lysaker, P., & Cicchetti, D. (1992). The positive and negative syndrome scale and the brief psychiatric rating scale *Journal of Nervous Mental Disability, 180,* 723–728.

Benowitz, N.L. (1999). Tobacco use and cessation. *Primary Care: Clinics in Office Practice, 26,* 611–631.

Best, A.J., & Hakstian, A.R. (1978). A situation specific model for smoking behavior. *Addictive Behaviours, 3,* 79–92.

Coombs, D.R., & Advokat, C. (2000). Antipsychotic medication and smoking prevalence in acutely hospitalized patients with chronic schizophrenia. *Schizophrenia Research, 46,* 129–137.

Dalack, G.W., Healy, D.J., & Meador-Woodruff, J.H. (1998). Nicotine dependence in schizophrenia: Clinical phenomena and laboratory findings. *American Journal of Psychiatry, 155,* 1490–1501.

de Leon, J. (1996). Smoking and vulnerability for schizophrenia. *Schizophrenia Bulletin, 22,* 405–409.

DeLisi, L.F., Buchsbaum, M.S., Holcomb, H.H., Dowling-Zimmerman, S., Pickar, D., Boronow, J., Morhisa, J.M., vanKammen, D.P., Carpenter, W.,

Kessler, R., & Cohen, R.M. (1985). Clinical correlates of decreased anterioposteria-metabolic gradients in position emission tomography (PET) of schizophrenic patients. *American Journal of Psychiatry, 142,* 78–81.

Desai, H.D., Seabolt, J., & Jann, M.W. (2001). Smoking in patients receiving psychotropic medications. *CNS Drugs, 15,* 469–494.

Farnam, C.R. (1999). Zyban: A new aid to smoking cessation treatment—Will it work for psychiatric patients? *Journal of Psychosocial Nursing and Mental Health Services, 37*(2), 36–44.

Forchuk, C., Norman, R, Malla, A., Vos, S., & Martín, M.-L. (1997). Smoking and schizophrenia. *Journal of Psychiatric and Mental Health, 78,* 95–97.

Glassman, A.H. (1993). Cigarette smoking: Implications for psychiatric illness. *American Journal of Psychiatry, 150,* 546–553.

Glynn, S., & Sussman, S. (1990). Why patients smoke. *Hospital and Community Psychiatry, 41,* 1027–1028.

Goff, D.G., Henderson, D.C., & Amico E. (1992). Cigarette smoking in schizophrenia: Relationship to psychopathology and medication side effects. *American Journal of Psychiatry, 149,* 1189–1194.

Gorell, J.M., Rybicki, B.A., Johnson, C.C., & Peterson, E.L. (1999). Smoking and Parkinson's disease: A dose-response relationship. *Neurology, 52,* 115–119.

Hughes, J., Hatsukami, D., Mitchell, J., & Dahlgren, L. (1986). Prevalence of smoking among psychiatric outpatients. *American Journal of Psychiatry, 143,* 993–997.

Ikard, F.F., Green, D.E., & Horn, D. (1969). A scale used to differentiate between types of smoking as related to management of affect *international Journal of the Addictions, 4,* 629–639.

Ikard, F.F., & Tomkins, S. (1973). The experience of affect as a determinant of smoking behavior: A series of validity studies. *Journal of Abnormal Psychology, 81,* 172–181.

Jha, P., & Chaloupka, F. (2000). The economics of global tobacco control. *British Medical Journal, 321,* 358–361.

Kay, S.R., Fiszbein, A., & Opler, L.A. (1987). The positive and negative syndrome scale (PANSS) for schizophrenia. *Schizophrenia Bulletin, 13,* 261–276.

Kay, S.R, Opler, L.A., & Lindenmayer, J.P. (1988). Reliability and validity of the positive and negative syndrome scale for schizophrenics. *Psychiatry Research, 23*(1), 99–110.

Kay, S.R., Opler, L.A., & Lindenmayer, J.P. (1989). The positive and negative syndrome scale (PANSS): Rationale and standardization. *British Journal of Psychiatry, 7*(Suppl.), 59–67.

Kramer, T. (2000, July 13). *Psychiatric comorbidity in smokers: Epidemiologic aspects.* XXIInd Congress of the Collegium Internationale Neuro-Psychopharmacologicum, Brussels.

Lasser, K., Boyd, J.W., Woodhandler, S., Himmelstein, D.U., Mc-Cormick, D., & Bor, D.H. (2000). Smoking and mental illness. A population-based prevalence study. *JAMA, 284*, 2606–2610.

Leventhal, H., & Avis, N. (1976). Pleasure, addiction and habit: Factors in verbal report oh factors in smoking behaviour. *Journal of Abnormal Behaviour, 85*, 478–488

Lohr, J.B., & Flynn, K. (1992). Smoking and schizophrenia. *Schizophrenia Resource, 8*(2), 93–102.

Lyon, E.R. (1999). A review of the effects of nicotine on schizophrenia antipsychotic medication. *Psychiatric Services, 50*, 1346–1350.

Malla, A., Norman, R., Aguilar, O., Carnahan, H., & Cortese, L. (1995). Relationship between movement planning and psychopathology profiles in schizophrenia. *British Journal of Psychiatry, 167*, 211–215.

Malla, A., Norman, R., Williamson, P., Cortese, L., & Diaz, F. (1993). Interrelationships between symptoms in schizophrenia. *Schizophrenia Research, 10*, 143–150.

McEvoy, J.P., & Brown, S. (1999). Smoking in first episode patients with schizophrenia. *American Journal of Psychiatry, 156*, 1120A–1121A.

Niavra, R, Goldstein, M.G., Ward, KD., & Abrams, D.B. (1989). Reasons for smoking and severity of residual nicotine withdrawal symptoms when using nicotine chewing gum. *British Journal of Addiction, 84*, 681–687.

Norman, R., & Malla, A. (1991). Dysphoric mood and symptomatology in schizophrenia. *Psychological Medicine, 21*, 897–903.

Norman, R., & Malla, A. (1994). Correlations over time between dysphoric mood and symptomatology in individuals with schizophrenia. *Comprehensive Psychiatry, 35*, 34–38.

O'Farrell, T., Connors, G., & Upper, D. (1984). Addictive behaviors among hospitalized psychiatric patients. *Addictive Behaviors, 8*, 329–333.

Russell, M.A., Petro, J., & Patel, V.A. (1974). The classification of smoking by factorial structure of motives. *Journal of the Royal Statistical Society, 137*, 313–342.

Statistics Canada. (2001). *Lifetime probability of developing and dying from cancer.* Retrieved January 18, 2002, from www.statcan.ca/english/Pgdb/People/Health/health25a.htm

Tate, J., Pomerleau, C.S., & Pomerleau, O.F. (1994). Pharmacological and non-pharmacological smoking motives: A replication and extension. *Addiction, 89*, 321–330.

Tate, J.C., Schmitz, J.M., & Stanton, A.L. (1991). A critical review of the reasons for smoking scale. *Journal of Substance Abuse, 3*, 441–455.

Tomkins, S.S. (1966). Psychological model for smoking behaviour. *American Journal of Public Health, 56*(Suppl. 2), 17–20.

Van Dongen, C.J. (1999). Smoking and persistent mental illness. *Journal of Psychosocial Nursing and Mental Health Illness, 37*(11), 26–34.

Weinberger, D.R., Berman, K.F., & Illowsky, B.P. (1988). Physiological dysfunction of dorsolateral prefrontal cortex in schizophrenia: III—A new cohort and evidence for a monoaminergic mechanism. *Archives of General Psychiatry, 45*, 609–615.

West, R.J., Hajek, P., & Belcher, M. (1986). Which smokers report most relief from craving when using nicotine chewing gum? *Psychopharmacology, 89*, 189–191.

West, R.J., & Russell, M.A.H. (1985). Preabstinence smoke intake and smoking motivation as predictors of severity of cigarette withdrawal symptoms. *Psychopharmacology, 87*, 334–336.

World Health Organization. (1999). *Leave the pack behind.* Geneva: Author.

4.07

FOLLOW-UP EXPLANATIONS DESIGN

The Effects of Pacing on the Academic Testing Performance of College Students with ADHD: A Mixed Methods Study

Kathryn S. Lee,* Randall E. Osborne,* Keith A. Hayes,* and Richard A. Simoes*

ABSTRACT: Minimal research has been conducted contrasting the effectiveness of various testing accommodations for college students diagnosed with ADHD. The current assumption is that these students are best served by extending the time they have to take a test. It is the supposition of these investigators that paced item presentation may be a more beneficial accommodation than extended time. To test the effects of paced item presentation, the investigators designed a mixed methods sequential explanatory study to explore the relationship between computer-paced and student-paced item presentation on the academic test performance in college students diagnosed with ADHD. The participants were randomly assigned to 1 of 2 testing conditions. Half of the participants were provided a computer-paced testing condition, and half were provided a student-paced testing condition within a computer-based environment. Interviews were conducted after the test administration to discern the students' perceptions of the value of the various components of the testing environment. No significant differences were found in performance scores between the students tested under the two conditions; however, the interview data illuminated the quantitative findings in that the students reported that the computer-based testing environment itself, as well as other environmental variables, provided a beneficial structure and format conducive to their overall successful performance under both accommodations. The practicability of university disability offices offering a computerized format for students diagnosed with ADHD is also discussed.

INTRODUCTION

Attention-Deficit/Hyperactivity Disorder (ADHD) is not outgrown during adolescence as was once thought (DuPaul, Guevermont, & Barkley, 1991). It is

*Texas State University–San Marcos

considered a valid adult disorder (Kessler, Adler, Barkley, Biederman, Connors, Demler, et al., 2006), and approximately 2% to 4% of college students are affected by it (Weyandt & DuPaul, 2006). Studies examining the academic performance of college students diagnosed with ADHD show that these individuals typically earn lower grade point averages, are on academic probationary status more often, report more academic problems, and have greater difficulty managing time and conforming to schedules than their non-ADHD peers (DuPaul & Weyandt, 2006; Heiligenstein, Guenther, Levy, Savino, & Fulwiler, 1999).

Dowrick, Anderson, Heyer, and Acosta (2005) powerfully present the rationale for the providing educational support for adults with disabilities in the United States:

> Postsecondary education is becoming increasingly important in obtaining quality employment for people with disabilities. Significant relationships exist between disability, level of education, and employment outcomes. While employment rates for people with disabilities have a dramatically positive correlation with educational level, their postsecondary enrollment remains low in comparison to the general population. Individuals with disabilities in postsecondary education enroll in postsecondary education at a rate that is 50% lower than their non-disabled counterparts. Furthermore, only 12% of individuals with disabilities graduate from college as opposed to 23% of their non-disabled counterparts. For full participation in society, people with disabilities need increased levels of participation and completion in postsecondary education programs (p. 41).

Literature addressing the legal and educational contexts of accommodating students with disabilities is abundant. The reauthorization of the Individuals with Disabilities Education Act in 1997 and the passage of the No Child Left Behind Act in 2002 emphasizing the inclusion and accountability of students with disabilities in high stakes testing have spurred increased emphasis in this area (Elliott, McKevitt, & Kettler, 2002; Fuchs, Fuchs, & Capizzi, 2005; Niebling & Elliott, 2005).

There "is a glaring need to expand the types of strategies to enhance academic performance among students with ADHD" (DuPaul & Eckert, 1998, p. 79). Although few studies have targeted the performance of secondary school students (DuPaul & Eckert, 1998) and college students (Tindal & Fuchs, 2000; Wallace, Winsler, & NeSmith, 1999), several studies have examined other types of academic interventions to assist college students with ADHD. Various investigators have examined the effectiveness of course-specific strategy training, training in learning strategies and self-advocacy skills, coaching, and peer tutoring, to name a few (Allsopp, Minskoff, & Bolt, 2005; Getzel, McManus, & Briel, 2004; Quinn, Ratey, & Maitland, 2000; Swartz, Prevatt, & Proctor, 2005; Zwart & Kallemeyn, 2001). Students with disabilities are routinely counseled to advocate for themselves and take advantage of educational services provided by university disability offices (Dowrick et al., 2005).

The most consistent educational service to be offered for persons with disabilities in post-secondary education is testing accommodations (Tagayuna, Stodden, Chang, Zeleznik, & Whelley, 2005). Although the most frequent testing accommodations provided by disability services in university settings are extended time for tests and the ability to take exams in minimal disturbance testing rooms away from peers (Farrell, 2003; Lancaster, Mellard, & Hoffman, 2001), few studies examining these routine accommodations have been conducted, particularly with college students diagnosed with ADHD. In order to situate this study within the existing literature, this review will focus primarily on research investigating:

a. the routine postsecondary testing accommodation of extended time;
b. paced item presentation; and
c. computer-based presentation.

Extended Time

Studies exploring an extended time accommodation for college students with learning disabilities have inconsistent findings. For example, Alster (1997) found no significant difference in algebra test scores between college students with learning disabilities in an extended time condition and students without learning disabilities in both timed and extended-time conditions. Medina (2000) found that although extended time benefited all participants in the study, extended time did not benefit college students with learning disabilities as compared to their non-disabled peers. Zuriff (2000) also found that although extended time benefited both learning disabled and non-disabled college students, the analysis of the five studies examined did not support the theory that only students with learning disabilities benefit from extended time. In contrast, Weaver (2000) found that postsecondary students with disabilities made significantly higher gains on their reading test in an extended time condition as compared to students without learning disabilities.

Extended testing time may not be sufficient to "level the playing field" for this population (Wallace et al., 1999). In fact, some college students with ADHD report that extended testing time may actually hinder their performance and "that the pressure to finish the test quickly is what gives them the stimulation they need to focus" (Farrell, 2003, p. 51). It is our hypothesis that providing a paced item presentation of the test will enhance the testing performance of this population by regulating their attention as they respond to test items at a specified rate. The computer served as the tool for providing our participants a paced item presentation.

Paced Item Presentation

Few studies have addressed paced item presentation as a testing accommodation for students with disabilities (Thompson, Blount, & Thurlow, 2002; Tindal & Fuchs, 2000) and those that have vary widely in the type of technology used as well as the method of pacing. In one study focusing on projected methods of test administration, Curtis and Kropp (1961) compared the administration of a School Ability Test under two conditions with 29 9th-grade general education students. Students who took the test with each test item projected on a screen in a teacher-paced manner performed better than those who took the test using a traditional paper and pencil format. Hoffman and Lundberg (1976) compared the administration of a test under similar conditions with 136 general education pharmacy students in their second year of study, but with different findings. They also compared a standard paper and pencil administration of a test with test items visually projected on a screen and verbally read to the participants. They found the general scores were equivalent under both conditions; however, decreased performance was noted for matching items. Helwig, Almond, Rozek-Tedesco, Tindal, and Heath (1999) compared the math test scores of 33 students from 6th-grade classrooms. Half were administered the test via a standard test booklet format and half were presented the test via a video monitor with an administrator reading and pacing the test. The investigators analyzed the data on various subgroups related to reading and math ability and found only one statistically significant finding—the more verbs presented in a passage increased the success rate in favor of the video accommodation. Tindal, Glasgow, Helwig, Hollenbeck, and Heath (1998) compared the results of a video paced read aloud administration of a math test with a standard paper and pencil multiple choice test with 2000 students, 1000 elementary and 1000 middle school students. Significant effects were found for the elementary students and not the middle school in favor of the video paced read aloud administration. Finally, Hollenbeck, Rozek-Tedesco, Tindal, and Glasgow (2000) compared the effects of student-paced computer presentation versus teacher-paced video presentation of a large-scale math test with 50 seventh grade students, consisting of special education and general education students. The investigators found that both student-paced and teacher-paced accommodations significantly impacted the scores of both special and general education students. The student-paced computer accommodation resulted in slightly higher scores than the teacher-paced video presentation.

Computer-Based Testing as an Accommodation

Although our focus was on paced item presentation, using the computer as the tool to deliver this accommodation merits a review of the literature. Computer-based testing (CBT) "generally refers to using the computer to administer a conventional (i.e.,

paper-pencil) test" (Wise & Plake, 1989, p. 5). Since the research employing computer presentation as a test modification is extensive, the focus in this literature review will be on recent studies using secondary school students as the participants. The studies investigating computer-based presentation as a testing accommodation has had mixed findings (Thompson et al., 2002). Brown and Augustine (2001) found that computer use had no significant effect on the scores of 206 12th-grade students. Hollenbeck, Tindal, and Almond (1999) found no differences between stories written with computers and those written without. In contrast, Burk (1998) found that the performance of students with disabilities was significantly higher on a computerized administration of a test as compared to a paper and pencil format. Calhoon, Fuchs, and Hamlett (2000) also reported computer use had a positive effect on performance of 9th-through 12th-grade students with math and reading learning disabilities, as well as Russell and Plati (2000) with a group of 8th and 10th grade students writing compositions via a computer.

Research Summary

Synthesizing the studies exploring testing accommodations for students with disabilities is a complex endeavor for a number of reasons. Often the studies differ substantially in terms of the ages and range of disabilities of the students sampled, the research methodologies used, as well as the type of technology used to deliver the various accommodations in which technology is a factor. In addition, the various accommodations investigated are often packaged with other accommodations and are seldom investigated in isolation (Tindal & Fuchs, 2000). Nevertheless, one can see that investigating the relationship between computer-paced and student-paced item presentation on the academic test performance in college students diagnosed with ADHD deserves attention. In this study, we compared the performance of students who manually self-paced their progression through the computerized test with students who were paced automatically through the computerized test as designed within the computer program.

METHODS

This exploratory study utilized a mixed-methods quasi-experimental design to explore and explain the effects of paced item presentation for college students diagnosed with ADHD. This sequential explanatory strategy was appropriate, because our goal was to analyze two testing conditions and interpret their impact on a small number of participants who participated in the study.

Participants

Twenty-one students enrolled in a mid-sized public university in the southwestern United States who were registered with the Office of Disabilities with a diagnosis of ADHD participated in the study. Participants were solicited through advertisements posted around the university campus. After numerous unsuccessful scheduling attempts and unsuccessful follow through on scheduled appointments, the investigators offered an all-day "open lab" on the day between the last class day and the first of the final exams for the students to come by the university psychology computer lab and take the test at their convenience. After completing the computerized test and a follow-up interview, each participant was given $20 as an incentive to participate.

The average age of the participants was 26.8 years old with a standard deviation of 9.3 years. Five participants were classified as Freshman, nine were Sophomore, two were Junior, and five were Senior (see Table 1).

Of the 21 participants, 11 were males and 10 were females; 15 were Caucasian, 4 Hispanic, 1 African-American, and 1 Island Pacific/Other. Although 13 participants were prescribed medication to manage their ADHD symptoms, only six participants used medication on the day of the experiment (see Table 2).

Materials

The software program designed for the study was a Microsoft Windows application written in the programming language Visual Basic NET. The application recorded test results to a database located on a separate, designated computer. Additionally, an administrator's interface was written as an interactive Web document in the PHP scripting language. By using the interface to access the database, a test administrator was able to monitor the results as they came in and also export these results to a raw text file for the purpose of data analysis.

The program displayed all screens in a simple grey color, had a clock display in the upper right hand corner of the screen for the timed portions of the

experiment, and provided an auditory tone when a screen was advanced. Test items were displayed in a controlled sequence; the participants were unable to return to previously answered questions. Participants wore headphones during the experiment in order to hear the tone alerting advancement to the next question. Upon completion of the test, participants were interviewed about their testing experience.

In order to simulate testing conditions in a university setting as closely as possible, a passage from a college psychology textbook was selected as the prompt for the participants. The students were allowed 5 minutes to read the short passage (see Figure 1)*.

Multiple-choice questions from the college textbook test bank were administered to assess the students' learning. The text and 11-item multiple-choice test were taken from a textbook routinely used in introductory psychology classes (see Figure 2)*.

Immediately following completion of the computerized test, each student participated in a face-to-face interview with the primary investigator. The guiding questions of the interview consisted of two open-ended questions:

1. Were there any conditions in the testing environment that helped your performance? and

2. Were there conditions in the testing environment that hurt your performance?

Procedure

Participants were randomly assigned to one of two treatment conditions. In the computer-paced

Table 2. Participant Demographics

	Computer-Paced		Student-Paced	
	Total	%	Total	%
Gender				
Male	6	60.00	5	45.50
Female	4	40.00	6	54.50
Ethnicity				
African American	1	10.00	0	0.00
Caucasian	6	60.00	9	81.80
Hispanic	2	20.00	2	18.20
Other	1	10.00	0	0.00
Medication				
Prescribed, but not used on experiment day	1	10.00	6	54.50
Prescribed and used on experiment day	4	40.00	2	18.20
Not prescribed	5	50.00	3	27.30

Table 1. Participants Age and GPA

	Computer-Paced		Student-Paced	
	M	SD	M	SD
Age	25.8	7.10	27.7	11.2
GPA[a]	2.53	1.04	2.78	0.93

[a]Freshman students with a GPA of "0.00" were not included in the Mean or Standard Deviation results as those scores would have unfairly skewed the results. Those students had no official university grades at the time of the experiment.

*Figures 1 and 2 omitted for this edition.

testing condition (CP), the students were allowed 90 seconds per question and were forced to move on to the next question when the time expired. The clock on the screen counted down the 90-second time limit for each multiple choice question. If the student answered the question before the maximum time allowed, s/he could manually advance to the next question. In the student-paced testing condition (SP), students were allowed an average of 90 seconds per question but were not forced to move on to the next question. They paced themselves by using a clock on the screen that counted down the total time (16.5 minutes) allowed for answering the 11 multiple choice test questions.

The computer software program first displayed a demographic questionnaire screen. Participants completed the brief questionnaire on demographic information and whether or not medicine for ADHD had been prescribed and whether medicine had been used the day of the experiment. After providing the online demographic information, the participants were given instructions regarding the upcoming text passage. Participants were instructed that they would have 5 minutes to read the brief text passage. After reading the instructions, the students indicated they had read and understood the instructions by selecting an option given on the screen. After reading the text passage, the participant could either manually advance the screen, or the screen was advanced automatically after the 5-minute time limit for reading the passage had expired. After reading the text passage, a screen with instructions for the multiple-choice questions was presented. All instructions were presented on a single screen and were not timed. After reading the exam instruction page, participants indicated that they had read and understood the instructions by selecting an option to proceed. They were then instructed to begin answering the multiple-choice questions.

The computer-paced testing condition (CP) was achieved by restricting participants to a 90-second time limit for each multiple-choice question, for a total of 16.5 minutes to complete all questions. A clock in the corner of the screen counted down the 90-second time limit for each question. The test question automatically advanced to the next question after the 90-second limit had expired, unless the participant manually advanced the screen to the next question if he/she submitted the response prior to the 90-second limit. The student-paced testing condition (SP) was achieved by allowing participants to self-manage the amount of time spent on each question. The SP also allowed the participant a total of 16.5 minutes to complete all questions; however the participants paced themselves by referring to a clock in the corner of the screen that counted from the 16.5-minute maximum time to answer all questions.

Upon completion of either the computer-paced or student-paced test, each participant was individually interviewed face-to-face by the primary investigator to explore the student's perception of the testing experience. After completing the interview, the participant received his/her monetary incentive.

RESULTS

The data of primary interest to the study were mean differences in the two treatment conditions (computer-paced and student-paced) and the student interview data. The results will be presented in two parts. The quantitative data will be reported first, followed by the qualitative data provided by participant interviews.

Data Screening

Prior to conducting the quantitative data analysis, we screened the data for the assumptions of normality and equal variances (Kirk, 2008). For both, the data met the requisite assumptions to conduct an independent t-test of means.

Quantitative Data Analysis

Means were calculated for each participant in the two conditions and the mean scores were recorded. Mean differences and standard deviations were calculated for each of the two treatment groups, and an independent t-test of significance was employed. We found no significant difference between the treatment groups. Group one (CP) had a mean score of 8.10 with a standard deviation of 2.68, and group two (SP) had a mean score of 8.18 with a standard deviation of 2.75. Results are reported in Table 3.

Qualitative Data Analysis

Upon completion of the computerized test, each participant was individually interviewed face-to-face by the primary investigator in a room adjacent to the computer lab. The purpose of the interview was to explore the student's perception of the testing experience. To ensure open inquiry and an emerging design, the guiding questions of the interview were open-ended. The guiding questions were:

Table 3. Mean Scores on Reading Comprehension Test for Computer-Paced and Student-Paced Testing Conditions

	Computer-Paced		Student-Paced	
	Mean	SD	Mean	SD
Reading compre-hesnsion score	8.10	2.68	8.18	2.75

1. What conditions in the testing environment helped your performance—in what ways; and

2. What conditions in the testing environment hurt your performance—in what ways?

Each interview lasted approximately 15–20 minutes. The primary researcher wrote the student responses verbatim in the form of notes and read back the written responses to ensure that the student had communicated what he/she intended.

After all student interviews were completed, the participant responses were reviewed and organized into two general categories: helpful testing conditions and unhelpful testing conditions. Three general themes emerged upon organization of the data: format, time, and physical environment.

Formatting

One theme that emerged was the formatting of the text and the questions presented on the computer screen. Of the 21 students, 15 reported that the structure of the reading passage enhanced their performance. Several participants commented that the text reading passage was spatially organized so that they could easily focus on content of the reading passage. For example, one participant said:

> It was easy to see how it's organized. The first paragraph explained one type of motivation. The second paragraph explained the other type. The third paragraph gave examples of each. Having only three paragraphs gave me the confidence that I could read easily.

Another participant said:

> The text was clearly written and broken up well.

Another said:

> The bold letters in the passage helped. The bold font emphasized the main ideas.

Although most of the participants emphasized a perceived benefit of the formatting and succinctness of the reading passage, a few students found the text passage difficult to read.

> The text clumped together in the reading passage made it hard. I see a big jumble of words. I can read it over and over but it doesn't help. The more information that's presented, the harder it is. Testing is really a crapshoot for me.

Another student said:

> Lots of big words in succession—too many in a row—the academic wording—made it hard.

Another said:

> The long passage of text was difficult to process and organize.

Over one-half of the participants reported that having only one question on the screen at a time helped them to focus and increased their confidence. For example, one student said:

> Paper tests that are pages full of questions make me nervous. I liked having each question, one at a time.

Another participant commented:

> I liked seeing one question at a time. Lots of questions on a page makes me anxious.

Timing

A second theme that emerged was the structure and visibility of the time component within the test. Whether testing under the computer-paced experimental condition with the 90-second maximum time limit per question or testing under the student-paced condition with the 16 minute overall time limit, most participants reported that the timer was an added distraction. One student said:

> Timers make me feel rushed. I hate timed tests.

Another said:

> Timers make me feel nervous. I need to time to think. The timer made me feel pressured.

said another. Although most of the students in both the computer-paced and student-paced conditions reported a distaste for timers, a few in the student-paced condition only said knowing they had 16 minutes to complete 11 multiple-choice questions relieved them.

> The timer scared me at first, but when I realized I had 15 minutes for 11 questions, it didn't affect me at all.

Another said:

> I liked the timer telling me how much time I had left to take the test. It was nice not worrying about the time.

Physical Environment

A third theme that emerged was the students' overwhelming emphasis of their need for a distraction-free testing environment. Most of the students emphasized a preference for an isolated and quiet environment.

> I liked the quiet and calmness, the lack of sound and no other people in the room.

Another said:

> It was quiet—no cell phones.

Another said:

> Any background noises really distract me. I give equal attention to everything around me.

It should be noted that students completed this test in a computerized research lab with fewer than two or three other students present. This, of course, more closely mimics the accommodated testing conditions available to most students via disability services than conducting such research in a classroom setting with multiple participants completing the exam at the same time and in the same room.

DISCUSSION

Finding no significant differences in the mean scores between our treatment groups was surprising. Our quantitative data suggested that forcing students to advance at a computer-prescribed pace (CP) did not enhance their performance as compared to allowing students to pace themselves (SP), as we had predicted. Information gleaned from the student interviews suggested that for many of the students in the computer-paced condition, the 90-second time limit structure for each test question actually increased their anxiety. It is interesting to note, however, that this self-reported increase in anxiety was not associated with decreased performance on the test in comparison to the student-paced test takers.

The qualitative data analysis revealed that the computerized testing environment itself provided structure for the students through the formatting of the reading passage and test items—displaying only one question on the screen at a time. This may account for the average of 8/11 correct responses for participants under both conditions, allowing them to perform equally well. Perhaps the reported increased anxiety was "washed out" by the structure provided by computerizing the exam, providing a sufficient advantage, resulting in no quantitative differences in total correct responses under both conditions. Although the quantitative data do not allow us to validate this assumption, the qualitative data appear to be rich for making such connections and for suggesting future avenues for research.

Our findings suggest that this exploratory study is useful as primary research and that future research needs to investigate our unanticipated finding that computerized testing, in-and-of-itself, appeared to improve performance of ADHD students regardless of other types of accommodations. Although we did not have a non-ADHD control group to compare performances, the interview data suggested that computerized testing for college students diagnosed with ADHD may "balance the playing field" in comparison to students without ADHD. A future study may test this assumption directly by including both a non-ADHD control group and an ADHD control group that takes the exam via paper-pencil as well as a non-ADHD

experimental group that takes the exam via the computerized format. Comparison of these added conditions may not only support the qualitative results found by the present study, but may also yield significant quantitative findings. The additional data may also illuminate the potential benefit of computerized testing to non-ADHD students as well as the ability of computerized testing to accommodate the needs of ADHD students better than the traditional accommodations of paper-pencil testing and extended time.

Based on our qualitative findings, we anticipate improved performance for students with ADHD in the computerized conditions in comparison to any non-computerized conditions. Students with ADHD taking the exam paper-pencil, for example, would not be expected to perform as well as the students with ADHD in any of the computerized conditions. Comments from participants strongly suggest that the focus of being at the computer and being presented one question at a time alleviated much of the anxiety they typically experienced in testing situations. Although extended time may assist students with ADHD in performing more effectively, our findings suggest this may be due more to pacing. If a student with ADHD in a traditional time paper-pencil condition were "paced," we would expect improved performance in comparison to traditional paper-pencil conditions.

Implications

What is the feasibility of university offices of disability providing computerized testing to accommodate students diagnosed with ADHD? Approaches to creating test administration software may be divided into three broad groups: commercial/proprietary; open-source; and custom-written software. All of these approaches are practicable, and each has its own positive and negative aspects. The following briefly examines each approach, along with some of its relative advantages and disadvantages.

Commercial/proprietary software is software that is usually licensed to an educational institution for a fee. Examples include Blackboard, WebCT, and Desire2Learn. The widespread use of these software packages makes them easily accessible to many English-speaking educators, including grade-school level (Blackboard, 2006a). While many of these products are "closed-source," meaning that the software may not be edited (or in some cases, not even be viewed) by a licensee, some packages include the ability to extend the basic features, such as by augmenting its built-in online test administration component. Thus, depending on the package, features may be added to the online test-facilitating component by a licensee to accommodate the various needs of special population students. Universities using this type of software routinely employ staff skilled in programming that could easily make modifications to the online test-facilitating component. One possible drawback to using commercial/proprietary software, at least in the United States, is a presently hostile legal climate due to efforts by Blackboard, Inc. to protect its patent on "Internet-based education support system and methods" (Blackboard, 2006b).

Different than commercial/proprietary software packages in several ways are open-source packages such as Sakai, Moodle, and A Tutor. Both commercial and open-source types of software packages are typically Internet-based e-learning systems, and all major packages include computerized testing components (although at varying levels of sophistication). Open-source projects offer many advantages over their commercialized counterparts. The former are almost always usable without costly licensing fees (Sakai, 2004). A package's source code being "open" means the entirety of the code may be viewed and edited to suit the needs of a given educational agenda. It also indicates that an online development community exists for the software. For example, Sakai has a large non-profit organization backing it. Such a community can be sought after for assistance and feedback in the development of electronic test-facilitating modules designed to meet the needs of students with disabilities. Universities using these open-source packages routinely employ staff skilled in customizing components of the groupware to meet the stated needs of the institution, including online test administration. Finally, open-source software seems to be safe from the hostile legal climate that Desire2Learn is currently experiencing, as Blackboard, Inc. has pledged not to file patent infringement suits against those developing and using open-source projects (Carnevale, 2007).

The last of the three approaches, and the one utilized in the present study, is custom-written software. Perhaps the most salient advantage is the ability to "custom-tailor" the software directly toward meeting the needs of a specific student population. The ability to avoid Internet congestion issues that may arise using either of the previously discussed approaches is also a significant advantage. Custom-written software can be designed to simply operate on a local area network (LAN) that would be linking desktop machines together in a student computer lab. With the exception of a remote backup database to which test results were sent, this is how the present study's software was designed. Another advantage of the custom approach is that it does not require a large, pre-existing e-learning software package used by an educational institution. This means that while some institutions may use Desire2Learn and others, all would still be able to use a small, custom-written, test-facilitating application that accepts Microsoft Word files containing test questions.

A disadvantage of the custom approach requires the utilization of technically proficient personnel to design, write, and further customize the software. Further, the software would be unfamiliar to anyone not involved in its design or use. This is not the case when simply adding onto pre-existing software such as Blackboard or Sakai—software with which many educators and institutions are familiar. However, whether familiar to educators and institutions or not, each of the aforementioned approaches requires available, proficient technical personnel in support of its software package.

In conclusion, each of the three approaches allows for modification of testing procedures with the assistance of technical personnel skilled in programming. When comparing the advantages and disadvantages of the three approaches to computerized testing, custom computer software seems a viable and beneficial solution to the problem of meeting the needs of a specific student population, such as those diagnosed with ADHD. The current study has demonstrated that fully modular test-facilitating software packages can be custom-designed at low cost, and with ease-of-use in mind for both the testing administrators and students.

CONCLUSION

In an effort to understand appropriate testing accommodations for college students with ADHD, this exploratory study illuminated several important issues:

a. a continued need for a distraction free testing environment;
b. further investigation of benefits and drawbacks of formatting on exam performance; and
c. the effects of the structure and visibility of the time component within the testing environment.

Clearly, there is a need to investigate the perceived usefulness of various accommodations by the students themselves. The interview data in this study was rich in insight. Numerous participants expressed a long history of academic difficulty and frustration, using a "trial and error" approach in attempting to discover effective academic strategies to help them deal with the limitations of their ADHD symptomology. Many of the participants expressed a willingness to add to the knowledge base in hopes to help others avoid their "hit and miss" approach in trying to successfully learn the necessary skills and competencies required to be successful in an educational setting. Although conducting studies exploring testing accommodations for students with disabilities is complex, it certainly merits our attention and study. Clearly it is our responsibility as educators to provide accommodations to this underserved and underrepresented population of college students with ADHD to increase their chances of graduating from college and contributing to and participating fully in society.

REFERENCES

Allsopp, D., Minskoff, E., & Bolt, L. (2005). Individualized course-specific strategy instruction for college students with learning disabilities and ADHD: Lessons learned from a model demonstration project. *Learning Disabilities Research and Practice, 20*(2), 103.

Alster, E. H. (1997). The effects of extended time on algebra test scores for college students with and without learning disabilities. *Journal of Learning Disabilities, 30*(2), 222–227.

Blackboard. (2006a). Michigan leads the country with new K-12 e-learning initiative. *Blackboard Media Center.* Retrieved February 1, 2008, from http://www.blackboard.com/company/press/release. aspx?id=872036

Blackboard. (2006b). Blackboard awarded patent on e-learning technology. *Blackboard Company Press Releases.* Retrieved February 1, 2008, from http://investor.blackboard.com/phoenix.zhtml?c=177018&p=irolnewsArticle&ID=887622&highlight=

Brown, P. J., & Augustine, A. (2001). *Screen reading software as an assessment accommodation: Implications for instruction and student performance.* (ERIC Document Reproduction Service No. ED458273) Retrieved February 2, 2008, from ERIC database.

Burk, M. (1998). *Computerized test accommodations: A new approach for inclusion and success for students with disabilities.* Paper presented at Office of Special Education Program Cross Project Meeting "Technology and the Education of Children with Disabilities: Steppingstones to the 21st Century."

Calhoon, M. B., Fuchs, L. S., & Hamlett, C. L. (2000). Effects of computer-based test accommodations on mathematics performance assessments for secondary students with learning disabilities. *Learning Disability Quarterly, 23*(4), 271–282.

Carnevale, D. (2006). Blackboard sues rival over alleged patent infringement. *Chronicle of Higher Education, 52*(49), A30.

Carnevale, D. (2007). Blackboard pledges to ease enforcement of controversial patent. *Chronicle of Higher Education, 53*(23), A35.

Curtis, H. A., & Kropp, R. P. (1961). A comparison of scores obtained by administering a test normally and visually. *Journal of Experimental Education, 29*, 249–260.

Dowrick, P. W., Anderson, J., Heyer, K., & Acosta, J. (2005). Postsecondary education across the USA: Experiences of adults with disabilities. *Journal of Vocational Rehabilitation, 22*, 41–47.

DuPaul, G. J., & Eckert, T. L. (1998). Academic interventions for students with attention-deficit/hyperactivity disorder: A review of the literature. *Reading & Writing Quarterly, 14*(1), 59–82.

DuPaul, G. J., Guevermont, D. C, & Barkley, R. A. (1991). Attention deficit-hyperactivity disorder in adolescence: Critical assessment parameters. *Clinical Psychological Review, 11*, 233–245.

DuPaul, G. J., & Weyandt, L. L. (2006). School based interventions for children and adolescents with Attention Deficit/ Hyperactivity Disorder: Enhancing academic and behavioral outcomes. *Education and Treatment of Children 29*(2), 341–358.

Elliott, S. N., McKevitt, B. C., & Kettler, R. J. (2002). Testing accommodations research and decision making: The case of 'good' scores being highly valued but difficult to achieve for all students. *Measurement & Evaluation in Counseling & Development, 35*(3), 153–167.

Farrell, E. F. (2003). Paying attention to students who can't. *Chronicle of Higher Education, 50*(5), 50–52.

Fuchs, L. S., Fuchs, D., & Capizzi, A. M. (2005). Identifying appropriate test accommodations for students with learning disabilities. *Focus on Exceptional Children, 37*(6), 1–8.

Getzel, E. E., McManus, S., & Briel, L. W. (2004). An effective model for college students with learning disabilities and attention deficit hyperactivity disorders. *LD Online.* Retrieved January 20, 2007, from http://www.txstate.edu/education/sped/

Heiligenstein, E., Guenther, G., Levy, A., Savino, F., & Fulwiler, J. (1999). Psychological and academic functioning in college students with attention deficit hyperactivity disorder. *Journal of American College Health, 47*(4), 181–185.

Helwig, R., Rozek-Tedesco, M. A., & Tindal, G. (2002). An oral versus a standard administration of a large-scale mathematics test. *Journal of Special Education, 36*(1), 39–47.

Helwig, R., Almond, P. J., Rozek-Tedesco, M. A., Tindal, G., & Heath B. (1999). Reading as an access to mathematics problem solving on multiple-choice tests for sixth-grade students. *Journal of Educational Research, 93*(2), 113–125.

Hoffman, K. I., & Lundberg, G. D. (1976). A comparison of computer-monitored group tests with paper-and-pencil tests. *Educational and Psychological Measurement, 36*(4), 791–809.

Hollenbeck, K., Rozek-Tedesco, M. A., Tindal, G., & Glasgow, A. (2000). An exploratory study of student-paced versus teacher-paced accommodations for large-scale math tests. *Journal of Special Education Technology, 15*(2), 27–36.

Hollenbeck, K., Tindal, G., & Almond, P. (1999). Reliability and decision consistency: An analysis of writing mode at two times on a statewide test.

Educational Assessment, 6(1), 23–33. Retrieved February 25, 2008, from Academic Search Complete database.

Kessler, R. C, Adler L., Barkley, J., Biederman, J., Conners, C. K., Demler, O., et al. (2006). The prevalence and correlates of adult ADHD in the United States: Results from the National Comorbidity Survey replication. *American Journal of Psychiatry, 163*(4), 716–723.

Kirk, R. E. (2008). *Statistics: An introduction* (5th ed.). Belmont, CA: Thomson Learning.

Lancaster, S., Mellard, D., & Hoffman, L. (2001). *Experiences of students with disabilities in selected community and technical colleges. The individual accommodations model: Accommodating students with disabilities in post-secondary settings.* Lawrence, KS: Kansas University, Center for Research on Learning (ED452617).

Medina, J. G. (2000). Classroom testing accommodations for postsecondary students with learning disabilities: The empirical gap. *Dissertation Abstracts International Section A: Humanities and Social Sciences, 60*(7-A), 2372.

Niebling, B. C., & Elliott, S. N. (2005). Testing accommodations and inclusive assessment practices. *Assessment for Effective Intervention, 31*(1), 1–6.

Quinn, P. O., Ratey, N. A., & Maitland, T. L. (2000). *Coaching college students with AD/HD.* Silver Spring, MD: Advantage Books.

Russell, M., & Plati, T. (2000). Mode of administration effects on MCAS composition performance for grades four, eight, and ten. A report of findings submitted to the Massachusetts Department of Education. *NBETPP Statements World Wide Web Bulletin.* (ERIC Document Reproduction Service No. ED456142) Retrieved February 2, 2008, from ERIC database.

Sakai. (2004). *MIT helps break ground in educational software collaboration.* Retrieved February 1, 2008, from http://sakaiproject.org/index.php?option=com_content&task=view&id=93&Itemid=547

Swartz, S. L., Prevatt, F., & Proctor, B. E. (2005). A coaching intervention for college students with attention deficity/hyperactivity disorder. *Psychology in the Schools, 42*(6), 647–655.

Tagayuna, A., Stodden, R. A., Chang, C., Zeleznik, M. E., & Whelley, T. A. (2005). A two-year comparison of support provision for persons with disabilities in post-secondary education. *Journal of Vocational Rehabilitation, 22*(1), 13–21.

Thompson, S., Blount, A., & Thurlow, M. (2002). *A summary of research on the effects of test accommodations: 1999 through 2001. Technical Report.* 67 pp. (ED475047) Full Text from ERIC.

Tindal, G., & Fuchs, L. (2000). A summary of research on test changes: An empirical basis for defining accommodations. 125 pp. (ED442245) Full Text from ERIC by Ebsco Host.

Tindal, G., Glasgow, A., Helwig, B., Hollenbeck, K., & Heath, B. (1998). *Accommodations in large scale tests for students with disabilities: An investigation of reading math tests using video technology.* Unpublished manuscript with Council of Chief State School Officer, Washington, DC.

Wallace, B. A., Winsler, A., & NeSmith, P. (1999, April). *Factors associated with success for college students with ADHD: Are standard accommodations helping?* Paper presented at the Annual Meeting of the American Educational Research Association, Montreal, Quebec, Canada.

Weaver, S. M. (2000). The efficacy of extended time on tests for postsecondary students with learning disabilities. *Learning Disabilities: A Multidisciplinary Journal, 10*(2), 47–56.

Weyandt, L. L., & DuPaul, G. (2006). ADHD in college students. *Journal of Attention Disorders, 10*(1), 9–19.

Wise, S. L., & Plake, B. S. (1989). Research on the effects of administering tests via computers. *Educational Measurement: Issues and Practices, 8*(3), 5–10.

Zuriff, G. E. (2000). Extra examination time for students with learning disabilities: An examination of the maximum. *Applied Measurement in Education, 13*(1), 99–118 (AN 3341986).

Zwart, L. M., & Kallemeyn, L. M. (2001). Peer-based coaching for college students with ADHD and learning disabilities. *Journal of Postsecondary Education and Disability, 15*(1), 1–15.